from CONVICT PRINTERS
to BOOK ARCADES

a HISTORY *of*
the BOOK *in*
AUSTRALIA
VOLUME I: 1788–1890

A History of the Book in Australia

Volume I: From Convict Printers to Book Arcades (1788–1890)
Edited by Wallace Kirsop, Elizabeth Webby & Judy Donnelly
Ancora Press 2024

Volume II: A National Culture in a Colonised Market (1891–1945)
Edited by Martyn Lyons & John Arnold
University of Queensland Press 2001

Volume III: Paper Empires (1946–2005)
Edited by Craig Munro, Robyn Sheahan-Bright & John Curtain
University of Queensland Press 2006

from Convict Printers to Book Arcades

a History of the Book in Australia
Volume I: 1788–1890

Edited by Wallace Kirsop, Elizabeth Webby
& Judy Donnelly
with the assistance of Meredith Sherlock

Ancora Press

MONASH UNIVERSITY
with the support of the
Bibliographical Society of Australia and New Zealand
2024

250 copies have been reserved for members of the Bibliographical Society of Australia and New Zealand in lieu of their subscriptions to volumes 47 (2023) and 48 (2024) of *Script & Print*.

First published 2024 by Ancora Press, Monash University, Melbourne, Australia

Compilation Wallace Kirsop, Elizabeth Webby and Judy Donnelly © 2024
Essays and case-studies © individual authors

This book is copyright. Except for private study, research, criticism or reviews, as permitted under the Copyright Act, no part of this book may be reproduced, stored in a retrieval system, or transmitted in any form by any means without prior permission.
Enquiries should be made to: Ancora Press c/o School of Languages, Literature, Cultures and Linguistics, Monash University, Clayton VIC Australia 3800

Distributed by Monash University Publishing, 40 Exhibition Walk, Monash University, Clayton VIC, Australia 3800
Typeset by Lynn Smailes
Printed in Australia by Jossimo Print, Rowville VIC 3178

ISBN 978-0-6487385-4-1 (v.I: hbk)
ISBN 978-0-6487385-5-8 (v. I: ebook)

First Nations peoples are advised that this publication contains an image of an Indigenous person and the names of people who have died, and includes previously published discussions and descriptions of First Nations cultures.

*In memory of John Percy Holroyd (1911–2000),
veteran bookseller and indefatigably generous
chronicler of the trade*

Contents

Acknowledgements	ix
Note on Pre-Decimal Currency	xi
General Introduction to the series of three volumes *Wallace Kirsop*	xiii
Preface *Wallace Kirsop*	xxi
Chapter 1 A Book by Any Other Name? Towards a Social History of the Book in Aboriginal Australia †*Penny van Toorn* Postscript *Leonie Stevens*	1
Chapter 2 Printing Technology *Stephen James Herrin*	27
Chapter 3 Australian Print Workers To 1890 *Rae Frances*	66
Chapter 4 Illustrations *Thomas A. Darragh*	75
Chapter 5 Australian Colonial Binding *Carol Mills*	103
Chapter 6 The Use of Paper in Nineteenth-Century Australian Publications *Carol Mills*	112
Chapter 7 Colonial Type: Imported and Australian-Made *Dennis Bryans*	122
Chapter 8 'The laurels in the pit were won': Authorship in Colonial Australia †*Elizabeth Webby*	139
Chapter 9 The Beginnings of Australian Publishing *Ian Morrison*	148
Chapter 10 The Significance of Colonial and Imperial Copyright for Australian Authors, Publishers and the Book Trade to 1890 *Clive Turner*	176

Chapter 11 'The Land of Newspapers' *Wallace Kirsop*	188
Case Study: Andrew Bent — Father of the Free Press *Sally Bloomfield & Craig Collins*	211
Chapter 12 Magazines †*Elizabeth Webby*	222
Chapter 13 Bookselling *Wallace Kirsop*	258
Chapter 14 Australia's Public Libraries in their Infancy *David J. Jones*	292
Chapter 15 Mechanics' Institutes *Wallace Kirsop*	316
Chapter 16 Commercial Circulating Libraries *Wallace Kirsop*	330
Chapter 17 Private Libraries *Wallace Kirsop*	338
Chapter 18 The Print Culture of Colonial Music from its Beginnings *Graeme Skinner*	348
Chapter 19 Textbooks †*Jeff Prentice*	365
Chapter 20 Australian Directories to 1890 †*R. Ian Jack*	372
Chapter 21 Australian Almanacs 1806–1890 *Maureen Perkins*	382
Chapter 22 Australian Printing and Publishing in Pacific Islands and Indigenous Languages 1814–1900 *Susan Woodburn*	388
Chapter 23 Official Printing *Tony Cavanagh*	406
Chapter 24 After the 'toil of a long day': Reading in Colonial Australia †*Elizabeth Webby*	417
Conclusion: Coming of Age *Wallace Kirsop*	455
Notes on Contributors	461
List of Illustrations	466
List of Abbreviations	470
Select Bibliography	471
Index	483

Acknowledgements

A volume that has been so long in joining its two companions covering the twentieth century carries an even heavier burden of debts to those who — despite all — continued to believe in its necessity. Our first duty, therefore, is to thank our contributors for their forbearance and patience. Even those who decided finally that they could not embark on the process of updating and hence withdrew their texts deserve our gratitude for their participation in the ongoing dialogue that was essential to the shaping of this still provisional history.

From the start in the 1990s, discussion and the exchange of points of view, not least in mini-conferences, were a central part of the work of the collective responsible for the project. The original committee, composed of the editors of volume I together with Martyn Lyons and John Arnold (volume II) and Craig Munro and John Curtain (volume III), was able to shape the enterprise in the light of what was contributed in the formal series of meetings. In the early years we had the invaluable contribution of Elizabeth Morrison as Project Officer. Later, after the death of John Curtain in 1999, Robyn Sheahan-Bright joined the group, and Meredith Sherlock took on the role of Project Officer. From time to time the committee had input from Paul Eggert and Bryan Coleborne. Although each volume followed a somewhat different path, awareness of the whole picture was maintained.

Martyn Lyons's success in obtaining a Large Grant from the Australian Research Council was critical in supplying research support, especially to volumes I and II. In our case we were assisted by Stephen Herrin, who worked on a database of trade personnel. Earlier, with a research grant from Monash University, he had completed a comprehensive bibliography of primary and secondary sources relating to the book trade in Australia from its settler beginnings.

Most of the editorial labour in the early stages of volume II was done by Elizabeth Webby and Meredith Sherlock. After the publication of volume III in 2006, it was clear that the available funds were exhausted and that our efforts had to be suspended for a time. Much later, we had to face the fact that the University of Queensland Press had decided to bow out. Worse, long illness and death removed both Meredith and Elizabeth in 2020 and 2023 respectively. Judy Donnelly's acceptance of the position of Editorial Assistant in 2021 and two years later of co-Editorship gave new stability and energy to the team. The Ancora Press accepted total responsibility for steering the text through the press and covering all costs. The agreement by Monash University Publishing to ensure distribution to the trade and the decision by the Bibliographical Society of Australia and New Zealand to subscribe for copies for all its members have meant that the volume will reach the audience we believe it deserves.

Lynn Smailes, as Technical Editor, has guided us through all the problems of setting and laying out a quite complicated book.

Several colleagues have provided much-appreciated advice on and critical scrutiny of the various chapters: Dennis Bryans, David Jones, David McKitterick, Robert McLaren, Ian Morrison and Ian Wilson.

Barbara Nicholls, Meredith Sherlock's successor as Secretary of Ancora Press, has not only looked after administrative matters but undertaken numerous research tasks. Various ancillary jobs were undertaken by the editorial team in concert. Judy Donnelly took major responsibilities for illustrations and the index. Wallace Kirsop, assisted by Barbara Nicholls, prepared the Select Bibliography.

Libraries and archives across the country have been generous in giving access to material. Specific debts in relation to illustrations are set out in the captions and in the List of Illustrations.

Note on Pre-Decimal Currency

The following is offered as a guide to give the contemporary reader an understanding of the currency used in the period.

12 pence (12d) = 1 shilling (1/-)
20 shillings (20/-) = 1 pound (£1)
1 guinea = 1 pound and 1 shilling (£1/1/-)
crown = 5 shillings
half a crown = 2 shillings and sixpence (2/6d)

General Introduction

Wallace Kirsop

The decision to undertake *A History of the Book in Australia* was made at an informal meeting of bibliographers and historians at the University of New South Wales in November 1992. Strong encouragement had come from Ian Willison and Don McKenzie to embark on a parallel to the national histories of the book taking shape across the English-speaking world in Britain, the USA, Canada, Scotland, Wales and Ireland. For some at least of these enterprises the impetus had arisen from the four volumes of the *Histoire de l'édition française* produced between 1982 and 1986. Indeed two members of the Australian group had participated in the French effort, and others again in the local specialist community had been called upon to write for some of the volumes that issued from a genuine international movement. It is hardly an accident that the same decade saw the emergence of the Society for the History of Authorship, Reading and Publishing (SHARP), which has brought together — with an English-language emphasis, it is true — scholars from many countries to pursue a common cause. Although the main annual conferences take place in the Northern Hemisphere, there have been regional gatherings elsewhere. In 2018 the official meeting took place in Sydney, or more precisely at the University of Western Sydney campus in Parramatta, a gesture of recognition of the part that Australians and New Zealanders have played in the Society's affairs more or less since its inception.

More important as a background to the Australian project was the Bibliographical Society of Australia and New Zealand (BSANZ), founded in 1969 to co-ordinate and encourage research in the broad field in both countries. Quite predictably our New Zealand friends, again challenged by Don McKenzie, were not slow in joining — in 1993 — a push towards a new-style history of the print culture of their own country. The overall framework was provided by the now classic study of Lucien Febvre and Henri-Jean Martin, *L'Apparition du livre*, first published in 1958, but not translated into English until 1976. However, it is worth recording the fact that French is read and understood by some people in this corner of the world and that BSANZ has not ignored the lessons of the French school. At the same time we are conscious of our debt to, and, in the case of our colleagues across the Tasman, our solid contributions to British traditions of bibliographical scholarship.

Short articles on both the Australian and New Zealand book-history programmes appeared in the last number of the *BSANZ Bulletin* for 1993. In both cases wide consultation and the involvement of the many interested people in meetings and small conferences were envisaged. Over the next few years this happened, with the resulting papers often being published, especially but not exclusively in the *BSANZ Bulletin*. It is not hard, therefore, to measure the stimulus given to the research area in both countries.

Nobody anywhere was claiming stridently that the series being planned would be definitive, given in particular the already observable effects of the digital revolution. Some teams were more cautious than others. The Welsh contribution — *A Nation and its Books: a history of the book in Wales*, edited by Philip Henry Jones and Eiluned Rees (Aberystwyth, The National Library of Wales in association with Aberystwyth Centre for the Book, 1998) — was avowedly a first step made necessary by the complexity of the country's bilingualism. A similarly tentative approach was taken in New Zealand, another proudly bicultural society, a year earlier. The resultant volume — *Book & Print in New Zealand/A Guide to Print Culture in Aotearoa*, edited by Penny Griffith, Ross Harvey & Keith Maslen, with the assistance of Ross Somerville (Wellington, Victoria University Press, 1997) — is a remarkable achievement that we Australians should have imitated, if only because the formula allows more of the ground to be covered.

Despite the relatively recent publication of a collection initiated by Dietrich Borchardt on the occasion of the Australian Bicentenary — *The Book in Australia: Essays towards a Cultural & Social History* (Melbourne, Australian Reference Publications, 1988) —, it was decided to press ahead with a sequel intended to coincide with the Centenary of Federation in 2001. With three volumes planned it was clear that something more ambitious was being attempted. Two editors were allocated to each of the three parts. To our great regret John Curtain died prematurely in 1999 and was eventually replaced by Robyn Sheahan-Bright in the preparation and completion of volume III. Reports on progress coupled with thoughts on what the product should be were carried in the last numbers for 1994 and 1995 of the *BSANZ Bulletin*. Subsequent news was reported in the *HOBA Newsletter*, of which nine numbers were printed between 1994 and 2003.

A research grant from Monash University in 1995 enabled the compilation of a comprehensive in-house bibliography of relevant secondary material by Stephen Herrin. An Australian Research Council Large Grant for 1996, 1997 and 1998 ($204 000 in total), obtained under the leadership of Martyn Lyons, made it possible to appoint research assistants in Sydney and Melbourne to collect some of the indispensable data, especially for volumes I and II. A part-time Project Officer was also employed to co-ordinate what had become a quite complex undertaking in the years around the turn of the century.

The team considered it important to work with an all-Australian publisher. We were happy to have the support of the University of Queensland Press for volumes II and III. The long delay after the issue of the latter in 2006 saw a decline in interest in the production of serious books in the Australian field. As a consequence, the Ancora Press, affiliated with Monash University, has taken over responsibility for volume I, but with due attention to maintaining uniformity in presentation.

In the interest of accessibility to a wider non-specialist audience it was decided at the outset to dispense with footnotes or endnotes and to provide instead a note on sources at the end of each chapter as well as a thematic select bibliography to conclude each volume.

For the academic authors involved in particular in volumes I and II this procedure was not without problems. Discreet use of parenthetical references has helped to alleviate the difficulty. In passing it should be recorded that the various national histories, some of them sold to the public at much higher prices than our series, have adopted several solutions in this respect.

The first edition of the French history is the most lavish in its illustrations. Elsewhere there have been different approaches. As readers will have noticed, our volume III, with photographs grouped between pp. 210 and 211, is quite distinct from its predecessors, which try to integrate images with the relevant parts of the text.

A History of the Book in Australia, with appropriate emphasis on an indefinite article that speaks of a modest and provisional stance, has as its subject the introduction and perpetuation of a European-style print culture at a recent date in an ancient continent. The time-span is very short, as one can understand if one remembers that there are Australians still living whose great-grandparents were born in the reign of George III. If one puts it in another way, some of us bought books from James Tyrrell (1875–1961), whose career covered all three volumes of our series. Yet human communication was being practised in diverse ways over tens of thousands of years in this land. In the early 1990s it was perhaps possible to skate over this contrast. However, in the 2020s, it cannot be ignored any more than the criticisms that have been made of the grand international project in which we have been engaged. Even if there are answers to some recent objections, the fundamental point is there as a huge challenge.

That we were not unaware of our dilemma is suggested by a paragraph that was included in the first 1993 statement of the project's aims:

> The scope of the volume(s) would be inclusive rather than exclusive insofar as all aspects of print culture would be considered. Indeed it would be desirable to examine communication before the arrival of Europeans, oral culture, scribal publication and pictorial aspects as well as the impact of film, radio, TV and electronic possibilities in more recent times. Production, distribution and reception would need to be given equal weight, in other words all the technologies used since 1788, trade networks of every kind (including direct

selling, colporteurs etc.) and the evidence for reading/consumption would have to be carefully considered. The history of the newspaper press (so crucial in colonial societies) and of the provision of libraries would be an integral part of the story. The development of publishing could be expected to be given special attention. On the model of the *Histoire de l'édition française* produced in the 1980s chapters could be expected to be devoted to such categories as books for children, atlases, women's magazines, Bibles, reference works and the literature on food, wine and cooking.

In the event we veered away from the temptation to treat in depth pre-1788 Indigenous Australia, oral culture, scribal publication and the full impact of new media throughout the twentieth century and on into the twenty-first. In other words we stuck to our brief of examining the print civilisation that arrived with the Europeans at the end of the eighteenth century. This did not preclude a chapter designed to sketch one of the missing elements: communication among the continent's First Nations.

It is obvious that the next synthesis — in 2038, perhaps — will have to come to terms with these broader questions. Leaving aside the theoretical fashions to which book history is as subject as the humanities in general, it is appropriate to tackle one charge levelled at some of the national series. The present Australian effort can hardly be accused of neglecting the transnational dimension that has in any case been prominent in the diffusion of print culture since the fifteenth century. From 1788 to the 2020s Australians — printers, publishers, booksellers and readers — have been involved in a constant dialogue with a world outside, especially in the Northern Hemisphere. Books in Australia have always been imported in greater numbers than they have been produced locally.

New preoccupations with scribal publication, oral communication and 'the writing culture of ordinary people' have not been absent from Australian discussions in recent decades. It is enough to cite the work of the late Harold Love, Alan Atkinson's *The Commonwealth of Speech: An Argument About Australia's Past, Present and Future* (Melbourne, Australian Scholarly Publishing, 2002) and recent books by our HOBA colleague Martyn Lyons to indicate that an agenda is ready for a fresh departure. Anyone familiar with the enlarged scope of the researches of Henri-Jean Martin (1924–2007) towards the end of his life and with the themes of some French book-history investigations in this century will know that the time is ripe for innovation.

For the moment, however, we have to be concerned with what we are offering our readers in our three volumes. By and large we have kept to the programme drawn up in 1993 and cited above. Production, distribution and reception have been given equal weight. The special interest of some editorial team members in the history of reading has helped to reinforce this aspect of our endeavours. Newspapers have been given their due, especially in volumes I and II. The role of libraries of all kinds has been a constant throughout. None the less there are differences dictated by the nature of the periods treated.

The division of the volumes was determined not by the calendar but by discernible changes in the way the book trade operated. The boundaries could not be watertight, but they correspond to shifts in emphasis and not to political events. After the consolidation of distribution methods in the post-gold-rush decades, a major subject of volume I, there came in the 1890s the gradual tightening of British control of supplies linked paradoxically to an expansion of local publishing. The Second World War marked a turn to American influences as well as further reinforcement and diversification of what was being initiated and manufactured in Australia, although one should not forget a growing recourse to offshore printing in a more overtly global context.

The volume editors, in consultation with their team colleagues, had a certain freedom in shaping and organising their material. Volumes I and II are closer to the classical model developed worldwide in the late twentieth century. Volume III, like the supplementary text issued by the French in 1998 to deal with the years after 1945 — on an unmatchable scale, be it added —, had to contend with the problems of assessing still unfolding developments. Academic studies are available, but it was important to collect testimonies from living trade participants. Perhaps inevitably there is a particular emphasis on publishing, a field in which both the relevant editors had long been engaged.

Our readers can judge how successful we have been in presenting a leisurely and yet summary overview of a critical part of Australian literary, intellectual and social history from the European beginnings in 1788. It is, despite all, a provisional account with gaps of which the editors are well aware, all the more so since they saw the *History* as a first step towards two more enduring publications.

The 1995 *BSANZ Bulletin* report on the project named the later proposals as a *Dictionary of the Book in Australia* and a *Historical Dictionary of Newspapers and Journals in Australia*. Both are more ambitious in scope and will require — in our Federation with its fragmentation of resources — much more time and larger teams of dedicated researchers, both salaried and volunteer. There exist already admirable models for both apropos of *ancien régime* France. That country knows how to organise teamwork and has institutions that are capable of carrying it through in the long term. We, with short-term research grants and an inexplicable disdain for compiling basic inventories for future scholars, find ourselves in an almost impossible situation. It is true that the *History* has quite deliberately collected relevant material and that independent researchers have published several monographs, in particular on regional newspapers, that can feed into the collective enterprise. We must end then with a challenge. Can a future generation turn our tentative essays into solid monuments?

Preface

Wallace Kirsop

The long-delayed first volume of *A History of the Book in Australia* has suffered from the inevitable consequences of not appearing at the appropriate moment. The time necessary to supplement a publication fund exhausted by the cost of the second and third volumes has posed serious problems for the editors and their assistants. One editor and three authors have died. Three other contributors, unable to do the updating they considered necessary and therefore unwilling to see their original texts in print, have had to be replaced. The University of Queensland Press decided, to our regret, to withdraw from the project, which now appears under the imprint of the Ancora Press.

Although this is no excuse for our failure to produce the volume in close proximity to its fellows, we note that some other similar enterprises in the English-speaking world have not escaped the difficulty of holding to a tight publication schedule. The compensation for our readers is that the various chapters, and in particular their notes on sources, have made a serious effort to reflect the state of research in the early 2020s. This has been all the more necessary since writing on many, but not all, aspects of the nineteenth-century Australian book world has continued apace over the last three decades.

As is set out in the General Introduction to our series, perspectives have changed considerably in the last quarter of a century. None the less, consistency required that we stick to our original plan of presenting the introduction of a European mode of print publication into the Australian continent after 1788. A few discreet references are made to other approaches, but the essence of the volume is a traditional and conventional book history as the subject was understood at the end of the twentieth century.

Early in our planning we agreed that a serious attempt should be made to take account of the pre-existent system of communication in Indigenous Australia as a prelude to the three projected volumes. This did not preclude appropriate attention to the role of Aboriginal writers and presses in the modern industry, a topic taken up in volume III, the study of the period 1946–2005. Almost two decades further on, that presence is even more obvious. In 2000 we invited the late Penny van Toorn to contribute a chapter that covers the whole of our more than two centuries and that suggests some of the themes we could have developed if we had had the prescience to conceive the task differently when we started out. Her essay and the postscript by Leonie Stevens are, we hope, more than a gesture to a more comprehensive view of the many ways in which people interacted and sent messages to one another in the Australian world over millennia.

Another point that needs to be made strongly is that what was imported in 1788 was based on a complex centuries-old technology that had become an integral part of the culture of the newcomers. The glib assertion that Australia is a 'young' or 'new' country must be rejected. Apart from being wrong in geological terms it is patently absurd in relation to tens of thousands of years of Indigenous civilisation. Even if one accepts the formula 'of recent European settlement', it is essential to grasp the fact that language and tradition define what people are. For those of European heritage location is simply irrelevant. The first arrivals in 1788 and thereafter were in their mass transported English persons and others who brought with them their customs, institutions and literatures. Allowing that what they had to offer was much more recent than what they found at the Antipodes — and thoroughly misunderstood —, it was still of considerable antiquity. Shakespeare and Milton were as much their property as of the populations they had left behind. Being absent from headquarters, from centres in the Northern Hemisphere, did pose problems. All provincials and 'colonials' are well aware of this. It is a constant and dominant theme in Australian book and literary history to this day, with all sorts of responses and reactions on view.

However, short of total integration in Indigenous society, nothing can change the reality that outside settlers in Australia are defined ultimately by their origins. That they could modify and inflect their approaches by virtue of their position on the periphery and construct a distinct identity is a fundamental aspect of the story to be told with an Australian accent.

More obviously perhaps than our colleagues charged with the other volumes in the series we have followed the late twentieth-century categorisation of production, distribution and reception in an unbroken succession of specific topics. The table of contents shows this clearly. Six relatively brief studies of genres that for various reasons were prominent in Australian book publishing in the course of the nineteenth century are inserted between the chapters on distribution and reading. Overlapping could not be avoided altogether. It was in any case characteristic of a trade that before the 1900s often linked manufacture closely to distribution. The specialist publisher, for example, appeared on the scene more recently. There is a certain ambiguity in the treatment of newspapers, a topic to which this volume gives special attention because of their overwhelming bulk in people's reading. Alongside local production, importation continued to be a major source of supply. Like magazines sent from Europe and North America they joined books themselves in keeping the colonists abreast of what was being done and thought in the wider world. The role of libraries of all kinds throughout the period is treated with some care. In these and other areas the aim has been to make the reader acquainted as far as possible with the latest state of research. However, it has to be stated that even now some subjects have been more effectively explored by historians than others. The volume is, therefore, in part an invitation to undertake new investigations.

We have not departed from the intention to make the series accessible to readers other than specialists. As a consequence there are no footnotes, but a more or less brief statement at the end of each chapter about the sources used and available. Given the amount of writing about some topics this has posed problems for authors desiring to give precise references to documents quoted. Parenthetical notes in the texts and careful lists of the relevant sources have attempted to get over this difficulty for interested users without interrupting the flow of the narrative and analysis. The Select Bibliography at the end of the volume brings together and lists much of this material chapter by chapter. It also provides a guide to general documentary and bibliographical works on a subject with a rapidly expanding secondary literature. Judiciously chosen illustrations inserted in some chapters seek to enrich the reader's understanding of the points being discussed.

The limits on space decided for this volume, as for the others, have imposed a sort of straitjacket on our authors. This is not, and was not intended to be, a comprehensive or exhaustive treatment of the various aspects of print culture in the Australian colonies. We have aimed to offer more than a mere digest or synopsis, but we are acutely aware of details that are omitted or skated over. More substantial expositions have to be sought in the quoted sources or, not infrequently, in treatises that remain to be written. The dilemma is not just ours. In his preface to volume VI of *The Cambridge History of the Book in Britain*, covering the period 1830–1914, David McKitterick insists on the 'tentative' nature of conclusions based on incomplete exploration of available sources, notably the huge corpus of publications in the British Isles in the Industrial Age. Thanks to Ferguson and others we have better bibliographical control of the much smaller output of nineteenth-century Australian presses, but on many topics our findings are approximate because more basic research has to be done. Then, too, there are omissions like children's books and in-depth grappling with parallel book cultures like that of the German immigrants who were so numerous and influential in several regions.

The basic problem is the diversity of European Australia, something that is glossed over in crude descriptions of supposedly national characteristics. Separation came before Federation, and the temptation for Australian States to follow different paths has persisted right up to the 2020s. An unavoidably rapid synthesis can perhaps do no more than hint at these complexities. At all events we can propose ways of coming to grips with what newcomers did and thought they were doing in the lands they occupied.

CHAPTER 1

A Book by Any Other Name? Towards a Social History of the Book in Aboriginal Australia

†Penny van Toorn

Europe and 'the People Without Books'

Books have often served as icons of Western civilisation, and their fate has reflected the progress of empire — or the threats thereto. While some Australian literary landscapes are dotted with the bodies of lost explorers and ailing stockmen, others are littered with torn, rotting, coverless, or broken-spined books. In the novels of canonical authors such as Patrick White, Randolph Stow and David Malouf, the wilderness is a place where books and papers are manifestly vulnerable, and where cultures of writing and reading are difficult to sustain. The explorer's exhaustion and disorientation are reflected in the deterioration of his journal. Violent rainstorms wash ink from paper and turn it back into pulp. Pages, whole or in shreds, flutter away in the searing wind, or lie scattered in mouldy drifts on the floors of abandoned buildings. The lonely settler's degeneration is manifest in acts of bibliocide that involve tearing the covers off once-cherished books to prop up wobbly furniture, or ripping out printed pages to light the fire or mop up spills. The literary motif of the damaged or annihilated book functions as part of a grand narrative of the dangers posed to Western civilisation by the ravages of a hostile environment, natural and/or social. Books are exposed to the devastating effects of wild wind and weather in regions inhabited by 'wild', bookless peoples.

The British and European settlers who came to Australia from 1788 onwards brought with them a firmly established sense of what a book was. The business of making and selling books had been going on long enough in England and Europe for people to have achieved a clear perception of what kinds of objects could legitimately be called books. Many convicts and free settlers in Australia did not know how to read, and may not have been very familiar with the contents of books, but they knew a book when they saw one, and they saw nothing resembling books in Aboriginal cultures. Books were defined Eurocentrically in a manner that excluded the objects Aboriginal societies had developed to serve as sign-carriers. To colonial European eyes, books were bound gatherings of writing(s), usually on paper, and the paradigm of writing was alphabetic script. Non-Western peoples' textual objects that did not contain alphabetic script were therefore not categorised as books, unless (like certain Mesoamerican 'books of the devil') they bore a close physical resemblance to European book forms such as the medieval codex or the Renaissance printed book.

That pre-contact Aboriginal societies were without European-style books and alphabetic writing was in itself a politically neutral fact of Indigenous cultural history. This historical fact became politically charged, however, by the symbolic values Europeans attached to books. Europeans viewed books and alphabetic writing as signs of their own cultural superiority over Indigenous societies, whom they deemed to be without history, without writing, without books. Books and alphabetic literacy were taken to be a sign of cultural advancement. They were one of the many material and cultural benefits that European philanthropists and missionaries believed Indigenous peoples needed, in order to be 'raised up' to the level of Europeans.

These Eurocentric understandings of what a book was, how it might function, and what its very existence said about its culture of origin remained largely undisturbed in Australia until the later decades of the twentieth century when Aboriginal stories and songs previously collected by anthropologists were incorporated into major poetry anthologies. This assimilation made it possible for non-Indigenous Australians to understand that, in certain respects at least, Indigenous oral narratives and songs performed functions comparable with those of certain kinds of texts in Western print cultures and created the conditions under which the question of 'What counts as a book?' could be reopened.

By the late 1990s, it became feasible for members of settler societies to entertain the possibility that, far from being exclusively a European artifact, books were and had always been a cultural universal. In his 1998 Garnett Sedgewick Memorial Lecture, the eminent Canadian poet Robert Bringhurst lamented the Eurocentricity of literary historians who focused exclusively on books and writing in the narrow European sense. These historians were leaving out of account the rich tradition of Indigenous oral narratives preserved in the manuscripts and publications of anthropologists, and in the narrative practices of contemporary Indigenous communities. Every language, Bringhurst argued, has its own distinct literature, whether or not it is 'lettered' in the European sense. Nor do books necessarily have to exist in material form. While acknowledging that the verbal dimension of these narratives remained intangible until anthropologists wrote the words down and published them, Bringhurst sought to add prestige to Indigenous oral texts by calling them 'books'. He urged that the Indigenous storytellers whose words Franz Boaz transcribed in the 1890s, for example, should be regarded not as native informants but rather as authors. Conversely, Boaz should be known not as the author of the book version of these stories, but rather as the scribe, translator and editor.

Accommodating as it is, the view that books are a cultural universal substitutes one mode of Eurocentrism for another. The Eurocentric perspective remains, only now it works through a process of inclusion rather than one of exclusion. Like Bringhurst, Germaine Warkentin has urged that books be defined in terms of their functions rather than by their physical characteristics. Arguing that Indigenous writing systems and sign-carriers should come within the purview of book history, Warkentin shifts the focus away from the book as object. 'The choice is not between objects that are books and objects that are not', she maintains, 'rather it is the much more interesting difference between cultures that exhibit "bookishness" and those that don't'. Warkentin warns against 'reduc[ing] a Native category to a European understanding of it', yet concentrating on bookishness rather than books does not necessarily solve the problem of understanding non-European cultures in terms of European paradigms and terms of reference. To define all artifacts that perform 'bookish' functions as variants of 'books' is to obscure material, cultural and historical differences between cultures.

Warkentin endeavours to stretch the meaning of the word 'book' by stressing that 'it is the individual culture that determines, inflects, and reinvents what it wishes to be its books'. The question cannot be 'What is a book?' but rather 'How does a given culture define what a book is?' Some Indigenous communities, however, might not be concerned with the question of whether or not their traditional textual artifacts are, as we say in English, 'bookish' in form or in function. They might not be pleased to see their artifacts as 'inflections' or 'reinventions' of a European category. Despite the incursions of global capitalism, and the many legal and other contexts where power and authority are effectively monocentric, it is still true to say that the world has many alternative centres of cultural authority. If members of traditional Aboriginal cultures were to address the question of how different sign-carriers can be compared, they might well do so from their own distinctive directions, asking, for example, how a book compares to a message stick, or a ritually painted body, or an elaborately prepared ceremonial ground. The question, then, would not be 'How is an Aboriginal message stick bookish?' but rather 'How is a book "message stick-ish"?' It might even be conceded that it is up to non-Aboriginal cultures to decide what they wish to be their message sticks. And as well as seeing the prestige of books and writing as *leading to* a denigration of cultures that lacked these markers of 'advancement', one might also calculate the extent to which the prestige of books and writing *grew out of* an imperialist ideological need to construct European cultures as superior to the cultures of those whose lands they were usurping.

Faced with the multicentredness of cultural authority, and a desire to move beyond a facile celebration of cultural relativity, Walter D. Mignolo has argued for a philological and comparative approach to book history. Mignolo has stressed the need to consider the locus and politics of scholarly enunciation, a consideration that might begin by focusing on the word 'book' itself:

Book is neither the universal name nor the universal concept associated with solid surfaces in which graphic signs are inscribed, preserved, and transmitted. It is only from the point of view of a culture capable of applying its regional concept to similar practices and objects of other cultures that could see Middle East clay tablets and Egyptian papyrus [or other inscribed objects] as forerunners [or variants] of Western and Christian books.

When practitioners of Western academic disciplines bring non-Western textual artifacts within the purview of a field called 'book history', they perpetuate colonial power relations by demonstrating a continued desire to understand non-European cultures in terms of European categories and concepts. And yet, when Indigenous peoples engage with (European) books and writing within their own terms of reference and protocols of communication, they often demonstrate the degree to which they remain culturally unassimilated. Books, in other words, may cease to function as (European) books when they move across cultural boundaries. A book by any other name may not be a book. At the same time as book historians are assimilating non-European sign carriers into the category of the book, non-European cultures have reinvented and recontextualised books in a manner that transforms them into something not entirely bookish (in the European sense).

How might Indigenous Australians be included in histories of the book without being characterised (Eurocentrically) as peoples traditionally without books, or (equally Eurocentrically) as peoples whose traditional means of communication are bookish in function or form? Both forms of Eurocentrism — the exclusive, and the assimilative — are made possible by a tendency to imagine cultures as discrete, bounded domains located on an abstract, ahistorical plane. In historical reality, in ex-colonial societies, Indigenous and non-Indigenous cultures have become entangled in complex ways. To pretend otherwise is to perpetuate what Johannes Fabian has called 'the denial of coevalness', and to practise a mode of book history that approaches questions of cultural difference in ahistorical terms. Without imagining that the biases and blind spots of my language and locus of enunciation can be avoided, this chapter focuses on a series of moments in the history of this entanglement between Indigenous and non-Indigenous Australian cultures. These moments open up a range of questions such as: To what classes of objects did books (and pieces of books) correspond in the minds of Aboriginal peoples during the early contact period? How might these correspondences have shaped Aboriginal peoples' engagement with books and writing, and their early negotiations of the social roles and relations that centre around books and writing? How have Aboriginal peoples developed their own book cultures today? How do the social relations within which they write, publish and read books differ from those that prevail in European book cultures? And finally, how have Aboriginal and non-Aboriginal peoples gone about the process of making books together?

White men's message sticks and Black men's letters

Henry Reynolds has shown that Aboriginal peoples living considerable distances beyond the outskirts of white settlement felt the impact of European presence in the form of biological pathogens, animals and material objects. Those who survived the ravages of introduced diseases found uses for the settlers' goods and chattels, some of which were transported across vast distances along Aboriginal trade routes. Aboriginal peoples collected iron implements such as tomahawks, knives, pots and pans, as well as glass bottles, clothing, blankets, sewing implements and, occasionally, written and printed texts. Amongst the diverse array of articles contained in an Aboriginal camp in Gippsland in 1841, for example, were two children's copybooks, a bible, and newspapers from London, Glasgow and Aberdeen.

While books and writing were almost synonymous in the minds of Europeans, Aboriginal peoples in the early contact years would have encountered alphabetic writing on a wide variety of European sign-carriers in addition to books and papers. Writing and books, for them, may not have been bound so closely together in conceptual terms as they have been in post-Renaissance European cultures. As I have suggested elsewhere, the nature of early Aboriginal inscriptions of alphabetic characters carved on wooden objects suggests that they were probably not copied from printed books, magazines or newspapers, but from surfaces other than paper, for example, from carved, painted, stamped or stencilled objects such as milestones, coins, ships, packing crates, flour bags, barrels, china, and metal weapons, tools and utensils. In comparison with these sign-carriers, books and papers are fragile objects. If books came into Aboriginal hands in areas remote from white settlement, they are unlikely to have been in anything like mint condition.

Aboriginal peoples who encountered alphabetic writing before becoming literate in the European sense would not necessarily have engaged with alphabetic characters as a phonographic code for (the English) language. From the little evidence that is available, their engagement with alphabetic writing was more likely to depend on the degree to which it resembled the shapes of their own traditional inscriptions. The same principle applied to Aboriginal engagements with European sign-carriers such as papers and books (or pieces of books). Aboriginal and settler societies each assimilated the other's textual artifacts into their own cultural categories, and integrated them into their own structures of social relations.

There is evidence to suggest that Indigenous and non-Indigenous societies saw the other's communication technologies as analogous to their own. For example, the popular white perception of Aboriginal message sticks was that they were the 'blackfellows' letters', and there are some recorded cases where message sticks were read as a series of sentences, or where the recipients had been able to decipher the message without the aid of the messenger. Ethnologists, however, saw the equation between message sticks and letters as misleading. They maintained that message sticks carried ideographic signs, the primary function of which was to aid the messenger's memory, not to preserve a script for a given set of words. The message lived not in the message stick but in the messenger's memory and voice. Unlike books, message sticks were not the primary locus for a verbal text, but a means of recycling information from one oral context to another.

As well as serving as a memory aid, message sticks also functioned as a type of 'passport'. They were '*bona fides* of the bearer' and 'a guarantee of good faith to show that there was no gammon'. Dawson emphasised that 'As the office of messenger is of very great importance, the persons filling it are considered sacred while on duty; very much as an ambassador, herald, or bearer of a flag of truce is treated among civilized nations'. When written documents initially came into Aboriginal peoples' hands, they were sometimes made to serve in this manner as passports, flags of truce, or badges of office. Despite the disparity between the kinds of signs carried on message sticks and written texts, *as objects* the two could be made to perform similar functions.

In the early 1840s, for instance, George Augustus Robinson, Chief Protector of Aborigines at Port Phillip, made extensive excursions throughout what is now the State of Victoria. When contacting unfamiliar tribes for the first time, Robinson used known Aboriginal people from nearby areas as go-betweens or messengers. He issued the messengers with visiting cards something like those used in polite British and colonial social circles. Without these messengers and their paper message sticks, Robinson would in all likelihood have been attacked by the 'wild natives' he wished to befriend and defend.

Some of Robinson's visiting cards were signed by himself; others were signed by Superintendent Charles Joseph La Trobe. Many were merely printed pro formas, and had nothing hand-written on them at all. However, what was written or printed on the cards was of no consequence, as the cards had ceased to function as phonographically written texts as soon as they passed into Aboriginal hands. Although they called the cards 'letters', the Aboriginal messengers and recipients engaged with the cards as alien *objects* that could serve the same functions as message sticks in their own culture(s). As objects, Robinson's visiting cards were inserted into Aboriginal cultural categories, where they functioned not only like message sticks, but like the special spears, balls of clay, hairnets, feathered branches, body paintings and other tokens traditionally carried and/or worn by messengers to signify their special status, indicate the nature of their message, and guarantee them safe passage through foreign country. Robinson's visiting cards may also have enhanced his standing in the eyes of the Aboriginal communities he contacted. In some areas, message sticks were usually sent by men of some seniority. By sending out visiting cards, which Aborigines saw as white man's message sticks, Robinson may have elevated himself to a high rank in the eyes of the Aboriginal groups he visited.

Robinson's practice of sending cards was imitated by Aboriginal groups. Aborigines living on Edward Stone Parker's station on the Loddon River near Mt Franklin received 'letters' from Aborigines living to the south, inviting them to visit Melbourne. Like Robinson's visiting cards, these 'letters' were written documents that were not deciphered phonographically, but were treated rather as badges of the messengers' office. The message was delivered orally by memory, not read verbatim off the paper. What was written on the paper was in Aboriginal cultural terms completely unimportant. During the 1840s, Parker recorded in his journal that one such 'letter' was simply 'a dirty fragment from the log book of a ship. The natives however accepted it as a formal proposal for them to visit their Melbourne friends'. Here the dismembered book has been transformed in its new cultural context into something radically other than a (European) book.

Forty years after Robinson was sending out his visiting cards, Aboriginal people at Coranderrk Reserve were writing their own petitions to government officials. Under Woiwurrung law, William Barak, the clan-head on the land on which Coranderrk was established, was the rightful spokesperson for the reserve community. One of Barak's 'speakers' — men to whom he 'gave his words' — was Thomas Dunolly, a literate younger man. When Barak wished to write petitions and letters on behalf of the Coranderrk community, Dunolly's status as a 'speaker' entitled him to act as scribe. The Coranderrk residents thus generated written texts from within a traditional Indigenous, orally grounded structure of authority.

In important communications with powerful government officials, the Coranderrk leaders appeared to believe that writing was no substitute for lawfully authorised, properly witnessed, face-to-face dialogue. While the senior men of Coranderrk knew they had to put their complaints on paper to make white authorities take notice, under the leadership of William Barak delegations of men from Coranderrk would walk to Melbourne to hand-deliver their written petitions to government and Protection Board officials. A measure of the Coranderrk men's belief in the importance of face-to-face communication can be seen in the fact that the round trip from Coranderrk to Melbourne and back was well over 100 kilometres. The men often travelled through the night and had little or no food. Barak walked with a limp from a broken leg that had never healed properly. What the men were doing was using written texts according to their own traditional protocols of communication. By speaking directly to the individuals to whom their petitions were addressed, Barak and the other senior men were using written documents as though they were message sticks or other badges of office that authorised their spoken words. Only when these written petitions passed out of the Coranderrk men's hands and into the white bureaucracy did they cease to work as ancillary aids to oral enunciation and become instead the primary locus of the men's message.

In parts of central and northern Australia, written texts functioned in a manner akin to that of message sticks until well into the twentieth century. Spencer and Gillen observed the use of 'paper yabber' as a badge of office in the Northern Territory. Seeing 'two strange natives coming into our camp' carrying letters in a cleft stick, they noted that:

> Though the natives had come through strange tribes . . . yet so long as they carried this emblem of the fact that they were messengers, they were perfectly safe . . . Such messengers always carry a token of some kind — very often a sacred stick or bull-roarer. Their persons are always safe, and so the same safety is granted to natives carrying 'paper yabbers' . . .

Books as a technology of power

For many Aboriginal peoples, the word 'book' is a foreign word, part of the language of the 'gubbas', the 'migloos', the 'balanda', the 'kardiya', or the white man. Books have functioned historically as part of a harsh, externally imposed technology of power. The meaning of 'book' in Aboriginal English carries the memory of oppression. Used as a noun or adjective, the word 'book' denotes 'European law or laws, characteristically written down, as opposed to Aboriginal law which is contained in oral tradition'. 'Book' is used metonymically as 'the icon of literate culture, significant because it is from this written tradition that the laws used to control Aboriginal people are drawn'. In the Northern Territory, for example, Mudburra man, Hobbles Danayarri, used the word 'book' to explain the position of Aboriginal trackers ordered to kill other Aboriginal people: 'They got that book all over from Captain Cook [the government]. "You might see blackfellows anywhere longa this country, you'll have to get them together and if them too wild, and shoot [the] whole lot." Captain Cook got the order from book'.

Secular book law was backed up by the 'Holy Book', invoked by missionaries and reserve managers as a source of Christian morality and a path to spiritual salvation. This book loomed so large in the lives of Arrernte people at Hermannsburg Mission in the Northern Territory that they referred to everything associated with Christianity — church buildings, church sermons and meetings, as well as the Bible — as 'pepe' (paper). This tendency not to discriminate between books and other textual forms is not confined to Central Australia. For instance, 'bihbar' in Western Bundjalung, and 'piipa' in Wangkumara refer to books, paper, letters or mail.

Books were also part of the daily administrative apparatus of reserve life. Superintendents used books to carry out roll-calls, to record the distribution of food, clothing and tobacco rations, to keep track of the work carried out by the adults, and to record the children's attendance at school. Rations, monetary payments and certain privileges were dispensed or withheld on the basis of information recorded in books. If disputes arose, information contained in the record books was often used to settle the matter. Many discrepancies existed between Aboriginal peoples' recollections and the facts as recorded in the superintendents' documents. Books were therefore regarded with suspicion if not hostility. The information they contained was written, read and acted upon by white authorities. On the authority of book records, white officials denied the accuracy of Aboriginal memory, undermined the truth value of Aboriginal peoples' spoken words, and subverted the structures of authority that bound Aboriginal societies together.

A white man could make a book say whatever he wanted it to say. Sometimes the same book could say different things on different occasions of reading. Accordingly, a significant proportion of Aboriginal peoples' attribute little authority to books. For example, in the late 1980s, Australian artist and Aboriginal advocate, Chips Mackinolty, recalled having:

> explained to Wainburranga the non-Aboriginal account of Captain Cook. When Wainburranga relayed this account to the people back at Beswick, it was greeted with some hilarity. How did white people know about Captain Cook? Only through books, of course: books are notoriously changeable.

Oral narratives, on the other hand, are more likely to be viewed as reliable and permanent, especially if they are lodged in the land. Wandjuk Marika says, 'Many are the stories I could tell you — *already there in the land*'. Bill Neidje likens the land to a reliable, indestructible book: 'Our story is in the land . . . it is written in those sacred places . . . Dreaming place . . . you can't change it, no matter who you are'. Books that are based on oral narratives may be reliable, however, if they are produced in proper, lawful ways. Neidje tells Stephen Davis: 'I give you this story. This proper, true story. People can listen. I'm telling this while you've got time . . . time for you to make something, you know . . . history . . . book'.

Why do stories 'already there in the land' need to be transferred into books? Usually this need is explained with the aid of framing narratives about the imminent extinction of fragile oral traditions, or the vulnerability of Aboriginal lands to destruction by white development. Yet books can intensify the dangers they ostensibly attempt to alleviate. When given material existence and mass-produced in book form, stories once lodged in one unique place are disseminated indiscriminately over large expanses of space and time. Books pose a potential threat to the differential rights to certain kinds of knowledge that pertain in Aboriginal cultures. How might one decide what goes into a book in a culture where the transmission of information is restricted according to age, gender, kinship, mortuary practices, and affiliations to Country? How might one transfer an oral narrative into a book in a culture that observes strict laws governing how, where, and when certain kinds of knowledge must, and must not, be transmitted? How might book publishing — a form of mass reproduction and mass circulation — be adapted to the needs of Aboriginal cultures that are rooted in specific places, and bound together through face-to-face social interactions? Aboriginal peoples are well aware that books have the potential to violate traditional ownership and inheritance laws. By disseminating stories previously lodged in specific sites, books can transform owned textual territories into a *terra nullius* that belongs simultaneously to no one and everyone.

A number of books have been published that contain secret, sacred knowledge that should never have passed into the public sphere.

Wandjuk Marika, for example, recalls how upset he and his family were to see information they had divulged to anthropologists being broadcast indiscriminately in books. In recording his own life story for publication in book form, Wandjuk Marika points out that he has been careful not to include any secret, sacred knowledge. Unable to control the circulation of the book, he includes nothing that children, women, Balanda (whites) and other unauthorised people may not lawfully know: 'I'm not going to say it . . . The book will spread out too far'. By contrast, in oral contexts of transmission, Wandjuk would have been able to tailor each story to the knowledge-rights of each different audience he was addressing. His published narrative of sacred events is merely 'one for the books'. In Standard English, something that is special, noteworthy, important, deserving of fame is said to be 'one for the books'. For Wandjuk Marika, however, 'one for the books' would mean something altogether different — a version of a story designed to keep certain kinds of information secret, an abridged, secular rendition of a larger, more powerful, potentially more dangerous story.

Some Aboriginal communities in central and northern Australia have actively resisted assimilation into European book cultures. Research by Jennifer Biddle at the Warlpiri community at Lajamanu in the Northern Territory suggests that, in that particular community, alphabetic writing is perceived as a threat to traditional, orally grounded structures of authority. Against those who have seen *kuruwarri* signs (or Warlpiri iconography in Nancy Munn's terms) as a precursor of European writing, Biddle argues that the painting of these symbols is a 'redressive writing', a mode of inscription aimed specifically at preserving differential rights to knowledge and authority, both amongst the local Warlpiri people and between them and Kardiya (whites). As Jimmy Jampijimpa Robertson puts it, 'Kardiya . . . can't read it. No. (laughing) They got to look that paper. They got to read from a book, not from painting'. While *kuruwarri* painting reinstitutes Warlpiri structures of authority, writing and books are seen at Lajamanu as a province of white authority. Outside the school, most of the writing produced in the community is addressed to Europeans. Although literacy levels are high in all but the older age groups, many Warlpiri people appear not to feel authorised to generate alphabetically written texts. They therefore tend to seek white people to act as their scribes or to witness, authorise, or check the texts they produce.

Books and social relations

Like other elements of material culture, books are a focal point around which social roles and relations are organised. These roles and relations change not only across time, but also as books move from one cultural context to another. Yet, as Alison Ravenscroft has pointed out:

> Dominant western conceptions of the written text tend to assume that the book carries the same relations across cultures and indeed this is the assumption that commonly shapes the encounter between western publishing structures and Aboriginal writers. White readers, editors and publishers tend to apprehend Black writers' texts according to a singular notion of the book and its powers.

As noted above, books and writing were integrated into traditional Aboriginal cultural practices and social structures during the nineteenth century. What kinds of social roles and relations are forming around books at different points on the spectrum of Aboriginal Australian cultures?

Looking first at the moment of writing, European and Aboriginal authorial practices are shaped by disparate cultural values, laws and conceptions of the addressee. In Western book cultures, the qualifications for authorship and readership differ from those in traditional Aboriginal cultures (among which there is considerable variety). In Western cultures, any person who can find a publisher is potentially the author of a book on any topic. Any literate person is potentially a reader. In traditional Aboriginal societies, by contrast, one's authority to divulge and receive certain kinds of information may be determined by one's connections to specific sections of country, one's place in the kinship network, one's gender, age and/or stage of initiation. By such criteria, for example, Wandjuk Marika could lawfully speak about his country, culture and history in *Wandjuk Marika: Life Story* (1995).

In Western print cultures, book authorship is usually conceptualised as a solitary, individual activity, even though the process of producing a book involves editors, designers, and many other people whose input affects the experience of the reader. This romantic individualist model is not appropriate to the circumstances under which many Aboriginal peoples have produced written texts. During the nineteenth century, Aboriginal peoples participated in translation work, and related stories, songs and other cultural knowledge to ethnologists and linguists. If their role was acknowledged at all in the resulting publications, these Aboriginal collaborators were called 'native informants' rather than co-authors. This exclusion of Aboriginal people from the category of (co-)author continued in some instances into the middle decades of the twentieth century. In 1962, Waipuldanya was not named as the author of his own autobiography *I, The Aboriginal*. Despite the book's title, and the fact that the narrative was written in the first person, the front cover and title-page of *I, The Aboriginal* named Anglo-Australian journalist, Douglas Lockwood, as the author. Douglas's role had in fact been to interview Waipuldanya and to transcribe and edit his story for publication. In his own autobiography, Waipuldanya had been relegated to the role of native informant rather than author or co-author.

Since the 1960s, a growing number of Aboriginal people have authored books of various kinds, some working alone, others in collaborative relationships either with non-Aboriginal people or with members of their own families or other Aboriginal associates. Black-white collaborations have been seen both as a process that 'dilutes' the authentic Aboriginality of the resulting books, and as a means by which an Aboriginal author can gain a greater degree of control over the final published text by 'in-sourcing' part of the editorial process. Depending on the book's intended readership or market, the role of the 'white hand' may be either obscured or highlighted. This is usually a decision made by the publishing house. Books aimed at tourist and overseas markets tend to play down white involvement in an effort to appear 'authentically' Aboriginal. In academic and other markets where cultural *métissage* is viewed as an asset, the collaborative production process may be partly what the book is about.

If books structure social roles and relations differently in different cultures (and in different intra-cultural spheres), what kinds of relations develop between authors, co-authors, editors and readers in contexts where Indigenous and non-Indigenous peoples work together in the making of books? How do these relations shape the content and language of Aboriginal-authored books? Alison Ravenscroft has broached such questions in relation to her work on *Auntie Rita* (1994) with Rita Huggins and Jackie Huggins. She suggests that, unlike most Western authors who address a readership of strangers, Rita Huggins was writing in large measure for an existing community of family members and friends. Her sense of readership was based 'largely in the face-to-face, in corporeality, and a shared life, rather than in technologically extended communications such as print, although of course Aboriginal communities use these technologies'. Rita wrote the book with the assistance of her daughter Jackie Huggins, and with editor Ravenscroft who was inserted into the family by being 'asked to call Rita "Auntie", the customary term of respect for Aboriginal women elders'.

Rita Huggins's sense of the people she was writing for, and of what kind of work her book would do in *their* world, shaped both the form and content of *Auntie Rita*. As Ravenscroft has noted, Rita addressed her readers in quiet, intimate tones, as a known, familiar 'you', as 'someone whom she knows and loves . . . someone who is standing close by'. Because she wanted her book to entertain and give enjoyment to this readership, she left out some of her most disturbing experiences: 'Her Aboriginal readership already knew the painful and unexpurgated life. It was their own'. When, at the launch of the book, Rita met members of her unknown white readership, she drew them into a relationship of community. She spoke with each person at length, and continued that 'conversation she had started in the flesh' by writing 'a veritable letter on the flyleaf' of each book as she signed it. Each copy of the book she sent out into the world at the launch carried on it a tangible trace of her bodily presence.

While Rita Huggins's authorial practices were grounded in a paradigm of face-to-face communication with family and friends, those of her daughter Jackie Huggins were shaped by a print-based sense of the reader as a white stranger. Jackie Huggins saw the book as a political document that could open the eyes of white readers to unknown or misunderstood aspects of Australia's Black history. For this reason, she wanted to include painful incidents that Rita herself wished to omit. While Jackie used a gentle, loving voice, and departed from standard English when addressing her mother in the book, she addressed the reader-as-stranger in a more academic, public voice, providing background information that placed her mother's life in its historical context.

Ruby Langford Ginibi's *Haunted By the Past* (1999) was also produced through a process of collaboration between Aboriginal family members with white editorial assistance — Ruby and her son Nobby (the biographical subject), and myself. Nobby began to write his story while in prison, but found the task too difficult, so Ruby decided to write Nobby's story herself. She did a good deal of writing while Nobby was still behind bars, but when he was released in March 1996 he was able to sit down with Ruby and record some of his early memories and later experiences on tape. Ruby and Nobby had been separated for years at a time by prison walls. Making the book together gave them both a chance to share certain parts of their lives for the first time.

In an important sense, *Haunted by the Past* is a gift from Ruby to Nobby, an assertion of her enduring love, trust and faith in her son. It is also an attempt both to retrieve and to change the meaning of Nobby's life as previously recorded in the police, court and prison records. The book is dedicated to Nobby and to 'every mother's son or daughter who has fallen foul of the Westminster system of justice that came with the first squatters and settlers in 1788'. These people, like Rita Huggins's family and friends, are already familiar with the kinds of difficulties Ruby and Nobby have lived through. Yet the content and tone of *Haunted by the Past* are shaped by Ruby's desire to reveal to (mainly white) readers a dimension of life most would not have directly experienced themselves. Ruby wanted to confront an unknown, unknowing readership of white Australians whose lives were unlikely to have been touched by racial prejudice or the legal justice system.

Although, like Jackie Huggins, Ruby addressed a readership of strangers, like Rita Huggins, her primary paradigm of social relations was based in the face-to-face. Paradoxically, she wanted to have a stranger — or someone who could anticipate the needs of strangers — physically present to serve as a sounding board. This was one of my roles. Reading over her drafts, I would identify points in the narrative where Ruby needed to add extra information to make the story clearer. Like Alison Ravenscroft with Rita Huggins, and Jennifer Isaacs with Wandjuk Marika, I was privileged to be incorporated into Ruby's network of familial relations. She made me her 'tita' (sister). As well as being Ruby's 'tita', however, I understood that, as Ruby's editorial assistant, one of my roles was to be a surrogate stranger, a representative of the person who does not know Ruby's family history.

The question of the imagined reader was complicated by the fact that Ruby was assuming that some, but by no means all, of those who would be reading *Haunted by the Past* would already have read parts of Nobby's story in Ruby's autobiography, *Don't Take Your Love to Town*, a book that has remained continuously in print since 1988. As a story, *Haunted by the Past* had to stand on its own; it had to be addressed to a reader presumed to have no prior knowledge of Ruby's family history. Whenever Ruby rewrote events already covered in the earlier book, she would acknowledge that this was the case, in order to avoid being accused of the cardinal literary sin of repetition. To complicate matters further, Ruby and Nobby were acutely aware that some of their potential readers were not strangers at all, but individuals involved in events recounted in the book. Their names had to be suppressed in order to avoid possible legal action or more direct reprisals.

As well as being a sounding board, I was asked by Ruby to tidy up aspects of the text such as spelling and punctuation, but under no circumstances was I to sacrifice the sense of her voice speaking through the text. Ruby may have seen herself as addressing a readership of strangers, but she wanted them to be able to hear her voice in their mind's ear. She positioned herself imaginatively in the bodily proximity of readers, while also addressing them as strangers. This dialogic, face-to-face relation is reflected in Ruby's use of the word 'aye?', a word which Ian Henderson has described as 'a hand held out to the reader'. Strangers they may have been, but Ruby's readers were also urged to be with her, standing by her, *at* her side and *on* her side.

In *The Darker Side of the Renaissance*, Mignolo has argued that, in colonial contexts, writing has been used as an 'instrument to tame the voice'. Part of my work with Ruby involved adding punctuation and paragraph breaks without taking away from the oral feel of the text. Ruby's first drafts included very few full stops. Sections of her draft did not contain discrete sentences, but long chains of compound sentences joined together with the word 'and'. If a sentence is a grammatical concept grounded in writing and print rather than in oral utterance, Ruby's sentenceless prose reflected an oral paradigm of enunciation, an escape from the prison house of grammatically correct writing. One of my jobs was to add full stops to Ruby's prose where appropriate. Yet when Ruby reads from her books, she usually puts the 'ands' back in. Her readings are a process of re-voicing, an implicit reclaiming of the voice's freedom to break out of the bounds of the sentence. The voice has primacy over the book as a source of authority. Although Ruby takes full political advantage of the book's ability to disseminate knowledge to strangers dispersed over time and space, the primary home of her story is perhaps not in the material artifact of the book, but in the social contexts in which it is re-voiced. This re-voicing may be actual, as in the case of 'live' readings, or imaginary as when readers 'hear' her voice as carried to them through the medium of the book. In either case, the book is not the main locus of the story, but rather a means of recycling the text from one (real or imagined) oral context to another.

The challenge of historicity

In emphasising this oral paradigm, I do not essentialise Aboriginal cultures in the pre-contact oral tradition. The manifold shortcomings of the oral-literate binary are by now well established, and it is clear that parts of Indigenous Australian society are no more or less 'oral' than sections of non-Aboriginal society. It is possible, however, to see patterns of connection between early and more recent phases of Aboriginal book history, for example, in the tendency to work collaboratively, in the wariness towards books and writing as technologies of an alien power, in the practice of textually positioning readers as physically present to the author, and in the use of books and writing as a means of carrying stories from one (actual or imagined) context of oral enunciation to another.

The obvious challenge to those concerned with book history in Aboriginal Australia is to retain a cultural materialist focus that distinguishes between books and other textual artifacts without dismissing Aboriginal cultures as inferior to European ones. If the twin temptations of equating booklessness with primitivity and of seeing books as a cultural universal can be resisted, it is historically valid and politically neutral to say that Aboriginal book history begins with the arrival of European material culture on Australian shores. Like Nobby Langford's life, contemporary Aboriginal engagements with books are manifestly haunted by the past — not a cloudy universal past of human semiosis, but a finite history of entanglement between practitioners of specific cultures at specific moments in particular physical, social and political environments.

NOTE ON SOURCES

The images of damaged and destroyed books are found in Patrick White's *Voss* (1957), Randolph Stow's *Tourmaline* (1963) and David Malouf's *Remembering Babylon* (1993).

There is an extensive literature dealing with non-European systems of graphic signification. Most useful in the present context has been Walter D. Mignolo's *The Darker Side of the Renaissance: Literacy, Territoriality, and Colonization*, Ann Arbor, University of Michigan Press, 1995, which is the source of all quotations attributed to Mignolo.

Transcribed Aboriginal songs are published as poetry in Rodney Hall, ed., *The Collins Book of Australian Poetry*, Sydney, Collins, 1981; Leonie Kramer, ed., *My Country: Australian Poetry and Short Stories*, Sydney, Lansdowne, 1985; Les Murray, ed., *The New Oxford Book of Australian Verse*, Melbourne, OUP, 1986; and Ken Goodwin and Alan Lawson, eds, *The Macmillan Anthology of Australian Literature*, South Melbourne, Macmillan, 1990.

Robert Bringhurst's Sedgewick Lecture, 'Native American Oral Literatures and the Unity of the Humanities', was presented at the First Nations House of Learning, University of British Columbia, Vancouver, 17 July 1998. Germaine Warkentin's discussion of 'bookishness' appears in 'In Search of "The Word of the Other": Aboriginal Sign Systems and the History of the Book in Canada', *Book History*, vol.2, 1999, pp. 1-27.

Johannes Fabian explores the mechanisms and consequences of the 'denial of co-evalness' in *Time and the Other: How Anthropology Makes its Object*, New York, Columbia University Press, 1983. The concept of 'entanglement' is developed by Nicholas Thomas in *Entangled Objects: Exchange, Material Culture, and Colonialism in the Pacific*, Cambridge, Massachusetts, Harvard University Press, 1991. Regular contact and entanglement between Aboriginal and settler societies occurred at different times in different parts of Australia, beginning at Sydney Cove in 1788 (and spreading west after 1813), in Tasmania in 1803, in Victoria, South Australia and in the south-west of Western Australia in the 1830s, and in central and northern Australia in the second half of the nineteenth century and the early decades of the twentieth century. The list of European articles found in the Aboriginal camp in Gippsland is from Henry Reynolds, *The Other Side of the Frontier*, Townsville, Queensland, History Department, James Cook University, 1981. I offer a theoretical exploration of initial Aboriginal engagements with alphabetic and numerical scripts, and with textual objects other than books, in 'Transactions on the Borderlands of Aboriginal Writing', *Social Semiotics*, vol.11, no.2, 2001, pp. 209-27.

Information about message sticks, especially the question of whether or not they carry phonographic signs, is derived from F. N. Bucknell, 'Message Sticks and Their Meanings by Mr Bucknell', *Australasian Anthropological Journal*, 27 February 1897, p. 10; R. Hamlyn-Harris, 'On Messages and "Message Sticks" Employed Among the Queensland Aborigines', *Memoirs of the Queensland Museum*, vol.6, 1918, pp. 13-35; W. W. Thorpe, 'Aboriginal Message Sticks', *Australian Museum Magazine*, vol.2, no.12, 1926, pp. 423-25; C. P. Mountford, 'Aboriginal Message Sticks from the Nullabor Plains', *Transactions of the Royal Society of South Australia*, vol.62, no.1, pp. 122-26; James Dawson, *Australian Aborigines*, Melbourne, George Robertson, 1881; and A. W. Howitt, *The Native Tribes of South-East Australia*, London, Macmillan, 1904.

Mention of Aboriginal use of alphabetically written and printed documents as badges of office and passports is made in Jan Critchett's *A Distant Field of Murder: Western District Frontiers 1834–1848*, Carlton, Victoria, MUP, 1990; Edgar Morrison, *Early Days on the Loddon Valley: Memoirs of Edward Stone Parker 1802–1865*, [Yandoit, Victoria, The Editor, 1965]; as well as in Howitt and Dawson. Critchett's *A Distant Field of Murder* also describes G. A. Robinson's use of visiting cards.

The Coranderrk residents' assimilation of alphabetic writing into their own social protocols of communication is discussed in Diane E.

Barwick, *Rebellion at Coranderrk*, Laura E. Barwick and Richard E. Barwick, eds, Canberra, Aboriginal History Inc., 1998; and Penny van Toorn, 'Authors, Scribes, and Owners: The Sociology of Nineteenth-Century Aboriginal Writing on Coranderrk and Lake Condah Reserves', *Continuum*, vol.13, no.3, 1999, pp. 333-43.

The words 'gubba' (in south-eastern Australia), 'migloo' (in Queensland), 'balanda' (in northern Australia) and 'kardiya' (in central and western Australia) are used by Aboriginal peoples to refer to white people. Information about Aboriginal usage of the word 'book' comes from J. M. Arthur, *Aboriginal English: A Cultural Study*, Melbourne, OUP, 1996. Hobbles Daniyarri's use of 'book' is recorded and discussed in Deborah Bird Rose, *Hidden Histories: Black Stories from Victoria River Downs, Humbert River and Wave Hill Stations*, Canberra, Aboriginal Studies Press, 1991. In many Aboriginal stories, white men are referred to as 'Captain Cooks'. See, for example, Chips Mackinolty and Paddy Fordham Wainburranga, 'Too Many Captain Cooks', in D. B. Rose and T. Swain, eds, *Aboriginal Australians and Christian Missions*, Bedford Park, South Australia, Australian Association for the Study of Religions, 1998, which is the source of the Paddy Wainburranga quotation.

Information on the Arrernte word 'pepe' was provided by Diane Austin-Broos (unpublished lecture, University of Sydney, 16 March 2000). The meaning of the Western Bundjalung word 'bihbar' is listed in Margaret Sharpe, *Dictionary of Western Bundjalung*, 2nd ed., Armidale, NSW, The Author, 1995. The meaning of the Wangkumara word 'piipa' comes from Carol Robertson, Wangkumara Grammar and Dictionary, [typescript], Sydney, Department of Technical and Further Education, Aboriginal Education Unit, 1984.

Wandjuk Marika's view of the readability of the land, his distress that secret stories have been published by anthropologists, and his intention not to let the same thing happen again are articulated in *Wandjuk Marika: Life Story*, as told to Jennifer Isaacs, St Lucia, Queensland, UQP, 1995. Bill Neidjie's statements about land, oral narrative and books come from Bill Neidjie, Stephen Davis and Allan Fox, *Kakadu Man*, Queanbeyan, NSW, Mybrood, 1985.

Jennifer L. Biddle's work on the use of *kuruwarri* signs is described in her article 'When Not Writing is Writing', *Australian Aboriginal Studies*, vol.1, 1996, pp. 21-33. Nancy Munn refers to *kuruwarri* as 'Walbiri iconography' in her seminal book of the same name (Ithaca, New York, Cornell University Press, 1973).

Much inspiration for the 'Books and Social Relations' section of this chapter was gained from Alison Ravenscroft's account of her work with Rita and Jackie Huggins, in 'Strange and Sanguine Relations: Aboriginal Writing and Western Book Culture', *Meridian*, vol.16, no.2, October 1997, pp. 261-69. I have written about other aspects of my work with Ruby Langford Ginibi in 'Indigenous Australian Life-Writing: Tactics and Transformations', in Bain Attwood and Fiona Magowan, eds, *Telling Stories: Indigenous History and Memory in Australia and New Zealand*, Crows Nest, NSW, Allen & Unwin, 2001. As each collaboration is unique, the account of my work with Ruby Langford Ginibi on *Haunted By the Past*, St Leonards, NSW, Allen & Unwin, 1999, should not be taken as indicative of the nature of the Huggins/Ravenscroft collaboration. Ian Henderson's reflections on Ruby Langford Ginibi's use of the word 'aye' (spelled 'eh' in non-Aboriginal Australian English) are in his review of *Haunted by the Past* entitled 'The Getting of Wisdom', *Southerly*, vol.60, no.1, 2000, pp. 224-29.

In 'Early Aboriginal Writing and the Discipline of Literary Studies', *Meanjin*, vol.55, no.4, 1996, pp. 754-65, and in 'Authors, Scribes and Owners', cited above, I endeavoured to show how the romantic individualist model of authorship worked alongside other institutionalised assumptions about 'Literature' to obscure the fact of Aboriginal participation in the making of written texts since at least as far back as 1796. The potential financial consequences of Aboriginal peoples' exclusion from the category of 'author' are perhaps most dramatically illustrated in [Waipuldanya]/ Douglas Lockwood, *I, The Aboriginal*, Adelaide, Rigby, 1962, which won the first Adelaide *Advertiser* Festival of Arts Award for Literature in 1962 and went on to be reprinted many times, including a 'school edition'. Jack Stillinger's *Multiple Authorship and the Myth of Solitary Genius*, New York, OUP, 1991, has contested prevailing models of authorship from a different perspective, showing how important collaborative relationships have been in the composition and editing of a range of canonical English and American literary texts.

The argument that Black-white collaborations dilute the Aboriginality of texts has been put forward by Mudrooroo in *Milli Milli Wangka [The Indigenous Literature of Australia]*, South Melbourne, Hyland House, 1997. In 'Indigenous Texts and Narratives' in *The Cambridge Companion to Australian Literature*, Elizabeth Webby, ed., Oakleigh, Victoria, CUP, 2000, pp. 19-49, I have counter-argued that, under certain circumstances, such collaborations can enhance Aboriginal control of the final published text.

POSTSCRIPT

Leonie Stevens

Penny van Toorn's work on Australian Indigenous writing cultures is well placed to open this volume of the *History of the Book in Australia*. It marks the crucial moment when, to borrow the metaphor of groundbreaking, the hard shell of more than a century of academic lack of interest and discrediting was irrevocably cracked. Van Toorn in her work credited authorship and authenticity to the women and men who held the pen and dictated the narrative. It says something about the colonising nature of the academy that it took the meticulous and insightful work of a non-Indigenous writer to confer credibility on Indigenous texts and their authors.

The impact of van Toorn's work has been significant. When I mention her name, Indigenous and non-Indigenous colleagues respond with unhesitating fondness and respect. *Writing Never Arrives Naked: Early Aboriginal cultures of writing* was, and continues to be, a marker; a node in the general discourse; when the *Macquarie PEN Anthology of Indigenous Writing* came out shortly afterwards, the two formed a kind of roadmap and fuel for scholars. Van Toorn's work emerged from, and contributed to, the cultural shift of the late twentieth century. Previously, Indigenous-authored texts were viewed as ethnographic curiosities, signalling from beneath the shroud of a doomed race, or *not really* the work of the authors. This chapter, 'A Book By Any Other Name? Towards a Social History of the Book in Aboriginal Australia,' does exactly what it sets out to do, as a rigorous intellectual overview of a complex and often vexed series of events, ideas, attitudes and changes. This remains an important and timely essay, two decades after it was first penned.

There are, of course, points of departure. Van Toorn urges us to guard against what she sees as the dangers of equating Indigenous writing systems and books: this, she suggests, is another form of Eurocentrism. I would argue this is a false equivalence. Globally, there is a strong tradition of First Nations writers claiming, for Indigenous literacies, the status of writing systems commensurate to abstracted symbolic systems like the alphabet and the book. This is a conscious act of resistance, and a subversion of stereotypes of Indigenous peoples as illiterate, uninterested in education, and in need of cultural rescue.

It is a self-evident truth that Indigenous writing systems in Australia predated European systems by millennia. People had literacies, and were having literacies, when, to borrow from I. C. Campbell, Europeans stumbled in. Indigenous texts and archives include writing on message sticks, possum skin cloaks, tools, weapons, rocks, trees, arranged stones, sand, land and bodies. In terms of global First Nations literacies, this extends to birchbark, petroglyphs, wampum, Inukshuks, marked trees, carvings, tattoos or ta moko, quipu and weave. European alphabets, and the printed book, merely added to these suites of existing literacies. The question should not be *How do Indigenous literacies relate to books*, but *How do books relate to Indigenous literacies?*

Van Toorn's chapter has highlighted the radically changed nature of the Australian literary landscape. I write this in 2023 in a period of what has been termed Indigenous efflorescence — a time of Indigenous prosperity and cultural renaissance. Scholarship is interdisciplinary, nation-to-nation, and Indigenous led. 'Nothing about us without us' is the emerging cultural standard across fiction and non-fiction, film, academic research and popular culture. Writers and essayists such as Alexis Wright, Anita Heiss, Tony Birch, Bruce Pascoe, Kim Scott, Melissa Lukashenko, Clare G. Coleman, Evelyn Araluen, Tara June Winch and Debra Dank, to name just a few, feature prominently in both retail sales and in prestigious literary awards. Publishing houses such as Magabala Books promote Indigenous authors and maintain an extensive back catalogue. The largest book of all — the Land itself — is being continually re-inscribed with Indigenous place names and identity.

Decolonisation is probably *structurally* impossible under the permanent system of settler colonialism. But if we reorient our perspective to embrace the full range of archives — if we hear Ruby Langford Ginibi's voice in our mind's ear — we are infinitely enriched as readers, writers and citizens.

NOTE ON SOURCES

The general sources cited are: Penny van Toorn, *Writing Never Arrives Naked: Early Aboriginal cultures of writing in Australia*, Canberra, Aboriginal Studies Press, 2006; Anita Heiss and Peter Minter, eds, Nicholas Jose, gen. ed., *Macquarie PEN Anthology of Aboriginal Literature*, Crows Nest, Allen & Unwin, 2008. On recognising the authenticity of early Indigenous authorship, see Leonie Stevens, '*Me Write Myself*': *The Free Aboriginal Inhabitants of Van Diemen's Land at Wybalenna, 1832–47*, Clayton, Monash University Publishing, 2017. I. C. Campbell wrote that Polynesian societies '. . . had a history and were having a history when Europeans stumbled in', in 'The Culture of

Culture Contact: Refractions from Polynesia', *Journal of World History*, vol.14, no.1, March 2003, pp. 64-82, esp. p. 72. Regarding Indigenous texts and archives being written on message sticks, possum skin cloaks and other materials, there is a wide scholarship: see for example Paul S. C. Taçon, Sally K. May, Ursula K. Frederick & Jo McDonald, eds, *Histories of Australian Rock Art Research*, Canberra, ANU Press, 2022; and for similar practices employed by global First Nations, see Elizabeth Boone & Walter D. Mignolo, *Writing without words: alternative literacies in Mesoamerica and the Andes*, Durham, Duke University Press, 1994; and Marie Battiste, 'Print Culture and Decolonizing the University: Indigenizing the Page', in Peter Stoicheff & Andrew Taylor, eds, *The future of the page*, Toronto, University of Toronto Press, 2004, pp. 111-124. On Indigenous efflorescence, see Gerald Roche, Hiroshi Maruyama and Åsa Virdi Kroik, eds, *Indigenous Efflorescence: Beyond Revitalisation in Sapmi and Ainu Mosir*, Canberra, ANU Press, 2018.

CHAPTER 2

Printing Technology

Stephen James Herrin

Printing was invented out of a necessity to communicate ideas and information to a wide audience. The importance of the new technology grew as the reading public increased. From the time of its invention the printing process remained relatively the same for around 350 years. In the early nineteenth century numerous technological advances began a series of developments that were to change the process from labour-intensive hand composition and hand-presses through to keyboard-operated typesetting on Linotype machines and web-fed rotary presses capable of extraordinary speeds. Australia's printing trade was just beginning at this juncture and witnessed these momentous developments, although in a limited capacity as Australian printers did not mass-produce for international audiences as was done in the Northern Hemisphere.

The first press in Australia came with the First Fleet in 1788. Amongst the supplies planned for the settlement was a printing plant consisting of an old and rather small wooden hand-press with an assortment of type. Ink and paper are listed in the inventory of the fleet's stores, but these were not distinguished as printing materials and could have been the more common items used for writing. It is not surprising that a printing press was considered a necessity for starting a colony in the Antipodes. Government printing had long been used in Western Europe to communicate proclamations and orders to the populace. In the early years of the Australian colonies the population — 7000, of whom only 1000 were free, in 1803 — was small enough not to have merited this attention. The press remained idle and all communications from the Governor were carried out either in manuscript or orally.

Not until 1795 did anything appear in print, thanks to the convict printer George Hughes. The earliest extant example of his work, and to date also the earliest extant item printed in Australia, is a playbill dated 30 July 1796 advertising a performance in Sydney of *The Tragedy of Jane Shore*, likely printed on the original First Fleet press. It was 1803 before the first newspaper sheet was issued by George Howe. The advance of printing technology in Europe at the beginning of the nineteenth century did not play a large role in Australia. The newer hand-presses — the Stanhope, Columbian and the Albion — offered a better impression than the common wooden press, but did not speed up the rate of production to any great degree. A single pull of the bar rather than the two pulls needed on the wooden press did make it less labour-intensive. Until the introduction of cylinder presses a rate of 250 impressions could be expected per hour. Hand composition of two to three hours was required to set a 22-inch column (a compositor setting three to four columns of eight-point type in a 10-hour day). But for pre-gold-rush printers the acquisition of labour and supplies was a larger concern than speed of production.

A second press arrived in Port Jackson before 1801, but it is not known if it was used there. A press was included in the stores that accompanied David Collins to Port Phillip and Van Diemen's Land in 1803. A bill for printing type from Collins requested he be sent a small pica roman letter of 80lbs with limited other small fonts for jobbing, 20lbs of pica italic, 40lbs of double pica roman, a dozen lengths of brass rule, one dozen skeins of thick and thin scabbard, and two dozen [casks] of good printing ink. He must have received some advice on what a small printing office might need as he details sorts, weights and style of font when asking for either Caslon or Figgins type. Collins's party spent the months of October 1803 to January 1804 at Sullivan Bay, Sorrento, in Port Phillip. The press was employed there by Matthew Power, who printed government orders for the temporary settlement that preceded the installation at Hobart Town on the Derwent in February 1804. The equipment was used over the following years by Power, Francis Barnes and George Clark, the last of whom produced the short-lived *Derwent Star* — Hobart's first newspaper — in 1810. The same or similar presses later served the enterprises of Andrew Bent in Hobart and John Pascoe Fawkner in Launceston.

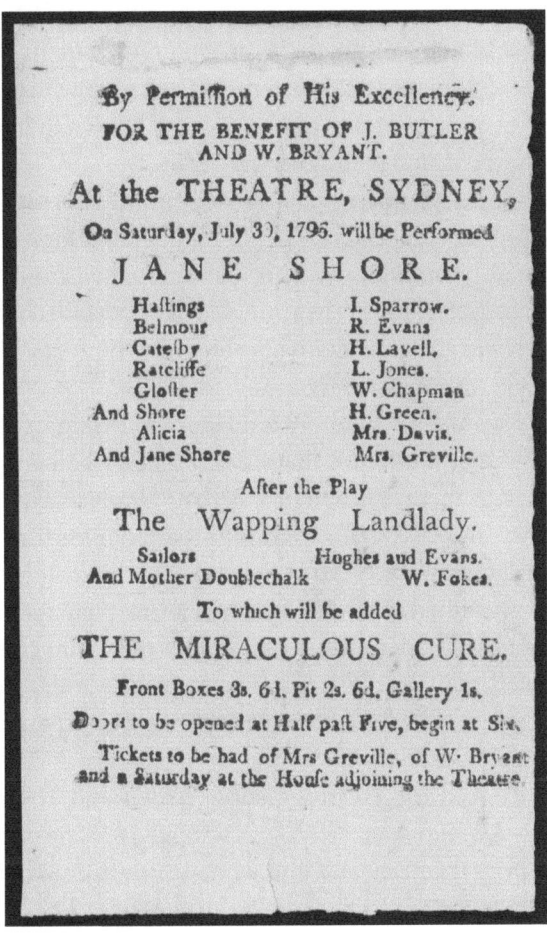

Playbill advertising three theatrical performances on 30 July 1796 in Sydney. Australia's earliest surviving printed document, the playbill was produced using the small wooden screw press and type (likely Caslon) brought over on the First Fleet. The printer — convict George Hughes, whose name appears in the cast list for *The Wapping Landlady*, — served as Australia's first 'Government Printer' until 1800, but little is known about him. The verso was annotated and signed by Philip Gidley King, later the Governor of New South Wales. Discovered by a librarian reviewing ephemera at Library and Archives Canada, the playbill was formally presented to the people of Australia by the Canadian Government in 2007. It is listed in the UNESCO Australian Register for the Memory of the World. Single sheet; 20 x 12 cm. (National Library of Australia)

The early papers in Sydney began publication on hand-presses, but how many of these were wooden is now uncertain. We know that at least two of the Sydney presses made their way south after they were discarded: it was not unusual for printers to update their equipment and sell an old press to another printer just starting out. Two of the early Sydney presses we know of are the one that went to Tasmania with Collins and another for the *Port Phillip Gazette* in Melbourne. Another inter-colonial press transfer was Fawkner's which came from Van Diemen's Land. A total of five presses are known to have come to Victoria from the island colony by the 1850s.

Fawkner's misadventures with his *Melbourne Advertiser* in 1838 — the need to produce the early issues in manuscript, then suppression because official permission had not been obtained from Sydney — were not uncharacteristic of the time. The lack of skilled compositors and pressmen was also an ongoing problem for the *Port Phillip Patriot and Melbourne Advertiser* as it became in 1839.

Fawkner's type was acquired from Henry Dowling in Launceston. It was in such poor condition that Fawkner described it as 'swept up from the floor'. A further problem was that there was no pearl ash to clean the type. The press was a common wooden press that T. L. Work had estimated as manufactured at the end of the seventeenth century. The carriage was lined with zinc and had a tiny platen adjusted with hooks fastened with rope. It took all day to print 300 copies on the old press given the two pulls required to print a full sheet and the necessity of inking with balls. Later the paper was expanded and the staff was raised to six.

In opposition to the *Patriot*, George Arden and Thomas Strode began the *Port Phillip Gazette* on 27 October 1838. Strode had been trained as a printer in England and came to South Australia in 1836. He left Adelaide for Sydney, where he met Arden. After deciding to establish their own paper in Melbourne they encountered difficulties in getting a press and plant in Sydney. It seems the master printers there feared competition, but when it was known that Arden and Strode were going to Melbourne, they acquired the necessary equipment. The plant consisted of a wooden hand-press — possibly an American Ramage — that arrived at Williamstown together with some cases of brevier and bourgeois in October 1838. The type was in poor condition and mostly in pie, but was cheap at 2d. per pound. The press was in such a state that, in order to achieve a uniform impression, Strode had to put a blanket on the carriage of the press underneath the forme and plane down the new letters. The common problem of supply shortages required him to manufacture his own lye from wood ashes. Again the press was not the only concern, since Strode was always looking for printers. The *Gazette* was forced to offer to pay steerage passages from Sydney or Van Diemen's Land for two compositors. Strode was even known to go on newly arrived emigrant ships to approach printers. Over six weeks in 1839, he set the biweekly *Gazette* himself, over a fortnight sleeping only two hours in order to accomplish this. Resourcefulness was required: Strode cut all his poster type himself from New Zealand pine and made a roller out of India rubber. When the newspaper moved to Collins Street, he had two workmen to assist him, one of whom was William Strode, presumably a relation. As there was a lack of journeymen, Thomas Strode trained many apprentices. They would roll for the pressman in turns and also fly (remove sheets from the press). All hands would deliver the paper in four rounds. Arden himself was known to help: in July 1840 he distributed the newspaper with two messengers. Though the paper was growing, with 81 new subscribers in its last quarter, Arden was forced to declare insolvency in 1843. In 1844 the *Gazette*'s copyright was sold for £50.

There were few wooden presses in Australia. These were considered quite old technically when printers here were beginning, but the earliest newspapers used them because they were relatively cheap second-hand from Europe, where they were being discarded for the new iron presses manufactured in Great Britain and the United States.

Iron presses

Around 1800, the Stanhope press, the first hand-press completely made of iron, was produced. The design was refined in 1806. These presses were large and very heavy but improved the hand-press to the point where a full page could be done in one impression. This was achieved by replacing the screw with a series of levers that increased the pressure exerted on the platen while reducing the stress on the press's frame. Although iron presses began appearing in Australia, it was still possible to operate a printing office with a wooden press up to the 1840s.

Despite Governor King's encouragement of George Howe's work, the printer was not to receive a Stanhope press till the beginning of 1812 under Governor Lachlan Macquarie. The printing process was not accelerated, but there was less labour and the impressions were crisper. Even as late as 1819 Howe was not producing more than 400 copies of the *Sydney Gazette and New South Wales Advertiser*. He claimed in that year that 700 was thought in England to be a break-even circulation.

It is important to note that most of the problems Howe faced were not mechanical but centred around the challenges of obtaining supplies such as paper and ink. Numerous pleas for paper of any sort appeared in the newspaper. Paper ordered from Great Britain was expensive: the cost of a sheet in England was 1d. but after shipping, it rose to 2d. in Australia. As late as 1833 the *Australian* was forced to stop publication for three months as there was no suitable paper available. Ink shortages proved problematic as well. Howe is reported to have made his own ink at times, probably using whale oil, charcoal and tree resins.

About the same time as the Stanhope was produced, a number of people in both Great Britain and the United States were working on improved designs for the iron press. Several were introduced, but only one stands out, that of Clymer, who developed the Columbian, which was lighter but still created the same pressure as the Stanhope. A further differentiation was made through the use of copious ornamentation on the press itself in the iron cast. The first Columbian appeared on the market in 1813. Its driving principles were a fulcrum and lever rather than the screw. Most of the later presses followed this design, some more successfully than others. In Australia it seems that many experimental designs were discredited before being offered on the market, for only examples of the Columbian, Albion and at least one Ruthven appear in the historical record. The Albion, designed by R. W. Cope in 1822, operated with a lever joint called a toggle, allowing for simplicity, which was the reason for the press's commercial success. This was especially important for Australian printers, who were far removed from the manufacturers. The Albion was probably the most popular iron hand-press in the nineteenth century.

Robert Howe, George's son, and successor in 1821, was able to expand his print shop. The Stanhope press was replaced in April 1824 with a Columbian that only seems to have been used for one year. An Albion press was ordered shortly after the Columbian was in use and it arrived in 1826 at a cost of £1000 including printing materials. Howe had not been satisfied with the Columbian. Although it was powerful enough, he questioned its manufacture, having trouble with several broken parts and being concerned that a serious break would render it useless and delay essential printing. Thus the Albion was either a backup press or could altogether replace the Columbian. At this time Robert Howe was paying £500 a year to a London agent for supplies and to keep him informed of printing developments. He had found that the local government officials he had been dealing with caused too many delays, not only for printing materials but for books, magazines and reviews necessary for the *Gazette*'s content. The newspaper became a daily for a short time in January 1827. In that year, its press and type were valued at £1000. The Albion was reported to have had good use at another office in Sydney. In the 1840s it was passed on to Alonzo Grocott, engraver, letterpress and copperplate printer, and was still in limited use up to the 1860s in that office.

Howe's first competition came in 1824. William Charles Wentworth and Robert Wardell, both lawyers, brought a press and materials from England. Their paper, the *Australian*, was printed by George Williams and first appeared on 14 October 1824. This new rival may explain Howe's fears of the Columbian being out of service and the *Gazette* going biweekly in the same month. Further competition was added when in mid-1825 the *Sydney Monitor* appeared, printed by Alfred Hill for the proprietor Edward Smith Hall.

In the 1830s more newspapers were published in New South Wales, with the main consequence being the lowering of prices to around 6d. or less per copy. Concurrently, invested capital for printing offices was on the rise. The *Gazette*, probably the best equipped plant in Australia at the time, was sold to Robert Howe the younger for £1000 in 1829. Growth in the 1830s can best be shown by the rise of the *Sydney Herald*, printed on an Albion imported in 1831, which had circulations of 750 in May 1831, 1100 in 1832 and 1600 in July 1836 when it was a biweekly. The *Herald* became a daily paper in October 1840 and had grown to a value of £10 000 when it was sold to Charles Kemp and John Fairfax. By 1847 the value had doubled to £20 000.

Most newspaper offices of the 1830s were not of this size, and skilled labour was still in short supply. In 1836 the *Gazette* had four pressmen (presumably working two presses), four compositors and one engraver. In 1838 the Sydney *Colonist* was operating two Columbian presses: a double demy size worth £80 and a demy worth £55. In these offices the type was much more valuable than the presses.

Adelaide's first printer, Robert Thomas, brought with him from England a somewhat dated Stanhope press, which he set up in a rush hut in Glenelg and then slightly later moved to a mud structure in central Adelaide. On the Stanhope he printed the *South Australian Gazette and Colonial Register*. He also brought a rough wooden press for jobbing work, as he did not want to use the Stanhope for anything but the newspaper; however, Thomas stated that he had used the Stanhope to print the first two South Australian pamphlets — the *Constitutional Signing* and the *Announcement of the Establishment on 28 December 1836 of The Governor in South Australia* in 1837.

Two Stanhope presses also made their way to Western Australia. The first was imported by Governor James Stirling in 1833 and leased to Charles Macfaull for £75 a year with the stipulation that government printing needs were attended to. Macfaull's own concern was the *Perth Gazette*. Almost all jobbing printing was sent out of the colony. The second Stanhope arrived around 1847 and was used to print the *Perth Gazette*, which was now under Government Printer Arthur Shenton's control. The *Gazette* by this time also possessed a Columbian for jobbing work.

By the 1830s jobbing printers were establishing themselves in Sydney, Hobart and Launceston. They still found it necessary to produce some sort of newspaper in order to maintain a steady flow of work. Later this trend was more prominent in Melbourne than elsewhere. The jobbing printers had small concerns, and many of them brought a plant or stock with them from Europe. John Sands arrived in Sydney in 1837 at the age of 19 and established a printing and stationery business on George Street with the limited stock of £500 worth of stationery that had accompanied him. As his family were engravers in England, it would have been possible for him to send home for necessary supplies. Another early Sydney jobbing printer was William Moffitt, whose business was eventually to become W. C. Penfold and Co. In the 1830s this was a bookbinding, stationery, engraving and copperplate printing establishment. The early Sydney trade still suffered from lack of supplies: it has been reported that, for printing, the artist John Carmichael at times used copper sheets stolen from the hulls of moored ships.

Later, although Sydney had become the largest town, it was still possible to begin a newspaper with little equipment. The *Empire* was established on 28 December 1850 with only a hand-press that was later displayed at the NSW Technological Museum.

Melbourne's printing trade began developing in the 1840s. George Cavenagh left Sydney for Melbourne in 1840 to start the *Port Phillip Herald*, the first eight-page newspaper to be printed in that city. He brought with him a whole office including type, press, compositors, reporters and editor. John Ferres, later Government Printer, acted as superintendent, and his foresight instigated the installation of the *Herald*'s first steam printing machine later in the 1850s. The *Herald* became a daily in January 1849 and by 1850 it claimed to be the largest circulating newspaper in Melbourne. It was sold in 1855 to Levey, Robson and Franklyn of London. Francis Burdett Franklyn had come to Australia as a printers' supplier a few years earlier and probably saw possibilities for the *Herald* in the quickly growing city.

Although the Melbourne jobbing market was served by several establishments that appeared in the mid-1840s, J. P. Fawkner's *Patriot* was still sending contracted jobbing work to Launceston, presumably because its plant was fully occupied with printing the newspaper. The delays caused by this arrangement would have been quite annoying to customers and perhaps were responsible for their looking to local firms capable of in-house production. Among Melbourne printers to make a start in this decade were Samuel Goode and James Shanley. Goode was the first printer in Melbourne not to begin a newspaper straightaway, although in 1844–1845 he brought out the *Melbourne Courier* in association with William Kerr. Goode made another venture into journal publishing in 1847 when along with Kerr and Curtis he printed the *Melbourne Albion*. Shanley, rather than publishing a newspaper, found a niche working for Melbourne's Catholic community.

Of all the Melbourne printing offices the *Herald* had the most extensive jobbing office mainly owing to the efforts of James Harrison, who was later to start the *Geelong Advertiser*. The success of the jobbing department was due to a specific and concerted effort to undertake this kind of work, which was done by a manager, one journeyman and one apprentice using one dedicated press and display types. This focus declined in the mid-1860s when the *Herald* allowed the jobbing arm to deteriorate: a newspaper office once it reached a certain size had no need for jobbing as all its capital had to be invested in new machinery. The *Herald*'s jobbing office was bought by A. Henriques in 1869 to add to his one-journeyman plant.

The last major area to develop printing in the colonies was the Moreton Bay district in what became Queensland. The *Moreton Bay Courier* appeared on 10 June 1846. Although convicts had been sent there since 1824, the then outpost of New South Wales had earlier lacked the population necessary to justify publishing a newspaper.

The Australian gold rushes of the 1850s transformed colonial printing into a thriving industry. Populations exploded in the established cities, and towns appeared wherever any substantial strike was made. With the huge immigration came numerous skilled workers, who, shortly after becoming disillusioned with digging, returned to their trade. Capital, skilled labour and an expanded reading public all bolstered the newspaper and jobbing printing trade.

Presses were installed to print newspapers in the new settlements in Ballarat, Bendigo, Castlemaine, Maryborough and Beechworth in Victoria. Plants were usually acquired in metropolitan centres and brought to the new town in a cart. The presses were usually a Columbian or an Albion. It is interesting to note that the popular lightweight presses that helped to open up the West in the United States — the Ramage and the Washington — found little use here. Even though British presses were favoured, Hoe rotaries and treadle platens still came across the Pacific from North America. The most popular press for these provincial printers was the Albion, which was much more reliable and lighter than the Columbian. The only known variant was a Ruthven brought out to print early newspapers in Van Diemen's Land. This press was later bought by a Mr Weavell, who transported it to Western Australia and leased it to Shenton and Macfaull to print the *Fremantle Observer* in 1831–1832.

The gold rushes bolstered the Melbourne jobbing trade as well. Many printing firms that grew into large establishments found a start during this period, prime examples being Walker, May & Co., Sands & McDougall, and Fergusson & Moore. All were hand-printing establishments. Walker & May experienced a fire in 1861 that completely destroyed their £300 plant, for which they were uninsured. The low value of the plant they owned suggests a single press and some type. Fergusson & Moore, established in 1854 as Goodhugh & Hough, suffered a fire during a printers' strike — the fire rumoured to have been caused by strikers in revenge for Goodhugh setting up type for the *Argus*. When Goodhugh & Hough became Fergusson & Moore, William Detmold joined them as a partner. Detmold sold his share in the concern early on to go into the printers' supply business. James Fergusson and William Moore had been shipmates on their voyage to Australia. This firm was renowned for its skilled workmen. In 1880 McCarron, Bird, Püttmann and Stewart left Fergusson & Moore to start their own business. This company eventually became Edgerton & Moore.

The lack of firms in Melbourne devoted specifically to repairing printing equipment meant that businessmen such as Stephen Charlwood had to make do when presses were damaged, as happened when the leg of his press broke when it fell from the dock into the water. He was forced to have a blacksmith fix it as best he could.

Up to 1860 almost all printing offices started with a hand-press which continued to be used; even the introduction of cylinder machine presses did not mark the end of the iron hand-press. These were employed in many country districts until the twentieth century and were retained in larger offices as proofing presses or presses for small runs. Gibbs, Shallard & Co. in Sydney are known to have used an Albion for runs under 250 in the 1870s. It is difficult now to establish how many Australian printers still relied on hand-presses in the 1880s and 1890s: figures in statistical registers name the operative power employed by printers, but the terms 'manual' and 'hand' in these documents more commonly refer to printers operating cylinder presses by hand rather than to hand-presses.

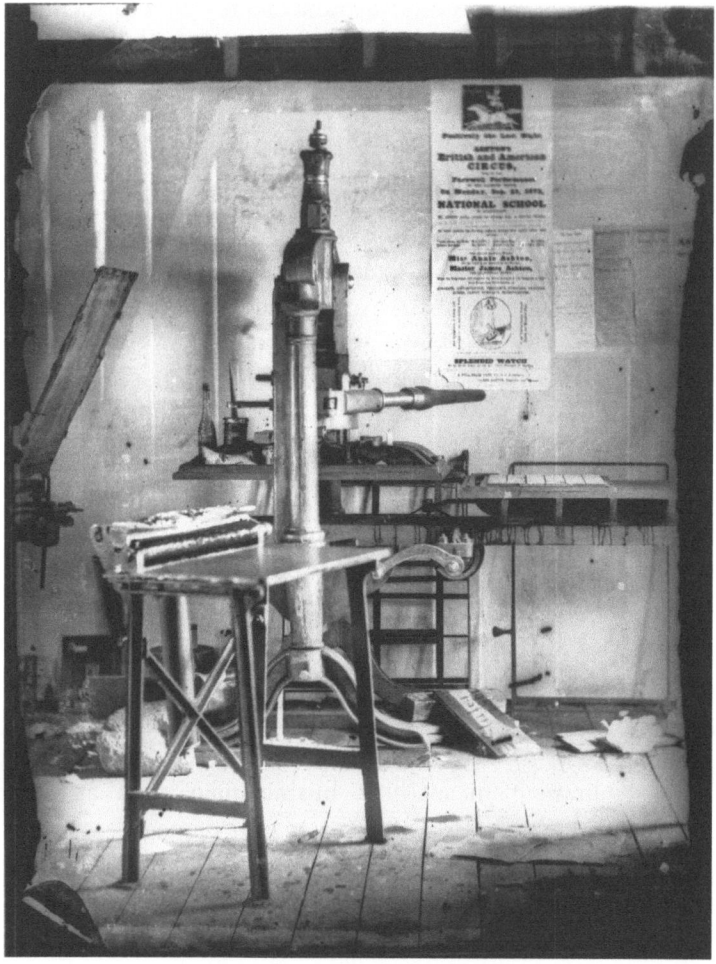

Photograph of Albion press in the somewhat disorderly pressroom of the *Border Post and Stannum Miner*, Stanthorpe, QLD, 1872. Established by Henry Beauchamp Unwin (d. 1874) and printed by Joseph William Pillar, the newspaper began publication on 20 July 1872. Another image in the State Library of Queensland collections taken the same year shows the exterior of the newspaper office, with seven men (presumably including Unwin and Pillar) and a boy standing in front of a bark and slab building. In the image shown here, the Albion press is prominently displayed along with the two broadsides — likely printed in-house — advertising performances by 'Ashton's British and American Circus'. The newspaper was initially printed on foolscap-size paper, later becoming a broadsheet. Pillar became its sole owner upon Unwin's death. The current *Border Post* originates from Unwin's original publication. (State Library of Queensland)

Machine presses

The concept of using the pressure of a cylinder for printing dates back to the early seventeenth century, but it was not practically applied until 1811 when Friedrich Koenig and Andreas Bauer developed a cylinder machine for Thomas Bensley's printing office in London. With the introduction of the cylinder came the capacity to apply a power source to the printing process, which increased speeds over fourfold compared to the screw and platen hand-presses. Later it was possible to attach a power source to the treadle platen. In between the transition from hand-press to cylinder was the bed and platen press. Craft prejudice and the imprecision of the early cylinder presses created a place in the market for this development. The principle of the bed and platen press was closely related to the hand-press, but power could be employed rather than the pulling of a bar. The press retained the tympan and frisket of hand-presses but mechanised the rest of the process with a reciprocating bed, a platen that provided a downward force through the use of a toggle joint and automatic inking.

The first mechanical presses came to Australia well after they had found their market overseas. We know that by October 1840 the *Sydney Morning Herald* (*SMH*) had replaced its Columbian with a bed and platen press, in the style of the Napier later constructed in Sydney for the *Herald*. The Columbian could only print two pages at a time amounting to around 500 pages an hour, i.e., 250 impressions. At this time the *Herald* was a daily newspaper with a circulation of 3000. The Columbian would have taken at least 24 hours to print so many copies of the four-page paper, so the new 'Splendid Cylindrical Machine' was needed in order accommodate this print run. This press was constructed by Frederick Michael Stokes, who had been the printer at the *Herald* in the 1830s and then worked his own shop in the 1840s and 1850s. Some newspapers are known to have printed issues concurrently by adding another press. Although this would cut the time in half, two further pressmen would be required to operate it and, depending on the way the work flow was organised, the entire paper might have to be set again, which added further costs. Another Napier is known to have been at Walker, May & Co. in 1858. A much later press of the Napier style was installed in the New South Wales Government Printing Office in 1887, when a double platen was set up to print postage stamps.

The bed and platen press was soon superseded by cylinder presses, especially in Australia where there was little demand for the quality bookwork the earliest versions of the new machines could not achieve. The press consisted of a cylinder that took a sheet of paper and exerted pressure as it rotated on the type forme laid on the bed of the press, the two working simultaneously. Inking was accomplished automatically by rollers. The *Times* in London was the first to adopt this machine for printing a newspaper in 1814. It was fed from both ends of the press, an operation which increased the speed twofold. Australian newspapers were rather slow to install cylinder machines: initially the cost and speed would not have been justified given the low circulation figures.

Many different cylinder presses came on the market during the nineteenth century, some better than others. All operated on the same basic principle of a bed of type and a cylinder for impression, but how these two interacted could vary. Basically, the four different types were the drum, two-revolution, stop-cylinder, and reversing. The drum cylinder press had a large cylinder, only part of which was used for impression. The remainder allowed the bed to return to its original position as the cylinder continued to revolve. The two-revolution had a cylinder that revolved twice for every one impression: as the bed returned the cylinder was raised. The stop-cylinder arrested the rotation of the cylinder as the bed returned for the next impression. The reversing press had a cylinder that moved with the bed and then raised and returned to its original position. For printers who employed these presses, this nomenclature was not as important as the size of the impression cylinder. Advertisements for new and used presses in the *Australasian Typographical Journal* and in newspapers usually only described the press as a 'double royal' or 'double demy' machine rather than a 'drum' or 'reversing' one. Regardless of the specifics of these presses most were capable of 600 to 1200 impressions per hour.

The most popular cylinder press in Australia was the Wharfedale, which appeared first in Britain in 1858. These medium-sized stop-cylinders employed simple workings which rendered them reliable and moderately priced. In the 1870s additions were made to the press so that different size sheets could be printed without changing the cylinder. This versatility made the press suitable for both smaller newspaper offices and jobbing printers of all sizes. Other presses used in Australia were the Belper, Quadrant and, later, the American Miehle.

The first cylinder press in Melbourne was at the *Melbourne Daily News*. This newspaper was originally printed on a Columbian by a pressman and a compositor who assisted him at press. By 1849 the staff had grown to include an overseer, sub-overseer and 16 compositors. The hand-press was replaced in July of that year with a Belper machine, sent from Sydney and reportedly capable of 1000 copies per hour although British reports gave a figure of 500 impressions. The Belper was a cylinder press that worked on the principle of a rolling cylinder. The type forme was placed on a bed and remained stationary at the impression as the cylinder passed over it. Belpers lost favour in the 1850s as the speed of other cylinder presses overtook them.

The largest Melbourne newspaper in the 1850s was the *Argus*. After only four years it claimed a circulation greater than all other Melbourne papers combined. Initially produced on Columbians, in the early 1850s the newspaper installed a machine press to generate 6150 copies. Each issue took 26 reams of paper to produce. The growth of the *Argus* was significant, necessitating the installation of a second press in August 1852. By the end of this year the newspaper had four Victoria machine presses and a staff of 140. With four presses printing the paper, it is most likely that stereotyping was introduced into the *Argus* office at this point.

Steam, gas and other motive power

The application of steam to printing came to Australia in 1853 when the two largest newspapers, the *Herald* in Sydney and the *Argus* in Melbourne, introduced it to their plants. The *Argus* first printed with steam in January 1853. At this stage the paper had a circulation of 10 000; by July it was claimed to be 17 000 and later still 23 000. The proprietors still found the speed inadequate, and were waiting for an Applegath type revolving press ordered in September 1852.

Until this press arrived the publishers were limited to a small format four-page paper. The transition to steam power was not a smooth one. By March the *Argus* had received a number of complaints concerning the amount of smoke emitted from its plant, claimed to be creating a public nuisance. It was forced to construct a new boiler to cut down emissions. Only three months later, a boy was charged with attempting to sabotage the press. The lad, Bryan Ward, was first caught trying to wedge a block of wood between the platen and cylinder, then attempting to place a bolt between two wheels of the machine. Conspirators were suspected, either within the office or from a competitor, but this suspicion could not be substantiated. The *Argus* claimed that if the attempt had been successful the press would have taken the night to repair, which suggests spare parts and a mechanic were not far away.

Although it has been stated a number of times that the *Sydney Herald* was the first to print by steam in Australia, this is difficult to establish as no fixed date has been put forward. However, considering the *Argus* had steam from 27 January 1853 and the *Sydney Herald* installed steam and a new press in 1853, if the *Herald* was indeed the first to have recourse to motive power its use by the *Argus* was almost simultaneous. In 1852 John Fairfax of the *Herald* went to England expressly to buy new machinery, and ordered a two-feeder Cowper printing machine (which had yet to be constructed) and a steam engine. These arrived in Sydney in 1853, at which point the publishers were near desperate as their subscriptions had increased substantially (to 6620 in 1854). Applegath and Cowper working at the London *Times* as machine engineers were credited with improvements to the *Times*' two-feeder that increased its speed to 1800 impressions per hour in the 1820s. Fairfax had been quoted a rate of 2000, which suggests further improvements had been made by the 1850s.

The *Argus* installed the Applegath Patent Victoria Printing Machine — an English press — in 1854. Before its arrival the newspaper had announced it as a fast printing machine from America, which leads one to believe they had instead expected a Hoe rotary. The Applegath model (patented 24 December 1851) was on the smaller scale of the company's type-revolving cylinder presses, the largest being a 10-feeder installed at the *Morning Herald* (England). It had two vertical type cylinders of 69 inches in circumference. The forme was divided on the two cylinders and printed two pages per revolution. Although capable of producing 6000 copies of the paper per hour, speed was dependent upon the skill of the feeders. After initial problems it was working by July 1854 and in September the price of the paper was raised to 6d. to cover increased production costs that in total amounted to £12 000 per year. There was the normal increase in wages and prices, but the new press added the expense of nearly a ton of coal per day plus repairs. Circulation was now 15 000. Less than a year later the publishers complained of the press's speed, stating that it could not cater to a circulation of more than 25 000 which was 5000 below what they believed their market to be.

The *Age* in Melbourne followed the *Argus* shortly after installing a four-feeder steam driven machine, imported for the newspaper by F. B. Franklyn and Co. and displayed in 1854 at the Melbourne Exhibition. The specifications indicate it was capable of 5500 impressions per hour, with laying-on stations in two tiers. It had four impression cylinders with the type cylinder placed in the centre. One may well assume that the other daily papers in the metropolitan centres had installed steam cylinders at least by the mid-1860s: by 1856 the *Empire* in Sydney was calling itself a general steam printing office.

The *SMH* updated its printing press again in 1860, when its six-cylinder Hoe rotary press was installed. This relatively late installation of the large press was probably due to its investment in the two-feeder Cowper earlier on. The new press was imported from New York at a cost of £6000. It was much the same as the press at the *Age* but with two extra impression cylinders that increased its output. The Hoe was constructed differently from the Applegath in that it had a horizontal type cylinder rather than vertical. The six-feeder was capable of 12 000 one-sided sheets per hour. When this was up and running, the publishers found that there was now a surplus of press time, so they employed it for their new publication, the weekly *Sydney Mail*, soon to gain a circulation of 5000.

Steam appeared later in the country newspaper offices. In New South Wales only the *Maitland Mercury* (est. 1843) and the *Goulburn Herald* (est. 1848) were printing with the aid of steam in 1864.

These papers were exceptional for their size, both having Sydney advertising agents. The *Goulburn Chronicle* was incorporated into the *Herald* at this time, thus giving it the highest circulation in the southern region of New South Wales.

Jobbing printers of the 1850s did not require the extensive machinery of their newspaper counterparts but had installed a number of cylinder presses and hand or steam power by the 1860s. Many of them did print a newspaper to supplement jobbing work, especially in Melbourne. Statistics for New South Wales show that in 1863 eight printers were operating on steam. This rose to 17 in 1876 and 24 in 1880. Not until the 1880s was gas to gain favour over steam. In 1885, 28 printers were operating on steam and 49 on gas in NSW. South Australia had 12 gas and five steam at this time.

As the larger papers transferred to steam machine printing, a number of second-hand presses became available for journeymen willing to venture out on their own in a small printing establishment. The Melbourne trade expanded from six jobbing printers in October 1852, to 25 in 1858 and to 41 by 1860.

One of the first jobbing printers to transfer to steam was F. Cunninghame in Sydney. He began his office around 1853 as the Albion Printing Office, presumably with an Albion press. The business expanded, and by 1858 at least he had installed a steam-operated cylinder. He was then advertising himself as a general letterpress printer, with recent additions to machinery and type, which included a set of Greek type. Varied type fonts were to become more important later in the century for advertising purposes. The widespread acceptance of steam is suggested by the name in the late 1860s of the Caxton Steam Machine and General Printing Office in Sydney.

Not all transitions to a motive source went smoothly. One of the less successful cylinder press installations in Australia was that of the *Bulletin* in Sydney. This illustrated journal began in January 1880 when a German cylinder press displayed at the International Exhibition in Sydney in 1879 was acquired. The press was arranged vertically and was an uncommon size (the impression cylinder being 17 x 10 ¾ inches). Gas was installed to run the press, which the printer described as 'the quaintest gas engine ever built'. The press initially failed to work, and the first two issues of the *Bulletin* were printed on another journal's press. Once the initial problems were solved circulation soon grew from 5000 to 10 000 and a hand wheel was attached to the cylinder for those times when power was unavailable.

It was not absolutely necessary to have steam or gas power to run cylinder presses. This was true for newspaper offices but more particularly for jobbing printers, many of whom employed cheap labour in the form of boys or unskilled workers to operate the press. H. L. Bullen, a Ballarat (then Melbourne) printer, told of his first experience with a cylinder press, a Wharfedale constructed by Dawson and Payne in England. It took three boys to work the machine: one to feed, one to turn the crank and one to fly the sheets. Each boy took 20-minute intervals at each station. In Bendigo a man of Chinese extraction was hired solely for the purpose of turning the wheel of the press. The *Observer* in Adelaide in the early 1850s ran two hand-operated machines which required two men to turn the handles; at times of extra work, two additional men stood by as replacements so that the presses ran continually. This was hard work and the pressmen were bathed in sweat at times. On these machines they produced 800 copies of the paper per hour.

Even as late as the 1880s and 1890s some printers chose not to install motive power. New South Wales still had at least nine printers operating manually in 1883. This figure, presented in the *Statistical Register of New South Wales, for the Year 1885*, only surveyed two districts, so a higher figure for all of NSW can be assumed. By 1885, only four New South Wales printers operated manually. In the same year South Australia had eight. Even a decade later, Victoria still had 31 printing establishments being operated manually.

An alternative to manual labour was water power, which Sands & McDougall and the *Armidale Express* are known to have employed. In 1867 Sands & McDougall replaced their hand-presses with a water-powered printing machine. This seems to have been very successful because the printing side of their business became more important than the production of stationery, and additional machines were acquired. In 1873 Robert Brown Fraser bought into the partnership for £10 000, which indicates the extent of the establishment by then. The importance of machinery to this firm can be shown by the fact that, between 1868 and 1871, Dugald McDougall was acting as a purchasing agent in England. The firm expanded in 1872 to a three-storey brick building, and later a four-storey building was added.

The *Armidale Express* began publishing with an old hand-press and hand composition in 1856. The newspaper began as a weekly of four pages with five columns each in either eight or 10-point type. As its frequency and subscriptions grew, a tumbler press powered by a water wheel was installed.

Gas and steam were eventually superseded in the twentieth century by electricity, which was more efficient, cleaner and safer. Electricity made its way into Australian manufactories in the 1880s, at first in the form of lighting fixtures. By the 1890s only some of the largest establishments were operating on electricity. In 1891 there were six printers in Melbourne employing electricity for motive power. Most firms waited until the early 1900s to change over. The *SMH* is a good example of this transition, as it introduced electric lighting in 1882 but delayed running the presses via electricity until 1902.

Web-fed rotary

Web-fed rotary was introduced in 1882. In this year the *SMH* installed a new Hoe rotary press. This was an advance as it printed from a web (large reel) of paper, making the hand-feeders obsolete, and perfected each page (printed both sides of the paper at the same time). A further time-saving device was the introduction of a mechanism that cut and folded the paper. Prior to this, all folding was done laboriously by hand. This machine enabled the Fairfaxes to expand to eight pages. In the 1880s newspapers increased both in size and circulation. The *SMH* had grown to 28 pages for its Saturday issues by 1886. The *Age* was able to offer the same at 1p., half the cost of the *SMH*. The *Age* circulation had grown to an enormous figure of 80 000 by October 1888.

The smaller metropolitan centres were slower than Sydney and Melbourne in their change to web-fed rotary. Not until 1893 was the *South Australian Register* able to install its Hoe stereotype web printing and folding machine. It was still considered newsworthy when the *Launceston Examiner* and *Weekly Courier* went to rotary in 1900. The *Examiner* changed its size to eight pages, just as the *Sydney Morning Herald* had done. The *Examiner*'s illustrative work was still carried out on a two-revolution cylinder press. By 1891 the *SMH* had updated its machinery to a double-web capable of 24 000 newspapers per hour. The price was lowered from twopence to a penny as a result of the Depression in the early 1890s and competition with the *Daily Telegraph*, but any potential loss caused by the price reduction was offset by increased revenue from advertising.

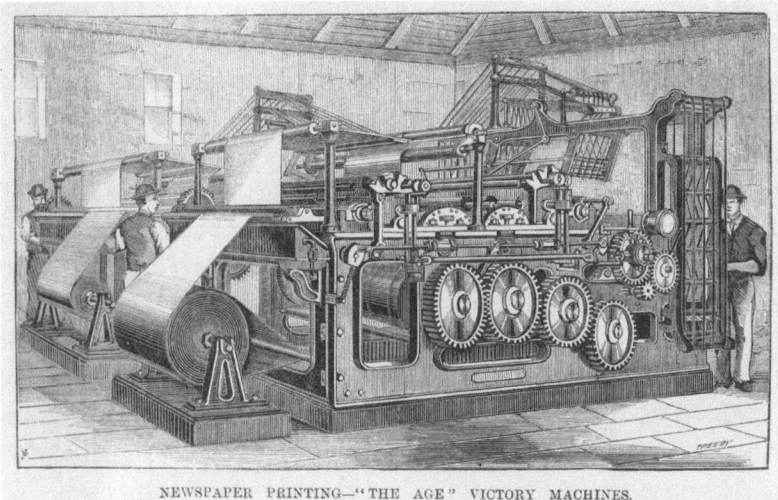

Wood engraving depicting the 'Victory Printing and Folding Machine', a web rotary printing press, used to produce the *Age* (1872–88), as published in the *Illustrated Australian News*, (Melbourne: Ebenezer and David Syme), 10 June 1878, p. 104. Designed in Liverpool by Duncan & Wilson for the *Glasgow Star* circa 1870, the press was the first machine that could print, cut the paper and fold the sheets. It was purportedly capable of printing 9000 complete, folded 8-page newspapers per hour, which greatly increased the speed of production. The image is signed 'Treeby', likely George Treeby, Australian illustrator, cartoonist and writer, who may have augmented earlier known versions of this image by adding the workers and the building surrounds. (State Library Victoria)

Labour and supply

The most significant change in the Australian printing industry of the 1850s was not the importation of modern presses, which came in the 1860s, but rather the huge influx of skilled labour mainly from Great Britain and the United States. Conditions overseas certainly justified the risk of displacing the family. Some came first to try their hands on the goldfields, others emigrated to escape the depressed trade in Britain, bringing with them a press, usually a hand-press, and type. Walker & May began in 1854 in Sydney, bringing a hand-operated letterpress and a lithographic printing plant, and relocated to Melbourne in 1855. Thomas May trained at Blaikie's printing house in Glasgow as pressman; his brother John trained as a stereotyper. Owing to this expertise, Walker & May were the first to carry out stereotyping and electrotyping work in Melbourne.

It was possible to set up as a printer without bringing along a press. A. H. Massina arrived in Melbourne in 1855 with half a crown. In England he had broken his indentures in 1850 by marrying, which would have limited his prospects there. After returning from the goldfields he worked at W. H. Williams's jobbing office, where he was known as a good machinist. By 1859 he had enough money to join Clarson, Shallard and Gibbs in partnership. In the early 1870s Gibbs and Shallard went to Sydney, and Massina carried on his own business.

Immigration of this kind culminated in the mid-1860s when the London Typographical Society was sponsoring emigration in order to alleviate conditions in a trade beset with unemployment. Many compositors in Britain were lent large sums of money: the Emigration Allowance entitled any unemployed member to receive the sum of £5 to aid him in emigrating, £6 if he had been member for three years, £7 for four years, £8 for five years, £9 for six and £10 for seven or more years. In addition, members were able to use their strike pay.

Beginning in the later 1850s when jobbing printers began installing machine presses, suppliers to the printing industry became more prominent. Presses and materials formerly difficult to get were now available. Paper, ink and type made up the bulk of these supplies with the occasional press appearing. Import statistics for Melbourne in 1864 showed that Great Britain was by far the largest point of supply for the colonies. Of the £20 394 worth of printing materials imported, only £513 were from all other ports; similar figures apply to NSW. The opposite was true for presses. Victorian statistics for 1850–1859 show that in this decade ten printing presses came from Great Britain, worth £240, five from Tasmania worth £180, while 56 came from the United States for a total value of £4500. Some of these materials were not for the Victorian trade, since suppliers such as F. B. Franklyn and W. Detmold acted as distributors to the other colonies as well as New Zealand.

These suppliers played an ever-increasing role in the Australian printing trade. Francis Burdett Franklyn arrived in Melbourne in the early 1850s and set up as a printers' broker. Aspects of his career as an importer of type and the vicissitudes of his business dealings are treated by Dennis Bryans in Chapter 7. Selling presses and other materials for printing remained a central part of his activities, which included from 1855 ownership of the *Melbourne Herald* with his London partners and participation in local exhibitions in 1854 and 1866. These displays covered the range of printers' needs and featured items of local manufacture.

William Detmold arrived in Australia in the early 1850s and first set up business as a bookbinder and stationer but moved into the supply business as a sideline. As well as arranging imports he acted as a financier to the printing, stationery and bookselling industry. He was either assignee or trustee for no fewer than 13 insolvent companies and held a number of bills of sale for various Melbourne printers.

Other companies which later entered into the printers' supply business included F. T. Wimble, Cowan & Co. (established in Sydney in 1868), Gordon & Gotch (1853), S. Cooke & Co., Robert Bell, Oliver Levey, Edwards Dunlop and Freemantle & Co. (formerly F. B. Franklyn).

Edwards Dunlop was established in Sydney in 1868, originally as suppliers of paper, stationery, inks, type, printing machinery and books. A purchasing office was set up in London by Frederick Lewis Edwards, and wholesale was handled in Sydney by William Phillip Dunlop. The partnership flourished and by 1885 it had £97 718/17/10 in assets. It became a private limited company in 1886 with £107 000 in capital. F. T. Wimble arrived in Melbourne in 1866, aged 20, with printing ink materials. In the next year he set up his factory in the rear of an undertaker's shop. His father in England, an ink maker, supplied him with materials, dry colours and gold bronzes, equipment and formulas. An ink mill and steam engine arrived in 1868, and in 1878 he moved to Sydney, as it was more centrally located. There he began selling printing machinery as well. Gordon & Gotch were printers' agents in Sydney in the 1860s. Also there in 1871 were E. Greville & Co. and L. Sharwood & Co. Subsequently, Greville moved into the telegraph business.

There was also a trade in used printing supplies. Thomas Stubbs, a printers' broker in Melbourne, supplied the trade with new and used materials after relinquishing his printing business. His reputation was not entirely honourable: in one instance he was accused of mixing new type with used stock. Harry Davenport was a printers' pawnbroker in South Melbourne operating in the 1850s. By the 1860s most major newspapers had their own printers' joiners, who made everyday necessities such as galleys, furniture and brass rule.

1861 marked the appearance of Australia's first printing manual. The need for such a publication probably arose from the industry's transition from a craft-based trade to one technically oriented with complex machinery and chemical processes. *The Art of Printing* was written by John Degotardi, a Sydney printer and photographer, who had always taken an interest in technical developments and was well acquainted with the European trade. For the newest advances he corresponded with Alois Auer, Director of the Imperial and Royal Court and State Printery in Vienna. The book provided descriptions of the various types of printing with sections on letterpress, engraving, lithography, galvanoplasty and photolithography, as well as examples of each type, and of nature printing. Since Degotardi stated photolithography was not yet practised in the colonies, he was apparently not aware of the work of John Walter Osborne in Melbourne.

Osborne was funded by the Victorian government to solve the problems of adapting photography to printing. In 1859 he was granted a Victorian patent for a process involving the development of a light-sensitive gelatine that could be applied to the stone or plate and when exposed to the photographic negative, would render the image on the stone. It was then printed in the same way as normal lithography.

Photography in the commercial market began to be used in the same year in Melbourne via the process of projecting the image onto a wood block as a guide for engravers. The practice was later taken up in Ballarat by Hermann Deutsch, who operated from 1860 to 1865. This kind of work and the developments for reproducing illustrations are discussed by Thomas A. Darragh in Chapter 4.

Another recognition of the technical difficulties facing the printer was the establishment of the Melbourne Printers' Library, begun in the late 1850s. This had grown to the quite impressive figure of approximately 1600 volumes by 1880. It had been set up as a reference library primarily at the instigation of the Melbourne Typographical Society (MTS), which had always followed a policy of embracing new technology. Its magazine ran extracts from overseas trade journals describing new techniques and inventions. Most of these inventions did not threaten the compositor-dominated Society until Linotype appeared in the 1890s. Cylinder presses did affect the printing industry as they became more prominent, since less skilled labour was needed and more boys employed. It required little expertise to turn the crank or fly the sheets, which led to labour abuses here much as in Britain, where Karl Marx found them so disturbing. By the 1870s the trade was inundated with boys, who were for the most part unindentured. The *Sydney Mercantile Advertiser* was able to operate its plant with men from the poor-house and a contingent of non-Society labour from Melbourne, when hands went on strike in 1871. But for the MTS the situation regarding boy-labour was not a question of the threat of new technology, but rather one of the morality of exploiting children.

Stereotype and electrotype

Overseas printers began to use electrotyping and stereotyping in the first half of the nineteenth century. These processes increased production through their durability and the saving of type. Electrotyping was developed in the first quarter of the nineteenth century for reproducing both type and illustrations. The relief is achieved by taking a mould of the original in beeswax, resin and turpentine with a copper plate. Once dusted with graphite and electrically charged, the copper reacts by growing, which develops into a duplicate of the original. This was mostly used for illustrative work, because when applied to letterpress the type could be damaged through the extreme pressure required in making the mould.

Stereotyping had been used since the early eighteenth century but did not find acceptance in larger European offices until the 1820s. A stereotype was made by taking a mould of the type-set page, originally in plaster, but later papier mâché, and by pouring an alloy of tin, antimony and lead into it. The plate was then mounted onto wood at type height ready for printing. The benefits of this process were that type could then be distributed. It did not have to remain standing if more impressions were needed later. This effectively reduced the wear on the type. However, the added expense of stereotyping was only recovered if the print runs were sufficiently large and so it received little employment in Australia outside newspaper offices. Newspapers found this most useful, since the plates could be curved and fitted onto the cylinders in rotary presses.

The first tangible evidence of electrotyping in Australia came in 1858 when Walker, May & Co. advertised this kind of work. In 1861 this firm won a first-class certificate at the Melbourne Exhibition, and a silver medal at the Exhibition of 1872–73. As noted earlier, training of the masters in Glasgow proved very important to the success of the firm in Melbourne. John May had trained as an electrotyper and stereotyper in Scotland. His skill in this field coupled with his brother's training at Blaikie's, a printing house working for large book publishers, enabled the firm to form a close relationship with bookseller and publisher George Robertson. Throughout the 1850s and 1860s Walker, May & Co. were printers to Robertson and in 1874 further consolidated the connection by moving into Robertson's McKillop Street factory. Presumably, since Robertson was the largest publisher in Australia at this time, much of the book work he required could need stereotyping. In 1871 Nicholas Duffield in Melbourne developed a process of engraving with an oxide of zinc plate, with a special hardening ink, as a preparation for electrotyping. A decade later T. H. Flere was working on a photo-electrotype process with glass and gelatine.

As few other printers, at least in Melbourne, had experience with stereotyping, John May was forced to train one of his employees, Joseph Bickle, who later went to the Government Printing Office. But it was not until 1889 that stereotypers were sufficiently numerous or motivated to form their own union. In 1886 they had combined with press machinists and feeders in Sydney to form the Pressmen and Stereotypers Union. One who had been trained as an electrotyper and stereotyper was John Markby, who arrived in Victoria from Tasmania in 1861. By 1870 he had sufficient capital to set up a typesetting business on his own, and the next year wood engraver Angelo Azzopardi joined him in partnership. In 1888 Markby employed seven hands to carry out both electro and stereo work for most of the larger printing establishments in Melbourne. The demand was considerable, and in the twentieth century the company added a type foundry.

Outside of these examples there was little demand for stereotyping in Australia, owing to the rather small amount of book production in the 1870s. Most of the fiction, which had the largest runs, was imported from England even when the authors resided in Australia. In these works the title-page only was changed to indicate colonial or Australian editions. Another practice was to make extra stereo plates or moulds in England and to send them to Australia for printing.

That said, the publisher David Reid in Melbourne found sufficient use for stereotype plates in the late 1880s and early 1890s to attempt to improve them. He applied for five separate patents related to mounting stereos and electros on their bases. At least by 1883 the *Register* and *Advertiser* in Adelaide employed stereotyping for their larger advertisements and illustrations, as this process was cheaper than hiring compositors at penalty rates. In Sydney electrician Gustaf Dillberg and journalist J. A. Philp were working on stereotypes created with matrices from a machine operating in a similar fashion to the typewriter.

The production of stereo plates in Australia was essentially for newspapers. In the 1860s many found the use of plates more economical. In 1866 the Launceston *Examiner* proprietors were so proud of their stereotyping they displayed it at the Exhibition of that year. It was not until the 1870s, with the introduction of rotary machine presses that required stereotype plates to wrap around the impression cylinder, that they found extensive use. These presses were of course limited to the larger offices. The *Age* and *SMH* were the first to introduce web-fed machinery, but later, owing to increased circulation, the *Argus* (1882) and the *Sydney Daily Telegraph* (1885) soon joined the ranks. In Adelaide the transition was delayed until 1892 with the *Register* and *Advertiser*.

Jobbing platens and larger factories

Jobbing printers of course did not require larger presses capable of 5000 impressions an hour. They needed a number of presses that could obtain a reasonable rate for smaller run jobs executed at the same time. For this reason the equipment in jobbing offices was not as homogeneous as that of their newspaper counterparts. There was no set standard of appropriate machinery required. Some printers employed the latest machine presses available while others were content with one or two treadle jobbing presses, while still others remained hand-printers. Alternatively, any combination of presses could be employed to best suit the type of work carried out in a given office. A printer of the mid-nineteenth century had a number of options for equipment: hand-presses, jobbing platens, and various cylinder presses that could employ any power source.

As the new machine presses became commonplace in the 1860s there was a shift in the labour force. More and more boys were being employed, but the nature of jobbing printers' output remained pretty much the same. It consisted mostly of handbills, cards, newspapers, periodicals, pamphlets and to a lesser extent books. A significant change came in the late 1870s that bolstered the printing industry: the advent of aggressive advertising. In addition to the established printers' production, packaging and the demand for design work for such items as Christmas cards and calendars rose, and this required more display fonts and wood engravings. This trend extended to experiments with colour printing. In 1867 Thomas Stokes tried to develop a system for label printing in colour, then in the 1880s and 1890s experimentation became more prevalent. In 1882 J. T. B. Gibbs of Gibbs & Shallard in Sydney was exploring the possibilities of printing with different colours formed by parallel lines and printed in a single impression. H. C. A. Ffrost came out with his parti-coloured printing in 1887. This involved mixing colours on the forme to create an effect. In 1891 C. W. Burford offered a more sophisticated multi-colour idea that utilised partly covered inking rollers.

Other ideas arose to print on metal (J. M. Thompson, 1869, and S. L. Parker, 1892) and celluloid (M. W. Fergusson, 1889). Here also should be mentioned a patent of the Melbourne printer R. D. DeLittle for white-letter poster type in 1887.

There was a steady rate of growth in the printing industry in the 1870s. In Victoria the number of extensive printing establishments rose from nine in 1865, to 17 in 1870, to 34 in 1875, and then to

55 in 1879. Queensland had 42 printers by 1880, 14 of whom were located in Brisbane. This expansion created a larger demand for printing materials, and printers' brokers began acting as agents for overseas manufacturers. Oliver Levey advertised in 1870 that he was the agent for Figgins hard-metal type, Harrild's printing materials and machines, Shacknell & Edwards's inks, and Hughes & Kimber's lithographic materials. In the same year Gordon & Gotch advertised that they were agents for Miller & Richard's type and A. B. Fleming & Co.'s inks, while also offering new and used printing presses.

In addition to the large manufacturers' materials being available, a small manufacturing industry was beginning locally. The most important of these was Robert Bell, printers' engineer and broker, who died in 1876. Not only did his business supply new and used presses, type, machines and furniture, it also carried out repairs. Bell began manufacturing when he patented his Victoria Press in 1874. The *Talbot Leader* installed Bell's Patent Eclectic Printing Machine in December 1874.

There are examples of other presses manufactured in Australia. In 1860 DeGruchy & Leigh, printers in Geelong and Melbourne, designed a press with a chemical band that was used to strike off impressions. Also in Melbourne was the aforementioned Thomas Stokes, who in 1872 developed a lever embossing press. In 1884 a home printing machine was introduced by the printer Frederick Puech, who had emigrated from Canada. This was a wooden case with an ink roller and a hinged lid. In the ensuing two years, Puech made further refinements, one of which was to replace the platen with a wooden mallet. Finally, in 1890, A. O. Whiting sought a patent for a press that tackled the difficulty of consecutive numbering on printed matter such as cheques and tickets, a staple of the jobbing trade.

Manufacturing of materials in Australia for the printing industry continued to grow. Oliver Levey was by this time making brass rule for printers, and the machinist for the *South Australian Register* had designed a self-acting fly-boy to lay sheets on the depressing table of the press. Climatic differences between Australia (with its high temperatures and great temperature swings) and Europe and the United States, forced some technical adaptations for printers in Australia. Rollers used on cylinder presses are the best example: the composition used in Europe was not satisfactory here and so had to be changed to a harder composition of India rubber for the presses to work properly. In 1885 the Melbourne confectioner Richard Miller offered a composition of gelatine, glycerine, Russian glue and erythrosene for the rollers. One of the most knowledgeable press manufacturers to live in Australia was Thomas Main, although it does not appear that he used this expertise in this country. Main was a partner in the English firm Main & Conisbee. He was the inventor in the 1850s of the Main Tumbler Machine Press, which utilised a rocking cylinder, considered a precursor to the popular Wharfedale. Main fled England because of financial difficulties, and died as a Melbourne printer on 8 July 1856.

In the 1880s newspapers were still the main source of printing employment. The jobbing industry had also grown and was diverse. Offices ranged from the very small with only one or two employees to the very large, Sands & McDougall having 320 employees in 1888 and a nominal capital of £300 000, with offices in Melbourne, Adelaide and their affiliate Robert Sands & Sons in London.

The smaller offices were made viable by the treadle platen. A number of these had been around since the 1850s, but did not truly find their place in the Australian printing scene until the 1870s and 1880s. One of the earliest to import a treadle platen was James Curtis in Ballarat, who established his firm in 1863. The model was a Minerva constructed by H. S. Cropper & Co. in Nottingham. Such platens were also found useful in the 1870s by larger firms that had also the space and capital to install a number of them specifically for smaller-run jobs. In the 1880s, however, one could establish a printing firm and have as its sole printing press one of these ingenious machines. In 1888 Cowan's was offering new Pearl Platens for £41 that were capable of 2000 impressions an hour without the use of steam or gas. This became such a trend that in 1889 Gordon & Gotch offered only small presses in their advertisements: these were Josiah Wade's Anglo-American Arab printing machines and J. M. Powell & Co.'s Empire and Quadrant machines. All were treadle platens except for the Quadrant, which was marketed as a 'small jobber' cylinder press. Thus it was possible to own and operate a printing business for under £100, in a limited capacity.

The West Australian industry lagged behind the east coast. Only the Government Printing Office was well equipped and steam-powered. By 1881, only one treadle platen was operating in the jobbing offices. As for cylinder machines, there was a Double Royal, a Light Demy, and an older machine press, which was in a state of disuse.

At the other end of the scale, older established firms in the metropolitan centres became quite large, and capital investment played a major role. Only a limited number, such as John Fairfax, Sands & McDougall, W. C. Penfold, and Mason, Firth & McCutcheon, could boast over 100 hands and capital over £100 000. Machinery was very important to these big firms, and agents were employed overseas to keep them abreast of new developments and technology. The Victorian statistics for 1885 show that the 139 extensive printing establishments were valued at a total of £731 609, which included plant, machinery and buildings. The average plant value then was just over £5000.

This large capital investment did not necessarily have to be paid outright as arrangements could be made with manufacturers, distributors, and other printers. Foremost of these was the time lease or payment arrangement, but financing from banks in the form of an overdraft account or from another printer was possible. An example was the firm of Hanstein & Ellingworth, jobbing printers who also published three suburban papers. Its total assets were £10 354 with machinery rented from F. Brendt (£112/10/0), Wimble & Co. (£400/10/0), and S. Cooke & Co. (£2106/12/6). In addition, there was always the possibility of acquiring used machinery. Presses could change hands a number of times because of the diverse operations among businesses. Insolvent estate sales were common occurrences in the printing trade. Melbourne printers Dunn & Wilkinson were forced to sell their gas-powered plant valued at £1840 for just £250 in 1892 for this reason. Leasing or purchasing second-hand were good options because of the rate at which presses became obsolete, having a depreciation value of 10 per cent. Serious consideration had to be given by printers as to what kind of machinery they wanted. There was always the danger of over-capitalisation, especially if a large portion of profits was to go towards paying leasing debts.

Large capital investments were needed to house extensive plants, which could necessitate the design and construction of new buildings. Much of this cost related to the intricate belting systems that ran along the ceiling and brought power to individual presses. Thus the arrangement of the factory was dictated by the alignment of the presses and work flow through the shop. Departments were set out for letterpress, lithography, and treadle platens. James McDougall, of Sands & McDougall, is known to have visited the United States in 1888, and to have contracted an architect there to design the firm's Spencer Street factory. On this voyage he also visited England, France and Germany to appoint agents to relay information back to Australia on stock and any new machinery available.

Typesetting machinery

While remarkable developments were occurring, with great speeds being obtained in the nineteenth-century printing industry, typesetting remained unchanged. Hand composition was always a big expense. Large Australian newspapers of the 1850s employed upwards of 50 compositors. This number rose at its height in the 1880s to around 120 at each paper. Numerous machines were devised to perform the task of composing individual type pieces into lines of words, justifying them, and then redistributing them once they had been printed. None of these inventions were satisfactory enough to effect a major change until Ottmar Mergenthaler devised the Linotype in 1886. This machine abandoned the principle of individual pieces of type and so solved the problems of line justification and redistribution at the same time.

The Linotype is believed to have replaced two thirds of the compositors wherever it was installed. It came as a surprise to the printing trade in Australia because earlier machines had posed little concern to compositors. Three of the most popular early typesetting machines were the Hattersley, Kastenbein and Thorne, but only a few are known to have been used in Australia.

The earliest recorded typesetting machine used here was at the *Sydney Evening News*. In 1887 this paper installed two Simplex machines developed by Joseph Thorne. These were used to set individual pieces of type. Each letter had a nick on its back, which gave it a distinct shape and corresponded with a specific channel on the lower of the two vertical cylinders. When a letter key was depressed, the matching type letter dropped into place. Projections of the speed of this machine stated that 10 000 pieces could be set in an hour, or roughly four times faster than a hand compositor. Not until 1900 were these popular, and in Britain only provincial printers used them. The only other known Australian installation of a Thorne was at the *Bendigo Independent* in 1891.

The *SMH* installed five Hattersley machines in 1895, a rather surprising choice. Linotypes had by this time proven their worth overseas and made their first appearance in Australia in 1894, and Hattersleys can be considered basic when compared with later inventions. The first of these was patented in 1857. The type pieces were placed in grooves and each individual piece dropped when a key was pressed. To complete composition the line then needed to be justified. These were known in Australia at least by June 1871 when an article appeared in the *Australasian Typographical Journal*, which was far from enthusiastic about the machine's capabilities. Despite the limitations of the Hattersley, the *Herald* was able to reduce its compositorial staff from 41 to 21. Eight machines were installed to overcome the expense of redistributing the type. Formerly it was common practice to hire 'grass' for redistribution (in the 1860s the rate for this was a shilling per hour). Women were more commonly employed in jobbing offices, mainly as stitchers, in the nineteenth century, and outnumbered men in the printing firms of A. W. Schuhkrafft and Andrew Jack in 1883. (Australian print workers are discussed by Rae Frances in the Chapter that follows.)

Several Australian attempts at overcoming the expense of typesetting should be mentioned even though little came of them. As early as 1868 Charles E. Reeves was working on a scheme which replaced composing sticks with a system of rods, and type that slotted onto them. In the 1880s concentration turned to mechanical typesetting. In 1885 Phineas Pearson Craven took out a Victorian patent for 'an improved type-setting machine' and, a year later, one for 'an improved type-distributing machine'. The typesetting machine set individual pieces of type through a system similar to that of a piano with rows of like characters, and the distributing machine was treadle-operated. The Melbourne printing and stationery firm, Ellingworth and Hanstein, is known to have held a quarter interest in this invention. The total invested in these machines was £1000. A Melbourne civil engineer Joseph Fielding Higgins designed a series of machines for typesetting, distributing and justifying using a letter fingerboard and normal type. A combined effort of journalists in Melbourne and Sydney was that of Watkin Wynne, J. R. Topliss and J. A. Kay; in 1890 the Universal Compositor Company in Melbourne took on their mechanical typesetting system that was a case and race system for loose type. A type distribution machine developed to be used in conjunction with this was a cabinet with vertical tapered channels and a ward plate that sorted the letters automatically. For these machines a special type needed to be developed called Quadrate Self-Adjusting Type. This was machine-manufactured type with the spaces for commas, full stops and thin letters being of equal size. This type also needed to be nicked for distribution. But, on a trip to the United States, Wynne inspected the Linotypes and cabled back to his partners to stop work on their invention. He was responsible for Linotypes being installed in the *Daily Telegraph*. Another system, based upon the introduction of the typewriter, came from Joseph Snowball and John Warde in 1889. This avoided type composition altogether, but limitations in fonts on the typewriter hindered its application to real printing.

The first installation of a Linotype in Australia occurred after the cut-off date for this volume and cannot therefore be discussed in any detail. However, it is essential to note that the machines were a critical technological advance. Not until they were introduced was printing a mechanised industry. The effect on the labour force was particularly dramatic, — especially in major newspaper offices.

It is necessary too to add that although mechanical typesetting made such an impact in the 1890s in Australia, there are many examples of printers continuing well into the twentieth century with hand composition. The *Leader* Newspapers Group delayed the change-over until the 1920s, while smaller newspapers and jobbing printers prolonged the transition even further.

Conclusion

The nineteenth century was the most productive era for technical development in the printing industry. Changes came quickly and printers needed to follow developments in order to stay competitive, even if they decided not to adopt certain techniques or machines. Industrialisation meant that invested capital became much more important as bigger and faster presses came on the market. Printers needed to be shrewd and balance financial investment in new equipment against the prospective profit new technology might bring. For the large metropolitan daily newspapers, capital concentration became necessary because of the costs of purchasing and running machinery capable of handling circulations approaching 80 000. As this happened, joint stock companies were formed to create that purchasing power. For jobbing printers this was not so simple: they needed to weigh the benefits of modern equipment against what could be generated by that capital investment.

Australian printers remained somewhat behind their overseas counterparts. Wooden presses continued to be used after iron presses had confirmed their utility in Europe and the United States. There was a delay of 25 years after its invention before the first cylinder press was installed here. The treadle platen failed to have an impact on the trade until the 1870s, while web-fed machines and Linotype installations were ten years behind. The main reasons for these delays were Australia's small population — print runs were too small to justify the expense of new presses — and the tyranny of distance that caused delays in communications and shipping.

In 1890 printed material looked much as it had in 1800 despite all the technological advances. What was changing was an industry where journeymen printers were moving from being craftsmen to factory hands and their masters were becoming industrialists. Following chapters show this evolution and the slowness of Australia to develop manufacturing in such fields as paper and type. Shortages and outmoded techniques were to prevent Australian printing from being highly profitable, qualitatively superior and adventurous. The ingenuity and inventiveness of certain people in the trade were not fully represented in the end-products.

NOTE ON SOURCES

The literature available to printing historians in Australia is small given 200 years of the trade's existence. Much of what we need to know must be pieced together as new research from extant sources such as statistical registers, directories, newspaper articles, bills of sale, probate papers, insolvent lists, etc. The two main monographs are James Hagan's *Printers and Politics: A History of the Australian Printing Unions 1850–1950*, Canberra, ANU Press in association with the Printing and Kindred Industries Union [PKIU], 1966; and Robert Fitzgerald's *The Printers of Melbourne: The History of a Union*, Melbourne, Pitman in association with PKIU, 1967. Both are labour-union histories but contain notes on firms and developments within the industry. Commissioned histories are James Churchett's *One Hundred Years of the Printing Union in South Australia, 1874–1974*, [Adelaide], PKIU, 1974; Fred C. Humphrey's *From a Rush Hut . . . a Chronicle of the First 100 Years of Organisation of Master Printers and Allied Trades in South Australia, 1885–1985*, [Adelaide], Printing and Allied Trades Employers Federation of Australia, SA Region, 1985; Harold Hunt's *The Master Printers of Sydney: the Story of the Printing and Allied Trades Employers' Association of New South Wales, 1887–1971*, Sydney, Printing and Allied Trades Employers Association of NSW, 1976; and *PATEFA Victoria Region: One Hundred Years: profile 1982*, Hawthorn, Victoria, Printing and Allied Trades Employers' Federation of Australia, Victoria Region, [1982]. Also focusing on the labour side of printing is Kenneth Eric Eckersall's *Young Caxton: A History of the Aims in Printing Education in Melbourne 1870–1970*, North Melbourne, Melbourne College of Printing and Graphic Arts, 1980.

Two early printing historians were Herbert Norman and John Gartner. Gartner wrote *The Premier Victorian Pamphlet*, Melbourne, Hawthorn House, 1937; and Herbert Norman, *The Development of the Printing Industry in Australia*, [Melbourne, The Author], 1934. Trade journals, produced from very early on, are of great use. The first of these was *The Australian Typographical Circular* (1858–60) which became *The Australasian Typographical Journal* (1870–1916). Both discussed new developments in the trade in general, and carried advertisements. T. L. Work's 'The Early Printers of Melbourne' appeared in twelve issues of the *Australasian Typographical Journal* in 1898. Later publications — *Cowans* (Melbourne, Alex Cowan, 1904-30), the *Australian Printer* (Adelaide, Hussey & Gillingham, 1911–13?), and the *Australasian Printer* (Sydney, Lawson Publications, 1950–87) — all ran historical articles. Articles in

Twelve Point (the journal of the Craft Printers' Union in Melbourne), Melbourne, The Division, 1934-19-, are historical and technical. The two printing historical societies in Australia fostered important work in their journals in the 1980s. The Printing Historical Society of Australia issued the *Journal of the Australian Printing Historical Society (JAPHS)* (Pyrmont, NSW, The Society, two volumes, 1986 and 1990), which included D. W. Barrett's 'Some Aspects of Early Printing in New South Wales', *JAPHS*, vol.2, 1990, pp. 1-29; and Sandra Blair's 'George Howe and Early Printing in New South Wales', Wayzgoose: *The Australian Journal of Book Arts*, no.1, 1985, pp. 2-22. The Victorian Printing Historical Society produced *Inklings* (Melbourne, The Society, 1987-). This latter journal included Tony Cavanagh's work on the early stages of the Victorian Government Printing Office (as discussed in more detail by that author in Chapter 23 of this volume) and included John Holroyd's article, 'Walker, May & Company, Book and General Printers, 1855-1924', no.5 (April 1988), pp. 3-10. General historical articles on printers have appeared in the *BSANZ Bulletin*, now *Script & Print*, and other historical journals.

There has been more work on the early nineteenth century than on later periods. Sources include D. H. Borchardt's 'Printing Comes to Australia' in *The Book in Australia: Essays Towards a Cultural and Social History*, Melbourne, Australian Reference Publications, 1988, pp. 1-15; and Sandra Blair's 'Australia's First Printery', *Heritage Australia*, vol.4, 1985, pp. 2-4. Early government printers are highlighted in Tony Cavanagh's significant research, including 'The Victorian Government Printer and Early Scientific Publishing in Victoria: Ferdinand von Mueller, the Royal Society and R. Brough Smith', *Riverina Library Review*, vol.5, no.4, 1988, pp. 263-76; 'The Victorian Government Printing Office', *BSANZ Bulletin*, vol.16, no.2, 1992, pp. 67-73; and 'The Victorian Government Printing Office', *ALJ*, vol.38, no.4, 1989, pp. 282-95. Also relating to Victoria must now be added Peter Marsh's output of imposing documentary volumes including *The Fawkner Press: Unravelling the Images*, Emerald Hill, Kitchen Table Press, 2018. For Queensland see Dennis Cryle's 'Growing Pains: the Queensland Government Printery 1860-1900', *Journal of the Royal Historical Society of Queensland*, vol.13, 1989, pp. 349-58.

Other important articles are Ruth Johnston, 'The Printing Industry Before and After Automation', *Westerly*, vol.25, no.1, 1980, pp. 73-82; Rosslyn Reed's 'From Hot Metal to Cold Type Printing Technology', in Evan Willis, ed., *Technology and the Labour Process: Australian Case Studies*, 1988, pp. 30-50; Kevin Molloy and Katie Flack, 'James Shanley of Clonmel: Printer to the Population of Port Phillip, 1841–1857', *Script & Print*, vol.42, no.2, 2018, pp. 69–93; and Philip Parr, 'A History of Hobby Printing in Australasia', *BSANZ Bulletin*, vol.4, no.3, 1980, pp. 203-11. The sole biographical work in monograph form is John Fletcher's *John Degotardi: Printer, Publisher, and Photographer*, Sydney, Book Collectors' Society of Australia, 1984. The website andrew-bent. life, compiled by Sally Bloomfield and Craig Collins, focuses on the Tasmanian newspaperman and is comprehensive and regularly updated. Additional sources are Geoffrey Farmer's 'Three Women Printers', *Biblionews and Australian Notes and Queries*, vol.8, no.3, 1983, pp. 86-89; Jürgen Wegner's 'The Australian Printers' Keepsake', *Brandywine*, vol.2, 1990, which contains information on the Melbourne Printers' Library; 'The History of Print in Australia: Bi-Centennial Supplement', Prahran, VIC, Peter Isaacson Publications, 1988, *Graphix*, 1988, 24 pp.; and Alan Ives, ed., *Images of Australia: The Faces of Printing: Essays from the* Australian National Review, Wagga Wagga, RMIHEARS, Riverina/Murray Institute of Higher Education, c1987. Sheena Coupe compiled a history of the Penfold firm titled *W. C. Penfold, Printer and Stationer, 1830–1980*, Kingsgrove, NSW, W. C. Penfold & Co., 1980. Other company histories include: H. P. Down, comp., *A Century in Printing: the Story of Sands & McDougall Pty. Ltd. During its First Hundred Years 1853–1953*, Melbourne, Sands & McDougall, 1956; *The History of the House of Wimble in Australia: being the commemoration of the diamond jubilee of the establishment . . . in 1868*, Sydney, Wimbles Ltd., 1928; and Sidney Cooke Limited, although some of these are quite short.

Reference works include Jürgen Wegner, *BPA: Bibliography of Printing in Australia*, Beecroft, NSW, Brandywine Press and Archive, 1998–1991; Thomas A. Darragh, *Printer and Newspaper Registration in Victoria 1838–1924*, Wellington, New Zealand, Elibank Press, 1997; and his *Engravers and Lithographers in Colonial Victoria: A Directory*, Melbourne, Ancora Press, 2023. See also Don Hauser, *Printers of the Streets and Lanes of Melbourne*, Melbourne, The Nondescript Press, 2006.

Theses concerned with printing are: Lishi Kwasitsu, Printing and the Book and Newspaper Press in Bendigo, PhD thesis, Monash University, 1989; Patricia Bratulic, Economic Development in the Book Printing/Publishing Industry in Victoria in the 1850s and 1890s, MLib thesis, Monash University, 1988; John Gilbody, Craft to Computers: the Impact of Technological Change on the Printing Industry, MSci, Griffith University, 1978; and my own theses: The Development of Printing in Nineteenth-Century Ballarat, MA thesis, Monash University, 1995, published under that title by BSANZ, 2000, and Printers and Printing in Australia to the Early Twentieth Century: Personal and Business Pursuits, PhD thesis, Monash University, 2004.

Newspaper histories, generally published to mark a milestone in the paper's existence, can contain valuable information regarding printing technology. Elizabeth Morrison's *Engines of Influence: Newspapers of Country Victoria 1840-1890*, Carlton, VIC, MUP, 2005, has tables and establishment dates of printer firms that are extremely useful, as are two works by R. B. Walker: *The Newspaper Press in New South Wales, 1803-1920*, Sydney, SUP, 1976; and *Yesterday's News: A History of the Newspaper Press in New South Wales from 1920-1945*, Sydney, SUP, 1980. Other helpful publications are: Gavin Souter, *Company of Heralds: A Century and a Half of Publishing by John Fairfax Limited and its Predecessors, 1831-1981*, Carlton, VIC, MUP, 1981; Elizabeth Morrison, *David Syme: Man of The Age*, Clayton, VIC, Monash UP, 2014; and Ann Clarke 'Advertising, Rising Circulation and Steam Printing: The *Argus* in the Early 1850s', BSANZ Bulletin, vol.19, no.4, 1995, pp. 256-66.

Many overseas studies discuss technical developments in printing. James Moran's *Printing Presses: History and Development from the Fifteenth Century to Modern Times*, London, Faber, 1973, is probably the most comprehensive, but there are additionally books and articles that deal with single aspects of printing or of certain firms. The *Journal of the Printing Historical Society* (London) provides a long run of papers for over fifty years on all matters pertaining to printing.

CHAPTER 3

Australian Print Workers to 1890

Raelene Frances

In the first sixty years of colonisation, the Australian printing industry was mainly restricted to the publication of newspapers and official notices, with a small jobbing industry producing invitations, programmes, stationery, pamphlets, handbills, and the very occasional book. The first print workers in Australia were, like most of white society at the time, immigrants from Britain. A few came unwillingly, as convicted felons. Indeed, Australia's first newspaper, the *Sydney Gazette*, was run by a convict printer, George Howe, under the patronage of Governor Philip Gidley King. Subsequent colonial newspapers also relied heavily on convict labour, especially as compositors and printers, but also occasionally as reporters and editors. They were employed alongside freemen and received the same rates of pay. According to historian Sandra Blair, convict print workers in no sense formed a separate class in these establishments and were involved along with free colleagues in organising the first major strike action of Australian workers in 1829 and in establishing the first union of printing workers — The Australian Society of Compositors — in Sydney in 1835. It can be argued, however, that convicts were less deferential than freemen and so contributed to the militant character of the early printing workforce. Employers certainly preferred free workers and offered to pay the passage of suitable persons from Britain.

Whether convict or free, all printers shared in the customs of the trade which provided a structural basis for the emergence of trade unionism. Each printing office had its own chapel, established by 'the Custom of Time out of mind', to which all workers belonged. Chapels operated according to an agreed set of rules, enforced by the 'Father of the Chapel'. Initially the chapels served a largely social purpose, binding print workers together in a tightly knit group through the exercise of workplace rituals and after-work socialising. In theory, offences such as swearing, or making weak puns (perhaps an occupational hazard) were punishable by 'solacing' — a beating across the buttocks. In practice, the solace was bought off by a donation to the chapel funds. Newcomers had to be ritually initiated and pay a 'benvenue', or entrance fee. The birth of a son, a marriage, or other domestic event also required payment of a fee to the chapel funds which were used to defray the cost of collective social gatherings. These workplace groups, unique to the printing trade, over time began to assume industrial as well as social functions, with the Father of the Chapel representing workers in negotiations with employers. Eventually, the Father became the union delegate and ancient customs were modified to fit the changed industrial relations climate. 'Ralph', the obligatory chapel 'ghost', for instance, often put pressure on non-unionists to join the union by pieing their type while they were out of the composing room.

The majority of print workers who arrived in Australia came of their own accord, hoping to find more and better opportunities than those in Britain. Although printers in Britain had for 300 years enjoyed the income and status of élite craftsmen, by the nineteenth century their social and economic position was under threat. The increasing tendency to employ boys rather than skilled workers meant that those with experience were losing control of their trade: unemployment was more common and it was easier for employers to undermine wages and conditions. Many print workers left, often with financial assistance from their unions, to seek their fortunes in the colonies. Conditions in Australia, however, although sometimes better than any dared hope, were by no means uniformly favourable and often disappointed workers' expectations, especially during the Depression of the 1840s. Whereas British unions tried to export their surplus workers, Australian unions were from the outset involved in political agitation to control the entry of labour to the colony and end the convict system. The use of excessive numbers of apprentices was an equally burning issue for printing workers in Australia and the earliest industrial campaigns were directed at limiting the employment of boys to a fixed ratio of journeymen.

The gold rushes of the 1850s transformed the printing industry of eastern Australia. The populations of New South Wales and Victoria tripled in the space of a decade, bringing about a boom in the production of newspapers. Wherever gold prospectors set up substantial camps, printing presses quickly appeared. Almost as quickly, trade societies were formed as workers took advantage of the shortage of wage labour to improve their lot. By 1858 there were over a dozen such societies in towns throughout New South Wales and Victoria, the largest — the Melbourne Typographical Society — based in Melbourne. As the demand for newsprint increased, proprietors installed steam-driven engines to power the machines, and machine minders were employed to operate and maintain them. The work of compositors, however, could not be so easily mechanised and employers relied on longer hours and higher wages to increase production. For many, especially those employed on daily newspapers, such demand for their labour, along with collective bargaining, meant very high earnings — higher, probably, than those of any other skilled workers at the time. Unlike other craftsmen, such as stonemasons, who took the opportunities offered by prosperity to limit their hours of work as a long-term strategy to ensure steady employment for all, compositors were happy to labour for long hours provided higher piece rates ensured them good incomes. Indeed, many trained like athletes in order to attain greater setting speeds. They looked forward to self-employed independence rather than a more comfortable wage-earning life: gold-rush conditions created opportunities for enterprising workers to set up in business on their own and many became proprietors in the new gold townships. The prospect of self-improvement encouraged more sober habits and even total abstinence amongst printers, many of whom spent their leisure hours in 'rational amusements' aimed at bettering themselves. They read widely, learnt to play musical instruments and wrote learned letters and poetry for their trade journals. Compositors generally felt themselves a superior class of worker and never tired of citing the achievements of their colleagues who had attained distinction in politics and industry.

Like the general prosperity brought by gold, however, these boom conditions had faded by the end of the 1850s. As the gold towns declined or disappeared, their newspaper offices discharged hands or closed their doors. The unemployed and bankrupt drifted back to the larger centres where their presence increased the downward pressure on wages already being exercised by a slowing economy and the employment of boys. Although some workers resisted wage cuts by striking against the new rates, the employers generally were able to win by drawing on the local unemployed as well as importing 'blacklegs' from other colonies and even from Britain. As the economy stagnated in the 1860s, workers were increasingly unemployed and less able to defend their pay and conditions. Craft unions, which at best had only ever represented half the workers in the printing industry, completely folded in the 1860s.

Other print workers, however, found employers keen to use their services. Comparatively untrained colonial youths were in high demand in the growing number of weekly periodicals where their lack of skill was not a problem as they were only required to set simple text without the pressure of daily deadlines. Employers made up for the boys' slowness by keeping them at their jobs for up to sixteen hours a day. There was also more of a demand in the jobbing trade where a small market opened up for locally produced advertising brochures, labels and packaging. There was still, however, no significant colonial book-publishing industry. As noted in more detail by Carol Mills later in this volume, bookbinders found little scope for their skills beyond the binding of receipt books and ledgers for commercial enterprises and the binding of parliamentary papers.

As the economy revived in the 1870s, so too did the printing industry and the bargaining position of employees. By the middle of 1873 the Melbourne Typographical Society, established in 1867, had struck the first agreement with employers in the Australian printing industry. Most importantly, this agreement provided for the control of boy labour by apprenticing all youths and fixing a ratio of apprentices for every journeyman employed. However, the agreement only applied to daily newspapers and large, 'fair' employers, and several major firms broke the conditions during the slump of 1874–75. The bargaining position of the union was constantly undermined by the instability of the trade, which caused high levels of mobility in the printing workforce. Unionists toyed with more radical strategies, such as legislation and trade union councils, to control boy labour and the problem of unemployed tradesmen, but these schemes bore little fruit in the 1870s and workers lost interest in them once prosperity returned in the last three years of the decade.

The 1880s saw major changes to the printing workforce and its industrial organisation in all Australian colonies. The decade of relative economic buoyancy brought continued expansion in the industry with the burgeoning of country and suburban newspapers as well as expansion in the jobbing trade. With this expansion came a diversification of print workers as compositors and printers were joined by increasing numbers of lithographers, stereotypers, machine minders, oilers, reelers and bookbinders. Women and girls also began to be employed in the industry in significant numbers, particularly in the bookbinding and stationery divisions. Firms became larger and were often able to offer their employees better wages, conditions and more stable employment. The 1880s were a creative decade in which print workers developed new strategies to deal with old problems and in some cases responded boldly to new challenges.

The most obvious development to occur in these years was the growth in numbers and strength of typographical unions. In the colonies where unions were already established (New South Wales, Victoria and South Australia), the 1880s saw them consolidate their positions, recruiting new members from amongst the formerly spurned sections of the trade (those workers who had not served a formal apprenticeship yet were able to hold down skilled jobs) and offering members new unemployment and mortality benefits. Societies were formed amongst typographers in Queensland (1884), Western Australia (1889) and at the Barrier in New South Wales (1888). By the end of the decade, the Australian Typographical Union — a federation of these societies and some New Zealand unions — was assuming increased importance as a body able to defend the craft status of its members at an intercolonial level. Other print workers, in most cases refused membership of the typographical societies, also formed unions and waged industrial campaigns. Along with the typographers, they joined with other unions to promote co-operation amongst working-class organisations for mutual protection and advancement.

Traditionally, compositors had attempted to protect their craft by controlling the numbers and types of workers who could practise it. Specifically, they tried to insist on formal apprenticeship indentures and a limit to the number of boys entering the trade. These policies continued in the 1880s, but the way in which they were achieved changed to take advantage of the better economic conditions and union organisation. Instead of relying on the goodwill and pressure of 'fair' employers, unions increasingly sought to exert industrial pressure through use of the closed shop and the threat of strike action. Indeed, major strikes did occur in Brisbane and Adelaide in the late 1880s.

In some cases industrial muscle was combined with political pressure: in Victoria typographers were prominent in the agitation for factory legislation which effectively curtailed the employment of boys (and women and girls) on daily newspapers by limiting their employment to daytime hours. The Queensland Typographical Society was from the outset interested in political issues, and advocating for the election of labour members to the legislature.

The position of female employees in the printing industry became a new issue for male workers during the 1880s. Typographers almost universally opposed women and girls joining the workforce and successfully persuaded the few employers in the jobbing section who showed an interest in taking on female compositors to abandon the practice. The newspaper section was not so easily controlled and at least two newspapers in Sydney employed significant numbers of women in the late 1880s. In both cases the New South Wales Typographical Association mounted an unsuccessful opposition. The attitude of outright hostility to female labour, which continued until well into the twentieth century, was clearly established during these years, with typographical societies refusing to admit qualified women even when they were being paid the same rates as men.

The other major section of the industry which sought to expand the use of female labour was bookbinding and stationery. In Britain, women and girls had worked in the trade since the eighteenth century and were employed in similar kinds of work in Australia from the 1850s. This 'line of demarcation' between highly paid, male work and poorly paid, female work was rigidly maintained by the male craftsmen who were able to keep the workplace effectively a closed shop because the largest concentration of bookbinders worked in relatively large establishments.

Photograph of Sewers' Room, NSW Government Printing Office, Sydney, c.1890. From an album of images of the printery dating from 1871 to 1910. These women were among the many employees in the large Binding Section. Other images from this album show the gender division of the labour: women are shown using traditional sewing skills while men worked in the exclusively male binding room where the backing, covering and finishing stages were carried out (see also image in Chapter 5). 12 x 10 in. (State Archives and Records Authority of NSW; State Library of NSW)

The reasons for this hostility are more complex than the purely industrial concern to limit the competition of cheaper labour. For most printing craftsmen, the spectre of female labour in the composing room represented a threat to the whole culture of the workplace and their sense of masculinity. Compositors prided themselves on the manliness of their occupation, requiring them as it did to work in the dirty, often poorly ventilated, atmosphere of the composing room. The rights of passage of the apprentice as he evolved into a journeyman were often sexual in overtone, deriving from longstanding customs brought to Australia from Britain. It was very much a man's world, in which men often worked into the small hours of the morning and drank on the job as well as afterwards at nearby pubs. They prided themselves on being amongst the most well-paid, well-educated and well-respected of workers, taking a lively interest in world affairs. In the men's view, to admit women into this 'élite' circle would severely curtail the more boisterous aspects of workplace interaction and undermine the status of the craft as a whole. If a woman could do the job, the feeling was, the work could not be seen as being so skilled nor the male workers so manly. And while printers in many British workplaces were forced to accept working alongside women, colonial conditions ensured that the male artisan kept control of his craft. It remained to be seen whether economic depression and technological innovation after 1890 would challenge his supremacy.

NOTE ON SOURCES

For the convict period, Sandra Blair's 'The "Convict Press": William Watt and the *Sydney Gazette* in the 1830s', *The Push From the Bush*, no.5, 1979, pp. 98-119; 'The Felonry and the Free? Divisions in Colonial Society in the Penal Era', *Labour History*, no.45, 1983, pp. 3-15; and 'Patronage and Prejudice: Educated Convicts in the New South Wales Press', *The Push From The Bush*, no.8, 1980, pp. 75-87, remain the most useful generally, while R. W. Connell and T. H. Irving (*Class Structure in Australian History: Documents, Narrative and Argument*, Melbourne, Longman Cheshire, 1980) and Stephen Nicholas and Peter Shergold ('A Labour Aristocracy in Chains', in Stephen Nicholas, ed., *Convict Workers: Reinterpreting Australia's Past*, Cambridge, CUP, 1988, pp. 98-110) offer interesting discussions of the status of convict printers and other craftsmen within colonial society. See also L. J. Hume, 'Working Class Movements in Sydney and Melbourne Before the Gold Rushes', in M. Beever and F. B. Smith, eds, *Historical Studies: Select Articles*, Melbourne, MUP, 1967, pp. 30-50; and Ian Turner, *In Union is Strength: A History of Trade Unions in*

Australia 1788–1978, Melbourne, Thomas Nelson, 1978. For the post-convict period, J. Hagan, *Printers and Politics: A History of the Australian Printing Unions 1850–1950*, Canberra, ANU Press, 1967, is an invaluable source of information about changing technologies and labour processes in the printing industry as well as the development of industrial organisation. It is, however, heavily focused on the typographical unions. R. T. Fitzgerald's *The Printers of Melbourne: A History of a Union*, Melbourne, Pitman & Sons in association with Printing and Kindred Industries Union, 1967, is similarly limited. Raelene Frances, *The Politics of Work: Gender and Labour in Victoria: Case Studies of Three Victorian Industries, 1880–1939*, Sydney, CUP, 1993, provides some corrective to this, with discussion of female printing workers and gender politics in the industry as a whole for the 1880s.

The role of printers based in Australia in the global network of the English-speaking trade in the nineteenth century is treated in a recent monograph by David Finkelstein, *Movable Types: Roving Creative Printers of the Victorian World*, Oxford, OUP, 2018.

CHAPTER 4

Illustrations

Thomas A. Darragh

During the nineteenth century the market for books printed in Australia was relatively small. Illustrations were generally expensive to produce in small numbers so they were used very sparingly, except in books and newspapers printed in large numbers, or in government publications where a commercial return was not so important. Most of the common processes used for printing illustrations were well established in Europe by the time the first books were printed on this continent. Accordingly, these processes were used with little, if any, modification for Australian conditions.

Several of the main processes in use in the nineteenth century are discussed below.

Copper or steel line engraving

This was an intaglio process in which lines were cut into a copper or steel plate with an engraving tool called a burin and a thick ink was then rubbed into the engraved lines. Printing was undertaken on dampened paper using a rolling press to push the paper into the engraved lines to absorb the ink.

Copperplate line engraving was developed in Europe about the middle of the fifteenth century, originally to produce prints, but it superseded woodcuts for book illustration in the sixteenth century and became the principal means of book illustration through to the early part of the nineteenth century. A disadvantage of copperplate engraving was the small number of prints that could be taken before the soft copperplate started to wear. In the first half of the nineteenth century, this problem was overcome by the use of steel plates. The engraving was carried out on a softened steel plate, which was then hardened, enabling printing runs of 10 000 or more.

Plates produced by this method were expensive and could not be printed with letterpress as they were not type high. They needed to be tipped into a book by hand, thus adding to the expense. For these reasons copperplate engraving was not much used for books in Australia, except in the first half of the nineteenth century. Steel engraving, which was especially suited for large press runs, seems to have been rarely used, though several Australian-themed books were published with steel-engraved plates produced in England, for example, *Victoria Illustrated*, published by Sands & Kenny (Melbourne, 1857) and *Victoria Illustrated: Second Series*, published by Sands, Kenny & Co. (Melbourne, 1862). Some steel-engraved plates were said to have been used in the *Picturesque Atlas of Australasia* (1886–89), as discussed later in this chapter.

Mezzotint engraving was developed in the seventeenth century and extensively used in England in the 1800s for the reproduction of oil paintings and photographic portraits because it gave the impression of continuous tone. In this process, a copperplate was first finely textured all over with small pricks or pits by means of a tool called a rocker, and the design was then developed by scraping and burnishing the plate to remove the pricks or pits where the lighter parts of the picture were to be. The plate was then inked as in a line engraving. The ink remained in the pits, and the plate was then printed in a rolling press. Because of the delicate nature of the pitting, mezzotint plates were susceptible to even more wear than a conventional copperplate.

Most engravings produced in Australia were line engravings. Mezzotint was very rarely used in books, and then usually only for portraits, either because of the expense or possibly because there seems to have been only one engraver of any such ability in Australia — Henry Sadd — who worked both in Sydney and Melbourne. An example is Sadd's mezzotint frontispiece of Queen Victoria in *Smith's*

Medical Almanac for 1863. Even Sadd could not make a living from this technique and turned to wood engraving as an alternate source of income.

Woodcuts and wood engraving

Woodcuts were used as a means of book illustration from the very beginning of printing in the fifteenth century, but gave way to line engraving in copper in the sixteenth century. To produce a woodcut, the lines of the image to be printed were cut out of a plank of wood along the grain with a knife, leaving the lines in relief. Wood engraving is also a relief printing process, developed in the late sixteenth century. In this technique the end grain of a hard wood (usually box wood), rather than the plank was used to engrave lines, with tools similar to those used for metal engraving. The area of the design to appear in white is cut away leaving the parts of the design to be printed in black standing in relief to take the ink. Large illustrations could be printed by bolting several woodblocks together. The design was traced onto the composite block and the block engraved. In the middle of the nineteenth century, a method of placing an image on the block by photography to guide the engraver was developed. Where rapid production was required, for example for periodicals or newspapers, the composite block was engraved across the joins by a master engraver and then the block was disassembled and distributed among several engravers. When finished, the individual blocks were bolted together again for printing. The height of the block exactly matched that of ordinary metal type. The process was much cheaper than metal engraving and probably more expensive than lithography, but had the great advantage that an engraved woodblock could be printed with ordinary lettertype on a common press, so illustrations could be inserted at any convenient place in the text. Stereotyped or electrotyped copies of these blocks could be made easily and distributed widely or could be used to print several copies at once. This was the most common method of book and newspaper illustration during most of the nineteenth century.

Wood engraving enabled much finer work to be undertaken than with woodcuts. In the late eighteenth century Thomas Bewick revived this technique in England and wood engraving soon superseded line engraving as a medium of book illustration. A good Australian example of illustrations reproduced by this technique, undertaken by a number of engravers, is Henry Kendall's *Orara: An Illustrated Poem*, published by the Art Union of Victoria in 1881.

Lithography

This is a planographic process in which the design is drawn with a greasy medium, lithographic ink or crayon, on a clean, dry, flat plate with a slightly porous surface, usually a fine-grained limestone or a zinc plate with a thin coating of zinc oxide. The image is fixed by washing with a mixture of gum arabic and dilute nitric acid. The lithographic stone or plate is then dampened with water and inked with a greasy ink. The dampened surface repels the greasy ink but this adheres to the greasy design and so the design can be printed onto paper using a special lithographic press. This press has a scraper rather than a roller. The inked stone bearing the paper is passed under the scraper, which exerts considerable pressure to transfer the ink from the stone to the paper.

Lithography was developed by Alois Senefelder, a Bavarian actor and playwright, in the 1790s and seems to have been perfected in 1798 or 1799 in Munich. Lithographic printing then spread quickly from Bavaria to other parts of Europe, the first country outside Germany being England, where Senefelder was granted a patent in 1801. However, it was not until 1817, when Rudolph Ackermann and then Charles Hullmandel in 1819 started to use the technique, that it became more widely known and appreciated in Britain. It was introduced into Australia shortly thereafter.

This process was much cheaper than copper and steel engraving and could produce large numbers of prints without deterioration of the image on the stone or plate. It could be used for printing from engraved copperplates in large numbers by means of the lithographic transfer process, for example to produce maps which could then be used in a book. The transferring of an image from a copperplate involved the image being printed onto lithographic transfer paper, thin paper covered with a gummed surface. The paper was placed image side down on a clean dry stone and run through a lithographic press several times. The paper was then dampened, pulled through the press again and lifted off the stone. The stone was then inked in the usual way. Transfer paper was also used by artists, who could draw on it without having to reverse the image, as they would have to do if drawing directly onto the stone.

Lithography was often used for book illustrations, particularly where colour was required. More rarely, whole books such as *The Travels and Adventures of Mr Newchamp* by H. J. [Henry J. Le Plastrier], printed and published by Stringer, Mason & Co. (Melbourne, 1854), and even newspapers, such as *L'Echo*, a French-language newspaper published in Melbourne in 1870, were produced in Australia by lithography. This process can reproduce hand-written material using lithographic transfer paper. Facsimiles of letters or autographs have been used as illustrations with this method.

Lithography was also utilised to reproduce shorthand symbols in specialised journals such as the Melbourne publications *Southern Phonographic Harmonia* (1859–1860) and *Coo-e-e: An Illustrated Shorthand Magazine* (1878–80).

Some botanical illustrations were produced lithographically, not by having an artist draw images on the stone, but by a technique of nature printing in which the plants themselves were treated with lithographic ink, laid on the plate to produce the image, and the plate was then inked up and printed in the usual manner.

Plates produced by lithography must be tipped into a book by hand. This disadvantage was eventually overcome in the early twentieth century by the development of offset lithography, using rotary presses and flexible metal plates, in which text and illustrations were printed together.

Process- or photo-engraving

This relief process uses photography to project an image onto a metal block with a sensitive coating. For images with continuous tones, such as a photograph or wash drawing, the image was projected through a fine screen to break it up into a series of dots. The finer the screen used, the finer the grade of reproduction. The coating on the block was then developed, washed and the block coated with an acid resist that adhered to the image. The black areas of the image retained the resinous coating, whereas the light areas remained clear.

The block was then etched with acid to produce a series of raised lines or, in the case of a screened image, graded dots which carried the ink. These blocks could be printed with ordinary lettertype, but fine screened blocks needed to be printed on good quality coated paper. This process had the great advantage that it could faithfully reproduce photographs or other images and thus superseded most other processes at the end of the nineteenth century. Some firms of wood engravers, who may have used photography to place designs on their woodblocks for subsequent engraving, successfully made the transition to process-engraving.

The earliest engraved blocks for line work using photography were developed in Europe in the late 1850s and early 1860s; however, it is not clear if this process spread to Australia at this time. The development of the halftone process to reproduce continuous tones was complex and awaited the invention of a reliable method of breaking up continuous tones into a series of separate printing elements. Gauze netting was tried, but it was found that parallel lines etched into a glass plate gave the best results. Various kinds of screens were patented in Europe, but not until the 1880s were they perfected to allow the process to compete satisfactorily with other methods of illustration.

Process-engraving is said to have been introduced to Australia in Sydney by W. H. Traill, publisher of the *Bulletin*, in 1884 to reproduce the work of his cartoonists. However, photo-engraving using zinc plates was being used at the New South Wales Government Printing Office and also in at least one private Sydney firm in the late 1870s. Whatever the case, photo process-engraving was quickly taken up for illustrated periodicals. Halftone plates followed shortly after. George Sutherland of Adelaide developed a process for reproducing engravings direct from photographs suitable for being worked by the ordinary printing press. He sold the rights to the process to Cassell & Co in England and patented the process in 1885 in Australia. His process halftone illustrations were first published in the Adelaide newspapers *Adelaide Observer* and *Evening Journal* issues of 19 March 1887. Sutherland transferred his patent to the Fairfaxes in Sydney in 1886 and probably to other newspaper proprietors. Halftones produced by the Electric Photo Engraving Company, established in

Sydney by 1885, first appeared in the *Illustrated Sydney News* and the *Sydney Mail* in July 1888. Use of halftones in other journals, for example in the *Journal and Proceedings of the Royal Society of New South Wales* (vol.22, 1889) and newspapers quickly followed. A halftone by the Melbourne Photo Engraving Company appeared in the *Sun* (Melbourne) in March 1889. Colour printing, using coloured filters to produce three blocks to be printed with coloured ink plus a fourth black ink key block, was introduced in the 1890s.

A number of other photographic processes, such as collotype and photolithography, were relatively little used for book production because of slow rates of printing and the precise environmental controls needed to get good results. The exception was F. W. Niven's extensive use of the Crisp Photo Process developed in his establishment at Ballarat in the 1890s for book illustration.

Collotype or heliotype

This process, a planographic process like lithography, was also based on greasy ink being repelled from a moist surface, but in this case a gelatine plate was used as the printing surface. The sensitised gelatine was exposed to light through a superimposed negative. The light passing through the negative hardened the gelatine underneath in proportion to the amount of light penetrating it. After treatment with glycerine, which was absorbed into the non-printing areas, the plate was inked. The softer portions of the gelatine retained moisture and so rejected the greasy ink, whereas the hardened portions which were not moist retained it. The inked plate was then printed in a flat bed press. Colour printing could be done by making separate plates for each colour as in lithography.

Because it is a photographic process, collotype can render very fine detail and was used in scientific publications and to reproduce works of fine art. However one could only print about 1000 copies before a new plate had to be made from the negative. Precise humidity controls were also needed to ensure that the soft parts of the plate retained moisture.

Collotype was first developed in France in 1855 by Alphonse Poitevin, but not until further experiments were undertaken by Joseph Albert in Germany (1866) and Ernest Edwards in England

(1869) was a practical process developed. It quickly spread through Europe and to the United States of America. It seems to have arrived in Australia directly from Albert's workshop. John Degotardi of Sydney, a printer and lithographer who later turned to photography, arranged to have his sister Josephine trained in Albert's workshop in Munich in 1872, just before she came to Australia. As a result of her acquired knowledge, Degotardi was able to produce collotype plates in April 1873.

Collotype was used for a short period both in New South Wales and Victoria, employed in the latter area as early as January 1885 by the Imperial Photographic Company. Publications of the Victorian Mines Department from late 1887 to 1896 contained heliotype plates, but it is not known who produced them. One such report was A. W. Howitt's *Notes on the contact of the metamorphic and sedimentary formations on the Upper Dargo River* (1892), in which photomicrographs of rock slices were reproduced. Collotype plates were also used to illustrate photomicrographs of blood cells and the structure of the venom gland of the tiger snake in G. B. Halford's *Thoughts, Observations, and Experiments on the Action of Snake Venom on the Blood* (Melbourne, Stillwell & Co., 1894). These are the earliest illustrations of photomicrographs by a photographic process so far located in Australia. Earlier reproductions were usually of drawings reproduced by wood engraving or lithography.

Fergusson & Mitchell, one of the largest printing firms in Melbourne, used a form of collotype to produce plates for George Mackay's *History of Bendigo* (1891). The previously-mentioned Crisp Photo Process patented by Niven & Co. was a collotype process in which the plate was so hardened that 10 000 copies could be taken. Bryans has suggested that this process was probably a pirated form of A. D. Edward's Photophane Process. Collotype printing was also undertaken by James Taylor and his son Donald, firstly in Port Augusta in 1901 and later the same year in Adelaide when Donald set up business in that city.

Woodburytype was patented in England in 1864 by Walter Woodbury, a photographer who had previously worked in Australia. Woodburytype has some similarities to collotype. A sensitised gelatine plate was exposed to light through a negative, but then washed with water to remove the gelatine not hardened by the light. The gelatine sheet was then placed between a plate of steel and a sheet of lead and subjected to intense pressure in a hydraulic press. The lead was forced into the irregular surface of the gelatine and produced a perfect cast of its surface. A special ink containing gelatine was then poured into this lead cast and paper placed over it in a press. When the gelatinous ink set, it adhered to the paper. The paper was placed in an alum bath to harden the gelatine, washed and dried. This process can reproduce very fine detail, so that the prints look like the photographs they replicate.

The Woodbury process was introduced into the New South Wales Government Printing Office in December 1877 but does not seem to have been used very much. Two plates in the first edition of the *Railway Guide of New South Wales* (1879) were Woodburytypes, but these plates were printed by collotype in later editions.

These various photographic processes came into use late in the nineteenth century, though photolithography had been invented in 1859 in Victoria by John Osborne at the Victorian Lands Department for the reproduction of line drawings such as maps. Because of its limitations, it was not taken up by commercial firms for printing illustrations until much later, though in 1865 the Melbourne Public Library arranged for John Noone, Osborne's successor at the Lands Department, to produce a facsimile edition of a set of reproductions of Albrecht Dürer's prints from an album acquired by the library from the Prussian government. The major disadvantage of photolithography in its early manifestation was that it could only reproduce dark solid lines and not continuous tones images such as photographs. Various improvements were attempted to adapt the process, but these met with little success, including efforts in the 1880s by the Phillips-Stephan Photo-Litho and Typographic Company in Sydney. The results were poor and this and the other photolithographic processes were rapidly superseded by process-engraving.

During the transition period from about 1875 to 1895, as photomechanical processes were being commercially applied, some interesting mixtures of illustrative techniques were used. For instance, volume one of the *Records of the Australian Museum* (1890) had heliotype plates of drawings and photographs, while volume two (1891 to 1895) included heliotype plates, lithographs and line drawings reproduced by both the Electric Photo Engraving Company's process and the Photoline Printing Company's process.

Photographs

Photographic prints were also used in some publications. The prints were pasted on thick paper and then tipped into the book. Photographs had the disadvantage that each single print had to be processed by hand, and unless properly fixed, readily faded. Examples of books with photographs are *The Horse: Its Treatment in Australia* by George Hamilton, with 17 photographs (Melbourne, 1866), and *The Gawler Handbook* by George E. Loyau (Adelaide, 1880). Hamilton's *Experiences of a Colonist Forty Years Ago* (Adelaide, 1880) includes photographs of sketches that have not reproduced very well.

Colour printing

Colour illustrations could be produced by all these methods but were expensive and not generally used except in large editions such as children's books or in deluxe editions and some government publications. In the first half of the nineteenth century, plates were coloured by hand and this was very expensive. Colour printing became common in the 1850s. Usually only three or four colours were printed to keep costs down, because the paper had to pass through the press as many times as there were colours. Often plates were merely tinted with one or two colours. Garnet Walch's *Victoria in 1880* has a mixture of tinted lithographs, and plain and tinted wood engravings. True chromolithography for colour illustrations does not seem to have been attempted for book illustration very often because of the cost, but examples include Nicholas Chevalier's garish productions in his album of Victorian scenery printed in ten colours in 1865 and the plates in the *New South Wales Album* published by Charles Troedel in 1878. These plates were lithographed in about seven colours by the lithographic artist Richard Wendel. Probably the best example of such illustrations are the 28 plates in J. H. Maiden, *The Flowering Plants and Ferns of New South Wales*, published in seven parts between 1895 and 1898 by the New South Wales Government Printer. The plates were lithographed in about eight colours by E. W. Minchen and H. J. A. Barron.

William Calvert, brother of the wood engraver Samuel, produced children's books in the 1870s with brilliant colour, using metal or wood blocks. Examples include *The Young Australian's Alphabet* and *This is the Hut that Jack Built in Australia*, both published in 1871.

Costs

The cost of producing illustrations is not easy to determine. The few examples given here are from Melbourne and may not be typical either of the trade in general or of the charges for similar work in other colonies.

Wood engravings were costed by the area of the image. In the 1870s, wood engravers working for illustrated newspapers received 2s per square inch, irrespective of the amount of work involved, hence the quality of work in many of the images in those newspapers was not very high. In April 1885, Rudolph Jenny, one of Melbourne's best wood engravers, charged £2 to engrave the head of a lizard, from a sketch by J. J. Wild, which appeared on page 79 of Decade 10 of Frederick McCoy's *Prodromus of the Zoology of Victoria*. A comparison of wood versus glass engraving for a large engraving one foot square was given in the prospectus of the Patent Engraving Company in 1882. The cost of the wood at 3d per inch was £1/16/6, drawing was £4, engraving at 3s per inch was £21/13/-, total £27/9. This compared with a glass and metal block at 16/-, drawing £4, engraving at 6d per inch £3/12/-, totalling £8/8.

In 1858, at a time when wages were rather high in Melbourne, Ludwig Becker was charging £8 per octavo plate to draw and lithograph plants in black and white for Ferdinand Mueller's *Fragmenta phytographiae Australiae*. The cost of printing 500 impressions of these plates by Hamel & Locher was £5/12/6. At the same time, Becker charged Frederick McCoy £10 per plate for drawing and lithographing fossils and animals. Hamel & Locher's printing rates were £1 per 100 if some hundreds were involved, but they charged from 12s to 15s extra for providing chalk, lithographing the title and figures (if necessary) for small numbers. Hand colouring of these plates cost £17/6/- per 100. In 1859, Becker's successor, Friedrich (Fritz) Schoenfeldt charged £9 per plate for similar work. He later charged 3s per hour. In the 1860s when wages and salaries had fallen, McCoy was able to get his plates printed at prices varying from 10s to 16s per 100 depending on how many colours were used. He cut out the cost of hand-colouring by having his plates printed in colour. In 1885, J. J. Wild charged £10 a plate for drawing and lithographing plates in four colours, with the costs of printing borne by the Government Printer.

It should be noted that the colourists used by publishers are generally not known. Often the colouring was done by the artists themselves. We do know that for his natural history plates, McCoy employed a Mrs Poole of Sandridge (4s per dozen), F. W. Woodhouse (£1 per hundred), John Kelly (£1 per hundred) and J. Riegg (27/6d per 100). In the case of Alexander Walker Scott's *Lepidoptera* the plates were produced by his talented daughters, Harriet and Helena, and were subsequently hand-coloured in London.

Some costs of commercial printing can be obtained from the ledgers of Troedel & Co. In 1898, Troedel charged £2/10/- for printing 650 copies in black and white of plates 9 and 10 in volume 11, part 2 of the *Proceedings of the Royal Society of Victoria*.

The expense of producing illustrations was certainly a limiting factor in their use, especially in small editions. Canon Marcus B. Brownrigg, the author of *The Cruise of the Freak* (Launceston, 1872), commented that the illustrations 'have been drawn on stone by an amateur and lithographed, wood engraving being too expensive a mode of illustration for the object in view'. Very few authors were like Thomas Shearman Ralph, a gifted amateur lithographer with his own press able to draw and lithograph the 24 plates in his *Elementary Botany (Australian Edition) for the Use of Beginners* (Melbourne, 1862). Some professional lithographic artists published their own illustrated books, like Cyrus Mason who wrote and illustrated *Australian Christmas Story Book* (Melbourne, 1871 and 1872). Artists Frederick Woodhouse senior and junior published their highly successful *Record of the Melbourne Cup* with 14 chromolithographs in 1889 and lithographic artist Charles Turner wrote and illustrated *Zoology and Things* (Sydney, n.d.). However, lack of capital, the cost of paper and letterpress printing and the risk of failure seem to have prevented most illustrators from self-publishing.

Tinted lithographic plate in three colours of the frog *Ranoidea aurea* (Lesson), the Golden Bell Frog, drawn and lithographed by Arthur Bartholomew, printed by Troedel & Co., plate 53 in F. McCoy, *Natural History of Victoria. Prodromus of the Zoology of Victoria; or, Figures and Descriptions of the living Species of all Classes of the Victorian Indigenous Animals*, Government Printer, Melbourne, Decade 6, 1881. 145 x 235 mm.

The outlines of the images and the lettering were drawn in lithographic ink on a clean dry lithographic stone by the lithographic artist, Arthur Bartholomew. This stone was to be printed using black ink. He then painted on three separate stones, one for each colour, the areas to be printed in the respective colours, grey, green and yellow/orange. The four stones were then sent to the printers, where each piece of plate paper was printed from each of the four stones to produce the final image. (Private collection)

Experimentation

During the late nineteenth century, many experiments were undertaken in Australia to improve existing processes or to invent new ones, though very few led to the introduction of practical processes. The most important exception was John Osborne's invention of photolithography referred to above. Many of these attempts remain unknown, but a few resulted in patents being taken out and some techniques were actually introduced. Some innovators were so desperate they published their own illustrated newspapers in competition with existing newspapers that were still using traditional wood engravings.

Melbourne wood engravers Frederick Grosse and Rudolph Jenny patented bismuthography in 1861 for the reproduction of line drawings by means of bismuth lines standing out on a zinc plate. Presumably this process was meant to replace wood engraving, but we do not know whether it was ever applied to book or magazine illustration. In 1871, Edward Roper patented his graphotype process. When it failed to attract users, he founded his own illustrated newspaper, *Graphic News of Australasia*, but it was unsuccessful and ceased after a few issues.

George Sutherland patented a lithographic process in 1879 for surface printing of illustrations, then published in 1880 the illustrated *Australian Pictorial Weekly*, which apparently used the technique. Although the newspaper failed after eight issues, his halftone process, patented in 1885 as mentioned above, was highly successful.

In 1881, Samuel Crocker patented a process to produce etchings on glass blocks. A company was formed to work the process and a few blocks were used in the *Australasian Sketcher* in 1882. Though the technique was said to be much cheaper than wood engravings, proprietors of illustrated newspapers did not take it up.

In desperation, the company founded its own illustrated newspaper, the *Australian Graphic*, published in Sydney in 1883, but this also failed and the company foundered.

Other patents for illustrative processes were applied for but whether these were ever used is unknown. Charles Nettleton and Fernand Desroziers applied for a patent for a process called photogravure or zincography in 1879. George William Levy's process of 1866 produced relief blocks using French chalk. In 1885, W. C. Norman and others of Sydney patented a process to produce an engraved block. This may have been used by the Electric Photo Engraving Company of which Norman was manager. Patents were taken out by Leon Joubert and Felix August Ratte for a black ink heliographic process in 1886, and by George Edward Walker and Jean Bonnard for a method of producing zincographic copies of photographic designs in 1887. Henry Sutton of Ballarat patented Suttontype, a form of collotype printing. It was never used in Australia, except for some sample images in a supplement to the *Ballarat Star* and failed to be successful after he took the process to England in 1890.

Personnel

The artists who drew the illustrations sometimes also engraved them on wood or copper, or lithographed them on stone or zinc, but more often these tasks were undertaken by specialist wood engravers and lithographic artists or lithographic draftsmen. Portraits were often engraved or lithographed directly by the engraver or lithographic artist from photographs. Most of the illustrators were reproductive artists, who copied the work of others.

Wood engravings could be printed by letterpress printers, but copperplates or lithographs involved highly specialised tasks undertaken by craftsmen called copperplate or lithographic printers. Transferring and colour printing, particularly, required a high degree of experience and skill.

Most illustrations were produced by specialist firms, as book printers usually undertook only letterpress printing. As the century progressed and some companies expanded, specialist artist departments developed to produce illustrations in-house. Firms such as John Sands and S. T. Leigh & Co. in New South Wales and, in Victoria, Sands & McDougall, Fergusson & Mitchell, Mason, Firth & McCutcheon, and Niven & Co. had the necessary artists and craftsmen to undertake illustrative work in-house. Most illustrated newspapers had engravers on staff, but complex work involving, for instance, particularly large blocks or colour printing was contracted out to experts such as Samuel Calvert.

During the early period of the use of halftones, most were produced by specialist firms such as the Electric Photo Engraving Company or the Melbourne Photo Engraving Company, though newspapers quickly developed their own departments to do this work.

Initially the artists and craftsmen involved in book illustration in Australia were all immigrants from Europe, mostly from Britain, but later from Germany and the United States of America. By the late 1860s personnel were being trained in Australia.

Most illustrations used in books were produced in the capital cities of the colonies. Provincial towns were usually too small to sustain a viable graphic arts industry. There were, however, exceptions in the two large towns of Victoria: Geelong and Ballarat. Ballarat firms, Rider & Mercer and F. W. Niven & Co., produced illustrations of a very high standard. Niven & Co., in particular, developed a highly successful book-publishing programme by shrewd marketing, and employed the best artists and craftsmen to sustain it.

History

Looking at the development of illustrations in Australia very generally, it can be said that copperplate engraving was used initially in most colonies and was the usual method up to the 1830s when lithography gradually came into use. Wood engraving seems to have been introduced in the late 1830s but did not have widespread use until the 1850s and then quickly became the most common method of reproduction for illustrations. Copperplate engraving virtually disappeared as a method of book illustration in the 1850s and from then on was confined to maps or commercial uses such as billheads and bank notes. Lithography continued as an important technique right through the century. Wood engraving declined rapidly in the late 1880s and early 1890s to become obsolete as photomechanical processes superseded it. Western Australia is an exception to this general history. The colony was too small to have the expertise necessary to produce illustrations of good quality, but with the rapid development in the early 1890s as a result of the gold rushes, the situation changed quickly and the latest photographic techniques were introduced.

New South Wales

The first book illustrations produced in New South Wales were a series of plates engraved by the artist John William Lewin, who arrived in 1800, for the Sydney edition of his *Birds of New Holland* (1813). Other engravers, entering Sydney either as freemen or as convicts, also set up in business or were engaged by printers or publishers to produce engraved plates. Walter Preston, an engraver, came as a convict to Sydney in 1812 and was assigned to the publisher Absalom West. Preston created a series of engraved plates for *Views of New South Wales*, published by West in 1813 and 1814.

The first lithographic press to arrive in New South Wales was purchased by the Governor, Sir Thomas Brisbane, from Rudolph Ackermann some time between December 1821 and December 1825. It was entrusted to James Dunlop, the assistant at Brisbane's private observatory. It is not known whether the press was used, but on Brisbane's departure, it was given to Augustus Earle who employed it for lithographic prints and also commercial work. As a result, by the late 1820s it was possible to produce illustrations in Sydney either by copperplate engraving or lithography, although such book illustrations as do appear, mostly in almanacs, seem to have been done by engraving.

The first permanent lithographer in Sydney was apparently John Gardner Austin, who arrived in 1834 and published his *A Series of Twelve Profile Portraits of Aborigines of New South Wales* and *Lithographic Drawings of Sydney and its Environs* in 1836. Austin sold his business the next year to David Edward Barlow, who in turn sold it to William Kellett Baker in 1840. Raphael Clint had also set up a lithography firm in Sydney in March 1837.

The first woodcut produced in Australia was the masthead for the *Sydney Gazette*, 5 March 1803, that Butler suspects was the work of the convict copperplate engraver John Austin, who arrived in 1800.

Other simple wood engravings or woodcuts are known from the 1820s and early 1830s, possibly produced by William Wilson. Butler believes Wilson also executed a somewhat later wood engraving in *Bell's Life in Sydney and Sporting Reviewer*, 18 January 1845. Wood engraving for books seems to have commenced with Dublin-born Robert Clayton who undertook some plates in James Maclehose's *Picture of Sydney* (1838). Clayton's son Thomas, who had arrived in 1835 with his father, became Sydney's leading wood engraver in the 1840s, providing illustrations for the journal *Atlas* in 1846 and William Baker's *Heads of the People* in 1847–48. Baker's publication is notable in that it contains illustrations produced by lithography, wood engraving and copperplate engraving, and is possibly the last Australian publication to use all three processes under the one cover.

Most Sydney engravers and lithographers of the 1840s worked well into the 1850s, but gradually new arrivals changed the face of the trade. Wood engravers Charles Mason and George Mason arrived in 1850, followed in 1852 by Walter George Mason, who was proprietor and illustrator of the *Illustrated Sydney News* (1853–55) and also engraved for *Sydney Punch*. Two hundred of his engravings appeared in the *Australian Picture Pleasure Book* (1857). His sons Edward and Frederick also became well-known wood engravers. In Sydney, amateur lithographers played an important role in book illustration, possibly because the authors could not afford commercial artists, but also possibly because they were not as talented — at least in scientific illustration — as the amateurs. Harriet and Helena Scott, excellent artists in their own right, provided lithographic plates for James C. Cox's *Monograph of Australian Land Shells* (1868), Gerard Krefft's *Snakes of Australia* (1869) and his *Australian Mammals* (1871). As noted previously, the sisters also illustrated their father Alexander Walker Scott's *Australian Lepidoptera* (1864, 1890). The lithographic artists S. T. Gill and Edmund Thomas were also involved in this latter publication.

Thomas Richards, the New South Wales Government Printer, introduced a number of photomechanical methods into the Government Printing Office in the late 1870s. At the Sydney International Exhibition, he exhibited illustrations produced by photoxylography, a technique whereby photographs were produced on wood for engraving. He introduced this process in 1878.

Other illustrations produced by 'Woodbury, heliotype, Albertype, Obernetter, Waterhouse, photoxylography, photo-skytography, photo-engraving and autotype' were also displayed. The first edition of the *Railway Guide of New South Wales*, published that year, included a very elegant chromolithographed and photolithographed title page, wood engravings of flowers, ferns and views, collotype plates, two plates produced by Woodburytype and two coloured maps produced by lithography.

The 1880s saw some of the largest illustrated publications of the nineteenth century issued in Sydney. In 1886, John Sands published *The New Atlas of Australia* by Robert McLean, in five parts, one for each of the mainland colonies. This was a major undertaking: in addition to 99 maps, there were plates of illustrations and decorative titles and covers by lithographic artist Charles Turner, formerly of Melbourne. Despite the level of sophistication of the graphic arts in Sydney at this time, it apparently was not good enough for the proprietors of the proposed *Picturesque Atlas of Australasia*. The Picturesque Atlas Company brought its own artists from the United States of America under Frederic B. Schell and wood engravers under the supervision of Horace Baker, to undertake the work, but also used many local artists and engravers. Issued in 42 parts making up three volumes, the *Atlas* included over 800 wood and steel engravings, ranging from full page to small vignettes. Steel engravings were used for some full-page plates for portraits where the image was not interspersed with text. The *Picturesque Atlas* was published from 1886 through to 1889. The text and plates were reissued without the maps in 1892 under the title *Australasia Illustrated*. The illustrations in the *Picturesque Atlas* were drawn by the artists in Indian ink on a large scale, then the image was reduced and printed by photography onto a woodblock to guide the engraver. Electrotypes were made both of the engraved blocks and the set text and the electrotypes printed on Hoe & Co.'s stop-cylinder presses. W. S. Calvert in Melbourne also made some photo-engraved zinc blocks for The Picturesque Atlas Company.

G. J. Broinowski published *Birds and Mammals of Australia* in 1885. It had 16 coloured plates of birds and 15 of mammals all drawn and lithographed by the author. The final large work of the period was his *Birds of Australia*. Published in six parts between 1887 and 1891, it included 303 plates drawn and probably lithographed by Broinowski; as a result they are not as good as other natural history plates by more talented artists. The plates were printed in six or eight colours by S. T. Leigh & Co. or Geo. Murray & Co.

Victoria

The earliest illustrations known to have been produced in Melbourne were lithographs and an engraving that appeared in the *Port Phillip Magazine* early in 1843. The lithographs were executed by G. A. Gilbert and Henry Lingham and the engraving by Thomas Ham. Both methods were used in the district to reproduce illustrations throughout the 1840s. The first book known to have had lithographic illustrations was William Henry Mortimer's *Warning Voice, and some important considerations on the observance of the Lord's Day* (October, 1844). This had two lithographs executed by Thomas Ham, but no copy of this work has been located, so the nature of the illustrations is not known.

William Hull's pamphlet *Remarks on the Probable Origin and Antiquity of the Aboriginal Natives* (Melbourne, 1846) has unsigned lithographs in three colours. There is no imprint, but they were probably undertaken by Thomas Ham. In the 1840s the only other illustrations produced were mostly in the form of trade cards engraved by Ham, inserted in the few almanacs published at that time, plus the odd plate of signals. This situation changed when he began to publish the *Illustrated Australian Magazine* (1850–52), which contained both engraved plates and lithographs executed by himself, David Tulloch and William Strutt.

The rapid increase in population resulting from the gold rushes not only created a bigger market, but also led to an influx of very talented craftsmen and artists, so that the quality of work produced in Melbourne improved dramatically. Wood engraving was introduced into Victoria by James Andrews in 1851, followed by Samuel Calvert, then Charles Winston, and later Frederick Grosse and Rudolph Jenny. Their work was widely used in books, magazines and newspapers. Lithographic artists such as Edmund Gilks, Henry Glover, Edmund Thomas (later of Sydney), S. T. Gill, Cyrus Mason, Ludwig Becker and Friedrich (Fritz) Schoenfeldt provided a pool of talent for the production of lithographs.

Some of Victoria's most significant illustrated books were published by the Government Printer and most were of a scientific nature. Ferdinand Mueller's larger botanical monographs, such as *Iconography of Australian Species of Acacia* (1887–88), were well-illustrated with quarto lithographic plates. Though the letterpress was set and printed at the Government Printing Office, the plates were lithographed by freelance lithographic artists and printed by private enterprise until the 1880s because the Government Printer did not have a lithographic printer until 1878.

Professor Frederick McCoy began his large project to describe and illustrate the zoology and palaeontology of Victoria in 1858, using the same artists who were working for Mueller: Ludwig Becker and Friedrich (Fritz) Schoenfeldt. Though many plates were accumulated, it was not until 1874 that the first part of the aforementioned *Prodromus of the Palaeontology of Victoria* appeared; it ran to seven parts of ten plates each, the last part appearing in 1882. At first the plates were coloured by hand, but later they were printed in four to six colours. The *Prodromus of the Zoology of Victoria* did not commence publication until 1878 and continued until 1890, making 20 parts in two volumes of 200 plates. From 1878, the plates were printed at the Government Printing Office.

Two other significant publications of the Victorian Government Printing Office were both compiled by R. Brough Smyth. The *Gold Fields and Mineral Districts of Victoria* (1869) had so many wood-engraved illustrations that Frederick Grosse was especially recruited into the Government Printing Office to undertake the work. The lithographed maps in the book were printed by the Lithographic Branch of the Mining Department, formerly the Lithographic Branch of the Geological Survey of Victoria. Grosse also did all the wood engravings for the two-volume *Aborigines of Victoria* (1878).

Private enterprise also produced significant illustrated publications. Garnet Walch's *Victoria in 1880*, published in 1880 by George Robertson, consisted of lithographs by Charles Turner and wood engravings from Turner's and H. J. Woodhouse's drawings engraved by Frank Appleton, Samuel Calvert, Rudolph Jenny and R. B. Smith.

The end of the 1880s saw the publication of the last of the large illustrated books, with the appearance of *Victoria and its Metropolis* in two volumes (1888). Nearly every wood engraver working in Melbourne at the time, plus one or two from Sydney, was used for this publication, the last significant work to be produced in Melbourne using wood engravings. Subsequent encyclopaedic works used photomechanical processes to produce illustrations.

Tasmania

Though the printer Andrew Bent commenced copperplate printing in April 1820 using existing plates, it was not until 1824, with the arrival of the convict engraver and miniature painter Thomas Bock, that engraved illustrations could be produced in the colony. Hobart publisher James Ross hired Bock and later Charles Bruce to create illustrations for his *Hobart Town Almanacs* from 1829 to 1836. Ross's successor, W. G. Elliston, employed Bruce for his almanacs of the same title in 1837 and 1838.

Lithography was introduced in Hobart in November 1829 by the lithographer James Wood and his wife Eulalie, their firm being run in her name. The Woods printed Charles Atkinson's *Views through Hobart Town* in September 1833.

From 1838 through 1839, Henry Dowling's pirated edition of Charles Dickens's *Pickwick Papers* was published, complete with rather crude copies of the original illustrations reproduced by lithography. It is not known who undertook this work, but it was likely the Woods or perhaps Henry Melville, who practised lithography in Hobart from 1833. Thomas Bluett, an experienced lithographic printer, came to Hobart in 1843. After working for publisher James Thomson, he set up on his own account and, amongst other things, printed plates for John Skinner Prout's *Sydney Illustrated* (1842–43) and *Tasmania Illustrated* (1844).

Robin Vaughan Hood, a lithographer who arrived in Hobart in 1833, purchased Prout's lithographic press in 1848. In 1851 his business passed to his son Robin Lloyd Hood thereby placing lithography in Hobart on a permanent footing.

Wood engraving was established in Launceston as early as 1836 by William Lushington Goodwin, and in Hobart in 1846 by a

'Mrs Rogers'. The technique does not seem to have been used to the same extent as copperplate engraving or lithography.

The population of Tasmania was too small to justify sophisticated printing establishments, so much of the quality work seems to have been contracted to firms in Melbourne. The largest and most prolifically illustrated book to be undertaken in Tasmania was Robert M. Johnston's *Systematic Account of the Geology of Tasmania* (1888). Though it was printed and bound by the Tasmanian Government Printer, with lithographs printed at the Tasmanian Lands Department, the wood engravings were undertaken by George Collingridge, an engraver living in Sydney from 1879. Many of the lithographs were very crude because they were executed by amateurs: Mrs C. P. Sprent, W. H. Cundy and Alice Hudson.

Queensland

No craftsmen in Brisbane could undertake illustrations either in engraving or lithography until the arrival of the aforementioned Thomas Ham and his partner William Knight in 1861. Even so, their work appears to have been mostly of a commercial nature. Ham does not seem to have undertaken any book work except for the provision of engraved maps for the *Atlas of Queensland* published by the Queensland Government Printer in February 1866.

The most significant illustrated book published in the colony during this period was Silvester Diggles's *The Ornithology of Australia*. It was issued in parts from 1866, each part having six hand-coloured lithographic plates. The lithography was undertaken by Eaton & Wilson. Henry Green Eaton was a lithographer in Tasmania in the 1840s, but later moved to Brisbane and then Rockhampton.

Other illustrated natural history books included botanical texts by Queensland botanist F. M. Bailey, lithographed by H. G. Eaton, Warwick & Sapsford, and H. J. Diddams & Co. In two of Bailey's books, *Lithograms of the Ferns of Queensland* (Brisbane, 1892) and *An Illustrated Monograph of the Grasses of Queensland* (Brisbane, 1879), the illustrations were produced by lithography using a variety of nature printing from the plants themselves. In the book on grasses, the illustrations were electrotyped by K. T. Staiger (of the Queensland Museum) and lithographed by Warwick & Sapsford.

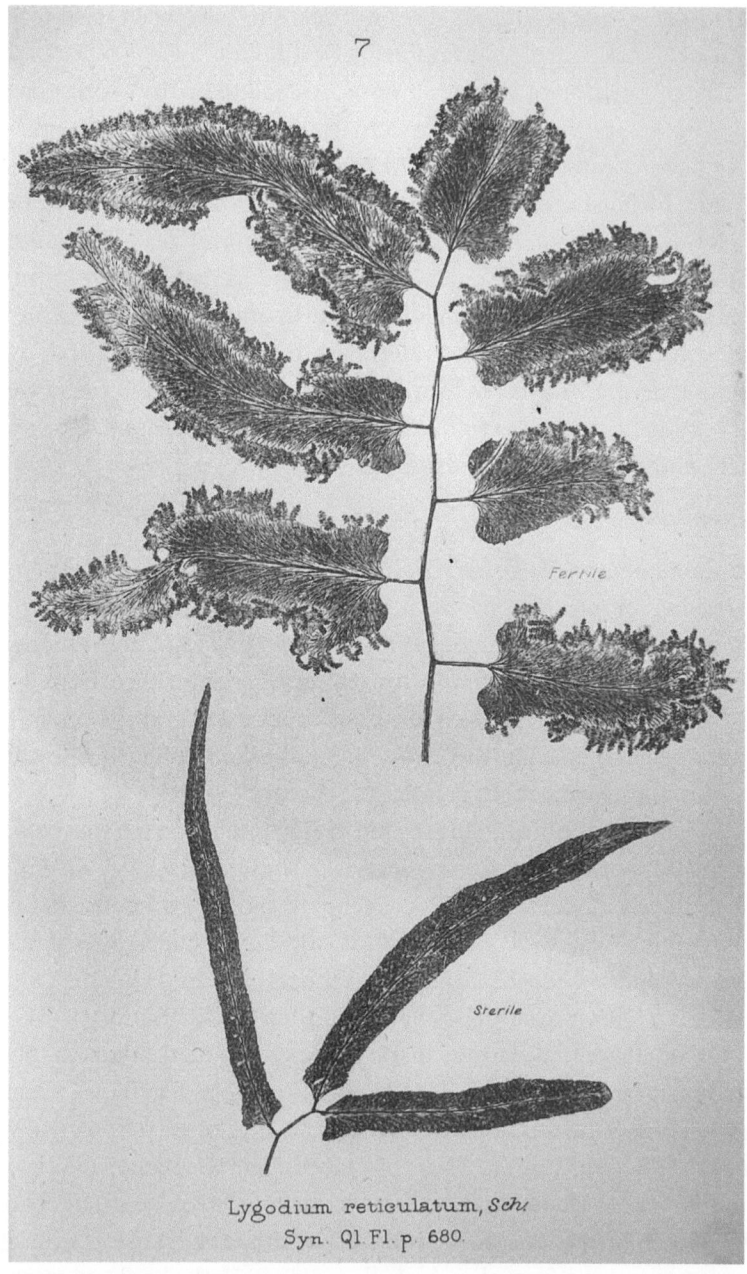

Nature printed plate of a fern *Lygodium reticulatum*, printed by John Thomas Costin, Government Lithographer, at the Government Printer, Brisbane, Plate 7 in F. M. Bailey, *Lithograms of the Ferns of Queensland*, Department of Agriculture, Brisbane, 1892. Printed at the Government Engraving and Lithographic Office. Dimensions of printed area 120 x 200 mm.

The fern was coated with lithographic printing ink then carefully laid on a clean dry lithographic stone. It was then covered and the stone with the fern in place run through a lithographic press to transfer the ink onto the stone. The fern was removed, leaving the image of the fern in ink on the stone. The stone was first wetted and then inked, the ink only adhering to the fern image and being repelled by the clean areas of the stone. The stone was now ready for printing, put in the lithographic press, paper placed on the stone; and paper and stone run through the press to produce the fern image on the paper. (Royal Botanic Gardens, Library, Melbourne)

Joseph Augustus Clarke, Queensland's most important artist of the period, was a co-founder of *Queensland Punch* in 1866, contributing to its illustrations then and later when it was re-founded in 1878. He also provided illustrations for the *Queenslander*, including the elaborate front cover illustration engraved in Melbourne by Samuel Calvert, and for the few books published in Queensland, such as James Brunton Stephens's *Marsupial Bill* (Brisbane, 1879).

By the 1880s, Brisbane printers could produce illustrated periodicals similar to those of the larger colonies: *Queensland Figaro* and *Queensland Punch*, illustrated by Arnold Vivian Thomas, a Lands Department lithographic draftsman, and printed by Warwick & Sapsford, and *The Boomerang*, printed by Alfred Walker. In the latter case, photographic processes were used, overcoming the need to have skilled wood engravers. Even so, it seems that many illustrations in Queensland publications were furnished by artists living in Sydney and Melbourne.

South Australia

In the 1840s, a number of prints or collections of prints were produced in Adelaide by skilled amateurs such as Nathaniel Hailes or professionals such as Henry Cooper Jervis (before he moved to Sydney), but there was no sustained commercial production. With the arrival of lithographic artist Samuel Thomas Gill and wood engravers Samuel Calvert and Charles Winston, high quality work began. There were, however, still no commercial firms with craftsmen who could capitalise on this talent to undertake sophisticated illustrative work on a larger scale until the arrival of the lithographic printers John Penman and William Galbraith, who set up in business in Adelaide in 1848. They printed S. T. Gill's *Heads of the People* in three series in 1849.

The exodus from Adelaide to Victoria at the beginning of the gold rush was a serious set-back for the trade, because most craftsmen and artists left, never to return. Through the latter half of the nineteenth century, only a few firms in Adelaide were capable of producing sophisticated illustrations. Nevertheless, a number of illustrated periodicals were established, some of which appear to have used artisans imported from Melbourne, including wood engraver W. Hart, who was active in Adelaide in the mid-1860s and illustrated the Handbook to the City of Adelaide [1867]. Adelaide Punch, issued in the late 1860s, seems to have had at least some of its illustrations made in Melbourne, using artist Thomas Carrington and wood engraver Rudolph Jenny.

The limited talent available to produce good lithographic plates to illustrate scientific works, and the cost involved, can be seen in the difficulties experienced by Professor Ralph Tate in finding lithographic artists to illustrate his specimens for publication. In 1879 and 1880 his artist was G. H. Strother, with plates lithographed by J. Williams; from 1886 to 1889 the artist was W. J. Chidley, but when Chidley left to go to Sydney, there was no one to undertake this work so the letterpress of one paper was issued with the comment that the plates were delayed. They were issued a year later in 1892 with plates by the artist 'A.T.A.' and H. Barrett of the South Australian Government Printing Office. Most of Barrett's work for Tate is of a high standard, but he had considerable difficulty when it came to reproducing small specimens, and the results are not of the same quality as the earlier illustrations.

The major nineteenth-century illustrated work of South Australia was J. E. Brown's *Forest Flora of South Australia*, published in 1882 by the South Australian Government Printer. The illustrations, mostly drawn by Rosa Fiveash, were lithographed by H. Barrett and printed at the Government Printing Office in four or five colours. Though technically of a high standard, artistically the illustrations do not match those produced in Melbourne or Sydney.

Western Australia

The population of this colony was so small that illustrated works were almost entirely confined to government publications. Robert Austin's *Journal of an Expedition to Explore the Interior of Western Australia* was published in Perth in 1855 with lithographs of W. A. Sanford's sketches by A. Hillman. William Müller, an engraver and die-sinker, resident in Perth from 1864, did some illustrative work for the *Inquirer*. Cartoons for the *Goldfields Courier* were apparently sent to the eastern colonies to be engraved. With the increase in population as a result of the discovery of gold at Coolgardie and Kalgoorlie in the 1890s, craftsmen from the east were recruited and photoengraving was established in Perth to produce good quality illustrations, for instance in the weekly *Western Mail*.

NOTE ON SOURCES

Roger Butler's *Printed Images in Colonial Australia 1801–1901*, Canberra, National Gallery of Australia, 2007, provides an overview of the history and development of illustrations in Australia, but there are no histories for individual colonies except for Tasmania, well covered by Clifford Craig's three books: *The Engravers of Van Diemen's Land*, Launceston, Tasmanian Historical Research Association, 1961; *Old Tasmanian Prints*, Launceston, Foot & Playsted, 1964; and *More Old Tasmanian Prints*, Launceston, Foot & Playsted, 1984; and by Butler's chapter, 'Thomas Bock, Engraver' in Diane Dunbar, ed., *Thomas Bock. Convict Engraver, Society Portraitist: Exhibition and Catalogue*, Launceston, Queen Victoria Museum & Art Gallery, 1991. Thomas A. Darragh's chapter '"The desert shall rejoice and bloom": Botanical prints in Colonial Australia' in Gordon Morrison et al, *Capturing Flora: 300 Years of Australian Botanical Art*, Ballarat, Art Gallery of Ballarat, 2012, provides a survey of botanical illustrations published in Australia. Peter Dowling has published several papers on Australian illustrated newspapers and their illustrations.

The first lithographs in New South Wales were studied by Butler, 'Sir Thomas Brisbane, Augustus Earle and Australia's First Lithographs' in *The Australian Connoisseur and Collector*, no.3, 1982, pp. 94-99, 130. Darragh has summarised the beginnings of engraving and lithography in New South Wales and Victoria in *The Establishment and Development of Engraving and Lithography in Melbourne to the time of the Gold Rush*, Willow Bend, Thumb Creek, NSW, Garravembi, 1990. Early printmaking in South Australia is dealt with by Alison Carroll, *Graven Images in the Promised Land: A History of Printmaking in South Australia, 1836–1981*, Adelaide, Art Gallery of South Australia, 1981.

Entries on various artists, engravers and lithographers in Joan Kerr, ed., *Dictionary of Australian Artists: painters, sketchers, photographers and engravers to 1870*, Melbourne: OUP, 1992; as well as contemporary illustrated books, were used to draw up the history of the various colonies. Marguerite Mahood's *The Loaded Line: Australian political caricature, 1788–1901*, Carlton, VIC, MUP, 1973, provides information on illustrators and illustration in newspapers and magazines. Vanessa Finney's *Transformations: Harriet and Helena Scott, colonial Sydney's finest natural history painters*, Sydney, NewSouth, 2018, treats two of the most important artists of the period.

Also relating to individuals in the trade, the author of this chapter is the compiler of *Engravers and Lithographers in Colonial Victoria: A Directory*, Melbourne, Ancora Press, 2023.

A few contemporary descriptions of techniques and processes were published in Australia. John Degotardi, who pioneered collotype printing, published a popular account of other printing techniques in *The Art of Printing*, Sydney, 1861, (reprinted Sydney, Officina Boronia, 1982). John Fletcher has provided further background on Degotardi and printing processes in *John Degotardi*, Sydney, Book Collectors' Society of Australia, 1984. An account of Woodburytype is given by the man who introduced it to Australia, Ludovico W. Hart, in 'The rise and progress of photography', *Journal and Proceedings of the Royal Society of New South Wales*, no.12, 1879, pp. 145-64. A lecture by Cyrus Mason gives useful background on the traditional techniques of reproduction in 'The "Multiplying" Art', *Industrial and Technological Museum, Melbourne. Lectures . . . Autumn 1871*, Melbourne, Samuel Mullen, 1871. Photomechanical processes in use towards the end of the nineteenth century were summarised by John J. Horrocks, who worked on the *Illustrated Sydney News*, in his 'Modern methods used for the reproduction of pictures', *Report of the first meeting of the Australasian Association for the Advancement of Science*, 1889, pp. 537-43.

There is a complete bibliography of all books using actual photographs as illustrations in Robert Holden, *Photography in Colonial Australia. The Mechanical Eye and the Illustrated Book*, Sydney, Hordern House, 1988.

Useful modern technical references on nineteenth-century illustrative processes are Estelle Jussim's *Visual Communication and the Graphic Arts*, New York, R. R. Bowker Co., 1974; and Luis Nadeau's *Encyclopaedia of Printing, Photographic and Photomechanical Processes*, Fredericton, [the author], 1990.

Lastly, the author would like to express his gratitude to the following for their assistance in providing information for this chapter: Dianne Byrne, John Oxley Library, Brisbane, Queensland; Jenny Carew, Toowoomba, Queensland; and Joanna Sassoon, Curtin University, Western Australia.

CHAPTER 5

Australian Colonial Binding

Carol Mills

We do not know how the first edition of that near-icon of Australian children's books, *Cole's Funny Picture Book* (1879) was bound, as it seems that no copy survives. The second edition, published in about 1882, was a red cloth volume. The editions which followed for the next century were black, decorated with Cole's familiar arching rainbow. The second of these was decorated in black and gold, with a gilt rainbow, and a gold frame line around the cover design. In the bottom right-hand corner of its frame line can be read: 'W. Detmold, Binder'.

There are more known nineteenth-century Australian bindings by the German-born William Detmold (1828–1884) than by any other binder. Detmold came to Australia during the gold rushes, returned to his trade and established a successful business in Melbourne from about 1852, with agencies or branches in several colonies. Surprisingly, he trained as a binder not in Germany, but in New York. He became wealthy through financial speculation, mostly in book-trade enterprises, where he was known by some as 'the great debt-moulder'. His business, taken over about 1890 by the Spicer paper firm, continued bookbinding until at least 1956.

In the earliest period, almost certainly most binding was done for the stationery trade — in the production of cash books, journals and the like. Ledgers, not printed books, sustained the skills of colonial bookbinders. For much of the nineteenth century, Australian bookbinding was practised in firms encompassing a blend of book trades such as printing, bookselling and stationery. In Adelaide in 1866 we find Charles Platts's book, music and stationery warehouse offering 'music, harmoniums, mourning, photograph albums, archery and cricketry ... [binding and more]'. William Moffitt (1802–1874), a Liverpool binder who arrived as a convict, began binding in Sydney in 1830 but diversified into stationery, bookselling and engraving to make a living. His business continued as W. C. Penfolds into the early 2000s. Detmold was unusual in concentrating on binding from the start. With increasing specialisation, the book trades gradually — but never fully — drew apart, or developed into specialist departments of larger businesses.

The early binders were mostly of British extraction, bringing their training with them. Unfortunately we know very little about their lives and work. Although there appear to have been no women craft-binders until the early twentieth century, 'respectable' women were working as folders and sewers at an early date, no doubt following a tradition going back to the eighteenth century in Britain. In New South Wales, Van Diemen's Land, Western Australia, and probably Queensland, the first binders were convicts, one of whom was working in Sydney by 1796. The first binder we know by name is Thomas Broughton, *alias* William Smith, who arrived in 1799 as a convict, was binding by 1803, had given up by 1811, and possibly died in 1815. As with all binders before Moffitt, none of Broughton's work has been definitely identified.

Binders and binding firms flit in and out of Australian book history, totalling hundreds throughout the country by the end of the century. Edward Welsh and John Boyland were Sydney convict binders in government service at the time of the Bigge Commission in 1820, joining forces when free, to form Boyland and Welsh by 1828. This was also the year that the *Sydney Gazette* was scathing about the quality of the binding of that year's *New South Wales Pocket Almanack*. Welsh, who as a convict worked under Boyland, carried on alone; Boyland disappears from the record. The aforementioned William Moffitt was the first prominent Sydney binder. He became a wealthy man from land speculation in the city area and was described in the *Gazette* in 1831 as 'that excellent bookbinder'.

Also in Sydney, Charles Harwood, an 1850s binder, was a convict assigned to Moffitt before working for himself. George Springate or Springquart, another Moffitt-assigned convict, was originally a copperplate printer. He received a colonial sentence and ended up as a binder in Van Diemen's Land, via Norfolk Island. James Conyber, a master binder working in Sydney from the 1850s, shared an address for several years with engraver and bookbinders' toolmaker Alfred Flack, who thus may have made Conyber's tools. A Sydney binder of the 1850s and 1860s, Newman Sapsford, by the 1870s had become a Brisbane printer (continuing to offer binding) and was prominent in the wrangles between print trade unions and employers there at the end of the century.

Along with William Moffitt, perhaps the most consistently competent of Australian colonial binder-craftsmen was Glasgow-born George Rolwegan (1812–1866). A free settler of Hobart Town, he sent some much-praised exhibits to London's Great Exhibition of 1851, decorated with tooling of California gold, beaten in Van Diemen's Land by Hobart picture-framer Robin Vaughan Hood, and bound in local skins prepared by J. G. Reeves. Rolwegan was lost at sea in the foundering of the SS *London* in the Bay of Biscay in January 1866. Some of his tools are in collections of the State Library of Tasmania.

South Australia had two unnamed binders by 1840, working in the offices of the *Register*. Bookseller E. S. Wigg advertised binding by 1851. As previously noted, Adelaide's first bookseller, Charles Platts, offered a bookbinding service by 1848, although it is not clear if in the early years this was carried out by his employees.

In Melbourne, George Cooper was almost certainly the first binder, working out of the *Port Phillip Patriot* office by 1842. George Robertson, a bookseller by trade, established a bindery in his new 1872 building on Little Collins Street. Melbourne binders of the 1880s and 1890s, James and William Wrigley, began as apprentices to Detmold. Bernard Stein of Perth, a German-born convict and binder by trade, achieved notoriety when he escaped from Western Australia in 1874 by walking to Adelaide. The unfortunate Stein was caught, and returned to Perth, with his sentence extended. He later married a widow of some means and became a prominent Perth and goldfields binder, bookseller, printer and stationer.

Photograph of employee working on books in the Binding Section, NSW Government Printing Office, Sydney, c.1890. From an album of images of the printery dating from 1871 to 1910. See also image in Chapter 3, from the same album, showing women in the Sewers' Room. 12 x 10 in. (State Archives & Records Authority of NSW; State Library of NSW)

Until the eighteenth century, the printed book was most commonly bound in plain calf or sheep. Time has proven these to be less durable than the more expensive goatskin, vellum or tanned pigskin. In the early 1800s publishers continued to sell their books as folded sheets wrapped in plain paper to protect them, or in light paper and card covers held together by simple stab-sewing. The book buyer commissioned a binding to his or her own requirements from the bookseller, or from a bookbinder. Signing bindings — in gold, with stamps or with tickets — was not particularly common until the eighteenth century, or even the nineteenth. The earliest signed Australian work seems to be Moffitt's, perhaps dating from the first half of the 1830s.

Craft-binding never became strong in Australia, largely because the age of the industrially cased book had arrived by the time binding in any quantity was needed. In the first decades of settlement, book production was negligible. There was little to bind, as most books were imported as already-bound volumes, and binding work was limited to local publications, repairs, newspapers and periodicals. Even at the 1879 Sydney and the 1880 Melbourne exhibitions a number of European bookbinders exhibited, indicating that the practice of binding before shipment continued; this was certainly still the case with new books bought by libraries, although by the end of the century the major libraries had well-developed binding policies and practices.

The earliest Australian printed books were published in the old way, ready to be bound by the buyer, or with printer/publisher/booksellers such as George Howe, the only one in New South Wales for many years, accepting orders which included a request from the purchaser for a particular style of binding. Most of these publications were functional: almanacs, government orders, handbooks, scriptures (some in Pacific languages for the missions based out of Sydney, as Susan Woodburn discusses in Chapter 22), spellers, and so on.

It was not until 1813 that the first 'non-functional' Australian title, John Lewin's *Birds of New South Wales* (Sydney, George Howe), appeared, in a very limited edition. It would be interesting to know when and where the copies of this title were bound, but, if bound locally in 1813, it was presumably by an unidentified convict, perhaps Charles Clark(e), who arrived in 1807 and was due for release in 1814, when he was working as a binder. There is no mention of bookbinders in musters, nor are there any advertisements in the *Sydney Gazette*, for binders who can be confirmed as working in 1813. Broughton, the first known binder, was no longer active. It was not uncommon for a book to be bound well after printing, so possibly Lewin's work was bound by the next known binder to arrive in 1814, a free man, H. Tindell, who does not seem to have stayed long in the colony. In 1818 the *Sydney Gazette* advertised itself as offering binding, with no tradesman named. The situation was similar in Van Diemen's Land, where Andrew Bent's *Hobart Town Gazette*, founded in 1816, offered a binding service. Although advertising in his own right after he arrived in 1818, the earliest named Tasmanian binder,

Robert Drysdale, was a convict working under Bent's direction, and was not emancipated until 1831.

The nineteenth century saw the rapid technological advance of many industries, including book production. Papermaking was mechanised; steam was harnessed to drive printing and other equipment. Binding machinery evolved to keep up with these innovations. This was the era of the rise of the great publishing houses; the creation of a new industry. The introduction of this technology meant that by the 1880s there was a marked separation between craft-binding and edition-binding. Increasingly more books, even in Australia, were being bound using machines. However, the introduction of this equipment was slow and uneven in its application. '[In New South Wales] up to nearly the middle of the present [nineteenth] century almost anything in the [binding] trade was done by hand', wrote the *Australian Town and Country Journal* in 1873. Even though most binding done in the Australian colonies occurs during the period of increasing industrialisation which began in the 1820s and was flourishing by the 1860s, nineteenth-century Australian binding remained embedded in the pre-industrial age until later in the century. Hand-binding, or at least casing by hand rather than by machine, continued after mechanisation was in use abroad. Even so, by the 1880s the hand tools and ploughs (for trimming edges) of the past were being supplanted by the new equipment, which handled in mass everything from pressing, gluing, cutting, trimming, sewing and stapling to 'forwarding' and 'finishing' (covering and decorating).

Case-binding — attaching a complete cover made separately from the book — replaced lacing-on of boards that were then covered in leather. Book cloth was used on case-bound covers in England from about 1825, particularly on edition or publisher's bindings. Cloth made an early appearance in Australia, although even in the 1890s libraries regarded it as inferior to leather. Craft-binding became a luxury service, one of several pursuits fostered by the Arts and Crafts Movement of the early twentieth century. Most binding moved from craftspeople to machine feeders or technicians.

For most of the nineteenth century, the greater number of tools and materials used were imported. In Victoria such items were subject to reduced duty, recognising the lack of a local product. Some gold leaf was locally made after the gold rushes. Binders' skins (though the local product was considered inferior) were prepared from local calf and sheep or from imported raw goat skins. Some tools were locally made, perhaps most notably by Charles Roeszler of Melbourne, who set up in 1869. Complete engraved cover designs, meant to simulate tooling but 'fly-embossed' onto covers in one process by the binder, were among Roeszler's work. *Cole's Funny Picture Book* of circa 1882, selling at 1/6d, aimed at the cheaper end of the market and was almost certainly produced using any labour-saving device then available. The fact that Detmold, one of the best-equipped binders of his time, was named in the cover design makes it clear that the cover decoration was specially made for fly-pressing, although the design itself, which could not have been made with binder's tools, also makes this clear. Roeszler is the likely maker; he is known to have done such work well, and his workshops were not far from Detmold's bindery. His firm is still operating, but not making tools.

'Some well-executed specimens of colonial marble-paper', possibly from George Robertson's bindery, were noted at the Victorian Exhibition of 1875. In 1876 Melbourne stationers Evans and Campbell were using paper which 'they found surpassed all other kinds for book-binding' from Samuel Ramsden's Melbourne mill, which is discussed in the next chapter. It was seemingly insufficient. In 1872 a binders' deputation, which included Detmold, representatives of Sands & McDougall and of George Robertson, called on the Victorian Commissioner for Customs seeking suspension of import duty on certain papers, including surface-coloured and marbled.

The use of book cloth, never made locally even in the twentieth century, demonstrates one problem that could result from reliance on imports. It was common practice to bind up a portion of a publisher's edition, binding more printed copies only when the first batch was sold. This has resulted in identical texts having different colour or texture cloth covers, and occasionally even slight variations in size.

With increased use of industrial binding, public perception of the distinction between binding and casing became blurred, with 'binding' coming to be understood more in terms of embellishment than structure. In the 1890s D. M. Angus, of Angus and Robertson, as a witness for the defence, gave a flamboyant demonstration of the difference in court. The publishers of the rather bulky vanity publication (still to be found in numbers out of all proportion to its importance), *Australian Men of Mark* (1889), advertised as being bound in half morocco, were suing customers for refusing to pay for their copies. Walter Stone told the story in 1961 of Angus who, 'holding a volume of *Men of Mark* by the covers [...] gave it a shake, and out fell the inside and all the men of mark therein. "That ... is what is known as a 'cased book' unless it has been properly stitched into its covers". No doubt some 'men of mark' regretted placing orders. The defence argued that the book was not bound. In a significant comment on then-current appreciation of what constituted binding, they lost.

Men of Mark was bound by Detmold. It is lavish in appearance, half red morocco, half red grained cloth, with gilt and black decoration and lettering on the covers, the edges and the spine. It was machine cased. Machines would have folded, pressed and trimmed it; a machine bevelled its boards. Its headbands were pre-made, not plaited onto the text. Most, if not all, of its decoration and lettering was done with engraved plates, rather than being a design devised using the individual tools from the binder's bench.

Not all of the earlier Australian binders were tradesmen, as binding of a sort was frequently offered by printers, particularly in country areas. Most of their work is unsigned. We have names, if we have anything, but rarely can we link these to specific works. There is much to learn about this integral part of the history of Australian books. By the end of the century, hand-binding was becoming expensive for collectors, who were beginning to prize edition binding, further reducing opportunities for good tradesmen. John J. Troy stated in *Art in Australia* in 1925 that 'We must be thankful that the modern binder is content to receive less than a rabbit-trapper and almost as much as a Cremorne gardener'.

NOTE ON SOURCES

The history of Australian bookbinding is diffuse, with very little detailed information being readily available about most of the binders, the perception of their work, or the work itself. The longest discussions are those regarding binding in the library context: Redmond Barry, *Two Papers Read . . . at the Conference of Librarians held at The London Institution . . . 1877 on Binding, and on Lending Libraries*, London, printed by G. Norman & Sons, [1877?]; J. S. Battye, 'Bookbinding in Public Libraries', *Library Association of Australasia. Transactions and Proceedings of the . . . Second General Meeting . . . 1900*, Adelaide, C. E. Bristow, Govt. Printer, 1901, pp. xxi-xxiii; and F. S. Bryant, 'Bookbinding for Public Libraries', *Library Association of Australasia. Proceedings of the Sydney Meeting, October, 1898*, Sydney, Hennessey, Harper & Co., 1899, pp. 121-27. In modern reference sources, accounts of individual binders include: 'William Moffitt', in *Dictionary of Australian Artists*, Joan Kerr, ed., Melbourne, OUP, 1992, pp. 542-43; and the website of Sally Bloomfield and Craig Collins, andrew-bent.life [accessed 16 June 2023], with detailed information about early Tasmanian bookbinders, including Drysdale and Rolwegan. There is a short account of the early history in H. W. H. Huntington, 'History of the Stationery Trade in Australia', *Australian Printer, Stationer and Bookseller*, 30 January 1904, pp. 24-25; and a brief historical account in Carol Mills, 'Towards a History of Australian Craft Bookbinding', *Australian Exhibition of Contemporary Bookbinding, 1992*, Canberra, Canberra Craft Bookbinders' Guild, 1992, pp. 7-10. Walter Stone's 'Old-Time Book-Canvassers and an Act of Parliament', *Biblionews*, January 1961, p. 2, describes the *Australian Men of Mark* case. K. Turnell, 'The Canisius College Finishing Tools Collection', *Morocco Bound*, vol.8, nos 3-4, 1987, pp. 41-56, discusses and illustrates some older tools located in Australia. George Rolwegan's bookbinding tools are in the W. L. Crowther Library, State Library of Tasmania. Peter Marsh's *Bookbinding Tools from the Government Printing Office of Victoria*, Melbourne, [the author], 2016, provides a detailed inventory of the equipment gathered from the 1850s onwards and surviving till the Victorian Government Printing Office abandoned its traditional role at the end of the twentieth century.

CHAPTER 6

Paper in Nineteenth-Century Australian Publications

Carol Mills

The issue of the *Sydney Gazette* for 29 July 1820 included a one-leaf supplement devoted to the death of George III. Its appearance and page size differed from those of the regular folded two-leaf issue. The coarse, faintly greenish paper with flecks of brown discolouration was probably the product of Australia's second paper manufacturer, the Macquarie Paper Mills. The first, operated by Frederick Fisher and George Duncan, was worked at John F. Hutchi[n]son's Bank Mill, very likely commencing operations in late April or May of 1818, and financed by subscriptions from prominent citizens. Fisher and Duncan were both convicts, Duncan a papermaker by trade. Fisher later went farming, and was murdered in the winter of 1826, achieving historical notoriety as Fisher's Ghost. This first mill would have closed down by the time the Macquarie Paper Mills, financed by Thomas Clarkson, who employed Duncan as papermaker, began working some time in 1819. Both water-driven mills were on the Lachlan Swamps, south-east of the town of Sydney. A third mill is thought to have started up in the same area a little later. Most of this colonial production was almost certainly destined to be used as writing paper. Clarkson, a freed convict baker and publican, went bankrupt in 1821, and died three years later. By the mid-1820s there was no papermaking activity in the colony; nor would there be again until the late 1860s.

Although the papermaking machine was by then in use in Europe, these first Australian mills must have been vat mills, with paper made by hand. Twelve leaves in two sections of the *New South Wales Pocket Almanack ... 1820* (Sydney, George Howe, 1820) are printed on paper from the Macquarie mill.

George Howe, as printer and publisher of the *Sydney Gazette* and the *Almanack*, had to perform a constant financial balancing act between the cost and availability of paper, and delinquent subscribers. By 1807 the price of paper had risen dramatically from eight shillings a ream (then 480 sheets) to eight shillings per quire (24 sheets). Howe, the colony's sole printer, obtained paper from the government (when available), and from ships' captains and Sydney merchants. He also exchanged paper to obtain a better stock for printing. The *Gazette* changed colour, was reduced in size or failed to appear, sometimes for lengthy periods. Edition sizes of the newspaper and of the *Almanack* were reduced. Some Howe publications are recorded as requiring subscribers to supply their own paper — which must have been a nightmare for the printer to handle. By December 1811 Howe was importing his paper directly from England.

The paper in individual copies of early colonial publications could vary. Paper used in the plates of John Lewin's *Birds of New South Wales* (Sydney, George Howe, 1813), for example, carries varying watermarks, and dates as early as 1802. No doubt Lewin obtained his paper from Howe. Sir John Ferguson in his *Bibliography of Australia* does not record any watermarks in the earlier (London, 1808) edition, although he notes that the plates were completed, printed and coloured by Lewin whilst in the colony. The bibliography of Lewin's *Birds* is notoriously complicated. A sample of copies held in public institutions indicates unpredictable variations in the presence of laid and wove paper for the plates.

In the next-established colony of Van Diemen's Land, and to some extent in the very first years of the Port Phillip settlement, local publications provide evidence of the same erratic paper supply as occurred in New South Wales in their variable paper colour, weight and quality, and variation in the paper used within a single copy, particularly in the earlier years. The later-settled colonies experienced fewer difficulties, as they had the more established paper trade of the older colonies to fall back on. However, there was no fully developed paper trade in any Australian colony until the second half of the nineteenth century.

The makers of the paper on which nineteenth-century Australian publications were printed are mostly unknown. In the earliest period, the paper, reflecting the trading patterns of the vessels which put in at the colonies, could be from Britain, Spain, India, Ceylon, China and other places. 'China paper' was advertised for sale in the *Hobart Town Gazette* in 1817 (24 May and 16 August) and was at times used to print the newspaper itself. In 1819, the publisher, Andrew Bent (profiled in Chapter 11 by Sally Bloomfield and Craig Collins), even had to paste together scraps of 'China paper' to make up the *Gazette*'s usual sheet size. Later on, the lines of supply became almost exclusively British. With the exception of the watermarked paper used for government publications (probably all made in the United Kingdom), almost none is watermarked. Even when Australian paper became available, its use as book printing paper was apparently not common; local mills focused more on newsprint and wrappings as the most significant part of their production. Some of the reasons for this emphasis are embedded in the complex tariff regulations of the time, which favoured cheaper types of paper. That manufacture of book-printing paper was less common was also due to cost: the local product was more expensive because of the price of essential imported chemicals, higher Australian wages and the longer distances which incurred freight charges including costly trans-shipment. Further impediments to production were local printers' preferences for imported paper, home government paternalism and the poor local supply of fibre. When paper was being made, fibre supplies (rags, old bagging, ropes and sails, imported jute and local rushes being the main sources) were frequently inadequate, and in some cases unsuitable for white paper. As late as 1907 the cover of some issues of the Melbourne *Native Companion* proclaimed it 'THE ONLY Magazine Printed on Australian-Made Paper', namely paper made at the Barwon mill. At the same time it needs to be remembered that, with its small colonial population, the scale of book production in Australia remained insignificant until the latter half of the nineteenth century.

The most detailed information available on local paper relates to the production and use of newsprint. The rise of newspapers in Australia in the second half of the nineteenth century meant that newsprint was required in large quantities, making it the most economically attractive printing paper to produce locally and the most important of all types of paper other than wrappings. Newspaper owners were at times vociferous in their published demands for a reliable paper supply. The long delivery times involved in importing paper from across the world tied up scarce capital, so newspapers were quick to support local papermaking ventures. As a sign of the interest in local paper production, at least two real-estate advertisements in Launceston in the 1850s mentioned the potential of properties as water-driven paper mills. In Victoria there were at least three different ventures in the 1850s and early 1860s. The Tasmanian Government Printer, James Barnard, encouraged experimentation with local fibres and acclimatisation of esparto grass (the commonest non-textile papermaking fibre before the introduction of wood pulp) and commissioned the design of a mill in 1862, which he proposed would be run by convicts under supervision. It seems that a mill was imported into Tasmania in 1825, but apparently never put to use.

There were also experiments in Hobart with barks of trees. These trials were not an isolated phenomenon. In the nineteenth century the colonies seem to have been almost seething with would-be inventors seeking to facilitate independence from imports in any number of commodities. In the case of paper these included such well-known personalities as Ferdinand von Mueller and Alexander Tolmer, who experimented with barks, grasses, sugar cane waste, New Zealand flax and tussock, bunya pine, cereal waste, reeds, seaweeds and rushes. There was even a proposal in New South Wales to grow the giant native Gymea Lily (*Doryanthes excelsa*) in plantations as a fibre source. Experimentation was supported by grants and prizes offered by the British government, colonial governments, and the major exhibitions which followed the Great Exhibition in London in 1851.

The colonies sought not only self-sufficiency, but exports. In the mid-nineteenth century, the demands on the European industry were not being met, because of limited supplies of fibre. Indeed, for a period the colonies exported rags to British papermakers. This trade was short-lived as the European fibre shortages began to abate in the 1860s with greater use of softwood pulp. By the end of the century the European paper industry was no longer interested in alternative fibres.

Because the predominant local timbers were hardwood species, Australia lacked a major fibre source to make wood pulp. It was not until the late 1920s that experiments began to yield economically successful methods of using hardwood fibre. Consequently, fibre experimentation continued in Australia until softwood pulp began to be imported early in the twentieth century. The impetus to work on hardwood fibres came with the isolation of Australia from imported paper fibres during the First World War.

The first economically viable mill in Australia was the Australian Paper Company's Collingwood mill, begun at Liverpool, New South Wales, in 1867. The second was that of Samuel Ramsden in Melbourne in 1868. The Barwon mill near Geelong, which began production in 1878, was the third major mill. The fourth was the board mill (for book-cover boards) of James McDougall, established at Broadford, Victoria, in 1890. There were other manufacturers with shorter success: Joseph Wearne near Liverpool in the 1870s and 1880s; James Bryant at West Maitland in the 1860s and 1870s and George Adams (of 'Tattersall's' fame) near Sydney in the 1890s. William Daniel Hughes built a mill near Geelong in 1891, but it never went into production.

Ramsden's mill was based on equipment he acquired from two separate enterprises, those of Thomas Kenny and Samuel Fieldhouse. After Kenny's aborted attempt to start a mill in the early 1860s on the upper Yarra, his equipment was purchased by Ramsden and became Ramsden's Number One machine, which operated until the 1960s. In the 1870s Ramsden bought a second papermaking machine, which he acquired when Fieldhouse lost his new Melbourne mill through bankruptcy in 1874. Fieldhouse's equipment became the Melbourne Number Two machine. Collingwood, Ramsden, Barwon and Broadford survived for decades, not always running at a profit. None of them is now operating. All went through ownership changes and mergers and were antecedents of the Australian paper and packaging giant, AMCOR.

Kenny's Irish papermaker Nathaniel Kerr and Scots engineer Alexander Steele joined Ramsden, who lacked papermaking experience. Ramsden was probably advised by J. Cosmo Newbery, the Analyst of the Geological Survey of Victoria, one of the experimenters with paper fibres. Ramsden's mill ran successfully on 2 May 1868, following a dry run in late April. The Melbourne *Evening Star* of 4 May 1868 and the Bendigo *Advertiser* of 22 May 1868 were printed on its buff newsprint. In 1872 Ramsden paper was being used for the Victorian *Government Gazette*, the *Ballarat Evening Mail*, and by other newspapers. Some covers of the Melbourne *Australasian* were printed on Melbourne paper.

Woman sorting rags at the Barwon Paper Mill, Fyansford, Barwon River, Geelong. c.1880. A visitor to the 'rag-house', writing in the *Age* (22 June 1889), noted the mill employed approximately 70 to 80 employees, 'about equally divided' between men and women. The mill operated from its opening in 1878 to 1923. The mill and adjacent buildings were restored and now operate as an arts and cultural precinct. Photograph by J. H. (John Henry) Harvey. Glass lantern slide, toned; 8.5 x 8.5 cm. (State Library Victoria)

In 1871 Warren Weedon of the Australian Paper Mills (formerly Collingwood) described the Brisbane *Courier* as 'still on our paper'. In 1872 the *Illustrated Sydney News* said of this steam-driven mill:

> ...we consider this manufactory one of the most, if not the most, important in a young colony such as this ... it carries along with it the march of progress, education, and enlightenment of the people. We, in the printing and newspaper trades, can fully appreciate at this time its great importance, and desire its success, as, owing to the advance of the price of paper in the home markets, and consequent short supply to the colony, some of the leading city and country journals have been hard pressed for want of supply of paper, and who, in some instances, have had to pay as high as 50, and even as high as 75 per cent. advance on the usual price. Had the dearth continued much longer it is not at all improbable some would have had to discontinue their issues till supplies came to hand.

The *Australian Town and Country Journal* from its first issue in 1870, and sometimes the Melbourne *Age*, were printed on Collingwood paper. In 1884 the Fairfax *Echo* commented:

> An order was made this week for a quantity of paper measuring over 300 miles long. In less than 24 hours ... the first instalment was made in reels four and a half miles long and placed in railway trucks for delivery. Mr Murray has supplied the whole of the paper for the *Echo* for nine years ... The *Melbourne Age* last month received a quantity 500 miles long with every satisfaction as to quantity and price.

The *Sydney Morning Herald* and the *Empire* were Liverpool customers. George Murray & Co Paper Mills Printing Works were Sydney manufacturing stationers, lithographers and printers and paper importers from the 1880s. Ferguson lists 17 books printed by this firm. These included Broinowski's *Birds and Mammals of Australia* (1885), Arthur Jose's *Growth of Empire* (1897), W. Frederic Morrison's *Aldine History of Queensland* (1888), his *Aldine History of South Australia* (1890) and also his *Aldine Centennial History of New South Wales* (1888). The first edition of Edward Dyson's *Rhymes from the Mines* (1896) was printed by Murray. It would be a reasonable assumption that some of these publications were printed on Liverpool paper, some of which was considered quite fine, the quality attributed to the inclusion of fibre from rushes growing on the river bank at the mill.

In one week of 1888, Barwon sent 180 reels of newsprint to Melbourne, all of which were sold in that year. Included in the sale was the transfer of a contract with the *Age* for the supply of 150 reams of paper weekly. Barwon production ceased in 1923. One of the last jobs was making paper to print the New South Wales Forestry Commission *Report* for 1922–23 (New South Wales Government Printer, 1923), the paper of which was made from 65 per cent New South Wales blackbutt, 25 per cent imported pulp and 10 per cent waste paper.

In 1889 a pamphlet on the 'Bounty' story appeared, entitled *The Mutiny*. It was described as being printed on the first 'toned' paper manufactured in New South Wales. As Liverpool was the only mill then operating, the pamphlet was presumably printed with its paper. The present-day beige colour of the paper, some of which may be caused by breakdown, makes it difficult to determine what 'toned' meant.

By the 1880s, nineteenth-century Australian papermaking had achieved a peak in production. It was estimated in 1882 that 50 per cent of the world's paper production was for printing, one sixth for writing and the rest for other purposes. If New South Wales is typical, by 1883 Australia was a heavy user of paper. Using 16½ lb *per capita* per year, New South Wales was second only to the United States at 17 lb, with England, Germany, France, Italy, Spain and Russia coming after. Papermaking in New South Wales, which was not protected by the colonial government, was adversely affected by tariff protection in Victoria. After 1884, apart from the Broadford machine, no new capital equipment was purchased by Australian mills during the rest of the century. This failure to keep up with technology led to poor production, which in turn probably induced the lack of capital for large equipment. Shortages favoured the more active local marketing by British papermakers evident by the 1880s. Apart from a brief period during the First World War, reliance on British paper did not ease until the late 1930s when large Australian mills using hardwood pulp, and mills supported by softwood plantations, came into production. Right through into the twentieth century, British paper was imported for book work and regarded until after the Second World War by many printers as superior to the local product.

NOTE ON SOURCES

The writing on Australian papermaking history is diffuse. Titles which provide substantial overall coverage in one source are Jacqueline Rawson's excellent MA thesis, *A History of the Australian Paper Making Industry 1818–1951*, University of Melbourne, 1953; and E. K. Sinclair, *The Spreading Tree: A History of APM and AMCOR 1844–1989*, Sydney, Allen & Unwin, 1991. The earliest ventures in colonial Sydney are extremely well documented in Jean Murray, *Convicts and Ghosts: The Story of our First Papermakers*, Presidential address, Library Association of Australia, New South Wales Branch, 1962 (Mitchell Library MSS 5213). Coverage of specific mills can be found in Walter Randolph Brownhill, *The History of Geelong and Corio Bay . . . with postscript 1955–1990 by Ian Wynd*, Geelong, Geelong Advertiser, 1990; and Peter Milner, *The Water Turbine at the Barwon Paper Mill, Fyansford*, Parkville, University of Melbourne Department of Engineering, 1983 (Technology address T-83/5) for the Barwon mill; Christopher Keating, *On the Frontier: A Social History of Liverpool*, Sydney, Hale & Iremonger, 1996 for both the Collingwood and Wearne mills at Liverpool; and 'Works of the Sydney Paper-making Company, Liverpool', *Illustrated Sydney News*, 21 December 1872, pp. 7, 17 for the Collingwood mill. Discussion of fibres can be found in W. A. Hargreaves, *An Investigation into the Prospects of Establishing a Paper-Making Industry in South Australia*, Adelaide, Government Printer, 1916; Gerald Lightfoot, *Paper-Pulp. The Possibilities of its Manufacture in Australia*, Melbourne, Government Printer, 1919; J. Cosmo Newbery, 'The manufacture of paper from native plants', *Royal Society of Victoria Transactions and Proceedings*, vol.8, 1867, pp. 47-52; and Alexander Tolmer, *Reminiscences of an Adventurous and Chequered Career at Home and at the Antipodes*, Volume 1, London, Sampson Low, Marston, Searle & Rivington, 1882. There are few sources relating to specific publications and the paper on which they were printed. However, Andrew Bent's use of 'China paper' and other paper available to early Tasmanians is discussed in detail by Ian Wilson in 'China paper Usage in Early Van Diemen's Land Printing', *The Quarterly: The Journal of the British Association of Paper Historians*, no.72, October 2009, pp. 1-7. For the general reader, a useful source is the website 'Papermaking in Australasia to 1900', http://home.vicnet.net.au/~paper, maintained by Alexander Romanov-Hughes [As of May 2024, the URL of this website was no longer supported by its original host, but the site could still be found by searching the author's name and the website title]. It provides images and information about individual mills and papermakers, and includes Anne Pitkethly's detailed essay, 'Paper Manufacturing in Victoria, from European Settlement to Federation', privately published, Melbourne, 2017.

CHAPTER 7

Colonial Type: Imported and Australian Made

Dennis Bryans

Until the 1840s, more than half a century after the arrival of the first European colonists, types for printing had to be brought from the Northern Hemisphere, essentially the British Isles. This suggests a natural division of the subject-matter of this chapter: first, the history of the importation of the necessary materials; second, the emergence of local manufacture alongside the strong competition from the multi-national firms servicing the much expanded printing industry after the gold rushes of the 1850s.

Imported Type

Before 1851

The discovery at Library and Archives Canada of the *Jane Shore* playbill of 30 July 1796 and its subsequent presentation to the Australian Government by the Prime Minister of Canada in 2007 was an event of note for local bibliographers and book historians. Here was the earliest known sample of the printing of George Hughes, the first person employed by the colonial government — from late 1795 to the end of 1800, and perhaps a little longer — to use the press and related material that arrived with the First Fleet in 1788. Once again Hughes, the poorly documented convict predecessor of George Howe, whose tenure as official printer ran from 1801 to 1821, was in the limelight. A number of *Script & Print* in 2007 explored some aspects of the gift and of Hughes's rather shadowy activity.

However, interest subsided before the dossier was fully examined. We know that Governor John Hunter did not bother to send very much of Hughes's printed work to the Colonial Office, in other words to be preserved in Britain's National Archives. The loss for students of the earliest Australian printing is huge. Hunter's successor, Philip Gidley King, did send copies to London, and these require careful study before we can make definitive pronouncements on the work done in Sydney in the late 1790s.

On the evidence at present available it is clear that Hughes was hardly adventurous in his printing. All the specimens — playbills, notices, proclamations and forms — were inked, not always satisfactorily, on one side only of the paper. If the Caslon type that came in 1788 contained ornaments, Hughes did not bother to use any of them, apart from some ruling on forms, until late 1800. A General Order of 31 October 1800 concerning the conditions of employment of assigned servants (Ferguson 316), has a royal coat of arms headpiece and rules. This style of presentation becomes normal in 1801, although we cannot be absolutely sure when George Howe took over the printer's function from Hughes. One can assume that these ornaments were very likely in the original 1788 consignment.

Howe's first ambitious production, *New South Wales General Standing Orders* of 1802, took colonial printing to a new level, but it seems to have relied on the type passed on from Hughes. It is, therefore, hardly surprising that Howe pressed for new supplies in late 1802. Any new type required had to be ordered through government channels. King sent 'A Bill of Printing Type' to London in December 1802. His request suggests that Howe submitted a list of wants to the Governor, for King's letter stipulates: 'This type must be had from the foundries of either the late Messrs Caslon or Mr Figgins'. 'Paper for printing' was also ordered.

The first issue of the *Sydney Gazette and New South Wales Advertiser* on 1 March 1803 uses the same type hitherto employed by George Hughes, but inked better with the lines of type leaded. Thereafter there is little change except for swelled rules until 2 April when a small ornament is inserted above the heading 'State of the Barometer and Thermometer', an experiment not repeated.

New type is used in the *Gazette* in 1804. A Caslon ship in full sail in an oval frame and an apparently new cut of a brig appeared, as did ornamental rules not seen in earlier issues, with an identifiably Caslon border, substituted for a rule, a design first occurring as 'long primer flowers' (No. 14) in William Caslon III's 1798 specimen book, and still sold in their 1870s specimen book as 'No. 71. Old-Fashioned Border, 3/6'. On 24 June 1804 the *Sydney Gazette* received a new masthead replacing the original one 'Thus We Hope to Prosper' with the Royal Arms (supporters rampant) and larger type.

A fresh request for a new press and type was dispatched in October 1810. This order included new types: '4 cwt long primer roman and italics with a double complement of caps, small caps, figures and celestial signs, 1 lb of capital S extra, 30 lb of double pica, 10 alphabets, 2-line long primer caps full force [possibly an interpretation of full face], 8 pairs cases, 6 dozen brass rule . . . Royal Arms in brass, supporters couchant, about the same . . . as the Arms that head His Majesty's speeches to Parliament: 2 metal ditto, 6 lines pica. Ornaments, various small sizes in wood or metal, but metal preferred; 4 ships, 4 brigs, 3 schooners, 3 slops, 2 horses, 2 do. with grooms, six houses'.

Official type imports into the colonies of New South Wales and Van Diemen's Land up to the gold rushes formed a complex web of direct official orders for type replacements to the existing stock in the possession of the government printers and, later on, orders to appointed agents such as type sought through Rev. Robert Bourne, political agent, in 1829. The provision of type in South Australia and Western Australia in the 1830s was also subject to arrangements made in London or to emergency help from other colonies.

Identifying the vendors who supplied the type is inconclusive and perhaps they may never be known with certainty. The classic Caslon type-face included with the first printing press sent out in 1788 is by general consensus beyond dispute. The firm of Caslon, however, was at this time in a state of flux. From 1778 to 1809 management of the firm was in the hands of a whole series of family members.

Private enterprise also played a part in broadening sources of supply of type in New South Wales. A consignment of 'NONPAREIL TYPE of a beautiful face, cast on purpose for the *Sydney Monitor*, according to the pattern transmitted to *Figgins & Co. of London*' is mentioned in the *Monitor* in December 1833, and in January 1834 the *Gazette* published the rejoinder that they too had received 'A LARGE supply of NEW TYPE . . . by the *Brothers*, [and] the Proprietors . . . will have no objection to dispose of a quantity of their superabundant stock of PRINTING MATERIALS, which, though now designated *old* are yet in very excellent condition — '.

The growing number of colonial newspapers encouraged exchanges of second-hand type between printers. From about 1830 to 1840 greater competition between British letter founders increased sources of materials arriving in the colonies. Of these the following foundries deserve mention: Blake & Stephenson (designated thus 1830–41) later renamed Stephenson Blake was active from 1841 to 1905 and continued until the later part of the twentieth century; Thorowgood and Besley active 1838–49; Caslon & Son, 1840–50.

Reselling quantities of surplus type as mentioned above was a natural development once fresh supplies arrived. For instance a notice in the *Hobart Town Gazette* announcing the arrival of new type direct from the letter-foundry of Messrs Caslon & Livermore, London, in July 1823, can be compared in February 1830 with a consignment of type, printing ink and a case of pearl ash being exported by Andrew Bent of the *Hobart Town Gazette* to Edward Smith Hall, publisher of the Sydney *Monitor*.

More generally the emergence of colonist partnerships acting as importers in speculative ventures and sometimes as licensed local agents representing British foundries began to occur around 1840: in Sydney, Lamb & Parbury General Merchants, 1841; Thomas Trood's Albion Printing Office, 1841; Lyall, Scott & Co., New South Wales agents for Duncan Sinclair & Son, Edinburgh (March 1842).

At the end of the decade we have records of type ordered direct from London by NSW Government Printer W. W. Davies, delivered to Sydney in August 1850: '. . . the Type, &c. from Messrs Thorowgood & Co., of London, have been unpacked and found correct. That the Materials from Messrs Stephenson, Blake & Co. Sheffield, have been unpacked and found correct. That the Printing Materials from Messrs Figgins, London, although correct as regards quantity, quality, and price, were improperly packed in London and . . . are much damaged.'

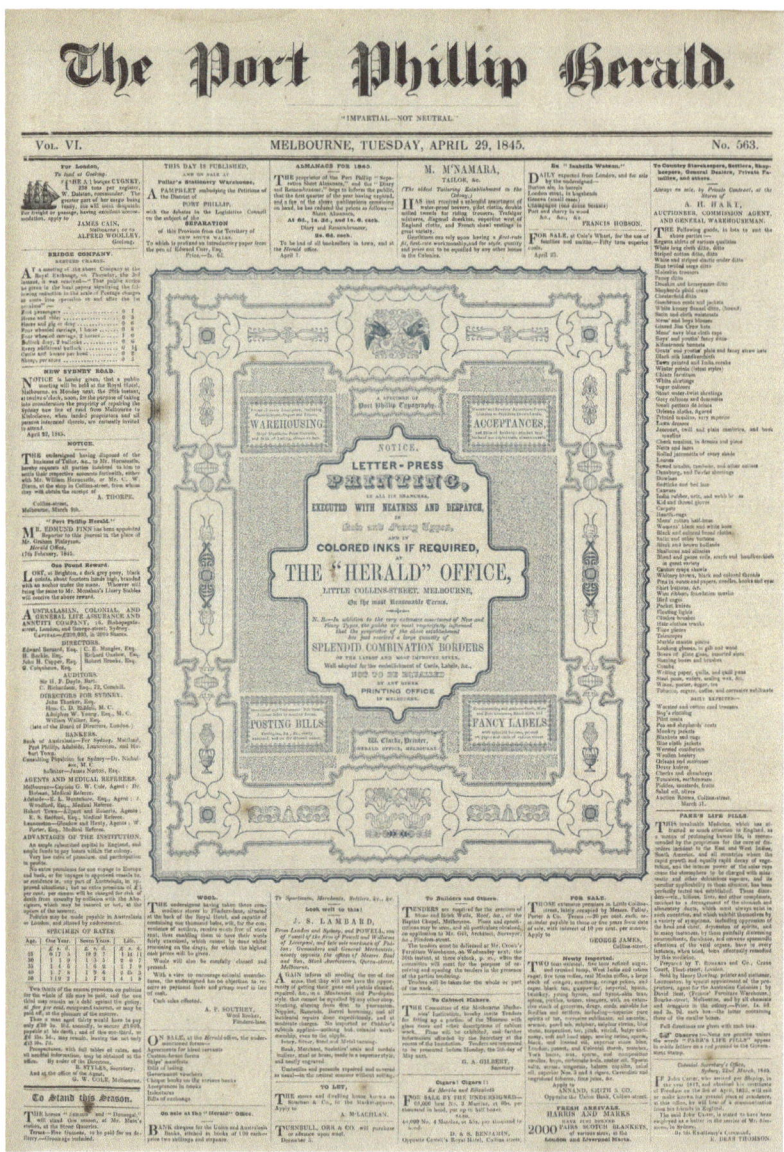

A specimen of Port Phillip typography produced by William Joseph Sayers Clarke (1813–1855), as printed in the *Port Phillip Herald* on 29 April 1845. The paper had first circulated the specimen on 3 April 1845. Clarke, the newspaper's owner, who had briefly been entrusted with government printing, deservedly holds the distinction of being Melbourne's first significant typographer. This specimen is a masterly example of decorative typographic composition employing extensive groundwork and ornamental border designs. Clarke's skills are also evident in a supplement honouring Ludwig Leichhardt (1846) and in the decorative border Clarke designed for 'Fawkner's Epitome of Victorian History' (1850). (State Library Victoria)

The United Kingdom was not the only source of printing material in this early period. The story of the importation of a press and German type to Adelaide at the end of 1847 has been told by Miriam Gilson and Jerzy Zubrzycki, followed later by Joyce Graetz. Unfortunately the source of the type is not specified. The material was soon used for producing Australia's first German-language newspaper, *Die deutsche Post für die australischen Colonien* (1848–1850).

One of the very few issues in Sydney of *The Voice of Jacob* in 1842 deplores the 'want of Hebrew type'. This problem does not seem to have been solved for the Jewish newspaper press till three decades later.

The gold rushes and after

The rush of immigrants to the goldfields of New South Wales and Victoria shifted the balance between colonial firms dealing in small consignments and newly arrived printers' furnishers importing type and machinery from Britain on a large scale to supply the demands of an explosion in newspaper publishing in the colonies. There are obvious parallels between this and what was happening in other industries in Australia in the second half of the nineteenth century.

A central figure in this massive expansion was Francis Burdett Franklyn (1814–1869). He was one of three partners trading in London as Robson, Levey & Franklyn and is first mentioned in the Melbourne *Argus* in February 1853. Trading as Franklyn & Co. he advertised an odd assortment of goods: Roman Catholic books, type cases and printing materials, a copperplate press, a Super-Royal Albion press, a lady's saddle and bridle, a cart and harness, axle-trees and guns.

Franklyn's career in London and Melbourne calls for a detailed presentation that is not possible here. However, his efforts in supplying type and printing materials — apart from his role as one of the proprietors of the Melbourne *Herald* — do need to be noted.

By 1854 Franklyn was established as the sole agent for H. W. Caslon's and Alexander Wilson's Letter Foundry in Victoria, operating from 20 Queen Street. Customers were enticed with a stock of 'Guinness's Stout and Bass's Ale in bottles' and 'Lithographic Presses, Stones, Inks, and all Materials' from premises in Fulton's Chambers, opposite Cole's Wharf.

Franklyn wrote to John Ferres, the Victorian Government Printer, on 9 June 1854 declaring that 'almost every Printer in the Colonies is constantly purchasing from our stock & admit the benefit of dealing with those who have a practical knowledge of the business' to persuade Ferres that his was the right tender to supply the government's needs. An agreement was reached to equip the printing office with a Scandinavian super royal press, a cylinder perfecting machine, two super royal inking tables and a galley proofing press, together with a four-horsepower steam engine (with boiler and apparatus complete) to power the machines. J. Moore of the Colonial Secretary's Office granted approval for Franklyn to receive the sum of £1200 to obtain and deliver the goods with a commission of 20 per cent.

Subsequently Franklyn extended his firm's commitments so far that financial disaster ensued. On a visit to London in 1863 the Australian-resident partner was confronted with the enterprise's difficulties and removed from his position. Bankruptcy for the London members followed in 1864. Franklyn played a minor role later once back in Melbourne, whereas Levey's son Oliver was to continue in business until F. T. Wimble took over.

As we move towards the last third of the nineteenth century, the range of foundries supplying the Australian market increases considerably. Among the British firms were H. W. Caslon, the last of the original line and active from 1850 to 1874, Reed and Fox 1861 to 1877, J. & R. M. Woods Austin Type Foundry, first mentioned in the colonies in 1863, and Miller & Richard from 1855. Foreign foundries, mostly American, also began to appear in the record, for example, Bruce's New York Type Foundry, 1882–1900. Recorded in Cowans' 1893–1894 Ledger Book (Baillieu Library, University of Melbourne) is a list of transactions representative of the American foundries' types available in Australia at the end of our period: American Type Founders (formed 1892); Conner Type Foundry (1829–92); MacKellar, Smiths & Jordan (1881–96); Barnhart Bros & Spindler (1873–1925); Boston Type Foundry (1860–89); Central Type Foundry (1856–93); Keystone Type Foundry (1890–1919); Dickinson Type Foundry (1856–93). The list is not exhaustive, as type supplied by Farmer, Little & Company of New York (1862–92) is also known to have been sold in Australia.

Typefounders Miller & Richard of Edinburgh initially dealt with various distributors: John Davies, Hobart *Mercury*; F. B. Franklyn, Melbourne; Arthur Cubitt, Sydney (1855–68). As the printing trade grew and communications between the colonies and Britain became more rapid and reliable, larger printers' furnishers became Australia-wide agents. The Gordon and Gotch offices in Melbourne, Sydney and Brisbane eventually had the Australian agency of Miller & Richard. Surviving specimens from this time have the Gordon and Gotch imprint.

In 1863 Levey and Robson endeavoured to recover their position as distributors of type to the trade by obtaining the agency for Vincent and James Figgins under the management of Oliver Levey. Freemantle & Co. took over the stock owned by F. B. Franklyn after his death and advertised as agents for H. W. Caslon and Reed and Fox between 1872 and 1881. A Caslon type specimen issued in Melbourne in 1863 has the 20 Queen St address and the imprint of the Freemantle firm.

In 1876 Frederick Thomas Wimble (1846–1936), printing ink manufacturer of Sydney and Melbourne, visited the Philadelphia International Exhibition, where he obtained the agency of typefounders MacKellar, Smiths & Jordan before crossing the Atlantic to London, where he did a similar deal with Vincent and James Figgins. In addition, the *Australian Typographical Journal* reported that Wimble had acquired the agencies of Miller & Richard, Figgins, Stephenson and Blake and Besley. In 1880 he purchased Oliver Levey's business, thus acquiring the agencies of Figgins, H. W. Caslon and Sir Charles Reed and Sons in Victoria. The extent of his type-importing business is indicated in the ledger below. In 1890 Wimble became a member of the Queensland Legislative Assembly, leaving his printing ink manufactory and printing agencies temporarily in the hands of others.

Stephenson Blake advertised in the *Hobart Town Courier* in 1847, and Brush and MacDonnell of Sydney advertised their type between 1854 and 1858. In the early 1850s Scottish papermakers Cowans acquired the British export agency of typefounders Stephenson Blake and appointed Callender, Caldwell & Co. as their Victorian agents from 1855 to 1858. James Callender stocked a broad range of stationery and books. Beside Cowan & Co.'s papers, account books, envelopes and Stephenson Blake and Co.'s type and printing furniture, Callender also stocked A. B. Fleming and Co.'s printing and lithographic inks and presses. According to Laurence Bunn, Cowan & Co. opened their first Australian Branch in Sydney in 1868, expanding to New Zealand in 1884, Adelaide 1885, Brisbane 1889 and Perth 1898. Throughout this period Cowans remained sole agents for Stephenson Blake.

Private Ledger — F. T. Wimble & Co., Sydney.

Year	Type on order or in stock	Liabilities	Balance (all goods) @ 30 June each yr.
1884			£5,114-15- 3
1885	Mackellar	£690-12-11	
	Figgins a/c	£1,000 - 7- 0	
	Figgins	£364- 1- 6	
	Figgins	£58-19- 7	£15,504- 8- 7
1886	Mackellar	£590-16-11	
	Figgins a/c	£1,399-10- 1	
	Figgins	£227- 9- 8	
	Dickinson & Co.	£761-12- 4	
	Schelter	£2-13- 5	£19,637-10-11
1887	Mackellar	£528- 1- 4	£21,669-10- 0
1888	Mackellar Smiths & J	£274-16-11	
	Dickinson & Co. Chicago	£306-10- 5	
	Dickinson & Co. a/c	£306-10- 5	
	Figgins, V. & J	£1023-19- 8	
	Jolly & Co	6- 1	£18,449- 2- 8
1889	Figgins & Co.	£2153-13-11	
			£22,910- 7- 5

For three further decades the sources of type for the quite numerous German newspapers produced in the colonies were not named. This was even the case for John Degotardi's *Australische Deutsche Zeitung* (Sydney, 1856–1858), of which only two numbers survive. Despite being the author in 1861 of *The Art of Printing*, Degotardi was not concerned with the questions future historians would ask.

Things changed in the 1880s. Even before Schelter appeared in Wimble's purchases, the importer was advertising the type of J. G. Schelter und Giesecke in the Adelaide *Australische Zeitung* in 1883. Benjamin Krebs offered Greek and Hebrew types in the same newspaper in 1884. The following year there were advertisements from Wilhelm Gronau of Berlin and Sachs and Fischer of Mannheim. Wilhelm Woellmer of Berlin had won an award at the 1880 Exhibition, whose role in revealing Australia to European manufacturers is well known. The market for Classical Greek and Hebrew types has yet to be explored thoroughly. The former was certainly in use by several Australian printers from mid-century.

It was to be expected that by the late nineteenth century the colonial printing industry was being offered such a range of types from the Northern Hemisphere. Trade members, advertisers and the general reading public were used to seeing the mass of printed material — books, magazines, newspapers — imported into the colonies. It was natural that there should be interest in the constant developments in presentation absorbed by typefounders on both sides of the Atlantic. Apart from Thomas L. Work, Australia in the later nineteenth century perhaps lacked a figure as widely informed as Robert Coupland Harding in New Zealand, but there is no doubt that aesthetic concerns — in line with the vogue of bookplates and with the beginnings of enthusiasm for private presses and fine printing — had begun to emerge in pre-Federation Australia. The imports of type played their part in this necessary advance.

Australian Type Foundries

Although type manufactured in Australia was always outweighed by imports — a situation familiar in many local industries — it was not disregarded by colonial printers. In the 1851 correspondence of Edward Khull, Ferres's immediate predecessor as Victoria's Government Printer, with his opposite number in Sydney, the possibility of obtaining locally cast type is mentioned. From the early 1840s onwards the colonial option existed, even if it did not encompass all the variety being introduced on the other side of the Equator.

Alexander Thomson (1814–1856), the first Australian typefounder, began his business in Sydney in the early 1840s after emigrating from Scotland. His brother-in-law, James Swan (1811–1891), formerly a printer's apprentice and then journeyman at the *Scots Times*, had worked for John Dunmore Lang's *Colonist* in Sydney. Later Swan was to be the foreman printer and eventually proprietor of the *Moreton Bay Courier* after 1848. Such family and professional connections were important to Thomson at a time when steam navigation made intercolonial travel and trade easier.

In 1847 Thomson's business transactions became a little clearer, because for the first time some scattered references to his terms of trade can be found amongst the records of the NSW Government Printing Office. In March, W. W. Davies, Acting Government Printer, and John Chambers reported to the Clerk of the Legislative Council that 'according to our usual custom, we have this day supplied Mr. A. Thomson Type-founder with (80) Eighty pounds of old type, for the purpose of having it recast'.

In December 1841 Hobart's *Colonial Times* claimed it had received 'a specimen of Type' from Thomson's foundry. If there were a printed document, it has not survived, and it is possible that what was being discussed was a sample of metal type. In any case it is certain that L. E. Threlkeld's *A Key to the Structure of the Aboriginal Language* (Sydney, Kemp and Fairfax, 1850), sent to London's Great Exhibition of 1851, did duty quite expressly as an extended model of Thomson's work.

The first firm evidence of Thomson sending exports south is in 1848. He was engaged in this trade until the last two shipments of type destined for Melbourne in 1852–53: the first, per *Eagle* on 11 February 1852, the last on 2 November of the following year. No further type exports are known until after Thomson's untimely death.

> A KEY
>
> TO THE STRUCTURE OF THE
>
> ## ABORIGINAL LANGUAGE;
>
> BEING AN ANALYSIS OF THE
>
> PARTICLES USED AS AFFIXES, TO FORM
>
> THE VARIOUS MODIFICATIONS OF THE VERBS;
>
> SHEWING THE
>
> ESSENTIAL POWERS, ABSTRACT ROOTS, AND OTHER PECULIARITIES
> OF THE LANGUAGE
>
> SPOKEN BY THE ABORIGINES
>
> IN THE VICINITY OF HUNTER RIVER, LAKE MACQUARIE, ETC.,
>
> NEW SOUTH WALES:
>
> TOGETHER WITH COMPARISONS OF POLYNESIAN AND OTHER DIALECTS.
>
> By L. E. THRELKELD.
>
> SYDNEY:
> THE BOOK FOR PRESENTATION AT THE ROYAL NATIONAL EXHIBITION, LONDON, 1851,
> UNDER THE AUSPICES OF HIS ROYAL HIGHNESS PRINCE ALBERT.
> THE TYPE COLONIAL, CAST BY A. THOMPSON.—THE BINDING
> WITH COLONIAL MATERIAL.
> PRINTED BY KEMP AND FAIRFAX,
> LOWER GEORGE STREET.
> 1850.

Title-page of L. E. Threlkeld's *A Key to the Structure of the Aboriginal Language* (Sydney, Kemp and Fairfax, 1850) composed of type from Alexander Thomson's Australian Type Foundry, and bound in local materials. The page displays six sizes of type, set in capitals. The book was exhibited by the colony of New South Wales at the Royal National Exhibition, London, 1851. Rev. Lancelot E. Threlkeld (1788–1859) and his collaborator, Indigenous man Biraban, are discussed further by Susan Woodburn in Chapter 22. 83 pp. [1] leaf of plates; 1 portrait; 23 cm. (National Library of Australia)

On 3 May 1856 the 'first and only type-founder in the Australian colonies, aged 40 years' died suddenly at Fairy Meadow 'of disease of the heart'. Probate was granted in the Supreme Court of New South Wales on 17 June 1856 to his widow Sidney Thomson, the estate being assessed at £1400.

After her husband's death Mrs Thomson resumed casting and exporting type. She managed the foundry until shortly before her own death in 1864, demonstrating considerable tenacity in the face of colonial hardship. Type continued to be exported to the other colonies, but increasingly Mrs Thomson turned to her brother-in-law James Swan at the Brisbane *Courier* for orders. At her death the foundry was bequeathed to her daughter, but the affair was soon taken over by Archibald Wright, who continued casting type for the Government Printer on the same terms as those agreed to by Thomson. Later Wright introduced the electrotyping process. However, he was bankrupted in 1878–79. The type foundry was broken up, partly purchased by the NSW Government Printer, Thomas Richards, and in part also by John Davies.

The Davies Brothers Type Foundry sometimes styled Davies Brothers Australian Letter Foundry had been set up in Chippendale in 1857 and later moved to Redfern. The new Government Printer, William Hanson, was keen to make a good impression as an innovative and progressive manager. From Davies Brothers he commissioned dies and matrices for a long primer Clarendon on a pica body and a pica 'erased'. John Davies, who took over when his brother Thomas died in 1869, had been trained in London and worked for leading firms there as a punch cutter. At the end of the 1860s the firm was vaunting its type-casting machine. The survival of some Davies Brothers specimens from these decades shows the sophistication of their work, notably in the 1873 'New South Wales Special Horse and Cattle Brands' printed or lithographed by J. A. Engel, 105 York Street, Sydney.

In Victoria two typefounders started in business. Robert Dale arrived in 1853 and continued his activity for two decades. The evidence available suggests that his work was somewhat limited in scope and that he made little impact on the trade. On the other hand Henry James Thitchener (1841–1911), who arrived in Melbourne late in 1876 with a long stint at V. & J. Figgins as part of his background, made a much stronger impression. His Victoria Type Foundry was situated at 3 Stanley Buildings, Moray Street, South Melbourne. His types were noticed at the 1880–81 Melbourne International Exhibition and awarded the Second Order of Merit by the judges. He maintained his establishment till 1885 — complaining bitterly, in particular, to the 1883 Victorian Royal Commission on Tariffs, that he had not received the bonus he had been led to believe was payable to innovating manufacturers. This had not prevented him from working and supplying many printers in Melbourne as well as some in other colonies. It was not astonishing that he decided to join John Davies in Sydney in the Australian Type Founding Company, which he managed from 1893 to 1898–99. In 1899 the business was sold to F. T. Wimble and Co. Thus it can be seen that in this area at least Melbourne played a subsidiary role to Sydney. The domination of the specialised trade by Australia's two major cities was all in all predictable.

Other typographic materials made in Australia

Wood type, in demand for the execution of handbills and posters, also found its exponents. American-born Charles Boyd settled in Ballarat in 1857 and became a leading printer. Praised as a letter cutter, he reputedly introduced the first font of Greek type and polychrome printing to Ballarat.

Earlier still, Thomas Strode, founder of the *Port Phillip Gazette* in 1838, claimed to have cut his own wood letters from Kauri pine. More tangibly, Christopher Furse cut wood type in Richmond, from 1874 to 1888, and was commended at the Melbourne 1880–81 Exhibition. In 1889, James Northey, typecutter, took over Furse's premises.

Wood letter manufacturer William V. Lambert was in business in Melbourne from 1859 to 1882. The *Yeoman and Australian Acclimatizer* described his type as 'very accurately [and] neatly made' noting the advantages of having a local maker who could quickly replace broken letters and provide type at a price lower than that of imported products.

Robert Duncan DeLittle, employed by lithographic printer Charles Troedel in the late 1880s, devised and patented a modular white-face wood letter prototyped in Melbourne and registered in London in 1887. Leaving the prototypes in Melbourne he began manufacturing wood type in York, exporting his first order to Wimble back in Melbourne. This singular event blurs the distinction between Australian-made and imported goods, but henceforth DeLittle of York was an exporter into Australia with Frank Middows as his Sydney agent.

Robert Bell's *Chinese Advertiser* (1856), later re-named the *English and Chinese Advertiser* (1857–1860), was first printed lithographically, but subsequently wood and metal blocks were cut and inserted by Bell, and presumably then lithographed. A second Victorian Chinese newspaper, *Fi-Pao*, was issued in Melbourne in 1868, edited by the Rev. William Mathew, published by the Chinese missions of the Presbyterian Church of Victoria and lithographed by the printing and engraving firm of E. Whitehead and Co. The nature of the types, blocks and hand lettering employed in preparing this sheet remains unknown. In the same way there are several questions to answer about the Chinese-English phrasebooks used by immigrants on the goldfields.

Other classes of typographic material were also produced. The electrotype process (used by Thitchener to make matrices for type and electrotype blocks and ornaments) was employed to copy and distribute electrotypes taken from wood-engraved blocks. Prominent Sydney firms included John Sands and F. T. Wimble and, in Melbourne, John May (Walker May & Co.), Azzopardi & Markby, and Mason Firth & McCutcheon.

In Melbourne in 1871 the talented wood engraver Angelo Azzopardi partnered with John Markby, an electrotyper and stereotyper who had started his firm in 1870. They received first prize for electrotypes and stereotypes at both the Melbourne and Philadelphia Exhibitions in 1875–76. Azzopardi was also commended at the 1880–81 Melbourne Exhibition 'for poster blocks of Kauri and Huon pine' and for 'Electro and Stereo; also wax and other moulds, facilitating the reproduction of the finest lines with clearness and distinctness'.

NOTE ON SOURCES

Information about early type imports is drawn from *Publicity and Printing* and also from H. W. H. Huntington's series of articles in *The Australian Printer, Stationer and Bookseller* in 1904. Documentation about types used in early Australian newspapers is from notes made in the St Bride Printing Library and from the newspapers themselves. American imports into Australia are mentioned in *Wimbles Reminder*, Diamond Jubilee Number, May 1928. The *Jane Shore* playbill is discussed in detail by Elaine Hoag, 'The Earliest Extant Australian Imprint, with Distinguished Provenance', *Script & Print*, vol.31, no.1, 2007, pp. 5-19.

Statistical information relating to imports is drawn from various sources including this author's article, 'The Beginnings of Type Founding in Sydney: Alexander Thomson's Type, His Foundry, and His Exports to Inter-Colonial Printers', *Journal of Design History*, vol.9, no.2, 1996, pp. 75-86; from *British Acts of Parliament, The Colonies, Australia* and from the Wimble Ledger. The ledgers referred to are in the possession of the Powerhouse Museum, Sydney, and The University of Melbourne archives. I thank Steve Saxe for explaining that the reference to Phelps, Dalton & Co., Boston, in the Cowans ledger represented the official name of the Dickinson Type Foundry. From this source I was able to compare more accurately values of type imported by Cowans with those imported by Wimbles.

Interest in Australian type founding was revived in 1967 with the publication of *The Spread of Printing: Eastern Hemisphere: Australia* (ed. C. Clair). Earlier references to Australian type founding may be found in *A Century of Journalism 1831–1931* (John Fairfax & Sons Ltd, 1931) and various nineteenth-century international and intercolonial exhibition catalogues as well as in the Sydney and Melbourne trade directories of John Sands and Sands and McDougall. John Holroyd first drew my attention to Alexander Thomson's exhibit at the Great Exhibition of 1851. Other sources include *Twelve Point, Wimbles Monthly Reminder, Men of the Times, The Australasian Typographical Journal*, with a series of articles by Thomas L. Work, and the records of the Victorian, New South Wales and South Australian Government Printers held by public records offices and state archives. The only type specimen books known to have survived are housed in the State Archives and Records of New South Wales, and the Powerhouse Museum, Sydney. See also Dennis Bryans, *A Survey of Australian Type-founders Specimens*, Blackburn South, Victoria, Golden Point Press, 2014. On German printing see Joyce Graetz, *An Open Book:*

The Story of the Distribution and Production of Christian Literature by Lutherans in Australia, Adelaide, Lutheran Publishing House, 1988; and the relevant sections of Miriam Gilson and Jerzy Zubrzycki, *The Foreign-language press in Australia, 1848-1964*, Canberra, Australian National University Press, 1967. The essential references on John Degotardi are Johann Nepomuk Degotardi, *The Art of Printing*, Sydney, Degotardi, 1861, facsimile edition in 2 volumes, ed. Jürgen Wegner, Sydney, Brandywine Press, 1982; and John Fletcher, *John Degotardi, printer, publisher and photographer*, Sydney, Book Collectors' Society of Australia, 1984. On Chinese type see Dennis Bryans, 'A Tolerable Interpreter: Robert Bell and the Chinese on the Ballarat Goldfields', *LTJ*, no.92, December 2013, pp. 126-43.

In addition to the above sources relating to type produced in Australia, mention should be made of Gordon and Gotch's annual *Australian Handbook and Almanac and Shippers' and Importers' Directory*. A family history pamphlet, *Lambert Family Tree* by Peter Coad, led me to more information about William Lambert. Details about Robert DeLittle's Melbourne sojourn are drawn from Claire Bolton's book, *DeLittle: The first years in a century of Wood Letter Manufacture, 1888-1988*, Oxford, Alembic Press, 1988. On the significance of Robert Coupland Harding see D. F. McKenzie, 'Robert Coupland Harding on Design in Typography' in *An Index of Civilisation: Studies of Printing and Publishing History in honour of Keith Maslen*, Melbourne, Centre for Bibliographical and Textual Studies, Monash University, 1993, pp. 187-205.

Readers should be aware of the important documentary studies being produced in extremely limited editions by Peter Marsh, notably in this connection his *The Establishment of the Government Printing Office Melbourne: The Golden Fifties*, Emerald Hill, Kitchen Table Press, 2018.

CHAPTER 8

'The laurels in the pit were won': Authorship in Colonial Australia

†Elizabeth Webby

Henry Lawson's well-known essay 'Pursuing Literature in Australia', together with the actual suicides or otherwise premature deaths of several leading writers, helped to establish a view of nineteenth-century Australia as something of a cultural desert, certainly no place for anyone with aspirations to authorship. For Lawson, writing at the end of the century, a talented young Australian writer had only two sensible options — to leave for overseas or to shoot himself. The alternative, staying in Australia, meant that his genius would turn to 'gall or beer'. Lawson's own subsequent history seemed almost designed to reinforce his argument. In 1900, with considerable financial help from others, Lawson and his family left for London. Just over two years later, prompted in part by his wife's illness, they returned to Australia and Lawson's genius did, indeed, turn to gall and beer.

In referring in his essay to the writer shooting himself, Lawson clearly had in mind — and knew his readers would also recall — the fate of Adam Lindsay Gordon, in the 1890s by far the most famous Australian poet. In June 1870, the day after the publication of the best-known of his volumes of poetry, *Bush Ballads and Galloping Rhymes*, Gordon shot himself on Brighton Beach near Melbourne. While financial disappointments, including the loss of a possible family estate in Scotland, and poor health, no doubt contributed to

Gordon's suicide, legend has it that he was in despair over his inability to pay the printer's bill. An equally famous poetic suicide — though of a much less famous poet — Barcroft Boake, who hanged himself with his own stockwhip in 1892, would also have been well known to Lawson and his readers.

Two earlier poets had gone down the gall and beer route. Charles Harpur, the first to aspire seriously to the mantle of Bard of Australia, died in 1868, aged 55. There had been plenty of beer along the way and the gall is only too apparent in the epitaph he penned for himself in 1867, which begins 'Here lies Charles Harpur, who at fifty years of age came to the conclusion, that he was living in a sham age, under a sham Government, and amongst sham friends, and that any world whatever must therefore be a better world than theirs.' Although a prolific poetry and prose writer, whose work was widely published in local newspapers, Harpur never achieved his dream of book publication in Britain. Even in Australia, a collected poems eluded him; the posthumous volume finally published in 1883, with funds raised by his widow, was heavily edited by another hand. This was especially ironic given Harpur's own obsessive rewritings of his poems, in preparation for the longed-for volume that was to establish his poetic reputation in England and Australia.

Harpur was, initially, the mentor of Henry Kendall, another self-christened 'Native Australian Poet' who also went down the gall and beer path. Kendall is the source of the quotation in the title of this chapter — 'the laurels in the pit were won' — and his life, too, was one of unrealised ambitions, debt, illness and despair. As the 1995 biography of Kendall by Michael Ackland demonstrates, however, Kendall was not quite the put-upon Romantic victim that he and others have chosen to depict. Unlike Gordon and Harpur, Kendall attempted for some years to support himself and his family through writing, rather than through farming and other more commercial pursuits. As with Lawson and others, it is difficult to determine how much bad luck, temperament and family difficulties contributed to his failure and to what extent it actually was impossible to earn a living as an author in colonial Australia.

The case of Marcus Clarke, possibly the most talented of this group of hard-livers and early diers, might appear to weigh heavily against any such possibility. Clarke died youngest of all — at only 36 — after having already written what is now recognised as the major nineteenth-century Australian novel — *His Natural Life* (1874) — as well as several others, besides plays, short stories, essays and a host of other journal articles. For *His Natural Life*, Clarke was paid £100 for its initial 1870–72 serialisation in the Melbourne *Australian Journal*, a further £25 when the shortened version was published in book form in Melbourne, and another £50 when it was published in London. In the late 1860s, apparently, he had been earning up to £750 per year from his journalism. For the last eleven years of his life, he also held a salaried position at the Melbourne Public Library. Yet he twice became insolvent, in 1874 and not long before his death in 1881.

These, then, are some of the sad histories that prompted Lawson's end-of-century cynicism. How accurately do they reflect the fates of the majority of authors or would-be authors in colonial Australia? It would certainly be true to say that, of all the people who came to Australia voluntarily, no-one who arrived before 1850 came with the intention of becoming an author. But many of those who came to the colonies, from the officers of the First Fleet onwards, were able to become published authors by exploiting the continuing intense interest in Australia from readers in Britain and Europe. This was also true of some convict arrivals, such as Thomas Watling, artist and forger, whose *Letters From an Exile at Botany-Bay, to his Aunt in Dumfries*, was first published in Scotland in 1794. While most of these publications were works of non-fiction, some writers, including Charles Rowcroft and Alexander Harris, drew on their Australian experiences for successful novels, written, however, after their return to England.

The discovery of gold in the early 1850s created an even stronger surge of interest in Australia, with established authors now being among those attracted to the colonies. Some, like William Howitt, made only a brief stay before returning to England to write successful fiction and non-fiction based on their Australian experiences. Others stayed longer — Richard Henry 'Orion' Horne, who arrived in Melbourne in 1852, was the colonies' first real 'literary lion'. He remained until 1869, working at various government and non-government jobs besides writing for many local publications. The fate of Charles Whitehead, an English novelist who migrated to Melbourne in 1857, and died penniless five years later, would seem yet further evidence in support of Henry Lawson's views on the futility of pursuing literature in Australia. But Whitehead came to Australia partly because he had been unable to make a living in Britain; he had been drinking heavily and in financial embarrassment for years before his departure. An author who could not succeed in the London marketplace certainly had no hope of making a living with his pen from the much more restricted opportunities available even in Melbourne, the largest Australian literary centre in the second half of the century.

But it was possible, as some other case histories demonstrate, to earn a living by one's pen in nineteenth-century Australia, especially in Melbourne after about 1860. One needed, however, to have a strong constitution and considerable determination and industry, as well as a modicum of talent. A case in point is Garnet Walch, born in Tasmania in 1843 into a bookselling family, who died in Melbourne in 1913, aged 70. For most of his life, Walch supported himself, his wife and eight children, through a combination of writing, editing and publishing, mainly for the stage and the popular press. Another successful man of letters, James Smith, migrated to Melbourne at the height of the gold boom in 1854. He had already had considerable success as a journalist and editor in England and managed to make a good living through a combination of leader writing, editing, and art, music, dramatic and literary reviewing for the leading Melbourne newspapers and many other publications. In 1888, as Lurline Stuart records in her biography of Smith, he claimed to have earned £40 000 from his literary efforts over the 34 years he had been in Victoria, an average of £1200 per year. Although his income did not remain at this high level, Smith survived to 89; he also supported a large family. Another success was David Blair, who arrived in Sydney at the age of 30 as a trainee clergyman. Soon tiring of this life, he went into journalism without any prior experience. Although he spent some time in the public service, and as a politician, most of Blair's income came from journalism and from compiling reference works such as the *History of Australasia* (1878) and the *Cyclopedia of Australasia* (1881). He survived to 79, supporting his wife and six children largely through his pen.

What of the women of letters? For many years this term was believed to be an oxymoron in relation to nineteenth-century Australia, but work by Lucy Sussex, Patricia Clarke and others has established that there were indeed some women who earned a living by their pens, though none achieved the high profile of a James Smith or David Blair. In part this was because the types of official or semi-official positions and publications through which Smith and Blair supplemented their journalistic incomes and did their networking were not then open to females. The most public woman of letters in Australia during the second half of the nineteenth century was undoubtedly Catherine Helen Spence, novelist, lecturer and journalist. It is, however, clear that Spence, who never married and did at times have to help support relatives, would not have been able to do so without family legacies. Like most women writers of her period, she initially tried her hand as a novelist but found the rewards too limited. As was the norm for most Australian novelists of her time, she published in Britain and suffered the disadvantages of not being on the spot. Not only was her first novel *Clara Morison* (1854) cut down without her permission, but she was charged £10 for the cost of doing this, so earning only £30 for the work. This was, however, still £10 more than she was offered for her second novel *Tender and True* (1856), even though it went through several editions. Spence, like other Australian novelists, often earned more when her novels were serialised in local newspapers than when they were published in Britain as books. Her third novel, *Uphill Work*, earned her £50 when serialised in the Adelaide *Daily Telegraph*, but only a further £35 when published as *Mr Hogarth's Will* (1865) in London by Bentley.

The even more prolific Mary Fortune was virtually unknown until the late 1980s, largely because she published only in serials, wrote all her work under pseudonyms, both male and female, and carefully avoided any publicity. Much of her writing was done for the popular fiction magazine *Australian Journal*, to which she contributed several serialised novels, many comic and other stories, and some observational journalism of the type particularly associated with Marcus Clarke, but her speciality was detective stories. Fortune was one of the first women in the world to take up this relatively new genre, turning out one 10 000-word story a month for about 30 years.

Although for much of her life she earned enough to support herself and to raise at least one child, she was forced to depend on a pension from the *Australian Journal* when her eyesight faded in old age. There were rumours that she also depended on the bottle to keep her pen oiled but, unlike many of the male authors, she did not die young, living into her seventies.

Ada Cambridge survived to 82, during her lifetime publishing over twenty novels, three volumes of poetry, two autobiographies and many stories and essays. She had arrived in Australia in 1870 with her clergyman husband; her fiction, serialised in the highly popular and successful Melbourne weekly the *Australasian*, while not her only source of income, added considerably to her and her family's comforts. In 1880 she was paid almost £200 for the Australian serial rights to her novel *A Marked Man*. Although this was an exception, paid in a boom year, like Clarke and Spence she appears to have made much more from her Australian serialisations than from publication in Britain. According to Elaine Zinkhan, Cambridge earned only £15 when this same novel was serialised in the *Manchester Weekly Times Supplement*, and a further £17/7/- from Heinemann in royalties on the 3/6d edition. Like most Australian authors of this period, Cambridge suffered from the very low royalties paid on colonial editions; her contract with Heinemann for her novel *Not All in Vain* (1892), for example, offered 15 per cent royalties on the three-volume edition, 10 per cent on the 3/6d edition and one penny per copy on copies sold for the colonial market. Like Mary Fortune, if not to the same degree, Cambridge experienced financial hardship in old age, her saviour being the Sydney publisher and bookseller George Robertson, who in 1924 gave her £100 for the rights to reprint any or all of her books. By then, her novels were seen as part of the old colonial past, genteel romances with nothing to say to the new Australia, and it seems clear that Robertson had no intention of reprinting any of them.

The most financially successful Australian woman writer of this period would seem to have been Rosa Praed, born on her father's station in Queensland in 1851. Her first stories appeared in a handwritten family magazine when she was still a teenager, but Praed did not become a professional author until 1880. By then she was living in England, having moved there in 1876 with her English husband, who had failed to make a success of his Australian pastoral ventures. While Praed may have begun writing more for occupational than financial reasons, her separation from her husband in the 1890s meant that she was thereafter dependent on her pen. At the height of her popularity she did quite well, receiving, for example, £275 from Chatto & Windus for *Christina Chard* (1893) and a further £250 for the serial rights. Like Cambridge and others, however, she suffered from the lower royalty paid on colonial editions; the royalty on English editions of *The Scourge Stick* (1898), for example, was one shilling per copy as against only fourpence on colonial editions. Praed published more than 45 books before her death at the age of 84.

Other Australian-born writers who went on to success in London included Guy Boothby, creator of the Dr Nikola crime series, author of over 50 novels between 1894 and his early death from pneumonia in 1905 at the age of 37. His income was said to be as much as £20 000 a year, suggesting that success as well as failure could be a health hazard.

As these last examples show, it was usually easier to make a comfortable living as a novelist in England than in Australia during the nineteenth century, given a certain level of talent, hard work and good luck. Those who succeeded in Australia did so by writing in a wide range of genres and across many topics and, with the exception of Garnet Walch, were primarily writers of non-fiction, especially journalism. One of the ironies of nineteenth-century Australian literature was that the more obviously 'Australian' a work was, the better chance it had of finding an overseas publisher. So most fiction and non-fiction were published overseas, most poetry and drama in Australia, at the author's expense. Ken Stewart's analysis of the verse and fiction titles listed in E. Morris Miller and F. J. Macartney's *Australian Literature; A Bibliography* (1950) shows that, for the decades up to 1890, 61 volumes of Australian poetry had been published overseas, as against 153 in Melbourne and 133 in Sydney. Conversely, 284 Australian novels had been published overseas as against 105 in Melbourne and a mere 51 in Sydney. These figures reflect the fact that almost all Australian book publication before 1890 was done at the author's expense. Clearly, it was easier to afford the cost of a slim volume of verse than that of a substantial novel. On the other hand, most Australian novelists did not earn a great deal from books published in England, especially if they lived in Australia and had to depend on agents and friends to negotiate with their publishers. For them, at least before 1890, serialisation in Australian newspapers and magazines was a much more dependable source of income. It is a mistake, therefore, to assume that authors like Ada Cambridge were primarily writing for an English market, merely because their books were eventually published there.

Much of the writing done in colonial Australia was, of course, never published. A good deal was never intended for publication, being in the form of letters, which during this period was the major means of communication between friends and relatives separated by long distances. Much writing was also in the form of journals or diaries, often kept by migrants on the voyage out, by explorers during their hazardous expeditions, and sometimes by others to record their everyday activities, their dreams and desires, even what they had been reading. More recently, a good deal of this personal material has found publication, quarried by scholars from libraries and archives for the insight it offers into life in the new British colonies. Some fiction and poetry, as the example of the manuscript magazine written by members of Rosa Praed's family demonstrates, also continued to circulate scribally in Australia during the nineteenth century.

Of published writing, by far the bulk of it appeared in newspapers and magazines, which flourished in the Australian colonies from 1803 onwards. As this chapter has demonstrated, for authors who remained in Australia, journalism and publication of stories and serial fiction in the large weekly newspapers of the second half of the century were the most reliable sources of income. In order to become a best-selling novelist or successful dramatist, however, it was necessary to move to London, as a number of Australian-born authors did later in the 1800s. But such a change of abode, as the example of Henry Lawson indicates, was not always a guarantee of success. To be an author in Australia was largely a labour of love, or an obsession, as it remains today: a 2023 survey by the Australian Society of Authors reported that 80 per cent of respondents earned less than $15,000 a year, well below the poverty line.

NOTE ON SOURCES

This chapter draws heavily on two chapters from Laurie Hergenhan, gen. ed., *The Penguin New Literary History of Australia*, Ringwood, VIC, Penguin, 1988, namely Elizabeth Webby, 'Writers, Printers, Readers: The Production of Australian Literature Before 1855', pp.113-25; and Ken Stewart, 'Journalism and the World of the Writer: The Production of Australian Literature, 1855–1915', pp. 174-93, for general information about literary life in nineteenth-century Australia.

Henry Lawson's 'Pursuing Literature in Australia' can be found in Colin Roderick, ed., *Henry Lawson, Autobiographical and Other Writings: 1887–1922*, Sydney, Angus & Robertson, 1972, pp.109–16. Charles Harpur's 'Epitaph' is reprinted in Adrian Mitchell, ed., *Charles Harpur*, Melbourne, Sun Books, 1973, p. 176.

Information on authors' earnings comes from Michael Ackland, *Henry Kendall: The Man and the Myths*, Melbourne, MUP, 1995; Lucy Sussex, ed., *The Fortunes of Mary Fortune*, Ringwood, VIC, Penguin Books, 1989; Lurline Stuart, *James Smith. The Making of a Colonial Culture*, Sydney, Allen & Unwin, 1989; Patricia Clarke, *Pen Portraits: Women Writers and Journalists in Nineteenth-Century Australia*, Sydney, Allen & Unwin, 1988; Patricia Clarke, *Rosa! Rosa! A Life of Rosa Praed, Novelist and Spiritualist*, Melbourne, MUP, 1999; Elaine Zinkhan, 'Ada Cambridge: *A Marked Man*, the *Manchester Weekly Times Supplement*, and Late-Nineteenth-Century Fiction', *BSANZ Bulletin*, vol.17, no.4, 1993, pp. 155-79; Chris Tiffin and Lynette Baer, *The Praed Papers*, Brisbane, Library Board of Queensland, 1994.

The marketing of pre-1890 Australian authors in America is discussed in David Carter & Roger Osborne, *Australian Books and Authors in the American Marketplace, 1840s–1940s*, Sydney, SUP, 2018.

The Australian Society of Authors' survey was released on their website, asauthors.org, on 23 December 2023.

The ongoing mystery surrounding the year of Mary Fortune's death was solved by Lucy Sussex, and described by Jason Steger in 'Solved! The case of Mary Fortune, the pioneering crime writer who vanished', *Sydney Morning Herald*, 7 July 2016, smh.com.au, [accessed 14 April 2024].

CHAPTER 9

The Beginnings of Australian Publishing

Ian Morrison

An audience

In June 1789, in a crude wooden hut near Sydney Cove, Royal Marine Lieutenant Ralph Clark directed a cast of prisoners in a performance of George Farquhar's *The Recruiting Officer*. One modern editor has commented on 'the intricate ironies of the situation . . . [Sergeant] Kite, impersonated by a convict, is busy enlisting jailbirds, and frequently equates a garrison with a prison' (Dixon, 27). For all that it was a safe choice. *The Recruiting Officer* was one of the most popular English plays of the eighteenth century, missing only five seasons on the London stage between 1706 and 1800 and being regularly performed in provincial theatres and the North American colonies (Ross, xxxiii). It was comfort food even for Clark's fellow-officers, who might easily have taken umbrage. Captain Watkin Tench saw the performance as an:

> escape from the dreariness and dejection of our situation . . . The exhilarating effect of a splendid theatre is well known: and I am not ashamed to confess, that the proper distribution of three or four yards of stained paper, and a dozen farthing candles stuck around the walls of a convict-hut, failed not to diffuse general complacency on the countenances of sixty persons . . . Some of the actors acquitted themselves with great spirit . . . a prologue and an epilogue, written by one of the performers . . . contained some tolerable allusions to the situation . . . and the novelty of a stage-representation in New South Wales. (Tench, 25)

Tench's remarks show that the colonists had both the inclination and the ability to make their own entertainment. Convicts at the auxiliary settlement on Norfolk Island ran a theatre around 1793–94, and ex-convict Robert Sidaway opened the first permanent theatre in Sydney in 1796. Each of these ventures clearly had access to published play scripts, and the talent and experience to translate them into theatrical performances. Sidaway also had access to a printing press: the government printer George Hughes was a member of his troupe. Sidaway might thus be considered Australia's first non-government publisher. The earliest surviving Australian printed document is a playbill printed by Hughes for Sidaway's production of *Jane Shore* in 1796; copies of Hughes playbills for two later Sidaway productions have also survived: *The Recruiting Officer* in March 1800, and *Henry IV* in April 1800.

The significance of these documents was much greater than the information they contained. In 1796 Sydney's population was a little over 4000, and Sidaway could surely have filled his theatre by word-of-mouth advertising. Just as the act of printing and displaying regulations is an assertion of the authority to promulgate those regulations, the playbill did much more than advertise a specific theatrical event. In its mundane, formulaic functionality, 'adhering to the established playbill formulae ... offered the reassurance of familiarity and continuity ... It encouraged a kind of suspension of disbelief, the temporary impression that life in a new land could still be the same as at home' (Russell, 103).

Arrivals

'Publication' takes many forms, and neither authors nor publishers can be understood in isolation from their audiences. Nor can colonial publishing be understood outside the contexts of colonisation, the structures and dynamics of empire, the relationship between the colonisers and the colonised. In the broadest sense of making something generally known, the history of publishing in Australia stretches back tens of thousands of years, encompassing the art and complex oral cultures of the Aboriginal peoples. In this sense it also embraces the imperial gestures that preceded the British invasion: the inscribed pewter plates nailed to wooden posts on an island off the west coast by Dutch explorers Dirk Hartog and Willem de Vlamingh in 1616 and 1697, the flag planted by British naval officer James Cook on the east coast in 1770. It would also include the pictorial signboards deployed by the British in Van Diemen's Land at the height of the Black War in 1829–30 to communicate to the Indigenous population 'the effects of hostility and the effects of peace' (Brodie and Harman, 13).

A history of 'the book', the printed codex, in colonial Australia is by contrast inherently Anglocentric. The vast majority of books produced in colonial Australia were made by English-speaking white people for other English-speaking white people; moreover, the books produced in Australia represented only a small portion of the books bought and read by the colonists.

Publishers' records for nineteenth-century Australia are practically non-existent. The principal exception is Tasmanian firm J. Walch & Sons, now held in the Tasmanian Archives. The earliest surviving Walch records are a day book and a library borrowing register (Kirsop 2011). The bulk of the Walch archive comprises pressed copy letterbooks from the 1860s to the early twentieth century: with faded ink on fragile paper, these volumes are challenging to interpret, let alone analyse. It remains a source of frustration for Australian book historians that the records needed for a clear understanding of the day-to-day workings of the early colonial trade have not survived. Most of the evidence comes from the publications themselves, and from ancillary sources such as newspaper advertisements, postal and commercial directories, and government records.

When the British landed at Botany Bay in 1788 they brought with them a print-based culture centred on the codex. They also utilised the written and printed word in a multitude of other forms and contexts, and maintained oral traditions and cultural practices developed over many centuries. The archaeological record of early colonial Australia is rich in traces of folk magic (Evans, 1).

Nor was oral culture ever the sole preserve of the illiterate. The fundamental purpose of a book is to share ideas and information, and that process of sharing is ultimately dependent on readers talking to other readers. The book-based high culture of Enlightenment Europe had a significant oral dimension, as ideas and opinions were contested and discoveries demonstrated in coffee houses, private soirées, and lecture halls. Étienne-Louis Boullée's unrealised vision for the Bibliothèque du Roi made the reading room a social space, devoid of desks, where people walked and talked and consulted books at the shelves (Wilkinson, 67-69). Colonial bookselling and publishing, too, proceeded in parallel with attempts to establish learned societies and cultural institutions — venues for sophisticated conversation.

There was no shortage of intellectual curiosity or literary ambition on the First Fleet. Watkin Tench signed a publishing contract before leaving England; his *Narrative of the Expedition to Botany Bay* (1789) preceded Governor Arthur Phillip's official account, *A Complete Account of the Settlement at Port Jackson*, which followed in 1793. Books by Surgeon General John White, Phillip's deputy and successor John Hunter and Judge Advocate (later Lieutenant-Governor of Van Diemen's Land) David Collins followed quickly, along with numerous plagiarised and fictitious accounts.

Britain's penal colonies were at once geographically remote places and central pillars of the criminal justice system. As such, they were lucrative for British publishers. Books about experiences there practically sold themselves, and the demand for books to be used there only ever seemed to grow. Richard Johnson, chaplain on the First Fleet, brought 100 bibles, 350 New Testaments and various other religious texts to the colony. His *Address to the Inhabitants of the Colonies Established in New South Wales and Norfolk Island . . . Written in the Year 1792* (London, 1794) was the first book produced specifically for distribution in Australia. Johnson clearly had a 'Home' audience in mind as well: the imprint names three London booksellers.

The First Fleet also brought a printing press, an indication that someone in authority valued the capacity to produce printed documents, but there was no one with the skills to operate it until the appointment of George Hughes as official printer in 1795. His work finished no later than 1801, when he was replaced by George Howe (1769–1821).

George Howe

The story of publishing in Australia in the opening decades of the nineteenth century is largely the story of George Howe, who was born in St Kitts, the son of printer Thomas Howe and his wife Anne, the daughter of a plantation owner. Christened Robert, he took the name George in early adulthood. Having learned printing skills from his father, Howe travelled to England. During the 1790s he worked on the London *Times*. In 1799, under the alias George Happy or Happy George, he was convicted of robbery and transported to New South Wales, arriving in November 1800 (Robb, 15ff). He must have been given the role of official printer soon afterwards: in 1802 he produced the first book printed in Australia, *New South Wales General Standing Orders*.

In discussing Howe's work, the distinction between 'printer' and 'publisher' has little practical meaning. He was a product of the eighteenth century, and worked all his career with a hand-press and hand-made paper. In that world, printers — especially outside metropolitan centres — commonly dealt with issues of finance, design and distribution that we now regard as the domain of the publisher.

Howe was granted a conditional pardon in 1803, and was fully emancipated in 1806. From 1810 he received an annual salary of £60 as Government Printer. This salary and other business interests (notably speculation in sandalwood) were critical factors in the survival of the *Gazette*. By 1819 the colony's population had grown to 30 000 and the *Gazette*'s circulation to some three or four hundred. It was, however, far from secure. Howe lamented:

> A Paper in England, under 700 in number, is sensibly a losing concern; and what must be a Paper here within half that number and half of that unpaid for? (*Sydney Gazette*, 25 December 1819)

Howe was almost certainly overstating his difficulties: when he died in May 1821 he left an estate valued at £4000. To put this sum into perspective: Sir George Arthur was appointed Lieutenant-Governor of Van Diemen's Land in 1823 with an annual salary of £1500; the double-storey rectory built for the chaplain and magistrate Samuel Marsden in 1816–17 cost £2750.

Howe's second publishing venture coincided with his emancipation in 1806. In October and November 1805 the *Sydney Gazette* advertised for subscribers to an almanac, noting that the scarcity of paper meant that the impression would necessarily be a limited one. In the event, paper was so scarce that the *New South Wales Pocket*

Almanack and Colonial Remembrancer for 1806 was issued in two parts: the first, containing a solar and lunar calendar, information on 'Gardening, Agriculture, and the Care of Sheep', notable events, and 'Arrival of Vessels', was issued to subscribers on New Year's Day 1806; the second, an 'Abridgement of General Orders', did not appear until May. The venture was presumably profitable, as it continued into the 1820s. As with his newspaper Howe worked assiduously to turn readers into buyers. An advertisement for the 1811 issue warned, 'The Subscription List does not exceed 47. Unless 100 copies shall be subscribed for it will not be printed' (*Sydney Gazette*, 17 November 1810).

Howe also printed missionary texts in Pacific languages (as is discussed in more detail by Susan Woodburn in Chapter 22), the poems of Michael Massey Robinson and Barron Field, and the 1813 Sydney edition of John Lewin's *Birds of New South Wales*, but his financial security rested on his position as Government Printer.

Consolidation and expansion

The mid-1820s mark a turning point in Australian publishing history. In 1820 the entire publishing scene consisted of two Government Printers — one in Sydney, one in Hobart — who ran quasi-independent newspapers and occasionally produced other work on the side. Ink and paper were expensive, often unobtainable at any price, and seldom of high quality. The convicts and emancipists who formed the majority of the colonial population were not uniformly poorly educated: however, few could afford to spend large amounts of money acquiring books.

Back 'Home', the Romantic writers and painters were changing the way the British intelligentsia looked at the world. Charles Babbage and Michael Faraday were at the beginning of their careers. The *Times* had installed a machine press, allowing speedier production of greater print-runs of larger newspapers. The Corn Law Act of 1815 was keeping the price of basic foodstuffs at the high levels induced by the Napoleonic Wars. Soaring unemployment in the wake of military demobilisation saw authorities cut the costs of poor relief 'by making the Poor Law ... harsher in administration, more humiliating, more repellent... to drive the poor out of relief' (Hobsbawm and Rudé, 76).

The agitation that would lead to the 1832 Reform Act was beginning to swell.

During the 1820s the environment for colonial publishing altered dramatically. First, the physical dimensions of the colonies grew. In 1813 a party led by Gregory Blaxland and Lieutenant William Lawson followed Aboriginal routes through the Blue Mountains, enabling the British to expand their colony beyond the narrow coastal fringe into what looked like inexhaustible grasslands. A period of intense exploration of the inland followed: in 1817 John Oxley ventured westwards from Bathurst until confronted by swamplands; in 1824 Hamilton Hume and William Hovell headed south, reaching Port Phillip; in 1827 Allan Cunningham went northwards, into the pasturelands of the Darling Downs; and in 1828–29 Charles Sturt pushed further west, travelling the Murray and Darling Rivers and reporting the existence of large Aboriginal settlements. By the end of the 1820s the British were extending their areas of control ever more deeply into the continent. Although many goods still had to be imported and supply lines were fragile (when Robert Wardell and William Charles Wentworth established their newspaper, the *Australian*, in 1824, they stocked up with enough paper to last three *years*) the essential viability of the Australian colonies was no longer in question.

The first generation of British born in the colonies were now of an age to become parents themselves, and *belonged* in ways unimaginable in the 1790s. Although most of the grand plans of the 1820s — the Philosophical Society of Australasia (Sydney, 1821-23), agitation for a 'Public Library and Literary Society' in Hobart in 1825, the abortive Van Diemen's Land Scientific Society (1829) — came to little or nothing, the decade did see the opening of the Australian Subscription Library, stocked with 1000 volumes, in Sydney in 1827.

As convicts worked their way through the system, colonial society became more complex, and a dramatic increase in free settlers fuelled rapid population growth. In the period up to 1820 the colonies were unambiguous penal settlements, under firm — often openly corrupt — military control. During the 1820s barely one quarter of new arrivals were free; in the 1830s, with the introduction of assisted passages, free settlers accounted for more than half of the new arrivals.

In Van Diemen's Land, in particular, government policy through the 1820s and 1830s aimed to establish a landed gentry supported by convict labour. In 1835 the total colonial population was approximately 110 000, by 1840 it was approaching 200 000.

Poetry, fiction and piracy

The first book of verse published in Australia was printed by George Howe 'for private distribution' in 1819. The anonymous author was the colony's second Judge, Barron Field. Self-consciously titled *First Fruits of Australian Poetry*, the volume contained two poems, 'Botany Bay Flowers' and 'The Kangaroo', and sported an epigram on its title page: 'I first adventure, follow me who list, and be the second Austral Harmonist'. It was actually Field himself who was the second: he was preceded by Michael Massey Robinson, whose series of twenty odes was published individually, each as a separate issue (Ferguson 506 being one example), and in the *Sydney Gazette* between 1810 and 1820. A second edition of Field's *First Fruits*, published in 1823, contained several more poems, including 'On Reading the Controversy between Lord Byron and Mr Bowles' and 'On Visiting the Spot where Captain Cook and Sir Joseph Banks First Landed in Botany Bay'. Field dismissed Australia as 'a land without antiquities', Sydney a 'spireless city and prophane'. He is now seen as instrumental in introducing *terra nullius* to Australian law, in an 1819 ruling against Governor Macquarie's power to raise taxes (Ford & Clemens, 15-16). He was an active member of the Philosophical Society of Australasia, and of the Society for Promoting Christian Knowledge, but against trial by jury and the establishment of a legislative assembly for the colony. Following John Thomas Bigge's report into the state of the colony, which singled the judge out for 'the effects of his violent and unforgiving temper, as well as of his personal prejudices', Field returned to England in 1824. A friend of Charles Lamb, Samuel Marsden, and William Wilberforce, his other literary activities included editing the *Memoirs of James Hardy Vaux* (1819) and *Geographical Memoirs of New South Wales* (1825).

Between 1823 and 1826 there was a sudden upsurge of original poetry in Sydney and Hobart newspapers. Prior to 1823 the *Sydney Gazette* typically carried three or four poems per year; in the eighteen months from June 1823 to December 1824 it carried on average one poem a fortnight. The *Australian* carried 40 poems during its first eighteen months (October 1824–March 1826). The *Hobart Town Gazette* carried some 41 poems between January 1824 and June 1825. Whilst the bulk of these poems were the work of a few regular contributors (Laurence Halloran and Charles Tompson in the *Sydney Gazette*, 'J. M.' and 'J. R. M.' in the *Australian*, H. N. Murray in the *Hobart Town Gazette*), it is significant that those regular contributors all emerged quite suddenly and almost simultaneously. Tompson's *Wild Notes from the Lyre of a Native Minstrel* (1826) was the first book of verse by an Australian-born poet to appear in Australia.

In Hobart in 1827 Andrew Bent published the first book of verse in Tasmania: *The Van Diemen's Land Warriors, or the Heroes of Cornwall*, by 'Pindar Juvenal', a satire on the failure of the military authorities to capture the bushranger Matthew Brady. Although Brady had in fact been captured and executed in 1826, the satire struck a nerve and the book was suppressed.

Printers who were geared for frequent, regular single-sheet newspapers could not easily adapt to book production. In 1826 Arthur Hill, of the Sydney *Monitor*, accepted the job of printing Congregational missionary Lancelot Threlkeld's *Specimens of a Dialect of the Aborigines of New South Wales*. A 32-page quarto, Threlkeld's book took months to complete and tested Hill's resources to the limit. Hill printed each sheet separately, distributing the type as he went. When the book was finally published, in May 1827, Threlkeld wrote to the London Missionary Society that 'a greater interest has been excited here . . . than I anticipated', and suggested that the Society consider a reprint: 'an edition could be run off much cheaper in England than here' (Ferguson 1147).

Literary works printed in Australia before the 1850s can almost all be classed as vanity publishing, in that the authors carried the costs. Writers who could not afford to pay their own printing costs needed to find a patron or subscribers. Charles Tompson signed up some 200 subscribers to his *Wild Notes*, the 'general minimum' required (Webby 1981, 47). Anna Maria Bunn's novel *The Guardian* (1838) was published anonymously and never offered for sale, apparently funded and then suppressed by the author's family (Webby 1988, 117).

Australia's first two novelists, Mary Leman Grimstone (1796?–1869) and Henry Savery (1791–1842), were both in Hobart in the 1820s and 1830s. Grimstone was the sister-in-law of Stephen Adey, a director of the colony's premier financial institution, the Derwent Bank. An associate of Robert Owen, Elizabeth Gaskell and Caroline Norton, Grimstone was an established author before coming to Australia. Her novel *Louisa Egerton* (1830) was begun on the voyage out in 1825 and completed in Hobart. *Woman's Love* (1832) was written in Hobart. *Cleone: A Tale of Married Life* (1833) and *Character, or, Jew and Gentile* (1834), completed after her return to England, drew on her experiences in Van Diemen's Land. Grimstone has been identified as the author of poems published in Andrew Bent's *Colonial Times* and Henry Melville's *Hobart Town Monthly Magazine*, but all of her novels were published in England.

Savery was the son of a Bristol banker. Convicted of forgery in 1825 he was transported to Van Diemen's Land. After his release from prison he worked as a farmer; the records of the Derwent Bank include a docket showing him delivering grain to the Adey household. His satirical sketches *The Hermit in Van Diemen's Land* (1829) and novel *Quintus Servinton* (1830–31) were both published anonymously. *Quintus Servinton* was the first novel to be published in Australia, and the British Library catalogue originally attributed it to Grimstone. The publishing history of Savery's novel is atypical of nineteenth-century Australian novels. It was printed in Hobart by Henry Melville, who appears to have borne most if not all of the costs, 'expressly for transmission to England', where it was issued in 1832 with the additional imprint of Smith, Elder and Co., Cornhill, London. According to Melville's advertisement (*Hobart Town Courier*, 22 January 1831), 'a very few copies only [were] reserved for sale in this colony' (Ferguson 1391). The more usual pattern was to do as Grimstone did and have the book printed and published in England. It was generally cheaper to do this than to buy the paper and ink and print the book locally: throughout the nineteenth century the cost of paper in Australia was approximately double the cost of paper in England. And, at least until the 1860s, the printing could be expected to be of a higher quality in England.

Melville was himself a prolific writer, interested in occult philosophy, astronomy and Freemasonry, and the author of the first play written and produced in Australia, *The Bushrangers, or Norwood Vale* (1834) (Fotheringham, 5ff).

The arrival of the Tegg brothers in Sydney in December 1834 marks the beginning of professional bookselling in the colonies. James and Samuel Augustus Tegg were sons of the London bookseller Thomas Tegg. James established a business in Sydney, Samuel settled in Hobart in 1836; between them they played a dominant role in the Australian book trade for most of the following decade, as is discussed further by Wallace Kirsop in Chapter 13. The core of their business appears to have been high turnover, low profit margin, British imports, and they had 'the enormous advantage of . . . being able to base their offerings on their father's extensive range.' (Kirsop 1995, 10). But James, in particular, was much more than his father's colonial agent: he was an active publisher in his own right.

James Tegg was associated with 122 publications. His output was extraordinarily varied. Besides two literary magazines, sheet and book almanacs, it included: William Bland's *Journey of Discovery to Port Phillip* (1837), Lady Darling's *Simple Rules for the Guidance of Persons in Humble Life* (1837, a servants' manual), Beverley Suttor's *Original Poetry* (1838, a lavishly produced vanity project that attracted instant mockery), Caroline Chisholm's *Female Immigration Considered* (1842), and John Lang's *Legends of Australia* (1842). Tegg was also a subscription agent for J. G. Austin's *Series of Lithographic Drawings of Sydney and its Environs* (1836). Many of Thomas Tegg's publications, notably *Tegg's Handbook for Emigrants* (1839–44), include 'J. and S. A. Tegg, Sydney and Hobart Town' in the imprint. The listing of London and colonial branches on the title-page of the *Handbook* cannot have failed to impress readers with the scale of the Teggs' operations.

That James Tegg lasted in business for twelve years and operated three branches outside Sydney (at Windsor, Maitland and Campbelltown) suggests that he was successful in at least maintaining a steady cashflow. But, equally, he failed to amass substantial profits: he died intestate in 1846, aged 38, and, in contrast with the comfortable fortune amassed by George Howe, left an estate of little over £100 (Hubber 1989, 57).

Other major figures during this period were William Augustine Duncan, Daniel Lovett Welch and William Moffitt. Duncan and Welch were primarily involved with newspapers and periodicals, but each published notable books: Duncan's output included Charles Harpur's first book of poetry, *Thoughts: A Series of Sonnets* (1845); Welch published *Brabazon's New South Wales General Town Directory* (1843), Maria Theresa Vidal's homiletic *Tales for the Bush* (1845) and Sir Thomas Mitchell's *Notes on the Cultivation of the Vine and the Olive* (1849).

The multi-talented Moffitt commenced business as a bookseller, stationer, printer, bookbinder and engraver in 1830, and remained a major figure in the Sydney book trade until his retirement in 1874. Contemporaries commented upon his plate-glass windows (believed to be the first in Sydney), and flocked to the rat, cock and dog fights, and boxing matches, staged at the rear of his shop. His reputation rests largely on his engraving and bookbinding, but he was an active publisher as well, issuing book and sheet almanacs (1834–53) and a range of other books, including John Lhotsky's *Illustrations of the Present State and Future Prospects of the Colony of New South Wales* (1835–36) and W. Wedge Darke's *Observations on Convicts and the Discipline to which They Have Hitherto Been Subjected* (1852).

Colonial booksellers also dabbled in piracy. An edition of the *Poetical Works of Robert Burns* was issued with a lithographed title-page 'printed for the booksellers in Australia' in 1832 (Butler, 124-25). A more sophisticated effort was the edition of Charles Dickens's *Pickwick Papers* published in Launceston by Henry Dowling. It was issued in 25 parts beginning in June 1838, and as a bound volume in 1839. The London edition first appeared in monthly parts from April 1836 to November 1837. Assuming that shipping took around five months, Dowling must have begun production almost immediately upon receiving the final part — implying that he conceived the project much earlier (Craig, 7ff). With illustrations by 'Tizz' in imitation of the London edition's 'Phiz', Dowling's *Pickwick* was an impressive technical achievement. It also shows that authors and publishers of original work had no effective legal protection at that time: neither Dickens nor his publishers took any action against Dowling — indeed any action probably would have failed.

Dowling was abetted by Samuel Tegg, whose father's unauthorised, cut-price reprints provoked Thomas Carlyle to petition the House of Commons in 1839. It is doubtful that Dowling's piracy affected Dickens to the same extent that Tegg senior's activities aggrieved Carlyle: *The Posthumous Papers of the Pickwick Club* was one of the runaway bestsellers of early Victorian England, selling tens of thousands of copies; Dowling's edition numbered in the hundreds, and was not marketed outside the colony in which it was printed. A similar exercise was attempted in 1842–43 by Sydney printer William Baker, who published an edition of Charles James Lever's *Charles O'Malley, the Irish Dragoon* (curiously, also illustrated by 'Phiz'): Baker's advertisement was headed 'Cheap Edition for the People', but stated that 'only a limited number of copies' would be produced (Ferguson 3438). The economics of the situation were all against colonial reprints of even the most successful British novels.

New colonies

The rapid growth of the original colonies, and the establishment of settlements in Western Australia (1826–29), Port Phillip (1835), South Australia (1836) and, more tenuously, subtropical Moreton Bay (1824–39), created a market large enough to sustain a modest local publishing industry — and a settler class with a political need to control the narrative around frontier conflict.

As with New South Wales and Van Diemen's Land, the first publications in the new colonies were newspapers and official notices, followed closely by almanacs and directories. Each of the new colonies, however, had profoundly different origins.

British incursion into the diverse Aboriginal nations in the northeast of the continent, which became the colony of Queensland, was initially haphazard. A penal colony was established at Moreton Bay in 1824 and abandoned in 1839. Meanwhile drovers had been enticed through the mountains into the rich pasturelands of the Darling Downs. Brisbane's first newspaper, the *Moreton Bay Courier*, was established in 1846.

Western Australia was officially established in 1826, when a contingent of British soldiers and convicts was sent to King George Sound to forestall the French. A second settlement followed in 1829, on the Swan River, but Western Australia remained a minor outpost until the discovery of gold in the 1880s. Local publishing was mostly limited to newspapers, almanacs and government notices.

South Australia was unique among Britain's Australian colonies in not being a penal settlement. A newspaper, the *South Australian Gazette and Colonial Register*, was published before the colonists embarked from London in June 1836; the second issue appeared a year later in the new settlement at Adelaide. The publishers were Robert Thomas, a bookseller who had been engaged as Government Printer for the new colony, and George Stevenson, a journalist. In 1839 the *Gazette* became the *South Australian Register*.

Thomas lost the government contract in 1840. His successor was Archibald Macdougall, who had been Launceston agent for the radical Hobart newspaper the *True Colonist*. Macdougall arrived in Adelaide with a printing press in 1838 and immediately established a newspaper, the *Southern Australian*. In August 1838 he published Rev. T. Q. Stow's sermon for the opening of the Wesleyan Chapel, *Redemption Interesting to Angels*, and in June 1839 Surveyor-General William Light's *Brief Journal* in an edition of 450 copies. Light died in October, with only 50 copies sold, still owing Macdougall £75. Macdougall also published William Williams's *Vocabulary of the Language of the Aborigines of the Adelaide District* (1839) and Christian Gottlieb Teichelmann's *Aborigines of South Australia* (1841), but largely concentrated on government printing (Woodburn, 7).

Macdougall was ruined in 1843 by a dishonoured Government bill for £1000 (Woodburn, 4). The *Southern Australian* was bought by Andrew Murray, who had arrived in Adelaide in 1839 and started business as a draper. Murray published several books, including his own pseudonymous *Commerce: Its Laws, Their Anti-Christian Spirit, Their Anti-Constitutional Character, Their Pernicious Consequences, and Their Demoralising Tendency* (1845) and the *South Australian Almanack and Town and Country Directory* (1845–52). Following the gold rushes, he moved to Victoria where he published the *Victoria Nautical and Commercial Almanac* (1855) and several commerce-related periodicals.

Victoria has its origins in the activities of a group of landowners and businessmen in Van Diemen's Land who formed the Port Phillip

Association in 1835. One of their number, John Batman, concluded a treaty with the Wurundjeri people, allowing the Association to occupy land in exchange for an annual tribute. Dubious as the exchange was, it remains the only formal agreement between the British colonists and Australian Aboriginal peoples.

Three newspapers were established in quick succession: the manuscript *Melbourne Advertiser* started in January 1838 by John Pascoe Fawkner, who had published a newspaper and operated a circulating library in Launceston; the *Port Phillip Gazette* in October 1838, by George Arden and Thomas Strode; and the *Port Phillip Herald* in January 1840, by William Kerr. Arden and Strode produced the first pamphlet published in Melbourne — *Articles and Rules for the Regulation of the Melbourne Union Benefit Society* (1839) — and the first book, Arden's *Latest Information with Regard to Australia Felix* (1840). Kerr became a significant figure in Melbourne's political and cultural life, campaigning for secret ballots, land reform in favour of small settlers, and cessation of convict transportation. His publishing ventures included *Kerr's Melbourne Almanac* (1841–42).

The Port Phillip District expanded steadily — especially into the pasturelands of the west — during the economically depressed 1840s, and newspapers, magazines and almanacs began to appear in towns such as Geelong, Port Fairy and Portland. In 1850 the district formally separated from New South Wales, becoming the colony of Victoria in July 1851. At almost the same moment the Governor of New South Wales, Sir Charles FitzRoy, announced that gold had been discovered near Bathurst.

After the gold rushes

It is impossible to overstate the effects of the 1850s gold rushes. Costs spiralled upwards, wages doubled and quadrupled as employers tried to lure tradesmen back from the diggings or stop them going in the first place (Cannon, 6, 19). Melbourne, the city hardest hit by the exodus and the one that would ultimately get the sharpest jolt of new wealth, embarked on building a series of cultural institutions — a public library, an exhibition building, a university — seeking to bring *gravitas* to what was essentially a frontier town devastated by the rush to the diggings. Few who joined the rush to the diggings transformed their lives for the better; the real wealth was to be made by supplying food and equipment. By the early 1860s most mines were in the hands of a few large companies. Wages and commodity prices fell back to pre-rush levels (Cannon, 138).

The colonies that emerged from the frenzy of the gold rushes had changed utterly in the space of a decade. Between 1851 and 1861 the population of Victoria grew from 97 500 to 538 000; New South Wales from 197 000 to 350 000; South Australia from 66 500 to 131 000; Queensland from 8000 to 34 000; and Western Australia from 7000 to 16 000. Tasmania was the only colony not to experience dramatic growth: the gold rushes drew away large numbers of former convicts and, despite the change of name from Van Diemen's Land and various schemes to encourage immigration, the population grew slowly, from 70 000 to 90 000.

By the 1890s Australia was one of the most highly urbanised societies in the world. The two principal cities, Sydney and Melbourne, were comparable in size with most of the industrial centres of northern Europe. Melbourne's major broadsheet newspapers, the radical *Age* (the 'Australian thunderer') and the conservative *Argus* (the '*Times* of the Southern Hemisphere'), had reputations that extended way beyond the colonies. A series of Great Exhibitions had brought Sydney (1879) and Melbourne (1880 and 1888) international attention. The Melbourne Public Library compared favourably with its counterparts in Boston and New York; most of the other colonial capitals had similar institutions, and practically every town had at least a mechanics' institute. As early as 1866 a French traveller, the Comte de Beauvoir, was 'much struck with the rapid civilisation' of the working classes of Melbourne, whom he had expected to find 'sinking a well in auriferous rocks, or washing gold on the banks of a solitary stream, or riding across endless deserts' (Beauvoir, vol.1, 36-37).

The influx of various nationalities following the discovery of gold accelerated the growth of publishing in languages other than English. The first German newspaper, *Die Deutsche Post für Australischen Colonien/German Australian Post*, appeared in Adelaide in 1848, and numerous other German-language publications were issued in South Australia and Queensland during the second half of the century.

Other non-English publishing included the French *Journal de Melbourne* (1858), the *English and Chinese Advertiser* (Ballarat, 1850s), the Welsh *Yr Australydd* (Melbourne, 1866–72), and the English and Hebrew *Calendar of All Days and Nights, Sabbaths and New Moons, Seasons, Holydays, and Feasts* (Hobart, 1853).

The rapid growth of the population created possibilities for both literary and utilitarian publishing. Textbooks and treatises were doubtless more beneficial to publishers' cashflows; on the whole, the colonial market remained too small to sustain even the most gifted and prolific literary writer. Colonial writers typically had other careers — the law and the civil service were common occupations. The few who made serious attempts to 'live by their pens' either succeeded in breaking into Northern Hemisphere markets, or found work as journalists or newspaper editors. The bush balladist George Loyau claimed to have written the equivalent of 40 volumes of fiction, as well as compiling successful reference books, the *Gawler Handbook* (1880) and *Representative Men of South Australia* (1883), but remained dependent on journalism and newspaper editing for a regular income (Cryle, 161-62).

The newspaper remained the dominant form for literary publishing throughout the nineteenth century. Many highly popular and acclaimed works appeared only as newspaper serials. Nevertheless, the decades that followed the gold rushes saw the emergence of a vibrant literary culture as the increasing sophistication of metropolitan centres and the broadening varieties of colonial experience allowed an extension of creative writing. During the 1850s and 1860s a Sydney lawyer, Nicol Drysdale Stenhouse, became the patron of an informal coterie of writers and intellectuals that included Daniel Deniehy, editor of the *Southern Cross* (1859–60), John Woolley, Professor of Classics at the University of Sydney, and the poets James Lionel Michael and Henry Kendall. The major poets of this period — Harpur, Kendall, Adam Lindsay Gordon — are generally remembered for their poems of the Australian bush, but each was equally at home with European and biblical mythology.

The 1860s were a period of extraordinary richness and diversity in Australian literature. Kendall's first book, *Poems and Songs*, was published in Sydney by J. R. Clarke in 1862. In 1865 the Melbourne publishers Clarson & Massina launched a new literary magazine, the *Australian Journal* (see Elizabeth Webby's case study in Chapter 12). The popular success of this journal (it ran until 1962) gave colonial writers a reliable local outlet. In its first year the *Australian Journal* published poetry and stories by Mary Fortune ('Waif Wander'), Ellen Davitt's innovative mystery story *Force and Fraud*, and actor turned horse-breaker turned journalist R. P. Whitworth's first novel, *Mary Summers*. Whitworth's first play, *Under the Holly*, was also published in 1865 by Reading & Wellbank, Sydney. In 1867 the Hobart publisher Charles Walch issued a collection of stories by his brother Garnet, who would soon emerge as a successful comic dramatist; and in Melbourne the precocious 21-year-old Marcus Clarke began his column 'The Peripatetic Philosopher' in the weekly *Australasian*. Clarke's first novel, *Long Odds*, was published by Clarson & Massina in Melbourne in 1869, and in 1870 he accepted the editorship of the *Australian Journal*. Meanwhile, in Sydney, a failed sheep farmer named Thomas Alexander Browne became — as 'Rolf Boldrewood' — a regular contributor to the *Australian Town and Country Journal*.

Edward Abbott's *English and Australian Cookery Book* (1864), addressed somewhat condescendingly to 'the many as well as the upper ten thousand', might also be regarded as a literary work in its belles-lettres-esque approach to food writing and its place in national mythology (Bannerman, 204ff). Abbott was a Tasmanian landowner, politician, and proprietor of the *Hobart Town Advertiser*. His book was published by a major London publisher (Sampson Low and Marston). The initial print run of 3000 looks cautious for an era when authors like Isabella Beeton and Alexis Soyer sold hundreds of thousands, and the British publishers may well have been pleasantly surprised when the Tasmanian booksellers J. Walch & Sons took the entire run. Even at home in Hobart, Abbott's book had stiff competition: *Walch's Literary Intelligencer* for the mid-1860s generally lists twenty or more British cookery books. Although most of Walch's stock was distributed to the trade by early 1865, retail sales appear to have been slow: it was still appearing in booksellers' advertisements well into the 1870s, and Abbott's attempts to generate interest in a second edition came to nothing.

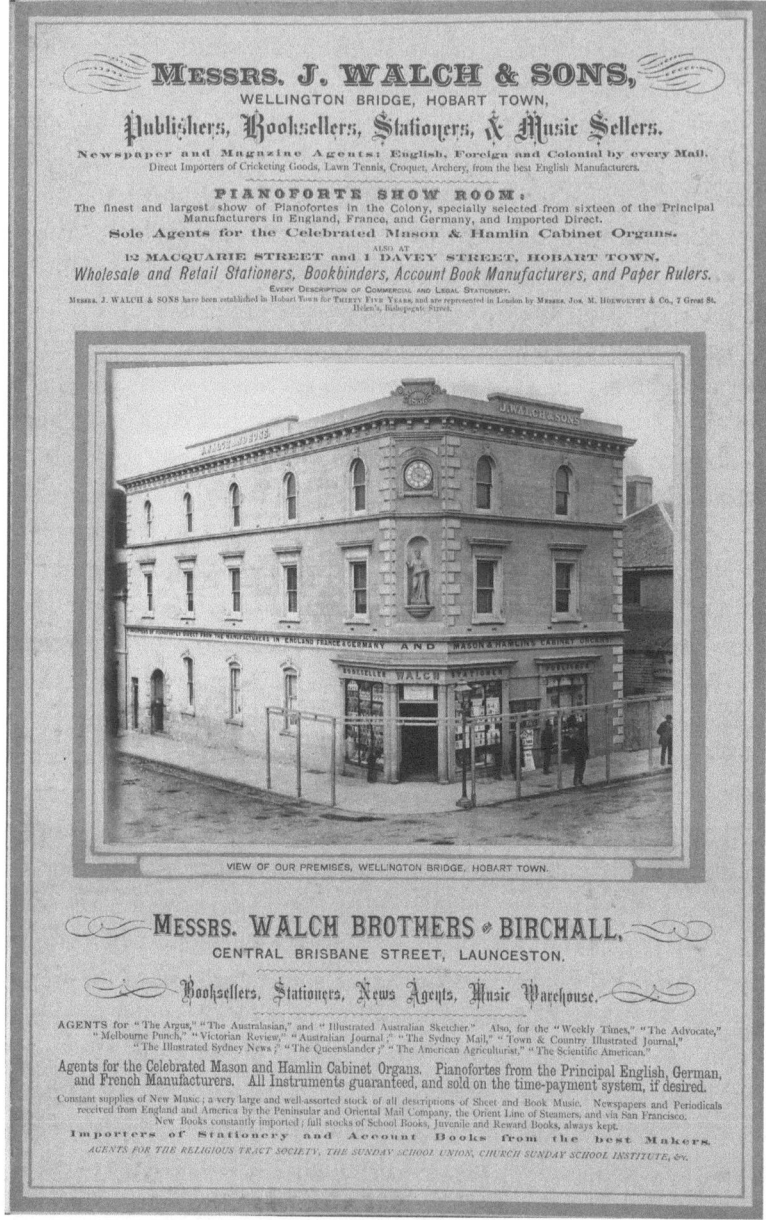

Advertisement for J. Walch & Sons, and Walch Brothers & Birchall, in *Tasmania Illustrated with Photographs* (Hobart: Anson Brothers, 1880). Tasmania's two longest-running bookshops both traced their origin to the business established in Hobart by Samuel Tegg in 1836. Tegg opened a branch in Launceston in 1844, but — facing multiple crises — sold his Hobart shop to James Walch in 1846, and the Launceston one to Robert Blake in 1847.

The Launceston shop went through multiple changes of ownership; in 1858 it was acquired by the Walches, who appointed Andrew Birchall as manager. Birchall bought into the business as a partner in 1867, and the partnership existed until 1893. Walch's and Birchall's continued as separate firms through the twentieth century, the last arm of Walch's going into voluntary liquidation in 2003, and Birchall's eventually ceasing trading in 2017. Although both were predominantly booksellers (Walch's also printers and publishers), they carried many other goods at various times: stationery, toys, musical instruments, sporting equipment, even bicycles. Their flagship stores occupied prominent positions in their respective cities: Walch's in what is now Elizabeth Street Mall ('Wellington Bridge' alludes to the Hobart Rivulet, the walls of which are visible at the right of the photograph), Birchall's in what is now Brisbane Street Mall. (Launceston Pictures Collection, Tasmanian Archives)

Marvellous Melbourne

'Marvellous Melbourne' became the major centre of the Australian book trade between the gold rushes and the 1890s Depression. By the 1860s there were more than 30 booksellers in the city, and at least half of them were involved in publishing. The most prominent were the elder George Robertson (1825–98), his friend turned arch-rival Samuel Mullen, E. W. Cole, H. T. Dwight, and F. F. Baillière.

Robertson, Mullen and Cole all arrived in Melbourne on the same day in 1852. Robertson brought a stock of books with him and set up as a bookseller immediately, Mullen briefly tried farming before taking a job with Robertson, Cole tried various occupations before becoming a bookseller in 1865. Like Robertson, Dwight and Baillière (a member of a French bookselling family) both arrived with a stock of books, Dwight in 1855, Baillière in 1859.

By 1860 Robertson was established as Melbourne's leading bookseller and had begun to make his mark as a publisher, having published James Bonwick's *Discovery and Settlement of Port Phillip* (1856) and H. L. Lindsay's *Industrial Resources of Victoria* (1856). In 1861 he began to distribute his *Monthly Book Circular*, which remained a key publication for the Australian book trade until the 1890s. Altogether he published some 600 titles, including such landmark books as Adam Lindsay Gordon's *Sea Spray and Smoke Drift* (1867), Henry Kendall's *Leaves from Australian Forests* (1869) and Marcus Clarke's *His Natural Life* (1874), James Dawson's *The Australian Aborigines* (1881) and E. M. Curr's *Recollections of Squatting in Victoria* (1883). His greatest commercial success was Alexander and George Sutherland's *History of Australia*, which became a standard textbook and sold 120 000 copies between 1877 and 1892 (Holroyd, 49). Robertson was a staunch Presbyterian, and his beliefs influenced his publishing decisions. One manuscript he rejected was an anti-religious tract, *The Real Place in History of Jesus and Paul*, by a first-time author called E. W. Cole.

Robertson was among the booksellers who opposed the importation of cheap American reprints of British publications; but he also published Australian editions of popular British and American authors in cheap paper covers. A more 'deluxe' publication was *Master Tyll Owlglass* (Kenneth Mackenzie's version of *Till Eulenspiegel*, 1869), issued as a Christmas book in elegant green cloth covers and illustrated with coloured lithographs produced by Robertson's own printing works. His most enduring contribution to the Australian book trade, however, was giving a start to his younger unrelated namesake George Robertson (1860–1933), who went on to establish Australia's most successful and widely recognised bookselling and publishing firm, Angus & Robertson.

Samuel Mullen had fallen out with the older Robertson in 1857, and the trade legend was that they never spoke again. Robertson established a London office and offered Mullen the position of manager. Mullen leapt at the chance, and set out for London with his wife and infant son — only to be informed, on arrival, that Robertson had changed his mind and given the position to his brother William Robertson. Mullen returned to Melbourne in 1859 and set up as a bookseller in competition with Robertson. He remained one of the few Melbourne booksellers who did not become dependent on Robertson for supplies, and although never matching the scale of Robertson's operations Mullen became a significant publisher as well. The bulk of his publications were sermons, textbooks, lectures and political pamphlets (often reprints of contentious articles from British and American periodicals), and an influential periodical, the *Melbourne Review* (1876–85). His list included Mrs Nugent Wood, *Woman's Work in Australia* (1862); Henry Britton, *Fiji in 1870* (1870) and *Lolóma, or Two Years in Cannibal-land* (1883); and an anonymous invasion-scare pamphlet *The Battle of Mordialloc, or How We Lost Australia* (1888).

E. W. Cole found his way to bookselling by a circuitous route. During a gruelling period of unemployment in the early 1860s he resorted to setting up a pie stall in the street outside Melbourne's Eastern Market. Meanwhile, unable to find a publisher for his aforementioned book *The Real Place in History of Jesus and Paul* he resorted to publishing it himself as a series of pamphlets. Customers at the pie stall read, but didn't buy. Hawking in East Melbourne in the Spring of 1865, Cole met a kindly householder who advised him to try selling more interesting books — and offered him a shelf-full of her books, which did indeed prove easier to sell. The handwritten sign on the street stall changed from 'Cole's Delicious Mixed Meat Pies' to 'Cole's Cheap Books'. Soon the young bookseller moved from the street into the Market proper and was busy enough to employ an assistant. In 1873 he signed the lease on a vacant building at 158 Bourke Street, a few doors down from the market, and the legendary Cole's Book Arcade was born (Broinowski, 78, 93-102).

After the bruising religious pamphlet experience, Cole turned to whimsy. In 1873, initially as an advertising gimmick, he published a serial in the Melbourne *Herald*, 'Discovery of a Race of Human Beings with Tails': inhabitants of 'the interior of New Guinea', the tailed people were named Elocwe — E. W. Cole spelled backwards. The serial ran from August to November, boosting both the *Herald's* circulation and Cole's profile as a bookseller (Broinowski, 97-99). Cole later published it in book form as *Account of a Race of Human Beings with Tails*. His greatest success came with *Cole's Funny Picture Book*, an instant children's classic full of wicked wit that also appealed to adults: first advertised in December 1879 it went through 70 editions up to 1965, selling 870 000 copies (Broinowski, 122). As the Book Arcade flourished Cole moved into general publishing. By the 1890s he had an extensive list of his self-branded editions (usually sheets from other publishers, with Cole's binding and title-page) of literary classics and popular reference books such as *Cole's Edition of Saxon's Everybody's Pocket Cyclopedia of Things Worth Knowing*, *Cole's Handbook of Etiquette and Home Culture for Ladies and Gentlemen*, and *Cole's Family Almanac*.

H. T. Dwight quickly established a reputation as a scholarly bookseller, becoming the first in the colony to issue regular catalogues (McLaren, xii). By 1868 he was the Melbourne agent for London bookseller Bernard Quaritch. His numerically modest publishing output, some 45 titles between 1860 and his death in 1871, ranged across fiction, poetry, history and philology, technical manuals, education texts, and *The Black and White List, or Electors' Handbook and Guide* (1868).

As a bookseller F. F. Baillière specialised in scientific and non-English language books. As a publisher he was responsible for at least 60 titles, mostly medical works and general English-language non-fiction, including gazetteers, directories, and an atlas of Victoria (Clark, 51-57).

Robertson, Mullen and Cole all featured in one of the most extraordinary publishing ventures in Australian history, Fergus Hume's *The Mystery of a Hansom Cab* (1886). Robertson rejected it, because of the 'coarse language it contained, as well as scenes of low life' (Holroyd, 56). It cannot have helped that the fatal cab journey begins at a Presbyterian landmark, Scots Church. Lucy Sussex notes that Robertson probably sent the manuscript to his regular reader, fellow Presbyterian David Blair: as co-editor of the *Age* newspaper, Blair would have taken additional offence that the opening sentence mentions the *Age*'s principal rival, the *Argus*. Sussex also notes that Robertson loathed crime fiction, and had been instrumental in excising the mystery element from the book version of Marcus Clarke's *His Natural Life* (Sussex, 99).

After multiple rejections Hume, like Cole twenty years earlier, resorted to self-publication. Also like Cole, Hume was in dire financial straits; unlike Cole he had a network of supporters. In partnership with Frederick Trischler he engaged the printing firm of Kemp & Boyce to print 5000 copies, an extraordinarily ambitious number at a time when the standard print run for a new novel was probably around 100 (Sussex, 118). Mullen and Cole both agreed to stock the book (Sussex, 131). Cole had by this time adopted a strategy of opening on Melbourne Cup Day, to take advantage of traffic from the races when most other city shops were closed — and that was the perfect day to launch a book with a horse on the cover. Hume and Trischler both later claimed that the first print run sold out within weeks: whether this was true or not — the details of their statements are inconsistent — *The Mystery of a Hansom Cab* was reprinted several times in 1886, possibly selling as many as 25 000 copies. Trischler, in partnership with Jessie Taylor, formed the Hansom Cab Publishing Company as a mechanism to publish in London. Hume sold them the copyright for £50. The London edition, launched for the Christmas market in 1887, sold 340 000 copies by August 1888 (Sussex, 134-35, 160).

Colonial publishing continued to expand through the 1870s and 1880s. The market for commemorative reference books seemed inexhaustible: *Australian Dictionary of Dates and Men of the Time* (George Robertson, 1879), the *Cyclopedia of Australasia*, edited by Robertson's friend David Blair (1881), and *Australian Men of Mark* (1889) are a few examples. The monumental *Picturesque Atlas of Australasia* (1886–88) was published by a company established specifically for that purpose. It commissioned dozens of expert contributors: 'geologists, botanists, ethnographers, historians, economists, cartographers and meteorologists', as well as — very discreetly, so as not to destroy the illusion of original drawings created on the spot — photographers to supply artists working in studios (Hughes-d'Aeth, 9, 168ff). The production itself involved a small army, organised into departments: art, cartography, engraving, electrotyping, printing, binding. Many of the supervisors were American. The bindery was staffed entirely by women. The advertising campaign went into detail on the sophistication of the printing machinery, the quality of the paper and ink, and the sheer complexity of the project, taking 'an almost Fordist joy in its organisational order' (Hughes-d'Aeth, 11). The British publisher Cassell's responded with *Cassell's Picturesque Australasia* (1887–88), edited by E. E. Morris, Professor of English, French and German Language and Literature at Melbourne University.

Paradoxically, perhaps, the increasing professionalisation of the Australian literary scene encouraged writers to look towards the larger markets of Europe and North America. In the 1890s, with imminent Federation fuelling an upsurge in literary nationalism, an estimated three quarters of novels written by Australian authors were published in Britain (Trainor, 199). G. B. Barton, writing in 1889, commented: 'all that an author can expect, when he publishes his book in Sydney, is that it will pay its expenses . . . the work that would make him famous in London would leave him very much where it found him in Sydney' (Barton, 90).

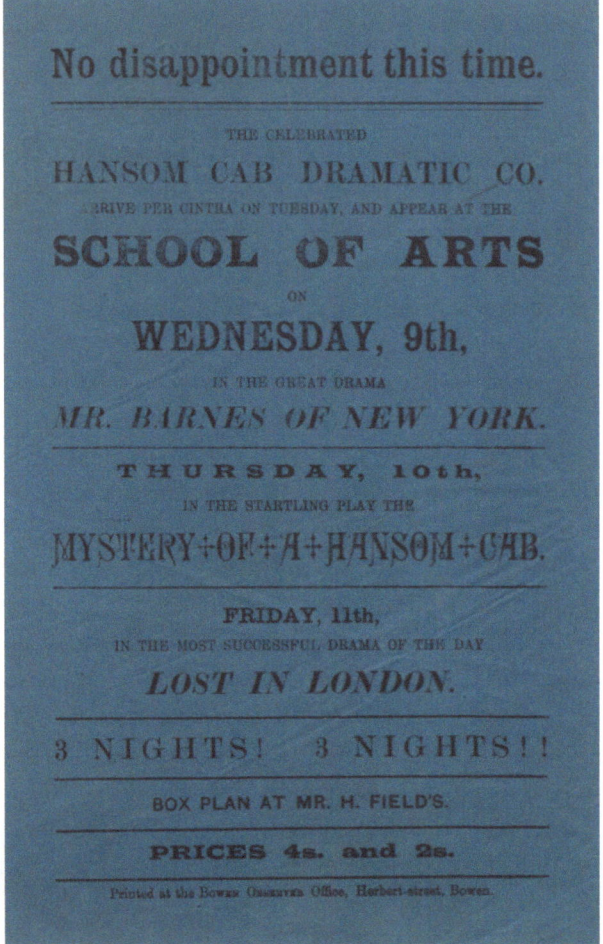

Handbill advertising performances by the Hansom Cab Dramatic Co., issued with the *Bowen Observer* (Bowen, QLD), 9 January 1889, 22 x 14.5 cm. International bestseller *The Mystery of a Hansom Cab* spawned many adaptations, including a stage play composed by Fergus W. Hume (the book's author) and Arthur Law, and another by George Darrell, both in 1888. The play was performed in London and in cities and towns around Australia. Capitalising on the book's success, the theatre company cited in the handbill not only performed the play but also took on its name. Their show a few weeks later in Rockhampton, QLD included, for the first time in that town, 'a REAL LIVE HORSE AND A HANSOM CAB' (*Morning Bulletin*, 15 February 1889, p. 1). A review the next day stated: 'The introduction of a real hansom cab and horse on the stage was doubted by a good many, but it was really carried into effect, and no inconvenience resulted in any manner . . .' The book's ongoing popularity also resulted in many screen adaptations, most recently as a telemovie in 2012.

The *Bowen Observer* (1888–1891) was published by Eugene William Keily and Joseph Smith. The handbill is a fine example of jobbing undertaken by a small-town newspaper office. (Pictures Collection, State Library Victoria)

Authors who built their careers overseas might be regarded as irrelevant to the history of book publishing in Australia; but it is also important to recognise the significance of the colonial market to British publishers. In 1850 British book exports to the Australasian colonies amounted to 2153 hundredweight, potentially around 175 000 volumes; in 1866 the figure for New South Wales alone was estimated at 100 000 volumes (Johanson, 268, 279ff). In 1879 the English publisher Edward Marston regarded Australia and New Zealand as 'by far the largest consumers of English books' (quoted by Hubber 1992, 20). In the 1880s, James Allen described the people of Victoria as voracious readers of 'the English, Irish, Scotch and American newspapers . . . the number of magazines, reviews, and other periodical publications, imported and read by them is very large' (Allen, 119). By the end of the century several British publishers — notably Cassell's and Eyre & Spottiswoode — had established branches in the colonies and were an important part of the local publishing scene.

NOTE ON SOURCES

In addition to consulting standard bibliographies, information in this chapter is derived from numerous sources, including: James Allen, *History of Australia from 1787 to 1882*, Melbourne, Mason, Firth & McCutcheon, 1882; Colin Bannerman, *The People's Cuisine*, Fremantle, Vivid Publishing, 2019; G. B. Barton, 'The Status of Literature in New South Wales: II. How the Publishers Look at It', *Centennial Magazine*, vol.2, no.2, September 1889, pp. 89-92; Ludovic, Comte de Beauvoir, *A Voyage Around the World*, London, Murray, 1870; Nicholas Dean Brodie and Kristyn Harman, 'Other Picture Boards in Van Diemen's Land: The Recovery of Lost Illustrations of Frontier Violence and Relationships', *Aboriginal History*, vol.41, 2017, pp.3-21; Richard Broinowski, *Under the Rainbow: The Life and Times of E. W. Cole*, Carlton, Victoria, Miegunyah Press, 2020; Roger Butler, *Printed: Images in Colonial Australia 1801–1901*, Canberra, National Gallery of Australia, 2007; Michael Cannon, *Melbourne After the Gold Rush*, Main Ridge, Victoria, Loch Haven Books, 1993; Laurel Clark, *F. F. Baillière: Publisher in Ordinary, Publisher Extraordinary*, Canberra, Mulini Press, 2004; Clifford Craig, *The Van Diemen's Land Edition of the Pickwick Papers*, Hobart, Cat & Fiddle Press, 1973; Denis Cryle, ed., *Disreputable Profession: Journalists and

Journalism in Colonial Australia, Rockhampton, Central Queensland University Press, 1997; Peter Dixon, ed., *The Recruiting Officer* by George Farquhar, Revels Plays, Manchester, Manchester University Press, 1986; Ian Evans, *Hidden in Plain Sight: The Search for Australian Magic*, Invermay, Tasmania, Australian Magic Research Project, 2021; Thomas H. Ford and Justin Clemens, 'Barron Field's *Terra Nullius* Operation', *Australian Humanities Review* 65 (November 2019), pp. 1-19; Richard Fotheringham, ed., *Australian Plays for the Colonial Stage 1834–1899*, St Lucia, QLD, UQP, 2006; Michael Hess, *Birchalls Bookshop, 1844–2000*, Canberra, ANU Open Research, 2019; E. J. Hobsbawm and George Rudé, *Captain Swing*, London, Pimlico, 1993 (first published London, Lawrence & Wishart, 1969); John Holroyd, *George Robertson of Melbourne, 1825–1898: Pioneer Bookseller & Publisher*, Melbourne, Robertson & Mullens, 1968; Brian Hubber, 'Bookseller to the City of Sydney: James Tegg in 1838', *BSANZ Bulletin*, vol.13, no.2, 1989, pp.57-59; and his 'A "Free Trade" in the Antipodes: American Reprints in the Australasian Colonies', *BSANZ Bulletin*, vol.11, no.1, 1992, pp.19-22; Tony Hughes-d'Aeth, *Paper Nation: The Story of the Picturesque Atlas of Australasia 1886–1888*, Carlton, VIC, MUP, 2001; Graeme Johanson, *Colonial Editions in Australia 1843–1972*, Wellington, Elibank, 2000; Wallace Kirsop, *Books for Colonial Readers*, Melbourne, BSANZ, 1995; and his *The Bookshop as an Index of Civilisation: The Case of the Walches in the 1840s*, Melbourne, Chaskett Press, 2011; Ian McLaren, *Henry Tolman Dwight: Bookseller and Publisher*, Parkville, VIC, University of Melbourne Library, 1989; Ian Morrison, comp., *The Publishing Industry in Colonial Australia: A Name Index to John Alexander Ferguson's 'Bibliography of Australia 1784–1900'*, Melbourne, BSANZ, Occasional Publication no.6, 1996; Gwenda Robb, *George Howe: Australia's First Publisher*, Kew, VIC, Australian Scholarly Publishing, 2003; John Ross, ed., *The Recruiting Officer* by George Farquhar, New Mermaids, London, Ernest Benn, 1977; Gillian Russell, *Australia's Earliest Printed Document: The Playbill and its People*, Canberra, National Library of Australia, 2011; Lucy Sussex, *Blockbuster!: Fergus Hume and The Mystery of a Hansom Cab*, Melbourne, Text, 2015; Watkin Tench, *A Complete Account of the Settlement at Port Jackson*, London, G. Nicol, 1793; Luke Trainor, 'Imperialism, Commerce and Copyright: Australia and New Zealand 1870-1930', *BSANZ Bulletin* vol.21, no.4, 1997, pp.199-206; Elizabeth Webby, 'Mr Beverley Suttor Publishes His Poems and Gets Laughed At', *The Push from the Bush: A Bulletin of Social History Devoted to the Year of Grace 1838*, no.10, Sept 1981, pp.47-57; and her

'Writers, Printers, Readers: The Production of Australian Literature before 1855', in *The Penguin New Literary History of Australia*, ed. Laurie Hergenhan, Ringwood, VIC, Penguin, 1988; Philip Wilkinson, *Phantom Architecture*, London, Simon & Schuster, 2017; and Susan Woodburn, *Printing and Publishing in South Australia*, Adelaide, Barr Smith Library, 1993.

CHAPTER 10

The Significance of Colonial and Imperial Copyright Law for Australian Authors, Publishers and the Book Trade to 1890

Clive Turner

Introduction

It was not until almost the last quarter of the nineteenth century that the Australian colonial legislatures enacted copyright legislation to provide redress against the unauthorised copying of books first published within their borders. During the preceding period, colonial authors and publishers were reliant upon Imperial copyright laws that, as will be seen, proved inadequate to meet colonial needs.

The development of United Kingdom copyright law

The recognition of the rights of authors has a long and interesting history. A landmark in the history of copyright in the United Kingdom was the Statute of Anne 1710 which 'represents the first clear legislative acknowledgment of the rights of authorship' (Copyright Law Review Committee 1988, p. 284). The Statute, entitled 'An Act for the Encouragement of Learning, by vesting the Copies of printed Books in the Authors or Purchasers of such Copies' was the product of petitions presented to Parliament by booksellers and publishers for the protection of their copyrights against piracy.

Under the Statute, the author (or assignee, e.g. the author's publisher) acquired the 'sole Right and Liberty of printing' a book published after the commencement of the Statute for a period of 14 years (s.I). The author was entitled to a further term of 14 years if still living at the end of the first term (s.XI). Infringing copies could be forfeited and a monetary penalty imposed (s.I), subject to the book having been entered in the register of the Stationers' Company, a guild of printers, publishers and booksellers (s.II). The applicability of the Statute to the Australian colonies raised complex legal issues which remained largely unresolved (Bond 2016, 373).

The Statute was only concerned with the unauthorised copying of *published* books. This was typical of copyright statutes throughout the eighteenth and nineteenth centuries. However, authors and their publishers were recognised at common law as having a right to prevent the unauthorised printing of their *unpublished* literary works. The right was enforced by an application for an injunction to the Court of Chancery to restrain the unauthorised publication of the work. This 'common law' right continued into the early twentieth century.

Following the Statute of Anne 1710, there was considerable controversy whether there was a perpetual common law right to prevent the unauthorised printing of *published* books and, if so, whether this right was in addition to the rights conferred on authors by the Statute. After a considerable difference of judicial opinion, the issue was finally resolved by the House of Lords in *Donaldson v Beckett* (1774) 4 Burr. 2408, 98 E.R. 257 which held that in respect of *published* literary works, the only protection against unauthorised copying was that provided by the Statute.

The Statute of Anne was subsequently amended by the *Copyright Act* 1814 (Imp.) to extend its term of protection to 28 years, or the life of the author, whichever was the longer. The 1814 Act also gave the author or 'other proprietor of copyright' a right of action in damages against a person who, in any part of the 'British Dominions', made unauthorised copies, or who imported or sold such 'pirate' copies (s.IV).

The Imperial Copyright Act 1842

A major development was the enactment of the United Kingdom *Copyright Act* 1842, which 'formed the basis of modern copyright law' (Seville 1999, 6). The Act repealed the Statute of Anne 1710 and the *Copyright Act* 1814: it remained in force until its repeal by the United Kingdom *Copyright Act* 1911.

The *Copyright Act* 1842 (Imp.) defined 'copyright' as the 'sole and exclusive Liberty of printing or otherwise multiplying Copies' of, *inter alia*, a 'book' (s.II). 'Book' was broadly defined to include 'every Volume, Part or Division of a Volume, Pamphlet, Sheet of Letterpress, Sheet of Music, Map, Chart, or Plan separately published' (s.II). The term of protection was extended to the life of the author and seven years after their death, or 42 years from the date of first publication of the book, whichever was longer (s.III).

A number of provisions were directed not only against the unauthorised reprinting of books but also against the importation of pirate copies which was an issue of growing concern. The 'proprietor' of copyright in a book was given a special civil action against a person who, 'in any Part of the British Dominions', printed the book, or imported for sale 'unlawfully printed' copies, without the proprietor's consent (s.XV). The unauthorised copies were also deemed to be the property of the copyright owner (s.XXIII). To reinforce the position, it was further provided, in effect, that pirated editions of books originally published in the United Kingdom and imported into the Dominions for sale, were to be forfeited, and seized and destroyed by customs officers. In addition, the importer or seller was liable for pecuniary penalties (s.XVII). Entry of the book onto the register of the Stationers' Company was necessary before the proprietor of the copyright could bring an action, although this did not affect the existence of the proprietor's copyright in the work (s.XXIV).

There is little evidence of the 'pirating' of English books in the Australian colonies with the notable exception of the unauthorised reprinting in 1838 of Dickens's *Pickwick Papers* by Henry Dowling, a printer and publisher in Launceston, Tasmania. Dowling's serialised version of the work, which was followed by his publication of a single-volume edition, appears to have had a wide circulation in the Australian colonies (Johanson, 151). A further example concerned the unauthorised serialisation of a novel by a Melbourne newspaper in 1848 (Johanson, 218).

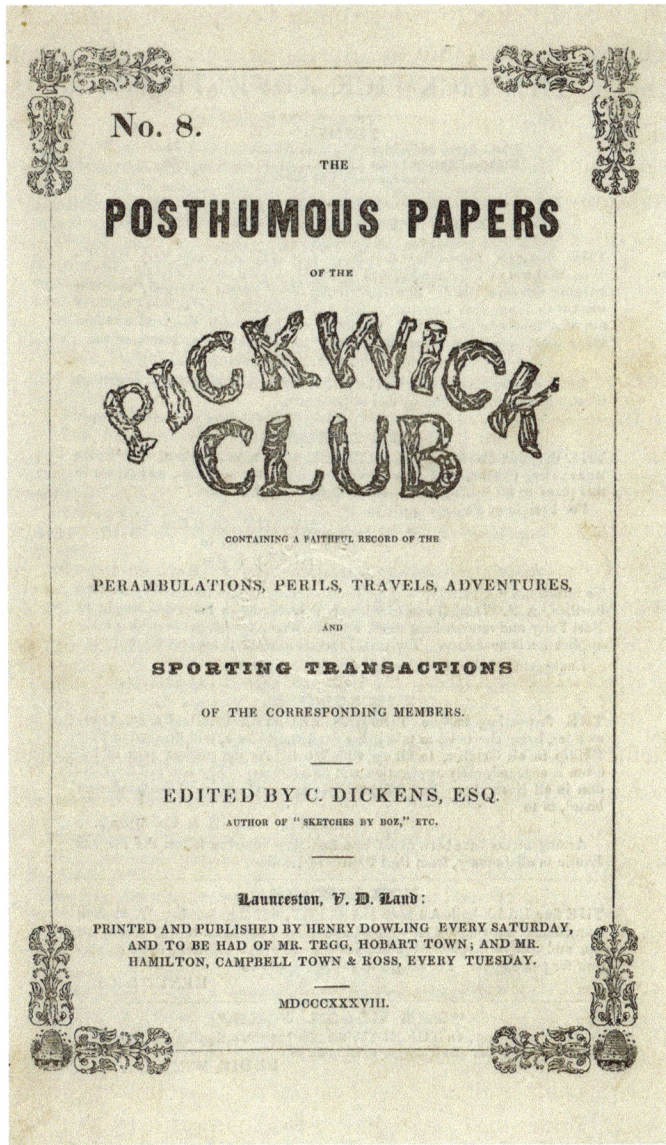

Cover of *The Posthumous Papers of the Pickwick Club*, Launceston, Henry Dowling, 1838. Also known as *The Pickwick Papers*, this was Charles Dickens's first novel, originally published in serial form in England by Chapman and Hall beginning in March 1836. Dowling boasted in his preface: 'The present reprint of the Pickwick papers is the largest publication which has issued from either the New South Wales or the Tasmanian Press'. It was published in 25 parts from June to December 1838, this being No. 8. The lithographed illustrations by 'Tizz' (thought to be Jack Briggs, a servant of Dowling) — appeared weeks later and were presented free to subscribers. Twenty-five parts, 588, xii pp., 23 cm. (State Library Victoria)

There is evidence of American pirated editions of British copyright books being imported into the Australian colonies (Johanson, 151-54, 218). In correspondence to the *Argus* newspaper in 1854 (26 April, p. 5), George Robertson, the leading Melbourne bookseller and importer, remonstrated against the practice in response to an earlier editorial, commenting that: 'There is not a bookstore in the city which does not offer these reprints for sale' (*Argus*, 22 April 1854, p. 4).

The significance of the decision in Routledge v Low (1868)

The *Copyright Act* 1842 (Imp.) was expressed to 'extend to the United Kingdom of Great Britain and Ireland, and to every Part of the *British* Dominions' (s.XXIX). '*British* Dominions' was defined to include, *inter alia*, 'all the Colonies, Settlements, and Possessions of the Crown which now are or hereafter may be acquired' (s.II). Some 26 years after its enactment, the Act was given a narrow judicial interpretation. In *Routledge v Low* (1868) L.R. 3 H.L. 100, the House of Lords held that the copyright protection provided by the Act in respect of books only applied where the book was first published in the United Kingdom.

The effect of the decision was that if a colonial author first published their work in the United Kingdom, it would be protected from infringement in any part of the British Dominions. On the other hand, if a colonial author first published their novel in New South Wales, no copyright could be acquired in the work except as provided by local legislation (Bond, 2010, 459-62). However, at the time of the decision in *Routledge v Low* (1868), none of the colonial legislatures in Australia had enacted copyright legislation. The reason is arguably that:

> [T]hose in the Australian colonies appeared to believe that Imperial law applied in those jurisdictions to protect authors who published books in either the UK or the colonies, until the decision of the House of Lords in *Routledge v Low* clarified that only the former was protected under the Copyright Act 1842. (Bond 2016, 380).

A contemporary comment on *Routledge v Low* (1868) was that:

> The result of this opinion of the House of Lords is very disastrous, and justly creates great dissatisfaction in the Colonies and India; it has either destroyed all copyright property in the numerous works which, since 1842, have been first published there, or rendered such property comparatively worthless. (*Athenæum*, 20 November 1869, p. 663).

The unfortunate effect of the decision in *Routledge v Low* (1868) for the colonial author was demonstrated by Marcus Clarke who first published *His Natural Life* in Victoria in 1874. In doing so, he lost any claim to copyright under the Imperial *Copyright Act* 1842 and, consequently, was able to make little profit on the subsequent publication of the novel in London (Finnamore, 720; Hergenhan, 56; Bond 2010, 456). A further example is Thomas Alexander Browne, who, on achieving fame as 'Rolf Boldrewood' after publication of *Robbery Under Arms*, found that 'one of his earlier serialized novels was promptly reprinted, legitimately but without his consent, in Britain' (Nowell-Smith, 94).

As early as 1 June 1870, in correspondence with colonial governments the Colonial Office expressed its disapproval of the effect of the decision in *Routledge v Low*: 'It appears to Her Majesty's Government very proper that this inequality should be removed, and I transmit to you the draft of a Bill which they are prepared to introduce into Parliament to effect that object' (Correspondence 1875, p. 653). The proposed Bill was intended to provide essentially the same copyright protection in respect of a book first published in a British possession as would have been the case had the book been first published in the United Kingdom. However, the draft Bill was not proceeded with.

The Royal Commission on Copyright handed down a report in 1878 that was highly critical of the existing state of copyright law in the United Kingdom. The complexities arising in respect of copyright and the colonies were highlighted by a Digest of the Law of Copyright, annexed to the report, which pointed out that:

> It is uncertain whether an author obtains copyright by publishing a book in the United Kingdom, after a previous publication thereof in parts of Her Majesty's dominions out of the United Kingdom.
>
> It is uncertain whether an author acquires copyright [...] in any part of Her Majesty's dominions out of the United Kingdom (apart from any local law as to copyright which may be in force there) by the publication of a book in such part of Her Majesty's dominions (Royal Commission 1878, p. 231).

To remedy the situation, the Commissioners recommended that where a work had been first published in any British possession, the proprietor of the work was to be entitled to the same copyright and to the same benefits, remedies and privileges in respect of the work to which they would have been entitled if the work had been published in the United Kingdom (Royal Commission 1878, p. 176). However, such reform was not effectuated until the Imperial *International Copyright Act* 1886.

Colonial copyright legislation

The decision in *Routledge v Low* (1868) demonstrated the inadequacy of Imperial copyright law in protecting authors and publishers from the piracy of books first published in the Australian colonies and the need for local legislatures to provide some measure of protection.

In 1869 Victoria enacted the first colonial *Copyright Act*. The Act was essentially a consolidation of earlier United Kingdom legislation. 'In fact the Bill is merely a transcript of the English Acts, with the addition of such provisions as will give speedy and inexpensive remedies to persons whose rights are infringed upon' (*Vict. Parl. Debs*, 9 June 1869, vol.7, p. 1005).

The *Copyright Act* 1869 (Vic) provided copyright protection for books that either had been, or would be, 'first published in the colony of Victoria' (s.14). 'Book' was defined to include 'every volume, part or division of a volume, newspaper, pamphlet, sheet of letterpress, sheet of music, map, chart or plan, separately published' (s.2). Remedies were provided against those who printed books in the colony without the consent of the proprietor of the copyright, or who imported for sale unauthorised copies of books first published in the colony (ss.21, 23). To enforce their rights under the Act, copyright proprietors were required to register their copyright at the Office of Copyright Registry of Victoria (ss.19, 20).

The introduction of the legislation has been criticised in that it 'reproduced the same hierarchy, privileging the commercial interests of publishers over the rights of authors working to create a national literature' (Ailwood and Sainsbury 2019, p. 3). The latter further comment: 'When they did publish local books — both before and after the introduction of the Act — the evidence suggests that ownership and protection of copyright was a comparatively minor consideration for both author and publisher' (Ailwood and Sainsbury 2019, 8; cf. Bond 2016, 387-89).

Almost a decade later, South Australia enacted the *Copyright Act* 1878, which was substantially identical with the earlier legislation in Victoria including provision for registration (ss.18, 19). The New South Wales *Copyright Act* 1879 contained provisions with similar effect in respect of books first published in that colony and requiring the copyright holder to register their 'proprietorship' at the Office of Copyright Registry of New South Wales (Hargrave, 438).

The scope of the colonial Copyright Acts was limited since they were confined to infringing acts in the colony where the book was first published. In his second reading speech on the South Australian Copyright Bill, the Attorney-General pointed out: 'By the Bill no copyright would be of any effect outside the colony, but it would amply protect the rights of authors [...] in the colony' (*S. A. Parl. Debs* [House of Assembly], 13 June 1878, p. 134).

An author whose book was first published in Victoria would have no remedy under the colonial legislation in respect of the unauthorised copying of the book in New South Wales, unless the pirated copies were imported into Victoria. The Victorian author would have had to publish their book first in the United Kingdom and rely on the copyright under the Imperial Copyright Acts to bring an action for the infringement in New South Wales. An 1883 Tariff Report appositely summed up the effect of the copyright position in Victoria:

> As that law at present stands, an author who wished to preserve an interest in his writings, would assuredly not print in the colony, but would probably send his MS. home, as in England his work would be published under a Copyright Law that covered not only Great Britain but all her colonies. Our Copyright Act extends to Victoria alone, and we do not think it unreasonable to ask that it be placed on a similar basis to the Imperial statute (Royal Commission 1883, vol.4, no.50, p. cxlii).

The original *Copyright Act* 1869 in Victoria was repealed and substantially re-enacted by the *Copyright Act* 1890 (Vic).

International copyright and the Berne Convention

During the course of the nineteenth century there was a growing recognition in the United Kingdom of the need to enter into reciprocal arrangements with other countries for the copyright protection of the works of British authors abroad. The *International Copyright Act* 1844 (Imp.) enabled the issuance of Orders in Council extending the protection of the United Kingdom Copyright Acts to books first published in designated foreign countries. Such Orders were made on a bilateral basis with a number of foreign countries that granted similar copyright protection to the works of British authors (Ricketson, 25-37).

The complexity and *ad hoc* nature of these arrangements led to a movement for a simpler and more unified system of international copyright protection. To this end a series of diplomatic conferences were held in Berne, Switzerland, between 1884 and 1886. From these meetings emerged the Berne Convention for the Protection of Literary and Artistic Works (the 'Berne Convention'), which was signed on 9 September 1886. In anticipation of this treaty, the United Kingdom enacted the *International Copyright Act* 1886 to enable it to comply with its obligations under the proposed Convention and to enable the Convention to be 'carried into effect in Her Majesty's dominions' (Preamble). The Berne Convention was ratified on 5 September 1887. An Order in Council was made on 28 November 1887 adopting the Convention in full. The Convention came into effect on 6 December 1887.

The original contracting States (Great Britain, Belgium, France, Germany, Haiti, Italy, Spain, Switzerland and Tunisia) constituted the 'Berne Union' for the protection of the rights of authors over their literary and artistic works (Art.1). Great Britain acceded to the Convention on behalf of her self-governing dominions, including the Australian colonies (Ricketson, 79). A principal feature of the Berne Convention was that, broadly, authors of a member country of the Berne Union enjoyed the same rights in respect of their literary works in other member countries as the laws of those countries granted to their own citizens (Art.2, 3). The Berne Convention ushered in a new era of international copyright protection and co-operation.

The United Kingdom *International Copyright Act* 1886 not only enabled that country to accede to the Berne Convention, it also removed the anomaly that had resulted from the decision in *Routledge v Low* (1868) regarding books first published in the Australian colonies. The Act provided that the United Kingdom Copyright Acts, including the *Copyright Act* 1842, applied to a literary work 'first produced in a British possession in like manner as they apply to a work first produced in the United Kingdom' (s.8(1)). The effect was that a book first published in, for example, Victoria in 1888 obtained copyright protection throughout the British Dominions. However, registration of the work at the Stationers' Company in London was still required unless the 'law of such possession provides for the registration of such copyright' (s.8(1)(a)).

The inconvenience of this requirement prompted the enactment in Queensland of the *Copyright Registration Act (Queensland)* 1887. As the Premier (Hon. Sir Samuel W. Griffith) pointed out: 'A man might now publish a book in Queensland and register it in England. But it was very inconvenient to do it; so inconvenient that it had not been done more than once or twice' (*Qld Parl. Debs* [Assembly], 27 July 1887, vol.52, p. 104). The Act provided for the establishment of a registration system for books first published in the colony. Its purpose was to obtain copyright protection for such books under the Imperial Copyright Acts without the further need to register them at the Stationers' Company (*Qld Parl. Debs* [Assembly], 21 July 1887, vol.52, pp. 84-85).

The Western Australia *Copyright Register Act* 1887 had been enacted a few weeks earlier than the Queensland Act for the same purpose. The 1887 Act was subsequently repealed by the more comprehensive *Copyright Act* 1895 (W.A.). As previously noted, Victoria, New South Wales and South Australia had already established registration systems under their respective Copyright Acts.

Conclusion

The combined effect of the *International Copyright Act* 1886 (Imp.), the *Copyright Act* 1842 (Imp.) and the Berne Convention 1886 was that towards the end of the nineteenth century, colonial authors and their publishers had essentially the same copyright protection throughout the British Dominions and in those countries which were parties to the Berne Convention as they would have had if their books had been first published in the United Kingdom. By this time, most Australian colonies had enacted comprehensive copyright legislation albeit limited by the confines of their borders and modelled largely but not exclusively on United Kingdom legislation (Bond 2016, 379). After Federation, this legislation was eventually subsumed by Commonwealth legislation enacted pursuant to the *Commonwealth of Australia Constitution Act* 1900, s.51(xviii) empowering the Commonwealth Parliament to make laws with respect, *inter alia*, to 'copyrights'.

NOTE ON SOURCES

Official reports and correspondence:

Copyright Law Review Committee, *The Importation Provisions of the Copyright Act 1968*, Canberra, Australian Government Publishing Service, 1988; Correspondence 1875: Correspondence between the Colonial Office and the Colonial Governments on the Subject of Copyright, *Brit. Parl. Papers*, (144), vol.LI, p. 635; Royal Commission 1878: Report of the Royal Commission on Laws and Regulations relating to Home, Colonial and Foreign Copyrights, *Brit. Parl. Papers*, [C. 2036], vol. XXIV, p. 163; Royal Commission 1883: Report of the Royal Commission on Tariffs, *Vict. Parl. Papers*, Legislative Assembly, vol.4, no.50, p. cxlii.

General history of copyright law:

J. P. Feather, *Publishing, Piracy and Politics: An Historical Study of Copyright in Britain*, London, Mansell, 1994; Martin Rose, *Authors and Owners: The Invention of Copyright*, Cambridge, Massachusetts, Harvard University Press, 1993; L. Ray Patterson, *Copyright in Historical Perspective*, Nashville, Vanderbilt University Press, 1968; Ronan Deazley, *Rethinking Copyright: History, Theory, Language*, Cheltenham, UK, Edward Elgar Publishing, 2006; Catherine Seville, *Literary Copyright Reform in Early Victorian England: The Framing of The 1842 Copyright Act*, Cambridge, CUP, 1999; and her *The Internationalisation of Copyright Law: Books, Buccaneers and the Black Flag in the Nineteenth Century*, Cambridge, CUP, 2006; Sam Ricketson, *The Berne Convention for the Protection of Literary and Artistic Works: 1886–1986*, London, Centre for Commercial Law Studies and Kluwer, 1987; Simon Nowell-Smith, *International Copyright Law and the Publisher in the Reign of Queen Victoria*, Oxford, Clarendon Press, 1968.

Copyright law in the Australian colonies:

Catherine Bond, '"Cabined, cribbed, confined, bound in": Copyright in the Australian colonies', in Isabelle Alexander and H. Tómas Gómez-Arostegui, eds, *Research Handbook on the History of Copyright Law*, Cheltenham, UK, Edward Elgar Publishing, 2016, pp. 372-90; and her '"Curse the Law!": Unravelling the Copyright Complexities in Marcus Clarke's *His Natural Life*', *Media and Arts Law Review*, vol.15, no.4, 2010, pp. 452-77; John Finnamore, 'Imperial Copyright Law as Affecting the Colonies', *Victorian Review*, vol.4, 1881, pp. 712-22; Sarah Ailwood and Maree Sainsbury, 'The Imperial Effect: Literary Copyright Law in Colonial Australia', *Law, Culture and the Humanities*, vol.12, no.3, 2016, pp. 716-40; and their 'An Old Law for a New Literature: Authors, Publishers and the Early Years of the Victorian Copyright Act 1869', *Law, Culture and the Humanities*, 2019, pp. 1-20, doi: 10.1177/1743872119885795; Jocelyn Hargrave, 'Printer in the middle: The Copyright Act 1879, the NSW Government Printing Office and Legal Deposit in Nineteenth-century Australia', *Media History*, 2020, vol.27, no.4, pp. 438-56, doi: 10.1080/13688804.2020.1833711

Relevant studies from the perspective of the book trade:

Graeme Johanson, *A Study of Colonial Editions in Australia, 1843–1972*, Wellington, New Zealand, Elibank Press, 2000; L. T. Hergenhan, 'English Publication of Australian Novels in the Nineteenth Century: The Case of *His Natural Life*', in *Bards, Bohemians, and Bookmen: Essays in Australian Literature*, Leon Cantrell, ed., St Lucia, Queensland, UQP, 1976, pp. 56-71; Brian Hubber, 'A "Free Trade" in the Antipodes: American Reprints in the Australasian Colonies', *BSANZ Bulletin*, vol.16, no.1, 1992, pp. 19-22; Clifford Craig, *The Van Diemen's Land Edition of the Pickwick Papers*, Hobart, Cat & Fiddle Press, 1973; J. A. Ferguson, 'Studies in Australian Bibliography: The Tasmanian "Pickwick Papers"', *JAHS*, vol.4, part VI, 1918, pp. 317-20.

CHAPTER 11

The Land of Newspapers

Wallace Kirsop

The omnipresent newspaper

The newspaper is a recurrent motif in the artwork of S. T. Gill, on the Victorian goldfields, and in Adelaide, Melbourne and Sydney. Over a period of forty years, Gill drew: the *Argus* being sold on horseback in the diggings; newspaper-boys offering their wares in the street, in one case identifiably the *Age*, the *Argus* and the *Herald*; a digger 'of high Degree' absorbed in reading while a sweating companion digs a hole; 'Bryce Ross's Newspaper and General Agency Office' and a notice next door pointing 'To Argus Office' at Forest Creek, Mount Alexander Diggings; a shoeblack with the sporting paper *Bell's Life* on his lap; and an 1855 interior view of the restaurant owned by John Alloo (Chin Thum Lock) with a copy of the *Ballaarat Trumpeter* lying across a table near an urn (Grishin, 171, 121, 192, 96-97, 221, 108-109). The last image is particularly interesting since it is one of the rare documents attesting the brief existence in the mid-1850s of an advertising sheet that has virtually disappeared from the record, with perhaps one surviving issue in a museum at Ballarat. Elsewhere one finds an illustration of William Stephens's Collins Street bookshop in 1864 commissioned from Gill showing newspapers being unpacked on the footpath and taken inside (Howard, 115-116). Overall one grasps the ubiquity of the press in a society that had not yet attained full literacy by the time of Gill's death in 1880.

'Interior of John Alloo's Restaurant Ballaarat, 1855' from *The Diggers and Diggings of Victoria as they are in 1855 / Drawn on stone by S. T. Gill*, Melbourne, James J. Blundell & Co, 1855, with inset showing the *Ballaarat Trumpeter*. Alloo (Chin Thum Lock, d. 1889) opened this restaurant on Bakery Hill in 1854 and also worked as a government interpreter in Victoria. Relocating to New Zealand in the 1860s he became a special constable-interpreter in Otago, assisting with court cases involving Chinese immigrants. Artist and lithographer Samuel Thomas Gill (1818–1880) worked in Adelaide from 1840 to 1852 producing landscapes, urban scenes, and portraits including *Heads of the People* (1849). He moved to Victoria in 1852 and executed many images of colonial scenes there and in New South Wales. Lithograph, 14.8 x 24.3 cm. (State Library Victoria)

The journalist Richard Twopeny's *Town Life in Australia* (1883) devoted a chapter to the colonies' newspapers. Twopeny's account of the local press reflects his professional preoccupations and offers quite detailed analyses of the contents of the publications he most esteems: the *Argus* and the *Australasian*. Critical assessments are made of further Victorian newspapers and of their counterparts in other colonies. Even if the tone approaches at times the boosterism characteristic of the literature designed to encourage immigration, Twopeny's picture of a society obsessed with news is unusually emphatic:

> This is essentially the land of newspapers. [...] Excepting the Bible, Shakespeare and Macaulay's 'Essays', the only literature within the bushman's reach are newspapers. The townsman deems them equally essential to his well-being. Nearly everybody can read, and nearly everybody has leisure to do so. Again, the proportion of the population who can afford to purchase and subscribe to newspapers is ten times as large as in England; hence the number of sheets issued is comparatively much greater. Every country township has its weekly or bi-weekly organ. In Victoria alone there are over 200 different sheets published. Nor is the quality inferior to the quantity. On the contrary, if there is one institution of which Australians have reason to be proud, it is their newspaper press. (Twopeny, 221)

Despite the stated difference in the proportion of the population able to afford to buy newspapers, it is important to remember that colonists from the British Isles and from North America were equally familiar with a free press and with societies in which print circulated widely and unhindered. Modern research, notably by Elizabeth Morrison, confirms and elaborates Twopeny's claim as to the number of sheets being produced in Victoria alone. The bibliographical record is complex, with many short-lived publications, not to mention mining towns that rose quickly and then disappeared. What was constant was quite obviously the impetus to start newspapers even when the projected audience was very small. Indeed occasionally manuscript had to replace print in the production process in order to meet expectations. The whole enterprise needs to be linked, as we shall see, to the emigrants' apparently overwhelming desire to retain connections with the 'Old World' and to be informed about what was happening elsewhere. Without doubt this attitude was not universal, but it was widespread enough to sustain the local press and to encourage massive importation of newspapers from the Northern Hemisphere. With the exception of stock arriving at Stephens's shop this aspect is absent from Gill's illustrations and from Twopeny's account.

As has been increasingly noticed in recent decades and analysed in a more comprehensive way by Martyn Lyons, the long weeks and months aboard ships sailing then steaming to Australia in the nineteenth century provided many incentives to produce newspapers that were circulated weekly and at times more frequently. Written by passengers, with active help and encouragement from the officers, these publications were, in general, manuscript for much of the period. Subsequently printed — and often edited — versions were issued in the colonies on arrival as souvenirs. There are examples of rival papers being written on the same ship. Despite gaps in the surviving record in major Australian libraries, the phenomenon, with its elements of imitation and sometimes parody, can be studied with some ease. What it demonstrates once again is how naturally people fell into writing in the style of a press that was familiar in metropolitan and provincial settings in their home countries.

If other examples of the vogue are required, they can be found in the newspapers or magazines that circulated — usually with the support of the teaching staff — in colonial schools. We are told that Louise Mack and Ethel Turner 'edited rival school papers' at Sydney Girls' High School in the 1880s (Griffen-Foley, 249). At Melbourne Grammar in 1871, Theodore Fink 'started a handwritten school newspaper' at a time when Alfred Deakin, who was long to combine journalism with his political career, was his 'admiring ally' (Brett, 26-27). An official impetus was given to this fashion by the educational Establishment. The *Newspaper Reader* published by Blackie in 1879 justified its 'novelty' by 'the fact that newspapers constitute so large a portion of the reading of the present day, it is deemed desirable that a work of this kind should form part of the educational course of the rising generation.' (Bussey and Wilson Reid, v).

The interconnection of reading and writing was widespread. Journalists, emerging in many cases from participation in amateur enterprises, provided and shaped the editorial columns. However, much of the matter carried in every newspaper issue was supplied by advertisers in mostly conventional, but sometimes eccentric ways. Then there were the correspondence columns in which readers found the views of their fellows. In the case of J. F. Archibald's *Bulletin* from 1880, the magazine/newspaper could become a co-operative project in which every reader was a potential writer.

It was sometimes said in the Paris of New Wave cinema in the late 1950s that would-be authors had the manuscripts of film-scripts rather than of novels in their drawers. One could almost suspect in late-nineteenth-century Australia that the literary dream was of contributing to a newspaper, not excluding in verse or in prose fiction, a tendency to which we shall have to return.

Overall in the Australian colonies the newspaper was the staple of reading for the literate public. Despite the necessary emphasis in this chapter on local production, it is essential to take account of what was imported. As a result we must first look at the availability of overseas newspapers, mostly from the Northern Hemisphere, before we turn to what was printed in the colonies from 1803.

News from elsewhere

In the digital world of the 2020s where post offices have been down-graded to shopfronts in suburban strips, it is sometimes hard to grasp the monumental dimensions of the buildings created in the nineteenth century for the receipt and distribution of mail. The Melbourne and Sydney GPOs are veritable palaces of communication, more prominent buildings than their counterparts in European capitals. There and here they are being repurposed as hotels and department stores, saved from demolition by their manifest value as jewels of the built environment. But why — in metropolitan centres and in provincial towns like Goulburn and Bendigo — are they so spectacular?

The simple answer is that they represented the link with 'Home' and with what was happening outside the Australian continent. Letters, newspapers, magazines and books were desperately sought. Shipping waits extended from several months in the early decades of the nineteenth century to twelve weeks or so in the 1850s and finally, as per a schedule established by the London publisher Bentley in 1885, to times between 36 and 44 days to the major Australian centres. The delay, however irritating it may have been, was tolerated, but once the objects had arrived people were impatient to lay their hands on them. When the cable connection with the Northern Hemisphere was completed in 1872 things changed. Expense dictated a quite sparing transmission of information, hence only major items of news, but any interruption — an occasional phenomenon for days at a time — was perceived as an intolerable deprivation. An editorial, headed 'THE BROKEN LINK', in the *Australasian* of 14 July 1888 states the case forcibly:

> The cable has created a desire, or rather a necessity, which did not formerly exist. In earlier days monthly communication with the outside world was sufficient, but now few men can sit down comfortably to breakfast unless they feel that they are informed regarding every portion of the earth (89).

Leaving aside the gendered assumptions about newspaper reading — often, no doubt, a reality — we can also note the assertion that 'The cable is the true antidote to provincialism'. Even if many colonists were content with the isolation into which they were more or less forced, it is important to recognise the countervailing desire of others, not necessarily the élite readers of the *Australasian*, to maintain connections, to participate in a wider world and to know what was happening elsewhere.

The literature aimed at encouraging emigration did not neglect this theme. Archibald Michie, Agent-General for Victoria in the 1870s, insists in his *Readings in Melbourne; with an Essay on the Resources and Prospects of Victoria, for the Emigrant and Uneasy Classes* (1879) that the settler in the southern colony does not 'leave civilization behind him' as he moves from place to place in the interior:

> In every little town and village and agricultural and mining settlement the newspaper is found, the Mechanics' Institute or the reading-room soon makes its appearance; the sound of the piano and of pleasant female voices falls on the ear of the passer-by everywhere; and we require no other evidence than the large piles of the *Times*, the *Spectator*, the *Saturday Review*, the *Athenaeum*, *Illustrated News*, and many other periodicals, weekly, quarterly, and monthly, which on the coming in of the English mail are forwarded to all parts of the interior, to convince us that the dwellers there are as retentive of their English tastes and sympathies as are the people of the city. (Michie, 153)

Can this inflow be quantified? Not so easily as one would like, but there are, from various sources, some credible reports. Geoffrey Blainey noted in 1978 that:

> In the year 1897, when personal links with England were shrinking, the British Post Office alone sent to Australian addresses a total of 9 million newspapers, or three newspapers for every man, woman, and baby in Australia. (Blainey, 13)

In a study of the Australian audience for the *Illustrated London News* Thomas Smits draws on an article 'The English Periodicals and Newspapers' published in the *Age* on 26 May 1863 and based on post office returns and reports from Melbourne booksellers. Whereas in 1851 some 40 400 British magazines and newspapers had reached the colonies, the 1862 figure was 1 330 000, a clear reflection of the population increase due to the gold rushes. Interestingly the anonymous author also cites the reverse traffic: 41 537 colonial publications sent to Britain in 1851 growing to 650 000 in 1862 (Smits, 88-89). The exports will have included such specialised titles as *News Letter of Australasia: Or Narrative of Events; A Letter to Send to Friends*, which appeared monthly in Melbourne from mid-1856 to the end of 1862.

A decade before the *Age* report, 'IRON' in a letter to the *Diggers' Advocate* of 10 November 1853 complained under the heading 'THE POST OFFICE AND THE NEWSPAPERS' that newspapers sent from Britain were not being distributed to their destinations in the colony. He quoted from an English newspaper:

> The last Australian Mail, *viâ* India, contained about 30,000 letters and 50,000 newspapers.

and then described his own arrangements:

> When I left England, eighteen months ago, I left with an understanding with my friends to send me four papers per week to Australia; and my brother, who arrived here a few days ago, informs me that not only four but a great many other newspapers have been sent according to promise.

Whether or not gold-rush confusion was responsible for non-delivery, it is clear that private deals, first in evidence in the colonies' early years, continued. The Reverend Robert Knopwood, pioneer Tasmanian chaplain, recorded in his diary, for example, that on 11 April 1825:

> Receivd three parcells of newspapers from England from Wm. Dalton Esqr., Bury St Edmonds. (Knopwood, 448)

Ad hoc contrivances of this kind would eventually be replaced by trade activity.

The letter traffic referred to by 'IRON' remained a constant. It even fed the columns of British newspapers, witness the letters sent by the bibliophile William Story to his son Edwin back in England in the late 1850s and reproduced in *Eddowes's Shrewsbury Journal* (Kirsop, 25, 28). This trend was obviously reinforced by the massive arrival of Australian publications in Britain with their news of what was happening in the colonies.

By the late 1840s trade sources, in Britain or in the colonial centres, were being used to obtain newspapers. A Walch advertisement in *Wood's Royal Southern Kalendar, Tasmanian Register, and General Australasian & East Indian Official Directory* of 1850 states: 'Orders for British and Foreign Books, Periodicals, and Newspapers, executed with promptness and care'. The *Illustrated London News* was seeking subscribers either directly or through its colonial agents in the second half of the 1840s. In the early 1850s two Sydney bookselling firms, W. R. Piddington and Waugh & Cox, each claimed to be receiving 1000 copies. A decade later Stephens in Melbourne was advertising that he sold similar quantities. When Stephens's stock was sold at the beginning of 1867, the newspaper and magazine side was taken over by Samuel Mullen. Despite this it seems that newspapers, as opposed to magazines, gradually receded from prominence in the offerings of mainstream booksellers. Newsagents, somewhat as they were understood in the twentieth century, were beginning to come into their own.

To back up the more specialised trade in periodical publications in general there emerged in 1853 the Melbourne-based multinational firm of Gordon and Gotch. The centenary histories produced in 1953 by the Australian headquarters, and by the then independent successor to the former London branch, list — on the basis of archives now lost — some of the weeklies distributed in the early years by the entrepreneurial newcomers: the *Illustrated London News*, the *Home News*, *Lloyd's Weekly News*, *Reynold's Weekly Newspaper*, the Dublin *Weekly Freeman* and, apparently the most in demand, the *European Mail*.

A small sample of institutional libraries indicates the spread of overseas newspapers taken for current use as well as for long-term retention. In 1876 the Free Public Library in Sydney had ongoing collections of the *Graphic*, the *Illustrated London News* and *Punch* alongside very short runs of a few other titles. The 1900 catalogue of the North Melbourne Free Library and Mechanics' Institute noted 'various volumes' between 1864 and 1894 of the *Illustrated London News* and the same between 1888 and 1893 of the *Graphic*. The Ballarat Public Library, Ballarat East, stated in the rules of its 1899 catalogue:

> The *Times*, as well as other English, Irish, and Scotch newspapers and periodicals, are received by each mail, to which the Subscribers and Public have free access.

Lists of 'Magazines, Journals, & Newspapers' occupy two pages at the end of the supplementary section. 'Graphic', 'London News' and 'London Punch' occur in the division for 'Illustrated Papers'. 'British Newspapers' contain six titles: 'Dublin Warder', 'Edinburgh Scotsman', 'Electrical Engineer', 'London Times', 'The Spectator' and 'Tyrone Constitution'. The selection reminds us that individual libraries can reflect the needs, and the nostalgia, of subscribers. A group of works in Swedish is another indication of unusual choices, or perhaps legacies.

In Bendigo the catalogue produced in the 1890s for the Mechanics' Institute and Free Library included a 'List of Periodicals and Newspapers supplied to the Reading Room' and therefore not necessarily bound for preservation. In the newspaper category there were 24 British titles, six American, one French (*La Semaine ou le Courier de l'Europe*) and one German (*Süd Australische Zeitung*). The quite eclectic British list shows, apart from the widely held illustrated weeklies, such publications as *Belfast Northern Whig*, *Manchester Weekly Times* and *Scotsman*. From America came in particular the *New York Herald* and the *San Francisco Bulletin*. Quite clearly the taste for illustrated papers is mirrored in the 1886 holdings of the Bendigo Deutscher Verein und Lesehalle. The *Graphic* was there as part of a limited English-language contingent. More important were the runs of German titles such as *Die Gartenlaube* and the *Leipziger Illustrirte Zeitung*.

The seriousness of the effort to be informed about the world outside the Australian colonies is most evident in the printed catalogue of the library of the Sydney Mechanics' School of Arts in 1901. Under the heading 'Periodical Literature (Europe, America, etc.)' there are over 250 entries. Although magazines and newspapers are mixed in together, the latter category is well represented, beyond anything in the other catalogues cited. Some runs are noted as 'incomplete', and in other cases, it is recorded that only 'current Numbers' are available. Even so the selection is generous and wide-ranging, for example: *Belfast Weekly News, Cape Argus, Cape Times, China Mail,* Boston *Daily Globe,* London *Daily Telegraph, Detroit Free Press, Freeman's Journal, Glasgow Herald, Harper's Weekly, Irish Times, Kölnische Zeitung, Le Figaro, Le Temps, Liverpool Mercury, Manchester Guardian, Montreal Gazette, Natal Mercury,* the *New York Herald, Observer* (1791–1831), *Reynold's News, Scotsman,* London *Times, Times of India, Yorkshire Post.* The ambitions of this well-endowed metropolitan institution cannot be overstated. A Sydneysider of the late nineteenth century could aspire — with a month or so of delay — to read authoritative news and opinion about the English-speaking world and some other major civilisations, if necessary in the relevant languages. What we see here is a trajectory that will be replicated in the local press aimed at an educated and discriminating public.

Informing, recording and entertaining a society of new settlers

An unavoidably summary account of the many hundreds of Australian publications begun before 1890 needs to adopt a simple periodisation that takes account of the different dates of foundation of the various settlements. The most convenient is to accept that conditions before the gold rushes represented a prolonged eighteenth century, in other words a pre-industrial age, and that from the 1850s to the 1890s one enters a time of rapid change and modernisation, including the 1872 cable link with the world outside.

However massive the importation of newspapers was in nineteenth-century Australia, it was eventually outweighed by local production and distribution in a quite dramatic fashion. As Alan Atkinson reports, postal records show that between 1838 and 1842 newspapers going inland, including by coastal ships, and essentially from Sydney, increased from 297 245 to 1 456 107. Even allowing for a third of this quantity to be made up of overseas titles, the audience of the Sydney press was considerable (Atkinson 1979, 21). This was on the eve of substantial development in the creation of country printing offices, a trend very much reinforced by the gold rushes of the 1850s.

Photograph of exterior of the *Argus* Newspaper & General Machine Printing Office, Belmore Street, Gulgong, NSW, 1870–75. The catalogue entry for this item indicates the newspaper, the *Gulgong Evening Argus*, began in April 1872, and identifies the owner John Bird Stormer standing fourth from left, and the editor George Dunmore Lang, sixth from left. The image was taken by the American and Australasian Photographic Company aka Henry Beaufoy Merlin, an outdoor, travelling photographer, and his associate Charles Bayliss. Many of their evocative images of cities, towns and residences were commissioned by Bernard Otto Holtermann and form the collection of that name at the State Library of New South Wales. Original: 1 negative, glass, quarter plate. (Mitchell Library, State Library of New South Wales)

In short the colonial newspaper was at the centre of the provision of printed matter for settler communities. It is important to remember the fundamentally parochial character of these early press organs. Intercolonial and intracolonial contacts, often by sea long after the establishment of railways in the second half of the century, were quite limited. The metropolitan dailies that evolved in the colonial centres were destined above all for their region of the Australian continent. Even the great weeklies launched from the 1860s onwards addressed themselves primarily to their New South Wales, Victorian or other territorial audiences in order that country readers could keep abreast of what was happening in the local capital as well as in the world at large.

The size of the continent and the huge distances to be covered dictated publishers' strategies. In addition, the long-held view in the United Kingdom that Australia, New Zealand and the South Pacific could be treated as one market reinforced the complications of providing for a widely scattered public. The consequences, which need to be studied in detail elsewhere, included: the existence of 'town' and 'country' editions of metropolitan dailies; special arrangements in certain regions and along borders, in particular the Murray River; the use of imported material, notably syndicated fiction, in local newspapers; and the frequent movement of trade personnel between the various separately administered centres.

The newspaper office occupied a special place in the country's printing — and cultural — history. Many of the century's advances in printing technology were first taken up by the larger press firms, which had the capital to invest in the machines that would allow them to produce more copies and to do this more rapidly. Similarly newspapers had the resources, along with government printers, to experiment with and develop new illustrative methods. The huge demand for paper, especially after 1850, dictated an interest in effective importation as well as in local manufacture. In the early decades newspapers played a critical role in book publication and indeed in the distribution of printed material before regular booksellers came on the scene. Apart from people employed elsewhere or enjoying lives of leisure — and these could be increasingly women as well as men — paid authorship was essentially the work of journalists. That many of these people, along with their proprietors, became politicians was a feature of Australian parliamentary life in the second half of the century and well beyond it. Readers were supplied not only with political, commercial, sporting and sensational news, but also with book reviews, reports on scientific subjects and works of imaginative literature — poetry and, more often as newspapers grew in size, serialised fiction. Present from the outset even in sheets whose primary ostensible purpose was to circulate official directives, advertising revealed as effectively as snippets of gossip and of local communications the everyday material preoccupations of a society intent on recreating a lifestyle it had enjoyed in another hemisphere.

In Sydney the beginning was slow. George Howe started his semi-official *Sydney Gazette* in 1803, the perfect moment to profit from expanding commercial activity. It was to have no rival till 1824, when the regime of 'official restraint' more or less ended under Governor Sir Thomas Brisbane. Despite difficulties under the next Governor, Sir Ralph Darling, the press was to emerge virtually free in the 1830s and with vigorous competition between proprietors and editors of differing political persuasions. From 1835 postage for newspapers was free. There were, however, other problems throughout the half-century: exclusive reliance on setting and printing by hand, shortages of paper, type and ink, small circulations, with only one title — the *Sydney Herald* — exceeding 1000 in 1836 (Walker, 56) and, consequently, quite high subscription and individual sale prices. Elsewhere deprivation could be more acute. Six of the short-lived titles launched in the Swan River colony — in Fremantle as well as Perth — were produced in manuscript between 1830 and 1833. John Pascoe Fawkner's *Melbourne Advertiser* first appeared in manuscript — up to 32 copies — for nine weeks at the beginning of 1838. His failure to register the publication correctly in Sydney resulted in an interruption of several months, another hazard of the early period when formalities were strictly policed. The first Indigenous newspaper, the *Aboriginal* or *Flinders Island Chronicle*, was handwritten at the Wybalenna Aboriginal settlement on Flinders Island by Thomas Brune and Walter George Arthur, who were 'overseen and controlled' by George Augustus Robinson, between 10 September 1836 and January 1838 (Rose, 2). More recent research attributes considerably more agency to Brune and Arthur (Finlay, passim, and Stevens, passim). Even after mid-century there were places with no access to a printing press: the *Argus* reported on 1 October 1856 from the *Ovens Constitution* the appearance of number 2 of the *Happy Valley Chronicle* '"written" for the edification of the miners in that locality'. Not surprisingly no registration document is known for the latter title.

Each settlement had its own story to tell about the provision of newspapers. The separate case study of Andrew Bent printed as an adjunct to the present chapter sets out the difficulties encountered in the early decades of Van Diemen's Land. The free settlers in South Australia arrived with the first number of the *South Australian Gazette and Colonial Register* already printed in London on 18 June 1836. The subsequent career of that paper and of its rivals over the next decade and a half was set out by George H. Pitt. Brisbane had the *Moreton*

Bay Courier (direct ancestor of the modern *Courier-Mail*) by 1846, later than some of the journals that had begun to appear in provincial centres, for example Launceston, Maitland, Windsor, Geelong and Portland. By and large the existence of multiple voices and points of view was a metropolitan phenomenon of the 1830s and 1840s.

A few general points can be made about the early colonial press. Material constraints ensured that issues would be small, often no more than one or two folio leaves in the first decades. Daily publication was the exception until the 1840s, and then often temporary. Weekly, twice weekly or thrice weekly issue was the norm. The titles that broke through this barrier in the 1840s were almost all destined for very long lives: the *Sydney Morning Herald* from October 1840, the *Melbourne Herald* from January 1849, the *Argus* from June 1849 and the *South Australian Register* from January 1850. Delivery posed problems, especially before the development of regular postal services — by road or by sea — in the later 1830s. In urban areas newspapers could be walked to their destinations. In 1821 the *Sydney Gazette* was distributed on Saturdays from 8am to local magistrates by constables traversing their own districts on foot to pass on the publication to neighbouring colleagues. The result was arrival as far away as Minto by 4pm and Richmond by 5pm (Blair, 13-14). Even in the 1860s Gordon and Gotch, who had the responsibility of taking the *Sydney Morning Herald* from house to house, used blind men and guide dogs.

Apart from the essential official notices in the early decades, local news and advertisements were a constant presence. However, the hunger for information from elsewhere ensured that planned or haphazard arrivals of newspapers from abroad were exploited generously. An analysis of foreign newspapers cited by the *Sydney Herald* and the *Australian* during two three-month periods in 1838 shows 191 for the former and 116 for the latter (Atkinson 1978, 86-87). The net was cast wide, but Sydney had become an important destination for ships from many parts of the world. The early newspapers did not neglect literature either. Verse started being included in the *Sydney Gazette* from 1804 (Webby, 1982). Space considerations precluded fiction in most cases, but the vogue of the *roman-feuilleton*, borrowed by the British from the French, began to appear in the later 1840s, foreshadowing the 'world of fiction' of the second half of the 1800s.

As the old convict and pastoral settlements approached mid-century, the newspaper press not only began to spread outside the colonial capitals, but also became the vehicle of a wider range of political, sectional and religious interests. Many of these publications were relatively short-lived, but their existence was testimony to a diversity of taste and opinion that reflected the whole of the British Isles and not just England in any narrow sense. Indeed the creation of *Die deutsche Post für die australischen Colonien* in Adelaide in 1848 signalled the arrival of a strong and mainly Lutheran German press and of a discreetly multicultural Australia that would grow in the second half of the century. Cultivated liberal Catholics like William Augustine Duncan, editor first of the *Australasian Chronicle* in 1839 and then between 1843 and 1845 of *Duncan's Weekly Register, of Politics, Facts and General Literature*, brought a touch of cosmopolitan suavity.

The paper known as the *Britannia and Trades' Advocate* from 1846 to 1851 belonged to the category representing special interests, in this case Tasmanian licensed victuallers, of whom there were claimed to be 500. By 17 September 1846, 250 of these innkeepers were listed as subscribers. Advertisers were reminded that the publication was 'at all times available for public information' in the subscribers' establishments. It is reasonable to assume that the number of readers, or indeed of people read to, was very much greater than that of purchasers.

After 1850 the 'reading and thinking classes', as they were designated in an 1846 Hobart advertisement, grew rapidly. Technological advances meant that newspaper printers and proprietors could keep pace with this change. More frequent publication, a move to broadsheets, a greater number of pages, the introduction of illustration, these were some of the characteristics of the titles produced after the gold rushes, especially in the colonial capitals. The major long-term addition to the range of durable papers was Melbourne's *Age*, founded in 1854 and controlled by David Syme from 1860. There were many other ventures before the 1890s in line with developments elsewhere in the English-speaking world, for example *Melbourne Punch* from 1855, various illustrated journals such as the first series of an *Illustrated Sydney News* between 1853 and 1855, followed under the same title by a paper that lasted from 1864 to 1894, the *Illustrated Melbourne Post* (1862–68) and the *Australasian Sketcher* (1873–89), Maurice Brodzky's *Table Talk* from 1885, and several attempts at scandalous and muckraking sheets.

Although there was intercolonial traffic, still mostly by sea before 1890, each separately administered part of the continent was self-contained in newspaper terms. This was a fundamental constraint on circulation figures. These are often unknown or imprecise, the object of boastful and not well substantiated claims. It was asserted that in the booming Melbourne of the late 1880s the *Age* had a circulation of 90 000 (Morrison, 2014, 239). If true, this was perhaps the highest in the colonies at that time. It was a Victorian market, not a national one.

To reach subscribers outside the metropolitan areas, mostly in country districts, but also in other colonies and even countries, the major dailies created weeklies that summed up what had appeared during the previous week as well as providing material of a magazine kind. Curiously the first of these companion weeklies seem to have been produced in Geelong (*News of the Week*), Ballarat (*Miner and Weekly Star*) and Bendigo (*Weekly Advertiser* and *Weekly Mercury*) in the 1850s. The prime examples, however, were published from the capital cities. The *Age* was first in the field in 1854, its various titles and experiments eventually settling down in the *Leader*. Alongside it one finds: the *Sydney Morning Herald*'s *Sydney Mail* from 1860; the *Argus*'s *Australasian* from 1864; the Melbourne *Daily Telegraph*'s *Weekly Times* from 1869 (later taken over by the Melbourne *Herald*); the Brisbane *Courier-Mail*'s *Queenslander* from 1866; the Sydney *Evening News*'s *Australian Town and Country Journal* from 1870; and the *West Australian*'s *Western Mail* from 1885. Much the same formula was used in the layout of these generous publications of up to 52 pages of four, five or six columns. In this respect the *Queenslander* and *Western Mail* were hardly to be distinguished from the *Australasian*. By the late 1880s the issues were commonly being sold for sixpence. All of these papers were to last well into the twentieth century.

The strengthening of the metropolitan press was accompanied by well-documented expansion into goldfields and country towns. Some in the former category were ephemeral, but many of the others lasted for generations and gave concrete expression to the need for local news and community cohesion. On the other hand their suburban contemporaries, quite numerous in these decades, have so far been neglected by historians. While some regional centres supported more than one paper and thus allowed for competing orientations, in most places there was a single title issued by what was effectively the local printing house, which did all the jobbing work required and occasionally might have produced a book. An 1885 photograph of the building of the *Horsham Times*, which did face a competitor two years after its foundation in 1873, shows the tell-tale 'GENERAL PRINTING OFFICE' under the newspaper's name (*ANHG Newsletter*, no.117, 1). The first Horsham building proclaimed even more clearly 'E.J. STEPHENS, JOB PRINTER.' (Kirkpatrick 2010, 61).

A prominent feature of the country press in the later decades of the nineteenth century was the regular inclusion of fiction in the form of short stories and serialised novels. Not infrequently the latter appeared as special supplements set and supplied from outside. The metropolitan model was the great weekly companion, where fiction, constantly present, occupied comparatively less space. The essential point is that for Australian readers newspapers were the most common and accessible source of novels, many of them of a popular character and not taken up in the regular publishing trade. Colonial writers, some of them anonymous, were well represented alongside authors from the rest of the world.

The ambitions and achievements of the Melbourne press in the 1880s are well summed up in Richard Twopeny's analyses. The *Argus* and the *Australasian* were not alone in the colonies in presenting themselves as journals of record, but, despite the Victorian-centredness noted by Twopeny, they did it better than their rivals. 'Marvellous Melbourne', which had rapidly overtaken Sydney after 1850 as the largest city in Australia, was not altogether unjustified in its sense of superiority. Agriculture, mining, sport, politics, legal matters, a rich selection of advertisements, theatre, literature, music and much more were reported daily and scrutinised weekly. Reuters and telegrams were bringing — selectively and at some expense — major news items from the Northern Hemisphere. The *Sydney*

Morning Herald had more overseas correspondents, among them Anna Blackwell, who sent reports from 1860 to 1890. Between 1874 and 1892 James Harrison, founder of the *Geelong Advertiser* in 1840, was contributing to the *Age* and the *Leader*, notably columns of 'Scientific Gossip'. There was therefore competition for the attention of cultivated readers, who were able to peruse in the *Australasian* in the late 1880s serious reviews of recent historical works in French supplied by Samuel Mullen.

One could argue that intellectually and artistically inclined newspaper subscribers were a small minority divorced from colonial society's get-rich-quick mentality. In the same way the public for a continuing German press and for the earliest attempts at Chinese and French publications in the 1850s and Melbourne Jewish titles in the 1870s could be seen as clearly apart. However limited in numbers, the educated élite, as perceived by Ada Cambridge in country Victoria during her clergyman husband's postings, had the influence to set the tone for a conservative, 'gentlemanly' and literate *Argus*. Cambridge, herself a consistent contributor to the *Australasian*, praised the colonial press almost unreservedly in the conclusion to her 1903 memoir, *Thirty Years in Australia*. Even Sidney Webb, on his return from the trip he and his wife Beatrice made to the colonies in 1898, expressed strong approval of the 'principal Australian newspapers' (Austin, 114). These notes of confidence explain the paramount position the press had in local publishing before 1890.

A query for historians and genealogists

Given that newspapers provided the largest body of information about what was happening in nineteenth-century Australia, it was to be expected that historians would use the relevant files as sources for their research. In this they could refer to whatever indexes were made available, rather fitfully, by the publications themselves or compiled in some of the country's leading reference libraries. What was covered in this way was exclusively the editorial columns and not the classified advertisements that bulked so large and were critical documents for economic, social and cultural history. As long as the emphasis was chiefly political, reports on campaigns, agitation, parliamentary debates and related correspondence, not to mention often partisan leading articles, were relatively accessible to diligent students. On the other hand, one has the impression that little attention was paid to the medium itself. In his 1964 *The Press in Australia* Henry Mayer was not inaccurate in claiming: 'Australian historians have shown little interest in our Press' (xiii). Since then the situation has changed markedly. There are still celebratory, commemorative and anecdotal pamphlets and volumes, but they are now outweighed by seriously documented studies by academics and independent writers. Are the lessons of these investigations always heeded by the people who fossick in newspapers for factual details about Australia's past?

The creation of the National Library of Australia's Trove database, a searchable digital index to all the monographs, periodicals and newspapers contained within it, has provided users with a remarkable key to a substantial part of what has been published in this country. It is not always easy to manipulate, notably because of the vagaries of Optical Character Recognition applied to poorly inked originals, often mediated through microfilms. Even so its coverage of metropolitan and country titles has been in advance of several similar enterprises elsewhere in the world. The somewhat incongruous result is that one finds scholars — or their research assistants — in the Northern Hemisphere quoting the *Colac Herald*, say, as the source of an item that manifestly appeared first in North America or Europe. Understanding how newspapers found their copy and resorted to fillers should still be part of careful documentation. It is one thing to pick up a welcome clue in an obscure provincial sheet, another to explore everything that surrounds it in other as yet undigitised publications or in less accessible manuscript and archival collections. Much now seems to be published, even on book-history topics, that relies almost exclusively on Trove. Is it too harsh to suggest that searching cannot be purely mechanical and that a sense of context and of other possibilities remains obligatory? The mass of what was printed after 1850 precludes working manually, as Elizabeth Webby was able to do on pre-1850 Australian newspapers. However, it is still important to be aware of the limitations of one's material. Collecting discrete facts has been made much easier, but this must not exclude broad knowledge of traditions and backgrounds or a capacity to deploy disciplined imagination. The quarry is open to all, but one cannot neglect other archaeological sites and the techniques that have to be learnt to explore them intelligently.

NOTE ON SOURCES

An account of Australian newspaper history in the nineteenth century that is deliberately not a rapid chronological synopsis but an exploration of a certain number of themes must still be based on the secondary literature of the last few decades. The important texts and authors are indicated summarily below, with details reserved for the Select Bibliography at the end of the volume. Texts cited are, however, listed here in alphabetical order. They extend into such areas as library catalogues. Some newspapers originally read intensively for other projects, for example the *Australasian* in the late 1880s and Hobart titles from 1846 and 1847, also appear. It should be noted that some of the work was done in Dunedin, where the Hocken Collections have partly unique holdings of the Tasmanian press up to the 1860s.

Ferguson's *Bibliography of Australia*, the *Australian Dictionary of Biography* and the National Library of Australia's *Newspapers in Australian Libraries: A Union List*, have to be constantly at hand. *A Companion to the Australian Media*, edited by Bridget Griffen-Foley, has much to offer even if the colonial period is not at the centre of its preoccupations. A comparative neglect of the work done by bibliographers and book historians can be corrected by consulting the files of the *BSANZ Bulletin* and of its successor *Script & Print*, not least on New Zealand, which provides an important parallel to the Australian experience. Indispensable to follow research done since the end of the last century is the *Australian Newspaper History Group Newsletter* founded by the late Victor Isaacs in 1999 and long edited by Rod Kirkpatrick. An important tool for historical research is Thomas A. Darragh's *Printer and Newspaper Registration in Victoria 1838-1924*, Wellington, Elibank Press, 1997.

In the absence of the comprehensive bibliographies of Australian and New Zealand newspapers that have been called for by book historians like Elizabeth Morrison and Ross Harvey since the 1980s, one must use the important monographs issued from the 1960s onwards. They include Miriam Gilson & Jerzy Zubrzycki, *The Foreign-language Press in Australia 1848-1964*; collected studies on journalism edited by Denis Cryle in 1997 and by Ann Curthoys & Julianne Schultz in 1999; several studies of country newspapers by Elizabeth Morrison and especially

Rod Kirkpatrick; Gavin Souter's history of the *Sydney Morning Herald* after 150 years and Elizabeth Morrison's biography of David Syme; Sylvia Lawson on J. F. Archibald and the *Bulletin*; Denis Cryle on the press of colonial Queensland; R. B. Walker on New South Wales newspapers to 1920; Sandra J. Blair's 1990 PhD thesis on early Sydney newspapers; Elizabeth Webby's body of work, which goes well beyond the pre-1850 period; the studies of serialised fiction in Australian newspapers by Elizabeth Morrison, Toni Johnson-Woods and, latterly, Katherine Bode and Carol Hetherington, with their Trove-assisted database of a substantial part of the corpus.

Among the older treatments of the press that must be consulted are Ferguson on the Howes, E. Morris Miller on Tasmania; and H. M. Green's *History of Australian Literature*. Despite its title Frank S. Greenop's *History of Magazine Publishing in Australia* contains interesting relevant material.

It is clear that there are gaps. The most notable one is a reliable account of the *Argus* and the *Australasian* from their beginnings, but the major obstacle is the absence of business records.

Titles cited in this chapter, in alphabetical order by author, are: *Australian Newspaper History Group Newsletter*, no.117, May 2022; *The Argus*, 1856; Alan Atkinson, 'A Slice of the Sydney Press', *The Push from the Bush*, no.1, May 1978, pp. 82-99; and his 'Postage in the South-East', *The Push from the Bush*, no.5, December 1979, pp. 19-30; A. G. Austin, ed., *The Webbs' Australian Diary 1898*, Melbourne, Sir Isaac Pitman & Sons Ltd., 1965; the *Australasian*, 1888; *Bendigo Deutscher Verein, und Lesehalle. Catalog der Bibliothek Sandhurst, im Juni, 1886*, Sandhurst, J. Brockley, 1886; Geoffrey Blainey, 'The History of Leisure in Australia: The Late Colonial Era', *VHJ*, vol.49, no.1, 1978, pp. 7-22; Sandy Blair, 'George Howe and Early Printing in New South Wales', *Wayzgoose: The Australian Journal of Book Arts*, no.1, 1985, pp. 2-22; Katherine Bode and Carol Hetherington, eds, 'To Be Continued...': *The Australian Newspaper Fiction Database*, 2017, http://cdhrdatasys.anu.edu.au/tobecontinued/, [accessed 24 April 2024]; Judith Brett, *The Enigmatic Mr Deakin*, Melbourne, Text Publishing, 2017; *The Britannia and Trades' Advocate*, 1846; H. F. Bussey and T. Wilson Reid, *The Newspaper Reader: the Journals of the Nineteenth Century on Events of the Day*, London, Blackie & Son, 1879; Ada Cambridge, *Thirty Years in Australia*, with introduction by Louise Wakeling and Margaret Bradstock, Kensington, NSW, New South Wales University Press, 1989; *Catalogue of the Ballarat Public Library, Ballarat East, September, 1899*, Ballarat, E. E. Campbell, 1899;

Catalogue of the Mechanics' Institute and Free Library, Bendigo, Bendigo, Bolton Bros, [n.d.]; *Catalogue of Books contained in the North Melbourne Free Library and Mechanics' Institute*, North Melbourne, March 1900; *Catalogue of the Free Public Library Sydney 1876: Reference Department*, Sydney, Thomas Richards, Government Printer, 1878; *Catalogue of the Libraries of the Sydney Mechanics' School of Arts, 1901*, Sydney, Ross, Mann & Co., Printers, 1901; Patricia Clarke, 'Anna Blackwell, *Sydney Morning Herald* Correspondent in Paris (1860-90)', *JRAHS*, vol.106, June 2020, pp. 29-48; *The Diggers' Advocate*, 10 November 1853; Grant Finlay, '*Good people always crackney in heaven.' Mythic Conversations in Lutruwita/Tasmania*, Hobart, Fullers Publishing, 2019; *Gordon & Gotch London: The Story of the G. & G. Century 1853-1953*, London, Gordon & Gotch Ltd, 1953; '*Years to Remember': The Story of Gordon and Gotch: Gordon and Gotch (A'asia) Limited Centenary 1853-1953*, Melbourne, Gordon & Gotch, 1953; Bridget Griffen-Foley, ed., *A Companion to the Australian Media*, North Melbourne, Australian Scholarly, 2014; Sasha Grishin, *S. T. Gill & his audiences*, Canberra/Melbourne, National Library of Australia/State Library of Victoria, 2015; Mark Howard, 'William Stephens: an innovative Melbourne bookseller', *Biblionews and Australian Notes & Queries*, 411th issue, September 2021, pp. 112-21; Toni Johnson-Woods, *Index to Serials in Australian Periodicals and Newspapers. Nineteenth Century*, Canberra, Mulini Press, 2001; Rod Kirkpatrick, *The Bold Type: A history of Victoria's country newspapers, 1840-2010*, Ascot Vale, VIC, The Victorian Country Press Association Ltd, 2010; and his *Dailies in the Colonial Capitals: A Short History*, Newmarket, QLD, Rod Kirkpatrick, 2016; Wallace Kirsop, *Books for Colonial Readers — The Nineteenth-Century Australian Experience*, Melbourne, BSANZ, 1995; *The Diary of the Reverend Robert Knopwood 1803-1838 First Chaplain of Van Diemen's Land*, Mary Nicholls, ed., Hobart/Launceston, Tasmanian Historical Research Association, 1977; Martyn Lyons, 'Ships' Newspapers and the Graphic Universe Afloat in the Nineteenth Century', *Script & Print*, vol.42, no.1, 2018, pp. 5-25; Henry Mayer, *The Press in Australia*, Melbourne, Lansdowne Press, 1964; Archibald Michie, *Readings in Melbourne; with an essay on the resources and prospects of Victoria, both for the emigrant and uneasy classes*, London, Sampson Low, Marston, Searle & Rivington, 1879; Elizabeth Morrison, 'Retrieving Colonial Literary Culture: the Case for an Index to Serial Fiction in Australian (or Australasian?) Newspapers', *BSANZ Bulletin*, vol.13, no.1, 1989, pp. 27-36; and her 'Grub Street inventor: James Harrison's journalism, old and new, in Geelong,

Melbourne and London', in Denis Cryle, ed., *Disreputable Profession: Journalists and Journalism in Colonial Australia*, Rockhampton, Central Queensland University Press, 1997, pp. 55-77; and her *David Syme, Man of the Age*, Clayton, VIC, Monash University Publishing, 2014; George H. Pitt, *The Press in South Australia 1836 to 1850*, Adelaide, The Wakefield Press, 1946; Michael Rose, ed. *For the record: 160 years of Aboriginal print journalism*, St Leonards, NSW, Allen & Unwin, 1996; Thomas Smits, 'Looking for *The Illustrated London News* in Australian Digital Newspapers: Colonial readership and the formation of imagined communities, 1842–1872', *Media History*, vol.23, no.1, 2017, pp. 80-99; Leonie Stevens, '*Me Write Myself*': *The Free Aboriginal Inhabitants of Van Diemen's Land at Wybalenna*, Clayton, VIC, Monash University Publishing, 2017; Richard Twopeny, *Town Life in Australia*, Ringwood, Victoria, Penguin Books, 1973 (reprint of the London edition, Elliot Stock, 1883); R. B. Walker, *The Newspaper Press in New South Wales, 1803-1920*, Sydney, Sydney University Press, 1976; Elizabeth Webby, *Early Australian Poetry: An Annotated Bibliography of Original Poems Published in Australian Newspapers, Magazines & Almanacks before 1850*, Sydney, Hale & Iremonger, 1982; and *Wood's Royal Southern Kalendar, Tasmanian Register, and General Australasian & East Indian Official Directory*, 1850, Launceston/Hobart Town, Henry Dowling, Jun./J. W. H. Walch, 1850.

Case-study: Andrew Bent — Father of the Free Press

Sally Bloomfield & Craig Collins

Andrew Bent (c.1791–1851) was inducted into the Australian Media Hall of Fame in 2018, hailed as Australia's first fighter for press freedom and first newspaperman to be jailed for libel. He was described as one of the giants upon whose shoulders Australian press freedom rests, and overcame not only professional, but also personal challenges. Bent's accent betrayed his low Cockney origins and although he was opprobriously described by a contemporary, J. E. (James Erskine) Calder, as 'lame, little and ugly', Calder's additional observation that Bent was 'a mass of brains, common sense and industry' foretold the pressman's future significance.

Bent's importance in establishing Tasmania's print culture has been well recognised, but the full impact of his more nuanced and complex role initiating press freedom is only now emerging. William Charles Wentworth and Robert Wardell, lawyers and men of capital, have conventionally been praised for establishing the first free and independent press in Australia, with the publication of the *Australian* newspaper in Sydney on 14 October 1824. Bent, with his more obscure convict origins and craftsman status, has been somewhat overshadowed. Yet it was Bent's outrageous assertion of rights, throwing off the shackles of official censorship in Hobart, which paved the way for the appearance of the *Australian* some four months later. Bent's actions triggered a chain of events which led Governor Thomas Brisbane to allow 'the full latitude of the freedom of the press' in the Australian colonies. Once colonial governors lost command and control of the public press there was no going back. Accordingly, the free press has been a feature of Australian society since Bent's assertion of rights on 4 June 1824.

Bent fought doggedly for the principles of a free press and showed resilience in the face of repeated attempts to silence him. He sacrificed much in making his stand, though the cost was often compounded by injudicious use of his editorial freedom. In the end, he was financially ruined and consigned to the margins of history.

Contribution to colonial print culture

Bent arrived in Tasmania in 1812 as a young man of twenty, transported for burglary. His career as a printer in Hobart spanned nearly a quarter of a century, from 1815 to 1838. For ten years he was Government Printer, and indeed the *only* printer operating on the island. Bent initiated the colony's first successful newspaper, the *Hobart Town Gazette* (later the *Colonial Times*), conducting it from 1816 until 1830. He compiled and published the first Tasmanian almanacs from 1824 to 1830. His monthly magazine, the *Colonial Advocate* (1828), was a significant typographical achievement. He printed and published numerous pamphlets, including *Michael Howe, the last and worst of the bushrangers of Van Diemen's Land* (the first work of general literature in Australasia, 1819), the ribald *Van Diemen's Land Warriors* (Tasmania's first book of verse, 1827) and *The Hermit in Van Diemen's Land* (an anonymous satirical publication and Australia's first book of essays, written by convict Henry Savery, 1829-30).

In the early years it was no easy task to combine ink and paper. Bent's only press was the small wooden hand-press brought out by Lieutenant-Governor David Collins at Hobart's first European settlement in 1804. Until 1824 the *Gazette* was just a single leaf. Bent was drastically short of type, made his own ink and occasionally pasted two sheets of inferior China paper together for each newspaper. He faced a constant struggle to get subscribers to pay up, whether in cash or kind.

Bent's capacity for innovation, and for doing a lot with not much, suggests he was well-schooled in his craft. In 1881, Calder noted that many of Bent's publications 'were, as far as the printers' art is concerned, superior to anything that is produced at this day in any of the Australian colonies'. Clues as to how Bent acquired his practical skill, nous and motivation can be found in the fragmented record of his early life.

London background

Bent was baptised in the church of St Giles-in-the-Fields, London on 24 October 1791, and orphaned at fourteen or younger. By his own statement, he followed the practical side of the printing business from 'infancy', but no apprenticeship indentures have been found. Calder suggested Bent was apprenticed at the *Times* while John Pascoe Fawkner claimed he was an errand boy at the *Public Ledger* newspaper. This latter association is supported by a prison record which describes Bent, at the time of his conviction in 1810, as 'a boy belonging to Mr. Crowder, printer of Ledger'.

The *Public Ledger*, a respectable publication with a strong commercial orientation, was one of three newspapers printed by John Crowder in Warwick Square, London. Crowder was a man of exceptional character, who became Lord Mayor of London towards the end of his life. According to his obituary in the *Gentleman's Magazine*, Crowder conducted his newspapers with 'the greatest impartiality, diligence and integrity' for a period of thirty years. The *Public Ledger* provided a model of a well-conducted newspaper and Bent later, perhaps over-optimistically, adopted its motto — 'Open to all parties, influenced by none' — for his *Colonial Times*.

In October 1810 Andrew Bent and Philip Street, both 'well-known characters', were caught trying to sell stolen goods (a coat, a 'tippet', two pairs of boots and two shoes) in the Sugar Loaf public house off Drury Lane. They claimed they bought the goods from a street vendor, but were charged with the capital offence of burglary. After a disastrous trial they were both condemned to death, spending four months in Newgate before their sentences were commuted to transportation.

Bent had little education beyond basic literacy and, by his own account, such knowledge as he acquired came from assiduous reading of newspapers. These mirrored the political turbulence of the times, with fractures in British society compounded by the pressures of the Napoleonic Wars. Joining Bent in Newgate were some printers from the *Times* sentenced to gaol for strike action. At the same time, William Cobbett, radical printer-publisher of the *Political Register*, was incarcerated in Newgate for libel, as was George Beaumont, editor of the *British Guardian*.

Born just as Thomas Paine's *Rights of Man* became a publishing phenomenon, Bent's London milieu encompassed the radical press, including Cobbett's articles promoting parliamentary reform and a free press. These influences were perhaps later echoed by Bent's stubborn stand for the free press in the Australian colonies.

Hobart

Bent had a rapid rise to success in Hobart. By 1815, three years after his arrival, he had supplanted the incumbent Government Printer George Clark, to whom he had been assigned. Supported by Lieutenant-Governors Thomas Davey and William Sorell, by 1824 he was well established. He was married to Irish convict Mary Kirk, with a growing family. He owned several town properties, a small farm at Glenorchy, and a newly built printery. Incoming Lieutenant-Governor George Arthur described Bent as a man of 'comparative wealth'. Around this time, an anonymous observer noted the printer's 'unexceptionable good character' and how after early struggles his newspaper had 'succeeded beyond all possible expectation'. Conditionally emancipated in 1816 and fully pardoned in 1821, Bent was a perfect exemplar of Governor Lachlan Macquarie's vision of a successfully reformed convict.

The *Hobart Town Gazette* was subject to official supervision. The proofs were vetted each week, although Sorell mostly delegated this task to his favoured clerk, Thomas Wells. There was little need for intervention as the paper consisted mostly of government announcements, advertisements, extracts from overseas newspapers and local chit-chat.

On the cusp of 1824 two things changed this settled dynamic. First, Wells made a sudden exit from the Secretary's Office. Sorell, needing an urgent replacement, appointed Henry James Emmett to the position of chief clerk and also made him editor of the *Gazette*. Bent agreed to pay Emmett £100 a year.

Second, the *Gazette* itself was evolving. Late in 1823 Bent moved into a new purpose-designed printery which he thought 'sufficiently large and commodious' to last for a hundred years, taking with him the new type and two presses which had arrived mid-year. The type, and one of the presses, had been ordered by Sorell, but Bent was permitted to purchase the equipment on his own account. He was advanced nearly £400 by the government, with twelve months to repay. In January 1824 he substantially expanded the size and scope of the newspaper and invited contributions from correspondents. His pages sprang alive with letters on topics as diverse as the new church organ, the potential of tobacco as a crop and whether Van Diemen's Land should become independent of New South Wales. Correspondents sparred with wit and barbs before a growing readership.

Policy shift and unsettled times

For some time, factions in England had felt that Governor Macquarie's leniency in granting pardons, land, government positions and opportunities to emancipists sent the wrong message to the criminal underclass in Britain. Recommendations from the Commission of Inquiry headed by John Thomas Bigge supported these views and triggered a policy shift in the Colonial Office in London. The popular Sorell was recalled. His replacement, George Arthur, was briefed to restore a sense of dread around the prospect of transportation. Under Arthur, emancipists would not so easily find favour with government or be allowed to forget their convict stain. Bent's success story was now bad news.

Arthur's arrival at Hobart on 12 May 1824 was calculated to unsettle the colonists. He defied custom by landing privately at the back of Government House, ignoring the official welcoming party. Change was afoot. Rumours swirled around town, including one that Bent's job was up for grabs.

While Arthur was still settling in, tensions escalated between Bent and Emmett, precipitated in part by the opening of the newly constituted Supreme Court. A correspondent's letter was the subject of a libel action and Emmett, anxious about his legal exposure, and with neither the capacity nor desire to help in court, urged Bent to employ a court reporter. They were also at cross-purposes over the editor's role. With his expanded paper, Bent needed a real editor who could give practical help, not just someone in a sinecure post who merely provided the government notices and acted as censor. In a testy exchange of notes Bent informed Emmett he 'could no longer sustain' having 'the sole fatigue of correcting and arranging' the newspaper's contents. A recent arrival, Evan Henry Thomas, had offered himself as both editor and court reporter, but Emmett refused to budge from his appointment unless ordered to do so by Arthur. Emmett's offer to provide court reports if Bent paid him extra received a withering response:

> as you never performed, nor until now by then your own confession understood the duties of an Editor to the Hobart Town Gazette, you will not by me either be expected to attempt, or paid for continuing to neglect them.

The pressure on Bent was immense. The Supreme Court had a full calendar of business which he felt obliged to cover. He was financially stretched from building his printing office and had ordered further expensive equipment. Repayment of the loan was looming and, to compound matters, he was also short-handed at press after a drunken brawl between two convict compositors left one dead and the other in jail charged with manslaughter. Perhaps no-one, least of all Arthur, foresaw what would happen next.

On 4 June 1824, two days after his last note to Emmett, Bent boldly put to press number 422 of the *Hobart Town Gazette* without submitting the proofs for approval. Emmett, watching the clock, heard that Bent was correcting the proofs himself. At 1.40 pm Emmett dashed off an urgent note to Arthur, stating there was 'no doubt that the proofs are purposefully withheld' and attaching the chain of correspondence. In tone and language, Bent's last note to Emmett must have shocked Arthur, who would have felt that this was no way for an emancipist printer to address — let alone purport to dismiss — his gentleman editor.

Arthur wrote to Sorell, who was still in the colony, seeking to clarify the arrangement between the printer and the government while privately confiding to his secretary, John Montagu, that Bent seemed to forget his 'situation in life'. Arthur asserted that the government 'decidedly objects to persons in [Bent's] station holding any responsible office ... immediately under the Government'. Sorell confirmed that the equipment belonged to Bent, but, puzzled by the latter's action, observed: 'Mr. Bent certainly has turned contumacious most abruptly — he has always been very humble, and seems to have totally changed his Character'.

Sorell met with Bent the following day. After attempts at persuasion both ways, Sorell strongly admonished Bent, advising him to see Montagu 'and place himself in his proper station as the Government Printer'. Sorell's view was that any attempt to conduct a paper without government supervision must fail. But for Bent there was no going back.

Press freedom

At first glance it might seem that the birth of the free press in the Australian colonies happened quite by accident. The printer, under pressure, lashed out at his editor, viewing him as an obstacle to producing the kind of newspaper Bent was striving to achieve. One could thus argue that any ideals about a free press were merely incidental.

But perhaps a more strategic hand was at play. Was it mere coincidence that, a day or so before Emmett's dismissal and a month before the due date, Bent fully repaid his government loan, in cash, making his ownership of the equipment impregnable? And was Bent influenced by others?

Arthur believed that, even before he stepped off the boat, a party had formed against him. If so, his most dangerous opponent was Robert Lathrop Murray, a man of imposing presence and forceful personality. Murray had been a military officer, as well as a notorious swindler and poseur, before being transported for bigamy in 1816. He relocated from Sydney to Hobart in 1821, once free, seeking fresh opportunities. He had connections to at least one radical London newspaper, the *Statesman*, and was already adept at manipulating the press to further his own interests and work political mischief. He loathed Arthur, privately calling him a 'wretched reptile'. As an emancipist under the new regime, Murray faced diminished prospects, and his dodgy land deals were exposed to Arthur's scrutiny. It is easy to imagine Murray (who was also the prosecutor in the upcoming libel case which so worried Emmett) fuelling Bent's anxiety about his business and dissatisfaction with his editor. Bent was a simple craftsman and his bold move to sack Emmett has the whiff of manipulation behind it, a view reinforced by Chief Justice John Lewes Pedder's later description of Bent as 'the tool of a faction'.

Just three weeks after arriving with a clear mission, Arthur was vulnerable, with the only printing press in the penal colony in the hands of an ex-convict operating outside Government control. Arthur hastily wrote to his superior, Governor Brisbane, urging press licensing powers to address this anomaly. Bent countered by sending his new editor, Thomas, to petition Brisbane in Sydney.

Thomas carried documents supporting Bent's ownership of the equipment and his establishment of the *Gazette* at his own initiative and expense back in 1816. An uneasy truce prevailed in Hobart pending Brisbane's response.

In Sydney, Brisbane's new Attorney-General, Saxe Bannister, advised that, as Bent clearly owned the equipment, he was 'entitled to the enjoyment of his ownership without control, subject only to his responsibility in a legal way for any abuse of it'. On 10 September 1824, the *Sydney Gazette* reported that Brisbane 'was pleased to consider Mr. Bent's claim to publish his said Paper, on his own account, completely indisputable'. Thomas returned to Hobart in triumph, editorialising in Bent's paper about a David and Goliath battle against a 'Gideonite of tyranny' (Arthur).

Over Arthur's head, Bent's right to publish an independent newspaper was now vindicated by higher authority. In New South Wales, with publication of the *Australian* imminent, Robert Howe, printer of the *Sydney Gazette*, applied for his paper to be released from censorship. Bannister agreed, mentioning his opinion on Bent's

Front page of the *Hobart Town Gazette and Van Diemen's Land Advertiser*, 8 October 1824, containing the Gideonite article. This copy was exhibited at Andrew Bent's 1826 trial and annotated in the upper right corner by the Clerk of the Supreme Court, Wm Sorell Jr. The annotation reads: 'Supreme Court of Van Diemen's Land Exhibited in the Case of the King agt Andrew Bent this 15 day of April 1826 W. Sorell'. Additionally, this copy is in a bound volume which, from its other annotations, was obviously Bent's own file copy. (Mitchell Library, State Library of NSW)

case as a precedent. And, when Wentworth and Wardell launched the *Australian*, Brisbane did not interfere.

Aftermath

Bent's newly independent paper soon began to snipe at Arthur's administration. Murray, who wrote carping, mischievous and supercilious letters under the moniker 'A Colonist', was toasted, along with freedom of the press, at public dinners. Arthur later complained that Brisbane's decision exposed him from the outset to the licentious attacks of Murray — 'the most able and most depraved Man living'. But Murray was too dangerous for Arthur to engage directly, and the printer presented a softer target. After a series of criminal prosecutions for seditious libel heard before military juries, Bent was heavily fined and imprisoned for six months. Unconscionable delays in legal process left him dangling in suspense and subject to official whim for long periods.

Arthur secured another press, sacked Bent as Government Printer and appropriated his newspaper title. Two rival *Hobart Town Gazette*s circulated for some weeks. Later, two of Bent's convict writers were sent, without due process, to the penal settlement at Maria Island. Another was removed from Hobart and convicts were banned from writing for the newspapers. In 1827, a local Act required newspapers to be licensed. In protest, the *Colonial Times* of 19 October appeared with heavy mourning borders and its news columns blank. Bent's repeated applications for a licence were refused. He was gaoled again, in 1828, for publishing the *Colonial Times* without a licence, even as a *gratis* advertising sheet. Vindication came when the British government ordered the Act to be rescinded as repugnant to the laws of England.

In the 1830s Bent remained associated with newspapers opposed to Arthur but, after years of political battles, court engagements and numerous libel convictions, he and his business became worn down. Early in 1839 he was sold up by the sheriff and took his large family to Sydney. Bent described his last years as a 'sad career of misfortunes'. His physical and mental health declined, repeated attempts to re-establish himself in business failed and a public appeal for charity gave only temporary respite.

Historian John West lamented that Bent, an 'undoubted benefactor to the colony, was left to an indigent old age, cut off from the prosperity to which his early labors contributed'. While Wentworth emerged as a colossal political figure for decades to come in New South Wales — along with wide acceptance of the *Australian* as the first independent newspaper — Bent slipped quietly into oblivion, his achievements largely forgotten even in his own lifetime. He died at the Sydney Benevolent Asylum on 25 August 1851. There was never a headstone and his remains were lost in excavations for Sydney's Central Station. But in Auckland, the grave of his daughter Elizabeth Warner commemorates Bent as 'Father of the Tasmanian Press'.

NOTE ON SOURCES

The conflict between Bent and Arthur is covered in general histories of Tasmania and biographies of Arthur. Joan Woodberry was the first to explore correspondence between Bent and Emmett in the Tasmanian Archives, CSO1/1/198/4725. Her book, *Andrew Bent and the Freedom of the Press in Van Diemen's Land* (Hobart, Fullers Bookshop, 1972) remains the only stand-alone account of Bent and his times, although it falls short of a full biography and much new material has since come to light. For Bannister's advice to Brisbane see S. Bannister, *Statements and documents relating to proceedings in New South Wales, in 1824, 1825, and 1826*, Bridekirk, Capetown, 1827, pp. 202-3. Additional sources are: James Erskine Calder, 'Something about old colonists – Andrew Bent', *Mercury (Supplement)*, 5 February 1881, p. 1; Herbert Heaton, 'The Early Tasmanian Press and its Struggle for Freedom', *Papers and Proceedings of the Royal Society of Tasmania*, 1916, pp. 1-28; and Craig Collins and Sally Bloomfield, 'Hobart Town, 1816: Andrew Bent and fermenting change', *Tasmanian Historical Research Association: Papers & Proceedings*, vol.64, no.1, April 2017, pp. 32-57.

More generally, this study draws on the as yet mostly unpublished research by the authors of this case-study across a scattered and fragmented archive of government records and private papers, Bent's own pamphlets about his affairs, and contemporary newspapers in Tasmania, Sydney and London. The authors have created a comprehensive and regularly updated website about Bent: *Andrew Bent: Father of the free press in Australia*, 2018: https://andrew-bent.life.

The site includes: Craig Collins, 'Andrew Bent and the birth of the free press in the Australian colonies,' Paper presented to the Australian Media Traditions Conference, Canberra, 24 November 2005; and Sally Bloomfield's *Andrew Bent: a bibliography of his printing 1815–1849*, [website and paper accessed 2 May 2024].

CHAPTER 12

Magazines

†Elizabeth Webby

The development of a mass reading public during the nineteenth century went hand in hand with a vast increase in printed material, including an enormous growth in the numbers of newspapers and magazines. The latter, with their inclusion of miscellaneous material on a range of different topics and, increasingly, in a range of different genres, typify the change in reading practices during the nineteenth century, away from intensive reading of a few books to extensive reading of a variety of printed materials. As the century progressed, magazines became more and more specialised. Quarterlies aimed at the educated gentleman reader were joined by monthlies and weeklies targeting a more popular family audience and then by a range of titles aimed more specifically at readers of differing genders, classes and ages, at members of various religious sects and other specific groups, or at those with a particular area of interest such as sport or drama. This development, of course, continued during the twentieth century so that there is now no longer anything resembling the general magazine of the earlier nineteenth century. Newspapers have also steadily become more magazine-like in response to challenges from other media, especially the internet, to their core functions of news gathering and reporting. In this respect they are in many ways returning to their origins, since, in nineteenth-century Australia it is often very difficult to distinguish between a newspaper and a magazine. In this volume, as discussed by Wallace Kirsop in Chapter 11, newspapers have been defined as such if their primary role was one of news gathering and reporting, even though they may also have included much other material, such as fiction and poetry, that one would normally associate with magazines. While the magazines discussed here may often, as with the many local imitations of London *Punch*, have been very much concerned with local and contemporary events, they did not purport to be offering an objective report on them of the sort then expected from a newspaper. Rather, they provided a comic or satiric slant on the events of the day, or reflected a particular religious or political opinion.

While magazines were attempted in Australia from 1820 onwards, most earlier publications failed to survive for more than a few issues. After the vast increase in population, in the colony of Victoria in particular, following the discovery of gold in 1851, some successful magazines were established. Initially these were very closely modelled on the British magazines with which, of course, they were also in competition. By 1880, with the establishment of the most popular of them all, the Sydney *Bulletin*, influences were coming more from the new journalism of North America.

This chapter aims to outline the main developments in the publication of magazines in Australia during the seven decades from the 1820s to the 1880s. For each decade there will also be a detailed case-study of a particular magazine, chosen to reflect general changes within that decade or because the magazine was an especially successful or influential one.

The 1820s: the beginnings of magazine publication

While newspapers were regularly published in the eastern Australian colonies from 1803 onwards, it was to be another 18 years before the first magazine appeared in 1821. This delay can be easily explained by the fact that magazines were much more of a luxury than newspapers. The earliest newspapers were established in large part to allow for easier distribution of government notices and general information. Despite difficulties in obtaining paper and other necessary materials, as noted in other chapters of this book, most survived because they soon became essential for the advertising of goods, land and other commercial enterprises. This was something that had to be done locally, even though most of the 'news' these papers contained was still coming from elsewhere. For magazines, however, there was no such commercial imperative. At the beginning of the nineteenth century few English magazines carried advertisements; quarterly publication was not especially attractive to advertisers and would, in any case, have been out of keeping with the tone of magazines like the *Edinburgh Review*. They therefore relied on the appeal of their literary contents alone. For a magazine to succeed in Australia, it had to offer something that could not be just as easily, and usually more cheaply, obtained from an English import.

Competing in terms of price was generally not possible, given the higher cost of printing in Australia during the nineteenth century. Some of the earlier magazines may have had the advantage of being more easily obtained than English imports, at a time when the tyranny of distance was more strongly in evidence and regular supplies not yet well established through booksellers. But by the 1840s this geographic separation was no longer a problem, with delays of no more than four to six months between publication in Britain and availability in Australia. So it did really come down to content. Australian magazines were offering literary works by local, usually unknown, authors while English ones featured the latest productions of the great names of the age: Dickens, Thackeray and so forth. But the colonial publications were also including reflections of local scenery, events and personalities which could not be found elsewhere; as the century progressed, and with the rise in numbers of Australian-born, there was a growth in demand for local content. Even so, few magazines survived for more than a year or two.

The 1820s was the only decade when quarterly publication was the most favoured magazine form in Australia. This may reflect the difficulty of getting any magazine off the ground at this time, though would also be strongly related to the prestige of the great English quarterlies. Most magazines were published in Sydney, then the largest city, though two appeared briefly in Hobart in 1828. All featured lengthy titles or subtitles drawing attention to the range of topics being covered; most also reflected their place of origin in their titles, even if not always in their contents.

The earliest of these publications, the *Australian Magazine; or Compendium of Religious, Literary, and Miscellaneous Intelligence*, first appeared in Sydney in 1821. As one might expect from the stress on religious material in its subtitle, its editors and proprietors were a group of Wesleyan missionaries. Publication of the magazine was no doubt seen by them as part of the encouragement of literacy and reading intrinsic to the Methodist ideal of individual salvation through personal contact with the scriptures and other uplifting literature. All Wesleyan missionaries were required to send detailed monthly reports back to London, many of which were edited down for publication in the *Methodist Magazine*. The *Australian Magazine*, however, included virtually no original material, though one of its initial aims had been to provide an outlet for local writers. Its other objectives were to defend the vital principles of Christianity and keep readers in touch with the most important developments in Britain in areas such as theology and philosophy. While articles on subjects like 'Life of the Eminent Missionary Swartz', 'The Truth, Importance and Design of Revelation' and 'Sixteenth Anniversary of the British and Foreign Bible Society' sound pretty unappealing today, the *Australian Magazine* was apparently quite successful. Its editor, Ralph Mansfield, told his brother on 13 October 1821 that its sale was 'very good, and we hope it will be a means of intellectual, moral, and spiritual improvement'. After issuing 14 monthly parts, however, the magazine ceased publication, apparently on the orders of the London Wesleyan Committee, who thought its missionaries should be doing other things with their time — clearly, they perceived local magazines as a luxury rather than a necessity.

Despite this, Ralph Mansfield and other Wesleyans, as well as the Presbyterian clergymen-poets J. D. Lang and John McGarvie, were associated with an unsuccessful attempt to publish another *Australian Magazine*, subtitled '*or Quarterly Journal of Literature, Science, Philosophy, Agriculture, Morals, and Religion*' in 1826. An Anglican clergyman, the Rev. C. P. N. Wilton, did manage to bring out a few issues of his *Australian Quarterly Journal of Theology, Literature and Science* in 1828. A contemporary reviewer correctly summed up this production as 'staid, didactic, and . . . highly respectable'. While only a few more issues appeared of another quarterly, the *South-Asian*

Register of 1827, it received a good deal of attention in the local press as discussed in the case-study below. Only one issue of the *Blossom* ever appeared. It was the first magazine to be edited by someone who had been born in Australia, John Walter Fulton. As one might have expected, it published more original material on local issues, including some of the political comment shunned by all other magazines at this time.

Both of the two magazines published in Hobart in 1828, Andrew Bent's *Colonial Advocate* and Robert Lathrop Murray's *Austral-Asiatic Review*, were actually newspapers put out in magazine guise to subvert Governor George Arthur's new newspaper licensing laws of 1827. The latter received a highly critical review in the Sydney *Monitor* for 3 March 1828, which indicated the problem local editors had in achieving the right mix of local and overseas, original and selected material:

> A Van Diemen's Land Magazine or Review should give information of Van Diemen's Land. The people of every colony like to read about themselves, better than of England or foreign countries. And the people of England, when they look into an Australian Magazine, would be disappointed to see it occupied almost entirely with matters which apply as well to Europe, as to the colony in which it is published... The only article worth our notice, or that of our readers, is Mr Murray's critique on the Sydney Journals. We here transcribe it for the edification of our readers. We had almost forgotten to state, that on politics Mr Murray is tame. Perhaps necessarily so. We had expected otherwise.

The last comment referred to the constraints under which Tasmanian publishers were operating during the regime of Governor Arthur. After his newspaper licensing legislation was disallowed by the British Secretary of State, Murray merged the *Review* with another newspaper, the *Tasmanian*.

Case-study: *The* South-Asian Register

One of the first noticeable things about this quarterly magazine, which ran for four issues from October 1827, is its very modern-sounding title. While not much of the magazine's content reflected this apparent recognition of Australia's links with Asia, it did include rather more original material than other local magazines of this decade. Its intention, according to the prospectus published in the *Monitor* on 30 July 1827, was 'to establish a permanent medium of Colonial information' as well as to provide an outlet for significant local writers:

> ... men of learning or experience have had no inducement to write, no sufficient stimulus to prompt their labours — nothing in which they could place any deliberated evidence of what they have seen or known or felt; any record of their existence.
>
> They, to whom this silent destitution, this confinement from the sociality of the mind, is the worst form of exile, are invited to witness our preparations for a more active scene; one in which, we trust, they may participate ...

Accordingly, the first issue featured an article on 'Aboriginal Dialect' by the Rev L. E. Threlkeld, an historical account of 'New Holland' and reviews of two volumes of poetry published in Sydney in 1826, Lang's *Aurora Australis* and Charles Tompson's *Wild Notes from the Lyre of a Local Minstrel*. The *South-Asian* also included a range of material selected from major English magazines: reviews from the *Edinburgh* and *Quarterly Review*s, prose extracts from the *New Monthly Magazine* and several poems and ballads. While it republished a piece about Scott's novels it did not, however, include any fiction.

The ratio of original to select material was criticised in a semi-humorous letter by 'XYZ' published in the *Monitor* on 18 October 1827. Its author complained of the magazine's high price and the amount of English Literature, 'for I have no acquaintances up the country to send it to; but I want to send it home as a put-off against several little invoices which have come out, to let them see what is going forward here'. This correspondent points to one of the difficulties faced by local editors of magazines: who was their main audience? Was the magazine going to be bought to be read locally or sent off to England as a sign of colonial advancement? Should it cater for readers 'up the country' who had no access to English periodicals and so would welcome selected material or to readers in the city who would want something new and different?

The subsequent three issues of the *Register* indicate another common difficulty faced by Australian magazine editors, especially in the earlier decades of the century: lack of good local material. There were no other new local publications to be reviewed and the gentlemen addressed so hopefully in the prospectus had apparently not been prepared to contribute. Issue No. 2 concluded the article on 'New Holland' and included another on theatrical performances in Sydney; No. 4 featured an essay on 'A Walk through Sydney in 1828'. Apart from some local poems, the rest of the material in these issues was selected from English publications. At 7/6d per issue, the price of the *Register* was indeed very high. While it received many favourable reviews, and apparently sold out its initial edition of 200, later issues may not have sold so well, once the novelty had worn off and the supply of original material diminished. The gap of eight months between issues 3 and 4 suggests a shortage of either cash or copy, and probably both. Mystery also surrounds the identity of the editor, said to be one Dr Roger Oldfield, though on 26 May 1828 the *Sydney Gazette* claimed that this was a pseudonym.

The 1830s: the growing demand for fiction

If the magazines published in Australia during the 1820s were predominantly quarterlies of serious tone and intent, those that appeared during the 1830s mirrored developments in Britain by being mainly monthly publications that included increasing amounts of fiction. While Sydney and Hobart continued to be the only two places of publication, nearly as many magazines appeared in both places and Hobart was the site of the best of them, the *Hobart Town Magazine*, which will therefore be the case-study for this section.

Of the seven magazines published in Sydney during the 1830s, the earliest, the *New South Wales Magazine* of 1833, was again edited by Ralph Mansfield. Having left the Wesleyans, he was now prepared to publish fiction as well as theology, from both local and overseas authors. The local material included fiction set in Australia, such as G. J. Macdonald's story about Indigenous Australians, 'Bremeba the Kharadjie' as well as a longer, serialised piece, 'The Pythoness: A Tale of the First Century', set in Corinth and dealing with the conflict between early Christians and those who still worshipped Apollo. The magazine also offered a range of essays, and poetry, both original and selected.

Much the same mixture can be found in *Tegg's Monthly Magazine*, published from March to July 1836 under the auspices of James Tegg, the Sydney bookseller. Here, however, one finds a number of Sydney-based tales, apparently the work of William Kerr, who was later to move to Melbourne and edit the *Port Phillip Patriot*. They include 'Fisher's Ghost: A Legend of Campbelltown', one of the first of many retellings of this story, and a longer piece, 'The Governess', based on another notorious event of a few years earlier, the seduction of an immigrant girl by a Sydney lawyer and her eventual suicide. Interestingly, the only story in John Lhotsky's equally short-lived periodical, *Illustrations of the Present State and Future Prospects of New South Wales* (1835–36), 'The Ten Sovereigns, A Tale Founded on Colonial Facts', dealt in part with the same case. On 9 March 1836, the *Monitor* noted that Dr Lhotsky had asked them to 'state that his tale was in type, in the office at which the *Governess* was printed, for a fortnight before the latter story appeared'. If there was any question of plagiarism, as a result of competing publications all being produced from the same printing office, then he was not the one at fault!

Despite its heavy seasoning of local fiction, *Tegg's Magazine* was not successful. Undeterred, Tegg was also the sponsor of a weekly which began publication in Sydney on 12 August 1837, the *Literary News; A Review and Magazine of Fact and Fiction; The Arts, Sciences and Belles Lettres*. It was edited by the lawyer William a'Beckett, who also wrote much of the original material, a pattern common to many of the magazines of this decade and later. The *Literary News* included a fair amount of selected material since a'Beckett believed it was necessary to create a taste for literature before one could expect much in the way of original work worthy of publication. Indeed, on 6 January 1838 he criticised the editor of a rival magazine for including too much original material in his publication.

The selling point of this competing publication, the second to be called the *Australian Magazine*, was, indeed, that it was almost entirely written by 'the *Sons of Australia*'. Unlike the *Literary News* and most other magazines from this period, it did not avoid discussion of local political issues, including in its first issue for January 1838 (the fiftieth anniversary of the establishment of an English colony in New

South Wales) articles on the future of Australia, the present financial situation of the colony and the administration of its then governor, Sir Richard Bourke. In addition, there was an essay on the need for freedom of the press, and even one on 'The Destructive Contagious Epidemic Catarrh' currently raging among local sheep, as well as agricultural and scientific reports and articles. Readers of lighter literature were not neglected, with several poems and stories set both in Australia and elsewhere.

The most successful Sydney magazine of this decade was the *Australian Temperance Magazine*, which ran from July 1837 to June 1840. According to the *Monitor* of 5 July 1837, it began with '2,000 copies already subscribed for' at a time when 200 was seen as the minimum number needed to start a magazine. This was, of course, a sign of things to come, as general magazines were gradually replaced by those targeting a special interest group.

Case-study: *The* Hobart Town Magazine

This periodical, subtitled '*An Interesting Miscellany of Literature*', was published monthly from March 1833 to August 1834, for a total of 18 issues. It initially concentrated on imaginative literature, particularly fiction, aiming to appeal not only to all classes in the colony but to their friends in England, so demonstrating that 'Tasmania is not devoid of individuals who have the means, as well as the desire, of cultivating Literature as well as Land'. In this, it was initially successful, attracting favourable comment from reviewers in both Hobart and Sydney. According to E. Morris Miller in *Pressmen and Governors* (1952), its editor Thomas Richards had contributed to the *Monthly Magazine* and other London literary journals and been friendly with such well-known English authors as William Hazlitt and Thomas Hood. Richards was a talented writer but, like many other colonial editors, had increasingly to supply most of the original material for his magazine. As well as many stories and serialised longer works, he also wrote genial, rambling essays on popular medical and scientific subjects, such as 'The Philosophy of Apparitions' and 'Eating and Drinking'. One of his best essays, 'A Day's Fishing in the Plenty', engagingly reveals Richards's delight in fishing as well as his appreciation of the Tasmanian countryside.

Richards's fiction tends to fall into one or other of the conventional melodramatic or sentimental styles then so popular. The most effective of his shorter tales are thinly disguised accounts of his experiences as surgeon on the female emigrant ship the *Princess Royal*. Like so many other local authors, Richards was also attracted to the topic of bushranging. Among his shorter pieces on this subject was 'An Adventure with Bushrangers', an account of a successfully laid trap for some of the gang of the notorious Michael Howe. The more humorous 'Peter Potter's Robbery by Bushrangers' dealt with the equally notable Matthew Brady. The longer 'A Tale of Blood' appeared over three numbers but was never concluded. Nor was 'Lost and Found; or, the Bushranger's Confederate. (A Tale of the Colony)'. Two other adventure stories set in England, 'Rob the Red-Hand' and 'The Confessions of Edward Williams' were, however, brought to satisfactory conclusions before the magazine folded.

The amount of original fiction published in the *Hobart Town Magazine* would appear to be one of the reasons for its relatively long run, though, because of this emphasis, some local reviewers accused it of being too much focused on attracting 'fair and feminine readers'. The Tasmanian *Colonist* for 21 May 1833 described the third number as a '"dear book" for the ladies, being with the exception of one or two very decently written serious articles, full of love, murder, and "the like of that"'. Whether because of criticisms such as these, or because of falling circulation, Richards and the magazine's proprietor Henry Melville decided to add articles on local political matters. Melville's *Colonial Times* noted on 12 August 1834 that 'The usual light reading for which this Work has been so celebrated, will continue as usual; but a more extensive portion will be spared to domestic intelligence, and Colonial information of every description.' But only one further issue was to appear; while it included two articles on current matters such as 'Free Representation by a Legislative Assembly', it was not noticeably more 'colonial' than the earlier issues.

The 1840s: the beginnings of specialisation

The 1840s saw a large increase in free immigration and the development of new colonies in South and Western Australia and Victoria, all of which began to publish magazines in this decade. It was also marked by the beginnings of magazine specialisation, with the first appearance of illustrated and sporting magazines as well as the spread of publications associated with particular communities, mainly different religious groups but also organisations like the Odd Fellows, which published a notable magazine in South Australia.

Most of the new magazines were issued in Sydney — 29 of them — a fourfold increase from the 1830s that would not be surpassed, and then only slightly, until the 1880s. Adelaide followed with seven periodicals and then Hobart with four. A large number of these new magazines appeared weekly, allowing them to claim some of the immediacy of a newspaper as well as to run advertisements in some cases. Apart from a slight hiccup in the unusual circumstances of the gold-mad 1850s, when a more or less equal number of new monthly and weekly magazines were issued, weekly publication was to be the preferred mode for the remainder of the century.

Many of the magazines attempted earlier in the decade failed, owing in part to the severe financial depression of 1843, and in part to the lack of sufficient reader demand for the material they were supplying. The *New South Wales Magazine*, published for a few months in 1843, was edited by men with impeccable literary credentials, initially by the Rev. T. H. Braim, a Cambridge graduate who was then headmaster of Sydney College, and afterwards by two other Oxbridge graduates, Thomas Walker and Henry John Hatch. They appealed for support from all classes of the community, promising that, before everything else, their magazine would not be '*controversial*'. Though this might now seem a sure way *not* to attract readers, initially the magazine received favourable reviews. The *Sydney Morning Herald* for 14 February 1843, however, noted that 'after some years of observation in this colony, we are disposed to think that a magazine, to become popular, if not useful, must be prepared to skirmish, if not to do something more, in the disputatious warfare which those ominous words, Politics and Polemics, invoke'. Ten issues of the magazine appeared, with some attempt towards the end to include more local and political material, though this was not enough to ensure its survival.

Even though the first issue of a rival monthly publication, *Arden's Sydney Magazine* of September 1843, stressed that it would not shy away from political matters or articles on '*colonial interests and resources*', it managed to survive for only two numbers. In the first issue, under the heading 'Review of Colonial Literature and Productions of Art', George Arden canvassed a number of reasons for the failure of earlier magazines: their editors had all had other professions and did not devote enough time to their magazines; they had tried too hard to encourage local talent and so included inferior material. While he promised not to make either of these mistakes, Arden could not do anything about two other problems he noted. Readers living outside of Sydney were more likely to be supporters of his magazine, but poor transportation meant that most of them were out of reach. In Sydney itself, there was 'a habitual apathy among the educated classes'; they were only interested in commercial matters, horse racing and going out to dinner.

The problem of finding enough able contributors as well as enough readers also plagued the *Colonial Literary Journal*, a weekly miscellany which began publication in Sydney in mid-1844. It attempted to attract a wide range of readers, not only combining original essays and articles with selected material but also carrying 'British, Foreign, and Domestic News — Articles on Trade and Commerce — and a summary of Local Intelligence, with such other items as may be recommended by their utility'. Given this emphasis, it is not surprising that the *Journal* was very like *Chambers' Edinburgh Miscellany* in its aims and appearance, as well as in its low cost — 16 pages for 4d. In some ways, too, it anticipated the weekly journals aimed especially at country readers that later in the century were to be attached to the large city daily newspapers, though of course it lacked their financial and other support. Initially, this first attempt to cater for the less well-off seems to have proved successful, with 500 subscribers after its first six months of publication. Its final issue, however, appeared at the end of March 1845 just before a proposed price rise, indicating that the previous price may have been too low to make the journal viable. A subsequent attempt to offer an even cheaper magazine, in the form of the *Australian Penny Journal*, was made in Sydney in 1848. While this consisted almost entirely of material selected from English publications, it too seems to have been unable to cover costs. The proprietors announced that from the beginning of 1849 it would become the *Australian Literary Journal*, priced at 2d. Only a few issues appeared.

A cheap magazine of this type, the *Adelaide Miscellany of Useful and Entertaining Knowledge*, was published for a full year in South Australia from 5 August 1848, but only because of a colonist's generous subsidy. He lost, it was claimed, over £400 on the venture and there was some understandable bitterness in the final issue for 28 July 1849:

> It will be wise for the South Australians to reflect, that although the pursuit of wealth is a justifiable object, in subservience to its proper application, yet the total abandonment to such pursuits can only constitute an ignorant, grovelling population, and will never maintain South Australia as an example of heightened moral feeling, intelligence and worth.

Given that the much more expensive *South Australian Magazine* had earlier managed to survive for over two years from July 1841, it was perhaps difficult not to resort to attacks on the apathy of those readers at whom cheap periodicals were directed, when explaining their failure in Australia during the 1840s. It should, however, be remembered that by this time the equivalent British publications were readily available, either for purchase or to be read at a mechanics' institute or other reading room. Those who desired to improve themselves through reading therefore had no real need to resort to local publications. On the other hand, cheap local publications, which consisted mainly of selected material, were not in demand by those wishing to send samples of colonial literary productions back to their friends in England.

The *South Australian Magazine* had been greeted with much admiration and not a little regret by Sydney newspaper editors. The reaction of William Duncan, in his *Australian Chronicle* for 8 January 1842, is typical:

> We opened this periodical with no slight feeling of shame at the reflection that a small community of yesterday should be enabled to send forth an elegant monthly magazine, while this extensive colony, is to this hour all but a blank in the republic of letters... The South Australian Magazine is in point of typography not inferior to any of the English monthlies, and many of the articles are extremely well written.

Monthly magazines of this type were also attempted in Hobart and Melbourne during the decade, but none managed to survive for more than a couple of issues. In Western Australia, two short-lived monthly magazines were begun by Wesleyan ministers; as with the earliest magazines in Sydney, their main interest was in religious instruction and education.

As mentioned earlier, the 1840s also saw the beginnings of more specialist magazines, aimed at or published by different reading communities. The Odd Fellows produced quarterly magazines in both Sydney and Adelaide, the latter, like the more general magazines of the decade, being the superior product. The *South Australian Odd Fellows' Magazine* commenced publication in July 1843 and ran for just over two and a half years, making it the longest lasting magazine of this period. Moreover, it ceased not for want of readers, it appears, but because 'the managers of the Order in England' felt that such a commercial undertaking was not appropriate. The monthly *New South Wales Sporting Magazine* commenced publication in October 1848; in its December issue it claimed to have received liberal support, even from those gentlemen not especially interested in sport, and accordingly proposed to enlarge its interests and change its name to 'the New South Wales Sporting and Literary Magazine, and Racing Calendar'. But even this move away from specialisation was not enough to save the journal, with the January 1849 issue being its last.

Case-study: Heads of the People

That even by the 1840s the populations of the various Australian colonies were still too small to support either general or specialist magazines for very long is further demonstrated by the relatively short life of the first extensively illustrated Australian magazine, *Heads of the People*. This Sydney weekly was issued for a year, from April 1847 to March 1848, making it the most successful of the 1840s Sydney periodicals. While in one sense the first of many local attempts at a *Punch*-style illustrated weekly comic miscellany, its more direct model was an English magazine of the same title. Pride of place was given each week to a portrait of a local notable, accompanied by a semi-humorous essay discussing him less as an individual than as a representative of a particular profession or type. Thus on 21 August

1847 Samuel Prout Hill appeared as 'The Poet'; a fortnight later Robert Lowe was profiled as 'The Orator'. While prepared to feature occasionally more mundane professions such as 'The Baker' or 'The Night Auctioneer', women appeared only twice, once as 'The Wife' (of the magazine's publisher, William Baker) and once as 'The Soldier's Wife'. In the 1840s being a wife was, presumably, the only respectable profession open to women.

As outlined in its prospectus published in the *Sydney Morning Herald* on 23 March 1847, the magazine, as a weekly, was also to feature a good deal of local news. Readers were promised:

> A compendium of the doings of the Court; the passing events of the day, and news of the hour; carefully selected extracts from the leading London magazines and newspapers, and every incident of interest in the examination of our own social (*not* political) economy.

Again one notices a refusal to engage with local political issues; while this might have been justified in terms of not alienating any potential readers, it did of course mean that some of the most vital local topics could not be canvassed. The more successful later localisations of *Punch*, in contrast, concentrated heavily on local politics, especially for their leading cartoons. Apart from the portrait of the particular person featured in each issue, *Heads of the People* carried few illustrations with specific local reference. Nor did it include any advertisements; reliance on subscriptions alone was presumably one of the reasons for this magazine being unable to survive beyond its first year.

During the first six months, quite a lot of local fiction and poetry appeared in *Heads of the People*, as well as a serialisation, with some of the illustrations, of Charles Dickens's *Dombey and Son*. During the second six months, serialisation of an additional popular English novel, Charles Lever's *The Knight of Gwynne*, appears to have been an attempt to compensate for the decline in original material. At no stage did the magazine live up to its promise to provide summaries of all the events of the day, though it did run occasional brief reports of Sydney-area theatricals and other such happenings. The declining amount of local material was presumably one of the reasons why subscriptions soon fell away.

The 1850s: Magazines proliferate

The rapid increase in the population of Australia following the discovery of gold in New South Wales and Victoria in 1851 was accompanied by a comparable growth in print culture, especially in Victoria. While this was mainly reflected in the development of newspapers, magazines also proliferated. Melbourne now became the main centre of production, with more magazines starting up there during this decade than in the rest of the country combined. While most proved just as short-lived as the earlier publications, several survived for many years, demonstrating that there was now a large enough population of readers to sustain some local periodicals. Of the less specialised publications, the most successful was *Melbourne Punch*, which in 1855 commenced a run of 70 years, and has been chosen as the case-study for this section. The 1850s also saw the rise of several long-lasting magazines connected with various religious groups, such as the *Melbourne Church of England Messenger* (1850–1910), the *Victorian Miscellany and Wesleyan Chronicle* (1857+), with various titles, and the Roman Catholic *Freeman's Journal* (1850–1942). Another magazine which survived into the twentieth century, *Walch's Literary Intelligencer* (1859–1915), published by the leading Tasmanian bookseller of this time, shows the associated growth of the book trade in Australia as a consequence of the discovery of gold.

One interesting, if short-lived, magazine was targeted specifically at the diggers: James Bonwick's *Australian Gold-Diggers' Monthly Magazine*, which ran for eight numbers during 1852–53. As its subtitle, '*Colonial family visitor*', indicates, however, Bonwick also wished to appeal to the diggers' families, and his was one of the first Australian magazines to run specialist women's and children's pages. As their titles suggest, too, this wider family readership was also targeted by other equally short-lived magazines such as the *Australian Family Journal* (1855) and the *Australian Home Companion* (1856–57). Others specialised in selected overseas material, such as the *Spirit of the Age* (1855–56) and *Crouch's Epitome of News* (1858–60). The *News Letter of Australia* (1856–62), which did the reverse, interestingly had the longest run. Subtitled '*A narrative of events, or a letter to send to friends*', it summarised local news and affairs, with a space left for personal messages, clearly a boon to those who were not practised in letter-writing or had little time or inclination for it, yet needed to stay in touch with their families overseas. All of these Melbourne magazines, in their various ways, had attempted to cater for the particular needs of the vast influx of new settlers into Victoria.

A number of the older-style monthlies, appealing more directly to the gentleman reader, continued to be attempted in Victoria and the other colonies. Some more highbrow magazines even continued to try to shun fiction. *The Month* (1857–58), a Sydney literary and critical journal, reported on the doings of local learned societies and initially did not carry fiction. A feature of earlier numbers, edited by the visiting English writer Frank Fowler, was 'The World of Books', a regular survey of contemporary literature not equalled until the *Bulletin*'s 'Red Page' of the 1890s. In his issue for December 1857, Fowler announced that *The Month* was a 'complete commercial success' with upwards of 2000 subscribers including 'the most distinguished residents in *all* the colonies'. He claimed 'a far larger circulation than that of "Bentley", the "New Monthly", the "Gentleman's Magazine" . . . we challenge a comparison with any *Shilling* periodical published in Great Britain'. But only two issues later he was begging agents and subscribers to pay their outstanding accounts (said to amount to £910) so that *The Month* could remain solvent. This was Fowler's last issue as editor; under J. S. Moore there was much more emphasis on serialised fiction and the journal ceased publication in December 1858.

The *Tasmanian Athenaeum, Or, Journal of Science, Literature and Arts* published in Hobart in 1853–54 by Richard Lee and William Coote, attempted to concentrate on science, also including reports of the meetings of learned societies as well as meteorological and astronomical tables. As the editors noted in the preface to their first and only volume, however, the difficulties of producing such a periodical in Hobart were enormous: 'One sheet had to be struck off ere another was set up; hence a complete revisal of even a single number was impracticable. Neither could any illustrations deserving of the name be procured. This to scientific articles was an insurmountable difficulty.'

In Melbourne, despite some early problems caused when printers and other workers joined the initial exodus to the diggings, magazine editors encountered no such difficulties. The first substantially illustrated magazine, the *Illustrated Australian Magazine*, had been published there from 1850 to 1852, while *Melbourne Punch* also relied heavily on illustrations. Gold had brought talented artists and engravers, as well as writers, to Melbourne and this was reflected in the high standards of some of these new publications.

Case-study: Melbourne Punch

Like the earlier *Heads of the People*, *Melbourne Punch* was a 10-page quarto weekly, which featured one full-page illustration each week as well as a number of smaller ones. Right from the first issue, however, its editors and cartoonists made clear that they were prepared to go in boots and all with both politics and personalities. The featured cartoon showed Mr Punch Junior setting off to Toorak to replace the already very unpopular Governor Charles Hotham. Both in this and subsequent cartoons, the governor was represented in a comic but far from complimentary fashion. Right from the first issue, too, the magazine carried advertisements. In addition, most of its contents were local: satirical accounts of the doings of the Legislative Council, supposed letters home which allowed for much humorous comment on local happenings and personalities, the occasional poem, and a cartoon which was, alas, to become something of a commonplace over the next fifty years: Indigenous Australians before and after the coming of 'Civilisation'.

Later editors and proprietors of *Melbourne Punch* were less daring and enterprising than its founders Edgar Ray and Frederick Sinnett. In 1857, Sinnett was succeeded as editor by the journalist, critic and all-round Victorian man-of-letters James Smith and the journal lost some of its initial *élan* under him and his successors, as it and they grew older and more respectable together. While local politics and politicians continued to be the main focus of the leading cartoon, the Queen's representative in Victoria was no longer the butt of jokes. The magazine's format remained very close to that of its London parent, and plagiarism sometimes extended to content as well, but over the decades something of a growing nationalist consciousness was reflected. By October 1864, the local Mr Punch was accompanied by a pet kangaroo as well as his traditional dog; by the final issues in 1925, the kangaroo had replaced Toby on a very much redesigned masthead.

An early cartoon, 'A very just complaint', attempted to suggest that *Melbourne Punch* appealed to all classes and to women as well as men. There was little in the journal itself, however, to suggest that its contributors, all male as far as one knows, had much sympathy for the plight of the lower classes, while women were more often than not figures of fun. But, in comparison with the later *Bulletin*, *Melbourne Punch* had an engaging cosmopolitan outlook, while its major cartoonists, Nicholas Chevalier and Tom Carrington, were in their own day just as influential as the better known Phil May and Hop of the *Bulletin*.

'A very just complaint', *Melbourne Punch*, 2 August 1855, p. 160. (State Library of NSW)

The 1860s: something of a lull

After the rapid comings and goings of both people and periodicals that marked the 1850s, the following decade saw something of falling back in both areas. A much smaller number of new periodicals was attempted in Melbourne and Sydney, especially in the latter city which saw its previous role as cultural leader well and truly passed over to its younger rival for the next few decades. Of the few new Sydney journals, however, two, both obvious copies of popular London periodicals, had relatively long lives: the *Illustrated Sydney News* (1864–94) and *Sydney Punch* (1864–88). The most successful of the 1860s magazines, however, was another Melbourne product, the *Australian Journal*, which ran from 1865 until 1962. It has therefore been chosen as the case-study for this decade.

The 1860s were especially marked by the spread of comic illustrated magazines throughout the colonies. Some acknowledged their model in their names and layout, with *Sydney Punch* even featuring a smiling Mr Punch proudly displaying his new baby Punch as the frontispiece to its first volume. Others in this vein were *Adelaide Punch* (1868–84) and the less successful *Tasmanian Punch* (1866–68) and *Ballarat Punch* (1867–70). A number of other magazines of a similar style if rather more original names were attempted. Marcus Clarke's short-lived *Humbug* of 1869–70 had several Melbourne rivals, including *Touchstone* (1868–70) and the locally named *Laughing Jackass* (1867–68). Among the more successful magazines of the period was another which met the needs of those who wished to send Australian news to England without too much exertion of their own. *Australian News for Home Readers* ran from 1862 to 1896, showing how continuous was the desire to let those in Europe know what was happening in Australia, something they were very unlikely to learn about otherwise. *George Robertson's Monthly Book Circular* (1861–97) met another long-lasting need, that of Australian readers to keep in touch with what was being published outside the country. More specialist periodicals also continued to be established for specific religious and other groups. The Melbourne Catholic journal, the *Advocate*, for example, began in 1868 and continued in publication until 1990.

While having less staying power than any of these publications, another Melbourne journal, the *Australian Monthly Magazine* (1864–70), was one of the more creditable of those general periodicals that tried to compete with such English titles as the *Cornhill*. One way it attempted to do so was via essays, articles and fiction on local subjects, with politics no longer the taboo it had been formerly. Hence the first number featured a discussion of 'The Political Crisis in Victoria' as well as the first part of an Australian serial 'Chick: The Story of a Waif and Stray'. The editor also noted that 'Several stories founded on Australian incidents, sketches of bush life and life at the diggings, are under consideration, and others have been promised'. This was clearly seen as an inducement to would-be subscribers. Some of Marcus Clarke's first contributions to Australian literature were published in this magazine, and he was later to edit it under its new title, the *Colonial Monthly Magazine*, from March 1868 to September 1869.

Case-study: Australian Journal

The peripatetic Marcus Clarke was also briefly the editor of the much more successful *Australian Journal*. Its success lay, it seems, in its lack of pretension, and value for money. Initially commenced as a weekly, priced 3d, its model was not the higher class London monthlies, but the popular *Family Herald*, and its forte was fiction. Like the editor of the *Australian Monthly Magazine*, however, its proprietors saw the wisdom of offering local as well as selected material; in addition, the journal, like its English model, appealed to all members of the family. Readers were told in the first issue, for 2 September 1865:

> The ablest COLONIAL pens of the day will be engaged on our staff. Historical Romances and Legendary Narratives of the old country, will be mingled with Tales of Venture and Daring in the new; Nouvellettes, whose scenes will be laid in every nation, varied occasionally with Fairy Stories for the Young, and Parlour Pastimes for boys and girls.

In keeping with these aims, the first issue featured two serials by local writers, Mrs Arthur Davitt's *Force and Fraud; A Tale of the Bush* and James Skipp Borlase's *Galfried of Arlington; A Historical*

Nouvellette. The *Australian Journal* continued as a weekly until February 1869, after which it became a monthly, now offering 64 pages of closely printed material for 6d. It differed from many other local magazines in that most of its contributions were signed, though often with pen-names, and in having contributors and readers in nearly all the colonies. According to G. B. Barton in his *Literature in New South Wales* (1866), the *Australian Journal* was then circulating an average of 5500 copies weekly, including 1750 in New South Wales. This was at least equal to the circulation of English magazines of a similar style and cost, again indicating that Australian readers were prepared to support local magazines if their contents and prices were competitive with the imported products.

The *Australian Journal*'s policy of printing original fiction with both local and overseas settings continued until 1871 when, under Marcus Clarke's period as editor, this notice announcing a more nationalistic emphasis appeared in the July number:

> The Conductor wishes intending contributors to understand that the AUSTRALIAN JOURNAL will publish no 'original' story, the scene of which is laid elsewhere than in the Colonies, or which does not — in some way — treat of Colonial life, or subjects of Colonial interest.
>
> Tales of the West of England, the North of Scotland, India, Baden-Baden, Venice, Kamschatcha, and other places favoured by novelists, can be culled from the English magazines and French Feuilletons, in much better condition than as manufactured here.
>
> The Conductor is willing to protect native industry in the matter of tale-writing, but the tales must be 'Colonial', and suited for 'Colonial wear', not bad imitations of the French and English imported article.

This change of policy may be one of the reasons why one of the most prolific and longstanding of the *Australian Journal*'s writers, Mary Helena Fortune, concentrated in the later decades on the long detective stories published in each issue under the heading 'The Detective's Album' and signed 'W. W.'. Earlier, she had contributed a range of material under the longer, and more feminine, pseudonym 'Waif Wander', including some of the peripatetic journalism usually the preserve of male writers like Clarke.

As a typical issue of the *Australian Journal*, one may examine the number for September 1870. There were the usual two serials, given one illustration each: an episode from Clarke's *His Natural Life* and another from *The Trapper's Last Trail* by Leon Lewis. While Clarke, in the passage quoted above, did not refer to stories set in America, they were a regular feature of the journal. This issue also carried three full-page illustrations, showing a characteristic nineteenth-century blend of the natural and the man-made: 'Waterfall on the Coliban'; 'Australian Railways — Viaduct near Goulburn'; 'Fitzroy Iron Works: Scene on the Tramway between the Works and the Coal Mine'. As well as 'W. W.'s 'The Evidence of the Grave', one of 'Waif Wander's comic Irish tales, 'Biddy Twohy's Adventures in Australia — Her Caper Sauce', and several other stories by local and overseas authors were included. There were also several poems, including a long one by Henry Kendall, and a number of scientific and other non-fiction pieces. Regular features included 'The Doctor'; 'The Cook'; 'News of the Month'; 'Gardening for September'; 'Answers to Correspondents'; a page of puzzles of various types; 'Facetiae and Scraps'; and 'Register of Births, Marriages, and Deaths in Victoria, during Aug., 1870'. There were seven pages of advertisements, though at least two of those related to the *Australian Journal* and other publications by its proprietors. Although the price had now increased to one shilling for single issues or ten for a year's subscription, readers were still getting great value for money and continued to do so until the journal was eventually killed off following the coming of television to Australia in 1956.

The 1870s: an attempt at higher things

While the number of new periodicals attempted in Melbourne during this decade continued to decline from their 1850s peak, there was a considerable increase in the numbers appearing in Sydney and Adelaide, with weekly publication now being clearly the favoured form. Only one really longstanding new periodical was established, the *Harbinger of Light* (1870–1956), the mouthpiece of those who followed the new form of belief called Spiritualism. A distinctive feature of the decade was the number of attempts to establish a more highbrow critical journal along the lines of the famous British quarterlies. The most successful of these, the *Melbourne Review* (1876–85), provides the case-study for this decade.

In one of the many unfortunate examples of wasteful rivalry which dog the history of cultural production in Australia, a competing monthly magazine, the *Victorian Review*, was established in Melbourne in 1879 by H. Mortimer Franklyn. It ran until 1886, edited for most of the time by that all-round littérateur James Smith. While the *Victorian Review* initially featured a serialised novel, later issues were aimed squarely at readers who preferred the more serious fare of essays on general and literary topics, accompanied by reviews and poetry. The first issue's 'Prefatory Note' opened with some of the usual high-sounding sentiments, though it can also be read as something of a backhander against the *Melbourne Review*: 'It is felt by many of the leading men in Melbourne that there is wanting in Victoria a first-class Magazine which shall reflect its highest culture and express the opinions of the best thinkers of the day.' Elsewhere in the preface there were signs of changing attitudes, as in the comment that the journal would be 'distinctively Australian in tone'. The old taboos against discussion of religion, politics and other controversial topics were also firmly renounced. In keeping with this change in policy, the first issue of the *Victorian Review* included Marcus Clarke's attack on conventional religion, 'Civilisation without Delusion', which argued that education was the surest way to an enlightened future. There were also several articles on local political issues.

Given the relatively restricted pool of literary talent in mid-nineteenth-century Australia, it was inevitable that the *Victorian Review* competed with the *Melbourne* for contributors as well as subscribers. As the *Victorian* had more financial backing and so was able to pay contributors, it was able to attract many of the writers who had earlier featured in the pages of the *Melbourne Review*, such as David Blair and Catherine Helen Spence, as well as Clarke. The *Victorian Review*'s demise apparently owed more to the loss of this financial support than to declining numbers of subscribers; they had already won the battle with the *Melbourne Review* but, as in so many other cases, were unable to go on and win the war against continuing strong overseas competition.

Many of those who contributed to the *Victorian Review* also had work published in a Sydney journal, the *Australian: A Monthly*

Magazine (1878–81), though it aimed for a more popular market, including much short and serialised original fiction. Its title-page, which featured many local flowers, including waratahs, as well as an emu, a lyrebird and a kangaroo, further suggests the greater emphasis on Australian content seen in magazines from this decade onwards. One of the most strident in its nationalism was another Melbourne journal, the *Austral Review* (1877–78), which in an article on 'Journalism' in its first issue attacked the *Melbourne Review* for 'admitting too many papers which might just as well be written anywhere else'. Another article in the same number, on the Melbourne Public Library, was similarly critical of the prominent place given to the classics 'on the pleasanter ground floor', while works by Australian writers were 'stuffed away upstairs in a horrible atmosphere on summer nights, ranging not seldom to 90 degrees'. Given these attitudes, it is not surprising to find an article on Australian Literature, in the February 1878 issue, which gives special praise to the *Australian Journal*: 'Year by year it has improved, and forms quite a torrent of purely native authorship in fiction. Its tales abound in local colour, which is everything.' Some years later, Henry Gyles Turner described the *Austral Review* much less kindly as 'A worthless, scrappy, and generally inaccurate repository'. In its shorter and more brightly written articles, as well as in its nationalism, the *Austral* can, however, be seen as a portent of things to come, even though its quarterly format was definitely a thing of the past and presumably worked against its achieving a substantial readership.

Few new journals were attempted in Tasmania after the 1860s, a sign of the island's general economic decline following the cessation of convict transportation and the gold-rush exodus of the 1850s. One of the brave few has the unusual title of *Quadrilateral: Moral, Social, Scientific, and Artistic*, a foursome which, though not usually spelt out as here, had by the 1870s come to replace the older trio of 'Literature, Science, and Art'. An unillustrated, 24-page monthly, *Quadrilateral* offered the usual mix of essays, fiction and poetry, and survived for ten issues in 1874. In some of the other colonies, the topicality offered by comic weeklies proved once again to offer a surer recipe for success. Adelaide's *Lantern: A Satirical Paper for Australians*, ran from 1874 to 1890, while Brisbane's *Queensland Punch* appeared between 1878 and 1885, before being incorporated into its later and more successful rival, *Queensland Figaro* (1883–1936).

Case-study: The Melbourne Review

A number of Melbourne's leading men of letters, including the banker Henry Gyles Turner, the writer A. Patchett Martin and the historian Alexander Sutherland, were among the 'literary gentlemen' who in 1876 launched this quarterly review, 'not as a financial speculation, but purely in the interest of literary development'. In its opening address 'To Our Readers', January 1876, the failure of earlier Australian monthly magazines was attributed to their over-concentration on the fiction and 'light literature' already abundantly supplied in English periodicals and 'our own excellent weekly papers', together with their 'practice of dealing too exclusively with local topics of no intrinsic interest'. In contrast, in the *Melbourne Review*, the emphasis would fall on 'articles on Philosophy, Theology, Science, Art and Politics'. Its English model was not to be *Blackwood's Magazine* or the *Cornhill* but the *Contemporary* and *Fortnightly Reviews*. Articles on local subjects would be admitted only if they 'derived their value from their style and treatment, rather than from their containing allusions to places and names familiar to the Colonial reader'.

Of the nine articles which made up the first issue of the *Review*, therefore, only a third were specifically focused on local topics or issues: Marcus Clarke, no doubt drawing on the research carried out for the later chapters of *His Natural Life*, wrote 'The Story of the Eureka Stockade'; the Rev. Robert Potter discussed relations between Church and State in Victoria, with a particular emphasis on their respective roles in education; Edward E. Morris, headmaster of Melbourne's Church of England Grammar School, was highly critical of the textbooks in History and Geography set for the Matriculation Examination at the University of Melbourne, describing them as boring collections of facts. Other essays dealt with such topical matters as 'The Political Future of Europe', with the strength of Germany seen, correctly, as a major issue, 'Labour and Capital' and 'The Basis of National Prosperity'. There was a nod to science in an essay on 'Brain Waves', and essays from two of the journal's founders on topics obviously dear to their hearts: Henry Gyles Turner on 'An

Episode in Californian Banking' and A. Patchett Martin on 'The Drama as a Fine Art'. Regular features in each issue were reviews of recent local publications and a summary of recent events of public interest entitled 'Public Affairs in Victoria'. There were of course no illustrations, but readers were offered a good range and amount of material for their 2/6d. The only advertisement was for the equally high-minded Melbourne Athenaeum.

Competition from the *Victorian Review*, as mentioned above, eventually resulted in a declining number of subscribers and in 1885 the *Melbourne Review*'s publisher, Melbourne bookseller George Robertson, decided that he could not afford to lose any more money on the venture. Correspondence between Robertson and Turner in October 1885, now in State Library Victoria's La Trobe Collection, shows that Turner was anxious for the *Review* to be placed on a more professional footing; he argued that it was no longer possible to attract the most 'prominent men' as contributors because of the journal's falling circulation. He felt, however, that 'a good canvasser could work up a list of nearly 1000 subscribers and a dozen pages of advertisements'. More money would also allow for some payment of contributors, attracting work from professional writers and also removing the 'element of amateurism' which Turner thought had caused the *Melbourne Review* to be 'coldly, if not hostilely regarded by the Australian press'. These arguments demonstrate an awareness that the disinterested principles which had motivated the founders of the *Review* were not adequate to ensure its survival in the changing economic circumstances of late-nineteenth-century Australia. Culture and commerce could no longer be kept at a respectable distance; even a high-class review must stoop to carrying advertisements and to being hawked about the countryside by canvassers. As George Robertson reminded Turner rather brutally in declining to throw any more money at the *Review*, literature was for him not a hobby but his livelihood:

> The loss on the publication is about £25 or £30 per ann. Perhaps I ought not to encounter this further, as I have a large family and no regular salary, but if you are willing to go on as hitherto, I, for my part, am willing for another year to sacrifice my family on the altar of 'littry enthoosm'.

Despite Robertson's generous offer, there were no further issues of the *Melbourne Review*.

The 1880s: new journalism arrives (so do women)

The year 1880 saw the establishment of the most famous Australian periodical of them all: the Sydney *Bulletin*. While its fame mainly relates to its association with the rise of Australian nationalism during the 1890s, leading to the federation of the Australian colonies in 1901, the success of the *Bulletin* of the 1880s rested on different foundations. The construction of an Australian national identity, especially from 1930 to around 1970, placed a special emphasis on the unique qualities of the Australian bush and the bushman; hence the *Bulletin* was seen primarily as 'the bushman's Bible', and the birthplace of a truly national literature as represented by the work of Henry Lawson and Banjo Paterson. While Sylvia Lawson's detailed study, *The Archibald Paradox* (1983) has presented a different image of the *Bulletin* during J. F. Archibald's time, that of 'the great print circus', she does not look in detail at the reasons why the *Bulletin* of 1880 was such an immediate success. In the accompanying case-study of this periodical during this decade, it will be argued that the initial appeal of the periodical needs to be seen in terms of its depiction of the city and presentation of images of modernity.

Another aspect of the *Bulletin*'s success can be attributed to its adoption of many of the principles of the 'new journalism' of the late nineteenth century, principles which had been developed largely in North America. They included a more complete packaging of news and other items into easily recognisable compartments; a greater use of illustration; and more headings and subheadings to break up the vast expanses of type found in earlier publications. In short, this was a recognition that publishers needed to cater to a wider range of readers, and a wider range of reading situations. While the more serious quarterlies of the first decades of the nineteenth century were clearly addressed to the gentleman at leisure in his study or club, many of the new weeklies towards the end of the century recognised the need to appeal to both men and women, including those who would now be commuting to work each day by train or tram, in situations where reading would be frequently interrupted.

The success of the *Bulletin* led to many attempts at imitation, often as blatant in their plagiarism as were the earlier imitations of *Punch*. One of the first was the *Melbourne Bulletin* (1880–86), which in its inaugural issue on 15 October 1880 outlined what it saw as the *Bulletin* formula:

> This paper has been started with the object of supplying news in a condensed form for those who do not care, or have not the time, for heavy reading. Life is short, and so are our paragraphs. Crystallised information of every sort will fill our columns. A few comments on current topics will occupy our first page, and we shall devote a large space to items for ladies, for at the present moment there is not a paper in Melbourne in which a woman can take any interest. The Church, Stage, Sport, fashionable and personal. Topics will be well represented, and we shall eschew politics as far as possible. They are hammered out thin enough by our contemporaries. Our motto is brevity.

The Bulletin, 19 June 1880, p. 9. (State Library of NSW)

It was, however, not just brevity alone that made the Sydney *Bulletin* a success. While the *Melbourne Bulletin* recognised the growing demands of women readers, its attempts to appeal to women may have been one of the reasons for its failure to thrive. In its second issue, 22 October 1880, it printed complimentary remarks from other periodicals, including the *Bendigo Independent*'s view that it 'had none of the smart vulgarity of its Sydney brother and consequently may be read without anyone's sensibilities being shocked'. In 1886, the *Melbourne Bulletin* was absorbed into *Melbourne Punch*.

Smartness and the desire to shock were, of course, two other characteristics essential to the new journalism. This was recognised by some of the more successful periodicals that adopted the Sydney *Bulletin*'s pattern of short paragraphs of news and comment, with a particular emphasis on politics, sport, the theatre and local affairs. They included Adelaide's *Quiz: A Satirical, Social and Sporting Journal* (1889–1930) and Brisbane's *Queensland Figaro: Titbits of Everyday about Everybody and Everything, with a Peep at Society, Sport and the Drama* (1883–1936). As this latter subtitle makes clear, another characteristic of the new journalism was its emphasis on journalism as gossip, allowing readers the sense of being 'in the know', giving them a peep behind the scenes of fashionable life. Like the *Bulletin*, these journals were also, however, following a pattern of a mostly male-centred emphasis on sport, scandal and satire, first established in Australia in the short-lived Sydney weekly, the *Satirist and Sporting Chronicle* (1843).

While one or two earlier magazines had had women editors, and many had attempted to include material designed to appeal to female readers, the 1880s produced the first Australian magazines to be directed specifically at women. First off the rank was the *Australian Women's Magazine and Domestic Journal* (1882–84), a monthly published in Melbourne that included much original long and short fiction as well as recipes, household hints and fashion pages. *Woman's World: Australian Magazine of Literature and Art* (1886–87), another monthly published in Melbourne, began with rather higher aims but after a few months its proprietors obviously saw the need to attract a wider and more popular audience. In September 1886 it became a weekly, with a drop in price from one shilling to threepence, and a change in title to *Australian Weekly Magazine of Literature, Art and Fashion*. A further change in title, to *Wide Awake: Illustrated Weekly of Pastimes, Fiction, Fashion, Science, Art, Drama* — reflecting, it would seem, another desperate attempt to attract male as well as female readers — failed to save the magazine from being merged with *Life: Fun, Fact and Fiction*, a Melbourne weekly aimed at a similar audience.

Undeterred by the failures of these two earlier attempts at women's periodicals, in May 1888 Louisa Lawson began producing a Sydney monthly called *Dawn: A Journal for Australian Women*. Her hard work and determination in the face of many difficulties were rewarded by the journal surviving until 1905. Like the *Australian Women's Magazine*, *Dawn* began as a 32-page quarto; unlike that earlier journal it was priced at 3d rather than 6d right from the start. And, unlike the two earlier women's journals, it was not only aimed at women but edited, written, typeset, printed and bound by them. This resulted in a dispute with the New South Wales Typographical Association, which refused to allow the women working on *Dawn* to become members, and attempted to place an advertising ban on the journal; but by June 1890 the Association had been forced to back down and allow the women to join. While many of Lawson's editorials dealt with such current feminist issues as rational dress, divorce reform, the evils of drunkenness and, of course, the need for full female suffrage, the *Dawn* was not exclusively political. Readers were also offered fiction and poetry, recipes and home hints, even fashion pages and dress patterns. As a result, it attracted a wide range of readers in both Sydney and country towns and had many subscribers in other colonies and in New Zealand.

Case-study: The Bulletin

The *Bulletin* as first published on 31 January 1880 was an eight-page illustrated weekly which sold for fourpence. Its editors and proprietors, John Haynes and J. F. Archibald, had previously worked on both country and city newspapers, and, most recently, together on the Sydney *Evening News*. Their disagreement over the title of their new paper can be seen in retrospect to signal their very different visions of its future: Haynes wanted it to be called the *Tribune*, Archibald preferred the *Lone Hand*, a name with strong associations with the bush life he had experienced as a Queensland goldminer. The compromise title, taken from a San Francisco paper, indicates that Haynes's vision of a modern illustrated newspaper along American lines initially held sway.

Despite some early problems with printers and equipment, and a reduction in price to 3d, the *Bulletin* was an almost immediate success. Circulation was claimed to have increased from 4000 in February to 10 000 in June, and then to 16 000 by October. Certainly, the paper was a success with advertisers; by September it had doubled in size to 16 pages, almost half of them devoted to advertisements. Many of its feature articles and illustrations could also be read as advertisements in another guise. Haynes, who had primary responsibility for business matters and advertising, each week wrote up a Sydney company, usually with illustrations of its new premises and sometimes its proprietors. He was an advocate of free trade, in marked contrast to the protectionist views of the nationalist *Bulletin* of the 1890s. There is little in the early issues of the journal, which featured fine engravings of noted men, city buildings and current news events rather than the political cartoons for which it later became known, to suggest the *Bulletin*'s subsequent incarnation as the 'bushman's Bible'.

As part of its 'modern' image, the *Bulletin* strove to expose hypocrisy and sham, especially with regard to sexual and other such 'vulgar' matters usually ignored by polite society. This led to a number of prosecutions for libel, most notoriously in 1881 when the proprietors of the Clontarf picnic grounds on Sydney Harbour sued over claims of scandalous orgies there on Boxing Day. Although damages were finally settled at one farthing, Haynes and Archibald both ended up in gaol, unable to meet the court costs. Another journalist, W. H. Traill, took over the *Bulletin* as proprietor and managing editor, though in August 1883 a limited company was formed, with Traill holding a half share and Haynes and Archibald one quarter each. It was Traill who recruited the outstanding cartoonists Livingston Hopkins and Phil May, who were to do so much to change the physical appearance of the *Bulletin*'s pages. Traill also increased its size and doubled its price to 6d; initially circulation fell, but then stabilised around 14 500.

By 1886 both Haynes and Traill had left the *Bulletin*, but before long its management was in the capable hands of William Macleod, who was to remain with the paper until the 1920s. The one constant in all this coming and going, J. F. Archibald, now had a freer hand to take the *Bulletin* down the more nationalistic line he had apparently envisaged from the beginning. During his time as editor, 1886 to

1903, the *Bulletin* was at its most influential, both politically and in terms of its publication of new Australian authors like Henry Lawson, Banjo Paterson and Steele Rudd, some of the first writers to attract a strong readership throughout the country. This was also true of the *Bulletin* itself, as it proclaimed with characteristic pugnacity on 30 August 1890:

> THE BULLETIN's red cover is equally familiar to the bushman of the Far North, the stockman of Central Australia, the pearl-sheller of Torres Straits, and the digger in the New Zealand Ranges. A paper which is at once the most popular city publication and the organ of the intelligent bushman must indeed be broadly based.

While the preferred promotional image of the *Bulletin* was now the lone stockman reading a copy on horseback rather than a train full of *Bulletin*-reading commuters, it is interesting that this paragraph does still acknowledge the city audience without which the journal certainly would not have survived. While much of the literary and pictorial content of the later *Bulletin* was increasingly focused on the bush, its popular social and dramatic columns remained city-based, of course, and the paper was read, and in part written, by women as well as men. The range of *Bulletin* readers by the late 1880s is beautifully conveyed in Charles Conder's well-known painting 'A Holiday at Mentone' (1888), where both the central woman reader and the sleeping man hold copies of a magazine with its very distinctive pinky-red cover. In contents, appearance, number and range of readership, Australian magazines had come a long way since 1821.

NOTE ON SOURCES

This chapter draws on earlier publications by this author: 'Before the *Bulletin*: Nineteenth Century Literary Journalism', in Bruce Bennett, ed., *Cross Currents: Magazines and Newspapers in Australian Literature*, Melbourne, Longman Cheshire, 1981; 'Journals in the Nineteenth Century', in D. H. Borchardt and W. Kirsop, eds, *The Book in Australia*, Melbourne, Australian Reference Publications, 1988; 'Australia', in J. Don Vann and Rosemary T. VanArsdel, eds, *Periodicals of Queen Victoria's Empire*, Toronto, University of Toronto Press, 1996, as well as on her unpublished PhD thesis from the University of Sydney, 'Literature and the Reading Public in Australia, 1800–1850' (1971). Lists of nineteenth-century Australian magazines have been compiled by Lurline Stuart, *Australian Periodicals with Literary Content, 1821–1925: An Annotated Bibliography*, 2nd ed., Melbourne, Australian Scholarly Publishing, 2003; and Alfred Pong, *Checklist of Nineteenth Century Australian Periodicals*, Bundoora, La Trobe University Library, 1985. Further information on the *Bulletin* can be found in R. B. Walker, *The Newspaper Press in New South Wales, 1803–1920*, Sydney, SUP, 1976; and Sylvia Lawson, *The Archibald Paradox*, Melbourne, Allen Lane, 1983. A wide range of magazines is discussed by Lurline Stuart in two papers in the *BSANZ Bulletin*, 'Nineteenth-Century English and American Literary Periodicals and their Australian Counterparts', vol.4, no.3, 1980, pp. 179-90; and 'Colonial Periodicals: Patterns of Failure', vol.13, no.1, 1989, pp. 1-10. A selection of cartoons and other material from *Melbourne Punch* has been reprinted in Suzanne Fabian, ed., *Mr Punch Down Under*, Melbourne, Greenhouse Publications, 1982. Information about nineteenth-century cartoonists can also be found in Marguerite Mahood, *The Loaded Line. Australian Political Caricature 1788–1901*, Melbourne, MUP, 1973. For examples of Mary Fortune's journalism see Lucy Sussex, ed., *The Fortunes of Mary Fortune*, Melbourne, Penguin Books, 1989. Extracts from the *Dawn* can be found in Olive Lawson, ed., *The First Voice of Australian Feminism*, Sydney, Simon & Schuster Australia, 1990. Henry Gyles Turner's accounts of earlier magazines are 'Some Magazines of Early Victoria', 'Some More Victorian Magazines', 'A Final Batch of Victorian Magazines', *Library Record of Australasia*, vol.1, 1901, pp. 49-52, 87-92, 130-35. See also the more recent study by Ken Gelder & Rachael Weaver, *The Colonial Journals and the Emergence of Australian Literary Culture*, Crawley, UWA Publishing, 2014. Mention must also be made of the Colonial Newspapers and Magazines Project (2009–ongoing): https://www.austlit.edu.au/austlit/page/5960612 [accessed 15 February 2024], within the larger AusLit online resource based at the University of Queensland and with teams from UNSW Canberra and the University of Sydney, uncovering new titles and indexing literary and print-culture content in periodicals dating to 1900.

POSTSCRIPT

Alongside the magazines of general interest published in the Australian colonies from the early 1820s onwards, there were, as was remarked earlier, more specialised periodicals directed to distinct and identifiable communities of readers and users. Many of these were produced for and by the various religious bodies. However, the aim of the present note is to draw attention to what was designed for professional, research and academic audiences across such fields as medicine, law, technology and the natural and social sciences. Although the first agricultural and horticultural societies were created in New South Wales in the 1820s, it is hardly surprising that the basis for regular proceedings and transactions had to wait till somewhat later in the century, with the gold-rush expansion of the 1850s as a particular defining moment.

Much interchange in the general scientific area took place in the bodies often known originally as philosophical institutes but eventually redesignated as royal societies. The Government Printer in Hobart published *The Tasmanian Journal of Natural Science, Agriculture, Statistics &c.* from 1842 to 1849. In the latter year it was succeeded by the *Papers and Proceedings of The Royal Society of Van Diemen's Land*. Similar enterprises began in the other colonies in the 1850s and 1860s, thus building up to a substantial corpus of material by the beginning of the 1890s.

Some early initiatives did not have a long life. *The Journal of the Agricultural & Horticultural Society of Western Australia* does not appear to have gone beyond a first volume in 1842. A Sydney *Australian Medical Journal*, the first venture of this kind, was confined to the years 1846 and 1847. On the other hand, *The Australian Medical Journal* launched in Melbourne in 1856 has survived different name changes and amalgamations to be the current *Medical Journal of Australia*.

Although reports of cases were a large part of legal publishing in the colonies, 'journal sections' were not unknown in the relevant titles. Examples are the two volumes — 1870–71 — of Stillwell and Knight's *Australian Jurist and Notes of Cases*, continued by J. and A. McKinley's *Australian Jurist* from 1872 to 1875. More durable was Charles Maxwell's *Australian Law Times* (1879–1927).

Especially as one moves into the 1870s and 1880s examples could be multiplied across a range of sciences and technologies. Societies and government departments were anxious to record their activities and researches, whether it be in entomology or engineering. Banking and insurance were not neglected either as in the *Australasian Insurance and Banking Record* (Melbourne, 1877–86) and the *Journal of the Bankers' Institute of Australasia* published in Melbourne beginning c.1866 and continuing under various titles until 1982.

Beyond the impulse to report on original investigations, to summarise advances made in other countries or to participate in debates current in international arenas, there was one fundamental incentive for the creation of journals in the colonies. Specialists are dependent on access to information, notably that contained in the periodical literature. Despite the collection efforts of major institutions, witness the 1880 printed catalogue of the Public Library of Victoria and the similar production of the University of Sydney in 1892, comprehensive coverage was extremely difficult. If a scientific society, a museum, a university or a government department had a publication to exchange it could hope to augment its resources. The trade was willing to help. It is not an accident that the Maxwell and Baillière dynasties set up in Melbourne in the decades after the gold rushes. However, then as now government allocations were never sufficient to acquire all desiderata, hence the importance of the exchange mechanism. The need to be up to date was paramount, and it is clear in the work of Australian-based scientists and inventors.

The size and complexity of the major Australian cities in the late nineteenth century have already been noted. One consequence of this situation was to provide union lists of specialist journals scattered across many institutions, not all of which were easily accessible to outsiders. The first in the field was T. P. Anderson Stuart's *Catalogue of the Scientific Serial Literature in the following Libraries in Sydney, N.S.W.* [. . .] of 1889. The Public Library of Victoria followed suit in 1899, with a second and more comprehensive edition in 1911: T. S. Hall, with E. R. Pitt, *Catalogue of the Natural Science & Technical Periodicals in the Libraries in Melbourne*. In some ways these compilations can be seen as a sign of the coming of age of the publishing industry and of the scientific society of colonial Australia.

W. K.

CHAPTER 13

Bookselling

Wallace Kirsop

Distribution sometimes looks like the stepchild of book history as it has been practised in recent decades. Although publishers are well aware, as their authors should also be, of the fact that getting books into the hands of buyers and readers is essential to the health and survival of the trade, the subject is often treated perfunctorily, usually because the relevant archival documentation has not been preserved. The odd 'character' or flamboyant self-publicist may attract attention, but the details of discounts, terms of trade, balance sheets and all the other elements that belong to economic history are skated over or missing. Attempts to understand the colonial Australian trade are especially hampered by these difficulties. Printed catalogues, advertisements, photographs or engravings of premises and people, obituaries, directories, records in the public domain, all of these can be used, even if they are silent about questions of profit and loss. Despite the problems it is necessary to try to grasp how booksellers brought their wares, for the most part imported, but also locally produced, to customers scattered across the continent's cities, towns and country districts. Unlike later times when oral historians went out in search of testimonies from veteran trade members, the nineteenth century rarely lets us read the words of the participants. Yet the story to be told is critical to understanding how successfully books were sold to an immigrant European population and to later generations that in their majority enjoyed greater literacy.

The three phases of colonial bookselling before 1890

One of the apparent paradoxes of the Australian scene almost from the beginning of European settlement in 1788 is that printing and rudimentary publishing preceded the development of bookshops and trade networks. Thus an unavoidably rough-and-ready chronology elaborated to explain what happened during the whole of the first century is best adapted to the various stages of distribution. Before the 1820s there was personal initiative of various kinds, missionary activity, government printing and the first auction marts, but no organised trade as such. Then, until the 1850s and the gold rushes, booksellers began to appear alongside the colonies' earliest cultural institutions, even though the market was occasionally flooded with more or less unsolicited consignments from specialised London houses. From the later 1850s to the 1890s, an era of free trade, the immigrant population expanded dramatically. This was accompanied by the establishment of wholesale businesses that directed material from overseas to Australian shops and retail customers in an orderly way. This period was also marked by the emergence of diversification and specialisation. During the 1870s and 1880s, British firms began to establish Australian branches and agencies. The 1890s saw tighter and tighter control by British publishers leading at the end of the decade to the Net Book Agreement, the instrument of resale price maintenance for a century to come. It will be obvious, too, that the chronology in its entirety applies only to New South Wales (in its present borders) and Tasmania. Western Australia, Victoria, South Australia and Queensland make their appearance in the second phase, in the 1820s, 1830s and 1840s.

Beginnings: improvisation

As could be expected, the first Europeans to arrive in New South Wales in 1788 brought books with them. Given that several of the officers and officials on board the First Fleet ships would later publish substantial accounts of their experiences, it is obvious that literary and scientific culture was a central part of the background to the venture on which they were engaged. At the time of the 1988 Bicentenary Colin Steele and Michael Richards set out an account of then identified surviving volumes from the voyage as well as of references to reading in correspondence and diaries. Apart from material brought by Richard Johnson, the first chaplain, for the edification of convicts and of Indigenous Australians, the total of practical and recreational works is quite meagre. Short of inventories of people's possessions it is impossible to be sure how much these ships and their successors in the 1790s brought with them. When Nicolas Baudin's French expedition spent a few months at Port Jackson in 1802, the commander's cabin on *Le Géographe* held an impressively large collection of general reference works that were listed and now have been identified (Fornasiero and West-Sooby, 215-49). Baudin's private treasure, which was rather resented by other members of the expedition, was in addition to the professional scientific collection on board. This curious revelation of quite extraordinary holdings that simply passed through colonial Sydney is a caution against assuming that privileged individuals could not bring whole libraries with them on the tiny cramped vessels of the time.

Private initiatives were to remain the principal source of the printed matter that reached the penal colony until after the Napoleonic Wars. Our knowledge of what was owned is unavoidably sketchy and usually anecdotal. Once the *Sydney Gazette* began to appear in 1803 there were occasional plaintive advertisements for the return of borrowed books. Similarly the *Hobart Town Gazette* of 6 and 13 July 1816 carried the notice:

> MISLAID, — One Volume of "HARRIS's MINOR ENCYCLOPEDIA." — Whoever may be pleased to return the same to MR. WALTER COLQUHOUN, Macquarie-street, will be rewarded.

The reference seems to be to John Harris's *Lexicon Technicum*, a work that went through at least five editions in the first half of the eighteenth century. Its absence from the late nineteenth-century printed catalogues of some of Australia's major libraries underlines the role private collections played in bringing significant material to the colonies.

Although concrete documentation is mostly missing, it is reasonable to assume that some settlers sought the help of family and friends back in Britain to obtain books. They could also deal with London, Edinburgh and Dublin booksellers. In all cases one has to allow for the several months required for travel in both directions. By 1818 Elizabeth Macarthur could write that 'we receive most of the new publications from England' (Scott Tucker, 247). In other words, those in privileged positions had managed to triumph over difficulties that were undoubtedly greater in the earliest years of the settlement. Ultimately evidence of what reached Sydney or Hobart must be derived from local Australian sources.

The aspect of importation that is perhaps best recorded is the provision of morally and spiritually improving literature for transported prisoners and for the original inhabitants now dispossessed of their lands by the new arrivals. The target audience for this material was not always receptive. At least one convict's prayer book ended up in the ocean, and was later found intact in the belly of a shark (Lt Ralph Clark's journal, 1 May 1792). We have figures for what Richard Johnson brought with him: 100 Bibles, 400 New Testaments, 100 prayer books, 200 catechisms, numerous tracts, spelling books and 12 copies of 'Bishop Thomas Wilson's *An Essay Towards an Instruction for the Indians*' (Steele & Richards, 3-4). The Auxiliary Bible Society of New South Wales, a branch of the British and Foreign Bible Society, was established in Sydney in 1817. Johnson's original suppliers, the Society for Promoting Christian Knowledge, followed in 1826. These early efforts were to be the forerunners of the major role religious publishing and bookselling played in the Australian colonies throughout the nineteenth century and beyond.

The best guide to what was being offered in the colonial market up to 1820 is to be found in the early newspapers, exclusively in this period the *Sydney Gazette* from 1803 and the *Hobart Town Gazette* from 1816. Elizabeth Webby's invaluable checklists of booksellers' and auctioneers' catalogues and advertisements from 1800 to 1849 have to be the starting point for detailed research on phases one and two of Australian book distribution.

Before there were bookshops in any meaningful sense there were auction marts. The first sale is recorded in 1805 in Sydney, and Hobart followed in 1818. Although the beginnings were modest, because most locally formed collections were not dispersed before the 1820s and in some cases remained intact in families for several generations, it has to be understood that auctions were the preferred method for disposing of deceased and bankrupt estates and for shedding the property of people returning to the Northern Hemisphere. A newspaper advertisement sufficed at a time before catalogues were printed. Very occasionally there might be in addition a brief editorial report. Some owners were not identified: 'Gentleman departed the Colony', *Sydney Gazette*, 4 May 1806; 'Gentleman leaving the Colony', *Sydney Gazette*, 11 January 1807. Other Sydney sales name the owners: William Cox, 13 January 1805; William Tough, 10 March 1805; Captain William Kent, 7 April 1805; James Larra, 15 September 1805; Captain David Dalrymple, 11 December 1808; William Blake, 14 May 1809; Ellis Bent, 21 October 1815 and 14 December 1816; Alexander Riley, 27 December 1817. Several of the names were not insignificant on the local scene. Almost invariably the Sydney auctioneers were Simeon Lord and David Bevan. Where the quantities sold were indicated, the figures shown are mostly not large. The highest quantity by far was '300-400' — that of the unknown Gentleman's collection — on 11 January 1807.

Three sales were all that were recorded for Hobart in the relevant period. One, advertised on 31 January 1818, concerned the 'Estate of the late WALTER LANG, Esq' and included amongst objects of all kinds 'A collection of books'. On 14 February the same auctioneer, Lewis, offered an unsourced mixture of goods that contained 'a great variety of choice books'. This may have been from one owner, but Lewis had advertised on 7 February a long list of articles, 'the Remains of several Consignments' with 'Lead Pencils' and 'Europe Letter Paper', but no books unless they came under the heading of 'a number of other articles too numerous to mention'. It is legitimate to suspect that such consignments, possibly speculative, were from overseas, an important part of the auction scene throughout the century. The third sale to mention books specifically was announced on 18 September 1819 by the Provost Marshal. In the action 'Sir John Jamison, Knt. *v.* Gordon, Esq.' one finds in the catalogue of goods 'a fine Edition of Burn's Justice, and 90 other Volumes on different Subjects'.

Outside the auction room, pickings for bibliophiles were even slimmer. Bookselling was quite incidental to other pursuits. The most frequent advertisers in Sydney were the *Sydney Gazette* office itself, Sarah Wills (wife of George Howe, proprietor of the *Gazette*), and Charles Tompson senior, emancipist shopkeeper and father of the poet (Charles junior's *Wild Notes from the Lyre of a Native Minstrel* was published by George Howe's son Robert in 1826). The largest quantity reported in Sydney was 167 volumes (Loane and Hall, *Sydney Gazette*, 23 September 1815). The *Hobart Town Gazette* occasionally advertised books for sale, including a set of A. F. M. Willich's *The Domestic Encyclopaedia: or a Dictionary of Facts and Useful Knowledge* (London, 1802, 4 volumes 8º) at the London price, 'The most useful book every printed' (27 July 1816), and 'A few ALMANACKS, containing 89 pages, for the present Year ... Price 6s.3d.' (31 January 1818). In March 1818 William Jemott, ex-convict turned trader and debt collector, advertised 'at considerably Reduced Prices, for Cash or Credit upon approved Security' an array of goods that included, amongst wine and spirits, farm equipment, firearms, stationery, clothing, spices and other household goods, 'a Variety of English Prints' and 'a quantity of Books' (*Hobart Town Gazette*, 28 March 1818).

Doubtless there were other transactions at the time, for example by general merchants and street traders, that escaped any sort of advertisement or public notice. None the less, it hardly needs to be stressed how rudimentary bookselling was in the colonies' first three decades.

Fitful progress towards a semblance of order

The period after the Napoleonic Wars saw a marked extension of the British presence in the Australian continent with settlements begun in Western Australia, Victoria, South Australia and Queensland, to use the modern designations for these territories. The consequences were multiple on the economic, social and political planes, but in a less obvious way they shaped the manner printed matter was produced and distributed. More numerous free settlers, the cessation of convict transportation to Eastern Australia (New South Wales 1840, Tasmania 1853), the recruitment — not just in Britain — of assisted immigrants to bolster the growing agricultural and pastoral industries, the dissident German Lutheran influx into South Australia, these were some of the factors that complicated the social and cultural scene. Remembering that the convict populations reflected the London melting-pot of the turn of the nineteenth century with, amongst others, enslaved Africans and Jewish exiles from Eastern Europe, and that the non-English-speaking peoples of the British Isles — Welsh, Irish and Scottish in particular — were very much in evidence, it is quite understandable that there was a discreet foreshadowing of the country's multicultural future. Public, religious and proprietorial institutions — museums, libraries of various kinds, churches, schools, scientific societies, even the first universities, clubs — provided a serious underpinning for the life of the mind and of the spirit. How were they to be supplied with reading matter? One grasps immediately that the authorities and private citizens were faced with a greater range of problems than in the earliest phase. Distance from the Northern Hemisphere and within the continent remained as tyrannical as ever. It was perhaps inevitable that the solutions sought and the resources available did not quite meet the colonists' needs.

Three aspects have to be explored: links with metropolitan suppliers, especially in the British Isles; the continuing and growing strength of the local auction market; the emergence of booksellers in colonial towns. Once again Webby's checklist has to be the basis of research, but there are enough printed catalogues and scattered business records to provide some precision and depth.

Given the absence of a trade on the spot apart from locally produced newspapers, it was to be expected that people and their newly created institutions in the 1820s would develop connections with businesses in the 'Old World'. Many of these are now undocumented, but there are enough survivals to suggest how things worked and how some booksellers in Britain came to understand that supplying 'colonials' was a useful and potentially lucrative specialism.

The minute books of the Bothwell Literary Society, founded in the Tasmanian Midlands in 1834, regularly record the titles of works ordered from an unnamed source in London and eventually received after long and inevitable delays. Even the local supply chain posed problems, since the Secretary noted in November 1846 that four volumes 'were carried away by the thieves who stole the case off the carriers Cart at Bagdad [Van Diemen's Land]'.

The Australian Subscription Library in Sydney sent its first order for books to the Colonial Agent in London in April 1826. In late 1831 Richardsons, of Cornhill, a firm founded in the eighteenth century, became the Library's agents. The stock was enriched, as often happened in these institutions at this period, by gifts and legacies from members.

Two libraries in Northern Tasmania — the Evandale Subscription Library, established in 1847, and the Launceston Library Society, which existed from 1845 to 1856 — used the services of Orger and Meryon, London booksellers who sought the custom of colonial institutions and individuals. The latter included the Tasmanian botanist Ronald Campbell Gunn. A small amount of publishing was done by the firm for Tasmanian authors at this time also. Yet our knowledge of this enterprise relies almost entirely on colonial sources including advertisements in the local press (Adkins, 9-16).

At mid-century the four major libraries of the newly separated colony of Victoria — the Parliament, the Supreme Court, the University and the Public Library — were persuaded to give their business to a London supplier, the Guillaume family. The sticker of the son, F. A. Guillaume, described him as 'Colonial Bookseller, Chester Square, London. Books delivered free in Melbourne, at London prices' (image in Reynolds, after p. 54). The style adopted underlines the fact that there were new markets beyond the seas. The promise on prices is at the heart of an ongoing struggle by colonial customers to acquire books at reasonable rates, and, if possible, cheaply. The Guillaumes had the disadvantage of being relatively minor figures in the English book trade, and by the mid-1860s it was clear that they were unequal to the complexities of supplying four connected but subtly different colonial institutions (Reynolds, 44-51, 64-7; Overell, 33-63; Gregory, 5).

All through the 1820s, 1830s, 1840s, and even beyond, auctions were a major opportunity for Australians to buy new and old books. On the one hand these were offerings of what was already in colonial towns and had been there for some time. On the other there were new arrivals sent essentially from the British Isles to tempt bookbuyers deemed to be deprived of adequate material in their remote outposts. These two categories must be treated separately.

During the 1820s and 1830s the number of auctions increased considerably, especially in Sydney. Beyond Hobart, other locations began to appear: Parramatta, Launceston, Perth, Adelaide and Melbourne. In some cases there were many more lots advertised than before; and for Sydney from 1828 one finds printed catalogues. Auctioneers were more numerous in the older centres, but their cataloguing was usually done in a summary and slapdash fashion that can make identifications difficult.

The three known catalogued collections up to 1830 were those of Henry Grattan Douglass (21 April and following days 1828), John Oxley (27, 28 and 29 August 1828) and Robert Howe (5 August 1830). The latter two had been formed in part in New South Wales in the early phase. Along with several other private libraries belonging to named notable citizens or to anonymous gentlemen and one 'Lady leaving the Colony' (Ferguson 1669a — sale on 25 and 26 November 1833) the works proposed added substantially to what could be acquired locally.

In the 1840s the quantities increased again, although catalogues were rare outside Sydney. Bathurst, Goulburn, Geelong, Portland, Port Fairy and Brisbane have to be added to the places where auctions were held. The most notable private libraries were those of Alexander McLeay (Ferguson 4232 — 1, 2, 3, 4 April 1845 — 4000 volumes) and John Dunmore Lang (Ferguson 4233 — 13, 14, 15 May 1846 — 2064 volumes), but there was much else to tempt buyers. In this period eighteenth-century imprints can hardly be rated as antiquarian, but there was a depth that was rarely encountered previously.

Another feature of what was drawn from local sources was bankrupt or abandoned stock of institutional and circulating libraries or of booksellers. Two early sales in Perth were of books from the Western Australian Institution (18 June 1833) and of discards from the Western Australian Book Society (22 September 1839). On 24 and 25 January 1831 Douglass sold in Sydney the stock of the bookseller, auctioneer and circulating-library proprietor J. Brennand who was 'returning to the Derwent'. On 19 April 1831 Brennand himself began the auction of the stock of his bookshop in Hobart. An amusing account of the tail-end of this sale appears in the diary of the public servant G. T. W. B. Boyes for 2 May 1831. Lithographs, misdescribed as copperplate engravings, of 'helligant butterflies' (Boyes, 428) were cried up by the vulgarian auctioneer. The whole episode is a reminder of the mobility of trade personnel in this period.

Later auctions of commercial holdings included the 'Circulating Library of Mrs John Solomon' (Sydney, 15 December 1840 — 700 volumes), 'Stock of a circulating library' (Melbourne, 27 July 1841 — 500 volumes), 'Stock in Trade of Shakespeare-Tavern' (Adelaide, 22 January 1844 — 1000 volumes), 'Stock of Mr W. Jones, Bookseller' (Sydney, 10 March 1845 — 4000 volumes), 'Remainder of Mr J. B. Edmonds' Valuable Stock' (Sydney, 12 and 13 September 1845 — 2000 volumes), 'Stock of Mr Charles Magee, Bookseller & Stationer' (Ferguson 4234 & 4235 — Sydney, 23, 24 & 25 July 1846 — 7105 volumes), 'Stock-in-trade of a Hobart Town Bookseller' (Sydney, 4 September 1846 — 700 volumes), 'Stock of Mr William Baker's Library' (Sydney, 19 February 1847 — 800 volumes), and 'Stock of U. B. Barfoot, Stationer' (Hobart, 1 March 1848 — 700 volumes), and 'Stock of Mr George Robinson, proceeding to the Mauritius' (Launceston, 23 March 1849 — 500 volumes). It will be noticed that collections could be sent from outlying places to the then centre of the auction trade — Sydney — and that the profession of bookseller and circulating-library proprietor was as uncertain in the first half of the nineteenth century as it would prove to be later.

What changed markedly after 1820 in colonial auctions was the amount of material sent directly from the British Isles. The consigners were not always named. John Blackman's sales in June and December 1836, the first of which was claimed to be 'about three thousand volumes' (Ferguson 2093b & 2093c), were possibly submitted by several owners. Those that are named at various times later: Henry G. Bohn; Constable & Co.; James Duffy; Fisher, Son & Co.; Longman, Rees & Co.; Edward Lumley; Murray, Baldwin & Cradock (Webby 1979, 150) show that the practice was becoming increasingly common in the British trade in the 1840s. London was not the only source even if it dominated. For some anonymous sales in Sydney in 1842 (3 September, 23 October, 7 December) large quantities — 5000 volumes, 10 000 volumes, 10 000 volumes — are advertised. One is forced to wonder how far private persons as opposed to trade personnel were successful bidders.

The rationale of speculative consignments is clear in a passage from the 1904 reminiscences of the veteran London publisher Edward Marston:

> I soon discovered that books were wanted in these Colonies, so I made a practice of going round among the publishers to whom I was already so well-known, and I selected, monthly, such books as I deemed suitable for these markets. I made them up into cases of the value of about £30 each, which I consigned to my correspondents in Sydney, Melbourne, and Adelaide.
>
> These little shipments invariably sold well, and paid me a very fair profit. (Marston, 51)

Opportunism played an important part in these efforts to serve a public that was inadequately provided with regular retail outlets. What a London trader thought 'suitable' may have coincided — happily — with the many remainders being disposed of by his colleagues at reduced prices. It has to be said, alas, that the English were rarely guilty of overestimating Australian taste, sophistication and intelligence. None the less it is important to see the British exports to the colonies as more than mere dumping. A full history of remainders, and indeed of optimistic over-production of books, has still to be written. The consignment trade was a consequence and a symptom of stresses in metropolitan publishing.

Edward Lumley (1806?–1874), who was the most inventive and dedicated of all the consigners, did not neglect the Australian market, although his invoices, variously to Adelaide, Sydney, Launceston, Port Fairy and Melbourne, were confined within the years 1844 to 1862. His North American ventures, to the United States and Canada, continued to 1871. The London bookseller's usual practice was to send to his agents and correspondents not only the cases of books and prints for sale, but also catalogues he prepared and had printed in England. These were much more accurate and informative than the crude lists done by colonial auctioneers, and they even extended to details of provenance. Lumley certainly dealt in remainders — sometimes superior ones like William Hunter's *The Anatomy of the Human Gravid Uterus* and Matthew Flinders's *A Voyage to Terra Australis* — but he also offered the people who attended his auctions interesting second-hand and antiquarian volumes and sets. In this way he enriched in the longer term the collections the colonists would pass on to their descendants.

As noted in the earlier chapter on 'Newspapers', not all aspects of supply from abroad were so haphazard. The demand for newspapers and magazines from 'Home' ensured that regular provision was organised. This presupposed that there were channels of distribution other than auction sales. The same was true of the one series launched in this intermediate period to cater specifically for colonial readers and buyers. John Murray III began his 'Colonial and Home Library' in the latter part of 1843. By mid-1844 it had been renamed the 'Home and Colonial Library' in recognition of the fact that the initiative had not had the desired impact on the book market in British North America, in particular Canada. Competition from cheap American reprints remained too strong and was in any case inadequately policed. In this sphere the move to cheaper and more affordable books from Britain did not go far enough.

On the other hand there is evidence of more success in Australia, where the claimed extent of illegal American competition after 1842 has never been thoroughly documented. Murray's collection was entirely of non-fiction, so it is hardly surprising that the cheap fiction series that were beginning to be published in Britain were more attractive to many readers. Murray's last title was issued in 1849, thus ending the experiment even if certain volumes continued to be reprinted for many years thereafter. The episode was an important but flawed step along the way to providing better services for colonial readers (Fraser, 339-408; Johanson, 211-53). Insofar as it worked it depended on the presence of genuine booksellers in major Australian centres by the 1840s.

The booksellers' advertisements listed by Webby are the most comprehensive guide to the people offering books for sale in the Australian colonies between 1821 and 1849. Her analyses decade by decade of the authors mentioned give the best account of what was proposed to readers. There are few shop catalogues extant for the whole period, and even fewer archival documents to back them up. Despite this one can see an organised trade beginning to take shape.

It was long believed that the first full-time bookseller was William McGarvie in Sydney. A brother of John McGarvie, who had joined

John Dunmore Lang as a Presbyterian minister in New South Wales in 1826, William was briefly a journalist in Glasgow. He arrived in Sydney in 1828 and went to work for the 'Australian Stationery Warehouse', associated with the Howes' *Sydney Gazette*. Two of the Warehouse's advertisements of books appeared in the *Sydney Gazette* in 1823 (9 and 16 October), so it is clear that McGarvie was joining a going concern. After a brief diversion as one of the founders of the *Sydney Herald* in 1831 and a voyage to Scotland, McGarvie returned to the Warehouse, before turning his attention to a land grant at Port Macquarie in 1835. Catalogues and various press advertisements between 1829 and 1835 are the chief documentary records of his bookselling activities. The last, in the *Colonist* of 1 January 1835, offered for sale the 1800 volumes of McGarvie's circulating library, a common accompaniment to a bookshop.

There is a counterclaim against McGarvie's priority. The musician John Philip Deane, who was in Hobart between 1822 and 1836, not only exercised his profession, but also ran a general store, which sold books on the side, with one advertisement appearing in 1823. Four years later Deane opened a dedicated bookshop with his wife, Rosalie (née Paine), whose particular responsibility was the Hobart Town Circulating Library. Their advertisements were published from 1827 to 1835. The failure of the business in that last year drove the Deanes to Sydney, where music occupied all their time.

In these early ventures till the middle of the 1830s there is a certain pattern. Businesses were often short-lived and their owners moved easily from one colony to another. Bookselling was often coupled with other pursuits. The celebrated surveyor George William Evans was, for example, active as a bookseller and stationer in Sydney from the early 1830s. Alongside the newspaper offices in various places one also finds Dowling in Launceston, and both there and in Melbourne John Pascoe Fawkner.

A more durable career in the trade was that of the emancipist William Moffitt, originally trained as a bookbinder in Liverpool, England. Although engraving, copperplate printing and stationery were the staples of his shop, he sold and advertised books through the 1830s and on into the 1840s. The firm was acquired much later by W. C. Penfold & Co, a major player in printing and stationery in twentieth-century Sydney.

Another recruit to Sydney bookselling in this pre-1850 phase was Jeremiah John Moore, a cobbler who arrived from Ireland in late 1840. From a bookstall selling stock from recently disembarked immigrants outside what was to become St Andrew's Cathedral, he eventually graduated to a substantial building on the opposite side of the street. He also developed connections with both Brisbane and Melbourne. As Kevin Molloy has shown, Moore was the principal figure in the Irish and Catholic trade that achieved substantial importance in and after the middle of the century. It was to be expected that there was a sectarian and denominational bias in Australian colonial bookselling, publishing and newspaper production up to Federation and beyond.

The Catholic convert William Augustine Duncan, a bookseller in Aberdeen before his emigration in 1837, sold books alongside his involvement in newspapers in Sydney in the first half of the 1840s. After his posting to a public service office in Moreton Bay in 1846 and his eventual return to Sydney, he distinguished himself more by promoting libraries and by writing based in part on a notable private collection. His compatriot John Carfrae, previously a bookseller in Edinburgh, arrived in Port Phillip late in 1841 to start in business as a commission agent. Initially he dealt in book consignments, but later, in Melbourne and after a move to Sydney in 1843, he was essentially an auctioneer.

Some other centres had a mixture of booksellers with a long commitment to the profession or people who engaged in the trade as a convenient adjunct to other work. Charles Platts, active in Adelaide for three decades from 1840, was an example of the former category. The journalist and inventor James Harrison sold books from the *Geelong Advertiser* office through the 1840s. This is one more reminder of the central position of newspapers in the colonies throughout the century.

The arrival of two sons of Thomas Tegg of Cheapside — James and Samuel Augustus — at the end of 1834 brought a new dimension to the trade in Sydney and, shortly thereafter, in Tasmania. As part of a family dynasty the Teggs were able, through their transnational networks, to improve supplies to the colonial market. There were many newspaper advertisements and at least three catalogues for the Sydney shop. It is therefore possible to define more precisely the character of the stock being offered to customers. There are no known business archives, but a surviving letter to a 'Mr Armstrong' from 1839 (Hubber, 57-62) gives a glimpse of James Tegg's way of doing business. Thomas Tegg specialised in remainders and cheap imprints, no doubt considered appropriate for Australian settlers, so his sons could hardly be expected to be operating at a high level of sophistication. In a way this is borne out by the negative remarks Charles Darwin recorded in his private diary about 'the emptiness' of 'inferior' Sydney bookshops when he visited with the *Beagle* in January 1836.

The Sydney shop was ceded to W. A. Colman in 1844, the year before James Tegg's death. W. R. Piddington, later a prominent politician, joined the firm in the same decade and eventually assumed sole control of it. In 1860 he was to sell copies of the 'fifth thousand' of Darwin's *On the Origin of Species* to what had become a more demanding public.

S. A. Tegg abandoned his Hobart business to Major James Walch at the beginning of 1846. Walch and his sons built up a concern that covered a great range of specialties relating to books, printing, stationery and artists' supplies. Their enterprise lasted till the beginning of the twenty-first century and, most significant, preserved a substantial part of its records. These include the invaluable borrowing register of the circulating library taken over from Tegg and maintained till the early 1850s as well as a day book of credit purchases from the shop from 1 July 1846 to 7 May 1847. The latter illustrates the nature of the sort of bookselling the Walches inherited from Tegg. It resembles what was happening in provincial England in the eighteenth century. Indeed, it can be argued that cultural life in the Australian colonies up to the gold rushes of the 1850s was a prolonged 'long eighteenth century' with characteristics that were not to disappear until the upheavals and the consolidation of the 1850s, 1860s and 1870s. What the Walches were selling, in line with the English provincial tradition, included books, periodicals, stationery, fancy goods, music, prints and patent medicines. Books represented barely a quarter of the monthly totals and stationery almost half. Local publications, apart from one or two political pamphlets, were rare. The fiction of the moment was Dickens's *Dombey and Son*, whose parts sometimes arrived out of order. The almost 400 listed customers had, like the shop's owners, to cope with all the vagaries of slow and long-delayed supplies. This was, in sum, the image of a trade struggling with its situation at the other side of the world.

Charles Platts's book and stationery shop, Hindley & King William Streets, Adelaide, *c.* 1866. London-born Platts (1813–1871) began selling sheet music soon after arriving in Adelaide with his family in 1839. He established South Australia's first bookshop and over the years also sold stationery and musical instruments and offered a bookbinding service. In 1845 he moved to the above-named location which became known as 'Platts's Corner'. He was a key cultural figure in Adelaide: an accomplished organist, pianist, performer and teacher, he also lectured on music, operated a circulating library and donated annual prizes to the Society of Arts. Upon his death the shop was taken over by E. S. Wigg. Photographer unknown. (State Library of South Australia)

Free Trade and virtual independence

Book distribution problems did not vanish overnight when the immigrant population ballooned during the gold rushes. On the contrary they became more acute in some ways. Speculative consignments of all sorts of goods, including books, increased so that, depending on the timing of the arrival of ships, there was an alternation of glut and dearth. A spike in the figures for British book exports to Australia in the mid-1850s reflects this situation with the various colonies receiving almost as much as the United States. It was not till the mid-1870s that Australia emerged consistently as the major export destination of British publications. Several other factors were in play by then: a massive increase in population (still very small by comparison with the United States and, of course, the British Isles); the introduction of universal primary education from the 1870s; the opening of the Suez Canal in 1869 and the consequent speeding-up of communications by mail steamer; the telegraphic link with Europe from 1872; the re-organisation of the colonial trade under the control of local wholesalers with London buying offices. It is this last aspect that has to be explored in describing the third phase. What needs to be recalled, however, is the quite extraordinary urbanisation of Australia compared with a more populous Canada. In round figures Melbourne had 491 000 inhabitants in 1891, and 494 000 in 1901. Sydney had 383 000 in 1891, and 488 000 in 1901, the substantial increase being explained by the great crash of the 1890s in the southern city. By contrast Toronto had 208 000 inhabitants in 1901 (rising from 181 000 in 1891) and Montreal 267 000. The very dimensions of the Australian cities must suggest that there was a complex book market running from the popular to the intellectually and culturally elitist.

Even an unavoidably schematic account of what happened between 1851 and 1890 encounters problems of access to sources. In theory something like Webby's index to newspapers for the earlier periods could be constructed from Trove, but the constant reprinting of advertisements, not to mention the great expansion of the press from the capital cities to country towns, has so far deterred any systematic effort. Some researchers have pursued mentions of individual trade members, at times forgetting that other documents are to be found outside Trove. A card file at Monash University lists auctions at which books were offered between 1861 and 1870 based on the Melbourne *Argus* and the *Sydney Morning Herald*. The records of firms relating to bookselling as opposed to publishing are regrettably scarce. The best resource lies in the printed lists and catalogues issued in quantity by booksellers thanks to cheaper postage charges, but it has to be admitted that these ephemeral productions have often not survived.

Auctions continued to be an essential part of the bookselling scene. After the 1850s speculative consignments from London appeared less frequently, but there is a rare preserved catalogue of such an offering by Chatto and Hughes in Sydney on 20 November 1862 (10 000 volumes — Mitchell Library 018.3c). The New South Wales capital was to see other ventures of this type throughout the decade. Much later — in the 1880s and 1890s — Bernard Quaritch tried a variant on the same formula to dispose of unwanted stock from his antiquarian business. Until we have a complete listing of auctions for the period beyond 1850 it is impossible to state whether British consignments went more frequently and later to other colonial centres away from Melbourne.

The Melbourne and Sydney sample for the 1860s is extensive enough to allow tentative conclusions about what was happening once local wholesaling arrangements were in place. Some 591 sales in Melbourne for the decade yielded, according to the newspaper advertisements, 202 printed catalogues. For Sydney the relevant figures are 977 sales and 137 catalogues. Sad to say, most of the more or less summary lists cannot now be discovered. The loss to bibliography and book history as elements of a cultural and intellectual map of Australia is huge. Without doubt the picture will be the same for the whole of the half-century.

Private and institutional/commercial collections — defunct mechanics' institutes and circulating libraries, booksellers' stock — continued to be sold off. The former category, including the large accumulations of doctors, lawyers, clergy and journalists, served to nourish a growing demand for second-hand and even antiquarian books. Simple advertisements have tantalisingly few details in many cases. More frustrating are the notices that indicate that printed catalogues — now lost — were available. Over three days in May 1861 the collection of Sir Charles Nicholson — some 6000 volumes — was dispersed. The books had been brought from Sydney for auction in Melbourne, a clear indication of the primacy of the rapidly expanding city in the south. No catalogue is known to have survived. The advertisement mentions a Second Folio Shakespeare, and the extensive purchases by Melbourne institutions — the Public Library, the Parliament and the Supreme Court — are documented.

Much, however, went to private buyers and still surfaces from time to time. Two decades later the catalogue of the sale of Sir Redmond Barry's books in March 1881 met with the same fate. Items occasionally appear in the stock of twenty-first-century booksellers, but this is no real substitute for an overall picture of the interests of a major promoter of Australia's book world. Other such losses could be noted, but what is important is that the books themselves were bought and continued to circulate.

Attention has to be paid to the auction market in other colonial centres and even to what could appear in country towns. As part of a successful attempt to save Terence Murray from bankruptcy, and thus to preserve his parliamentary seat, most of his books were sold at auction in Goulburn in 1865 — 580 lots, and many more volumes. A unique copy of the printed catalogue was to go eventually from the collection of his son Gilbert to the National Library of Australia. Its publication in facsimile is one of a number of efforts in recent times to reveal this facet of the nineteenth-century colonial trade by reproducing documents *in toto*.

The new element in the auctions of the third phase was the appearance alongside the waning speculative consignments from Britain of the trade catalogues of local wholesalers. In the Melbourne of the 1860s this meant George Robertson, one of three future major figures in the Australian trade to arrive in the colony on 12 November 1852. The other two were Samuel Mullen, also Dublin-trained, and E. W. Cole, who moved more or less by accident into bookselling in 1865. Robertson had already had his own shop in Dublin and was looking for greater opportunities in the rapidly expanding and now separate Victoria. He plunged straight into selling, but soon encountered the frustrations of unpredictable supplies. The freeing of the British trade from resale price maintenance by Lord Campbell's determination of 1852 provided precisely the opening that was needed to put colonial bookselling on a sound and attractive footing. By the end of the 1850s Robertson and the Walches had opened buying offices in London and were obtaining stock at favourable prices by paying cash to the English publishers. In addition they were choosing titles for a market they knew, rather than shopping around for remainders. One of the ways this material was offered to small retail booksellers in Melbourne and in country towns was through auctions reserved for the trade. In the 1860s the *Argus* carried advertisements for Robertson trade sales, stated to be accompanied by catalogues, on eighteen occasions between 19 March 1862 and December 1870. The highest number of volumes claimed was 50 000 for a three-day sale on 20, 21 and 22 October 1868.

Unfortunately only one of the trade-sale catalogues seems to have survived. The collection of Edward Augustus Petherick, Robertson's London manager from the early 1870s to 1887, holds the 19 March 1862 list of 30 000 volumes. There were 36 pages and 1638 lots. Single titles were typically scattered over several lots in smaller parcels. For example, 'Bonwick's Geography of Australia and New Zealand' was offered in five lots (25-29), each with 20 copies. Less sought-after items like 'Schleiermacher's Autobiography, 2 vols' appeared in two lots (265-266) with one set in each. Quite obviously, the needs of individual retail booksellers and of their customers had been considered in this division of what had been shipped. Calculations of saleability are in evidence throughout. There are many 'Cheap Novels', children's books, practical manuals, textbooks, religious texts (a total of 750 copies of 'Catholic Piety, 32mo' in various bindings over 12 lots (1467-1478), 'Mackenzie's Phrenology, 18mo, sewed' (200 copies in four lots, 1143-1146) as well as works of a more demanding character like 'Vestiges of the Natural History of Creation' (26 copies over 4 lots, 869-872), 'Macaulay's Miscellaneous Writings, 2 vols., 8vo.' (six sets over three lots, 887–889) and 'Guizot's Corneille and His Times' (two copies in one lot, 530). In what could seem a rather higgledy-piggledy mixture we are given a map of the tastes and inclinations of Robertson's clientele.

Moving outside the auction mart we can trace through a multitude of Robertson publications and newspaper advertisements how his wholesale and retail business was conceived. This is all the more necessary since there are no surviving business records. John Holroyd's valuable monograph of 1968 should be revised and extended, but the search will have to go well beyond Trove into all sorts of public archives, for example of bills of sale, because Robertson, like the binder William Detmold, did much to support minor members of the trade. Historians owe this labour to the dominant figure of the whole Australian book scene between 1852 and 1890, when he retired and the role of leader was assumed by the other George Robertson, of Angus & Robertson, in Sydney.

Although a respectable quantity of Robertson material is preserved at State Library Victoria, the largest, but still incomplete collection is in what went from Petherick to the National Library of Australia. A tabular account of the staggering amount produced can be found in Marie Cullen's PhD thesis on Petherick's career to 1887 (Cullen, 316-20). The essential division is between what was reserved for the trade and what was issued to retail customers. For the former there were 15 separate editions of a *Catalogue of Books Offered to the Trade* from 1859 to 1891, 1297 numbers of *George Robertson's Books & Stationery List* from July 1860 to December 1897, 86 numbers of *George Robertson's Trade List of Goods to Arrive* between December 1872 and October 1879, various other clearance and discount lists and the trade-sale catalogues. At the last-named, buyers paid the hammer price, whereas the trade catalogues and lists indicated the English published price and the varying discounts — up to 25 per cent — allowed. For retail purposes there were 16 editions of a *Select Catalogue of Books* from 1859 to 1891 corresponding to what was being proposed to the trade, many shorter catalogues covering separate subjects, Christmas and discounts and *George Robertson's Monthly Book Circular* in 420 numbers from March 1861 to December 1897.

By the 1870s Robertson's *Catalogue of Books Offered to the Trade* ran to over 300 pages and included 55 000 titles held in stock in his Melbourne warehouse. In a letter from Petherick published in the London journal *The Bookseller* on 2 June 1874 Robertson's mode of doing business was described. In 1873 he had imported £98 000 (approximately $10 000 000 Australian dollars in 2024) worth of books and issued 55 000 copies of his trade and retail lists. Despite the considerable costs of importation and then circulation within the colonies — Robertson's domain, visited by commercial travellers, encompassed all the Australian centres and New Zealand — retail booksellers were still normally able to sell at English published prices. Australian book-buyers were, it is immediately evident, better served in this respect than they were in the following century.

Robertson was not alone in importing books directly. Indeed, some of the financial difficulties he seems to have faced in the 1880s may be put down to the fact that some of his major confrères had made independent arrangements. At least in 1857, when he started in business in Melbourne, Alfred James Smith seems to have relied for supplies on his family's firm in Brighton, Sussex. The Walches had always run their own operation, but the relative decline of Tasmania after 1850 meant that it could not aspire to a dominating national position. Samuel Mullen, after being denied Robertson's London management, went his own successful way, not only in the circulating library field, but also in general high-class bookselling. A letter from E. W. Cole to his wife during his own London buying trip in 1886 refers to seeing — but not being seen by — Robertson and Petherick as he set up his own sources of supply (Broinowski, 163). Other booksellers, working in quite specialised fields, linked up with Northern Hemisphere networks relevant to them, even if Robertson made a considerable effort to be as catholic as possible in his approach.

The Walches were the first to publish an advertising journal based on their business. Charles Edward Walch, the younger son of Major James Walch, the firm's founder, not only organised the London agency office, but also launched and edited *Walch's Literary Intelligencer and General Advertiser* from June 1859 till its demise and his death in early 1915. The only known complete set is now in the Tasmanian Archives. It is the best of these publications and an important source for the history of the Australian trade and its British connections over more than half a century.

Samuel Mullen was quite late in this field. There had been earlier catalogues, but *S. Mullen's Monthly Circular of Literature, &c.* did not start till January 1884. Mullen himself retired in 1889 after three decades in his shop and library, but his successors (brother William Mullen, Scottish-trained Adam Graham Melville and Leonard Slade) continued the publication in the 1890s. The 1880s were a significant period for Mullen, who dealt in the high end of the trade and supplied monographs and scientific periodicals for the Melbourne Public Library, for which he also bid at auction. In this way he played an important role in the great John Macgregor sale in 1884. He also paid special attention to books in French, seriously cultivated and read by the Australian élite at this time.

E. W. Cole, pushed in this direction by his manager W. T. Pyke, issued *Cole's Book Buyers' Guide* from the late 1880s till his death in 1918. Library holdings are far from complete, which is all the more regrettable since the popular character of the Book Arcade distinguished it clearly from most of the rival firms in Melbourne, and in the 1890s in Sydney and Adelaide as well. The venture was continued from 1919 to 1928 under the title *Rainbow*.

When Petherick left Robertson's service and set up on his own in London in 1887, his Colonial Booksellers' Agency published a *Colonial Book Circular and Bibliographical Record* and eventually other titles. He had branches in Sydney, Melbourne and Adelaide of his distributing business. Bankrupted as a consequence of the crash of the early 1890s he lost his stock and Sydney and Adelaide premises to E. W. Cole, while his published series went to George Bell and Sons. He had taken over some of Robertson's wholesaling functions, so the fact that British publishers backing him allowed him to fail was a clear sign of the move into the 1890 phase of Australian bookselling. When a new trade magazine appeared after the First World War with a succession of different titles it was an independent initiative of D. W. Thorpe, who had been an employee of the Robertson house in the early twentieth century.

One of the strongest marks of George Robertson's preponderance before 1890 was the number of people trained by him who later went into business on their own. This process was reinforced by the wholesaler's presence in Sydney and Adelaide as well as Melbourne. The list is long and includes shops that went on into the twentieth and even twenty-first centuries: William Dymock, David Angus, the other George Robertson, G. B. Philip, E. J. Dwyer and William Maddock in Sydney; Richard Thomson in Brisbane; T. V. Carroll in Perth; W. J. Griffiths in Geelong; F. W. Preece in Adelaide. Given the strength of tradition in bookselling, it would not be too difficult to establish professional genealogies going back as far as the eighteenth century, since some of these people had worked for British houses before emigrating to the Australian colonies.

Robertson and Mullen were both strong over decades in condemning the importation of American 'reprints', technically piracies, into the Australian market in contravention of British copyrights established in 1842. The question is a complex and rather murky one, not least because of the disappearance of the customs records of colonial Victoria. There is no doubt that the phenomenon existed. Indeed one can add to the dossier an advertisement by Buzzard and Vale on 27 May 1854 for 'AMERICAN REPRINTS' in quantity. On the other hand the Gemmell McCaul and Co. auction on 15 March 1862 of an 'Elegant Library of American Works' (*Argus*, 15 March 1862, p. 2) lists briefly titles that are genuinely of United States origin. Benjamin Mortimer, the only authentic American bookseller operating in Melbourne in the 1850s, was careful to state in his 1855 catalogue that he was not proposing to import works prohibited by the British Government. Announcing his wares to 'his countrymen and the British public' in the *Bendigo Advertiser* of 1 January 1856 he urges the study of works on the American constitution, institutions and education system 'in an epoch in our history like the present inauguration of Australian self-government and, the projected confederacy of the colonies'. It is useful to be reminded of the melting-pot of the goldfields and of the ferment of ideas it provoked.

Booksellers like Robertson did not neglect to import American works as part of their normal business. 'GR' was not above producing Melbourne-printed editions of American authors like Bret Harte and Mark Twain as part of an effort to make the literature of the Northern Hemisphere accessible to the Australian public at affordable prices. Titles of more specialised interest could appear in the catalogues of booksellers who confined themselves to limited aspects of the trade. William Henry Terry, longtime editor of the *Harbinger of Light*, produced catalogues of spiritualist works with many American titles. In one of them he was manifestly assisted by the spiritualist convert Benjamin Suggitt Nayler (1796–1875), who brought to Melbourne in his last decade the experience of a publisher and notorious discounter in Amsterdam between the early 1820s and 1848.

The expense of English books, especially first-edition three-decker novels sold for a guinea and a half, was a perennial problem for the colonial trade, which was seeking much cheaper versions than those designed for circulating libraries. Murray's Home and Colonial Library had been confined to non-fiction as noted earlier. The 'colonial editions', comprehensively studied for Australia by Johanson, began to appear tentatively in the 1870s — Bentley's Empire Library, 1878–1881 — and then gathered pace from the middle of the 1880s. The key date in some ways was 1886, when Macmillan launched 'Macmillan's Colonial Library'. The new venture was welcomed in *Walch's Literary Intelligencer* of July 1886, but not without some rather caustic comments on the slowness of British publishers in coming to understand the realities of the colonial trade. This was not the stridency of the *Bulletin*, but Walch and Mullen did not hesitate to reject condescension and to stress the maturity of their Australian customers. Alongside the new formula there had been, and continued to be, shared editions and cheap reprints, notably by George Robertson. The complicated history of all this had Bentley, Robertson and Petherick in the foreground, and overall its heyday belonged in the period after 1890. There were other players, and especially around the turn of the century one sees editions printed by Walter Scott of Tyneside amongst others issued in great quantity with the address of E. W. Cole. Fiction was not the only category concerned, but its presence inspired a certain disdain for the taste of the numerous buyers of cheap books.

The major wholesalers should not monopolise an overview of the trade in the latter part of the nineteenth century. Some elements — bookstalls in outdoor or covered markets, itinerant sellers and so forth — are extremely hard to document. However, people keeping shops, advertising in the city and country newspapers and listed in the annual directories that became so important in the colonies can more easily be situated. Before 1850 the largest centres had no more than a handful of people selling books and many of these would have defined themselves as printers or bookbinders. Sydney, which experienced economic difficulties in the 1860s, had 31 listed booksellers and stationers in 1861 and the same number in 1870. Melbourne, on the other hand, grew from 39 in 1861 to 86 in 1870, the trade having long since spread from the central city to a few inner suburbs. James Tyrrell, whom some of us still remember from the 1940s and 1950s, had a career that spanned the three volumes of the present *History*.

In his *Old Books, Old Friends, Old Sydney* of 1952, he lists (185-186) the trade as it appeared in *Sand's Sydney and Suburban Directory* for 1889: six book importers, six wholesale booksellers (including J. J. Moore and Co. and George Robertson and Co.) and 62 booksellers (including the N.S.W. Bookstall Company with two city premises and stalls at railway stations). In order to complement Tyrrell's findings it is instructive to set out the comparative statistics of trade personnel at the end of our period in the capital cities of the various colonies. The year recorded is essentially 1890 with one or two minor variations. Launceston is grouped with Hobart in Tasmania whereas Fremantle is incorporated in Perth. The differences are stark and underline the predominance of the two major eastern cities with their numerous suburbs.

Adelaide: booksellers and stationers 35; stationers 6; newsagents 12.
Brisbane: booksellers and stationers 27.
Melbourne: booksellers and stationers 185; newsagents 81.
Perth: booksellers 4 (by 1893 this had increased to 7).
Sydney: booksellers 65; newsagents 113; stationers 110; law stationers 16; wholesale and manufacturing stationers 20.
Tasmania: Hobart: booksellers 12; retail stationers 7; wholesale and manufacturing stationers 3; Launceston: booksellers 6; retail stationers 7; wholesale and manufacturing stationer: 1.

Some long-established firms have left few traces both archivally and in the memories of customers, while others have preserved an aura that has survived for more than a century after the deaths of their founders. The prime example is Cole's Book Arcade. How a business that started as a stall in 1865 run by a man with no previous experience in bookselling and was finally installed in the heart of Melbourne's Bourke Street in 1883 remains in many ways mysterious. Cole would have known the omnium gatherum shops of provincial England and mid-century Australia as well as the stalls where customers had free access to the merchandise. On this rudimentary basis he built something that foreshadowed the book superstores of the late twentieth century. A flair for extravagant advertising — particularly in the Melbourne *Herald* — and for showmanship helped.

In articles in *The Booksellers, Stationers & Fancy Goods Journal* of 1928 W. T. Pyke set down some of his reminiscences of his half-century working for Cole and the Book Arcade. Cole's biographers have not paid sufficient attention to a text that does more than hint at the reasons for the business's success: stocking remainders and selling cheaply. In this way the Arcade disposed of the bulk of David Blair's *Cyclopedia of Australasia* (Melbourne, Fergusson and Moore, 1881) and many other languishing Australian publications. Given Cole's quite plausible claim that his Arcade was the biggest bookshop in the world, the analogy with James Lackington's late-eighteenth-century London 'Temple of the Muses' is quite appropriate. It was, in any case, a fitting monument for 'Marvellous Melbourne'.

Alongside many other shops with general stock, sometimes carefully catalogued, there were more specialised outlets. Denominational affiliations were important in the older Australia. The 'Glasgow Book Warehouse' of Robert Mackay and, later, Matthew Leighton Hutchinson started in Sydney in the 1850s, then moved to Melbourne in 1860. There was an explicit connection with Blackie & Co. Alfred James Smith issued catalogues of new and old books from successive premises in Swanston Street, Melbourne from the late 1850s to the 1880s, as well as having a branch in Bendigo. His bias was clearly Methodist. Other stores served Anglicans and Catholics across the country and are better documented in church newspapers than in the general press.

The Baillière dynasty of French medical and scientific publishers created its own global empire from a Paris base in the nineteenth century: London, New York, Madrid and Melbourne. Ferdinand-François Baillière (1831–1881) was in the last-named city as a bookseller and publisher from 1860 till his death in a railway accident. Apart from his activity as a publisher he produced three catalogues of his family's specialist field. This presence suggests the growing sophistication of the colonial market, which now needed easier access to the literature called for by a growing number of medical and scientific professionals.

Second-hand books were part of the stock-in-trade of many colonial booksellers, not least because of the vagaries of importation of current publications until around 1860. The one great, but not exclusive, specialist was Henry Tolman Dwight (1823?–1871). More than 20 catalogues produced between 1859 and 1871 contain both new and old books, but there is a respectable quantity of antiquarian material drawn in the main, one suspects, from local auctions. Dwight also engaged in publishing and his shop in Bourke Street was a meeting place for some of Melbourne's literati. After his early death, his stock was sold over 14 days from 28 August 1872 by Cohen & Co. (35 000 volumes). A residue of 2000 volumes was offered by the same auctioneer on 4 November 1872. Late in his career Dwight was advertising himself as the Melbourne agent of Bernard Quaritch.

The market for books in foreign languages is harder to define. French, more widely read than now by Anglophones, was in the mainstream and represented regularly in Robertson and Mullen lists, and not just in the form of school texts. German was on the whole apart, but since it belonged to the largest group of European non-British immigrants in the nineteenth century, its presence should not be underestimated. The preponderantly Lutheran aspect has been comprehensively treated by Joyce Graetz, with due emphasis on activities outside major urban centres. The colporteurs who carried about Gossner's *Herzbuechlein* on the goldfields and the bookseller Oscar Müller in Hochkirch (now Tarrington, near Hamilton in Western Victoria), were only part of a vast network of newspaper production, German-language publishing and book distribution that stretched from South Australia right across country Victoria, New South Wales and Queensland. There were also secular strands, for instance the Socialist and Forty-eighter Hermann Püttmann, who was a bookseller and stationer in Richmond, Victoria in 1859. Socialist commitments were to continue among some Australian German-speakers after 1890.

Present-day Australians are often unaware of the extent of the use of Celtic languages — Scots Gaelic, Irish and Welsh — in the nineteenth-century colonies. Much of this was confined to oral communication. People brought with them books in their native languages, but very little was produced in Australia, and trading is not abundantly documented. One of the exceptions was the dispersal in 1864 of the library of Edward Hayes, compiler of the two volumes of *The Ballads of Ireland*, first published in Edinburgh in 1855 and quite frequently reprinted thereafter. A catalogued auction by Gemmell McCaul & Co. of 3000 volumes, followed later in the same year by a substantial offering by Dwight based on it, represented the material that could be collected, essentially in the British Isles before his emigration to Victoria, by a scholarly student of Irish literature and history who sought out books and manuscripts in the traditional language of his homeland. This case, carefully analysed by Kevin Molloy, is far removed from the experience of the mass of Irish-speakers.

The Scots and Welsh could rely on Protestant churches that conducted services in their Celtic languages in the nineteenth century, even if the tradition was to fall away later for the former group. Not much was printed in Welsh in the colonies, but people brought with them the books they needed or wanted for religious and secular purposes, including guides for immigrants. The story to be told, therefore, is not equal to that for the United States or Patagonia, but there are relevant analogies. Churches and periodicals are an essential element of it, but there were also booksellers, notably Benjamin S. Evans of Sebastopol, near Ballarat, advertising in *Yr Australydd* in 1870 (Geraint Evans, 81). Despite the pre-eminence of Welsh congregations in Melbourne it is useful to remember that in the gold-rush decades provincial centres played their part in sustaining the civilisation of the printed word.

Curiously a recent serious study of Castlemaine in the decade 1851–1861 when it was 'poised precariously between a mining camp and a settled town' (Theobald, cover blurb) cites Charles E. Glass's directories for 1856, 1857 and 1861, but says nothing about his activity as a bookseller. Yet in 1859 and 1861 Glass, possibly a Canadian, published substantial *Price Catalogues* that bear comparison with what was being produced in Melbourne at the same time. In 1861 he offered 'Darwin's Origin of Species' for 16 shillings. In 1859 there was a generous selection of books in French far from the usual fare of elementary textbooks. Here is more than a glimpse of the cosmopolitan culture to be found in often transient goldfields towns that were anything but conventionally British. Something of this variety was to be contributed to the colonial capitals later in the century. By 1890 both Melbourne and Sydney were to have, despite the strictures of carelessly condescending visitors, a book world with unsuspected depth.

Cover of A. J. Smith's catalogue [1857]. Printed by Mason & Firth. [16] p.; 21 cm. Emigrating from Brighton, England, Smith operated his Melbourne bookshop from 1857 to 1889. He expanded his operations to Bendigo in 1884, purchasing W. A. J. Wenborn's business which he operated for 14 years before selling it to C.W. Hyett in 1896. Wenborn supplied books to the public and to local libraries. (State Library Victoria)

First small steps towards a closed market

The retirement of Samuel Mullen in 1889, followed a year later by his death in London, and the withdrawal of George Robertson in 1890 from control of his business marked more than a symbolic transition in Australia's trade. The Net Book Agreement was, it is true, ten years away, so free-trade conditions persisted for another decade. Even in the twentieth century it took fifty or more years for the market to be closed, in other words for Australian booksellers to be obliged to buy from the local branches of British publishers. Long before this, stock was indented on the publishers' terms. The old freedoms of the colonial wholesalers had gone, and sooner or later their businesses followed suit, leading to the gradual disappearance of London buying offices. All this took a long time, and it belongs in another volume.

What does need to be noted is that British publishers began to take a serious interest in the expanding Australian market as early as the 1870s. The Tegg experiment of the 1830s and 1840s and even Blackie's incursion at the end of the 1850s were outliers. Travellers started to explore possibilities and to seek orders on years-long trips to the Antipodes. These ventures were followed at varying intervals by the establishment of branches that replaced the agency arrangements previously concluded with local importers. William Collins was first in the field with a warehouse and showroom in Sydney in the later 1870s. Ward Lock set up a Melbourne branch in 1884, the same year as Cassell. John Lothian arrived in Melbourne in 1888 as 'the first independent British publishers' representative in Australia and New Zealand' (Sayers, 1) acting principally for his former employer Walter Scott, but also for other houses. E. R. Bartholomew began travelling for Oxford University Press and Hodder & Stoughton, as well as a number of other publishers, in 1890. This activity in the 1880s was in parallel to a general development of manufacturers' agents in the colonies bypassing local wholesalers. In this trend one sees before the end of the third phase of Australian bookselling history clear preparations for and announcements of the fourth.

NOTE ON SOURCES

The framework of the present chapter is in essence that presented in my Cambridge Sandars Lectures in 1981 — later published as *Books for Colonial Readers — The Nineteenth-Century Australian Experience* (Melbourne, BSANZ, 1995) — and in my chapter 'Bookselling and Publishing in the Nineteenth Century' in D. H. Borchardt & W. Kirsop, eds, *The Book in Australia: Essays towards a Cultural & Social History* (Melbourne, Australian Reference Publications, 1988, pp. 16-42, 174-81). However, a great deal of work has been done on aspects of the subject since the 1980s, and it was imperative to take due account of it. This is, therefore, a reworking using new secondary sources, but also going back to many of the primary documents. It is to be understood that the general reference works that will appear in the Select Bibliography at the end of the volume were constantly consulted, for example Ferguson's *Bibliography of Australia* and the *Australian Dictionary of Biography*, as well as monographs by others. Their details do not need to be set out here.

Many of the specific studies that supported the research are also left for listing later. They include contributions by Brian Hubber, Kevin Molloy, Laurel Clark, Alison Rukavina, Keith Adkins and myself. On the other hand, works mentioned in the text do need to be indicated here alongside the fundamental work that has to be the underpinning of any description of nineteenth-century Australian bookselling. This is all the more important since I have tried throughout to indicate how much students of the subject depend on what is available as original documentation and on clear understanding of what has been lost.

Leaving aside rare survivals of business records from the period, the central tools at our disposal are the newspaper press, with its invaluable advertisements, and printed catalogues, both of auctioneers and booksellers. For the years before 1850 the indispensable guide is Elizabeth Webby, 'A Checklist of Early Australian Booksellers' and Auctioneers' Catalogues and Advertisements: 1800–1849', *BSANZ Bulletin*, vol.3, no.4, 1978, pp. 123-48; vol.4, no.1, 1979, pp. 33-61 and no.2, pp. 95-150. Also relevant are her 'Sydney Auction Sales in the 1840s', *BSANZ Bulletin*, vol.5, no.1, 1981, pp. 17-28, and a series of articles published in *Southerly* in 1967 and 1976 on the place of English literary authors in the catalogues and advertisements of the 1820s, 1830s and 1840s. All this was based on her groundbreaking 1971 PhD thesis for the University of Sydney: Literature and the reading public in Australia 1800–1850.

The checklist allows consultation of the original material in reprints of early newspapers from Sydney and Hobart and in Trove.

After 1850 we have nothing comparable, but I have used the card file of auctioneers' advertisements in the *Argus* and the *Sydney Morning Herald* between 1861 and 1870 compiled at Monash University under my supervision in the early 1970s by Patricia Richards, Peter Freckleton and Joseph de Riva O'Phelan. A student report in 1997 by Angus Pearson on the year 1854 in Melbourne contains valuable data that deserve to be published. The discussion is taken a little further in my 'Selling books at auction in 19th-century Australia: The 2009 Ferguson Memorial Lecture', *JRAHS*, vol.95, 2009, pp. 198-214.

The most ambitious and rewarding monograph on the Australian trade in the nineteenth-century — and somewhat later — to have appeared since the 1980s is Graeme Johanson's *A Study of Colonial Editions in Australia, 1843–1972* (Wellington, New Zealand, Elibank Press, 2000). Although its title suggests — rightly – a specific focus, there is much on the general context of that phenomenon and on topics like pricing and statistics that could not be treated adequately in the space of an overview chapter like the present one. Anyone wanting to explore the subject further should read Johanson's book.

Other basic monographs that continue to serve well, even if recent or projected research can suggest modifications, are: John Holroyd, *George Robertson of Melbourne 1825–1878: Pioneer Bookseller & Publisher*, Melbourne, Robertson & Mullens, 1968; Cole Turnley, *Cole of the Book Arcade: A Pictorial Biography of E. W. Cole*, Hawthorn, Cole Publications, 1974; *The Early Australian Booksellers: The Australian Booksellers Association Memorial Book of Fellowship*, Sydney, The Australian Booksellers Association, 1980; and Ian F. McLaren, *Henry Tolman Dwight: Bookseller and Publisher*, Parkville, The University of Melbourne Library, 1989.

Sources cited, or specifically referred to, are, in alphabetical order:

Keith Adkins, 'Orger and Meryon: Booksellers to the Colony', *BSANZ Bulletin*, vol.28, nos 1-2, 2004, pp. 9-16; Bothwell Literary Society Minute Book — Tasmanian Archives NS 75/1/1 (1834–1855); Richard Broinowski, *Under the Rainbow: The life and times of EW Cole*, Carlton, The Miegunyah Press, 2020; Peter Chapman, ed., *The Diaries and Letters of G. T. W. B. Boyes*. Volume 1: *1820–1832*, Melbourne, OUP, 1985; Marie Joan Cullen, Edward Augustus Petherick: a Bio-Bibliographical Study to August 1887, PhD thesis, Monash University, 2000; Geraint Evans,

'Welsh-Language Publishing in Late Nineteenth-Century Victoria', *BSANZ Bulletin*, vol.17, no.2, 1993, pp. 79-84; Jean Fornasiero & John West-Sooby, 'Baudin's Books', *Australian Journal of French Studies*, XXXIX, 2002, pp. 215-49; Angus Fraser, 'John Murray's Colonial and Home Library', *PBSA*, vol. 91, no.3, 1997, pp. 339-408; Joyce Graetz, *An Open Book: The Story of the Distribution and Production of Christian Literature by Lutherans in Australia*, Adelaide, Lutheran Publishing House, 1988; Patrick Gregory, *Speaking Volumes: The Victorian Parliamentary Library 1857-2001*, Melbourne, Victorian Parliamentary Library, 2001; Brian Hubber, 'Bookseller to the City of Sydney: James Tegg in 1838', *BSANZ Bulletin*, vol.13, no.2, 1989, pp. 57-62; W. Kirsop, ed., *From Yarralumla to the Sale Room: Terence Murray's Library*, Melbourne, The Chaskett Press, 2011; Edward Marston, *After Work. Fragments from the Workshop of an Old Publisher*, London, William Heinemann, 1904; Kevin Molloy, '"Cheap Reading for the People": Jeremiah Moore and the development of the New South Wales Book Trade, 1840-1883', *Script & Print*, vol.34, no.2, 2010, pp. 216-39; and his 'HAYES, Edward (1816-1870)' in Charles Stitz, ed., *Australian Book Collectors. Some Noted Australian Book Collectors & Collections of the Nineteenth and Twentieth Centuries*, Second Series Part I: *A–I*, Melbourne, Books of Kells/Green Olive Press, 2013, pp. 343-52; Richard Overell, 'The Melbourne Public Library and the Guillaumes: The Relations Between a Colonial Library and its London Book Supplier 1854-1865', in F. Upward & J. Whyte, eds, *Peopling a Profession: Papers from the Fourth Forum on Australian Library History, Monash University, 25 and 26 September 1989*, Melbourne, Ancora Press, 1991, pp. 33–63; W. T. Pyke, articles with different titles on Cole in *The Booksellers, Stationers & Fancy Goods Journal*, 11 July, 10 August, 10 September, 10 October, 10 November, 3 December 1928; Sue Reynolds, *Books for the Profession. The Library of the Supreme Court of Victoria*, North Melbourne, Australian Scholarly, 2012; Stuart Sayers, *The Company of Books: A Short History of the Lothian Book Companies 1888-1988*, Melbourne, Lothian Publishing Company Pty Ltd, 1988; Colin Steele and Michael Richards, *Bound for Botany Bay: What books did the First Fleeters read and where are they now?*, Canberra, ANU Library, Australian National University, 1989; Marjorie Theobald, *The Accidental Town: Castlemaine, 1851-1861*, North Melbourne, Australian Scholarly, 2020; Michelle Scott Tucker, *Elizabeth Macarthur: A Life at the Edge of the World*, Melbourne, Text Publishing, 2018; James R. Tyrrell, *Old Books, Old Friends, Old Sydney*, Sydney, Angus and Robertson, 1952.

CHAPTER 14

Australia's Public Libraries in Their Infancy

David J. Jones

'In a colony which contains only a few hundred hovels built of twigs and mud, we feel consequential enough already to talk of a treasury, an admiralty, a public library, and many other edifices, which are to form part of a magnificent square', wrote Watkin Tench three years after the establishment of the convict settlement at Sydney Cove. For most of the newcomers, however, the concept of a public library containing books from which all people could freely draw information, entertainment, education or inspiration was remote. The English pattern of parochial libraries for the poor and subscription libraries for those with means was an irrelevance for people struggling to survive in a foreign and unforgiving environment. The First Fleet had of course carried some books: the treatises and manuals of the officers and the stocks of Bibles, prayer books and *Plain exhortations to prisoners* which the Chaplain, the Rev. Richard Johnson, had brought 'to promote education and piety' among those of his charges with a modicum of literacy. For the original owners of the Great South Land there were a dozen copies of *Instructions for the Indians*, although theirs would prove to be a different kind of literacy, sustained by oral tradition, artefacts, works of art, flora and fauna, and country.

As the white colony became less precarious, thoughts turned to the diffusion of useful knowledge as well as the saving of souls. In 1809 the Rev. Samuel Marsden advertised in England for donations to help found a 'Lending Library for the general benefit of the inhabitants of New South Wales'. The library would cover 'Divinity and Morals, History, Voyages and Travels, Agriculture in all its branches, Mineralogy and Practical Mechanics'. Although he did return to Australia with a number of book donations to a proposed 'Port Jackson Lending Library', some of which survive today in the library of Moore Theological College, no public institution actually eventuated.

A little later there was evidence of some public and official support for a library in Sydney: at a dinner in 1813 the guests toasted a new library: 'May every inhabitant of our Colony unite in promoting the general diffusion of useful Knowledge.' But a free public library for the colony was an unrealised ambition even during Lachlan Macquarie's productive governorship from 1810 to 1821.

For those able to pay, a number of commercial reading rooms and circulating libraries began to operate, first in Sydney and later in other centres of population. Meanwhile the most prominent members of Sydney society could borrow books from each other using a combined catalogue of their personal libraries. By 1821 special interest groups in Sydney could also use the Philosophical Society Library and a Biblical Library. Both circulating and private libraries are discussed by Wallace Kirsop in the chapters that follow.

Hobart was the site of what is believed to be Australia's first public, but not free, library. The Rev. Benjamin Carvosso set up a library in the Wesleyan Chapel in Melville Street in 1825. Subscriptions were ten shillings a year at a time when a clerk might earn a pound a week.

In 1826 the more ambitious Australian Subscription Library and Reading Room began in Sydney with a flurry of enthusiasm and gubernatorial patronage, much to the delight of the *Sydney Gazette*, which believed the library would 'ultimately become an elegant and substantial appendage to the extending empire of Australia'. It was for men only and its membership fees — five guineas to join and two guineas per year — were high enough to 'discourage social undesirables from applying'. It opened on 1 December 1827 with about a thousand volumes on the shelves of a temporary reading room in Pitt Street, but by 1830 was already in financial difficulties, a victim of its own exclusiveness. Its committee appealed to the Governor for help, claiming that 'the foundation of a Public Library' had been laid, a notion given statutory recognition in 1834, although the proprietors of the Library were never prepared to allow the general public free access. Financial problems persisted and by the 1860s the library was virtually bankrupt.

Unlike the earlier colonies, the infant settlement in South Australia had the nucleus of a public library almost from the moment of its conception: 117 volumes shared a metal trunk with the colony's Charter on the voyage to Adelaide in 1836 aboard the *Tam O'Shanter*. Again the motivation was one of 'diffusing useful knowledge among the colonists', but the first library services were available only to subscribers who joined what was successively known as the South Australian Literary Society (1837), Mechanics' Institute (1838–48), South Australian Subscription Library and Mechanics' Institute (1848–56) and South Australian Institute (1856–84).

Mechanics' institutes, schools of arts, athenaeums and literary institutes, most of which included a library for their subscribers, began to be established in all parts of Australia from the second quarter of the nineteenth century. The first, the Van Diemen's Land Mechanics' Institute, opened in Hobart in 1827. The Sydney Mechanics' School of Arts was founded in 1833.

In Victoria there were early examples of entrepreneurial spirit or genuine philanthropy which sparked lending libraries. In 1838 the colourful John Pascoe Fawkner set up a small lending library and reading room next to his hotel in Melbourne, charging five shillings per quarter for the privilege of borrowing. The following year another Melbourne resident, barrister (later Sir) Redmond Barry, was active in the foundation of the Melbourne Mechanics' Institute, which included a library for its members. In 1842 Barry, who would shortly gain greater prominence in the history of library development in Victoria, created a small lending library in his own house.

In Western Australia, as in the case of South Australia, the original plan for the settlement had included libraries: a parochial lending library for the working class and a literary institute for others. Institute libraries were sometimes known as 'public libraries' although this did not mean that they were free. Even an institution bearing the name Tasmanian Public Library, for example, founded in

1849 and foundering in 1867, was in fact a subscription library. Only members were normally permitted to make full use of the services of the institutes and to borrow, although as a condition of local or colonial government financial assistance, public access to their reading rooms was sometimes provided. These institutions were in the main the 'public libraries and mechanics' institutes . . . in one shape or another' which enthused Anthony Trollope when he visited Australia in the 1870s. By the end of the nineteenth century they numbered over a thousand, compared with a handful of free public libraries, all established after 1850.

By the mid-nineteenth century the concept of a free public library was already gaining ground in England and Wales — the Public Libraries Act of 1850 enabled local authorities to establish and maintain libraries from public funds, and similar permissive legislation would later be enacted in several Australian colonies. The impetus to establish libraries in England and Wales tended to spring not from mass manifestations of public demand, but from individual enthusiasm. This was certainly the case too with Australia's first government-funded library freely available to the public. It was in 1853 in Victoria, 'in the full flush of colonial pride', newly separated from New South Wales, quivering with gold fever and a booming pastoral industry, that the Melbourne Public Library (later called the Public Library of Victoria and now State Library Victoria) was conceived. Funds for books and a building were 'cheerfully voted by Parliament'.

On 3 July 1854 the foundation stones of both the Melbourne Public Library and the University of Melbourne were laid. Redmond Barry, by then one of the three judges of the Supreme Court of Victoria, was a driving force behind both institutions and greatly influenced their development. (He thus had a finger in four library pies, having also played a part in creating the libraries of both Parliament and the Supreme Court, and duplication of items across these libraries was deliberately minimised). Barry hoped the new Melbourne Public Library would draw attention to 'the achievements of men who enable us to achieve enlightened moderation and liberty'. He did not want books which would 'attract the idle and inquisitive, or entertain the frivolous, but invite the scholar, instruct the diligent inquirer and detain the serious'. The trustees 'abstained from displaying on the shelves works of injurious tendency, or from supplying an undue proportion of novels and of those usually classed as works of fiction and of the imagination, of those which in some catalogues are entered under the head of "literature for juveniles", of such as are purely ephemeral and of transient value'.

Literary curiosities, costly manuscripts and superseded voluminous publications were also avoided. Quality was to be prized above quantity, and Barry himself dominated the selection process for a quarter of a century. An early order was for all of the works cited by Gibbon in *The History of the Decline and Fall of the Roman Empire*. About three years' wages for a clerk — £140 — was spent on a set of Gould's *Birds of Australia*, signalling the Library's aspirations. By the end of the century its collections of nineteenth-century works in the humanities were described as 'probably still unrivalled in the country'.

In 1856 it opened the doors of its Swanston Street building to anyone aged fourteen and over, from all walks of life, on weekdays and Saturdays, free of charge and with no formalities whatsoever, although visitors might be asked to wash their hands before touching a book, and would be woken up if they fell asleep. 'Attention to the ordinary courtesies of life was all that was suggested'. Ladies were welcome, and a separate area was set aside for them, adjacent to works on theology, architecture and art, rural and domestic arts, prose and poetry. Readers could help themselves to all of its collection except rare books and some medical works, but could not borrow: a direct lending service would not be offered until 1892.

In 1859 opening hours were extended and by the end of 1861 there had been 595 143 visitors to the library. By then the building had been enlarged considerably to provide a bigger reading room and a 'Fine Art Room'. Liberality of access was a hallmark of Barry's approach, one well ahead of British practice and which saw Barry come under fire when he attended the first International Conference of Librarians in London in 1877. Early reservations about possible theft of or damage to books proved misplaced: in the first six years of operation, the Library reported only £7 worth of damage or theft.

Photograph of Queen's Reading Room, Melbourne Public Library [1859]. One of the earliest photographed interiors, believed to have been taken on opening day of the southern wing, 24 May 1859, or the day after. Sir Redmond Barry enlisted photographer Barnett Johnstone (1832–1910) to take the image. Johnstone wrote on the back of the photo: 'The day was fixed, and [Barry], the Attorney General, the Mayor of Melbourne, and [others] were present. The Chief Librarian ([Augustus Tulk], at the far end of the table) and [others] were . . . told that they must sit perfectly still for six minutes. The gentlemen [then] accompanied me to the "dark room", a cellar in which I had put my things, and there, on my knees, for there was no table, to the astonished delight of my distinguished audience, I developed the negative. Remember, I was a young man, only just beginning in Photography, & with a Judge, an Attorney General, and a Mayor looking on, – well, it was trying! My light was a naked candle.' Photograph; albumen silver, 14.8 x 17.1 cm, on mount. (State Library Victoria)

In Sydney the Victorian example was not immediately followed. The Australian Subscription Library limped on with declining membership and increasing debts, until in 1869 the New South Wales Government agreed to purchase its books and building for £5100, barely covering the Library's liabilities. In September that year, after 43 years as a private enterprise, the Library was officially reopened as the Free Public Library, Sydney, the first truly public library in New South Wales. (It was later known as the Public Library of New South Wales, then the Library of New South Wales and is now the State

Library of New South Wales). It began with about 20 000 volumes, two-thirds inherited from the Australian Subscription Library and a third from the library of the late Mr Justice Wise. The Wise collection was strong in Australian books, pamphlets and newspapers, and had been presented to the Government of New South Wales in 1865 and stored at the Australian Museum pending the creation of a 'free library'. Most works of fiction from the old library were discarded, and, echoing Barry's sentiments, the trustees were pleased to report that the Library now presented 'but few temptations to the idle and frivolous'. They were intent on 'stamping the Institution with an intellectual character' and, like their counterparts in Victoria, were well equipped to do so: their president was Charles Badham, Professor of Classics and Logic at the University of Sydney, and other members were drawn from the intelligentsia of Sydney. Though outshone academically by the trustees, the first librarian, Robert Cooper Walker, was a 'man of zeal and application' who would come to know 'the history and place of nearly every book in his library'. In a quarter century of service he saw his library collection grow fivefold, its building extended and remodelled and its users rapidly multiply.

Although visitor numbers were regularly reported, we do not have a clear idea of the social or occupational breakdown of readership in the reference libraries. Their long hours of opening meant that workers — and much industry and commerce was then within easy walking distance of the libraries — could spend fruitful hours at these institutions after finishing work for the day, not to mention weekend opening, whether they were clerks or artisans extending their education, or students supplementing reading matter available at their university. There is an indication that some citizens thought the Sydney library was 'simply a reading-room and a library for the working classes', a misconception which the trustees were quick to try to correct.

Tasmanians were served by a number of subscription libraries with some government subsidy, although by the mid-1800s there was also a small library associated with the parish church in practically every Tasmanian village. In 1870 the second institution bearing the name Tasmanian Public Library (now the State Library of Tasmania) was established in Hobart after the interest of the citizenry had been stimulated by the activist James Backhouse Walker (whose lobbying twenty years later would also help to establish the University of Tasmania). Like its counterpart in Sydney, the Tasmanian Public Library inherited the collection of a failed subscription library, in this case salvaged from a brewer's malt-loft and placed in the newly erected town hall. It became a joint venture between the Tasmanian Government and the municipal council. Over time it was neglected by both partners and was seriously under-resourced: a mid-twentieth-century commentator described it as 'for 70 years a slight, unmeritable institution'. Like its interstate counterparts, it was a reference library. Hobart had to wait until 1902 to see a lending library established. In Tasmania's second city, Launceston, a 'public' library was formed in 1889 by merging a mechanics' institute and a literary society, but it was still a subscription library. For this library, and others like it across Tasmania, 'all that was missing was the "free" — and the consequent membership of many thousands as compared with a few hundreds'.

Public reaction to the new reference libraries in Melbourne, Sydney and Hobart was enthusiastic. Even though its hours were initially from 10 am to 5 pm, the Melbourne Public Library welcomed 23 769 readers in its first ten months. Five years later, with longer opening hours and more seating, the library attracted over 160 000 readers each year. In Sydney 60 000 people signed the visitors' book in the Free Public Library's first year of operation. 'Hobart is behind the times', a visitor wrote, 'and as yet does not sufficiently appreciate the value of a Free Public Library'. Nonetheless 30 000 people a year were entering the Tasmanian Public Library by the 1880s despite its mediocre collection.

Users were, however, impressed by the Melbourne and Sydney libraries. A German doctor and amateur botanist rhapsodised about the Melbourne library in a letter home in 1859. 'A splendid building', he wrote. 'One signs one's name, takes off one's hat and goes in. And there before one is a large library. An excellent book collection is at the disposal of anyone interested, be he a learned man or the most humble worker ... I see books, can actually handle them and look at the maps and pictures inside books, for which at the Munich Library I presented call-slips week after week in vain'. He noted that from 7 pm to 10 pm almost every seat was taken, 'And I saw many people from humble walks of life who, you could see, had "dressed" for the library'. Using words which would have gladdened the hearts of the trustees, he added: 'Here you can quench your thirst for knowledge; learn what is necessary or useful in your life or position; raise your thoughts above the low, common path of daily life by reading sublime prose or poetry; fill in a useful, sober evening-hour instead of spending the last penny on the poisoning and consuming attraction of drink'. No less impressed was an English visitor to the Sydney institution: 'I have never been in a library where the difficulties of the searcher after knowledge are so well met, and where assistance is so quickly and willingly afforded'.

Although the British Museum Library has been seen as 'the central organisational and philosophical model for the major colonial libraries in Australia', other influences were also in play. There was awareness of library developments in other parts of the world, through education, reading or travel. Barry, for example, had first-hand experience of the library of Trinity College, Dublin. Badham was an alumnus of both Oxford and Cambridge. Augustus Tulk, Melbourne Public Library's first librarian, visited libraries in the United Kingdom. Although formal links between libraries of the Australian colonies did not occur, and even then fitfully, until the 1890s, there was knowledge of library practices in other colonies. In 1879, at the laying of the foundation stone of what would become the Public Library of South Australia, for example, Governor Jervois was familiar enough with the Melbourne Public Library to recommend its subject arrangement for adoption in the new institution. There may also have been an element of intercolonial rivalry in the establishment of cultural institutions, alongside universities, supreme courts and legislatures, as part of 'a process of intellectual and civic maturity'. Certainly there are instances of library development in one colony providing a stimulus or an inspiration, if not a model, for another.

There was commonality in the aspiration of the Melbourne, Sydney and Adelaide reference libraries to serve 'earnest students seeking intellectual improvement' with collections to match. From time to time, however, collection policies were criticised: in its early days the Melbourne Public Library, for example, was berated for not stocking novels by Dickens, Scott, Thackeray and George Eliot, whilst 'Milton, Byron, Tennyson and Swinburne are admitted'. Barry was unapologetic for 'admitting no works of a trivial or ephemeral character, which serve merely to dissipate the idle hours of the lounger, or, as far as they can be excluded, works having injurious tendencies'. Meanwhile the libraries were building research resources (including embryonic collections of Australiana) decades before the universities had begun to create library services on a useful scale for their students. Recent close examination of extant catalogues of public libraries in South Africa, Singapore, New Zealand and Australia suggests that the Melbourne Public Library had 'the largest scientific reference collection of any library in the southern colonies' and 'kept abreast with the latest developments in the evolving disciplines of ethnology, philology and anthropology throughout the 1860s'.

At the Free Public Library in Sydney, Robert Cooper Walker diligently acquired Australiana, building upon the Wise collection, and periodically compiled lists covering books and pamphlets relating to or published in Australia, New Zealand and their Pacific neighbours between 1869 and 1888. His compilation, covering 8000 items, eventually saw the light of day in 1893 as *Australasian Bibliography*, completed just in time to be proudly distributed at the World's Columbian Exhibition in Chicago that same year.

Much earlier his Victorian counterpart, Augustus Tulk, had overseen production of the Melbourne Public Library's lavish 1861 catalogue, with decorated initials and finials depicting Australian flora, illustrations which were claimed at the time to be 'the first of the kind published'. The effort and expense of publishing this catalogue — £500 was allocated for its production — served a threefold purpose: as an in-house search tool, as a guide for those elsewhere (in universities, institutes, parliamentary or court libraries), but also as what has been recently characterised as 'a promotional opportunity for both the library and the colony of Victoria'. It was seen at the time as 'ample proof that the colonists of Victoria are something more and better than a keenly money-seeking set of people'.

The reference libraries were open to all, old and young, educated and uneducated. They served gentlemen and ladies of leisure, people bent on improving themselves, new settlers keeping in touch with 'Home' by scanning newspapers and periodicals, and people who had fallen on hard times. But they could only serve patrons who were able to come into the colonial capital. To help those living outside metropolitan areas, schemes to lend books to distant institutes were established in South Australia, Victoria and considerably later in New South Wales. A book box service operated in South Australia from 1859, serving suburban and country institutes. Unlike later Victorian and New South Wales schemes it included light literature, mainly former bestsellers bought second-hand from English circulating libraries. The Victorian 'travelling libraries' consisted initially of duplicate items from the Melbourne Public Library, packed in oak cases, bound with brass, lined with green baize and covered in tarpaulins to protect them on their journeys. Over the years, various transportation methods were used, including coach, packhorse, boat and rail. The Public Library of New South Wales Country Circulation Department, similar in scope to Victoria's service, was established in 1883 and endured, with changes of name and modified formats, for almost a century.

Local councils showed little initiative in establishing free libraries, although by 1890 they were authorised to do so by local government legislation in all colonies except Western Australia. A New South Wales 'Act for Establishing Municipal Institutions' in 1858 failed to spur a single municipality to set up a public library. Some later responded to inducements: the Municipalities Act of 1867 in that State offered a non-recurrent government grant of £100 or £200, depending on population, to purchase books. Such libraries would also receive a set of the public statutes and copies of all of the publications of the Government Printer from the library's date of establishment. No items purchased or donated by the Government Printer would be available for loan. The first council to take up this offer was that of Newtown. Its free reference library was opened by Henry Parkes, author of the free public library clauses of the Municipalities Act, on 21 June 1869. The press was supportive, one editorial declaring 'it must henceforth be deemed inexcusable neglect for any municipality to remain without a free library'.

To receive grants-in-aid, councils had only to submit a list of book purchases for approval, certify that a free library was actually open in a room controlled by council (in many cases a back room and sometimes a cellar) and was reasonably available to the public. Over three decades, 67 such public libraries were established in New South Wales under this and later Acts. It was hoped that voluntary endowments and local rates would assure the future of these libraries, but the colonial government did not make any provision to maintain them. Parkes's hope that free public libraries would prosper, and that the system of grants to schools of arts — 'which had been so improvidently expended' — could be discontinued, remained unrealised for more than half a century. Once the excitement of an official opening was over, libraries were not high in council priorities. Few New South Wales councils purchased additional books and most libraries withered on the vine.

Had the New South Wales Act required the levying of a library rate, as in earlier English legislation, there may have been fewer but more viable free public libraries of this type. The quality of their collections was also questionable: selection was left to local authorities 'generally guided only by some bookseller, whose choices would naturally be more affected by the exigencies of his present stock than by altruistic consideration of the special needs of the young library'. Those established in rural New South Wales were doomed to failure, as farming families had little time to tarry in town reading in a reference library. If more local authorities had set up lending libraries and adopted longer opening hours, the institutions may also have proved more popular with users and stimulated further demand and support. Of the 67 local public libraries established under various local government acts in New South Wales in the nineteenth century, none survived into the twentieth.

Victoria experienced a flurry of partly free public libraries, many established owing to community pressure, often in competition with existing mechanics' institute libraries and athenaeums. Some free libraries operated in conjunction with an institute, such as that at Collingwood, opened in 1860. Richmond established a rate-supported library in 1873, replacing a failed subscription library. South Richmond's library opened two years later. They were well patronised and offered liberal admission: children under ten could use these libraries when accompanied by an adult. In 1875 some 17 per cent of Richmond's collection was for children.

Also in Victoria, when the Geelong Free Library opened its doors in 1876 after a lengthy public campaign, there were already free libraries in such prosperous towns as Bendigo and Ballarat, as well as in smaller localities like Steiglitz and Duck Ponds. Geelong's library was funded partly by the council and partly by public donations. It opened with '700 books, a good reading room and a splendid lavatory'. Thereafter, however, it 'lived "a parsimonious life" as the municipality's poor relation'.

These Victorian libraries were not completely free, however, as 'for most of the [nineteenth] century the privilege of borrowing books had to be paid for'. Free lending was finally introduced in 1891 by the Collingwood Free Library.

Meanwhile the capital city reference libraries came under early pressure to lend direct to the public. As early as 1871 there were calls to open a lending branch in Melbourne, but despite a pledge of financial support from Trades Hall, a shortage of funds and staff delayed this happening until 1892. The new century would arrive before a free lending library sprang up in Hobart, as a condition of a grant from the Carnegie Corporation.

It was Sydney's turn to be a pioneer in library services by lending to individuals. Even before it had opened to the public in 1869 the case was being put in the press for the Free Public Library in Sydney to provide a lending service, partly so as not to disadvantage the working class. 'As to a mere public library without a loan arrangement', a correspondent wrote, 'it would be of little use *to the masses*, in whose hands we have placed the franchise, and in whose hands we should place first-class books'. It was another eight years before 'A Reader' saw his or her wish come true. Despite misgivings from some of the Free Public Library's trustees that it would entice users away from the more serious literature in the reference library, a lending branch opened in 1877, available to people who lived in the penny post zone, within about a ten-mile (sixteen-kilometre) radius of the centre of Sydney. It was welcomed by the press, although its premises, formed by renovating a wine store and coal cellar in the basement of the Free Public Library, were 'not all that could be desired when we bear in mind the magnificence of the Public Library at Melbourne'. Premises notwithstanding, demand was so great that within three years its collection had grown fivefold. Borrowers checked the printed catalogue and staff collected items for them — open access to the shelves and card catalogue did not occur until the new century.

Interior of the Free Public Library, Sydney [1891?], Henry Ginn, architect. Seated at left is the librarian, Robert Cooper Walker (with white beard). The image, taken by a photographer from the NSW Government Printing Office, is from the album 'Photographs [of] New South Wales' dated [1879–c.1891] containing 51 albumen images, 32.5 x 45 cm. (Dixson Library, State Library of New South Wales)

By 1890, 50 000 people a year were visiting the Lending Branch, then occupying a prefabricated iron church next to Parliament House in Macquarie Street. This was an improvement on its former basement quarters, but subjected occupants to temperatures ranging in one year from 5° to 42°C.

The Free Public Library, Sydney was also the first to run the gauntlet of strict Sabbatarians, after a mild debate in a 'thin' Legislative Assembly in March 1878. By 25 to 7 the House voted to allow the Library to open from 2 pm to 6 pm each Sunday, hours chosen so as to interfere as little as possible with religious obligations. The decision was denounced from pulpits, petitions were presented to Parliament and outraged letters appeared in the press: as one observer later commented: 'There were those who advocated Sunday opening, those who strongly opposed it, while the masses remained indifferent'. On the first open Sunday there were only 70 people in the Reference Branch and 20 in the Lending Branch, but numbers grew steadily. By the 1890s over 500 people could be expected each Sunday by the officer in charge and four or five juniors working overtime. In Sydney, at least, the 'puritanical element' was by then 'practically extinct'.

In South Australia, Western Australia and Queensland free public library development occurred later, but followed similar patterns. The Public Library of South Australia (now the State Library of South Australia) established as part of a Public Library, Museum and Art Gallery conglomerate, succeeded a series of private subscription libraries. Its foundation stone was laid in 1879 and it opened in December 1884, and in a little over six months over 50 000 people had visited. Like its counterparts in Sydney, Melbourne and Hobart, it was intended to be an educational force, a reference library to 'meet the requirements of casual readers as well as those who pursue continuous studies'. The new library was 'a pure reference collection of scholarly works, with no quarter given to works of fiction or entertainment'. The lending services of its predecessors were hived off to a new subscription-based library, known as the Adelaide Circulating Library. Elsewhere in the state, well-coordinated institute libraries predominated long into the third quarter of the twentieth century. 'The story of free rate-supported public libraries in South Australia prior to 1955 can be told quickly and simply — there were none'.

In Western Australia the Legislative Council commemorated the Golden Jubilee of Queen Victoria's reign with a library. The Victoria Public Library (later renamed Public Library of Western Australia to avoid confusion with the Public Library of Victoria, and now known as the State Library of Western Australia) opened in temporary premises in Perth in 1889 with 1796 books on its shelves, seating for about 50 readers, and a recess reserved for ladies. It too was purely a reference library, excluding 'the more ephemeral works of fiction', but intended to be strong in science, history, biography, the classics, literature, agriculture and mining. It did not establish a lending branch, and 'the main source of books available for loan in Perth for most of the nineteenth and early twentieth century' was an institute which had been established in 1851 as the Swan River Mechanics' Institute (pictured on p. 323). The first free public library run by a local authority would not materialise in Western Australia until 1948.

Adelaide Public Library, Museum and Art Gallery (now the Mortlock Wing) c. 1885. Designed by E. J. Woods, amending an original design by R. G. Thomas, the building opened on 18 December 1884, constructed at a total cost of £36,395. The image was taken by Samuel White Sweet (1825–1886), a sea captain and surveyor who became a full-time photographer in 1875 and opened a studio in Adelaide. Travelling throughout South Australia in a horse-drawn darkroom, he captured images of towns, buildings and landscapes and is described as 'the colony's foremost documentary photographer of the 1870s' (*ADB*, vol.6. p. 231). Photograph, 20.6 x 15.5 cm. (State Library of South Australia)

In Queensland institutes abounded — there were over a hundred by 1890 — with funding from subscribers and some Government support. Queenslanders had to wait until 1902 for the opening of their state reference library, the Public Library of Queensland (now the State Library of Queensland). There were no truly free public lending libraries in Queensland until the takeover of the Townsville School of Arts Library by the local council in 1938.

With significant qualification, the decade to 1890 was an early peak in library provision for some parts of Australia. In the words of an English visitor in the 1870s, there were some 'institutions of the highest educational value'. Admittedly only a few were truly free and public, like the reference libraries in Sydney, Melbourne, Hobart and Adelaide, a small number of town hall-based reference libraries and a smaller number of free lending libraries. The majority remained subscription libraries within athenaeums, schools of arts, and mechanics' and literary institutes, with continuing colonial and occasionally local government subsidies to supplement membership fees. Many were at the time well run, resourced and patronised, but their membership represented only a small proportion of the local citizenry.

The capital city reference libraries, however, attracted much favourable attention from users and visitors. Despite the growing overcrowding and dinginess of its building, which he described as 'a very miserable place for such a city as Sydney', the Free Public Library impressed English industrialist Richard Tangye so much that he and his brother George later presented it with a First Folio of Shakespeare. British psychologist, critic and editor, Havelock Ellis, spending formative years in Australia, remembered the Free Public Library as 'an unfailing source of inspiration and delight . . . There were many good books, and few readers, and no formalities. I could wander where I would, and settle in some quiet corner to devour what I chose'. Ellis immersed himself in Stendhal, Landor, Brantôme, Quételet and Rabelais. 'No library', he declared, 'has been so influential in guiding and moulding my mental activities . . . Here in some beautiful dishes — for there were some fine editions on the shelves — the gods bountifully granted to me the nectar and ambrosia on which my spirit was fed'.

Ellis and Tangye were perhaps not typical visitors, but we know that the capital city reference libraries were used by all classes who lived or worked within convenient reach of them: people from salubrious suburbs rubbed shoulders with labourers and skilled workers from the booming local industries. The working classes were given special consideration: the 10 pm closing time of the Free Public Library, like its counterpart in Melbourne, was well beyond the end of the normal working day. The concept of 'university of the people' was not just rhetoric. A visitor to the Melbourne Public Library in 1884 saw it crowded with 400 readers, 'many of them quite of the poorest classes, and many horny-handed sons of labour'. In Sydney users of the Lending Branch were required to state their occupations, and these covered a very wide range. As the founding trustees would have hoped, there were many scholars, teachers and clergymen. But there were also butchers, bakers, cabinet-makers, japanners, coopers, undertakers, balloonists, billiard-markers, brush-makers, drivers and drovers, lift boys, tea blenders, telegraph-hands and typewriters. University students were certainly heavy users — university libraries were small and sometimes, as in the early days in Melbourne, only professors were allowed to borrow. Library users were generally respectable and orderly: 'Among them is not one alongside whom I would be shamed to sit', Hugh Wright said of his clientele in Sydney. They were awed perhaps by the vision of floor to ceiling books and studious fellow readers, or by the vigilance of library staff who viewed them from a dais or peered down at them from a gallery. If they were dirty, disorderly, drunk or led a dog into the reading rooms they were shown the door, but incidents were rare. Thefts and mutilation were infrequent offences, punishable by hard labour in serious cases, or by a parental thrashing for erring juniors.

The variety of reading matter was as diverse as the occupations and backgrounds of those who visited. As Hugh Wright recorded a little later, they might be reading Galton's *Fingerprints*, Brothers's *Photography*, Scheiner's *Astronomical spectroscopy*, Nansen's *First Crossing of Greenland*, Farrar's *Early Days of Christianity*, Heine's works, Swedenborg's *Arcana Coelestia*, Graham's *Socialism Old and New*, or Spender's *State and Pensions in Old Age*. The few novels would be very well read and more Dickens would be read on a Sunday, Wright opined, than Thackeray, Scott, Kingsley, Fielding and Stevenson put together. He noted that people who began to use the Library 'for the little fiction it contains, cannot help dipping into other deeper and more useful works'. Even the desultory readers, browsing aimlessly among the thousands of books would before long be following a purposeful course of reading. Not everyone came to settle down for extended reading: many people would run in to check a reference, verify a date in history, confirm the meaning of a word, or find an address in a directory or the location of a town.

The major libraries were beginning to offer a measure of reader assistance and reference service. The staff of the capital city reference libraries was exclusively male, self-trained or learning from others on the job. Their leaders were sometimes scholarly, like Melbourne's Augustus Tulk, and often enthusiastic, methodical and hard-working like Sydney's Robert Cooper Walker. None had set out to become librarians: had Tulk not lost all his money in the goldfields he would not have been one of the 48 applicants for the position at Melbourne. If author Marcus Clarke had not needed the money, he would not have spent eight years enduring the 'drudgery of routine work' at the same library. Librarianship in Australia was by the end of the period beginning to assume some stature as an occupation and there were stirrings of professionalism: within a few years representatives from libraries in Australia and New Zealand founded an albeit short-lived association in a first attempt to band together to discuss common issues.

Interest was also being shown in improving library methods, such as the innovative Dewey Decimal Classification and the card catalogue as an alternative to expensive and frequently out-of-date printed catalogues. Particularly in the state libraries in Sydney, Melbourne and Adelaide there had long been awareness of overseas developments in library services — Redmond Barry had actually presented two papers at the first International Conference of Librarians in London in 1877 and library workers were able to read publications of the British and American library associations. The period of the enthusiastic amateur in librarianship was coming to an end with the recognition of the need for more professional approaches in the larger libraries in the capital cities.

So it was that, a century after Tench envisioned a metropolis with a library as one of the signs of civilisation, most capitals had, or would soon have, such an edifice. There were colonial government-funded reference libraries in Melbourne, Sydney, Adelaide, Hobart and Perth, all approaching library services, like their railway gauges, in a distinctively different way. These were the state libraries of the future, building research collections, including formerly neglected local publications, frequently aided by legal deposit under the copyright legislation of each colony and by judicious purchases, gifts and occasional bequests.

It was an uneven and imperfect pattern of library services, even in the capital cities with good reference libraries, and was generally worse in country areas. It was not destined to improve for some time. Surveying Australian libraries in 1934 Ralph Munn and E. R. Pitt wrote that 'as a whole Australia was better provided with local libraries in 1880 than it is today'.

In 1890, in the afterglow of commemorations of the centenary of white settlement and of the Queen's Jubilee, however, there was little evidence of serious dissatisfaction with the libraries available. Few people had been exposed to the concept of a rate-supported free public library. Hence, there was little public pressure to open new free libraries and consequently a lack of official and political interest. Some colonial governments could demonstrate that they were already funding a major library in their capital city, in some cases very generously, as well as giving subsidies to institutes and grants-in-aid to local authorities. Libraries were still generally seen as a colonial government-funded operation, and there remained a distinct reluctance on the part of most local authorities to take on increased responsibilities by developing and maintaining public libraries. In the most densely populated cities too, local councils could absolve themselves of responsibility, pointing out that library services were already available from the capital city reference libraries, the future state libraries. It could truly be said that these libraries were the backbone of the library system, but also that for many years they prevented free public libraries from developing their own backbones. There was little desire on the part of the trustees of even the most progressive state libraries to extend beyond the terms of reference of their own institutions, and the library profession had not evolved to the point where practitioners could clearly articulate the case for more extensive free library development. They would not begin to do so in earnest until well into the twentieth century, when key practitioners, lay people and prophets from abroad would so mobilise public opinion that governments, local and state, would be obliged to act.

NOTE ON SOURCES

Watkin Tench's rosy outlook for the infant colony is from *Sydney's First Four Years: Being a Reprint of 'A Narrative of the Expedition to Botany Bay' and 'A Complete Account of the Settlement at Port Jackson'*, Sydney, Angus and Robertson and the Royal Australian Historical Society, 1961. The views of English observers are from Anthony Trollope's *Australia and New Zealand*, Melbourne, George Robertson, 1876; C. W. Holgate's *An Account of the Chief Libraries of Australia and Tasmania*, London, Whittingham, 1886, and facsimile reprint, Adelaide, Libraries Board of South Australia, 1971; and Havelock Ellis's *My Life*, London, Heinemann, 1940.

Overviews of Australian library development are provided in Peter Biskup and Doreen Goodman, *Libraries in Australia*, Wagga Wagga, Centre for Information Studies, Charles Sturt University, 1995; Harrison Bryan, 'Libraries' in *The Book in Australia*, Melbourne, Australian Reference Publications, 1988, pp. 139-71; P. C. Candy and John Laurent, eds, *Pioneering Culture: Mechanics' Institutes and Schools of Arts in Australia*, Adelaide, Auslib Press, 1994; R. F. Doust and Harrison Bryan, 'State Libraries' in *Design for Diversity: Library Services for Higher Education and Research in Australia*, St Lucia, UQP, 1977, pp. 79-114; and Norman Lynravn, *Libraries in Australia*, Melbourne, F. W. Cheshire, 1948.

On New South Wales see F. M. Bladen, *Public Library of New South Wales: Historical Notes Commemorative of the Building of the Mitchell Wing*, Sydney, Government Printer, 1906; and his *Public Library of New South Wales: Historical Notes*, 2nd ed., Sydney, Government Printer, 1911; C. H. Bertie, *A Short History of the Sydney Municipal Library 1877-1927*, Sydney, Municipal Council of Sydney, 1927; Free Public Library, Sydney, *Australasian Bibliography (in Three Parts): Catalogue of Books in the Free Public Library, Sydney, Relating to, or Published in Australasia*, Sydney, Government Printer, 1893; David J. Jones, 'Public Library Development in New South Wales', *ALJ*, vol.54, no.2, May 2005, pp. 130-33; and his *A Source of Inspiration and Delight: the Buildings of the State Library of New South Wales since 1826*, Sydney, Library Council of New South Wales, 1988; Peter Orlovich, 'Antecedents of the Free Library Movement in New South Wales', in *The Variety of Librarianship: Essays in Honour of John Wallace Metcalfe*, W. Boyd Rayward, ed., Sydney, Library Association of Australia, 1976, pp. 114-33; and his 'The Decline of Schools of Arts Libraries in New South Wales', in *Australian Library History: Papers from* the Second Forum on Australian Library History, Canberra, 19-20 July 1985, Peter Biskup and Maxine K. Rochester, eds, Canberra, Canberra College of Advanced Education, 1985, pp. 50-60; and his Library Legislation in New South Wales 1867–1937, MLib thesis, University of New South Wales, 1971; Wilma Radford, 'Charles Badham and the Free Public Library of Sydney', in *The Variety of Librarianship: Essays in Honour of John Wallace Metcalfe*, W. Boyd Rayward, ed., Sydney, Library Association of Australia, 1976, pp. 134-45; G. D. Richardson, 'A Man of Zeal and Application', *ALJ*, vol.25, no.7, August 1976, pp. 242-43; and also his *The Colony's Quest for a National Library*, Sydney, Public Library of New South Wales, 1961. Hugh Wright wrote on 'Sunday opening of libraries' in *Account of the Proceedings of the First Australasian Library Conference held at Melbourne*, Melbourne, Government Printer, 1896, pp. 26-27.

On South Australian libraries see H. C. Brideson, 'The Public Library of South Australia', *ALJ*, vol.6, no.2, April 1957, pp. 61-64; Carl Bridge, 'The South Australian Library Story', in *BLRCA Forum, 1984*, Elizabeth Morrison and Michael Talbot, eds, Clayton, VIC, Graduate School of Librarianship, Monash University, 1985, pp. 35-38; and his *A Trunk Full of Books: History of the State Library of South Australia and its Forerunners*, Netley, Wakefield Press in association with the State Library of South Australia, 1986; W. G. Buick, 'Central Government Agencies in the History of Libraries in South Australia', *ALJ*, vol.11, no .1, January 1960, pp. 1-9; Charlotte Henry, 'Cultural Collecting Institutions as a Reflection of their Society: Libraries in Nineteenth Century South Australia', paper presented at *Libraries for the People: the 11th Australian Library History Forum*, State Library of New South Wales, 18-19 November 2014, https://www.sl.nsw.gov.au/sites/default/files/alhf2014_charlottehenry.pdf [accessed 24 April 2024]; Brian R. Howes, *Public Library Services in South Australia: The Story to 1976*, Wagga Wagga, School of Library and Information Science, Riverina College of Advanced Education, 1982; Michael Page, *Port Adelaide and its Institute 1851–1979*, Adelaide, Rigby, 1981; A. Grenfell Price, *Libraries in South Australia: Report of an Inquiry Commissioned by the South Australian Government into the System of Management of Libraries Maintained or Assisted by the State*, Adelaide, Government Printer, 1937; *The South Australian Institute, comprising the Public Library, Art Gallery and Museums: Addresses Delivered at the Laying of the Foundation Stone . . . November 7, 1879*, Adelaide, W. K. Thomas & Co., 1879; M. R. Talbot, *A Chance to Read: A History of the Institutes Movement in South Australia*,

Adelaide, Libraries Board of South Australia, 1992; and his 'A Reevaluation of the South Australian Literary and Scientific Association Library', *AARL*, vol.39, no.4, December 2008, pp. 269-90.

For Tasmanian libraries see A. E. Browning, 'History of the State Library of Tasmania', *ALJ*, vol.8, no.2, April 1959, pp. 85-90; Heather Gaunt, Identity and Nation in the Australian Public Library: The Development of Local and National Collections 1850s–1940s, using the Tasmanian Public Library as Case Study, PhD thesis, University of Tasmania, 2010; John Horner, *Public Library Services in Tasmania*, Sydney, James Bennett, 1966; John Levett, 'James Backhouse Walker, the "Mope-Hawk", and the Tasmanian Public Library — a Cautionary Tale from 1870', in *Tasmanian Insights: Essays in Honour of Geoffrey Thomas Stilwell*, Gillian Winter, ed., Hobart, State Library of Tasmania, 1992, pp. 113-26; his *The Origins of the State Library of Tasmania*, Hobart, Australian Library Promotion Council, Tasmanian State Committee, 1988; and his The Tasmanian Public Library 1849–1869: The Rise and Fall of a Colonial Institution, MLib thesis, Monash University, 1984; and his 'The Tasmanian Public Library in 1850: Its Members, its Managers and its Books' in *BLRCA Forum, 1984*, pp. 11-21.

Accounts of Victorian libraries are in T. F. Bride, 'The Public Lending Library of Victoria', in *Account of the Proceedings of the First Australasian Library Conference held at Melbourne*, Melbourne, Government Printer, 1896, pp. 47-52; Jean Hagger, *Public Library Services in Victoria*, Sydney, James Bennett, 1966; Sue Healy, The Development of Libraries for the Community in Victoria, 1850–1885, MLib thesis, Monash University, 1983; Brian Hubber, 'Leading by Example: Barry in the Library', *LTLJ*, no.73, Autumn 2004, pp. 68-74; and his 'The Proto-profession of Librarianship: The Richmond Public Library, 1884', in *Coming Together: Papers from the Seventh Australian Library History Forum, Royal Melbourne Institute of Technology, 12 October 1996*, Melbourne, Ancora Press, 1997, pp. 3-13; Wallace Kirsop, 'Barry's "Great Emporium" in the Twenty-First Century: The Future of the State Library of Victoria Collections', *LTLJ*, no.46, Spring 1991, pp. 49-59; and his 'Redmond Barry and Libraries', *LTLJ*, no.73, Autumn 2004, pp. 55-67; Colin A. MacCallum, 'History of the Public Library of Victoria', *ALJ*, vol.8, no.4, October 1959, pp. 188-96; and his *The Public Library of Victoria 1856–1956*, Melbourne, Public Library of Victoria, 1956; David McVilly, 'The Acquisitions Policy of the State Library of Victoria, 1853-1880', *LTLJ*, vol.2, no.7, April 1971, pp. 58-63; his A History of the State Library of Victoria 1853–1974, MA thesis, Monash

University, 1975; and his 'Something to Blow About', *LTLJ*, vol.2, no.8, October 1971, pp. 81-90; Melbourne Public Library, *The Catalogue of the Melbourne Public Library for 1861*, Melbourne, the Library, [1862?]; Margery Ramsay, 'Concept of a Public Library: The Melbourne Public Library', in *BLRCA Forum, 1984*, pp. 22-27; Sue Reynolds, 'Libraries, Librarians and Librarianship in the Colony of Victoria', *AARL*, vol.40, no.1, March 2009, pp. 50-64; E. M. Robertson, 'A Century of Service: the Collingwood Free Library', *ALJ*, vol.9, no.4, October 1960, pp. 189-91; and R. W. E. Wilmot, *The Melbourne Athenaeum 1839-1939, History and Records of the Institution*, Melbourne, Stilwell and Stephens, 1939.

For Western Australia see Peter Biskup, 'The Public Library of Western Australia', *ALJ*, vol.9, no.1, January 1960, pp. 3-10; John Cook, 'The Public Library of Western Australia', in *BLRCA Forum, 1984*, pp. 28-34; and his *Information, Enrichment and Delight: Public Libraries in Western Australia*, Halifax, Nova Scotia, Dalhousie University Libraries and School of Library Service, and London, Vine Press, 1985; Claire Forte, 'From Strength to Strength: The Evolution of Western Australia's Library Service', *AARL*, vol.34, no.4, December 2003, pp. 251-64; Jack Honniball, 'The Public Library of Western Australia 1887-1955', in *Western Perspectives: Library and Information Services in Western Australia*, Perth, Australian Library and Information Association Western Australian Branch, 1990, pp. 31-34; and F. A. Sharr, 'Library Service for the Public in Western Australia', *ALJ*, vol.22, no.6, July 1973, pp. 212-16.

Insights into librarians and library users can be found in M. Askew and B. Hubber, 'The Colonial Reader Observed: Reading in its Cultural Context', in *The Book in Australia*, Melbourne, Australian Reference Publications, 1988, pp. 110-37; Lara Atkin et al, *Early Public Libraries and Colonial Citizenship in the British Southern Hemisphere*, Cham, Switzerland, Palgrave Macmillan, 2019; Brian Hubber, 'Libraries and Readers in Nineteenth Century Melbourne', in *BLRCA Forum, 1984*, pp. 55-63; John Adams, 'More than "librarie keepers"' from the same proceedings, pp. 93-101; and Peter Mansfield, 'The Issue of Access', in *Buildings, Books and Beyond: Mechanics' Worldwide Conference 2004*, 2nd ed., Windsor, VIC, Prahran Mechanics Institute Press, 2004, pp. 267-77.

CHAPTER 15

Mechanics' Institutes

Wallace Kirsop

It was in retrospect fateful that the first organised distribution of books in New South Wales and Van Diemen's Land in the 1820s coincided with the emergence of the mechanics' institutes movement in Britain. The colonial expedients of the decades between 1788 and the end of the Napoleonic Wars included gestures towards the development of parish libraries and collections designed to disseminate useful knowledge. However, the need to go beyond the book clubs, reading societies and subscription libraries that were set up after 1820 essentially for the benefit of Sydney, Hobart and country élites was obvious. A framework for the creation of free rate-supported public libraries lay quite far in the future. It is, therefore, hardly astonishing that a then-recent Scottish invention suggested to ambitious local communities across the Australian continent a way of bringing books and journals to much wider categories of readers and borrowers.

The model was one that was avowedly adapted to the circumstances of a Britain well embarked on the first Industrial Revolution. Founding texts like Henry Brougham's *Practical Observations upon the Education of the People, addressed to the Working Classes and their Employers* of 1824 make this clear. Since the intended audience was the growing body of artisans and skilled industrial workers rather than labourers at large, the emphasis was on classes in technical and scientific subjects and on the provision of laboratories and suitable libraries. In Brougham's view, the mechanics themselves 'should have the principal share in the management' of the institutions. This was not always the case, with the result that there were, not infrequently, quarrels about the direction to be taken. One can add to this the desire by some rich patrons to push the new creations towards literary pursuits. William Rathbone Greg (1809–1881), an early friend of Nicol Drysdale Stenhouse (1806–1873), long prominent in the affairs of the Sydney Mechanics' School of Arts, attempted precisely that at the beginning of the Bury Mechanics' Institute in Lancashire. In a letter to Stenhouse, then still in Edinburgh, on 19 December 1829 (Stenhouse Correspondence, Mitchell Library, vol. 2, A99, p. 241), Greg, later the son-in-law of James Wilson of *The Economist* and father of the great bibliographer Walter Wilson Greg (1875–1959), states:

> We have begun upon quite a new principle, of making our institution, less *useful* & more attractive — of attending less to science than to literature — & of seeking less to give *knowledge* to the lower classes than to sharpen their intellects and refine their minds.

This contrast was to become a leitmotiv in the history of mechanics' institutes in many places.

Given that the Australian colonies were — until the gold rushes of the 1850s — enjoying an unusually prolonged eighteenth century based on pastoral, agricultural and trading activities, the temptation to depart from Glasgow and Edinburgh orthodoxy could be quite strong. Although there is no direct evidence of conscious borrowings, it is curious that the designations used for mechanics' institutes in various countries and places echo the terms employed in France between 1780 and 1820 for societies set up to allow people beyond the restricted élites of learned academies to participate in an intellectual and cultural life that embraced both science and literature. American lyceums and Australian and New Zealand athenaeums in the nineteenth century shared something with the rather more patrician *lycées* and *athénées* of France before, during and after the Revolution. The wider aims suggested by the names were sometimes a better fit for what colonial communities removed from the industrial world hoped to achieve in bringing civilisation to their nascent European-style towns and rural districts.

It is striking how quickly the movement that started in Scotland spread to other parts of the English-speaking world. In the 1820s North America and Australia were following England itself in setting up mechanics' institutes. By 1830, a start had had been made in Newfoundland and Upper and Lower Canada, following the launch of the American lyceums in 1826. Thus Hobart in 1827 could claim to be in the vanguard.

In looking at the Australian scene it is appropriate to separate what was initiated before the gold rushes from what happened after the huge increase in European population that began in the 1850s. It is also necessary to look at each colony separately, because different traditions and legislative arrangements dictated the way in which mechanics' institutes were set up, financially supported and managed, not to mention the audiences they were able to attract.

Beginnings

Modern Australians are not used to thinking of Van Diemen's Land as a serious rival to New South Wales in the cultural and intellectual sphere in the first half of the nineteenth century. Yet Hobart, Launceston and small settlements in places like Bothwell and Evandale could at times set examples for the mainland. It was not an accident, therefore, that the Van Diemen's Land Mechanics' Institute, led by such people as James Ross, George Augustus Robinson and Chief Justice John Lewes Pedder, was the first in the field. Its history, recounted in various places by Stefan Petrow, was an uneven and ultimately unhappy one, with an ignominious end in 1871. The reasons go to the heart of the contradictions already noted for Britain itself. The strict prescriptions for an institution designed for the respectable working class ran up against the inclinations of an élite more interested in having something like another subscription library than in building an effective adjunct to technical and scientific education. The printed catalogue produced in 1839 reveals something of this character. The donations received from leading citizens — a constant feature of the founding years of many institutes — included the imperial folio with coloured plates of Humphry Repton's *Designs for the Pavilion at Brighton* of 1808, a work hardly to be found anywhere else in Australia in the whole nineteenth century.

Spasmodic government financial support, competition from other libraries and the disaffection of working people, these were the reasons for failure.

Despite tensions and conflicting initiatives of the kind noted in so many other places, the Launceston Mechanics' Institute, founded in 1842, proved to be a success over its long life. Even now, almost a century after the abandonment of its original name to claim identification as the Launceston Public Library, substantial parts of its stock of books have survived and are being zealously guarded by a society of concerned local citizens. Indeed community support can be seen as the key to the longevity and prosperity of a cultural centre set in a proud regional city. One of the important factors was the mobilisation of women as fundraisers even if they had a subordinate role in the institute's activities. The story of this unchallenged leader among Launceston's libraries has been expertly analysed by Petrow, who shows how traditional functions of a mechanics' institute — for example a museum and technical education — were eventually handed over to other bodies.

The Sydney Mechanics' School of Arts began its life in 1833 and has continued down to the present, but not on the same site, since it moved in 1989 and finally occupied new premises in the centre of the city in 2000. However, the path followed over nearly two centuries has mirrored that of many other colonial mechanics' institutes. Quite early it became obvious that its role — with paying subscribers — resembled that of a more democratic version of the Australian Subscription Library established in the previous decade. Notwithstanding this perhaps unavoidable shift in emphasis, there was a long-held commitment to some of the early aims. The School inaugurated its Working Mens' College as late as the end of the 1870s, only to have to cede it to government control and management in the middle of the next decade. What remained was the library with its cultural hub, which included a long-lived debating club and a room for chess players. At the end of the nineteenth century the library, as represented in a substantial printed catalogue of 1901, contained some 60 000 volumes for circulation — by no means swamped by fiction — alongside a reference collection of 4000 volumes and 500 newspapers and magazines. That the School managed to survive various crises like the 1840s depression in New South Wales and to achieve a quite solid position by the 1890s was due to support from the colonial authorities and from an influential group of backers, among whom Scots were quite prominent, and to the relatively late appearance of the Free Public Library and, in particular, of its lending branch in 1877.

Outside central Sydney the history of mechanics' institutes in those parts of New South Wales not hived off later to Victoria and Queensland is shadowy before mid-century. Various attempts were made at Parramatta and in the Hunter River Valley — Newcastle, Maitland and Singleton (Patrick's Plains) — in the 1830s and 1840s to launch viable libraries. Most of them failed after a relatively brief period, but the Newcastle one, not well documented in its early decades, does seem to have continued after its beginning in 1835.

South Australia offers a different situation altogether. The colony planned by people close to the founders of the mechanics' institutes movement was destined to have a library from the start. However, the collection landed at the end of 1836 in the Port River from the *Tam O'Shanter* was to remain untouched till 1838 when the South Australian Literary Association became the Adelaide Mechanics' Institute. By 1844 this had been replaced by the South Australian Subscription Library, which itself ran into difficulties. The Adelaide Mechanics' Institute was re-established in 1847 and merged the following year with the subscription library. The problems — caused by the colony's ideological commitment to voluntarist principles that precluded government subsidies — persisted over most of the ensuing decade until the South Australian Institute came into being in 1856 with proper public funding and a legislative basis. Five years later it moved into its own government-provided building in North Terrace. Membership was still on a subscription basis, but the Institute served what one might call a quasi-centralising function for institutions throughout the colony. As the outline of the succession of bodies in the first two decades suggests, the old tension between education for workers and cultural pursuits for the monied was well and truly in evidence. The activities and amenities recorded, apart from the libraries themselves, included classes, public lectures, conversaziones and musical performances.

In the light of the confused history of the original foundation of South Australia it was to be expected that the developments further afield in the colony would take time. There was briefly a subscription library at Balhannah in 1842–43, before rather faltering starts of mechanics' institutes at Hindmarsh and Bowden in 1847 and at Gawler in 1848. Many more efforts were made in the 1850s, but they were hampered by the massive exodus of the population to the diggings in Victoria. Complaints of the kind frequently aired in the other colonies about the deficiencies of the libraries were not lacking in South Australian publications. Progress, in short, was slow.

The Port Phillip District of New South Wales was almost as quick as South Australia in embracing the ideals of the mechanics' institute. Before Separation in mid-1851 and the inauguration of the Colony of Victoria, three institutes were set up. The first, the Melbourne Mechanics' Institution, began in 1839, four years after the first European settlers arrived. It is still on the same site in Collins Street, alongside the Melbourne Town Hall, in the fourth nineteenth-century iteration of its building, which includes a theatre, formerly a hall, as well as a library. As in Sydney, little of the original book collection has been preserved, but the cultural programme declared in the change of name in the early 1870s to Melbourne Athenaeum is unmistakable. The perseverance of what can be regarded as the oldest of the city's intellectual and artistic centres is in some ways remarkable. It was long in competition with Mullen's Select Library, the nearest Australian equivalent to Mudie's in London, and with the Melbourne Public Library, although the latter did not have a lending branch till 1891. A mooted Victoria Subscription Library — advertised in the *Melbourne Commercial Directory* for 1853 — gave way quickly to the Public Library. What sustained Melbourne's strength in the later nineteenth century as the country's headquarters of culture was its growth in a little over five decades to a population approaching half a million. Substantial suburban resources, some of them closer to the 'useful knowledge' aims of the mechanics' institutes, were part of this evolution.

The two other institutes established in Victoria before 1850 were in Portland (1844) and Geelong (1846). The dates are subject to some caution because in both places other moves were afoot in that decade. Nonetheless it is evident that there was a call in the two still small communities for libraries fitting the Scottish model. Portland survived with difficulty till 1880, whereas Geelong had a much longer life due to its gradual embrace of a middle-class general cultural orientation. Once again a common colonial pattern was reaffirmed.

In the Moreton Bay District, which became Queensland in 1859, there were two foundations at mid-century that, after a certain amount of shuffling of names and purposes, settled down as Schools of Arts. William Augustine Duncan (1811–1885), former bookseller and publisher in his native Scotland, Catholic intellectual, journalist and public servant, was the leading spirit in a body launched in Brisbane in 1849 as a 'Lyceum For Literary and Scientific Discussion, Lectures, Etc.'. In the long term it became the North Brisbane School of Arts and played an important role in the bookish life of the colony's capital till the end of the century, 'fulfilling [the] recreational needs' 'of the cultured middle classes'. Similar foundations in Ipswich as early as 1850 coalesced and assumed the style of Ipswich Mechanics' School of Arts in 1858.

There were aspirations in the tiny population of European settlers in Western Australia before mid-century to create libraries for the use of parts at least of the community. Nothing durable came of the first attempts in the 1830s and 1840s to organise parish libraries, literary institutions, book and reading societies and even a mechanics' institute. The birth of the Swan River Mechanics' Institute in 1851 was the starting point of a movement that, like its models in the eastern colonies, was to expand significantly in the second half of the century.

From a brief overview of developments in all the Australian colonies before the gold rushes it is obvious that, amid all the false starts and disappointed hopes, these were institutions destined to survive, albeit in forms not envisaged in the Brougham blueprint. The imports were shaped in ways that mirrored perhaps what was also happening in Britain, but that corresponded to the needs of colonial societies advancing in their own separate trajectories. It is always important to remember that Separation preceded Federation in Australian history and that local character, for example in as central a domain as education, has been jealously guarded right down to the twenty-first century.

Swan River Mechanics Institute's Mechanics' Hall, located at Howick (later Hay) and Pier Streets, Perth, 1861. The Hall, established in 1851, is described today as Perth's first cultural centre. Its founding and long-term president Captain John Septimus Roe (1797–1878), naval officer, explorer and the colony's first Surveyor-General, was a key figure in the development of Western Australia and had a keen interest in natural history. The above image was captured by Alfred Hawes Stone (1801–1873), an amateur photographer whose photographs are the oldest in the collections of the State Library of Western Australia, and were mostly taken in the Perth area. (State Library of Western Australia)

After the gold rushes

With limited competition in the decades between 1850 and 1890 from free public libraries, notably those set up for research and reference in the colonial capitals, and from the closed collections of universities, parliaments and supreme courts, the mechanics' institute, whatever its designation in particular places, could seem to be the prototype of an institution contrived for lending books to subscribers, for providing a public reading room and for offering a venue for lectures, concerts and community events. It is this that explains why, even in competition with commercial circulating libraries, mechanics' institutes had a peculiarly dominant position in Australia in the second half of the nineteenth century as compared with other

English-speaking countries. Nowhere was this pre-eminence more marked than in Victoria, a fact that helps justify the attention given by several researchers in recent decades to the institutions of that State and to their history.

Published lists of mechanics' institutes in modern times show quite clearly how difficult it has become to distinguish between the bodies of different origins and with divergent names that had as their central purpose the provision of reading matter for subscribers drawn from the public at large. The Government of Victoria subsidised all libraries that offered free access to their reading rooms, as distinct from borrowing privileges. Mechanics' institutes were foremost among these, but the statistical returns also included other libraries that met the 'free' intention. Thus German clubs in Ballarat, Bendigo and Talbot enjoyed financial support in the 1870s and 1880s. Blurring of these boundaries and the elastic nature of many of the foundations claiming to be mechanics' institutes do not make it easy to undertake a strict count of what is relevant to the present chapter. One thing is certain: the handful of bodies created before 1851 proliferated enormously up to 1890, and indeed for a few decades after that. This dictates a much more economical approach to discussion of them.

Population growth — roughly sixfold between 1851 and 1890 — is the first key to what happened. However, it was not equal across the continent. Tasmania receded from its earlier prominence even if the establishment of its University in 1890 and the Tasmanian Exhibition of 1891–92 held in Launceston — a city with suburbs of just over 21 200 inhabitants — spoke against any sense of relegation to a lesser rank. Western Australia did not begin its first mining boom until the 1890s. Mechanics' institutes appeared in number in both these less populous colonies and brought libraries to small and sometimes remote communities. South Australia developed its network of Institutes in suburban and country areas, but it did not share in the expansion brought by gold further east. There was more rapid growth in the European population of Queensland in these decades, with a still characteristic spread of substantial towns along the coast and with notable advances in mining, agriculture and the pastoral industry to attract immigrants. In the 1850s, 1860s and

1870s mechanics' institutes made their appearance both inland and away to the north from Brisbane.

Even by 1890 two thirds of European settlers were concentrated in Victoria and New South Wales. Thus it was in those two colonies, especially the former, that more institutes were created than anywhere else to fill the void caused in many small communities by the absence of other central meeting places. Mechanics' institutes by tradition eschewed political and religious debates, so they were distinct from churches, often warring in those times of prejudice, and they were not identified with partisan campaigns. A township, often a village or a mere hamlet in European terms, could acquire a weatherboard hall, with a small library room attached, and provide not only reading matter, but a place of entertainment and a locale for public meetings. The turn of libraries in the twenty-first century towards community hubs is in many ways a revival of functions perfectly familiar more than a hundred years before to people all across the Australian continent.

Just as there was a considerable variety of names for the new establishments of the second half of the nineteenth century — with mechanics' institute predominating in Victoria and school of arts in New South Wales — so too there were many ways to follow or depart from the Brougham template. Local conditions, which in most places were not those of industrial Britain, determined how an institute would be shaped. Generalisation becomes, therefore, very difficult. One can have the debate about alleged 'social control' of the working class by the bourgeoisie in the institutes, but, despite criticisms that were heard in Australia and the occasional launching of rival workingmen's clubs, the issue is often irrelevant to what was sought, particularly in rural towns. It is piquant to note that the circulating section of the Sydney Mechanics' School of Arts catalogue of 1901 included the 1892 edition of Friedrich Engels's *Condition of the Working Class in England* as well as Karl Marx's *Capital*.

Institutes in major mining centres could make a serious effort to follow the Scottish ideal down to 1890 and beyond. The beginnings of technical education in the Australian colonies are linked in this way to what was being done in the classes, laboratories and museums that were a feature of a few mechanics' institutes in the second half of the nineteenth century. It is perhaps not surprising that more was being done in Victoria than elsewhere, but the achievements of the Sydney Mechanics' School of Arts and of the North Brisbane School of Arts cannot be ignored. The contributions made in the gold-rush towns of Ballarat and Bendigo were predictably substantial. The role of a suburban Melbourne institute, that of Prahran, founded in 1854, falls outside the norm, but its 1870 venture into a school of art and design was to lead to a technical school that, like the goldfields schools of mines, eventually became part of fully-fledged tertiary educational institutions. The Burke Museum, the surviving component of the Beechworth body established in 1856, has the rare distinction of being one of only three such nineteenth-century creations by mechanics' institutes to be still functioning. The sad fate of the Rockhampton School of Arts Museum, launched in 1869 and disbanded in 1946, was a more typical development.

In essence most mechanics' institutes after 1850 followed a mainstream path that made them community cultural centres in the widest possible sense. Before the crash of the early 1890s they had enough financial support from government and other sources to fulfil this mission in a respectable way. There were, however, ups and downs in many places: unsympathetic local authorities, declining enthusiasm on the part of the volunteers who were essential to effective management, shifts in population and economic activities, reluctance of people to subscribe or to attend the classes, lectures and penny readings organised for them. Women were important members of the audience for public events, and some larger institutes had 'ladies' reading rooms'. However, the women were not in control and usually confined to auxiliary duties like fundraising. Bazaars helped bring the money to supplement subscriptions and, in particular, to finance buildings. Alongside the modest halls — necessary not only for the institutes' own programmes but also for income from hiring out — to be found in many townships, there were grand Victorian structures in larger centres. More space meant more possibilities: concerts, theatre, art exhibitions, rooms for chess and, ultimately, billiards as the institutes moved from instruction to recreation and entertainment to maintain their membership. Any collection of photographs of major or defunct institutions speaks of civic pride, witness Ballarat, Sandhurst/Bendigo, Bundaberg, Port Pirie, Rockhampton, Braidwood and others. How well were these aspirations realised?

When one turns to books and readers, it is essential to note that, whatever their deficiencies, mechanics' institutes provided in most places in Australia during the later nineteenth century the only accessible free reading rooms stocked with local and overseas newspapers and magazines as well as basic reference collections. Subscribers had the opportunity to borrow from a range that included serious material on most subjects as well as a growing corpus of fiction. In the latter field there was competition from commercial circulating libraries, but many of these were quite ephemeral. We know better what the mechanics' institutes held because they often printed catalogues of their libraries. In some cases, too, surviving archives document purchases and dealings with suppliers. In later times collections were weeded and turned over, but enough have been at least partially preserved, for example in Launceston, Ballarat, Bendigo, Chiltern and Stanley, to give some depth and precision to the record. Apart from donations, not always appropriate, there were regular acquisitions from local and overseas sources. The latter could be preferred to avoid costs associated with the wholesalers, i.e., middlemen, of the colonial capitals. Duplicates from Mudie's in London and Mullen's in Melbourne readily found their way to country districts in Australia. An ever greater reliance on fiction meant finding recent material as cheaply and quickly as possible.

Identifying readers and borrowers for the period before 1890 is another task again. The database being assembled by the Mechanics' Institute Resource Centre at Prahran Mechanics' Institute will be fundamental in this sort of research. In the interim we do know who the members of the Swan River Mechanics' Institute were in the 1850s. More significantly, borrowing records for the Braidwood Literary Institute have survived for eighteen months in 1861-1862. They are a useful parallel to what has come down to us from the Evandale Subscription Library near Launceston at mid-century. Even if borrowing is not necessarily reading and absorbing, the data cannot be ignored.

Articulate individuals offer us the most telling testimony about the place of the institutes in reading lives — and particularly in the lives of future authors. From the schoolgirl Henry Handel (Ethel) Richardson in Maldon and the young John Shaw Neilson in Nhill we have glimpses of local possibilities and limitations. On the other hand it is clear that Joseph Furphy profited mightily from the Shepparton Free Library and Workingmen's Club of which he was a committee member. It may not have been much frequented as a library over the years, but the hours 9am to 10pm were generous for readers as tenacious as the novelist. Lamentations about the decline of the institutes after 1890 and on into the twentieth century should not overshadow all the positives of the decades after 1850. It is no small thing to have nourished a work such as Furphy's *Such is Life*.

NOTE ON SOURCES

The literature on mechanics' institutes is very considerable. Paradoxically the many buildings scattered across suburbs and country settlements have — long after most of them were converted to other purposes — inspired a nostalgia expressed in commemorative and celebratory volumes. Alongside this the last four decades have seen a growth in serious historical studies, not all of them the work of professional academics. The series of forums on Australian library history begun in 1984 gave much attention to the institute movement in general and to specific foundations in the various States. Similarly the *BSANZ Bulletin* and its successor *Script & Print* have continued to publish interesting and well-documented articles in this field. *Pioneering Culture: Mechanics' Institutes and Schools of Arts*, edited by Philip Candy and John Laurent (Adelaide, Auslib Press, 1994), inaugurated a tradition of collaborative works exclusively on the institutes themselves. The papers given at conferences, starting with Kilmore in 1998, then 2000 in Melbourne, 2002 in Sydney, 2004 in Melbourne, but now Mechanics' Worldwide, as at Bath in 2009, Ballarat in 2018 and most recently hosted in Edinburgh in 2021, have been published as substantial volumes with a wealth of detailed information on institutes in Australia and overseas (as of April 2024, video presentations of the Edinburgh papers were available online: mivic.org.au/mechanics-worldwide.html, but a volume had not yet been published). Mechanics' Institutes of Victoria, which began in 1998, has played a central role in all this, not least through its regular newsletter,

Useful Knowledge, another contribution by Jim and Bronwyn Lowden to the cause.

It will be apparent that Victoria has been the national leader in this effort. Some of the major outcomes of the research will be found in Bronwyn Lowden, *Mechanics' Institutes, Schools of Art, Athenaeums, etc.*, 3rd ed., Donvale, VIC, Lowden Publishing Co., 2010; Pam Baragwanath and Ken James, *These Walls Speak Volumes: A History of Mechanics' Institutes in Victoria*, Melbourne, [the authors], 2015; Pam Baragwanath and Ken James, *Ubiquitous and Necessary: Australia's mechanics' institutes and schools of arts etc: A Research Guide*, Melbourne, [the authors], 2016. For other parts of Australia one could note in particular M. R. Talbot, *A Chance to Read: a History of the Institutes Movement in South Australia*, Adelaide, Libraries Board of South Australia, 1992; and Stefan Petrow, *Going to the Mechanics: A History of the Launceston Mechanics' Institute 1842-1914*, Launceston, Historical Survey of Northern Tasmania, 1998.

CHAPTER 16

Commercial Circulating Libraries

Wallace Kirsop

The trade began hiring out books well before 1700, but the commercial circulating library is generally accepted as being a creation of the eighteenth century. Both in the United Kingdom and in its colonies the institution was widespread in towns of any importance at the time Europeans first settled in Australia. Consequently it could be expected that as soon as booksellers were active in New South Wales and Van Diemen's Land circulating libraries established by and associated with them would appear. From the late 1820s on they played an important part in bringing books and magazines to an essentially middle-class clientele. Because of the relative slowness of Australia in developing an effective nationwide network of free public libraries, as discussed by David J. Jones earlier in this volume, the commercial lending library, sometimes coupled with a reading room, survived till the last quarter of the twentieth century. As a fundamentally private and profit-making enterprise it needs to be distinguished without equivocation from the cooperative and community-based ventures that took such forms as book clubs, reading societies, subscription libraries and mechanics' institutes, all of them present in colonial Australia as early as the 1820s.

Most circulating libraries were quite small, ranging from a few hundred to a little over a thousand titles. Right up to 1890 the number of volumes could be substantially larger because of the vogue of the three-decker, the consecrated physical form in which the first editions of novels appeared in London in the Victorian period. Subscriptions by the year or for shorter periods and fees for casual use of the reading room were the basis of the proprietor's income for this part of his or her business. Hastily compiled and bibliographically inadequate catalogues, usually mere lists of titles, were sold to subscribers for sums like sixpence or one shilling. Borrowers did not necessarily attend the library in person. It is clear from advertisements and the spelling out of lending rules that other family members or servants could be sent to fetch books selected from the catalogue. Apart from customers in the neighbourhood or within the town there were sometimes arrangements — at differential rates of subscription — for borrowers residing in quite distant country districts. Each title was allocated a number corresponding, one assumes, to its place on the shelves and certainly to the order in which it appeared in the manuscript borrowing register. The number of surviving Australian printed catalogues of these businesses is pitiful. What the documents reveal is the preponderance of fiction in the book stocks provided. For anyone familiar with what was happening at the same time in the Northern Hemisphere this is altogether predictable.

Despite the scantiness of the sources available to us, we are privileged in one way. Most European studies of the phenomenon have had to concentrate almost exclusively on catalogues and, where relevant, on government records of registration and licensing. Assessing public taste from the titles and authors present in catalogues is a tempting speculative exercise. However, where borrowing registers have survived, as is the case with the years from 1846 to the early 1850s when the Walch family took over the bookshop and Derwent Circulating Library established in Hobart in the late 1830s by Samuel Augustus Tegg, we can see how customers behaved. In 1846–47 more than 500 members of respectable Hobart society plus some people living at a distance frequented the Walches' establishment. For the most part they concentrated, men and women, on fiction to the exclusion of the more serious literature that was also provided. More important, they sought out in particular recent novels that had just been added to the library. Thus the presence in the catalogue printed in 1846 of authors from an earlier generation like Jane Austen and Walter Scott can be misleading. What people were borrowing — but not necessarily reading or digesting, or course — was in general the new writing of figures like Dickens, Charles Lever and Eugène Sue (in English translation). Common sense should tell us that things would happen in this way and that it is dangerous to compile statistics of the vogue of older and newer literary movements from catalogues reflecting a stock that is at least partly superseded.

The Walch example teaches us that to survive in the business of lending books one had to continue to invest capital in new titles. Although the Walches did this they ended up in the early 1850s abandoning the field to competitors, especially William Westcott, who in the 1860s ran a much bigger operation with several thousand titles. Many people who started out in a small way were unable to renew their stocks and quite quickly perished or turned to other, more profitable sides of the business such as bookselling or, especially, dealing in stationery, fancy goods and patent medicines. Few circulating libraries created before the 1860s proved to be durable.

In surveying the as yet largely unexplored domain of the nineteenth-century Australian circulating library, the distinction between the small ephemeral enterprises of early pastoral and gold-rush decades and the substantial metropolitan institutions of the later period is central. We may not always have quaint details, as for the Walches, of thieves, mutilators and slow payers. None the less it is possible to go beyond the fugitive newspaper advertisements or the goldfields photographs, like those in the Holtermann Collection, that are the only surviving evidence of the existence of many commercial libraries across suburbs and country towns. As has been recently demonstrated for New Zealand, progress in the identification and exploration of the relevant businesses will depend on systematic trawling through newspapers published after 1850.

Meeting early needs

Although there is no doubt that circulating libraries were present in Sydney at least as early as 1826, the first surviving catalogue — for the establishment attached to William McGarvie's Australian Stationery Warehouse — dates from 1829. For an annual subscription of £2 — a sum that would have been a decisive barrier for the bulk of the population — customers could borrow two volumes at a time for up to a week, or three days for new titles. The overdue fee was twopence per night. The library's stock is laid out alphabetically, essentially but not exclusively by title, over ten pages. Numbers are assigned to the fewer than 500 items. Many of the low numbers are for non-fiction. It is, therefore, possible to imagine that public demand pushed McGarvie into acquiring novels more and more for his collection. None the less Adam Smith's *The Wealth of Nations* in four volumes is no.425 and Charles Tompson, Jnr's *Wild Notes, from the Lyre of a Native Minstrel*, a local Sydney publication from three years before, is no.300. An early emphasis on Scotland gives way to fashionable fiction, including some of the Gothic novels whose original editions, present for McGarvie's readers, are now so hard to find.

Four years later a new edition of the catalogue included over 1800 titles and occupied 44 pages that had been written with more care. Yet, at the beginning of 1835, McGarvie sent his stock to be sold by auction when he turned to his new farming career. There is much in this that is typical of the commercial libraries of the period, including a short life determined by inability or unwillingness to go on investing capital. The choice of books, too, fell into a pattern that was repeated elsewhere. Restless entrepreneurs like John Pascoe Fawkner in Launceston and then in Melbourne were to try their hands at a library business that was about giving customers what they wanted.

The Mitchell Library holds a rare example of a catalogue printed in London in 1832 to accompany an invoice of books sent by A. K. Newman, successor of the Minerva Press, to form the nucleus of a lending library in Sydney. Under the general name of 'Australian Circulating Library' it offered well-heeled subscribers — the annual fee was three guineas — nearly a thousand titles, representing essentially fiction of the half-century between 1780 and 1830. Newspaper advertisements show it as operating from two different locations and with two proprietors between 1832 and 1837. Similar collections were sent to various parts of the English-speaking world, but few of them are as well documented.

The contents of the Derwent Circulating Library in 1846 and of Charles Platts's collection in Adelaide in 1848 were substantially the same. Indeed, as one sees auctioneers and publishers offering their wares explicitly to the proprietors of commercial libraries, one comes to recognise, as contemporaries did, that there was a sort of perennial stock-in-trade that kept changing only to the extent that novels and novelists went in and out of fashion. In the Australian colonies, as elsewhere, the circulating library performed the important function of bringing fiction to readers in a relatively affordable and accessible form when other, public institutions either did not exist or disdained a genre put out by publishers in a quite absurdly expensive way geared to the London carriage trade.

Given all the uncertainties of colonial bookselling before the market was properly organised in the late 1850s, it is not astonishing that many libraries were precarious enterprises. William Baker's Juvenile Circulating Library in Sydney between 1843 and the beginning of 1847 was an interesting, probably opportunistic and certainly undercapitalised experiment in a field that was beginning to emerge in Europe. Economic pressures later saw the same proprietor open in booming Bendigo 'Baker's gold-diggers' Go-a-head Library and Registration Office for New Chums' in competition with even more shadowy undertakings like 'Porter's Yankee Circulating Library'. There was a need to be met, and we know that the diggers were for the time more than ordinarily literate. However, once the frontier settled down and sought civilised amenities, other institutions were created and the hiring out of books had to be put on a firmer footing.

The metropolitan professionals

Whilst it is true that the Tegg brothers brought London professionalism and connections to the colonial trade in the 1830s and 1840s, their departure and the changes wrought by the gold rush in Australia and by free trade in Britain meant that there had to be a new start in the second half of the 1850s. This was to have a direct effect on the conduct and on the role of circulating libraries.

Small and temporary businesses continued to exist in suburbs and in country towns, but they found themselves hard pressed by mechanics' institutes and ultimately by free public libraries. In the metropolitan centres on the other hand there was a niche market for large commercial lending libraries on the model of Mudie's in

London. Irritatingly we do not have nearly enough information about institutions that survived in some cases well into the twentieth century.

The trade acquired new personnel after 1850, and much of it had been thoroughly trained in major book centres in the British Isles, notably London, Edinburgh, Glasgow and Dublin. Alongside the great wholesaler-importer George Robertson (1825–1898), Melbourne was served by his fellow-Dubliner Samuel Mullen, who established the premier lending library. His assistant — and eventual successor — Adam Graham Melville imported his Edinburgh expertise to the library side of the business. Unfortunately, the firm's archives have disappeared and with them the library catalogues. Melville's brief recorded account of his experience is not very helpful, so that the advertising magazine *S. Mullen's Monthly Circular of Literature, &c* — launched as late as 1884 — and some earlier bookselling catalogues listing retired stock from the library are the only sources we have at present to add to the anecdotes and picturesque reminiscences that circled round one of the major features of Melbourne's Collins Street 'Block'.

The Australia-wide reputation of Mullen's Library eclipsed that of most other larger establishments of the second half of the century, for example Westcott's in Hobart and T. M. Buzzard's Melbourne Circulating Library, a copy of whose substantial catalogue organised by genres was kept by James Edward Neild. In Sydney the leading name was that of William Maddock, whose business passed to William Dymock in the 1890s. Once again there is a lack of information. The few surviving catalogues are mostly for the bookselling side of the business. A four-page leaflet, *New Books added to Maddock's Select Library, 383 George Street, Sydney* of October 1878, gives some notion of the operations of a superior specimen of the type. Yet we can only guess at the composition of a clientele prepared to pay four guineas a year for 'Three works at a time and two Magazines'. It is perhaps appropriate to suspect that these were people more concerned with social distinction than with cheap books.

A paper by Paul Eggert wondered how much the colonial circulating libraries contributed to the demise of the three-decker in the 1890s. The evidence is too sparse, but the pressure for cheap and accessible fiction is so constant in Australia that some role cannot be ruled out. The institution was able to adapt to new circumstances and lived on well beyond the 1890s.

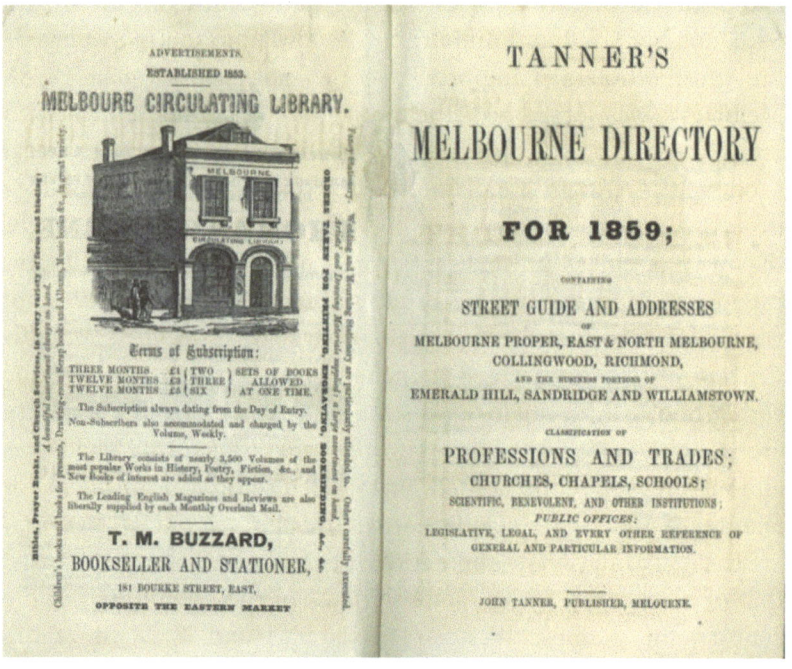

Advertisement for the Melbourne Circulating Library, and adjacent title-page of *Tanner's Melbourne Directory for 1859* (Melbourne: John Tanner, 1859, 331 pages, 22 cm.) Bookseller, stationer and publisher Thomas M. Buzzard operated in Melbourne from 1853. J. P. Quaine's article about early Melbourne booksellers (the *Age*, 10 February 1945, p. 13) quotes Buzzard's first advertisement as stating that his shop 'specialised in all articles needful for the camp of the digger... the latest books, divinity, history, Bibles, belles lettres, and a new stock of Witney blankets'. Buzzard was in business with William Vale selling books and stationery until the partnership ended in 1854. He also produced directories for Geelong in the 1850s and went on to publish the *Australian Medical Journal* from 1856 to 1895. (Private collection)

NOTE ON SOURCES

There is no systematic study of Australian circulating libraries in the nineteenth century, but the subject is treated in George Nadel's *Australia's Colonial Culture* of 1957 and in Elizabeth Webby's work on the period up to 1850. Wallace Kirsop has presented some of his research on the Walches in *Books for Colonial Readers*, chapter IV, in his contribution to the volume *The Flow of Culture: Tasmanian Studies* of 1987, and in other papers. He has also examined the cases of Samuel Mullen and William Baker in articles published in Northern Hemisphere collections.

Some questions of method are examined in Wallace Kirsop, 'Writing a History of Nineteenth-Century Commercial Circulating Libraries: Problems and Possibilities', *BSANZ Bulletin*, vol.27, nos 3 & 4, 2003, pp. 71-82. J. E. Traue, 'Commercial Circulating Libraries and Recreational Reading in Nineteenth-Century New Zealand: A Re-evaluation', *Script & Print*, vol.42, no.3, 2018, pp. 147-54, is an important contribution on a country viewed in the nineteenth century as part of the Australian sphere. Paul Eggert's text '*Robbery Under Arms*: The Colonial Market, Imperial Publishers, and the Demise of the Three-Decker Novel', in *Book History*, vol.6, 2003, pp. 127-46, raises important issues whose consideration depends on close study of widely scattered primary sources: printed catalogues, newspaper advertisements and commercial correspondence. Dirk H. R. Spennemann, *The Ten-Mile Creek (Holbrook, NSW) Circulating Library*, Canberra, Mulini Press, 2002, studies a country library from an extensive advertisement published in the Albury *Border Post* on 22 November 1871.

CHAPTER 17

Private Libraries

Wallace Kirsop

The earliest collections of books brought to Australia by Europeans were exclusively private. From Phillip's First Fleet till the 1820s this continued to be the case. Thus any study of the reading matter available to colonists cannot avoid considering what individuals owned, imported and eventually put on the local market. Efforts have been made — with some success — to identify what arrived in 1788. People quickly accepted that borrowing and exchanging were essential given the paucity of resources in the settlement. Plaintive advertisements in the *Sydney Gazette* after 1803 for the return of lent volumes show that the pattern persisted for decades. As late as the early 1820s a group of officials, merchants and professional men organised a collective catalogue of their own libraries as a means of collaborative provision of the infrastructure for scientific and intellectual work in the short-lived Philosophical Society. The launching during that decade of several lasting public institutions and commercial ventures made such efforts largely superfluous. However, the record of private lending by the young Redmond Barry in Melbourne in the 1840s and by Nicol Drysdale Stenhouse in Sydney in the 1850s shows that the practice could and did endure at times when the public had begun to have access to a variety of recognisable libraries.

Although some of the London consigners of books for speculative sale in the colonies — Edward Lumley in the 1840s and 1850s and Bernard Quaritch after 1880 — did not disdain to send antiquarian works, most of the material likely to attract collectors came from local sources. Private libraries were almost always dispersed at auction in the nineteenth century on the occasion of departures from the colony, bankruptcies or deaths. Collectors and the trade were active at the sales, as one can learn from memoirs and correspondence and from the subsequent catalogues compiled by booksellers like Henry Tolman Dwight, the most important specialist in the second-hand market before the advent of William Dymock and of Angus & Robertson in the 1880s. Knowledge of what was owned depends, therefore, in the first instance on surviving documents concerning the auctions themselves. Many sales were simply advertised in the press with rudimentary indications of the lots on offer. None the less, printed catalogues, often put together in haste and produced carelessly, were not uncommon throughout the period. The sad thing is that most of them, up to 90 per cent in certain decades, have not survived. In part their absence can be made good by manuscript lists or, quite exceptionally, printed inventories of private library holdings. Otherwise it is necessary to track the purchases of institutions, like the Melbourne Public Library, with good records or to consult relevant booksellers' catalogues in order to reconstruct, in part at least, the holdings of major nineteenth-century collectors. In a few cases the libraries of some great pastoral families like the Macarthurs and Winter Cookes have been maintained more or less intact in their original settings.

Despite all the gaps, we have enough evidence to characterise the collections brought to or formed in Australia in the first century of European settlement. We tend, of course, to use the words 'collection' and 'collector' in a rather elitist way that brings them close to 'bibliophily' and 'bibliomania'. Yet in our context it is perhaps more prudent to think inclusively, as G. Thomas Tanselle recommends, that 'collecting is the accumulation of tangible things'. A shelf of yellowback novels or of trade manuals or of devotional works is as assuredly a collection as rooms full of law treatises, of expensively bound examples of *belles-lettres* or of medical and scientific literature. The few may well have been more closely studied and more passionately loved than the many, but they are less often recorded for posterity because their commercial value is seen as minimal. Unavoidably, then, we are directed towards the larger accumulations. Some of them conformed to conventional nineteenth-century notions of bibliophilic pursuits, while the majority reflected the multitude of reasons — practical, intellectual and recreational — that people had to bring together quantities of books, pamphlets and magazines. Over time there were changes of emphasis and of fashion in all this.

Colonial bibliophiles

Collectors resident in the colonies do not bulk large in London accounts of the bibliophilic scene. Bernard Quaritch's *Contributions towards a Dictionary of English Book-Collectors* (1892–1921) has very few names associated with British possessions overseas. Apart from S. W. Silver, the London merchant whose York Gate Library was catalogued by E. A. Petherick in the 1880s and sold to the South Australian Branch of the Royal Geographical Society of Australasia early in the twentieth century, the only persons one can link in any way to Australia are the Rev. J. H. Gregory of Melbourne and Sir George Grey. Gregory's collection was dispersed in the 1890s, but Grey's much more substantial libraries went to Cape Town and to Auckland rather than Adelaide. Grey's interest in medieval manuscripts and in incunabula marked him out as a representative of the great tradition of European salerooms. Few people in the Australian colonies chose to emulate him in this trend, as Quaritch, who used Dwight as an agent around 1870, was in a good position to know.

One important reason was the absence of fortunes comparable to those of British and American tycoons in the nineteenth century. Another — especially before the advent of regular mail steamers and the completion of the Overland Telegraph Line — was the crippling effect of distance. It was difficult to compete in markets where time can be of the essence, so, outside infrequent buying trips to the Northern Hemisphere, collectors had to be content with leisurely supplies of standard and readily available books or with local opportunities, which existed because respectable private libraries arrived with their owners during the entire period.

The inclination to follow standard bibliophilic models certainly existed. Collecting is a strong passion and it had its devotees under

Southern skies. The curious coincidence that brought together at the first graduation ceremony of the University of Sydney in 1856 the Provost Sir Charles Nicholson, the graduand David Scott Mitchell and the student prizewinner George Salting, eventual benefactor of the Victoria and Albert Museum, was in some ways a defining moment. Is it altogether accidental that Sydney's libraries have a stronger tradition of private endowment than those of other Australian cities? At all events the small group of monied youths who constituted the undergraduate body of the day learnt that collecting and public service were desirable goals.

Before Nicholson, an Edinburgh medical graduate turned landowner and entrepreneur, left the colony in 1862 he sold at auction what was then the largest private library in the country. Surprisingly, unless one recalls the new gold-rush power and prosperity of Victoria, this happened in Melbourne. Over three days in May 1861 Fraser and Cohen disposed of 'upwards of 6,000 Volumes of Standard Works in English, French, Spanish, Italian, Latin and Greek' to 'the Literati of Victoria', according to the *Argus* advertisement of 21 May. Since the printed catalogue does not seem to have survived, we rely on the auctioneers' notice to know that there were 'several Rare and Valuable Works — scarce even in the Famous Libraries of England and the Continent of Europe', including the 1632 Second Folio Shakespeare. The second edition in 1852 of Godfrey Charles Mundy's *Our Antipodes* records that in 1848 the library of Nicholson's then residence Tarmons was 'well stored with books in all languages, many of them of a rarity only appreciable by a virtuoso' and was 'about forty-eight feet long by thirty feet high, with a ceiling of cedar in compartments' (III, p. 12). Individuals and institutions in Melbourne bought heavily, and in ways that can still be documented in part, at this liquidation of an altogether superior gentleman's collection. Nicholson's consistent purchases of medieval manuscripts and incunabula came during the decades he spent back in England. Many of them were to find their way to the University of Sydney early in the twentieth century.

After disposing of his law library in 1869, in other words when his father was dead and he was free to renounce any pretence of professional activities, David Scott Mitchell began his serious collecting career along Nicholson's lines. This is still reflected in the

Mitchell Library's unexpected holdings, but the happy systematic turn to Australiana under persuasion from George Robertson amongst others was to create something on an entirely different plane and to define a direction that came to predominate after 1890. It included the acquisition *en bloc* in 1906 of the collection of his Sydney rival Alfred Lee (1858–1923).

Older tastes and traditions allowed for variations. William Story (1801–1870), who brought the imposing remnants of a library auctioned in Shrewsbury and Hull in 1857 and 1858 when he emigrated to Australia, first to Adelaide then to Melbourne, in 1859, dabbled in the high spots of classical collecting like Hartmann Schedel's *Liber cronicarum* of 1493 (two imperfect copies), but he was restricted by the income of a solicitor's clerk. Nevertheless, his eclecticism masked the purposefulness of a collector fully aware of the intrinsic interest of eighteenth-century English literature, of travel and topography, of agriculture and even of Shropshire and Warwickshire provenances. Sales by treaty to various Melbourne institutions in the 1860s and an auction in 1870 enabled his adopted country to benefit from his skill.

John Macgregor (1828–1884), a solicitor who came to Melbourne as a child in 1840 and was a Parliamentarian between 1862 and 1874, provides another example of a collection formed from an Australian base. He was, however, a customer of Bernard Quaritch. His 10 000 volumes auctioned off over a week in August 1884 were described by the specialist firm responsible, Gemmell, Tuckett, and Co., as 'the finest private library in Australia'. Despite the trade's penchant for hyperbole this was accurate enough at the time. Macgregor's interest in Australiana was minimal, and he clearly did not seek out early printings as such. The focus of the material accumulated was in the broadest sense academic and scholarly. A wide range of subjects, standard editions printed in the seventeenth, eighteenth and nineteenth centuries, these were the backbone of what could have been seen as the nucleus of an ambitious research library. What was less usual was the emphasis on the history of science and philosophy. The solicitor imported, for the ultimate enrichment of the Australian book market, an ample selection of the minor and major classics of the Scientific Revolution, of the Enlightenment and even of the Ideologues.

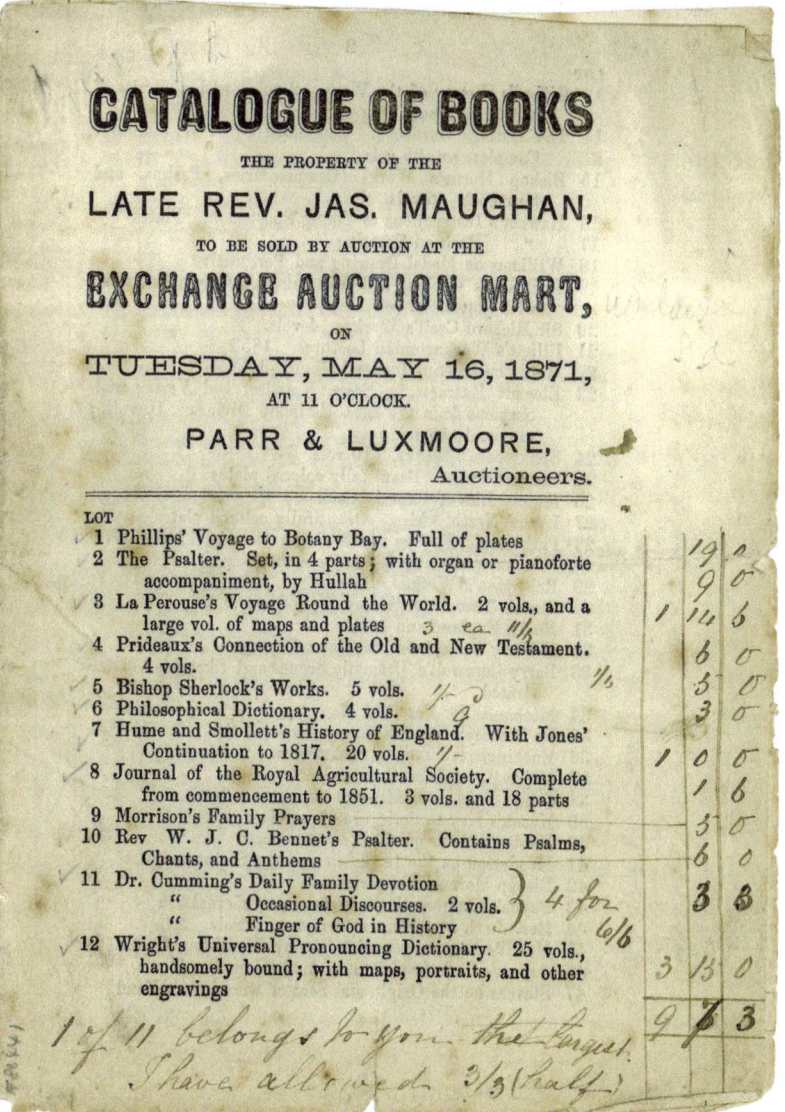

Page 1 of the 12-page sale catalogue of the estate of Rev. James Maughan on 16 May 1871. Maughan (1826–1871) (see *ADB*, vol.5, pp. 228-29) was a Methodist New Connexion minister who emigrated from England to Australia in 1862 and settled in Adelaide with his family. Prominent and well-respected by his colleagues and congregation, he suffered ill health for much of his life. The advertisement in the *South Australian Advertiser* (15 May 1871, p. 4) for the above auction held a few months after his death promised 'a large quantity of books' which included in its 402 lots historical and religious works as well as the *Journal of the Royal Agricultural Society*. The surviving copy of the catalogue is priced and annotated. (Private collection)

A Melbourne sale of the following year, that of William Cornell, offered a selection of 'grangerised' or extra-illustrated volumes. This fad also had its followers in the colonies. Inevitably one has to turn to the booksellers' catalogues of the post-gold-rush decades to see reflections of such tendencies, which also included the search for autographs and interesting provenances and the manufacture, already promoted in the eighteenth century, of de luxe editions distinguished by fine bindings, elaborate illustrations and large paper. H. T. Dwight's *A Catalogue of Books, comprising many Useful, Rare, and Valuable Works, in English and Foreign Theology; also, several scarce editions, printed by Elzevir, Stephens, Aldus, &c.* of 1865 not only showed the persistence of a certain antiquarian tradition, but also suggested to what extent the libraries of the clergy fed the local second-hand market. Canons of taste were more probably influenced by such trade priorities than they were by self-conscious monuments like the 1873 catalogue of the collection formed by William Rae of Happy Valley, Bendigo or the 1868 auction arranged by John Pascoe Fawkner near the end of his life.

Booksellers after the gold rush were also sensitive to the growing curiosity about books produced in or relating to the Australian colonies. Both Dwight and his successor John Brooks printed lists of the relevant titles in the 1860s and 1870s. Bearing in mind the vogue of Americana and the much longer established concern with travel, topography and local history and antiquities it is hardly astonishing that settlers in pre-Federation decades should turn their attention to those books and pamphlets it was easiest to collect in the various colonial cities. The emergence of bibliophiles like Edward Wise (1818–1865) and James Backhouse Walker (1841–1899) known to specialise in this field is another of the characteristics of the period. The triumphs of Mitchell and the following generation had been carefully prepared.

Professionals and amateurs

Most private libraries attested in the Australian colonies before 1890 mirrored the professional and leisure interests of their owners in more or less haphazard ways. The urge to be exhaustive or comprehensive in covering a field was usually not so strong, even though some people succeeded in bringing together quite impressive working collections in their offices or houses. In some instances we can glimpse the volumes *in situ*, as in the partial manuscript inventories of Redmond Barry's possessions in the 1870s, or in full bookcases like those of Charles Badham and George Russell transferred to institutions after their deaths, or again in private dwellings like William Lyall's Harewood at Tooradin overlooking Westernport. There are gaps in such survivals, although they are less dramatic than the dispersal of the library of the Allens' Toxteth Park in Glebe with remnants discoverable in the 1940s in the stables of a family property, South Wambo, in the Hunter River Valley. A full account has yet to be written of the breaking up of the Shoalhaven collections of Alexander Berry and Edward Wollstonecraft, two of the Philosophical Society group of the early 1820s. However, enough of the furniture and of the books — some of them bought in Edinburgh at the end of the eighteenth century — can still be found for the exercise to be worthwhile. More eloquent than any list or array of books on shelves is Joseph Elliott's meticulous description of his North Adelaide house and its contents in 1860. Here those volumes, pamphlets, magazine parts, music scores and prints that are identified situate a relatively modest family in a richly evocative cultural context. Images alone help us to grasp the role of books in the lives of the Sydney-resident French merchant Noufflard and of a series of colonial dignitaries of the Victorian era.

Quite predictably the collections about which we are best informed are those of professionals of various kinds. Robert Townson, the author of *Travels in Hungary* (1797), lived as a farmer in his twenty years in New South Wales (1807–1827) and had the mortification of seeing his polyglot scientific library disparaged by Governor William Bligh. By the time of Townson's death, Alexander McLeay, whose extensive collection was auctioned in 1845, was installed as Colonial Secretary and the age was much more propitious for savants. Sales, sometimes at later dates than 1890, give a clear idea of the resources available not only to university-based scientists like Frederick McCoy, but also to medical pioneers and entrepreneurs like John Maund, Richard Tracy and J. G. Beaney. The last-named's connection with F. F. Baillière is a reminder that Melbourne at least could support a specialist scientific and medical bookseller in the 1860s and 1870s.

Clergymen and lawyers are well represented among the serious owners of books in nineteenth-century Australia. Whereas the collections of the former group sometimes enriched diocesan, seminary and college libraries, the latter more often nourished the general market. John Dunmore Lang, Robert Cartwright and Richard Hill were among the early clerics whose books were catalogued and sold before 1850. The lawyers, who included barristers, solicitors, judges and academic teachers, were an even more diverse group with strong interests outside, notably in politics. Those for whom we have extensive records include William a'Beckett, Daniel Deniehy, Archibald Michie and W. E. Hearn. Typically they were people appointed in those times to oversee the major public libraries, which occasionally benefited from their largesse.

Other public figures whose collections were sold at auction included the scholar politician Charles Pearson, the journalist James Smith and the writers R. H. Horne and Marcus Clarke. The last case offers a special example of a library tailored to the documentary needs of its owner. Ultimately it is desirable to go behind mere catalogues and to see — if the evidence exists in the form of annotations or references in diaries or in letters — how books were used and absorbed. Private libraries run the full gamut from ostentatious furniture like that allegedly ordered by a Victorian country grandee from Melbourne booksellers and binders to impress Prince Alfred, Duke of Edinburgh on a visit that, in the event, was cancelled, to a handful of volumes that accompany inveterate readers through their practical problems and their dreams. The collections noted in Australia's first European century are, therefore, both essential parts of the national estate and invitations to penetrate the mysteries of individual readers.

NOTE ON SOURCES

There is still no comprehensive analytical study of the collecting of books in nineteenth-century Australia. Some suggestions were made by Jonathan Wantrup and Wallace Kirsop in the 1970s and 1980s. Elizabeth Webby's 'A Checklist of Early Australian Booksellers' and Auctioneers' Catalogues and Advertisements: 1800–1849', *BSANZ Bulletin*, nos 13, 14 & 15, 1978–79, pp. 123-48, 33-61, 95-150, provides a full list of printed documentary sources for the first half of the period. The five volumes of Charles Stitz's edited *Australian Book Collectors*, 2010-2016, offer not only numerous articles by him, but also reprints of individual studies published over several decades by many other people. It is an indispensable resource.

George Grey's Australian experiences are a minor part of Donald Kerr's *Amassing Treasures for All Times: Sir George Grey, Colonial Bookman and Collector*, New Castle, Delaware, Oak Knoll Press / Dunedin, Otago University Press, 2006. Eileen Chanin's *Book Life: The Life and Times of David Scott Mitchell*, North Melbourne, Australian Scholarly, 2011, is wide-ranging, despite some omissions (the 1869 sale of the law library), but it has not gone without criticism. On the general nineteenth-century context, see also Wallace Kirsop, 'Selling books at auction in 19th-century Australia: The 2009 Ferguson Memorial Lecture', *Journal of the Royal Australian Historical Society*, vol.95, 2009, pp. 198-214, and Wallace Kirsop, 'Bibliomania in Colonial Australia' in Jaynie Anderson, Max Vodola and Shane Carmody, eds, *The Invention of Melbourne: a Baroque Archbishop and a Gothic Architect*, Carlton, The Miegunyah Press, 2019, pp. 247-57.

On the First Fleet see Colin Steele and Michael Richards, *Bound for Botany Bay: What books did the First Fleet read and where are they now?*, Canberra, ANU Library, 1988. G. Thomas Tanselle's thoughts on collecting are in 'A Rationale of Collecting', *Studies in Bibliography*, vol.51, 1998, pp. 1-25. The essential reference on H. T. Dwight is Ian F. MacLaren, *Henry Tolman Dwight: Bookseller and Publisher*, Parkville, The University of Melbourne Library, 1989. Descriptive and iconographical aspects of private libraries can be found in Joseph Elliott, *Our Home in Australia. A Description of Cottage Life in 1860*, Sydney, The Flannel Flower Press, 1984; *Monsieur Noufflard's House: Watercolours by S. T. Gill, 1857*, Sydney: The Historic Houses Trust of NSW, 1983; Terence Lane & Jessie Serle, *Australians at Home: A Documentary History of Australian Domestic Interiors from 1788 to 1914*, Melbourne, OUP, 1990.

CHAPTER 18

The Print Culture of Colonial Music from its Beginnings

Graeme Skinner

Among the very earliest printed artefacts of Australian music are three versions of a single song, transcribed from the singing of the Sydney people. Future governor John Hunter noted in *An Historical Journal of the Transactions at Port Jackson* (London, 1793) that the settlers' interlocutor, Wangal man Woollarawarre Bennelong, 'sings a great deal, and with much variety: the following are some words . . . mangenny wakey angoul barre boa lah barrema'. David Collins recorded the same song ('Mang-en-ny-wau-yen-go-nah, bar-ri-boo-lah, bar-re-mah') in *An Account of the English Colony in New South Wales* (London, 1798) and described the Sydney people's singing, beginning 'at the top of their voices', and continuing 'as long as they can in one breath, sinking to the lowest note, and then rising again to the highest'. Bennelong and fellow Wangal man, Yemmerrawanne, in London in 1793, sang the same song for the musical antiquarian Edward Jones, who published both the words ('Barrabu-la barra ma, manginè wey en-gu-na') and his transcription of the melody, much as Collins described it, in his *Musical Curiosities* (London, 1811).

Other Sydney songs were musically notated by members of French naval expeditions in 1802 and 1819, and published in official reports in Paris in 1824 and 1839. In Paris in 1836, G. L. Domeny de Rienzi published the melody only of an Arnhem Land song, recorded on site in the late 1820s. A Sydney song, as sung by 'Harry' (Corrangie), was sent to London by Judge Barron Field, set in music type and published in his 'Journal of an excursion across the Blue Mountains' in the *London Magazine* (November 1823).

The earliest settler songs printed onshore took the form of lyrics, without musical notation, but indicating the tune to be sung. The first, 'Murtoch Delany's Description of the Races', to the Irish tune 'Ballinamona ora', appeared in the *Sydney Gazette* (20 October 1810), as notionally sung by a Hawkesbury Irish bushie attending the first Sydney Race Week. The making of such 'new songs to old tunes', which were then circulated in newspapers and magazines, was a popular mode of songwriting throughout the colonial era, outstripping in sheer volume new songs in notated sheet music format. Often, the tone of the new lyrics tended to be light-hearted or satirical. When Governor Ralph Darling retired and sailed out on the *Houghley* in October 1831, William Charles Wentworth held a *fête champêtre* at Vaucluse to which thousands came, and at which a topical parody of John Braham's *The Death of Nelson* was sung, and published in the *Monitor* 22 October 1831):

'Twas out of Sydney Bay,
The *Hooghley* sail'd away,
Each heart was bounding then!
The Tyrant wends his way,
On this auspicious day,
To England home again!

A 'South Australian Melody' sent to Adelaide's *Southern Australian* (8 May 1839) by the pseudonymous 'Timothy Short' was a parody of Thomas Moore's 'She is Far From the Land', and written for its melody. The subject was a green new chum:

... He lectures the blacks on their dear native plains,
His own little heart meanwhile quaking:
Ah! little he heeds, as his sweet voice he strains,
How the sides of the black men are shaking. . .

Among more serious early lyrics are those of the convict lament, 'The Exile of Erin on the Plains of Emu', by 'M. of Anambaba' (Presbyterian cleric John McGarvie), sung to *Erin go bragh*, published in the *Sydney Gazette* (26 May 1829), and the songs published in New South Wales papers by poet Eliza Hamilton Dunlop. Even her most famous lyric, *The Aboriginal Mother*, first published in the *Australian* (13 December 1838) without a tune indicated, was originally written for Handel's air *The Melancholy Nymph* (Händel-Werke-Verzeichnis 228/19), as she told Isaac Nathan (who later printed his own setting of it).

From as early as there were commercial presses in Australia, song lyrics were also occasionally printed in 'broadside' format (single sheets, letterpress but no music, printed one side only, and sold for 'a song' — a penny or halfpenny). However, surprisingly few examples survive. One of the earliest likely broadsides, now lost, was a new song, 'The Jackets of Green', advertised in the *Perth Gazette* in November 1834, on the 'late encounter with the Natives at Pinjärra', almost undoubtedly a partisan settler account of the massacre of Pindjarup people by the government militia. Another was a comic song, 'Billy Barlow in Australia', as 'written by a gentleman of Maitland', and advertised for sale at the *Maitland Mercury* office in 1843. No copy of the broadside itself is catalogued in any major collection, but the lyrics by the 'gentleman', Benjamin Pitt Griffin, had already been printed in the *Mercury*, and were widely disseminated thereafter. In December 1857 in Adelaide, 'two original songs' were printed in broadside format to celebrate the 'majority of the colony' (SSL).

To fill historical gaps left by the lack of more material of genuine early colonial provenance, twentieth-century folksong collectors and performers also turned their attentions to the many convict, emigration, and gold-rush broadside songs written, printed, and circulated in Britain. However, there is scant evidence that most of these ever found their way to the colonies as physical objects, let alone entered the sung repertoire of settler colonists; whereas almost all the genuinely local colonial songs that might otherwise have gone into print as broadsides survive because they were circulated in cheap local newspapers.

One exception is a run of seven songs in broadside format (200 x 130 mm) printed in Melbourne in 1854 by John Nutt Sayers (VSL). The songwriter was Charles Thatcher, a professional flautist from Brighton, England, who arrived in Melbourne in 1852 and had recently been singing his topical diggers' songs in 'free and easies' in Bendigo. He had earlier ventured into print with *Thatcher's Gold-digger's Songster*, the 'second edition' of which was advertised in October 1853 (no copy identified). No publisher was named, but the format was probably similar to Thatcher's later Melbourne songsters, most of which do survive, all produced by Charlwood and Son, and issued successively in separate 'numbers' (unbound 36-page pamphlets, 190 x 125 mm, letterpress both sides, with words only of 20–30 songs, no music, for a shilling). The first of five numbers of Charlwood's *The Victoria Songster* appeared in 1855, with popular and 'new local songs' by Thatcher and others, followed by two single-author collections, *Thatcher's Colonial Songster* (1857–58) and *Thatcher's Colonial Minstrel* (1859–61).

Songsters were also printed in other towns and cities. In 1847, Sydney stationer George Morley advertised the *Australian Harmonist*, 'a choice collection' of old, sentimental and comic songs (no copy identified). In Launceston in 1854, the first number of the *Tasmanian Songster*, including American 'plantation melodies' and 'several New Songs not yet published', was advertised at sixpence by bookbinder Alex Thompson (no copy identified). Another *Tasmanian Songster*, of 26 songs, was published by the singer-songwriter Marryat Hornsby in Hobart in 1867 (BL). In Ballarat in 1859, *Coxon's Comic Songster* was issued by John Coxon (VSL). Two important collections appeared in Sydney in 1865, the first and only number of *The Sydney Songster*, as written and sung by 'George Chanson', alias of George Loyau (VSL), and *The Queenslander's New Colonial Camp Fire Song Book* (NSL). In the latter, among several other 'new songs' attributed to 'REMOS', is the first appearance of the now-classic Australian folksong, 'The Overlander'.

The earliest religious music editions were also words-only. When news of the death of Princess Charlotte reached Sydney in April 1818, two hymns to be sung at a memorial service in St Philip's Church were printed in broadside format on the *Sydney Gazette* press; and in 1822, a four-page leaflet of *Hymns for the eighth anniversary of the Parramatta Sunday School* was also printed there (both NSL). In Sydney in 1828, the government printer issued the 88-page *Select portions of the Psalms of David* in the metrical versions sung in the colony's established (Anglican) churches. Largely identical books were printed in Hobart (1830) and Launceston (1844), and similar collections in Adelaide (1853) and for the Swan River District of Western Australia (1857). Complete printed wordbooks also survive for the consecrations of synagogues in Sydney (1844), Hobart (1845) and Launceston (1846), with Hebrew texts and English translations of all the sung portions of the ceremonies.

One of the earliest specific references to the sale of imported printed music is an advertisement in the *Sydney Gazette* in February 1815, when Mr Bevan, auctioneer, offered 'an extensive Assortment of Music in Sheets, just published, and a Copy of the Works of Handel', the latter probably volumes of Samuel Arnold's deluxe edition (London, 1788–97). The newly arrived Robert Campbell (not the Sydney general merchant, father or son, of the same name) opened the first dedicated 'music warehouse' in Sydney on 1 November 1825, 'with the most extensive and elegant assortment of . . . printed Music ever imported into this Colony'. In Hobart, musician John Philip Deane advertised imported sheet music for sale from 1825 onwards.

In the absence yet of skilled engravers, the first locally 'published' musical titles were new works advertised by composers for direct sale to the public in manuscript. In the Sydney newspapers on 28 April 1825, Sergeant Joseph Reichenberg, master of the band of the 40th Regiment, announced his *Australian Quadrilles* (probably first performed by his band at balls celebrating the King's birthday on 23 April), offering to arrange them to order 'for the Pianoforte, Flute, or Violin'. When his regiment moved on to Hobart, Reichenberg also offered manuscript copies for sale there in March 1826 (exemplars of neither 'edition' survive). Again, in Hobart, in January 1828, Deane advertised as 'Just published, the first set of Tasmanian Quadrilles', of his own composition; also lost, it was probably in manuscript. However, in the *Hobart Town Courier* on 20 June 1829, Eulalie Wood advertised that she had just imported a lithographic and a copperplate press, and in the *Colonial Times* on 30 April 1830 that she would print 'Music and Music Paper', though, if she did so, none has been identified.

Lost too, are the marches and other music that Sergeant Thomas Kavanagh, master of the band of the 3rd Regiment, offered for sale in Sydney in 1826, also usually presumed to have been in manuscript, although the artist Augustus Earle may already have been printing to order on his lithographic press. One title advertised by Kavanagh, *Currency Lasses*, survives elsewhere as the quadrille of the same name by 'a lady at Sydney' (amateur musician, Tempest Margaret Paul), engraved and printed for her in London by Joseph Cross in 1830–31 (NHH). Cross had recently published Augustus Earle's *Australian Scrap Book* (1830), and the lithographed cover of Paul's quadrille, with a vignette of a kangaroo, flute and sheet of music, is a variation on Earle's cover design.

The earliest surviving example of notated music printed onshore was *A Song of the Women of the Menero Tribe*, issued by the Polish explorer, natural historian and musical amateur, John Lhotsky. Advertised in Sydney in November 1834 as a pendant to his *A Journey from Sydney to the Australian Alps*, and sold at one shilling and sixpence. It consists of two separate versions of a corroboree song, for voice and piano and piano solo respectively, of which the melody and words were transcribed from Ngarigu singers on the Monaro Plains, and later arranged for publication by three professional musicians, George Sippe, James Pearson and Joshua Frey Josephson. The lithographer, John Gardner Austin, probably traced the music and words onto stone from a manuscript fair copy and added a title-page, drawn free-hand but imitating the decorative mix of copperplate fonts then typically found on engraved sheet music covers. The unique copy (NSL), printed on good, opaque paper, is a single, folded sheet of four pages, now cropped to 340 x 250 mm, but originally probably c. 360 x 265 mm.

Several other early pieces of printed sheet music were connected with the circle of the violinist, pianist and composer William Vincent Wallace, resident in Sydney from 1836 until 1838. As with Lhotsky's *Song*, and the majority of nineteenth-century sheet music in Australia and elsewhere, no year of publication is indicated internally in any of them. *Echo's Song*, to words by Sydney lawyer Robert Stewart, and composed and dedicated by Wallace to his Hobart cousin, Maria Logan, is, however, externally datable to early 1837. While the imitation copperplate title-page does not name a publisher, it does indicate that it was printed lithographically, again by J. G. Austin, in size and format as for Lhotsky's *Song* (unique copy at ANL). Another song, with music by Maria Logan and words by Robert Stewart, 'The Vow that Breathed in Solitude', was published in Hobart in April 1839 by William Gore Elliston, proprietor of the *Courier*, but no copy survives.

The earliest extant printed solo piano music is Wallace's *Walze favorite du Duc de Reichstadt*, a set of variations on a waltz by Johann Strauss I, in two separate Sydney editions (both at ANL). The authorised original has a genuine engraved copperplate title-page 'printed from zinc' by William Henry Fernyhough, either late in 1836 or 1837. The music, however, was probably drawn on stone. The second edition, by William Baker (date uncertain, but probably no later than the 1840s), was engraved on metal (both cover and music), evidently 'pirated' directly from a paper copy of Fernyhough's original.

In Tasmania, the earliest confirmed sheet music printing was a (lost) set of *Van Diemen's Land Quadrilles*, composed by a visiting naval bandmaster and advertised in Hobart in July 1838; the *True Colonist* saw 'the first proof sheet, lithographed . . . executed in a very creditable style'. The earliest surviving Tasmanian printed music is *A collection of psalms and tunes . . . arranged for the use of St. George's Church, Hobart Town,* edited by John Dickson Loch and lithographically printed, again by Elliston of the *Courier* in 1843 (NSL, VSL).

The first dedicated colonial music publisher who was himself a musician, Francis Ellard, arrived in Sydney in 1832 to set up a local branch of his family's Dublin music business. Ellard (who was Vincent Wallace's cousin) contemplated publishing music as early as 1833, but did not do so until 1835–36, when he issued two colonial compositions and one colonial-themed title, all three, however, engraved and printed in Dublin. Both local compositions are lost — *The Minstrel Waltz*, by native-born composer Thomas Stubbs, and a song, *The Parting*, to words by Frederick Hely (the New South Wales Superintendent of Convicts) and music probably by his eldest daughter Mary. But the colonial-themed issue — *The Much Admired Australian Quadrilles*, dedicated to the same Miss Hely — survives in two copies (one at NSL). The music for five quadrilles was arranged in Dublin by Ellard's brother, William, on popular European themes, but given localised titles, including 'La Wooloomooloo' [sic], and 'La Engehurst' (named after the Helys' Paddington house, on the tune of the song 'The Girl I Left Behind Me'). The cover (uniquely preserved at the University of Newcastle) has a view of Sydney Harbour, based on a drawing by Charles Rodius, but copied directly from an 1833 London engraving by S. G. Hughes. The Hely family may well have underwritten at least some of the Ellards' costs for the song and quadrilles.

Ellard advertised the first two sheet music editions published under his own name and from his Sydney address in August 1839. Since the cover of one is signed by Sydney engraver, John Carmichael, it is reasonable to assume that the music, too, was locally engraved, by Francis Ellard himself. Moreover, both were pirated from authorised imported editions, as were the bulk of Ellard's publications and those of his immediate Sydney rivals and successors (as was also typical in the United States of America at the time). After 1839, Ellard almost never advertised his pirated editions (perhaps to avoid detection by copyright owners when Sydney newspapers were read in Britain), and so it is impossible to date precisely 80 or more survivors bearing his imprint. Among the 30 or so exceptions, half can be dated by other means, while the rest were authorised editions of local compositions, and advertised as such — by, among others, Isaac Nathan (1841), Stephen Hale Marsh (1842), Florentine Dudemaine (1845), and his own son, Frederick Ellard.

Ellard also imported printed sheet music, though, because he didn't advertise his stock, the only certain evidence are surviving imported titles bearing his shop stamp. An album, bound to Ellard's order in the early 1840s for an amateur, Lilias Dowling (NHH), contains sheet music she collected over the previous decade, including several items from London publishers with Ellard's stamp. The album also includes two manuscript copies, both with his shop stamp, of 'All around my hat' ('a new comic song'), and Neukomm's descriptive song 'The Sea'. They appear to have been professionally copied 'in house' from the last print copy Ellard had in stock.

Declared insolvent in 1842 in the depths of the colonial depression, Ellard continued to trade on, but a second insolvency in 1847 marked the end of his business. His engraved plates were sold to James Turner Grocott, who used them to print new 'editions' under his own covers. He also contracted Ellard to engrave new titles on his behalf. In 1851,

Grocott again sold on the plates to his successors, the stationers Woolcott and Clarke, and Ellard similarly engraved new titles for them until his death in 1854.

Other specialist Sydney music publishers of the 1840s and 1850s who issued engraved pirate editions of imported titles and occasional locally composed works, included Thomas Rolfe (from the London firm of piano makers), George Hudson (master of the City Band, and a member of the theatre orchestra, who specialised in publishing polkas), pianist-composer Henry Marsh and organist W. J. Johnson. After terminating his partnership with Woolcott in 1856, Jacob Clarke traded on alone, occasionally still printing from Ellard's well-worn plates, and pirating many more recent imported titles. Clarke also regularly published local works. Like his colleagues, he must have come to some agreement with composers for sharing costs or profits, but no record survives of such arrangements.

Isaac Nathan, recently arrived in Sydney from London, issued his first Australian work, *Long Live Victoria*, in an Ellard engraved edition in June 1841, but then turned to self-publication, using general printers and the lithographer Thomas Liley for the rest of a series of 'Australian and Aboriginal Melodies' (1841–45). Nathan hoped it would be a colonial counterpart of his *Hebrew Melodies*, but few copies of the short-lived series survived. Nevertheless, it included some of his most noted Australian compositions, notably the Eliza Hamilton Dunlop setting, *The Aboriginal Mother*, and his arrangement of a Ngarigu song fragment, *Koorinda Braia*.

In 1842, W. A. Duncan, editor of the Catholic *Australasian Chronicle*, and a keen musical amateur, published an *Adoro te* and *Kyrie* that he had adapted from music by Rossini and Graun, printed using the first set of moveable music type in the colony. From 1845, Nathan used this same typeset, laboriously setting all of his musical publications himself. One remarkable project was a complete vocal score of his opera, *Merry Freaks in Troublous Times*, with the libretto by Charles Nagel interspersed in letterpress; printed by Thomas Forster, it was only ever intended to be a perusal score (Nathan hoped to arrange a performance in London) and was never advertised for sale (NSL). Another was *The Southern Euphrosyne*, a 170-page magazine-style anthology, with literary content in letterpress, interspersed with original music, including excerpts from Nathan's second colonial opera, *Don John of Austria*, and four arrangements of Aboriginal (Ngarigu and Wiradjuri) song fragments.

In 1854, Woolcott and Clarke first attempted to add value to their single sheet music editions by binding them together as albums. *The Australian Presentation Album* (Sydney, 1854), containing one song and four dances, including two locally composed by Charles Sandys Packer and Frederick Ellard, probably added little to their sales. However, their 1855 album, with more colonial content, was more widely noticed, not least for its illustrated covers with lithographed portraits and views by local artists. By a special arrangement with a fashionable composer of dance music in London, Charles D'Albert, Woolcott and Clarke also commissioned his *The Regatta Valse* for the volume and to celebrate the 1855 Sydney Regatta; but the full-colour cover illustrations of Sydney Harbour were executed in London by John Brandard from drawings supplied, and D'Albert's music was also engraved and printed there. After his partnership with Woolcott was dissolved, Clarke's *Australian Album 1857* was again completely lithographed, engraved, and printed locally in Sydney, by Allan and Wigley; sumptuously bound between gold-tooled and silk-backed boards, it sold for 30 shillings, and contained eight items, including seven locally-composed (by Edward Boulanger, Miska Hauser, Frederick Ellard, William Stanley, and the brothers Stephen and Henry Marsh) with pictorial covers by Sydney artist Edmund Thomas in two and three colours.

In June 1855 in Sydney, Henry Marsh launched the weekly series *The Australian Cadeau*, a music-only periodical which ran to 17 engraved titles — including colonial songs and piano pieces, many of which survive — before it foundered in September that year. In Hobart in 1854–55, the soldier and musical amateur, Henry Butler Stoney, edited two anthologies of locally composed music, the *Delacourt Bouquet* and the *Tasmanian Lyre*, lithographed and published by Huxtable and Deakin (both anthologies survive complete). W. J. Johnson's *Sydney Harmonicon* ran to ten issues by early 1856, and, though no copy of any survives, reviews mention literary content and otherwise-lost local compositions. Something similar was attempted on a more modest scale in Western Australia in 1864, when

The Minstrelsy of the West was published in Fremantle by George Barrow; the first number reportedly included a song and some literary content, though no copy survives. A single-composer album, *Boulanger's Keepsake for 1856*, was nominally published by bookseller Frederick Mader in Sydney, but almost certainly underwritten by Edward Boulanger himself or his patrons; consisting of six separate works over 53 densely scored pages (five of the six pieces survive complete in the unique University of Sydney exemplar), it demanded virtuosity not only from pianists, but also from the engraver, Abraham Western Chapman, who later produced New South Wales postage stamps. In Sydney in 1856, bookseller Jeremiah Moore commenced a series of pirated imported song titles, substantially cheaper than other local music sellers, with distinctive covers by a recent arrival, the well-known London illustrator, Archibald Alexander Park.

Other printed collections include several of notated religious music. Four chants sung at the opening of the Sydney Synagogue in 1844, though shorn of their words and arranged as piano solos by James Henri Anderson, appeared as *The Lays of the Hebrews*, engraved by Frederick Ellard (NLA). Likewise, eight chants from the consecration of the Hobart Synagogue in 1845 were arranged as piano solos by Joseph Reichenberg and printed lithographically as *Ancient Hebrew Melodies* (Hobart, 1847) by Thomas Browne (TSL). In 1857, William Dolman of Sydney published music for a selection of *Catholic Hymns, Litanies, &c.*, but no copy survives in the bibliographic record.

In Melbourne, two lost titles issued to celebrate the colonial Separation (from New South Wales) in November 1850 were probably the earliest music printed there: Thomas Reed's *Song of Victoria* and *The Separation Polka* by Joseph Wilkie, Melbourne's leading music seller. Through partnerships with John Campbell Webster and George Leavis Allan, Wilkie's business eventually became Allan and Co., the chief Victorian music publisher of the later colonial era and beyond. But in the 1850s, the most active Melbourne publisher was the printer and musical amateur William Henry Williams. With partners George Slater and Arthur Hodgson, he published the *Melbourne Vocalist* (1854–56), each number of which contained lyrics for between ten and twelve popular songs in songster format, and music for one song in moveable type that Williams had newly imported. Williams also typeset musical supplements to Slater's *Illustrated Journal of Australasia* (1857–58), and the same (or an identical) typeset was still being used for supplements to the *Illustrated Melbourne Post* in the mid-1860s. Between 1859 and 1861, the first three music editions issued by J. Walch and Sons, the major Tasmanian music publishers for the rest of the century, were also printed in Melbourne by Clarson, Shallard and Co., using Williams's typeset.

In Adelaide in 1857, composer Oscar Reyher advertised his *Kangaroo* and *Emu* polkas, the earliest documented music published in South Australia, but, as no copies have been catalogued at the State Library of South Australia, they have all likely been lost. They were presumably printed lithographically, as was the earliest surviving South Australian title, Carl Linger's *The Song of Australia*, by Penman and Galbraith in 1859. Walter C. Sims and Joseph Elliott published typeset musical supplements to their *Adelaide Musical Herald* (1862–63) and their 1868–69 revival of the *Adelaide Miscellany*.

Meanwhile, in Sydney from 1859 until the mid 1860s, most sheet music editions issued by the leading publishers appear to have been engraved in the workshops of John Degotardi, an Austrian-trained printer, using identical type elements laid out in closely similar formats. Degotardi also gave an example of his music engraving in his pamphlet, *The Art of Printing* (Sydney, 1861) and described his process of 'music punching... executed on plates composed of pewter and lead. The staves and general outlines are first drawn, and then the whole of the note-heads, signs, and lettering, each one of which is sharply cut on steel, in relief, like letter-press types, are hammered one by one into the Plate.'

By the 1860s, however, it was becoming cheaper to import music than to engrave (or typeset) and print it in the colonies. Increasingly, Australian publishers imported finished sheet music editions of British and European titles, though often disguising that fact by selling them under their own locally-printed or overprinted covers. Sydney's pirate print culture was in any event under attack. In 1863, music seller Robert Hammond Elvy, acting for Chappell's of London, took to the newspaper advertising columns to warn his competitors that they risked prosecution for infringing British copyrights.

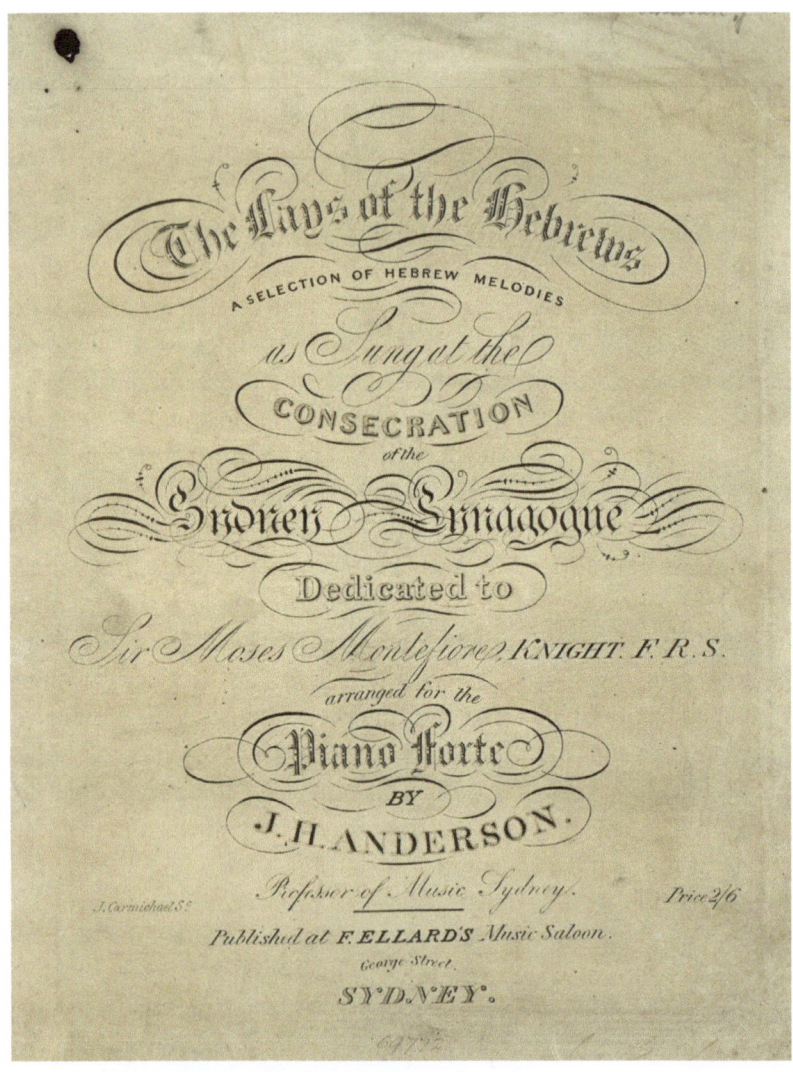

The cover (above), engraved by John Carmichael, and (right) fourth and final number, engraved by the publisher Francis Ellard, of *The Lays of the Hebrews, a selection of Hebrew melodies as sung at the consecration of the Sydney Synagogue . . . arranged for the piano forte by J. H. Anderson, professor of music, Sydney*, Sydney, F. Ellard, [September 1844]. (Uniquely surviving exemplar, State Library of New South Wales)

The Print Culture of Colonial Music from its Beginnings 361

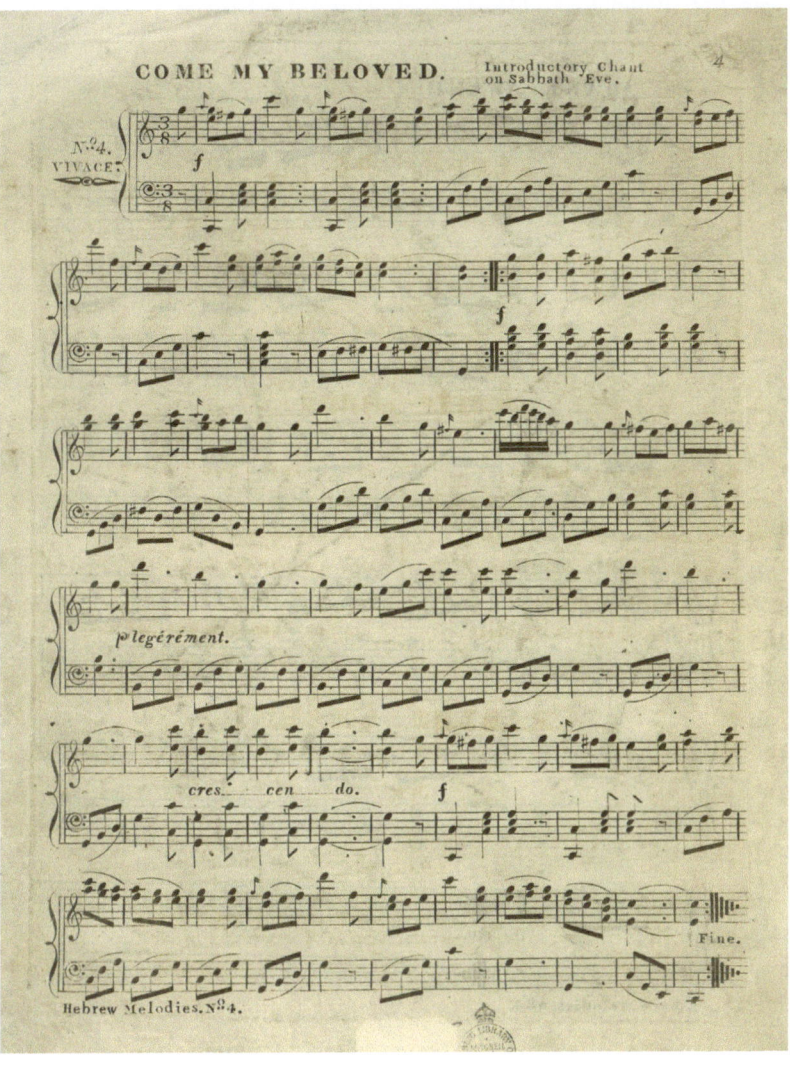

It was often also cheaper and more efficient to send Australian compositions to Europe for engraving and printing. An early example was *The Sydney Polka* (1861), by the young pianist-composer Alfred Anderson, which his father, the Sydney music seller James Henri Anderson, arranged to have engraved and printed in London by Joseph Williams of Cheapside. In the 1890s, W. H. Paling and Co. of Sydney regularly used the Leipzig printer C. G. Röder, as did Walch and Sons. In 1885–86, the late Charles Sandys Packer's oratorio *The Crown of Thorns* was sent to England to be engraved and printed by Novello, Ewer & Co. Likewise, in 1866, George Oswald Rutter's *Mass in D* (composed for St Francis's Church, Melbourne) was sent to Novello's.

Of music actually engraved and printed onshore in the colonial century, the great majority of surviving titles (a large proportion of them now digitised) are sheet music editions of single songs, mainly for solo voice and piano accompaniment; and short piano pieces, which until the 1850s were, overwhelmingly, arrangements of orchestral or band music rather than original piano works. Barely anything was printed locally for even the most common of other instruments, the violin and flute. Moreover, no nineteenth-century colonial printer ever produced a full score or set of parts of a large scale orchestral or instrumental chamber work, or work for wind or brass band, whether locally composed or otherwise, such as an overture, symphony, concerto or sonata.

Not all printed music was published commercially; cheaply lithographed materials were produced for use by choral organisations and classes in the 1850s. Notable documented cases are vocal exercises that John Adams reportedly composed and had printed for the Launceston Philharmonic Society in the 1850s (all lost); vocal music produced by Silvester Diggles in 1859 for the Brisbane Choral Society; and the *Singing Class Manual*, in tonic solfa notation, that James Churchill Fisher sold to his class members for sixpence in Sydney in 1855. In Melbourne in 1856, William Henry Williams reportedly used his music type to print a small collection of hymn tunes for use by a church singing class; no copy survives, but the contents were probably expanded into the undated

A collection of thirty standard psalm tunes for editor George Leavis Allan, also typeset and printed by Williams (ANL).

Printed 'books of the words' for music sung at concerts were also sold, though few survive in public collections. One wordbook (lost) was advertised for the oratorio festival at St Mary's Cathedral, Sydney in 1836; and the Melbourne Philharmonic Society advertised another (also lost) for sixpence, for its concert of selections from Handel's *Samson* in March 1855. Wordbooks were also printed for original musical plays. That for Charles Nagel's 'musical burletta', *The Mock Catalani, in Little Puddleton*, at the Royal Victoria Theatre, Sydney, was published by James Tegg in 1842, and included words of twelve musical numbers, most adapted to 'old tunes' (BL); Nagel himself set the remaining numbers to music, published separately as sheet music by Thomas Rolfe, though a single copy of only one, 'The Pretty Bark Hut in the Bush', survives. Nagel's second playscript, *Shaksperi Conglommorofunnidogammoniae*, a 'musical extravaganza' (Sydney, 1843), published by W. A. Duncan, includes lyrics for nine sung numbers all set to 'old tunes'. Nagel's libretto for Isaac Nathan's opera, *Merry Freaks in Troublous Times*, was also separately printed and advertised in 1844 (no copy is known, though the libretto itself survives separately in Nathan's later printed vocal score).

Librettos in English were published for opera companies. Two of the earliest that survive are for *Bellini's Norma, at the new Theatre Royal, Melbourne, as conducted by Lewis Henry Lavenu* (Melbourne, Wilson, Mackinnon & Fairfax, 1855), and in Sydney, for Verdi's *Il Trovatore*, again conducted by Lavenu (Sydney, 'Caxton' Printing Office, 1859). Similarly, wordbooks were printed and sold in the 1860s for the Lyster Opera Company. In the very first season, these books were also provided for 'local' content: resident Melbourne composer Stephen Hale Marsh's *The Gentleman in Black* (incorrectly billed the 'first original opera produced in Australia'), printed at the Melbourne *Punch* office (1861), and Vincent Wallace's evergreen *Maritana*, which Lyster spuriously advertised as having been 'composed in Sydney', thus inaugurating an ineradicable myth.

NOTE ON SOURCES

Some useful sources for study of colonial music publishing in Australia are: Prue Neidorf, A Guide to Dating Music Published in Sydney and Melbourne, 1800–1899, MA thesis, University of Wollongong, 1999; Robyn Holmes & Ruth Lee Martin, comps, *The Collector's Book of Sheet Music Covers*, Canberra, National Library of Australia, 2001; Prue Neidorf and John Whiteoak, 'Publishing Music', in John Whiteoak and Aline Scott-Maxwell, eds, *Currency Companion to Music and Dance in Australia*, Sydney, Currency House, 2003, pp. 550-53; and Graeme Skinner's *Australharmony (an online resource toward the early history of music in colonial Australia)*, https://www.sydney.edu.au/paradisc/australharmony/ [accessed 24 April 2024]; and see also his 'Eliza Hamilton Dunlop, Irish and Colonial Methodist: Her Songs for Music and Collaborations with Isaac Nathan', in Anna Johnston and Elizabeth Webby, eds, *Eliza Hamilton Dunlop: Writing from the Colonial Frontier*, Sydney, Sydney University Press, 2021, pp. 121-58; and, with Jim Wafer, 'A Checklist of Colonial Era Musical Transcriptions of Australian Indigenous Songs', in Jim Wafer and Myfany Turpin, eds, *Recirculating Songs: Revitalising the Singing Practices of Indigenous Australia*, Canberra, Asia-Pacific Linguistics, 2017, pp. 360-404.

CHAPTER 19

Textbooks

†Jeffrey Prentice

A definitive study of the publication of textbooks in nineteenth-century Australia, or indeed of the distribution of such material from overseas, has yet to be written. Most recent articles concentrate on later periods, giving some attention to the 1890s, when the school population expanded considerably and locally produced reading magazines began to flourish. School textbooks have always been a poor cousin of children's books, which have received strong academic attention, and yet the two fields have a common bond in their intended audiences.

As for tertiary textbooks, the limited market up to 1890, with just four quite small universities in existence, relied almost exclusively on British importations. Even Charles Badham, the University of Sydney classicist, and William Edward Hearn, Dean of Law at the University of Melbourne, published their serious contributions in association with British firms despite their commitment to colonial houses and to their adopted country.

Given the preponderance of imports at all levels, one must first sketch how they reached users. In 1788, Richard Johnson, chaplain to the First Fleet, had brought with him 100 copies of Dixon's *Spelling Book* and 200 copies of *Child's First Book*, parts 1 and 2. Forty-eight more copies of the former title arrived in 1789. The pattern thus established was to continue up to 1890 and beyond, ultimately under the control of the colonial book trade once it took shape.

THE

HISTORY OF AUSTRALIA

FROM 1606 TO 1876

BY

ALEXANDER SUTHERLAND, M.A., Melb.

AND

GEORGE SUTHERLAND, B.A., Melb.

George Robertson

MELBOURNE, SYDNEY, AND ADELAIDE

1877

Title-page of first edition of George and Alexander Sutherland's *History of Australia from 1606 to 1876* (Melbourne: George Robertson, 1877). 201 pp.; 17 cm. The Sutherland brothers emigrated from Scotland with their family in 1864. The history book — a collaboration between George (1855–1905), a successful journalist and author, and Alexander (1852–1902), also a journalist and a prominent Melbourne schoolmaster and educator, was a publishing success and remained a standard work for decades. (Monash University Library)

However, educational institutions had a role in distributing the various manuals and primers both through their direct links with religious publishers in Britain and via privileged connections with local wholesalers. An exchange of letters between a group of Melbourne booksellers, including Samuel Mullen and E. W. Cole, and George Robertson in October 1874 was published in the London *Bookseller* on 5 January 1875 (Holroyd, 34-35). Robertson's correspondents reproached him with selling textbooks on trade terms to schoolteachers. The wholesaler responded that he had done so for 21 years, i.e. virtually since the beginning of his business in Australia, and that he had no intention of changing his practices. This has to be seen as one episode in a battle over educational discounting and supply that would last well into the next century.

It is hardly surprising to find large quantities of textbooks in the one surviving copy of a George Robertson trade sale catalogue, that of 19 March 1862, for example 930 'Cameron's First Book of Reading' (lots 566–569), 1150 'Constable's First Lesson Book' (lots 766–770) and 200 'Walkinghame's Arithmetic, Mackenzie's edition, 18mo, sewed' (lots 883–886). Two dispersal sale catalogues give some notion of the part educational books continued to play in the Melbourne retail trade. The bankruptcy of William Stephens led to an auction of his stock in February 1867. Among the 1691 lots one finds, alongside much religious literature: 500 'National School Primer' (lot 1562); 'Seventy-two Stewart's First Lessons in Arithmetic; sixty Tegg's First Book' (lot 1565); 300 'National School Primer' (lot 1570); 'Two hundred and fifty M'Culloch's Reading; thirty Windett's Imperial Reading and Spelling; one hundred Bonwick's Grammar' (lot 1576). The sale of the estate of George Robertson's brother William on 7 March 1881 included in its 575 lots a substantial quantity of educational material. In a society where primary schooling predominated all through the nineteenth century, with the 'free, compulsory and secular' prescription making its appearance at various dates from 1872 (Victoria) to 1894 (Western Australia), it was to be expected that most of what was sold and used was of an elementary character. However, Robertson's stock extended — in smaller quantities — into what one can consider the secondary domain. Thus one finds 'Kenny's French Phrase Book' (25 copies — lot 275), 'Bossut's French and English Primer' (35 copies — lot 276) and 'Cicero's Cato *Major*' (101 copies — lot 312) among many others. On the other hand, one reaches a different dimension with 'Excelsior Table Book' (1278 copies — lot 487) and 'Small Preceptor' (1344 copies — lot 488). The textbook market was a potentially lucrative one in a trade where there was plenty of competition in the second half of the century.

The precariousness of supply lines from the Northern Hemisphere during the colonies' early decades led to almost immediate efforts to print textbooks locally. The notoriously poor survival rate of small books of this kind means that our knowledge of these productions up to the 1830s depends on the announcements made in their own newspapers by the relevant publishers. In chronological order we have four books printed by George Howe: a *Spelling Book* (1810) based on Lindley Murray (Ferguson 507); *Bowden's Tables* (1812) (Ferguson 532); Thomas Bowden's *Spelling Book for the Use of Schools in New South Wales* (1814) (Ferguson 572); *Catechism for the Use of Schools and Families* (1819) (Ferguson 735). These were followed by two books printed by Andrew Bent in Hobart: *Primer for Children* (1821) (Ferguson 837); and *Colonial Spelling Book* (1822) (Ferguson 878).

The colonial publications of the 1830s seem to have defied complete destruction better if one excepts T. W. Robinson's *Sydney Primer or Child's Manual* issued by James Tegg in 1838 (not in Ferguson). Again by date order we have John J. Davies, *Tables for the use of schools*, printed at the *Gazette* office in Sydney by Ralph Mansfield in 1831 (Ferguson 1426a); Rev. Henry Carmichael, *A Compendious Latin Grammar for the use of the students of the Australian College*, issued as a broadside by Ralph Mansfield in 1832 (Ferguson 1523); James Ross, *The Note Book of Useful, Experimental and Entertaining Knowledge*, part I, Hobart, 1833, the first and possibly the only one produced of a projected series (Ferguson 1699); *A Collection of English Exercises*, translated from the writings of Cicero for schoolboys to retranslate into Latin (Sydney, Stephens and Stokes, 1833) (not in Ferguson); *The Catholic School Book, containing Easy and Familiar Lessons*, part 1 (Sydney, W. Jones, 1834) (not in Ferguson); William Mavor, *The English Spelling Book — Australian Version*, printed for the Teggs and Dowling (Sydney, 1836) (not in Ferguson); and Rev. L. E. Threlkeld, *An Australian*

Spelling Book, in the Language as spoken by the Aborigines, in the vicinity of Hunter's River, Lake Macquarie (Sydney, Stephens and Stokes, 1836) (Ferguson 2192). The rarity of these editions is indicated clearly enough by the absence of some of them from the standard bibliography of Australiana.

After 1840, and especially 1850, there was gradual expansion of the local production of textbooks. This does not mean that everything printed has survived. One example is *Dowling's First Book for Children: a Popular and Progressive Primer on a simple and easy plan. Tenth Thousand* (Launceston, Henry Dowling, c. 1851) (Ferguson 9225; Craig, 57). Although Ferguson's *Bibliography* for the period 1851–1900 expressly excludes 'School books of elementary character' he allows for exceptions, of which this is one. On the other hand he does treat the growing number of texts for secondary schools. Special attention is given to James Bonwick's output in many fields as well as his early concentration on books for schoolchildren. After the first two editions of his *Geography for the use of Australian Youth* (Van Diemen's Land, sold by S. A. Tegg, James Dowling and W. A. Colman, 1845) (Ferguson 3994) and (Launceston, Henry Dowling junior, 1850) (Ferguson 5290) he tackled many other subjects listed by Ferguson (7188–7267) and earlier by E. E. Pescott. Bonwick can be seen as the first committed and longtime textbook writer resident in Australia.

Even though British educational material continued to bulk large in Australian schools in the second half of the century, it was partly naturalised. The use of books authorised by the Commissioners of National Education in Ireland was so widespread that they could appear with local imprints even if the sheets were imported. This is the case with the *Fourth Book of Lessons for the Use of Schools* (Sydney, John Ferguson, [no date], printed by Ballantyne and Company, Edinburgh and London). Ferguson, active between 1866 and 1887, described himself as 'Educational Publisher, Bookseller, and Stationer'. Victoria adopted Nelson's *Royal Readers* for its new school system in the 1870s, but, at the behest of Robert Ramsay, Minister of Public Instruction, 'insisted on a special Victorian edition [...] which omitted any reference to the name of Christ' (*ADB*, vol.6, 5). In 1887 some Australian content was introduced into an enlarged edition of the *Royal Readers* in Victoria. As early as 1876 the Collins branch in Sydney had launched *The Australian Reading Books*, and four years before that George Robertson had imported *Irish Readers* with some Australian content supplied by Archibald Gilchrist.

Public examinations and notably Matriculation provided a stimulus to the writing of textbooks in the colonies. In the two decades before 1890 the major publishers were the Melbourne firms of George Robertson and Samuel Mullen. The sections on 'English Literature', 'Classical Literature' and 'Modern Literatures' in Morris Miller's *Australian Literature from its Beginnings to 1935* provide an overview of what was being produced in these fields to meet the needs of a growing market. The attention to French language and literature reflects the priorities of an earlier age and the availability of native speakers locally to undertake the work. A substantial range of more elementary texts was being issued in Adelaide in impressive quantities by Edward Walter Wickes in the same period (Ferguson 18524-18533).

It was inevitable that there was rivalry in the trade for achieving prescribed status for books being planned. Archival records are sparse, but the occasional preserved document tells us how things were being managed. For example, the Charles Henry Pearson papers in State Library Victoria hold a memorandum of agreement between Mullen and the co-authors Pearson and H. A. Strong for the publication of an English grammar in 1876: 'Professor Strong undertakes that the Grammar shall be placed on the course of the Melbourne University' (Kirsop, 89).

At least one of the books written for schools in this time became a classic. Alexander and George Sutherland's *The History of Australia From 1606 to 1876* was published by George Robertson in 1877 (Ferguson 16447). Later extended to include New Zealand it went through numerous editions up to 1913 and sold more than 100 000 copies. A recent discussion by Anna Clark demonstrates how influential this text was in the Federation period (Clark, 79-97).

Writing about teaching and the purpose of schools also came to the fore in the colonies in the second half of the nineteenth century. Two prominent examples are William Wilkins, *The Principles that underlie the Art of Teaching* (Sydney, Thomas Richards,

Government Printer, 1886) (Ferguson 18571) and Ferdinand von Mueller, *Introduction to Botanic Teachings in the Schools of Victoria, through references to leading native plants* (Melbourne, John Ferres, Government Printer, 1877) (Ferguson 12935).

Alongside the continuing mass of importations, the Australian trade, including the official presses, had succeeded by 1890 in establishing educational publishing on a sound footing. The present author's unpublished *Bibliography of Australian Education* (with 6000 entries) reveals that 397 Australian school textbooks were published between 1810 and 1890, made up of 313 first editions and 84 new, revised, enlarged, second and subsequent editions. By contrast, during the same period 31 teacher education and technical education texts were issued, plus 22 university texts.

NOTE ON SOURCES

The basis for the chapter is to be found in Jeffrey Prentice, Bibliography of Australian Education (unpublished manuscript). Other secondary sources referred to explicitly are: John Holroyd, *George Robertson of Melbourne 1825–1898: Pioneer Bookseller & Publisher*, Melbourne, Robertson & Mullens, 1968; Clifford Craig, *The Van Diemen's Land Edition of The Pickwick Papers: a general and bibliographical study with some notes on Henry Dowling*, Hobart, Cat & Fiddle Press, 1973; Edward Edgar Pescott, *James Bonwick: A Writer of School Books and Histories, with a Bibliography of his Writings*, Melbourne, H. A. Evans & Son, 1939; Wallace Kirsop, 'From Curry's to Collins Street, or How a Dubliner Became the "Melbourne Mudie"', in Peter Isaac and Barry McKay, eds, *The Moving Market: Continuity and Change in the Book Trade*, Newcastle, Delaware, Oak Knoll Press, 2001, pp. 83-92; Anna Clark, *Making Australian History*, Melbourne, Vintage Books, 2022. On W. B. Stephens see Mark Howard, 'William Stephens: an innovative Melbourne bookseller', *Biblionews and Australian Notes & Queries*, 411th issue, September 2021, pp. 112-21.

CHAPTER 20

Australian Directories to 1890

†R. Ian Jack

In the early 2000s, an antiquarian bookseller in Sydney found it hard to attract a buyer for a collection of the first six directories published in New South Wales between 1832 and 1837. In the end, a consulting historian bought the series as a fundamental tool of his trade, but directories do not seem to have the same appeal to book collectors as works of exploration or travel, which have a more restricted use as sources for many historical inquiries. However, in more recent decades the importance of directories has been recognised by the wider community owing to the surge of interest in genealogy. Many libraries and archives have made these publications available online, often as part of a suite of family history research tools.

Directories were created for immediate purposes as instruments of commerce, making available to the more affluent public alphabetical lists of residents within a locality, large or small, with some form of address and, 'commonly', occupation. The genre had first appeared in London in 1677, concerned solely with wholesale trade, and the example spread and broadened its scope throughout Europe in the following century. The colonial government in New South Wales maintained its own manuscript lists of convicts, soldiery and settlers through regular musters, but did nothing to encourage a commercially published directory until 1831, when James Raymond, the Principal Postmaster, compiled *The New South Wales Calendar, and General Post Office Directory, 1832*. Raymond explained that this was 'begun with a view to extend the utility of the Department I have had the honor of being entrusted with' and 'compiled from the opportunities afforded by an anxious observance of my official Duties'. This directory was published to be 'of indisputable utility to the Post Office Establishment, and I trust — to the Public at large'.

Such a book was of only short-term use to government officials and the populace. As new editions appeared annually throughout the 1830s (except in 1838), earlier volumes became quickly redundant and it was only much later that their value as an historical record became properly appreciated. As a result, almost all nineteenth-century directories are rare, like the almanacs which reached a similar public in New South Wales as early as 1806. Despite their significance, neither directories nor almanacs are mentioned in works such as Jonathan Wantrup's *Australian Rare Books, 1788-1900* (1987). The almanacs, which contained lists of civil and military officials in the colony (unlike the comparable almanacs published in England in the early nineteenth century), had some affinities to directories, as they did also to emigrants' guides. Occasionally almanacs included full-scale directories, as for Port Phillip in 1847 or Newcastle in 1880. Another example is Andrew Bent's *Tasmanian Almanack* for 1825 which featured an alphabetical list of the names, occupations and streets of 149 residents of Hobart Town.

The early directories are composite volumes, both in New South Wales and Van Diemen's Land. The 1833 directory published in Hobart Town by James Ross constitutes, in at least one copy, only the second part, pages 49 to 83, of a work by Captain William Jacob which appeared under the title *Memoir on the Practicability of Establishing a Permanent Communication across the River Derwent by means of a pontoonbridge with a project for its construction.*

The New South Wales directories published between 1832 and 1835 included much civic information and a valuable 'itinerary of roads', with various illustrations from 1833 onwards, principally of Surveyor General Thomas Mitchell's new Victoria Pass over the Blue Mountains. The directories for 1833 to 1836 also contained attractive and informative engraved advertisements, as English directories had pioneered in the 1820s. These early New South Wales directories are unusually handsome books, though they are seldom seen in good condition because of their usefulness to their original owners, who consulted them often before discarding them for a new edition.

In the New South Wales series, up to 1837, the simple alphabetical listing of persons in the colony which constituted the directory proper was at the end of the substantial volume, either unnumbered or separately paginated. Each edition also had a fine map of Sydney executed in the Surveyor General's office. The compiler was justified when he presented the 1836 edition to the public, 'in the confident hope that it will be found an useful Book of reference to every Member of the Community, which has been the anxious object of the Publication', even though the guide to roads was permanently dropped in that year.

A significant change in the presentation of directories came in 1839, heralding innovations which were to become the norm in due course. In 1838 no New South Wales directory had appeared. Instead, a private entrepreneur, James Maclehose, diversified his business interest from umbrellas into publishing, with his popular *Picture of Sydney and Strangers' Guide in New South Wales*. This abundantly illustrated book (which reprinted William Wilson's engraving of Regentville, published in the 1835 directory) ran to two impressions in 1838 and 1839. Maclehose then published separately a modest, slim, unillustrated directory, the *New South Wales and Port Phillip General Post Office Directory for 1839*, which was essentially a supplement to the *Picture of Sydney*. Like the 1832 directory, Maclehose's 1839 publication was 'printed and published by permission of James Raymond, esquire, postmaster-general'. The 178 small, plain pages included Melbourne for the first time. This is the most workaday of all state directories and was also so highly expendable that only five copies are known to exist.

The first directory published in Melbourne, *Kerr's Melbourne Almanac, and Port Phillip Directory, for 1841*, two years after Maclehose, reverted to the older style of the Sydney directories of 1832–37, with the Port Phillip directory occupying the end pages, 233 to 257: for the first time the directory was now numbered as an integral part of the volume.

The first South Australian directory in the same year, 1841, was not a commercial publication at all, but an appendix, pages 322-29, to the report from the Select Committee on South Australia. It was arranged under the main geographical areas in South Australia, which was an innovation, but had something of the flavour of the unpublished New South Wales musters, showing in columns the quantity of sheep, cattle, horses and various crops owned by each settler.

These early directories clearly found a market and encouraged other entrepreneurs. E. M. O'Shaughnessy, who ran the *Gazette* office in Sydney with Ann Howe, had already competed unsuccessfully with the post office directories in New South Wales with his *Australian Almanack and Sydney Directory for the Year of our Lord 1834*, followed by the *Australian Almanack and General Directory for the Year of our Lord 1835*. These works pioneered the separation of city and country into two separate alphabetical sequences. This was further developed in 1843 by *Brabazon's New South Wales General Town Directory and Advertiser*, which introduced better addresses in the Sydney section by naming cross-streets for corner premises. Harry Brabazon also introduced separate directories for individual country towns, with particular attention to the Hunter Valley.

In the following year, 1844, and again in 1847, Francis Low further improved on listing house locations in Sydney by including many street numbers and, where relevant, cross-streets. His 1844 publication included 17 pages of advertisements and a great deal of useful public information about banks, churches, schools and transport. But Low targeted the city of Sydney at the expense of the country and was followed in this practice by W. and F. Ford in 1851 and by Waugh and Cox in 1855.

In contrast to New South Wales, Victorian publishers produced a series of directories including the rural areas in 1846 and 1847, followed by the first *Squatters' Directory* in 1849 and a *Victorian Directory* in 1851, although from 1853 until 1856 all five published directories catered exclusively to the city of Melbourne.

The rather sporadic nature of directory production, with a series of businessmen entering the game briefly, began to settle down in the late 1850s. The dominant firm, with premises both in Melbourne and in Sydney, was Sands and Kenny (which became Sands and McDougall in Melbourne in 1862 and John Sands in Sydney in 1863). Sands produced directories in Sydney until 1933, missing only six years, and continued as an institution in Melbourne until 1974. Sands, however, dealt only with the two major cities and their suburbs until 1901 (in New South Wales) and 1902 (in Victoria). The Melbourne and Sydney series are the best known of all Australian directories and the firm showed considerable professionalism in developing the layout of the ever-bulkier volumes, taking ideas from Kelly and Co., the major English publisher of directories.

The Sydney series of Sands' directories has been skilfully analysed by Joy Hughes. From the beginning in 1858, Sydney's streets were listed alphabetically, with occupiers listed by street numbers under each street. Pyrmont was separate until 1865 when its streets were incorporated into the Sydney sequence. Very conveniently, the names of many houses and terraces are also given. Until 1880 the Sydney wharves were in the street directory, but thereafter appeared in the separate business section.

The Sydney suburbs or municipalities were listed alphabetically with residents also alphabetically arranged under each section. In 1871 and 1873 (no directory was issued for 1872) the suburbs were integrated into Sydney under streets. Thereafter the suburbs were separate and were increasingly presented street by street, although some inner suburbs became absorbed into Sydney in 1884, as Pyrmont had been in 1865. The two topographical sections in Sands' Sydney directories were followed by a complete alphabetical listing of all occupiers in Sydney and the suburbs combined. The classified business directory, arranged under trades and professions in various forms, was a consistent additional feature, together with official, medical, clerical and legal lists reminiscent of the early almanacs and calendars.

The information presented so conveniently in Sands' directories was voluminous. The first Melbourne directory of 1857 was already 200 pages, plus 66 pages of advertisements. The directory steadily increased in size, to 408 pages in 1860, 806 in 1870, 874 in 1880 and 1296 in 1890. The number of advertisements, although an important part of the economics of such a publication, did not increase commensurately, peaking at 138 in 1885 but declining rapidly to 68 by 1890, virtually the same as in 1857.

The compilation of the information was a formidable undertaking. Sands' Sydney directory published in 1858 stated:

> as far as practicable information has been obtained from individuals, at their private addresses, or at their accustomed places of business, by competent parties, who have been both diligent and careful.

The method of compilation had long depended on competent agents. The days when William Bailey could claim that in assembling his *British Directory* in 1784 he had 'visited every town and personally waited on every house in the kingdom' had passed by 1811 when *Holden's Annual London and Country Directory of the United Kingdom and Wales* used as agent 'a gentleman of the first respectability'. This led in the 1840s in Britain to the employment of professional directory agents. Kelly started using 'selected whole-time agents' in 1845, when post office staff were prevented from collaborating in such commercial ventures.

In New Zealand, John Stone's surviving correspondence from the 1880s shows how the agent system operated in Australasia. Stone hired canvassers to work part-time in their own locality: thus a storekeeper in Portobello, a ranger of North East Valley and an insurance agent of Roslyn collected data in their home areas. Each had detailed instructions about the specific information to be systematically elicited from each resident. There was a powerful incentive of 5 per cent commission if the resident could be persuaded to subscribe to the directory.

Similarly it is known that Henry Wise, also in New Zealand, had sent Robert Seward as his agent all over the two islands in the first half of 1872 to collect data for Wise's New Zealand commercial directory for 1872–73. Wise made it clear that he did not simply borrow information from existing directories but, as for his New Zealand directory for 1875–76:

> over 4000 miles have been travelled in order to collect this information, every place of importance having been personally visited, and, to do this has occupied a period of twelve months.

The time involved depended on the number of agents employed and the distances that had to be travelled: Kelly's *London Post Office Directory* for 1840 had required only two to three months in 1839 to complete from start to finish.

In Sydney and Melbourne John Sands used a network larger than that used by Wise or Stone in New Zealand and probably comparable to Kelly's in London. Sands was obliged greatly to enlarge his team for his four country directories published in New South Wales between 1878 and 1889. The first two, for 1878-79 and 1881-82, were compiled by James Tingle on the basis of the agents' returns. Tingle organised these two directories in different ways. The earlier was arranged alphabetically by town, with inhabitants listed alphabetically under each locality. There were also various topographical and economic descriptions. By contrast, in 1881-82 Tingle provided only a single list of country dwellers, alphabetically arranged. It is, as a result, virtually impossible to discover from Sands who lived in, say, West Maitland in 1881, although this information was easily accessible for 1878. Probably as a result, Tingle was not employed to compile the 1884-85 country directory, which reverted to a topographical arrangement with classified business section. Yet in 1889-90 the country directory again listed all persons in one alphabetical sequence, as in Tingle's second compilation. Since Sands did not supply a Victorian country directory before 1902 and since the New South Wales country was so inadequately covered, there was an incentive for local publishers to produce localised directories and for other businessmen to fill a perceived gap in the states at large. In three states, the publisher F. F. Baillière met the general need with an *Official Post Office Directory of Victoria* in 1868, 1869, 1870, 1871-72, 1875 and 1880-81, for New South Wales in 1867 and for Queensland in 1868 and 1874. Greville and Co. (Sydney) succeeded Baillière in New South Wales. He excluded Sydney and its suburbs entirely in 1872, but included some of the city's suburbs in 1875-77.

Henry Wise from New Zealand stepped directly into Baillière's shoes in Melbourne after the publisher died in 1881. Wise obtained office premises in Melbourne and in 1884-85 published his first *Victoria Post Office Directory* in conjunction with Kelly and Co. in London. Wise's Victorian directories, covering separately, as he proudly claimed, 'over one thousand townships, boroughs, cities and districts', continued to appear biennially for the rest of the century and annually from 1900 until 1916.

Wise did not challenge Sands in New South Wales until 1886–87. In 1890 Wise expanded his portfolio, publishing his first *Queensland Official Directory* and *Tasmania Post Office Directory*, both of which ran well into the twentieth century. Wise is far less well-known than Sands, but anyone who has used both sets of directories has gained considerable respect for the New Zealand firm, which gave a much more consistent coverage of country Australia than any of its rivals.

The more localised directories are numerous and rarely appeared in long series. A notable exception is R. C. Knaggs's *Newcastle Business Directory and Hunter River District Almanac*, which first appeared as a single promotion sheet in 1862 and then as a slim annual volume from 1866 until at least 1889. By contrast, the gold town of Ballarat had seven directories between 1857 and 1886, produced by seven different compilers or publishers: Huxtable, Birtchnell, Dicker, Windle, Niven, Kerr, and Middleton & Maning, while Bendigo had a very similar experience.

In New South Wales there were local directories for the northern rivers in 1871 and 1872, for the Sydney suburb of Balmain in 1878, for the county of Cumberland centring on Parramatta from 1884 to 1887, for Dubbo in 1882, for Goulburn in 1882–83, for Bathurst and the west in 1886–87 and for the Wagga Wagga area from 1887 to 1895, while the Riverina around Albury had a certain amount of directory coverage over the whole period, principally in the *Border Post Almanac*.

In Queensland there was a *Maryborough Almanac and Wide Bay and Burnett Business Directory* for 1874–75 and a directory for Wide Bay and Burnett prepared by A. J. Ivimey in 1887, while Ipswich, Toowoomba and Drayton had a directory and gazetteer for 1885–86.

In addition to the first South Australian directory mentioned earlier, other titles for the area included the *Adelaide Almanack, Town and Country Directory and Guide to South Australia* (1864–83), compiled by government statistician Josiah Boothby. The first issue listed residents by district, covering over 50 communities.

Western Australia was served by various publications. In 1865 Stirling, Sholl & Co. at the *Inquirer and Commercial News* office, published the *Western Australian Almanack* which included a three-page, single alphabetical list of residents of Perth, Fremantle,

Guildford, Albany and Geraldton. Later that same year in a 'second edition', titled *Western Australian Almanack and Directory*, the listings had expanded to seven pages with individual lists for the aforementioned localities and for Geraldton and Champion Bay. It was offered at a price of 1/6d, or 2s 'with a map of the Colony'. By the late 1880s the directory section was over 50 pages and included many small farming communities. Post office directories for Western Australia did not appear until 1893, published by H. Pierssené and continued by the prolific Wise, again well into the twentieth century. Early issues listed postal addresses by town and those for metropolitan areas, by street.

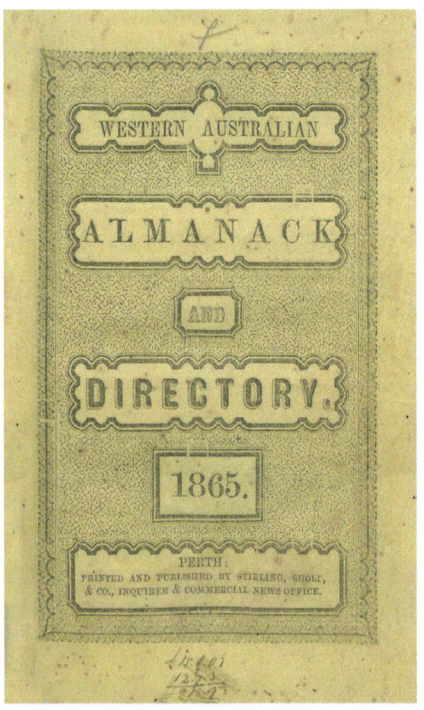

Several months after issuing the *Western Australian Almanack* for 1865, Stirling, Sholl & Co. (Edmund Stirling and Robert John Sholl) expanded the almanac's three-page directory to eight pages in a second edition with a revised title highlighting the added feature (cover shown above). They announced its publication in their newspaper, the *Inquirer and Commercial News* on 31 May 1865. In 1889 the publication — by then issued by Stirling Bros. (Edmund's sons) — changed to *Western Australian Calendar and Directory*. With Charles Macfaull and W. K. Shenton, Edmund Stirling had in 1833 produced Western Australia's first commercially printed newspaper, the *Fremantle Observer, Perth Gazette* and *Western Australian Journal*. (State Library of Western Australia)

The end of the first phase of Australian publishing, as defined by the title of the present volume, coincides with the appearance of the first telephone directory in 1889. Although the major firms, Sands and Wise, continued to produce directories well into the twentieth century, the telephone book was a progressive challenge. The rapid spread of the telephone among professional people and property owners by World War I meant that by 1920 the older street directory had lost much of its commercial appeal to those whose subscriptions and advertisements were essential to Sands and Wise. The future lay with the white pages and the yellow pages: the year 1890 is a meaningful stage in this determining switch in directory style, purpose and distribution.

NOTE ON SOURCES

As previously noted, many Australian directories can now be accessed online. General guides and bibliographies of directories and cognate publications in Britain and Australia are: Jane E. Norton, *Guide to the National and Provincial Directories of England and Wales, excluding London, published before 1856*, London, Royal Historical Society, Guides and Handbooks 5, 1950; C. W. F. Goss, *The London Directories, 1677–1855*, London, 1932; Maureen Perkins, *Visions of the Future: Almanacs, Time and Cultural Change, 1775–1870*, Oxford, Clarendon Press, 1996; Margot Hyslop, *Victorian Directories, 1836–1974: A Checklist*, Bundoora, La Trobe University Publication 18, 1980; and Joy Hughes, *New South Wales Directories, 1828–1952: A Bibliography*, bound with Christine Eslick, Joy Hughes and R. Ian Jack, *Bibliography of New South Wales Local History*, Kensington, NSW University Press, 1987. A list of pre-1890 Tasmanian directories can be found in Anne Bartlett, *Local and family history sources in Tasmania*, 2nd ed., Launceston, Genealogical Society of Tasmania, 1994, pp. 28–32.

For individual publishers of directories, see H. P. Down, *A Century in Printing: The Story of Sands & McDougall Pty. Ltd., during its first hundred years 1853–1953*, Melbourne, Sands & McDougall, 1956; K. I. D. Maslen, 'Wise's Directories: A Short History and a Checklist (1865–1922)', *BSANZ Bulletin*, vol. 12, no. 1, 1988, pp. 21–41; and Michael Hamblin, 'Kei hea ti whare? Titiro ki roto: John Stone's New Zealand Directories, Part One: 1884–1897', *BSANZ Bulletin*, vol. 19, no. 1, 1995, pp. 15–29.

CHAPTER 21

Australian Almanacs 1806–1890

Maureen Perkins

An almanac was the second book produced in Australia. There seems little doubt that George Howe's motivation in choosing to publish it in 1806, a year of scarce paper supplies, was the reliability of this publication as a source of income. Almanacs, or calendars, were considered essential household items. In Britain, at least one in seven people at this period bought a yearly book almanac, and many more than this number had access to almanac knowledge through the public display of broadsheet versions in shops and taverns. Australians experienced the same need to be reminded of the progress of the year. The title of Howe's almanac, the *New South Wales Pocket Almanack and Colonial Remembrancer*, testifies to the way in which calendars remind us of our temporal signposts, especially in an environment where 'everything is just the opposite of everywhere else'. One important remembrance that Howe's book highlighted was the list of seasons, to alert its readers that these were at a different time of the calendar year than they might perhaps have expected.

The first Australian almanac's division of the year marked a distinct break with tradition. Although many of the most famous London versions, like *Moore's*, were closely linked with astrology and prognostication, Howe included no astrological content at all. He avoided mention of the zodiac, even going so far as to record the seasons as coinciding with calendar months rather than with the sun's entry into celestial signs. Spring, according to Howe, began on

1 September, whereas for all British almanacs it began with the vernal equinox as the sun entered zero degrees Aries. It is likely that George Howe regarded this unusual interpretation of the year as striking a blow for rational knowledge, at a time when the responsibilities of publishers to a newly literate, impressionable readership were being widely discussed.

Other Australian almanacs were just as groundbreaking. Those of James Ross, compiler of the *Hobart Town Almanack* (1829–38), were much more than calendars. They were vehicles for detailed accounts of life in the colony, including various statistical compilations of 'useful' facts. By imagining a reader who was either new to Van Diemen's Land or considering emigration, Ross invented a cross between a calendar and an emigrants' guide. His almanacs caught the eye of the English publisher Charles Knight, who carried several extracts from them in the *Penny Magazine*, and lavished praise on them as models of rationality and literary achievement. Knight emulated Ross's style in the *British Almanac*, and this statistical approach, pioneered by both Ross and Knight, helped to transform the almanac into a compilation of data, the best-known manifestation of which is now *Whitaker's Almanac* (first published in London in 1869).

The purposes an almanac was expected to fulfil were fairly clear. There were the obvious uses of the calendar, giving a record of the past and an overview of the future, a function which was warmly welcomed as a service to the community. However, several other objectives were also well documented. Andrew Murray, for example, in the *Victoria Nautical and Commercial Almanac* for 1855 wrote (on p. 1): 'In submitting to the public the first Book Almanac for the Colony of Victoria, the Editor thinks it right to state that his chief aim has been — 1. To make it practically useful to the colonists.' The publication of times of tides, lists of government regulations, and directories of prominent businesses and citizens all made Australian almanacs sources of many different kinds of information. We know from Ann-Mari Jordens's account of Marcus Clarke's library that they provided much of the detail from which this author constructed his novels. Several compilers also noted that they expected a readership within both Australia and Britain. One of Murray's subsidiary aims was to 'exhibit both to the colonists and to persons at a distance an exact picture of the colony' (p. i). The second *Tasmanian Almanack* (Hobart, Andrew Bent, 1825, p. 1) listed its uses as being 'To regulate Mercantile arrangements, assist the unpractised Husbandman, inform the newly-arrived Emigrant, and develope [sic] to British Readers, the nature, description, and extent of this Island's peculiar Establishments, Civil, Military, and Marine.' (p. 1) Some nineteenth-century Australian almanacs, then, saw one function as convincing those in Britain that the 'advancement of knowledge and education' was proceeding at a due pace in the colonies.

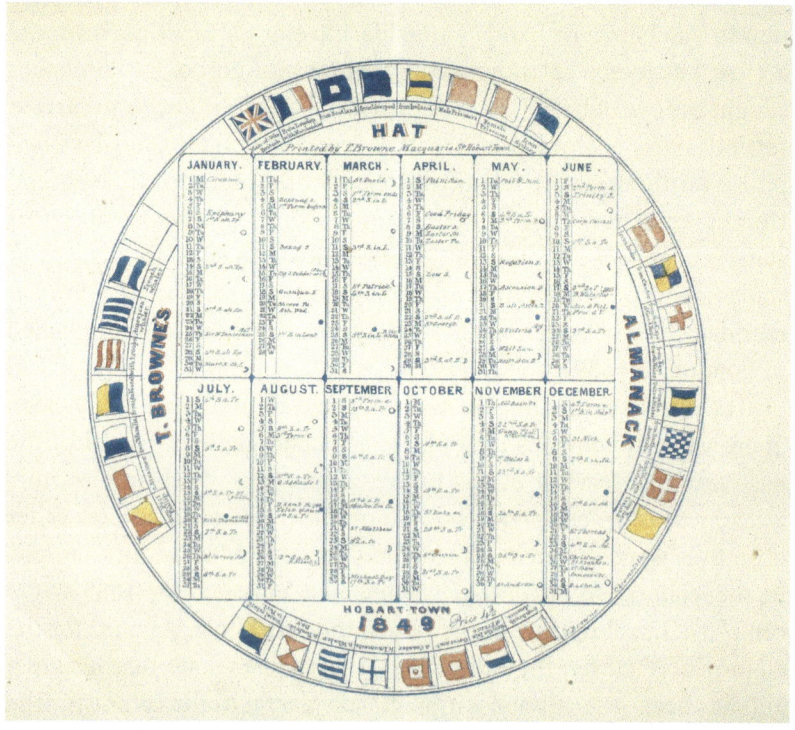

Hat Almanac for 1849, Hobart, T. Browne, 1848. Advertised in the *Hobart Town Advertiser* 17 November 1848: 'Just Published, price 4d . . . and with the signal flags beautifully printed in colours'. [Lithograph], one sheet, 229 x 283 mm. In his *London Labour and the London Poor* (1851), Henry Mayhew mentions 'diamond almanacks to fit into hat crowns' (i, 271). Such items would likely have been familiar to English-born Thomas Browne (1816–1870) who worked in Launceston at Henry Dowling's printing and stationery business before establishing his own firm in Hobart in 1844. He opened a daguerreotype studio in 1846 and was likely Hobart's first resident professional photographer, and also worked as a lithographer. In 1846 he was briefly the proprietor of the *Spectator* newspaper. (State Library of Tasmania)

Although the majority of Australian almanacs fitted this worthy utilitarian mould, there were some compilers, such as Henry Melville and Andrew Bent, who continued the popular astrological content, publishing planetary aspects, astrological weather predictions and advice for gardening according to the phases of the moon. Still others chose to perpetuate the tradition of listing natural wonders, monstrous births and vicious murders. The most curious example of the continuation of this popular appeal was in the almanacs of Robert Howe, son of George and inheritor of the *Sydney Gazette* office. In 1821 when Robert Howe took over the printing business at his father's death, he renamed the almanac the *Australian Pocket Almanac*, and on page one printed a list of the signs of the zodiac with their astrological symbols. Also, for the first time in Australia the calendar included a weather column, headed 'Usual State of the Weather'. This feature of almanacs was by far the most popular and most quoted characteristic of British and American equivalents. In Robert Howe's version, the entry for January advised the reader that 'Sol, while immersed in the Water-bearer, exerts his piercing and scorching energy, the heat being intense'. In later months the sun was 'stung by the Scorpion' or 'wounded by the Archer'. Planetary equinoxes were also included, marking the beginning of each season. Howe obviously either understood astrological terminology or, as so many compilers did, simply copied his material from some other source. However, there is no doubt about the originality of the changes he made to the almanac's chronology. In the *Australian Pocket Almanac* for 1829 he set aside the usual dates of historical discovery in favour of a list of local wonders and marvels, amongst which, for example, was the birth at Hawkesbury of a beautiful colt with the two forelegs totally missing, the death of four cows by one single flash of lightning, the appearance of a snake measuring 22 feet in length, and news of the compiler's own brush with death on the night of 15 June 1822, when he was nearly assassinated by a 'maniac' (p. 95). These 'Remarkable Occurrences' suggest an understanding of the popular interest in death, danger and the marvellous. However, when Howe died in 1829 ownership of the printery passed to his wife Ann, who appointed as editor the Rev. Ralph Mansfield, who quickly removed all astrological and sensational content from the following year's copy.

Most almanac compilers resembled Mansfield and Andrew Murray, the latter promising that 'speculations on the future have been diligently avoided'. By the middle of the century astrological almanacs had disappeared, with only the occasional faint allusion to older traditions embedded in what was almost always a rational, utilitarian publication. Occasional humorous references indicated that the memory of predictive content had not altogether disappeared, as in (Francis) *Hopkins' Rockhampton Almanac* of 1878 (Rockhampton, Queensland), which included a mock forecast, predicting the arrival of 'several hundred strangers . . . without passports', in a reminder to parents to register the births of new babies.

Despite Robert Howe's early example, chronologies continued to be a list of those historical events regarded by respectable compilers as of most value. As such, they provide a useful record of sanctioned communal memory, and furnish evidence of the creation of a sense of nationhood. As distribution of almanacs became more widespread, a sense of fraternal interest between regions was advanced in these chronologies in a way not evident in British almanacs, which generally remained non-specific in their sense of environment. The 1854 *Western Australian Almanack* (Perth, Arthur Shenton) noted, for example, that 17 May was the anniversary of the promulgation of the Charter of New South Wales in 1824, and that gas was first used in Sydney on 26 May 1841. Although earlier descriptions of place may have been included with the needs of emigrants in mind, by the end of the century a sense of the fostering of intercolonial links is evident, even in the new, non-English language versions that began to appear in the 1850s, such as the *Süd-Australische Deutscher Kalender* (Tanunda, Carl Kornhardt, 1851) and Phineas Moss's *Calendar of All Days and Nights, Sabbaths and New Moons, Seasons, Holydays, and Feasts* (Hobart, George Rolwegan, 1853) in both Hebrew and English.

Almanacs often provided substantial reading for the year. Articles on history, biography, political economy and agriculture were common. Some included works of fiction, poetry and travel. As the nineteenth century went on, several factors contributed to the increasing bulk of each volume: cheaper printing costs, increased use of illustrations, and emphasis on the role of statistical information as part of a useful education. Lists of references provided a miniature encyclopedia: ready reckoners, directories of local businesses, postal rates, cookery guides, and even dictionaries of Aboriginal languages as in the 'Native Grammar' appended to the 1842 *Western Australian Almanack* (Perth, C. Macfaull).

As in Europe, almanac publishing was increasingly neglected in the second and third decades of the twentieth century, as first the demands of wartime restrictions made them a luxury and then the subsequent spread of information and entertainment through broadcasting and periodicals rendered them superfluous. Throughout the nineteenth century, however, especially in the later years when railway distribution increased readership, almanacs were part of 'the standard furniture of the mind' as Ian Morrison has noted. They provide an historical record of elements of daily life and thought that might once have been dismissed as ephemeral but can now be appreciated as a fascinating insight into the experience of the passing of time, as well as the beliefs, both respectable and unorthodox, which helped to structure the memory of the past and anticipation of the future.

NOTE ON SOURCES

More detail can be found in Maureen Perkins, *Visions of the Future: Almanacs, Time and Cultural Change 1775–1870*, Oxford, Clarendon Press, 1996, chapter 5; Ian Morrison, 'A Bibliography of Australian Almanacs, 1806–ca. 1920: Notes on Work in Progress', *Biblionews*, 321st issue, vol.24, no.1, March 1999, pp. 3-12; and Ian Morrison, Maureen Perkins and Tracey Caulfield, *Australian Almanacs 1806-1930: A Bibliography*, Hawthorn East, VIC, Quiddlers Press, 2003. Ann-Mari Jordens's article, 'Marcus Clarke's Library' was published in *Australian Literary Studies*, vol.7, no.4, 1 October 1976, pp. 399-412. Andrew Bent's early Tasmanian almanacs have been investigated in detail by Sally Bloomfield on the website devoted to Bent which she created with Craig Collins, andrew-bent.life/2019/11/08/early-almanacs/ [accessed 2 May 2024].

Most helpfully for researchers, in recent years the full text of many Australian almanacs has been digitised and can be found on websites such as those of the National Library of Australia, state libraries, archives and record offices as well as on Trove.

CHAPTER 22

Australian Printing and Publishing in Pacific Islands and Indigenous Australian Languages 1814–1900

Susan Woodburn

Although printing and publishing in Indigenous Australian and Pacific Island languages in nineteenth-century Australia represent a relatively minor part of local production in the period, they have considerable bibliographical interest and encourage reflection on the reach (and limitations) of cultural transmission through the medium of the printed book.

Printing in Pacific Island languages

No fewer than five and possibly seven works in the Tahitian language and one in Māori were printed by George Howe in Sydney in 1814 and 1815, only four years after the first book in any Pacific language (a spelling book in Tahitian) was published in London. They were among Howe's earliest non-official publications in New South Wales and preceded by many years any Australian publication of works in a European language. Three Tahitian texts were printed by Robert Howe in 1821 and 1822. The first translation of the scriptures into Māori and the first publication in any of the Indigenous languages of Australia were printed in Sydney in 1827, and the following year the *Sydney Gazette* Office printed a lesson book in Tongan. Further portions of the scriptures in Māori and a Tongan primer and hymn-book followed in 1829–30 and additional scripture translations, service and lesson books in Māori in 1833 and 1834.

Thereafter, Australian printing in the languages of Oceania fell away almost completely for many years. When resumed in any volume from the 1870s it was principally in the languages of Melanesia rather than Polynesia and much more scattered, with Norfolk Island an unexpected new printing centre.

Distance from established printers in England, Europe and America and limited sailing opportunities from remote islands were obvious influences on the early Australian printing for the Pacific, but the most important factor was the mission origin of the translation endeavours. Then, and for more than a century, the history of printing in the Indigenous languages of Oceania was a mirror of Christian evangelical activity, and changes in the location, volume and focus of printing can be traced to the policies, fortunes and contacts of the various mission societies.

Missionary entry into the Pacific followed closely on the period of 'discovery' and economic exploitation of trade opportunities of the late eighteenth century. The newly established London Missionary Society began operations in Tahiti in 1797, the American Board of Commissioners for Foreign Missions in Hawai'i in 1820 and the Wesleyan Methodist Missionary Society in Tonga in 1822. In response to perceived success or new areas of 'need', each expanded progressively westward: the London Missionary Society into Samoa, Fiji, the Cook Islands and Loyalty Islands, New Caledonia and ultimately New Guinea; the Wesleyans into Fiji and the Bismarck Archipelago; the American Board into Micronesia. Missions to the Indigenous population of New Zealand were initiated from New South Wales: missionary activity from New Zealand itself then began with the establishment of the (Anglican) Melanesian Mission, which from 1849 ventured north into the Loyalty Islands, the northern New Hebrides (Vanuatu), the Banks and Santa Cruz Islands and then the southern Solomon Islands and Papua New Guinea. The Catholic missions of the French Picpus Fathers (Sacred Heart Mission) and Society of Mary (Marist Fathers) made their entry into the Pacific from 1827. They established themselves in the Gambier Islands, New Zealand, and Wallis and Futuna islands and expanded into New Caledonia, the New Hebrides, Solomon Islands, New Britain and Papua, generally obtaining a foothold on islands not yet approached by the Protestants though in some instances in direct and open confrontation with established missions. Presbyterian missions from Nova Scotia took as their particular field the southern New Hebrides from 1848, while Lutheran missions, Australian Methodists and the Anglican New Guinea Mission established sites in various parts of Papua New Guinea from the 1880s.

The earliest Sydney printings in languages other than English were for the Tahitian mission of the London Missionary Society and reflected the close association developed between the mission and New South Wales. The colonial chaplain Samuel Marsden had become the recognised correspondent of the Society from 1801 and it was to Marsden that the Society's John Davies — one of the 1801 group of reinforcements who had prepared the Tahitian spelling book published in London in 1810 — sent the manuscript of the scripture extracts and catechism in Tahitian for printing in 1813. The simple fact that Sydney was closer to Tahiti than was London meant that publication in the colony would reduce the time between preparation of the translation and printing of the final corrected work, even if the quality of the printing was not as good.

Sydney was similarly the obvious place for printing in Māori for the early missionary efforts in New Zealand by virtue of both proximity and the active pioneering work done among the Māori by Marsden and his subsequent close association with the first New Zealand-resident missionaries. Thus it was to Marsden that Thomas Kendall sent the primer *A Korao* that he prepared during his first year in the country, which was produced in Sydney by Howe in 1815 — the second of the Pacific languages to be printed in Australia. Further printings in Māori appeared in 1827 when the Rev. Richard Davis of the Church Missionary Society in New Zealand made a visit to Sydney with scripture translations, and in 1829, 1830 and 1833, when the liturgy and services, hymns and catechism were seen through the press by the missionary Rev. William Yate of the Church Missionary Society, sent to Sydney 'for that purpose'. Nathaniel Turner's Tongan *First lessons* and a second issue with the addition of a catechism, prayers and hymns were printed in 1828 by the *Gazette* Office on behalf of the Wesleyan Tongan Mission, which used the opportunity of a passing vessel to send the manuscript to Sydney.

The hiatus of more than twenty years that then occurred in Australian printings for the Pacific missions was the result of two developments: the progressive introduction of printing into the Pacific Islands themselves (commencing with Tahiti in 1817), and the establishment of facilities in New Zealand from 1835 for printing in Māori and, subsequently, in the languages of the Melanesian Mission field.

These ventures into printing and publishing were part of a conscious policy common to the principal Protestant missions, whose strategy was to send their missionaries into the islands to learn the language and use this knowledge to spread the 'Word of God' by preaching and by translating scripture, hymns and other devotional works into the local vernacular. After the first (often long-awaited) breakthrough, such as attendance at services, acceptance of new ways of behaving, or actual conversion or baptism, subsequent missionaries commonly took a press into the field or wrote to their parent organisation asking for one. A number of missionaries actively sought training in printing before they left their homeland or were already printers specifically recruited for the work. These presses and printers undertook the production in the field of simple vernacular teaching materials and translations of scripture, hymn, prayer and service books, the location of publishing operations moving with shifts in the power base of the local society. Together with the commercial presses that also began to operate in Polynesia and New Zealand the mission presses took over the majority of the printing that had previously been done in Australia, London and America, except for large editions of the complete New Testament and Bible.

When printing in Pacific Islands languages returned to Australia in any significant amount it was primarily in the languages of Melanesia, much of it on remote Norfolk Island — a reflection of the missionary activity of the New Zealand-based Melanesian Mission. Its strategy differed from the other mission bodies in that, rather than sending out its own missionaries, it sought to recruit and educate, in centralised training colleges, islanders who could then be returned to become preachers and teachers in their own or other islands. While it did ultimately set up European-staffed stations in the islands, the bulk of the Melanesian Mission-related printing, like the training, took place at College headquarters, first in New Zealand and then on Norfolk Island (St Barnabas) where the Mission removed in 1866–67 and remained until transferring to the Solomon Islands in 1920. Over some fifty years the Norfolk Island press of the Mission under Archdeacon John Palmer, Rev. Dr Robert Henry Codrington and, from 1880 to 1920, Henry Menges, a trained printer, turned out more than one hundred gospel and other scripture translations, hymn, prayer and service books, lesson and reading sheets, annual almanacs and a twice-yearly newspaper prepared by Codrington and other members of the Mission. Many publications were in the Banks Island language, Mota, which as a practical measure was adopted effectively as the *lingua franca* of the Mission for services and teaching on Norfolk Island. Overall, works in more than a score of different languages and dialects were produced.

Printing in Indigenous Australian languages

By contrast with the investment in mission printing for the Pacific Islands and the extensive Māori language publishing undertaken in New Zealand, the legacy of publications in Aboriginal Australian languages in the nineteenth century was limited, a reflection of the failure of early missionary endeavours and of the limited responsiveness of the Indigenous population to the printed materials offered.

Samuel Marsden in association with the Society for the Propagation of the Gospel had attempted to evangelise among Aboriginal Australians around Parramatta from 1795, but this and subsequent early Wesleyan, Presbyterian and Church of England Missionary Society undertakings in New South Wales and Moreton Bay (in present-day Queensland) had little impact. Lancelot Threlkeld, who had been one of the early missionaries to Tahiti with the London Missionary Society, commenced work with the Aboriginal peoples of the Lake Macquarie district on behalf of the Society and the colonial government in 1825. Just two years later, after collaborating with local Indigenous man, Biraban, he produced *Specimens of a dialect of the Aborigines of New South Wales* (Awabakal language) — the first publication of any of the Indigenous Australian languages (see illustration in Chapter 7) — followed by a small spelling book in the same language, published in Sydney in 1836. One of his stated objects was 'to pave the way for the rendering into this tongue the sacred Scriptures' and he began on a translation of St Luke's gospel. But Threlkeld's evangelical mission was less successful than his language work and with no converts after 17 years his mission too was abandoned. His gospel translation was not published until nearly 50 years later, long after his death. Another mission, to Wellington Vale in New South Wales, begun in 1832 by William Watson and John Handt under the auspices of the Church Missionary Society, reported undertaking translations in the language(s) of the local Wiradjuri people in 1836, but these were not published and the mission was relinquished in 1843. This pattern was repeated in other colonies. In Western Australia, George King at the Swan River Mission found it 'vain to attempt to convey to the mind of a native any idea of spiritual existence' and gave up his mission there after five years. In South Australia the German Lutheran missionaries H. A. E. Meyer, C. W. Schürmann and C. G. Teichelmann each prepared and had published vocabularies and grammars of the areas where they established their missions, but all of their stations closed within a few years in the face of 'insurmountable difficulties'.

A few later missionaries had more tangible success in the work of teaching 'The Word' in the vernacular. The Rev. George Taplin at the (Methodist) Point Macleay Mission in South Australia prepared some lessons, prayers and hymns and extracts from the scriptures in Narrinyeri for the mission school and had them printed in Adelaide in 1864 — the first scripture translations in any Aboriginal Australian language — and ten years later published the 12-page *Native Book of Worship*. Hermann Kempe at Hermannsburg produced and had published in 1879–80 a primer in Aranda and a reading book in the Finke River dialect, and Johannes Flierl at the Killalpaninna mission prepared some scripture portions and a reading book in the Dieri language/Aranda (published in 1880 and 1883) and with Meyer began in 1879 a translation of the New Testament in Dieri. A number of manuscripts like Threlkeld's translation of St Luke's gospel into Awabakal, William Watson's Wiradjuri translations and vocabulary and Carl Schoknecht's Dieri dictionary were never printed, and the first complete New Testament in an Aboriginal Australian language, the Dieri *Testamenta Marra*, was not published until 1897.

This comparative paucity of nineteenth-century Aboriginal Australian language publications was partly due to the number and complexity of the languages themselves and that (in spite of sanguine expectations to the contrary) they were unlike any others so far encountered in the mission field. In addition, there was the problem of regular contact with a traditionally nomadic population. Early missions were disheartened by what they saw as the scattered nature and (in their view) 'vagrant' or 'erratic habits' of people 'perpetually itinerating from place to place', and the consequent difficulty of 'instructing them'. Moreover, there were widespread assumptions by missionaries and others of the inherent inferiority ('degradation') of the Aboriginal Australian population, especially by comparison with the New Zealanders and other Polynesians with their recognisable chiefs, villages and cultivation. As in much of Melanesia, these perceptions often extended to despair of understanding, of 'arresting and engaging the continued attention of individuals of the tribes in an investigation imperfectly understood by them' (as reported by Redmond Barry in his preface to the *Vocabulary of Dialects Spoken by Aboriginal Natives of Australia* compiled for the Intercolonial Exhibition of 1866) or even a contempt for languages that to the newcomers appeared to lack words for the concepts of God, salvation and a future state. English was thus preferred by many missionaries for its ability to convey the message of Christianity. This was reinforced by the explicit belief of missions and colonial administrators in the role of the English language in their 'civilising' mission and the implicit assumption that English was most appropriate because they assumed Indigenous Australians would ultimately live as a minority in a largely English-speaking population.

The publishing ventures

With the Melanesian Mission largely looking after its own printing needs on Norfolk Island, language publishing on the Australian mainland in the latter half of the century essentially took up what the other missions could not have supplied locally. Even where there were dedicated mission presses in the field, the frequent shortages of paper and type, the poor quality of their equipment and the intensive labour involved in larger undertakings prompted missionaries to send work for publication overseas or to take the opportunity to have items published when returning home or on leave. Nonetheless the total of Australian commercial printings in Indigenous Pacific Island languages, while hard to measure exactly, was not large: some 100 titles over the period from 1814 to 1900 can be identified from contemporary sources and later bibliographies and catalogues (in particular D. G. Dance's 1963 compilation *Oceanic Scriptures* from the British and Foreign Bible Society Library). This total output was roughly equivalent to the number of publications of the Norfolk Island Melanesian Mission press. On the whole the mainland imprints were bulkier than the island publications and the languages more diverse, with printings in Fijian, Samoan, Gilbertese, Tongan, Rotuman and Niué(an) as well as in many of the languages of New Caledonia, the New Hebrides, Papua, New Guinea, New Britain and the Solomon Islands.

Some of the early ventures into publishing were documented by the individuals involved, and from their letters and diaries and the standard bibliographies and surveys into which much of this information has been collected we can get some idea of edition sizes, costs and problems. Compared with the 5000, 10 000 and even 20 000 copies known for the Island and New Zealand publications, the Australian printings were relatively modest: the Melanesian Mission Press issued editions up to 4000 for its Mota hymnbooks and primers, and a few Sydney publications were in editions of 3000 to 3500, but most editions were between 300 and 1000 copies. Most were plain and unpretentious in appearance, often in a two-column format typical of cheap colonial printing, with very little use of diacritics or phonetic symbols. Illustration was extremely rare in spite of recognition by many missionaries that visual representation of the Bible stories would greatly aid understanding: one exception was the 1864 prayer book published for the Fijian Catholic Mission by John Degotardi, illustrated with standard French Catholic religious publication woodcuts unmodified for the Pacific — but Degotardi, who engraved the frontispiece, was himself unique among contemporary Australian printers in being also a photographer and an early experimenter with photolithography, as discussed by Thomas A. Darragh in Chapter 4.

MARKUS.

———♦———

TA FASAO EREFIA O IESU KRISTO,

TA NONTARIKI O ATUA.

TERIKI SORE TSHOTE

MA

TATANE KAPARE ACITIA.

Rev J. G. Paton

Kofakairo Acitia Tafasao o Fanua Crisi i Tafasao Aniwa,
NIU HEBERITIS.

FAKOWA I MELBURNI VEKTOREA.
1877.

Title-page of *Markus. Ta Fasao Erefia O Iesu Kristo* [The Gospel of Mark in Aniwa language], J. G. Paton, transl., Melbourne, British Foreign and Bible Society (Melbourne Auxiliary), 1877. Printed by Fergusson & Moore, 72 pp., 18 cm. John G. Paton (1824–1907) — and, later, his son Frank (1870–1938) — were Presbyterian missionaries and translators in the New Hebrides, the colonial name for Vanuatu. Frank was born there, on Aniwa Island. (Mitchell Library, State Library of NSW)

Printing costs incurred by the various missions are difficult to assess. We know the details of some early undertakings: 400 copies of the first Māori language translation of 1827, a 32-page octavo, were printed at a cost of £41, and Threlkeld's 28-page quarto, *Specimens of a dialect of the Aborigines of New South Wales* (1827) was printed in a small edition of 273 copies at a cost of £31/1/- and sold at three shillings each or seven for £1. From the scattered evidence in both Australia and England the unit printing cost of an individual work seems on average to have been between 2/- and 3/-, becoming cheaper towards the end of the century with improved equipment and the use of stereotypes. Still, this could represent a significant sum, as only minimal returns were expected from the sale of publications, most of which were distributed below cost, free, or for payment in kind (a copy of St Luke's gospel in Tahitian traded for three gallons of coconut oil). In the 1890s, the peak activity period of the nineteenth century, the annual reports of the Melanesian Mission show printing expenditure ranging from £79 to almost £400, exclusive of salaries, but the Island presses, with low or no labour costs, could obviously print much more cheaply than commercial printers in Australia, England or elsewhere.

A major contributor to the funding of publications was the British and Foreign Bible Society, established in 1804 with the exclusive object:

> to diffuse the knowledge of the Holy Scriptures, by circulating them in the different languages spoken throughout Great Britain and Ireland; and also, according to the extent of its funds, by promoting the printing of them in foreign languages, and the distribution of them in foreign countries.

Throughout the nineteenth century the Society subsidised the costs of printing, supplied paper to many mission printeries, and occasionally supported the expenses of the translators in overseeing a work through publication. The Society paid for the whole of the 1897 *Testamenta Marra* (the New Testament in Dieri), and many Australian publications in the languages of the Pacific mission fields were assisted by support from the Society and its Australian auxiliaries, the Bible societies of the parent countries of individual missions, or the Society for Promoting Christian Knowledge (SPCK), usually on the basis of individual application by the translator. Occasionally, missionary translators themselves contributed directly to printing costs; for example, Frank Paton paid for his St Matthew in the Lenakel language printed in Melbourne in 1900. In an equally significant way, some Islanders, notably in the Cook Islands and New Hebrides, provided local marketable produce like coconut oil, pigs, cotton and in particular arrowroot, in exchange for the publications.

In the absence of contemporary company records, the monetary value of this publishing to the overall income of colonial printers is equally difficult to estimate. While it might have usefully supplemented a printer's income in the early decades, the mainstays of the commercial printing industry of the 1870s–1890s were newspaper and stationery and label printing. In this later period the direct income from the vernacular works was probably much less significant to the printers than the expenditure was to the mission, although the advantage to printers may have been the contacts for more regular printing orders from the parent organisation. We know very little also about the processes by which these vernacular manuscripts were published by Australian printers. Certainly the texts were demanding: in South Australia the printing of the *Testamenta Marra* took two years, every proof sheet having to be forwarded from the printer in Tanunda to Kopperamanna Mission — a distance of over 700 km of rough terrain — for correction and revision. Many authors and translators noted the problem of mistakes when there was no-one in the place of printing with a knowledge of the language to supervise a work through the press, but unlike the Island printers, commercial printers left no record of the difficulties they faced in composition and proofing in these unfamiliar languages.

Accounts by the first and subsequent printers to the Melanesian Mission Press, Henry Menges and F. R. Isom, reveal details about the Mission's first plant set up in New Zealand. This plant, consisting of a Columbian press with fonts of small pica roman and great primer, was enlarged in 1885 with a demy Albion press and good fonts of pica, long primer, brevier and nonpareil to supplement the original plant. In 1896 a Crown Wharfdale cylinder machine with a further collection of type was received as 'the gift of two or three friends in England, aided by a grant of £30 from the SPCK'. As in the case of the other Island printeries many problems were initially experienced because of insufficient type to set up more than a few pages at a time and from the lack of an adequate supply of letters like *a* — more frequent in some languages and dialects than in English — or italic *g* used to represent the common *ng* sound.

In mainland Australia no presses were established specifically to undertake the printing of or for a particular mission until the Seventh Day Adventists set up their first press in Melbourne in 1885. Nonetheless, particular printers did undertake work for specific missions. Joseph Cook, who would later print the Church of England *Chronicle* and *Australian Churchman*, also printed many books published for the Methodist Mission between 1868 and 1886 and then for the British and Foreign Bible Society (acting as publisher for the Australasian Wesleyan Methodist Missionary Society). Lee & Ross (later Edward Lee) printed for the London Missionary Society throughout the 1880s, Samuel E. Lees for the Australasian Wesleyan Methodist Missionary Society from 1888 to 1912, F. Cunninghame for the Presbyterian missions in the New Hebrides from 1877, and William Brooks and Co. for the London Missionary Society and the British and Foreign Bible Society from 1892 to 1911. All of these printers were based in Sydney. It is probable that religious affiliation played a part in the choice of printer. Samuel Lees was a prominent Wesleyan Methodist layman and honorary treasurer of the Wesleyan Methodist Missionary Society. At Tanunda, J. C. Auricht, a Lutheran pastor and father-in-law to the Killalpaninna missionary Johann Flierl, undertook with his son the printing of most of the translations into Indigenous Australian languages by Lutheran missions to Central Australia. Mainly, however, affiliations were not exclusive, and apart from the Melanesian Mission and later the Epworth Printing and Publishing House, the Australian printers did not take on the role of publisher or distributor/bookseller, returning the editions direct to the mission or individual author/translator for distribution.

Aims and reception

Belief in Christ's injunction to 'go ye therefore and teach all nations' (Matthew 28:19) was at the root of all missionary publishing, whether scripture translations, catechisms or simple readers. Learning the local language was a prerequisite both for effective teaching and for enabling the preparation of translations, while 'The Word' itself was seen as a potent influence on 'civilising' the people to whom it was brought. More prosaically, scripture translation was also a gauge of the success of the evangelising effort, expected from missionaries as concrete evidence of their progress in the field and looked for by their supporting Church or Society. Publication output was similarly seen as a measure of energy and enthusiasm, used competitively between the various Protestant bodies and by all of them as a weapon in combating Catholicism, prompting even reluctant Catholic missions into setting up their own presses and printing programs.

The often very large print runs produced in this battle for converts were readily distributed, even when charges in kind or cash were imposed, and the missionaries perceived this 'insatiable lust for books' as clear evidence of the desire for enlightenment. It should be kept in mind, however, that representations of the impact of books and writing are almost exclusively those of the missionaries, in reports written (or sometimes revised upon receipt) with the specific purpose of securing continued financial support of their endeavours — an incentive to interpret positively and a temptation to exaggerate. There are in fact indications of early confusion among Aboriginal peoples about this mystery of communicating by marks on paper, what books were, and their role in the purpose of the missions, and of a much more diverse, conscious and discriminating participation by the Islanders and Indigenous Australians in what was being offered. School and church often shared the same building and for many First Nations Australians the attraction was the teaching of letters rather than the formal Sabbath services: indeed, in many instances it was the demand for reading sheets and alphabets in local schools rather than for devotional material *per se* that prompted the establishment of local mission presses. Similarly, the major effort that went into the printing of hymn and prayer books was a tacit concession to local demand for words that could be sung and chanted as a group activity and to attract people to church services, although missionaries widely recognised that genuine understanding of doctrine was rarely advanced by this means and the British and Foreign Bible Society frowned on the diversion of resources.

Later observers, especially linguists and anthropologists, have viewed the cultural impact of the missionary efforts and their related translation and publishing ventures critically, citing in particular the corruption of languages and loss of language diversity in addition to more general cultural changes that resulted from the introduction of radically different material and spiritual value systems. The books generated by the missions, as a particular cultural manifestation and a means of persuasion and influence, also feature in discussions of shifting power and authority in developing societies. Certainly there were errors in the recording and interpretation of languages due to the complexities of the languages themselves, the use of translators who were untrained or, conversely, trained to look for structures based on known English and European or classical models, the publication of work before a language was mastered by the missionaries, and the imposition of an inadequate orthography for the convenience of missionaries and printers. There was also neglect of many languages as a result of assumptions of the similarity of the languages of a region or the inherent opposition of the mission purpose to what was seen as 'the curse of Babel', which, as previously noted, prompted economic and strategic decisions to use one particular language as the *lingua franca* of a mission or to adopt English or a pidgin. However, like the mission reports of the reception of their books, post-colonial criticism tends to ignore the very significant role of the people themselves in the acculturation process —as interpreters, translators, teachers, evangelists, printers and migrant labourers — even though they did not control what was taught, written and printed, or contribute to a vernacular literature beyond occasional hymns.

It is undoubted that, in the Pacific Islands at least, the missions largely achieved their evangelical purpose. Most Polynesians and many Melanesians ultimately professed Christianity and the vernacular Bible has a special place in this Christianity, while the mission teachings and the Bible itself influenced local language and culture. It may be, as Crowl argues, that 'book publishing introduced by the missionaries is the basis of political order in the Pacific Islands today'. In the very different situation of Australia, where most publications were vocabularies and grammars *about* the language, published with the aim of facilitating general communication with the local population by officials or missions and/or a scholarly interest in manners, customs and origins, rather than texts *in* the language for the people themselves, it would be difficult to make a similar claim for the role of missionary publishing, indeed of book publishing in general. When interest in Indigenous languages revived in the twentieth century, among linguists and anthropologists (increasingly with the aim of supporting literacy in those languages and the maintenance of cultural practices and social structures) as well as those intent on promulgating the 'Word of God' (including the American-based Christian evangelical Summer Institute of Linguistics), there would be a resurgence in publishing — largely in dedicated academic journals. Revival language programs concerned with cultural maintenance and identity, with the involvement of Indigenous linguists, have primarily focused on oral transmission through classes and using video and digital media rather than print publication. Just as the initial success or otherwise of both European and native evangelists in spreading 'The Word' throughout the Pacific Islands was at least as much dependent upon personality, language facility and oratory as upon the books they wielded, both evangelisation by Indigenous pastors and recent language restoration projects within Australia acknowledge that the voice is more effective than reading words off the printed page. Nonetheless, the mere dozen or so vocabularies, grammars and studies of Indigenous languages published in the nineteenth century by commercial printers under the auspices of a mission or other such supporting bodies (as the Aborigines Friends Association or colonial Bible auxiliaries), by government printers or in the proceedings of learned societies have provided vital documentation in later revival projects of a number of languages no longer spoken that would contribute to a new sense of community and identity.

NOTE ON SOURCES

Manuscript sources of particular interest for this period include R. H. Codrington's *Journals and Letters 1867–1882*, Canberra, Australian Joint Copying Project, microform; and the letters of Agnes and William Watt 1869–80 to the Glasgow Foundry Boys' Religious Society (NLA MS 8093).

The basic bibliographic sources in addition to Ferguson's *Bibliography of Australia* are D. G. Dance, *Oceanic Scriptures*, London, BFBS [British and Foreign Bible Society], 1963; T. H. Darlow and H. F. Moule, comps, *Historical catalogue of the printed editions of Holy Scripture in the library of the British and Foreign Bible Society*, London, The Bible House, 1903-1911; specific island and mission press bibliographies including: John A. Ferguson, *A bibliography of the New Hebrides and a history of the Mission Press*, Sydney, [the author], 1917-1943; Patrick O'Reilly, *Imprints of the Fiji Catholic Mission, including the Loreto Press, 1864-1954*, London, F. Edwards, 1958; George L. Harding and Bjarne Kroepelien, *The Tahitian imprints of the London Missionary Society, 1810-1834*, Oslo, La Coquille qui chante, 1950; T. M. Hocken, *A bibliography of the literature relating to New Zealand*, Wellington, N.Z., Government Printer, 1909; Herbert W. Williams, *A bibliography of printed Maori to 1900*, Wellington, N.Z., Dominion Museum, 1924; N. L. H. Krauss, *Bibliography of Niue, South Pacific*, Honolulu, [the author], 1970; Sally Edridge, comp. *Solomon Islands bibliography to 1980*, Suva, Fiji, Institute of Pacific Studies, University of the South Pacific, & Wellington, N.Z., The Alexander Turnbull Library, & Honiara, The Solomon Islands National Library, 1985; and the unpublished Check list of books printed 1855-1975 by the Anglican Church in Melanesia on the Mission Press, compiled by W. J. Pinson in 1976. Richard Lingenfelter *Presses of the Pacific Islands 1817-1867*, Plantin Press, Los Angeles, 1967; A. W. Murray, *The Bible in the Pacific*, London, James Nisbet & Co., 1888; Robert Kilgour, 'The Bible throughout the Pacific Islands', in his *The Bible throughout the world: a survey of scripture translations*, London, World Dominion Press, 1939; and J. W. Burton, *Missionary survey of the Pacific islands*, London, World Dominion Press, 1930, provide valuable surveys. Much additional information on translations, printing and publishing, and on the work, attitudes and motivations of the missions is contained in their annual reports and journal publications; the contemporary Mission Society histories of Joseph King, *Ten decades: the Australian centenary of the London Missionary Society*, London, London Missionary Society, 1895; Richard Lovett, *The history of the London Missionary Society 1795-1895*, London, Henry Frowde, 1899; E. S. Armstrong, *The history of the Melanesian Mission*, London, Isbister and Co., 1900, and Frances Awdry, *In the isles of the sea: the story of fifty years in Melanesia*, London, Bemrose and Sons, 1902. Other accounts are Niel Gunson, *Messengers of grace: evangelical missionaries in the South Seas 1797-1860*, Melbourne, OUP, 1978; David Hilliard, *God's gentlemen: a history of the Melanesian*

Mission 1849-1942, UQP, 1978; Hugh Laracy, *Marists and Melanesians: a history of Catholic missions in the Solomon Islands*, Canberra, ANU Press, 1975; Christine Stevens, *White man's dreaming: Killalpaninna Mission 1866-1915*, Melbourne, OUP, 1994. Other important sources are the journals and accounts of individual missionaries, notably William Ellis, *Polynesian researches, during a residence of nearly six years in the South Sea Islands*, London, Dawsons of Pall Mall, 1967 [first published 1829]; Aaron Buzacott, *Mission life in the islands of the Pacific : being a narrative of the life and labours of the Rev. A. Buzacott*, London, John Snow,1866; James Calvert, 'Mission History', in Thomas Williams, *Fiji and the Fijians*, London, Alexander Heylin, 1858; Walter Lawry, *Friendly and Feejee Islands: a missionary visit*, London, 1850, and his *A second missionary visit to the Friendly and Feejee Islands*, London, 1851; William Wyatt Gill, *From darkness to light in Polynesia*, London, 1894; Sarah S. Farmer, *Tonga and the Friendly Islands: with a sketch of their Mission history*, London, Hamilton, Adams & Co., 1855; Agnes Watt, *Agnes C. P. Watt: twenty-five years' mission life on Tanna, New Hebrides*, J. Paisley and R. Parlane,1896; W. G. Ivens, 'The printed word in the languages of Melanesia' in *The Church in Melanesia*, Stuart W. Artless, ed., London, Melanesian Mission,1936; J. N. Hey, *A brief history of the Presbyterian Mission enterprise among the Australian Aborigines*, Sydney, New Press, 1931; and E. R. Gribble, *Forty years with the Aborigines*, Sydney, Angus and Robertson, 1930. Two papers on Pacific printings by Susan Woodburn — 'Three Pacific mission presses' in *Expanding horizons: print cultures across the South Pacific*, BSANZ Bulletin 27, nos 3 and 4, 2003, and 'Making books for God: mission printing in the Pacific Islands and Australia' in *The making and keeping of books*, BSANZ Bulletin 27, nos 1 and 2, 2003, — were published subsequent to the original version of this chapter, as was Linda S. Crowl, *Politics and book publishing in the Pacific Islands*, PhD thesis, School of History and Politics, University of Wollongong, 2008, which provides an extensive survey of missionary publishing and its impacts and discusses theories of 'the ideological nature of power' in relation to book publishing. Also of note are H. M. Carey, 'Lancelot Threlkeld, Biraban, and the Colonial Bible in Australia', *Comparative Studies in Society and History*, vol.52, no.2, 2010, pp. 447-78; and Phil Parkinson & Penny Griffith's *Books in Māori 1815–1900 Ngā tānga reo Māori*, Auckland, Reed Books, 2004; and the recently completed thesis by Mathilde Dutertre: Le Développement de l'imprimerie en Océanie au XIXe siècle à travers l'exemple de la London Missionary Society, Mémoire de Master 2, École normale supérieure, École nationale des Chartes, PSL

Research University, October 2022; the Robert Howe imprints Dutertre cites are her no.32 (1821), no.42 (1822) and no.46 (1822).

The burgeoning study of the Indigenous languages of the region in the second half of the twentieth century can be traced through issues of *Pacific Linguistics* from its foundation in 1963, and is also surveyed in Graham McKay's *The Land still speaks: Review of Aboriginal and Torres Strait Islander language maintenance and development needs and activities*, National Board of Employment, Education and Training, Commissioned Report no.44, Canberra, Australian Government Publishing Service, February 1996; and William B. McGregor, ed., *Encountering Aboriginal languages: studies in the history of Australian linguistics*, Pacific Linguistics 591, Canberra, 2008.

CHAPTER 23

Official Printing

Tony Cavanagh

Although we still do not have a comprehensive history of printing in Australia, research undertaken in the last three decades and reflected in the present volume helps complement the picture presented in the collection of essays edited by D. H. Borchardt and W. Kirsop in 1988. The involvement of the early printers of New South Wales and Van Diemen's Land in all facets of the industry, including publishing, newspaper production and bookselling, is treated in the relevant chapters above. Before the 1820s these tradespeople were perforce official employees working on machines provided by the government, but they were also quite quickly allowed to take on private work like the playbills issued by George Hughes in Sydney in the 1790s. A similar situation was to be found initially, but for a briefer period, in Western Australia and South Australia.

Until the appointment of government printers was formalised on Governor Gipps's initiative in the 1840s the *ad hoc* arrangements made by the early autocratic administrators of the colonies continued. Before 1820 especially, those doing government work — in addition to whatever they undertook privately — were expected to print almost anything required for the functioning of the settlements. Governor King sent to the Colonial Office round the turn of the nineteenth century lists of goods received at the Sydney Store and samples of promissory notes as well as of the general orders issued by the Government. Most of this material is not listed in Ferguson, yet, on the Canadian model established in recent decades, what is not merely stationery should be included in the national bibliography.

Lists of the people designated as government printers need to take account of these varying circumstances and of a chronology that is not always precise in spite of records in the relevant government gazettes. Schematically the succession of officials in charge of the various colonial printing establishments can be set out as follows:

New South Wales:

> George Hughes, 1795–1801; George Howe, 1801–1821; Robert Howe, 1821–1829; Ann Howe, 1833–1836; E. H. Statham, 1835–1841; W. J. Rowe, 1841–1844; W. W. Davies, 1845–1854; W. Hanson, 1854–1859; Thomas Richards, 1859–1886; C. Potter, 1886–1896.

The decade following the early death of Robert Howe was confused, with others than his widow playing a role, for example Stephens & Stokes, then Kemp and Fairfax of the *Herald* office printing the New South Wales *Government Gazette*. Things settled down in the 1840s, and with the coming of responsible government in the 1850s official printers saw a considerable increase in their responsibilities, not least to the local legislatures.

Tasmania:

> [At David Collins's temporary settlement at Sullivan Bay, Port Phillip from October 1803 to January 1804 his official printer was Matthew Power.]
> Matthew Power, Francis Barnes and George Clark, 1804–1810; George Clark, 1810–1815; Andrew Bent, 1815–1825; James Ross and George Terry Howe, 1825–1826; James Ross, 1826–1836; W. G. Elliston, 1837–1838; James Barnard, 1839–1880; William Thomas Strutt, 1881–1893.

Western Australia:

> Charles Macfaull, 1831–1846; Elizabeth Macfaull, 1847–1848; Arthur Shenton, 1848–1857; 'convict establishment' or 'government press', 1858–1869; Richard Pether, 1870–1901.

South Australia:

> Robert Thomas, 1836–1840; Archibald MacDougall, 1840–1844; Andrew Murray, 1844-1847; John Stephens, 1848–1849; W. C. Cox, 1849–1878; E. Spiller, 1878–1888; H. F. Leader, 1889–1890; C. E. Bristow, 1890–1909.

Victoria:
>Edward Khull, January–October 1851; John Ferres, 1851–1887; Robert S. Brain, 1887–1906.

Queensland:
>T. P. Pugh, 1859–1863 (unofficial and on contract); James C. Beal, 1866–1867 (acting), then 1867–1893.

It is notable that in all six colonies there were men — Richards, Barnard, Pether, Cox, Ferres and Beal — who had long years of service in the second half of the century. Three of them — Richards, Barnard and Ferres — had reputations and influence beyond their own sphere as innovators and successful managers. Yet the paradox is that official printing in Australia has often been overshadowed by the achievements of private industry, in particular of the great metropolitan newspapers. Much of the material produced by the government's paid servants required sophisticated printing skills, the use of modern machinery, keen adoption of new practices, and the employment of hundreds of skilled staff. In open world competition at European exhibitions, they won gold, silver and bronze awards for printing, bookbinding and photography. It is rarely acknowledged that government printing offices published outstanding books and numerous other non-government items because they had the highly competent staff and equipment to produce these works at that time.

The diversity of the work of Government Printers

One of the best documented government printing operations was that of the Victorian office under John Ferres (1851–87). Largely through his two reports to Parliament in 1862–63 and 1874 and the three reports of a board of enquiry into the operation of the office we have a fairly complete picture of the workings of a large colonial printery in the latter half of the nineteenth century. Recent substantial documentary publications by Peter Marsh have made the mass of archival material much more easily accessible.

Although printing parliamentary and electoral material is usually thought of as the major work of the government printer, the offices in fact produced most if not all of the publications of government departments, various government and semi-government bodies and even organisations such as the National Gallery, the Museum, the Public Library and the University. The printing of government debentures was described in 1869 as 'tedious work . . . necessarily involving the greatest care and a large amount of responsibility'. Railway tickets were produced at the rate of 2000 per hour on an 'ingeniously contrived machine invented for the purpose', while the immense number of gold licences issued in the early 1850s prompted the purchase of printing machines, all work prior to this having been achieved on hand-presses.

In an era when quality type was scarce and was still cheaper to import from Great Britain than purchase locally, the large quantities of standing type required for reports of committees of enquiry, royal commissions and bills submitted to the legislature caused considerable hardship to the office. Ferres reported situations in which large documents of up to 100 pages were ordered to remain in type for as long as nine months awaiting the return of proofs. In 1869 he had 1683 pages of standing type, with another 120 pages of forms and also over 700 pages of bills standing to allow speedy amendments and alterations during their passage. The printing of electoral rolls became so critical in 1877 that Parliament authorised a special allowance for the purchase of more type.

The process of stereotyping was adopted in Victoria in December 1860, partly in answer to the problems referred to above; it proved to be especially time-saving in printing stock forms and forms where large quantities were needed. This was at a time when printing, responding to the steep growth in population, was expanding rapidly, a trend which continued into the 1870s (see Table 1).

Pricing was always set below the actual cost, with a uniform charge made for each page of printing in the various sizes of folio, quarto and octavo, whether the page was 'intricate tabular' work, straight text or merely a circular. As much as half of all government printing was of tabular forms, used for the census and statistical data for the colony, so the practice of setting a fixed, low price, irrespective of page content, meant that much of the work was heavily subsidised by government.

A special section was established by the Victorian office in 1854 for the binding of parliamentary votes and proceedings, government acts, government and police gazettes, mining by-laws and all books and pamphlets produced for all branches of the services. It also provided account books and books of ruled forms for all departments. The period of the 1850s to the 1870s was one of spectacular growth. Ferres in his reports emphasised the 'vastness of the operations continually going on in this department' and his figures for 1871–74 shown in Table 1 bear this out.

Table 1: Printing Quantities and Expenditure of the Victorian Government Printer 1871–74

Year	Copies Printed (Million)	Cost for Printing	Books Bound	Pamphlets	Ruled forms (Million)	Total Costs
1871–72	12.3	£ 27 881	29 756	65 985	1.60	£ 35 145
1872–73	13.6	£ 31 200	28 268	102 810	2.10	£ 38 517
1873–74	19.3	£ 33 548	32 017	201 200	2.68	£ 41 377

Innovations in official printing establishments

The New South Wales and Victorian Printing Offices were by far the largest and were fortunate in having as overseers far-sighted and skilled printers whose careers were remarkably similar in many ways. These were the afore-mentioned John Ferres in Victoria and Thomas Richards in New South Wales. Ferres had introduced steam printing to the southern office in 1855, stereotyping in 1860, and, in a world first, used steam power for the lithographic production of maps for the Geological Survey in 1862. Richards introduced photolithography in 1863 followed shortly after by stereotyping and electrotyping. In 1868, he applied a new fast process of photolithography developed by John Sharkey, whom Richards had assisted. At the 1870 Intercolonial Exhibition in Sydney, the Office was praised for the 'gems of photo-lithographic art' it displayed. Richards's other innovations included an ingenious system for numbering debentures during printing that was adopted by all other Australian colonies and the Bank of England, the introduction of heliotyping (a photomechanical process), and the invention of a new method of drying stamps using heat from gas. Both Ferres and Richards were 'active' printers, ambitious in producing many titles even if some had limited public interest. As early as 1854, Ferres had printed on hand-presses 5000 copies of the 278-page *Statistical Register of Victoria* by William Archer. His most outstanding work was probably R. Brough Smyth's *Gold Fields and Mineral Districts of Victoria*, published in 1869, which attracted international attention for the quality of its production. Richards compiled, edited and printed the highly-regarded *New South Wales in 1881* which was later translated into French, following it in 1883 with *An Epitome of the Official History of New South Wales*. It should also be noted that another New South Wales Government Printer, Charles Potter, proposed and printed the well-known *History of New South Wales from the Records* (1889).

As mentioned, the high quality of the printing, binding and lithographic work of both government offices was recognised in the international arena. Between 1862 and 1886 the New South Wales Office was regularly commended at exhibitions such as the 1883 Amsterdam Exhibition when it was awarded gold and silver medals. At the 1880 Melbourne International Exhibition, it received five high diplomas for printing, bookbinding and photography. Similarly, Ferres was honoured by the French Government through the University of Montpellier with a decoration for specimens of fine printing. Hence it is evident that the official printing offices had both the staff and equipment required to produce works of excellent quality.

Some publications of the Government Printers

Perusal of the entries under 'Government Printers' in Ian Morrison's *The Publishing Industry in Colonial Australia* (1996) reveals the incredible diversity of the work they undertook. Some examples of early and scientific works follow.

The first book published in Australia, *New South Wales General Standing Orders and General Orders*, was produced by George Howe in 1802. This was followed in 1806 by the *New South Wales Pocket Almanack*, which was to continue until 1835 under the Howes, except for 1807 when no almanac was published owing to scarcity of paper in the Colony. *Continuation of General Orders* also appeared in 1806. Howe was additionally responsible for the first textbook to be published in Australia — a spelling book in 1810 — followed by *Bowden's Tables* in 1812; copies of neither have survived.

The first natural history work, issued with hand-coloured illustrations, printed in Australia, John William Lewin's exceedingly rare *Birds of New South Wales with Their Natural History* of 1813 consisted of letterpress by Howe and plates produced by Lewin. Another primer for schools followed in 1814, along with three books in the Tahitian language, including a basic language text. These appear to be the earliest books printed in Australia in a language other than English and were followed by a Tahitian hymnal and a primer in the Māori language, its sub-title indicating that it was 'an attempt to compose some Lessons for the Instruction of the Natives'. Such texts were written by and intended for the use of church missionaries then attempting to Christianise the Pacific. As discussed in more detail by Susan Woodburn in the previous chapter, it was necessary to print these texts in the Colony of New South Wales rather than in England as those with a knowledge of the language were needed to revise and edit the works. Religious publications continued to be part of the output of government printers until late in the nineteenth century although it is not clear why. However, commercial topics were not forgotten and Howe produced in 1817 the *Rules and Regulations for the Conduct and Management of the Bank of New South Wales*, Australia's first bank. Literary and scientific publishing were also undertaken. Although 'Printed for Private Distribution', Barron Field's *First Fruits of Australian Poetry* (1819) was actually printed by George Howe. This was the first book of poems published in Australia; his son Robert was to produce in 1826 *Wild Notes from the Lyre of a Native Minstrel* by Charles Tompson, the first published book of poems by an Australian-born writer. The continent's first literary magazine, the *Australian Magazine*, also came off Robert Howe's press, in 1821.

Among early scientific publications, James Busby's pioneering works on viticulture are worthy of mention. Both *A Treatise on the Culture of the Vine* (1825) and *A Manual of Plain Directions for Planting and Cultivating Vineyards* (1830) were produced in government print shops. In Tasmania, Governor John Franklin allowed the Government Printer James Barnard to print the first volume of the *Tasmanian Journal of Natural Science* in 1842 'because there was not a private printing press with the necessary type' (Ferguson 3513). While many more examples could be given, it is clear that, in the early years at least, government printers published considerably more 'general' or non-government works than is generally perceived.

By the 1850s, the number of private printing establishments able to produce quality work had increased substantially. Government printers no longer had a monopoly and their output increasingly reflected their position as official departments focused on providing the government of the day with parliamentary and electoral material and the myriad of regulations, acts and forms needed for every-day administration. While official printers continued to produce other publications, these tended to be largely 'practical' in nature, mirroring the development and rapid expansion the country was undergoing, especially following the discovery of gold in 1851.

The driving force for many of these activities was the work of scientific societies such as the various colonial Linnean and Royal Societies. Much but by no means all of the scientific output of the period was channelled through government printers. In many cases, this was because the government employed professional scientists who then sought to have their work published. These scientists included the Victorian government botanist, Ferdinand von Mueller, the astronomer-scientists H. C. Russell in New South Wales, R. L. Ellery and George Neumayer in Victoria, and Charles Todd in South Australia, and the statisticians T. A. Coghlan in New South Wales, W. H. Archer in Victoria and R. M. Johnston in Tasmania, who sought to document quantitatively the economic progress of their colonies through regular survey publications. Several of these men were prolific writers and covered a range of subjects — Mueller's publications excluding letters probably exceed 1000, while Johnston and Russell each published over 100 papers. Other public servants whose work was produced through the government printers include officers who researched in areas outside their sphere of employment. Victorian Chief Mining Warden R. Brough Smyth, best known for his *The Gold Fields and Mineral Districts of Victoria* (1869), issued his ambitious two-volume compilation *The Aborigines of Victoria* in 1878, while the Chief Stock Inspector for Victoria, E. M. Curr, had his four-volume *The Australian Race: Its Origins, Languages, Customs, Place of Landing in Australia* published in 1886.

Between 1850 and 1900, the various government printers published nearly 1000 items of a scientific or technological nature. These ranged from pamphlets and reprints of scientific papers to substantial books. A breakdown by category is given in Table 2. The major position occupied by agriculture is probably not surprising as all states established departments of agriculture which adopted the philosophy of 'educating the farmer in the application of scientific principles' (Inkster and Todd). The scientists they employed undertook fundamental research, which resulted in such standard reference works as C. French's three-volume *A Handbook of the Destructive Insects of Victoria* (1891), as well as the investigation of basic problems affecting farmers. The information the scientists obtained was distributed to rural communities in the form of Department of Agriculture circulars. Reports were also issued on new and unusual crops such as beet sugar, olive growing and the cultivation of oysters, while in 1900 the Victorian office produced a 274-page translation of a French report on *Wine Making in Hot Climates*. Many government publications of this era were similar in their practical usefulness and were never intended as money-making ventures. Nevertheless their production was of high standard and they served the important role of providing access to new and important scientific and technological advances for the ordinary person and the intelligent layman.

Occasionally an official imprimatur was given to reports that fell outside what one would expect from a government. An egregious example is G. A. Tucker's *Lunacy in Many Lands* (Sydney, Charles Potter, Government Printer, 1887). In nearly 1600 pages of close print the author presented a comprehensive account of hospitals for the mentally ill across the world. The result is recognised by specialists as an almost unrivalled compilation of information on an international scale.

Table 2: Number of Items Published in Various Categories by Government Printers 1850–1900

Category	Number
Aboriginal Australians and Anthropology	50
Agriculture	112
Botany and Zoology	61
Communications and Transport	31
Education (especially Technical Education)	26
Exhibitions	127
Exploration and Travel	36
Medicine and Health	27
Military	51
Mining and Geology	75
Miscellaneous	111
Science — General (especially Astronomy, Weather)	63
Statistical Reports	58
Technology and General Engineering (water supply)	38

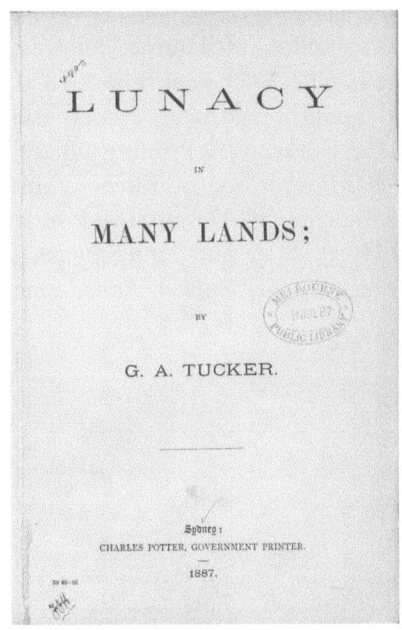

Title-page of George A. Tucker's *Lunacy in Many Lands*, Sydney, Charles Potter, Government Printer, 1887, xvi, 1564 pages, [17] leaves of plates: illustrations; 26 cm. (State Library Victoria)

NOTE ON SOURCES

Apart from general works by J. A. Ferguson, Ian Morrison and D. H. Borchardt & W. Kirsop, all listed elsewhere, the particular sources for this chapter are: Tony Cavanagh, 'The Victorian Government Printing Office; its Early History and its Publications', *ALJ*, vol.38, no.4, 1989, pp. 282-95; A. B. Davies, 'Notes on the Government Printing Office of Western Australia', *ALJ*, vol.18, no.7, (August, 1969), pp. 228-29; John Ferres, 'Report on the Government Printing Establishment for the years 1859, 1860 and 1861', *Victoria. Parliamentary Papers. Votes and Proceedings of the Legislative Assembly 1862–63*, no.27, Melbourne, Government Printer, 1862; and his 'Report on the Government Printing Establishment from January 1, 1871, to June 30, 1874', *Victoria. Parliamentary Papers. Notes and Proceedings of the Legislative Assembly*, V1874, no.73, Melbourne, Government Printer, 1874; Ian Inkster and Jan Todd, 'Support for the Scientific Enterprise, 1850–1900' in R. W. Home, ed., *Australian Science in the Making*, Sydney, CUP in Association with Australian Academy of Science, 1990, pp.102-32; A. B. James, 'Notes on the Government Printing Office of South Australia,' *ALJ*, vol.18, no.7, (August 1969), p. 230; and the *Victorian Government inquiry: Board Appointed to Enquire into and Report upon the Management of the Government Printing Office*, Government Printing Office, Melbourne, John Ferres, Government Printer, Reports nos 1 and 2, 1869; Report no.3, 1870.

Special attention should be paid to the recent substantial documentary works on the Victorian Government Printing Office by Peter Marsh: *The Government Printing Office*, Melbourne, Kitchen Table Press, 2013–2014, 6 vols; *Bookbinding Tools from the Government Printing Office of Victoria*, Melbourne, [the author], 2016; and *Establishment of the Government Printing Office Melbourne: The Golden Fifties*, Emerald Hill, Kitchen Table Press, 2018.

CHAPTER 24

After the 'toil of a long day': Reading in Colonial Australia

†Elizabeth Webby

'The British nation is characteristically designated "*a reading People*"; and wherever they spread themselves — however distant from their native land circumstances may carry them — their native attribute remains rather increased than diminished.' So wrote Hobart's Robert Lathrop Murray in the first number of his *Austral-Asiatic Review* in February 1828. This is just one of the hopeful paeans to an assumed British love of reading to be found in the introductions or prefaces of the many short-lived magazines attempted in Australia before 1850. Others, however, asserted that in a pioneering life there was no time for anything but money-making. Settlers were only concerned with material things and their sons were more interested in horse-riding than in reading.

If there was considerable disagreement about whether or not those who now lived in the Australian colonies had maintained their British heritage as a 'reading People', there is also no clear evidence as to how easy it was to obtain books in Australia at this time. Some writers claimed that hardly anyone could afford books, others that they were widely available. In May 1826, spending a few days in Hobart on his way to take up an appointment as a Presbyterian missionary in New South Wales, the Rev. John McGarvie noted in his diary that 'Books hardly pay, however cheap they may be. A copy of the British Poets 100 vols. has been offered for 7 Pounds — being bound and found no purchasers'. But only eight years later the *Tasmanian* newspaper for 26 September 1834 was proclaiming that 'it is to the credit of the country that you can go into no house, be it ever so small, but there are to be found books, in many instances where it would be least expected, in no inconsiderable amount'.

There was, however, general agreement that reading was a good thing, though, of course, some types of books were to be preferred to others. At a time of growing literacy, reading by members of the lower classes was no longer seen as a possible threat to society, in encouraging radical tendencies, but as a means of self-improvement and much preferable to other leisure activities such as drinking and gambling. While some saw any type of reading as worthwhile, others became increasingly concerned about the growing demand for fiction in preference to anything else. It was generally believed that women, in particular, were insatiable readers of novels, often to the detriment of their household duties. This debate became especially heated when it came to choosing books for the growing numbers of libraries established in Australia during the nineteenth century.

Without readers, books are of course nothing more than ink marks on paper. It is therefore impossible to trace the history of books in Australia without at the same time tracing the history of reading. But to do this, as has already been implied, is less easy than it may seem. While there is plenty of evidence relating to the presence of books in Australia from the time of initial European settlement in 1788, we usually need to infer that books owned meant books read. It is necessary to search much harder for representations of people reading or specific comments on what was read. And there is much conflicting evidence on who was reading, how much they were reading, and what they were reading.

It is possible, however, to make some generalisations. Most of the books read in Australia before 1890 would have originated in Great Britain. By the 1840s they were readily obtainable in the main cities but continued to remain in short supply in outlying areas until well into the twentieth century. By the end of the nineteenth century, however, a substantial majority of non-Indigenous Australians could read. The most read book was probably the Bible, though by 1890 fiction had long outstripped history, biography and travel as the favourite form of recreational reading. To read Australian authors was mainly to read newspapers and magazines rather than books. This chapter will take a broadly chronological approach in fleshing out these generalisations about Australian readers and reading in Australia from 1788 to 1890.

Reading before 1830

How many of those who arrived in New South Wales on the First Fleet were able to read and write? Clearly the 'gentlemen' — the ships' officers, the doctors and clergymen — could, as could some of the more educated convicts. What about the ordinary soldiers and sailors? Evidence of literacy rates in Britain at the time would suggest that at least half of them could read to some degree. In 1792, Major Grose, commander of the New South Wales Army Corps, instructed one of the men under his command to open a school; it appears that his fellow soldiers as well as their children would have been among the pupils. The first generation of colonists to be born and educated in Australia achieved a higher rate of literacy than those born elsewhere, perhaps because the ready availability of convict labour allowed children to stay longer at school. A survey of marriage registers kept in and around Sydney between 1804 and 1814 shows that 55 per cent of men and 24 per cent of women born outside the colony could sign their name as against 63 per cent of men and 44 per cent of women born in the colony. By 1821–24 the number of persons signing the register had, for those born in the colony, risen to 86 per cent for men and 75 per cent for women. Since it was the practice at the time to teach reading before writing, it is generally assumed that a number of those who did not sign the registers would still have been able to read.

The reading done by those who were able to read can be broadly categorised into two types: utilitarian and recreational. Most of the books that the first settlers brought with them were of the utilitarian type, though the prospect of the long voyage and the vast distance between their new home and any bookshop also encouraged some to bring recreational reading matter as well. For many years, books remained in short supply in the colony. The educated convict John Grant, for example, wrote to his mother and sister from Parramatta in January 1805 that 'Books are very valuable here, and any friend who would scrape together a few in a Box for me, I would make a collection of Insects for him in return'.

The distinction between the two types of reading, plus the need to have books for recreation as well as business, can clearly be seen in a letter sent by the nineteen-year-old George Allen to his brother in England in 1820. Allen was training to be a solicitor, so asked his brother to send him some law books, 'as they will be very useful and indeed essential to me in my profession'. He went on, however, to ask for other books as well:

> If you are comfortably situated in life and can spare the money (not else) I should have no objection to you sending the Books a list of which I have enclosed and marked No. 2. If you can't spare the Money for all and can for some, do the best you can for me as this place is not like London for amusements, here we have neither society nor places of amusement, there is not [a] library here to spend a few hours in; my only employment after the business of the day is to retire to my own room (for I am the only one of the family now left in Sydney) and read my books of which I am sorry to say I have but a slender stock. I am particularly fond of reading, to me it is the greatest of amusements and therefore a good Library would be a treasure — and such a one as could not be purchased in this colony at any price.

Allen, who was to establish one of the most famous of Sydney's legal firms, clearly maintained his love of reading, becoming a foundation member of the Australian Subscription Library in 1826.

Unfortunately, the two lists of books Allen sent to his brother are no longer extant. We do, however, have some idea of the books owned, and presumably read, by educated men of his class from lists of the contents of private libraries, usually drawn up when they were being advertised for sale. According to a list made in 1800, for example, the library of the surgeon and explorer George Bass consisted of around 100 volumes. There were, as one would expect, works on medicine and science, as well as on law, history, travels and theology. At a time when the classical authors formed so significant a part of a gentleman's education there were also volumes of Horace, Virgil and Homer. In addition to magazines and dictionaries, there were many of the standard English authors found in nearly all gentlemen's libraries of this period, such as Bacon's *Essays*, Dryden's *Works* and

Gay's *Poems*. But the only works of fiction were translations of *Don Quixote* and *Gil Blas*.

A few decades later, another famous Australian explorer displayed a decidedly stronger taste for fiction, indicating something of the shift towards novel-reading which began in this period, though still looked down on by many. When John Oxley's library was sold by auction in Sydney in August 1828 about half of the 330 or so lots listed in the catalogue were works of fiction. They included such recent publications as Scott's *Tales of the Crusaders* (1825), Fenimore Cooper's *The Prairie* (1827), Anne Radcliffe's *Gaston de Blondeville* (1826) and Mary Shelley's *Last Man* (1826). Oxley clearly was a regular purchaser of the latest English books, a surviving statement of account with the Sydney merchants Berry and Wollstonecraft showing that he spent nearly £41 on books and periodicals in November 1821 and a further £7/13/- in November 1822.

Another indication of the growing taste for fiction comes from the advertisements in early Sydney and Hobart newspapers for missing books, which before 1820 were far more numerous than advertisements for books for sale, showing that books were indeed a scarce commodity in this period, as George Allen had claimed. On 17 July 1803 the wealthy emancipist Simeon Lord advertised in the *Sydney Gazette* for the return of his copy of Clara Reeve's Gothic novel *The Old English Baron* (1777). In the next issue of the *Gazette*, readers were advised that 'The Old English Baron, advertised in our last, returned to his quarters on Monday; and we understand his presence was admitted as an apology for his absconding without leave of absence'.

Later advertisers seem not to have been so lucky. Again, fictional works and other types of recreational reading were in the majority, with the surgeon John Harris, on 20 November 1803, asking for the return of his volumes of *The Bee*, claimed to be the only set in the colony, and the first volume of Pope's *Homer*. Some volumes of Pope's *Works* and Smollett's *Adventures on an Atom* were among books advertised for on 30 September and 7 October 1804, complete with this appeal to their borrowers' better nature: 'As it is obvious to every intelligent mind that Sets of these valuable works are rendered incomplete by the detention of any of the volumes, and the Cause of Literature essentially hindered thereby, it is hoped that after this Public Requisition they will be forthcoming.'

Andrew Thompson, a settler at the Hawkesbury River, made a similarly gentlemanly plea on 16 December 1804. He had many missing books, including two volumes of the *Spectator*, Milton's *Paradise Lost*, Sterne's *Works*, and three volumes of Burns as well as two volumes of the *Newgate Calendar*. The latter work was, understandably, very popular in early Australia. Another prominent emancipist, Isaac Nichols, had advertised on 31 July 1808 for the missing first volume of his set 'in good binding, gilt, and lettered; with a coat of arms on the inside of the cover, the motto, Domini dirige nos'. By 28 April 1810, however, no fewer than three volumes of Nichols's *Newgate Calendar* were missing and he was losing patience: 'If not restored the person in whose possession either may be hereafter found will be prosecuted.' Others resorted to offering rewards for the return of their books. On 13 October 1805 George Howe, editor of the *Sydney Gazette*, requesting the return of the first volume of his edition of Shakespeare, said he would 'pay any reasonable reward that may be required; as will also be the case to any person who will give information that may recover it, as this very valuable work is rendered incomplete'.

On 6 July 1816, as already noted in Chapter 13, Walter Colquhoun of Hobart also offered a reward, via the columns of the *Hobart Town Gazette*, for the return of a volume of *Harris's Minor Encyclopaedia*. While few advertisements for lost or borrowed books appeared in Sydney after 1814, they remained plentiful in Hobart, testimony to the continuing scarcity of books in that city. On 8 December 1821 the owner of a number of missing recent publications, including Scott's *Ivanhoe* (1820), Lady Morgan's *Florence Macarthy: An Irish Tale* (1819) and Felix McDonough's *The Hermit in London; or, Sketches of English Manners* (1821), also threatened 'Recourse to Legal Proceedings'. This very telling testimony to the popularity of Walter Scott's fiction appeared in the *Hobart Town Gazette* on 10 May 1823:

> Lost, a few days ago, the Novel of 'Ivanhoe', in 3 vols. boards; also, in January last, a pocket Bible in 1 vol. bound in blue Morocco. — A Reward of 3 Dollars is hereby offered for Ivanhoe, and 2 Dollars for the Bible, upon delivering of the same to the Printer.

A few weeks later, on 7 June, the owner of a missing volume of Byron's *Works* offered an even more generous reward of one guinea for its return.

As these last advertisements suggest, among literary authors, Scott, Byron and Shakespeare were by far the most popular at this period and, at least in terms of the number of volumes advertised for sale, they remained so until the 1850s. While Byron was often seen as too radical and *risqué* to be safely read by young women, and the works of eighteenth-century novelists like Richardson, Fielding, Smollett and Sterne were increasingly condemned as crude and immodest as the century wore on, Scott was considered the least reprehensible of novelists. When the Sydney gentlemen, including George Allen, who had assembled together in 1826 to form the Australian Subscription Library, sent their first book order to London, the only novels included were those of Scott.

Working-class readers

Since the less wealthy members of Australian colonial society did not have large collections of books to be sold by auction, and did not come together to form book clubs, we know much less about their reading habits. Initial attempts to encourage reading among the convicts focused of course on collections of tracts, on the Bible and on other religious texts. The 4000 volumes of books sent with the First Fleet courtesy of the Society for the Promotion of Christian Knowledge included prayer books, psalters, testaments, bibles and hundreds of tracts with titles such as 'Plain Exhortations to Prisoners', 'Cautions to Swearers', 'Dissuasions from Stealing', 'Exercises against Lying' and 'Exhortations to Chastity'. These were issued to prisoners and others at the chaplain's discretion.

Missionaries were also active in early attempts to form lending libraries. In 1808 the Rev. Samuel Marsden had argued in his 'Proposals for Instituting a Lending Library for the General Benefit of the Inhabitants of New South Wales' that what the colonists needed was:

> a Public Library to consist of books carefully selected and confined to particular subjects it is obvious from the nature of the Colony should be Divinity and Morals, History, Voyages and Travels, Agriculture in all its branches, Mineralogy and Practical Mechanics.

Clearly, what Marsden had in mind was a library of mainly utilitarian works, which would help the colonists succeed in their pioneering pursuits while at the same time assisting them in overcoming the perceived moral disadvantages of a convict society. Of the 226 volumes he eventually assembled, through appeals in the *Evangelical Magazine* and his own purchases, about half were works classed as 'Divinity', with 'Agriculture' (27 volumes) and 'History' (18) being the next largest categories.

This was anything but a public library, however, since Marsden not only chose the books but their readers. On 5 March 1814 a 'Free Settler' wrote to the *Sydney Gazette* asking about the whereabouts of the library he had been told about in England 'consisting not only of a variety of useful School Books, but also of a large collection of Bibles, Prayer Books, Religious Tracts, Histories, Geographies, Travels, Voyages, Biographies, etc.'. After various other letters in response, Marsden himself wrote to the paper on 26 March, saying that the collection was not a public library, but books were lent to 'Settlers, Soldiers, and Prisoners, *at my discretion*'. When questioned further on this matter by Commissioner Bigge in 1821, he claimed that insufficient funds had been raised to establish the library in Sydney on the scale originally planned so he had built a room for the books at his home in Parramatta, where 'gentlemen and others' could read and borrow them.

Methodist missionaries, given their doctrinal emphasis on reading and writing as aids to individual salvation, were even more active in attempts to supply useful and uplifting reading material to early colonists. They were responsible for publishing the first Australian magazine in 1821 and also for establishing the first truly public, even if not totally free, library in 1825. In 1822 the Wesleyan missionaries Horton and Turner had offered to act as agents for the supply of books (other than those of a 'seditious or irreligious tendency') to the people of Hobart: 'through this channel heads of families may advantageously furnish themselves with good family Bibles, and other Works proper for a Domestic Library; and Schoolmasters with suitable Books of Instruction for their Pupils'. Four years later, the books in the Wesleyan Library bore a similar emphasis on Morality and Religion, with 'Publications that are either frivolous in their composition, or pernicious in their tendency . . . entirely excluded'. Subscriptions were ten shillings per annum in cash or books, though books 'on the plainest and most important subjects of doctrinal and practical Religion' were supplied without charge.

Despite the support given to the Wesleyan Library by Governor Arthur, himself a Methodist, it clearly did not fulfil all the reading needs of those in Hobart who were not able to join the very selective Hobart Town Book Society. On 20 March 1827 a general meeting was held in Hobart to establish the Hobart Town Mechanics' Institute. Among the resolutions, as reported in the *Tasmanian* on 22 March, was the establishment of a library, with 'donation of Books . . . urged upon the Gentlemen present, many of whom promised to contribute'. So, while the original idea for the Institute may have come from actual mechanics, 'gentlemen' were very prominent on its committee and remained so. As with the earlier libraries established largely through donation, the initial collection was far from ideal, though books were also soon ordered from England.

By the time the Sydney Mechanics' School of Arts was established in 1833, the one in Hobart had more or less ceased to function, though it was revived later in the 1830s. On 6 March 1834 the *Sydney Herald* was able to report that the School of Arts had opened its library and reading room: 'upwards of five hundred volumes already adorn its shelves, consisting of works on science, history and general literature, chiefly contributed by the liberal donations and loans of members and friends'. A year later, the *Alfred* for 10 February was urging further donations, implying that many gentlemen had large collections of books which 'in this busy Colony [are] mere food for worms':

> We trust the regard for literature which these persons have evinced as collectors, will lead them to aspire to the more honourable distinction of becoming patrons, and that they will remove from their dusty shelves works, of which they only peruse the titles impressed on the backs, and lay them open to the enquiring mechanic, who can find time to dive into their contents.

By this time, however, mechanics, like most others in the community, were showing a decided preference for fiction over other types of reading. Not that there were all that many mechanics among the School of Arts' membership: the *Monitor* for 7 February

1835 pointed out that, as in Great Britain, 'not more than a score of Members . . . fall under the denomination of Mechanics'. While the committee could do little about this, it was at pains in its annual report for 1836 to defend the number of literary works, especially recent novels, in its library:

> a taste for reading has to be formed before works of a more philosophical character will be relished or appreciated . . . if any book is likely to accomplish this more speedily than another, it is the works of Scott — containing, as they do, a vast fund of historical information, mixed up, in an agreeable shape, with the manners and customs of different periods.

Certainly, as the *Australian* reported on 7 February, by 1839 so many books were being borrowed from the library that an additional librarian had to be employed to cope with the demand.

By 1890 hundreds of mechanics' institutes had been established throughout Australia and, although never as successful in attracting working-class readers as had originally been hoped, they did cater to the reading needs of many thousands throughout the country. In Victoria alone, as outlined in *These Walls Speak Volumes: A History of Mechanics' Institutes in Victoria* (2015) by Pam Baragwanath and Ken James, over 500 were in existence by 1890. And the one at Shepparton was being heavily used by writer Joseph Furphy as he built up his *magnum opus*, the novel *Such is Life*.

The debate about fiction

As has already been indicated, by the 1830s the growing demand for fiction was beginning to be felt in other quarters besides the mechanics' institutes. The Hobart Town Book Society, also established in 1826 on principles just as exclusive as those operating with Sydney's Australian Subscription Library, was much less exclusive when it came to its books. Its members were concerned to obtain the latest and most popular English publications, many of which were novels, rather than more standard works that many presumably already owned. In 1831, having run into debt through their attempts to open a reading room, some members of the Book Society proposed to sell off their stock of books. Others, however, objected to this, including James Ross of the *Hobart Town Courier*, who in a long article on

8 October 1831 pointed out that 'many of the more instructive and standard works' had not yet been read by the majority of members. Earlier he had defended the members against the charge that their reading tastes were too 'frivolous', pointing out that their reading was a recreation after the 'toil of a long day in some official, public or private arduous occupation'. He put forward an even more interesting defence of recent fiction, however, in claiming that reading English novels was almost a patriotic duty on the part of colonists:

> the force of genius that is now devoted to works of a lighter character, to novels and other lively pictures of English life, must render the perusal of such productions to an inhabitant of a remote, isolated corner of the world like Van Dieman's Land, especially interesting and profitable, tending as it must do to keep alive in no small degree that *amor patriae*, that attachment of our mother country and that familiarity with the manners and relish for the habits of our countrymen which is at all times so desirable.

Despite this and much other evidence that it was not only women who read fiction, the assumption in most debates on the issue was that fiction was particularly a problem with respect to the 'weaker sex'. On 7 November 1833 Samuel Lyons advertised in the *Sydney Herald* a rare auction sale of a lady's library. While no specific titles were listed, it was said to consist of 'upwards of six hundred volumes, chiefly of standard works, by the most esteemed ancient and modern authors, forming altogether a collection of English Literature rarely to be met with out of Europe'. Yet any discussion of reading by women assumed that they read nothing but fiction. On 8 October 1839 the *Australasian Chronicle* published 'The Novel Reader', the first of many poems criticising women for spending too much time reading novels. And in an essay on 'Novels and Novel Reading' published in his weekly magazine the *Literary News* on 27 January 1838, William a'Beckett, while defending novel reading as an occasional recreation, had this to say about women readers:

> Woman ... all impulse and imagination herself, she flies to that which makes her a thousand times more so, till she half sighs to become the heroine she has been weeping over. What a wretch would she think you if you were to stop her in the midst of 'Ivanhoe' or the 'Scottish Chiefs', to bid her listen to a page of the Spectator or the Rambler!

Similar attacks on novel reading, especially by women and members of the working class, continued throughout the century, more or less keeping pace with the growing number of novels in local libraries. In 1869, for example, the *Advocate*, a Roman Catholic newspaper from Victoria, suggested that Catholic churches set up libraries containing sound moral works in order to wean readers away from the 'spurious, sensational and infidel trash' available so readily elsewhere. A few years later, a Protestant clergyman, the Rev. Andrew Cameron of Melbourne, recommended a similar scheme to drive out bad books via 'The systematic colportage of Bibles, wholesome books and periodicals'. But all such schemes came to naught and, by 1890, the writer Francis Adams was proclaiming:

> This is not a literary community. We are certainly voracious readers of novels, but a habit of novel reading scarcely implies the possession of literary taste any more than does the habit of newspaper reading.

Reading and periodicals

Intrinsically related to the rise of a mass reading public during the eighteenth and early-nineteenth century was the expansion of periodical publications. By their very nature, newspapers and magazines encouraged the sort of miscellaneous reading, with readers moving rapidly from one topic to another, which was condemned by some as promiscuous. Their rapid growth during the late-eighteenth and earlier-nineteenth century is therefore one of the clearest signs of the move from intensive to extensive reading that marked this period. So, too, is the development of cheaper monthly and weekly magazines which featured short stories and serialised fiction in addition to the essays and reviews that had been published in the earlier quarterly magazines.

As Wallace Kirsop has made clear in Chapter 11 on newspapers, this category was the most eagerly read of local publications. Australian readers were also avid consumers of newspapers from their countries of origin, mainly England, Scotland or Ireland. Imported magazines were even more popular. In the first fifty or so years of settlement, the major British quarterly magazines, the *Quarterly*, *Westminster*, and *Edinburgh Reviews*, were keenly sought after by members of the élite who wished to maintain contact with current ideas.

From the 1840s, pride of place was given to the new illustrated magazines, especially the *Illustrated London News* and *Punch*, and the monthlies like *Blackwood's Magazine* and Bentley's *Miscellany*. This change, reflecting similar developments in Britain, was, as noted above, a further sign of the move to a more extensive type of reading as well as of the growing popularity of fiction. As weeklies, both *Punch* and the *Illustrated London News* were also concerned to project an aura of contemporaneity, one especially attractive to those in the Australian colonies, anxious about losing touch with events in the motherland.

Most nineteenth-century private libraries included bound volumes of English periodicals and these were regularly advertised by booksellers. Before the advent of public libraries in the various colonies there were many attempts to establish reading rooms to cater to the demand for foreign newspapers and magazines. The newspapers, in particular, were of great professional interest to many local businessmen and merchants. Reading rooms were set up either commercially or by subscription but generally did not survive for very long. All later public libraries had reading rooms, with local and imported newspapers and magazines being in great demand. On 19 April 1861, for example, the Hobart Mechanics' Institute placed an advertisement in the leading local paper, the *Mercury*, informing readers of the facilities available there. Over a third of the advertisement was given over to a list of the magazines and newspapers regularly received for its reading room (see list next page). While the relatively large number of technological journals included here may reflect the supposed special interests of mechanics' institutes members, the list of magazines is otherwise made up of all the major British journals of the period. Significantly, the only Australian magazines included are technological ones, though many others were being published at this time. Likewise, the list of newspapers is heavily weighted towards London and Hobart, with nothing at all from the more outlying colonies of Western Australia and Queensland.

MAGAZINES
WEEKLY

All The Year Round	Journal of the Society of Arts
Athenaeum	Mechanics' Magazine
Builder	Leisure Hour
Chambers' Journal	Notes and Queries
Engineer	Punch
Colonial Mining Journal	

MONTHLY

Art Journal	Dublin University Magazine
Blackwood's Edinburgh Magazine	Fraser's Magazine
Civil Engineer and Architect's Journal	Macmillan's Cambridge Magazine
Colburn's United Service Magazine	Tait's Edinburgh Magazine
Cornhill Magazine	Tasmanian Journal of Agriculture
	Temple Bar

QUARTERLY

British Quarterly Review	National Review
Edinburgh Review	North British Review
	Quarterly Review

NEWSPAPERS
LONDON

Critic	Home News
Evening Mail	Illustrated News
	Spectator

EDINBURGH: — Scotsman

COLONIAL

Hobart Town Daily "Advertiser"	Sydney M. "Herald"
Hobart Town "Mercury"	"Argus" (Melbourne)
Hobart Town "Gazette"	"Punch" (Melbourne)
	Adelaide "Observer"
	Launceston "Examiner"

The enormous popularity of British periodicals, as reflected in this list from Hobart, was a major reason for the short life of the many periodicals attempted in Australia during the nineteenth century. In his 1866 publication *Literature in New South Wales*, G. B. Barton drew attention to this competition, providing figures on the monthly circulation in New South Wales of various British periodicals. These show that the quarterlies had the smallest circulation, 40 for the *Edinburgh Review* and 46 for the *Quarterly*, much less for the others, reflecting their appeal to a more specialist class of reader, many of whom perhaps also chose to read them in libraries rather than order their own copies. At the opposite pole were the magazines which specialised in popular fiction, such as *Good Words* with a circulation of 1750 copies, the *London Journal* with 1500 and the *Family Herald* with 900. None of these, interestingly, was purchased for the Hobart Mechanics' Institute reading room, reflecting the continuing distrust of fiction by the institutes, even though novels now had to be included in their libraries to attract subscribers. The most popular London newspapers, *Home News*, which circulated 1500 copies per month, and the *Illustrated News* with 1320 copies, were however to be found in the Hobart Institute as no doubt in most others throughout Australia. As Barton noted, '*Punch* and the *Illustrated London News* are read by everyone'.

Of course, in all towns and cities in Australia by the 1860s local newspapers would have formed a major part of many people's reading. One may compare the circulation figures for London newspapers given by Barton with his statement that the *Sydney Morning Herald* was then circulating 8450 copies each weekday, with 11 500 subscribers to its weekly edition, the *Sydney Mail*. In addition, another Sydney daily, the *Empire*, claimed a circulation of just over 4000 copies, while the Roman Catholic weekly, the *Freeman's Journal*, sold about 1600 copies. A country newspaper, the *Maitland Mercury*, which appeared three times a week, was said to sell about 3000 copies of each issue. Among magazines, the *Illustrated Sydney News* averaged sales of about 8500 copies per month and *Sydney Punch* no more than 1000. The Melbourne popular fiction magazine, the *Australian Journal*, a close imitation of the *Family Herald*, and then being published weekly, averaged around 5500 copies per week, of which 1750 were in circulation in New South Wales.

Many of those reading British periodicals in Australia, especially those living in remote areas where mail services were infrequent, did not of course purchase individual copies but bound volumes, either yearly or half-yearly depending on the frequency with which the magazine appeared. T. Willmett, a leading Townsville bookseller and stationer, also published the *Cooktown Almanac, Northern Queensland Directory and Miners' and Settlers' Companion for 1876*, which included many pages of advertisements for his own stock. One page was devoted to 'Serial Publications, Yearly and Half-Yearly Volumes' which could be ordered 'At a small advance on the published prices'. Of the 64 titles listed, only one was an Australian publication, the *New South Wales Medical Gazette*. A number of other medical journals, such as the *Lancet*, also appeared on the list, but generally it was directed at those in search of more recreational reading. Given the supposed ubiquity of *Punch* and the *Illustrated London News*, it is interesting that neither appears on this list. Perhaps these were so popular, and so topical, that readers ordered individual copies rather than waiting for the bound half-yearly volumes. Or perhaps they were not as popular with those living on what was then very much the colonial frontier as they were with readers in the more settled districts. It is notable that many of the other magazines purchased by the Hobart Town Mechanics' Institute are also absent. None of the quarterlies is listed, and among more general magazines only *All the Year Round*, *Chambers' Journal*, *Leisure Hour*, *Cornhill Magazine*, *Macmillan's Magazine* and *Temple Bar*. There were however plenty of the more popular journals mentioned by Barton, such as the *Family Herald* and the *London Journal*, as well as magazines directed at women and children, such as the *Young Ladies' Journal*, *Little Folks* and the *Infant's Magazine*.

An advertisement from a later Queensland almanac, the *Western Champion Almanac and Yearbook for 1890*, which circulated in the central west of the colony, shows that newspapers and periodicals continued to be among the most sought-after types of reading matter. In an advertisement, John K. Duncan of Barcaldine described himself not only as a bookseller and stationer but as a newsagent.

Furthermore, the advertisement stresses that he is an agent for 'All the principal Australian Newspapers', as well as English, Scottish, Irish and American papers. This appears to indicate a shift in demand away from overseas to local papers, which has a parallel in the enormous circulation of the Sydney *Bulletin* by this time. It is noticeable that Duncan's other highlighted offerings are 'Novels, Novelettes, Periodicals, British and Australian Poets', again indicating a growing interest in local material, and this even before the phenomenal success of Banjo Paterson's *The Man from Snowy River* in 1894.

Reading in the bush

While writing about the Australian bush is particularly associated with the work of Paterson and Lawson in the 1890s, both were drawing on images and ideas that had developed much earlier. By the 1840s at least, the bush was well established as a particularly Australian place, with bushmen being especially targeted by local booksellers. Though cities like Sydney had now progressed well beyond the stage described by George Allen, with regular theatrical programmes, concerts and lectures, in the bush reading remained one of the few forms of recreation available. There is conflicting evidence as to how popular reading was among bushmen but a general consensus that they all loved a good story or yarn. Where no books were available, or no one could read, then yarns were the order of the day. It was not much of a development to move from the yarn to the tale read aloud by anyone who could do so. By the 1890s, on the evidence of Joseph Furphy's classic *Such is Life* (1903), most bushmen were avid readers when they could get new books. A common method of doing this was by swapping one book for another.

The establishment of country newspapers during the 1840s allows us some information about what was advertised as available to readers outside the capital cities. Obviously, books would have been sold by country storekeepers well before this, especially the staples of bibles and other devotional works, almanacs and schoolbooks. All of these are featured in the 1890 advertisement by the Barcaldine bookseller John K. Duncan discussed earlier, along with other standard sellers like 'Dictionaries, Letter Writers, Fortune Tellers, Dream Books and Song Books', many being the successors of earlier chapbooks. William Lipscomb of Maitland in the Hunter Valley of New South Wales began selling books in 1839 as an agent for James Tegg of Sydney and remained in business all through the 1840s, despite Tegg's demise in 1844. A lengthy advertisement by Lipscomb in the *Australian* on 16 April 1840 gives a good idea of the range and strength of his stock at this period. Beginning with the standard series — such as the 48 volumes of Sir Walter Scott's *Waverley Novels*, the 88 volumes of Scott's *Complete Works*, the 38 volumes of the *British Essayists* — the list continues with histories, biographies, travel books, sermons, veterinary works and cookery books, Young's *Night Thoughts* rubbing shoulders with Ainsworth's *Jack Sheppard*, Collier's *London Stage* with Butler's *London Sermons*. In addition, there were 'Standard Novels' by Bulwer Lytton, the Porter sisters, Washington Irving, Fenimore Cooper, Lady Morgan, Godwin, Grattan and Mrs Gore, bibles, prayer books and other devotional works, not forgetting those indispensable ornaments of Maitland no less than Mayfair drawing-rooms, the 'Annuals for 1840'. Though perhaps a little deficient in the very latest works, apart from the Annuals, Lipscomb's stock catered for nearly every reading taste and need of the time. Of course, he did not live by books alone; he was a stationer, druggist and grocer as well, supplying such necessary 'fancy goods' as aromatic pastilles, patent inkstands, emery baskets and plated tea bells.

As in eighteenth-century America, there was a strong association in country Australia between bookselling, printing and newspaper proprietorship. In 1843 Lipscomb also began printing the *Maitland Mercury*, from whose columns one learns that auctions of books were held fairly regularly in Maitland throughout the 1840s. In at least one case, farmers were clearly expected to be among those purchasing. John Earnsey, who advertised a sale of 200 volumes of school, religious and other books on 7 December 1844, advised that he would 'take in exchange for goods bought privately Bacon, Butter, Eggs, Poultry, &c. &c.'

Like most country and many city booksellers in the 1840s, Lipscomb repeatedly advertised copies of the reprint series, the Novel Newspaper, 'the Cheapest Edition hitherto published'. On 8 May he advertised in his *Mercury* the arrival of 1300 volumes of this series, for sale at 1/3d each. A slightly later advertisement, on 21 June, included a little tale demonstrating the advantages of cheap books for the bush settler:

> 'These cheap works are just the sort I want', said a bush gentleman residing in a cottage of the primitive style of architecture, and covered with nature's own titles, as he was paying me £1 17s. 9d. for a lot he had just purchased. 'They will just do to lend to one's friends, who never return them, or, for a friend who walks into the cottage during my absence on the run, and walks off with a book, my ebony short pipe, a fig of tobacco, my pocket knife, my flint and steel, or any other trifle I have inconsiderately left on my solid circular table, which a matter of fact fellow who called one day styled a good big round stump.'

Copies of Novel Newspaper cheap reprints also featured in the stock of other country booksellers and newspaper proprietors, such as William Jones of the *Goulburn Herald* and James Harrison of the *Geelong Advertiser*, and were also for sale in Brisbane, Hobart, Melbourne and Sydney as well no doubt as in other places of which we have no record. The Sydney booksellers Colman and Piddington took advantage of the availability of country papers to advertise their books in those publications during 1849. On 7 March a list in the *Maitland Mercury* featured a number of Novel Newspaper titles at one shilling each, or ninepence to 'Storekeepers and others purchasing the above by the dozen'. A more extensive advertisement by Piddington in the *Goulburn Herald* for 16 June listed among 'Books of Light Reading for the Fireside' such recent successes as Eugène Sue's *The Mysteries of Paris* and *Matilda*, besides many other best-selling novels, for sale by mail order. The 'Country Gentlemen' who were seen as the most likely purchasers of these more expensive works were 'respectfully informed that all orders enclosing remittances, will be executed with fidelity and promptitude' — also, of course, with a mark-up for the bookseller, since the prices given are generally slightly higher than those in Piddington's advertisement of many of the same books in the *Sydney Morning Herald* on 1 August 1849.

As the above example demonstrates, when discussing reading in the bush it is important to distinguish between classes of readers. Many previous treatments of this topic have tended to focus on the gentlemen readers, especially those from the Western District of

Victoria who have left accounts of their libraries and their reading, such as E. M. Curr in *Recollections of Squatting in Victoria* (1883). Some historians, especially Russell Ward in his *The Australian Legend* (1958), have drawn on other memoirs to support their claim that 'bush workers had a passion for reading and versifying'. In particular, Ward quotes James Demarr's *Adventures in Australia Fifty Years Ago* (1893):

> At a certain out-station one day in the early 'forties, a man arrived 'with a joyful countenance' and a copy of Nicholas Nickleby. In the hut that night another man began reading to a company consisting mainly of old hands who, however, 'advised that the reading should be stopped, until the men of two or three stations near us, had been invited' to share in the feast. By the light of 'a piece of twisted rag stuck into a pint tin of melted fat' the book was read on successive nights to a full hut, and if the reader 'could have read till daylight' the audience would not have tired.

It is significant here that the audience is being read to, however, and also that the men are said to be mainly 'old hands', that is, former convicts. While by the 1890s literacy appears to have been much more widely spread among the non-Indigenous in Australia, in the 1840s many bushmen, and women, still could not read. In his *Analytical View of the Census of New South Wales for the Year 1846* (1847), Ralph Mansfield claimed that, of those over the age of 21, 78 per cent of the males and 77 per cent of the females in the colony could read, with inhabitants of Sydney being more literate than those in the country. It is possible, then, that only about half the bush workers could read in the 1840s. This would seem to be borne out by some other contemporary accounts, such as this description of two stockmen from Thomas McCombie's novel *Arabin* (1845):

> The two began to spell through the story, which was contained in a volume of 'Chambers's Edinburgh Journal'. The hero was Paddy O'Reardon, or some such name, who did many excellent things in a trip which he made to France. Neither of the characters could read, — the tale was so exactly to their taste, that they spelled it through, waiting occasionally to enjoy fits of inward mirth.
>
> 'I say, Bob,' said the guide, 'who wrote that? Was it Shakspeare?'
> 'Poh!' replied his companion, 'Do you think Shakspeare could write anything like that? Walter Scott wrote it in the 'Edinburgh Journal,' to be sure!'

Other contemporary accounts confirm that books were in fairly short supply in the bush at mid-century with the most common, apart from the Bible, being bound volumes of periodicals, sensational novels like Ainsworth's *Jack Sheppard*, and the equally sensational *Newgate Calendar*. According to some notes on 'Bush Society' published in the Sydney newspaper the *Atlas* on 11 March 1848, in the bush 'the Newgate-Calendar may be met with as often as the Bible, nay, they are often companions. Joe Miller forms a frequent addition'. The latter was a very popular joke book.

Later in the century, as mentioned earlier, when many bushmen could read, novels, along with newspapers and periodicals, seem to have formed their staple diets. An 1876 list of works available from the Townsville bookseller T. Willmett runs over nine closely spaced pages. The first seven are headed:

> General Alphabetical List of 'Railway Library,' 'Select Library,' and other series, issued in the 'Railway Library' style, comprising the Cheap Novels published by Routledge, Chapman & Hall, Ward & Lock, Smith, Elder, and Co., and others.
>
> The following Books are sold, retail, at from 9d. to 3s.6d. per Book; but where a quantity are taken, a considerable reduction will be made . . .

Perhaps, as with the earlier Novel Newspaper, country storekeepers took advantage of this discount to purchase stock from Willmett; perhaps the discount was also directed at those who only visited the town once or twice a year and would probably never get to read on a train. Willmett also advertised a number of other cheap fiction series, included Black's People's Edition of the *Waverley Novels*, Dick's English Novels, which included some titles by the Australian actor and novelist Eliza Winstanley, and Cameron & Ferguson's Novels and Romances. A less familiar and very interesting addition is Beadle's American Library 'Each 128 pages, foolscap 8vo., sewed', suggesting that cowboy tales were already popular in the Australian bush. Cheaply produced fiction, by now known as 'yellow backs', also seems to have been the reading matter favoured by those working in the Riverina district of New South Wales during the 1880s. Felix Furphy, the ten-year-old son of Joseph, accompanied his father on a bullock-driving trip in 1883. On 18 May he wrote to his grandfather: 'I have no books here but the third book and the story of the two dogs and father reads nothing but shakspere everybody carries books but they are yallow novels'.

Photograph titled 'Reading the paper in a Gympie garden, ca. 1871'. While it is impossible to be certain, the gentleman may be reading the *Gympie Times and Mary River Mining Gazette*, published from 1868 to 1919 by Alfred George Ramsey. The image was taken by Edward H. Forster, a studio photographer in Maryborough and Gympie during the 1870s and early 1880s, operating as the American & Australian Photographic Co. Photographic print: black and white. (State Library of Queensland)

Reading by children

From the earliest days of European settlement, immigrant children were being born and educated in Australia, ensuring a continuous demand for schoolbooks. Some had arrived on the First Fleet, under the care of the Church of England chaplain, the Rev. Richard Johnson, including 100 copies of Dixon's *Speller* donated by the Society for the Promotion of Christian Knowledge. Spellers were an essential tool for the abc method of learning to read, whereby the pupil progressed from recognising individual letters to recognising syllables and eventually to reading words and short passages. They therefore, besides the alphabet and selected syllables, included short extracts from religious and other works, and sections on grammar, punctuation, geography and history. In 1792 Johnson received a further shipment of a text called *Reading Made Easy* for use in the public schools operating under his supervision. But elementary texts remained in short supply, Rowland Hassall informing the London Missionary Society in 1801 of a great shortage of 'first and 2d Books as well as Spelling Books Testaments and bibles'. In 1804, after the establishment of his private academy in Sydney, the Rev. William Pascoe Crook also needed to write to a friend in England for supplies of 'pleasing as well as edifying reading books'. By this time some elementary schoolbooks were also being advertised by general storekeepers, but they were not widely and cheaply available before 1810, when a spelling book based on Lindley Murray's *English Spelling Book* was printed in Sydney by George Howe. Although no copies of this have survived, a notice in Howe's *Sydney Gazette* for 7 January informed readers that the speller had been printed mainly for use by students at the Orphans' Institution, but that additional copies were available for purchase by those 'studious of facilitating the first principles of instruction'. In 1822 Andrew Bent evidently printed some 'small spelling books' in Hobart as well, though no copies have come down to us of those either.

With the arrival of specialist booksellers, advertisements began appearing which listed books thought suitable for children's leisure reading. Most of these had not, of course, been originally written with children in mind. So, in his *Maitland Mercury* for 2 September 1848, William Lipscomb advertised cheap editions of *Robinson Crusoe*, *The Vicar of Wakefield*, *Don Quixote*, *Cook's Voyages* and *The Arabian Nights* as 'Juvenile Works, neatly Bound and suitable for presents'. But many works aimed especially at younger readers were also being imported. In Sydney in 1848, for example, the auctioneer T. S. Mort advertised, for sale on 13 April, 13 dozen copies of Maria Edgeworth's *Stories for Children* and 44 dozen copies of *Instructive Stories*. Copies of the first children's book to be published in Australia, *A Mother's Offering to her Children; by a Lady, Long Resident in New South Wales* (1841), otherwise Charlotte Barton, were also quite widely advertised, being available for example in Geelong and Portland in Victoria as well as in Sydney, where it had been printed.

Between 1872 and 1893 a series of Education Acts were passed in all the Australian colonies, establishing free, secular education for all, at least at the primary level. In 1875, William Wilkins, Secretary to the Council of Education of New South Wales, in association with those holding similar posts in Victoria and Tasmania, asked the English publishing house of Collins to adapt their graded *Progressive Readers* 'to fit them for use' in Australian schools. The new series, called *The Australian Reading Books*, began appearing in 1877. At the earlier levels Australian content remained fairly minimal, though Henry Kendall's poem 'The Last of His Tribe' was included in Book III, along with short essays on topics like 'The Emu' and 'Life of Captain Cook'. Designed for the most advanced readers, Book V was issued in separate editions for boys and girls, and included a series of accounts of Australian exploration, as well as some further essays on natural history and on regional geography. This localised material was common to both versions of Book V; boys, however, were given more scientific essays and instructions on how to behave in emergencies such as a fire, while girls got more poetry, some advice on first aid for common ailments and plenty of moral essays on topics like 'Plainness versus Beauty'.

Our other information about children's reading comes from diaries kept by children, mostly of course teenagers rather than younger, and all from élite and cultured backgrounds. One of the best examples is the diary kept by William Bunn, son of Anna Maria Bunn, who wrote the first novel to be published on the Australian mainland, *The Guardian* (1838), while living near Queanbeyan in southern New South Wales. The surviving volumes, now in the Mitchell Library, date from March 1845 to June 1848, with Bunn's age changing from around 15 to 18 over the period. Mrs Bunn does not seem to have been at all worried about what her son read, even allowing him to read her own novel with its gothic plot of illegitimate births, incest and untimely deaths. But she was herself an admirer of Byron from an early age, an author felt by many to be best kept locked away from young women. William, like many others at the time, read a large amount of fiction. As he seems to have had plenty of time for reading, evidently being required neither to attend school classes nor to work, as most other boys of his age would have been doing, he got through his books at quite a fast rate. Between April and August 1845, for example, he read eight of Scott's *Waverley Novels*, finishing some in four days, though taking up to a week for others. During this period he was also reading novels by other authors at much the same rate, including several that may not, unlike Scott's, have been tolerated by more conventional parents: Monk Lewis's gothic tale *Bravo of Venice* (1804) and Ainsworth's *Jack Sheppard* (1839) for instance. Charles Lever's *Harry Lorrequer* (1839) was read twice as was Bulwer Lytton's *Pelham* (1828), with Bunn on the second occasion staying up until 11 pm to finish it. While Bunn is disappointingly laconic in his critical comments on the books he read, he gave to *Pelham* his highest accolade of 'liked it exceedingly'.

Photograph of two boys reading in a garden, from an album [ca 1879–1882] which bears the signature of John Rae (1813–1900), public servant, author and painter. Rae was praised both for his professional work and his artistic talents as a painter and photographer, using these latter skills to capture images of colonial Sydney. The photograph may have been taken at his residence, 'Hilton', Liverpool Street, Darlinghurst; it is likely the boys are family members. Albumen print, 11.7 x 15.9 cm. (State Library of New South Wales)

Naturally, Bunn's reading was not confined solely to novels; he makes constant reference to reading current periodicals, many of which were borrowed from friends. Titles included the always popular *Punch* and the *Illustrated London News*, besides *Chambers' Journal*, *Bentley's Miscellany*, the *Saturday Magazine* and *Fraser's Magazine*. Further, he was not averse, at least when younger, to reading drawing-room annuals such as *The Forget-Me-Not*. He made two concerted attacks on Shakespeare, reading six of his plays in September and October 1845 and a further four about a year later. Also on Bunn's 'liked very much list' was Samuel Johnson's *Rasselas*, while the same author's *Letter to Chesterfield* was pronounced to be 'capital'. A more recent author much to Bunn's taste was Macaulay. On 15 April 1848 he recorded: 'Opened "Macaulay's Essays" at "Ranke's history of the Popes" began and never stopped till I finished it (nearly fifty pages)'. He clearly found poetry more difficult, on 17 April 1848 calling Longfellow's *Hyperion* 'a confounded book that I can't make out the meaning of yet', finding Scott's *Marmion* much less interesting than his novels and Wordsworth's *Peter Bell* 'good enough but exceeding bad some parts'. Bunn evidently retained a love of reading, later becoming a founding member of the Braidwood Literary Institute as well as proprietor in 1859 of the *Braidwood Dispatch and Mining Journal*.

Reading aloud

While the rise of extensive reading, especially of fiction, encouraged the practice of silent, individual reading, reading aloud remained popular throughout the nineteenth century. Those who worried about the amount of reading being done by women and young people, especially of supposedly dubious fictional works, were particularly keen to encourage the domestic practice of reading aloud. A father reading aloud to his family in the evening formed an ideal Victorian domestic scene: he could ensure that only correct works were consumed by his wife, sons and daughters; they had the advantage of his company and attention. Mothers could, of course, be just as censorious as fathers if the need arose. The young Annabella Innes, for example, noted in her journal that, during some months of isolated life in 1840, on the family property near Bathurst after her father's death, she 'read greedily such books as we possessed, chiefly the *Waverley Novels*, which then and always fascinated me. I read most of them aloud as well as to myself'. Her mother did not, however, allow them to read Shakespeare. In contrast, the aforementioned Anna Maria Bunn, another widow, thought nothing of reading 'The Borgias' from Dumas's *Celebrated Crimes* aloud to members of her family in 1848, reminding us that individual readers have always been free to set their own rules, ignoring the more restrictive norms of their times.

Among women, reading aloud was often encouraged as an alternative to idle gossip as they sewed or carried out other more sedentary household jobs. In 1843 the Innes family moved to Port Macquarie in northern New South Wales to live with Annabella's uncle. She recorded on 18 December 1844 that 'One of the party reads aloud while the others work. Our book is *The Old Curiosity Shop*. We are deeply interested in Little Nell, and enjoy it doubly when my aunt reads.' Dickens clearly remained a favourite for reading aloud, with Annabella noting on 31 August 1847 that 'Mr Smith has been reading aloud to us every evening from after tea till ten o'clock and has finished *Martin Chuzzlewit*. It is just the book for reading aloud, and he reads very well.' That reading aloud could be put to less innocent purposes is demonstrated by the journals of Annie Baxter Dawbin. While staying in a Melbourne boarding-house in 1864, with her husband absent, Mrs Dawbin carried on a flirtation with another boarder under the cover of his abilities as a reader of French. On 31 July she recorded: 'Every morning Mr Vernon reads aloud to me in French, and then we sing together, and indeed pass the best part of the day in each other's company'.

Reading, both aloud and silently, was also encouraged among bush workers as a more profitable alternative to gambling and yarning. Again, of course, there was some concern about what was read, with many commentators, as already noted, deploring the strong fondness for the *Newgate Calendar* and other works of that type. Thus, in 'A Nipping Super. An Original Bush Story, by a Bushman', serialised in the *Geelong Advertiser* between 1 and 18 July 1848, the narrator is forced to spend the night in a stockmen's hut, where he discovers that the only book is a life of the 'celebrated thief' Jack Sheppard. He advises the men to borrow other books from their master, mentioning in particular that 'improving' work *Chambers' Information for the People*. The previous year, the same paper had, on 27 August, published an article on 'Bush Libraries', which again recommended that employers help their men to acquire books, since 'that which will exclude a pack of cards from the bushman's hut and keep the pipe from continually adhering to his lips — which will set him thinking and help to strengthen his moral character, must tend to make him a better servant'. The diary kept by Alexander Finlay while at the Victorian goldfields in 1852 suggests that reading aloud was also practised among groups of men there. On 6 August he noted that 'Three parties have joined to read books which the storekeeper adjoining lets out at one shilling per vol. The "reader" Mr Buscombe is exempted from subscription. We have read one entitled "Fanny the Milliner", by Charles Rowcroft Esq.'

The latter half of the century saw the rise of the penny reading, so called because audiences paid a penny admission to hear readings from popular authors. In Australia they had forerunners in the literary lectures given at mechanics' institutes in Hobart and Sydney during the 1830s and 1840s, which were often little more than an excuse to quote extensively from the work of popular writers like Robert Burns. While Charles Dickens never managed to tour Australia reading from his own works, as he had in Britain and America, plenty of others were willing to step into the gap, with Dickens's novels taken up just as readily in these more public forums as in domestic ones. Penny readings were particularly popular in Victoria between 1865 and 1870, usually organised by bodies such as mechanics' institutes to raise funds, and held in town halls and other similar venues. Programmes consisted of readings from well-known authors, interspersed with musical performances and entertaining lectures. As with the earlier lectures at mechanics' institutes, however, the readings were criticised for an overemphasis on amusement at the expense of education. In 1866 B. S. Nayler published a pamphlet entitled *Penny readings; both what they now are ... and what they ought to be, namely, institutions for elevating the unlettered masses.* In it he complained that:

> Not one of the Penny Readings I have attended in Melbourne . . . seemed to have the remotest approximation towards informing the head or amending the heart. The best that I can say of the best of them is there was plenty of noise, abundance of merriment, and lots of fun, accompanied with deafening applause, long-continued clapping of hands, and execrable whistlings.

Some philanthropic souls also gave gratis readings to inmates of hospitals and prisons. The Melbourne man of letters, James Smith, for example, noted in his journal on 12 November 1863 that he had that day been out to Pentridge Gaol where he had read passages from Dickens's *David Copperfield* to some 400 prisoners:

> I felt that I never read so well or succeeded more completely in carrying the audience with me. It was interesting to watch the effect of the pathetic passage descriptive of Mrs Copperfield's funeral on the congregation of felons. The most profound silence reigned — broken only by the 'sniffing' of the attentive listeners. Numbers dropped their heads, & were touched with sympathetic grief, & at the end there was a general blowing of noses & clearing of throats. The humorous passages they appeared to enjoy hugely.

While some of Smith's audience were perhaps illiterate, the main function of communal readings such as his in the minds of the penal authorities would have been as cheap entertainment combined with a controlled use of fiction as a means of moral reformation. Smith testifies here to the continuing strong belief in the humanising value of literature as he describes the effects of the 'pathetic passage' on his presumably hard-boiled audience. At a time when many remained suspicious of private reading of novels, the reading aloud of passages selected by a well-known literary authority like Smith presented none of the dangers associated with an uncontrolled indulgence in fiction. For similar reasons, reading aloud in the family circle remained for many the preferred way of controlling fiction reading by women and children.

Reading groups

Reading aloud from favourite authors also formed part of the activities of the reading groups and literary societies that had existed in Australia from at least the 1820s, though initially their main function seems to have been to allow members to share book purchases by giving them access to a communal library. At a time when public libraries did not exist, and poor roads and inadequate transportation made visits to major towns a rare event, many reading societies sprang up, especially in Tasmania. Although information about these is as yet very scanty, groups underway there included the Campbell-Town Book Club, the Norfolk Plains Book Society (1830–34), the New Norfolk Reading Association (1835), the Richmond Reading Society (1835–37), the Bothwell

Literary Society (1834–) and the Pontville Reading Society, as well as the Hobart Town Book Society of the 1820s, discussed earlier in this chapter. While the conditions of settlement in other colonies did not lend themselves so readily to such a strong regional network, we know of at least one group operating in the Western District of Victoria in the 1840s. In his *The Present State and Prospects of the Port Phillip District of New South Wales* (1845), Charles Griffith refers to a book club 'established in the neighbourhood of the Grange and Warren, 200 miles west of Melbourne, where there are several married settlers, who thus obtain from England all the recent periodicals and publications'. This supports evidence from other sources that such groups were mainly interested in keeping up with the latest news and literature from home. A ledger kept by one of the book club's members, the squatter Acheson Ffrench, records activities from 1845 to 1850. Members paid an annual subscription of £3 and among the works purchased were volumes of the *Illustrated London News* and *Colburn's Magazine*, Dickens's *Dombey and Son* (1848) and many recent travel books. Of equal note, however, are a number of works in translation, including novels by Alexandre Dumas and George Sand and poetry by Friedrich Schiller.

By the 1880s, literary societies of a different type were flourishing, mainly in the cities. These allowed men and women to meet, usually in gender-segregated groups, to discuss their reading and debate topics of current interest. A manuscript journal, 'The Phoenix', compiled in 1874–77 to record the doings of the Redfern Literary Association in Sydney, is now housed in the Mitchell Library. Members evidently had some sort of joint library, since on 28 December 1874 the compiler lamented the fact that there were not more biographies in it, as 'knowledge of how great and good men have deported themselves' was essential for young men like themselves. He also lamented the lack of collections of speeches by famous orators like Fox since, 'if we are to turn out good speakers we can only do so by having good models to follow; and at the present time we have none'. While seemingly advocating a very instrumental view of reading, he was not, however, totally against fiction, believing that works like Dickens's *Oliver Twist* and *Nicholas Nickleby* had done much good in 'removing evils and abuse'. So, 'good, carefully selected works of fiction ought not to be neglected in replenishing our library'. An essay 'On the Acquisition of Knowledge. 1st By Reading', in the issue for 28 July 1875, however, was more critical: 'The proneness now a days for light reading which is only of use as a mere relaxation, tends to militate against the acquirement of solid knowledge.'

The subjects debated by members of the society at their weekly meetings included, on 11 August 1875, 'Was Charles Dickens the greatest novelist of his time?'. Recitations of speeches from Shakespeare's plays and well-known poems like 'Young Lochinvar' were also given and debates held against other similar associations, including the Cumberland Mutual Improvement Society and the Parramatta Literary Society. As this indicates, many such societies were running in Sydney at the time. A decade later, Hugh Wright, a member of the Woollahra Literary and Debating Society, recorded some of the talks he gave at their meetings in 1887. His exercise book, now also in the Mitchell Library, includes two essays of relevance to this chapter, one on 'The Free Public Library of Sydney' and the other on 'Novels and Novel-Reading'. He is critical of the fact that the Library kept locked away 'All the leading medical and anatomical works and several works in French', asking 'Is it feared that licentious individuals would be always gloating over them?' He is also critical of the books available through the Lending Branch of the Library as being 'more fit as babies' toy books than to be in a circulating library', though does not agree with the Trustees' decision to buy no more fiction. Fiction, if it has 'an elevating tendency', is approved of, as are 'the best of boy's books, such as written by Capt. Marryat, Henty, Capt. Mayne Reid and especially Jules Verne'. In 'Novels and Novel-Reading' Wright similarly points to the influence of the novels of Charles Reade in improving prisons and safety in mines and singles out novels by Verne as providing a way of acquiring scientific knowledge. Wright proves even more open-minded in not only defending the adventure stories published in magazines like *Boys of England* but the novels of Ouida and even Zola:

> If you skim them with a tainted mind, you may find sufficient to feed a licentious imagination; but by *reading* them carefully you are instructed about the whims and evils of society.

As he points out, the censoring tendency of the past fifty years is just as fatal to many of the classics of the past, from Ovid, Homer and others of their time, through to medieval drama and poetry and to the work of Swift, Fielding and Smollett. The lecture ends with a rousing plea for the extermination of 'all shams and hypocrisies no matter whether they be in our every-day life, or in prose, or verse'.

Despite its title, members of the 'Nil Desperandum Literary Society' were probably more circumspect in what they said and what they read, though they certainly did not steer away from contemporary issues. This society, also known as 'Lady Hamilton's Literary Society', met at Government House, Hobart from 1889 to 1892, with Teresa Hamilton, wife of the then Governor of Tasmania, as President. Members were required to present papers and 'to study the subject given in order to discuss the paper' when it was read at their fortnightly meetings. Their papers, as recorded in the minute book now in the Tasmanian Archives, generally dealt with an historical figure or a writer's work, though were sometimes more general, as on 13 March 1890 when the ladies discussed 'Woman's Influence'. This was perhaps a follow-up to an earlier meeting, 28 November 1889, when rather surprisingly the focus had been on the life and work of Henrik Ibsen. During the meeting one member read an essay on his plays, 'especially the "Doll's House"' while another gave an 'epitome and criticism' of *The Pillars of Society* and *Ghosts*. Unfortunately there is no indication of what the ladies thought about any of these plays, but that they were reading them, or at least reading about them, at all, is a sign of Ibsen's great notoriety at this time.

While most of the other literary papers dealt with standard English authors like the Brownings, Goldsmith and Thackeray, at least some members of this group clearly wished to keep up to date. George Meredith's *Diana of the Crossways* was discussed on 26 March 1891, the main point at issue being the obscurity or otherwise of Meredith's style, and on 14 May 1891 the diary of Marie Bashkirtseff.

On 13 August at a special meeting called to decide on papers for the Annual Meeting of the society, it was initially agreed that everyone should discuss 'the power and influence of the poets of Australia on its people' in comparison with the power and influence in England of Tennyson, Browning or any other two English nineteenth-century poets. But clearly not all members felt capable of discussing poetry, let alone Australian poetry, so eventually 'everyone was requested to choose their own subject'. The list of subjects actually chosen for the papers given on 26 August is revealing in showing the wide range of interests among this small group of upper-class women. While some spoke on such innocuous topics as 'Half Hour in My Garden' and 'From London to Melbourne', others ranged from 'Chaucer's Minor Poems' to 'Trade Unions'. Miss Chapman, the Hon. Secretary, clearly the source of the poetry topic pronounced too hard, spoke on 'Adam Lindsay Gordon'. Perhaps as a sop to her, other members read various poems by Gordon, including 'The Sick Stockrider'. After Lady Hamilton returned to England, the Society was renamed in her honour. The Hamilton Literary Society has continued to meet in Hobart to the present day.

The Hamilton Literary Society, at Government House, Hobart, 12 December 1889, at what is believed to have been one its first meetings. The Society was founded by Teresa Hamilton (née Reynolds, 1852–1932, seated centre in dark clothing), wife of Governor Robert Hamilton. A strong advocate for cultural and women's issues, she organised and gave lectures on health and related topics, formed an organisation that became the District Nursing Association, founded a women's refuge and took up related causes such as education for girls, women's sport and temperance activity. (Tasmanian Archives)

Conclusion

By the 1890s widespread literacy had been established in Australia, though for many reading would have been largely confined to religious texts, newspapers and magazines. By now the newspapers would nearly all have been local, as would many of the magazines, especially the highly popular ones like *Melbourne Punch*, the *Australian Journal* and, of course, the *Bulletin*. Most books read in Australia still came from elsewhere, especially from Britain, but Australian titles were beginning to find their way into private collections, having appeared in public and other libraries from the 1840s onwards: the heroine of Miles Franklin's *My Brilliant Career* (1901) is delighted to find copies of the works of Kendall and Gordon, as well as George du Maurier's *Trilby*, on the bookshelves at her grandmother's station. As we have seen, by the 1880s Australian poets, especially Adam Lindsay Gordon, were beginning to be admired by readers as far apart socially and geographically as the stockmen of North Queensland and the literary ladies of Hobart. Indeed, my own grandfather, born near Adelaide in 1891, was christened Lindsay Gordon in the poet's honour.

That it was Australian poetry rather than fiction that first caught the popular imagination is a sign of the extent to which the culture of nineteenth-century Australia was still a strongly oral one. While widespread literacy meant that there was no longer any necessity for reading aloud, this remained a popular pastime both within and outside the family circle. At a time when university education was restricted to the privileged few, literary societies and discussion groups provided an important means of self-improvement for young men and women living in cities and larger towns. Others, like the female members of Lady Hamilton's literary society, might perhaps have been more interested in displaying their cultural superiority, though it is clear that at least some members of that group were concerned with current issues like women's rights and the growth of trade unionism. In an age when radio, television and the internet were unthought of, even by Jules Verne, reading, along with lectures and group discussion, remained the only way in which Australians could learn about the past, and find out what was happening in the present both in their own country and in the world beyond its shores.

NOTE ON SOURCES

I am grateful to Ian Henderson for his research in Hobart and elsewhere, which I have drawn on for later sections of this chapter in particular. Material for the period before 1850 comes mainly from my unpublished 1971 University of Sydney PhD thesis, Literature and the Reading Public in Australia, 1800–1850. Information on education and literacy is taken from John F. Cleverley, *The First Generation: School and Society in Early Australia*, Sydney, SUP, 1971; and C. Turney, ed., *Pioneers of Australian Education*, Sydney, SUP, 1969. Material relating to George Allen, John Oxley and John McGarvie is held in the Mitchell Library, Sydney. Transcriptions of John Grant's letters may be found in Yvonne Cramer, *This Beauteous, Wicked Place: Letters and Journals of John Grant, Gentleman Convict*, Canberra, National Library of Australia, 2000. Brian Hubber discusses an early reading group in '"Entertainment for Many Solitary Hours": An 1840s Book Group on the Australian Frontier', *BSANZ Bulletin*, vol.22. no.2, 1998, pp. 81-92.

Much research remains to be done on reading in Australia, especially for the period from 1850 to 1890. Useful material has been found in Chew Chiat Naun, 'The History of Reading in Australia', *BSANZ Bulletin*, vol.19, no.2, 1995, pp. 101-14; Stefan Petrow, 'Reading in Launceston: The Case of the Launceston Mechanics' Institute 1842–1914', *BSANZ Bulletin*, vol.22, no.3, 1998, pp. 154-72; Patricia J. Alsop, 'A Study of Readership in Victoria, c. 1835–1865', *BSANZ Bulletin*, vol.17, no.1, 1993, pp. 17-32; Brian Hubber, 'Libraries and Readers in Nineteenth Century Melbourne', in Elizabeth Morrison and Michael Talbot, eds, *Books, Libraries and Readers in Colonial Australia*, Clayton, VIC, Monash University, 1985; and M. Askew and B. Hubber, 'The Colonial Reader Observed: Reading in its Cultural Context', in D. H. Borchardt and W. Kirsop, eds, *The Book in Australia*, Melbourne, Australian Reference Publications, 1988. Alexander Finlay's journal is in the Tasmanian Archives; for the quotation from Annie Baxter Dawbin see *The Journal of Annie Baxter Dawbin 1858–1868*, Lucy Frost, ed., St Lucia, UQP, 1998.

POSTSCRIPT

The long illness that preceded Elizabeth Webby's death on 6 August 2023 prevented her from updating the chapter on 'Reading'. Her unrivalled knowledge of the Australian book world in the first half of the nineteenth century was a guarantee of the solidity of her exposition, which, like all parts of the present volume, was constrained by strict limits on space. Given that the history of reading had come strongly into favour in the 1990s when our series was being planned, it was inevitable that important work was continuing to be done and that it needed to be reported. This brief note attempts to take account of some major contributions and to indicate a few of the newer directions now being followed.

As stated in the 'Note on Sources' above, much research remained to be done on the second half of the century, and it cannot be claimed that all the gaps have been filled. Indeed new evidence has come to light on earlier decades as well.

Tasmania has provided precious documentation on borrowing (not necessarily to be equated with reading) from commercial and subscription lending libraries. Analysis of the early years — 1846-1851 — of the Walch circulating library in Hobart is far from complete, but a report on problems and on progress made can be found in Wallace Kirsop's *The Bookshop as an 'Index of Civilisation': The Case of the Walches in the 1840s*, Melbourne, Chaskett Press, 2011. On the other hand Keith Adkins's *Reading in Colonial Tasmania: The Early Years of the Evandale Subscription Library*, Melbourne, Ancora Press, Monash University, 2010, offers a detailed analysis of borrowing between 1847 and 1861 from a small institution close to Launceston as well as a chapter on the Bothwell Literary Society founded in the 1830s.

The two halves of the century are bridged in a recent article by Paula Byrne on 'Women and Intellectual Life in New South Wales 1835-1868: Ann Rusden', *Australian Journal of Victorian Studies*, vol.26, no.1, 2022, pp. 42-62, giving due prominence to one of the female members of the Scott, Mitchell and Rusden dynasties. A great deal covering collector-readers of all periods is contained in the five volumes of Charles Stitz's *Australian Book Collectors* (2010-2016). William Bunn's reading in the second half of the century can be gleaned from Mary Anne Bunn, *The Lonely Pioneer: William Bunn, Diarist, 1830-1901*, Braidwood, NSW, St Omer Pastoral Co., 2002.

Borrowing from institutions, notably mechanics' institutes, is treated in articles by Tim Dolin on the later nineteenth century and early twentieth century: 'First Steps Toward a History of the mid-Victorian Novel in Colonial Australia', *Australian Literary Studies*, vol.22, no.3, 2006, pp. 273-93, and 'The Secret Reading Life of Us' in Brian Matthews, ed., *Readers, Writers, Publishers: essays and poems*, Canberra,

The Australian Academy of the Humanities, 2004, pp. 115-33. In much other recent work on borrowing the balance has shifted — for documentary reasons — to the twentieth century. For the proposal for an Australian Reading Experience Database aimed to begin from 1788, see Patrick Buckridge's chapter, pp. 340-47 in Katherine Bode and Robert Dixon, eds, *Resourceful Reading: The New Empiricism, eResearch and Australian Literary Culture*, Sydney, SUP, 2009.

The net is cast a little wider in studies on the reception of English novelists in nineteenth-century Australia. Sitting a little uneasily between literary history and book history in the strict sense one finds such works as Susan K. Martin and Kylie Mirmohamadi, *Sensational Melbourne: Reading Sensation Fiction and* Lady Audley's Secret *in the Victorian Metropolis*, North Melbourne, Australian Scholarly, 2011; and the same authors' *Colonial Dickens: What Australians Made of the World's Favourite Writer*, North Melbourne, Australian Scholarly, 2012. Diffuse sources feed into a corpus that will require extension for many years to come. For example, A. B. Piddington's anecdotal *Worshipful Masters* (Sydney, Angus & Robertson, 1929), mentions the fact that Sir George Long Innes (1834–1896), grandson of the emancipist entrepreneur Mary Reibey, politician and Supreme Court justice, was in the habit of buying French novels by the dozen from Angus & Robertson. This raises the interesting question of the audience for foreign-language books in a society that was far from uniformly Anglocentric in its tastes.

Towards the end of the last century a new vogue for the study of marginalia began in the Northern Hemisphere. The most substantial Australian contribution to this movement is the volume edited by Patrick Spedding and Paul Tankard under the title *Marginal Notes: Social Reading and the Literal Margins* (Palgrave Macmillan, 2021) with local-centred chapters by Patrick Spedding, Peter Pereyra and Patrick Buckridge. It can be argued, however, that investigations of this kind in Australia go back to G. A. Wilkes's work on Christopher Brennan in the 1950s. See Wallace Kirsop, *Sixty Years of Study of Marginalia: The Case of Chris Brennan* (Melbourne, The Chaskett Press, 2019). Brennan's intensive undergraduate work on Aeschylus falls within the period of the present *History*. Other annotators who have been examined in part include Redmond Barry. There is scope for further investigations of this type, for example on the scattered books from the library of Henry Keylock Rusden (1826–1910), another reader of French. It is easy to see a more systematic approach to Australian marginalia as a tool for exploring the country's intellectual history.

Beyond reading there is use, as David Pearson has emphasised in his *Book Ownership in Stuart England* (Oxford, OUP, 2021) and *Speaking Volumes: Books with Histories* (Oxford, Bodleian Library Publishing, 2022). To date that is a path that has not really been taken in this country, although possibilities undoubtedly exist.

W.K.

Conclusion: Coming of Age

Wallace Kirsop

By the end of the first century of European occupation of the Australian continent, a Western-style book industry had been effectively established. It was not exclusively British, since it is not hard to find influences and participation from North America and Continental Europe. The Asian presence, largely Chinese, was slighter at this time, and by 1890 the hostility that led to the White Australia Policy was beginning to take legislative shape. Indigenous Australians had a limited role in these new forms of communication. Their age-old traditions, disregarded and poorly understood, survived in areas mostly untouched by the newcomers and had to wait for a later period to be properly recognised. In other words the foreground was dominated by what had been inherited and imported from the other side of the world.

Given that the nineteenth-century Australian colonies were a small part of the Anglosphere, a certain subservience to what was being done and thought in the British Isles and the USA was inescapable. Even when the three million European inhabitants of 1890 are put alongside the 26 million (now counting the Indigenous) of the 2020s, the disproportion is obvious. Coming to terms with the advantages and disadvantages of a shared language is a perennial problem for those interested in national self-expression. None the less, it can be shown that the periphery was capable of looking critically at the centre and that submission to introduced ways was not universal and inevitable. Inventiveness, for example in developing a superior model of parliamentary democracy, and competitiveness, not to mention superiority, in the sporting arena are there to underline an Australian capacity for self-assertiveness and for moulding imports to suit local conditions. Similar remarks can be made about what has been seen in the world of books at the Antipodes.

Viewed in an international context the introduction of printing to Australia was remarkably rapid. It came less than half a century after the beginnings in what is now Canada, where Europeans had arrived to settle by the early 1600s. Even more striking is the fact that the first press in Sydney preceded vernacular printing in such parts of the Ottoman Empire as Albania, Bulgaria and even Greece. This situation can be explained in various ways, but it is important to acknowledge that the colonies established in the South Seas in and after 1788 were expected and equipped to participate in a relatively free and modern civilisation of print.

Despite many difficulties — lack of qualified personnel, shortage of materials, a severely limited population for several decades — there were obvious achievements when the colonies commemorated their Centennial in 1888. Foremost amongst them was the creation of durable newspapers, some of them of high quality that was recognised by English observers. After the gold rushes, distribution of books was solidly and efficiently organised, in particular by the great wholesaler George Robertson. A wide network of libraries, especially those of mechanics' institutes, brought books to many parts of the continent. Although heavy printing machinery continued to be imported, local manufacturing of type, ink and paper showed the colonies moving to provide at least part of their needs. Inventors were also at work, for example seeking patents for new illustrative processes.

Local writing carried in newspapers everywhere in the colonies complemented but did not replace the mass of fiction imported from the Northern Hemisphere. Certain genres had to be produced on the spot, notably directories, almanacs and the vehicles of government. The immigrants tried their hands at all sorts of subjects, but they were generally unsuccessful at sustaining magazines for long periods. Overseas competition was too strong in a small population. The paradox is that the Australian cities were exceptionally populous by 1890. Melbourne was the equal of Budapest and Warsaw and more than twice the size of Prague. From this flowed benefits that became more obvious in later decades. Easy access to what came in from the United Kingdom, the USA and even Continental Europe meant that ambitious and tenacious Australians could keep abreast of what was being thought and written elsewhere. David Scott Mitchell, the model of the cultured and scholarly collector, never left his native New South Wales. Beatrice Webb, a sharp and sometimes contemptuous critic of the people she met in Australia, wrote of Isaac Isaacs:

> He is the only man we have met in the colonies who has an international mind determined to make use of international experience. And this, in spite of the fact that he has never left Australia.

Exceptional cases? There were more perhaps than Old World condescension was able to discern, especially if, in the guise of governors and distinguished visitors, it confined its attention to the 'gross materialists' and vulgarians who peopled the colonial political world. What is essential to note in this context is that the well organised book trade of the 1880s made it possible to keep in touch, not just with cheap fiction, but with serious writing on scientific and intellectual topics.

How does the year 1890 mark a new stage in the story? One has to beware of noting breaks in continuity too neatly, but the late 1880s were the apogee of 'Marvellous Melbourne' with its domination of the Australian book world in the decades since the gold rushes. The crash that followed the 'irrational exuberance' of the Victorian boom changed the balance of forces for more than a century, despite the installation of the provisional federal capital in the southern city between 1901 and 1927. Federation itself, more actively proposed and debated throughout the 1890s, was less significant in the history of publishing and bookselling than a series of economic and cultural developments.

The discovery of gold was the impetus for the rise of Melbourne. The role of some earlier arrivals like Redmond Barry was critical alongside the skills brought by the would-be miners and those who presciently understood what else would be needed in an expanding economy. The 'cultural evangelists' who founded in the Victorian capital the Public Library, the Museum, the future National Gallery and the University were in effect joined by people whose focus was trade and manufacture. Prominent amongst them were the founders of George Robertson & Co. and Mullen's Select Library as well as the bookbinder and stationer William Detmold and David Syme, proprietor of the *Age*. Robertson retired from active direction of his business in 1890; Mullen sold his in 1889; Detmold died in 1884; Syme alone lived on into the twentieth century. In other words, the creative generation of gold-rush immigrants had largely disappeared. The two bookselling firms continued and, after various vicissitudes, ultimately merged in 1921 as Robertson & Mullens. Meanwhile leadership in Australian publishing had passed to Angus and Robertson in Sydney. That house's list, which was to become more clearly focused under the second George Robertson, was launched in 1888.

Financial collapse is only part of the explanation. From the 1870s, and then more strongly in the 1880s, British publishing firms had been setting up agencies and branches in Sydney and Melbourne. The understandable object was to profit as much as possible from the expanding market in the Australian colonies. Wholesaling firms like George Robertson & Co. were already under some pressure in the 1880s. By the end of the century the Net Book Agreement consolidated British control of the ways in which books were distributed and at what price, generally in advance of the London-equivalent rates that were offered, at least in the major cities, in the 1870s. The process was gradual, but 1890 can be seen as a tipping point. Outside Melbourne, the Australian population had continued to grow — with difficulties and uncertainties about the Indigenous component — to 3 772 583 by 1901. The discovery of gold in Western Australia contributed to this movement and to a greater role of that colony in the future nation's affairs.

The 1870s and 1880s had brought to Australia a number of important technological innovations. The cable link with Europe from 1872 hardly needs to be stressed in its contribution to rapid receipt of selected items of news. The telephone and the typewriter had appeared in the 1870s and made rapid advances towards the end of the century. Linotype, invented by Mergenthaler in the 1880s, was in regular production by 1890 and used in Australia from 1894. By reducing the number of hand compositors, it made huge changes in the printing industry. Cinema, eagerly taken up by Australians, had begun its incursion by the end of the decade. Sound recording was also being developed, to the point where Nellie Melba was one of the first major singers to embrace it, as early as 1904. Change was continuous in the second half of the 1800s, but 1890 can be seen without too much exaggeration as a watershed.

The latest inventions provided over time new ways of tapping into omnipresent oral culture. This stream was not absent from print. Popular Penny Readings had a clear connection with published literature. However, public lectures, speeches on the hustings, parliamentary debates, transcripts of evidence, sermons, theatrical performances and formal reports on enquiries could all be recorded in or related to printed texts. Some of them, well before 1890, were staples of the massive output of government presses or quite frequently produced by small publishers throughout the colonies. In this way some chosen community voices were heard. Eventually the innovations trialled in the 1890s were to bring many more of them into an accessible form.

The surge of Sydney's population in the 1890s aligned that city with Melbourne. Its opening to the Pacific, the Bohemian culture of which the *Bulletin* was one vehicle alongside its promotion of Bush myths, a stronger multicultural presence, witness the creation in 1892 of *Le Courrier Australien*, the expansion of a University enriched by the Challis Bequest, these were all signs of changes in the intellectual climate. Victoria and Queensland shared in this evolution, which had as its backdrop a growing national consciousness. Organised labour, soon to have substantial political representation, was a central element. All of this was reflected in the newspaper press, in magazines and in bookshops of a socialist or anarchist bent. The Melbourne Verein Vorwärts, meeting in the Turn Verein Building in Latrobe Street, offered a Continental European variant on the theme. Overall the flourishing of political, muckraking and sporting papers, not unknown before 1890, contributed to the different flavour of the century's last decade. The variety and the contradictions underline the difficulty of attempting a simplistic characterisation of Australianness.

There was much that was crudely materialistic and rawly uncaring about things of the mind in this society. Strident nationalism seemed to leave little room for nuance in some popular publications. However, as the universities emerged from a weakness that encouraged the rich to continue sending their sons to Oxford and Cambridge, other points of view became clearer. Women, after all, had begun to have full access to higher education in the 1880s and even to the franchise in South Australia and Western Australia before Federation. Two very large cities, in world terms, had to be the guarantee of a diversity of attitudes that went as far as sophistication and refinement in some quarters. Not that other less populous colonies did not share in this sort of quality in their élite, who could live in country towns as well as in the capitals. Separate centres of administration ensured, and continue to ensure, emulation and aspiration in all fields. The colonies went on being well served by their best journalists in this respect.

The extent to which the dismissive judgments of patronising visitors could be wrong can be illustrated in two examples from the 1880s. In July 1885 *Mullen's Monthly Circular* pointed out that the *Argus* and the *Australasian* had already published substantial critical articles on the Revised Edition of the Bible whereas nothing as exhaustive 'had as yet appeared in the British journals'. On 16 June 1888 the second editorial of the *Australasian* on English fears of a new Napoleon in the form of General Boulanger remarked, with perhaps the merest tinge of irony:

> The intelligent spectator who contemplates the old world from the armchair of Antipodean superiority is occasionally tempted to levity over the European situation.

The periphery could allow itself to make adult and informed critiques of the centre, something that can be demonstrated in other fields as well. Let us draw the conclusion that by 1890 the Australian print world had come of age.

Notes on Contributors

Sally Bloomfield BA (Hons), Dip Ed (UTAS); Grad Dip Lib (CCAE). Librarian (retired) and family historian. Research interests in Tasmanian history and colonial printing and publishing. Descended from Andrew Bent and Mary Kirk through their second daughter Catherine Hall (1820–1902).

Dennis Bryans was born at Ballarat, Victoria, and received a State School education. After full-time studies at the Ballarat School of Mines his career path led to television set design and then teaching graphic design, a BA and PhD. From 1995 he began writing articles about Australian printing history, first on the subject of Australian typefounding, but later on the broader topics of printing technologies, indexing and bibliography. In 2001 he published *Southern Invasion, Northern Conquest*, then books on local, sporting history, and family histories, and is author of *A Survey of Australian Type Founders' Specimens* (2014).

Tony Cavanagh was originally a metallurgist, After working in Birmingham then Geelong he lectured at the Gordon Institute of Technology (later the Engineering School, Deakin University, Geelong). After its closure he transferred to Deakin's library and retrained in librarianship at Monash University. His fascination with botanical history and a course in book-trade history made him aware of the Victorian Government Printer's role in producing non-Parliamentary material for botanists including Ferdinand von Mueller. The recognition that government printshops were often the only colonial facilities capable of high quality, complex printing using the latest printing techniques, often required to print almost anything necessary for the functioning of the settlement, led to the development of his *HOBA* 1 chapter.

Craig Collins LLB/BEc (ANU), LLM (Melb), GradCertHigherEd (NE), Australian Lawyer (Victoria 1992), specialised in defamation law as a litigation partner at Gadens Lawyers Melbourne. He has performed academic roles at the Australian National University and University of New England and is presently Deputy Director, Education Delivery at Leo Cussen Centre for Law. He is descended from Andrew and Mary Bent through Andrew Bent Jr (b. 1824) – who worked for some decades as printing foreman at the *Geelong Advertiser.*

Thomas A. Darragh worked at Museum Victoria, formerly National Museum of Victoria, as a Curator in invertebrate palaeontology and in administration from 1965 to 2001. On retirement he was appointed Curator Emeritus. He has had a long-standing interest in the history of the natural sciences, particularly geology, in Victoria, and in the people involved in engraving and lithography in nineteenth-century Victoria. He has also carried out research on nineteenth-century German scientists and intellectuals in Victoria and is one of the editors of the Ferdinand von Mueller Correspondence. *Engravers and Lithographers in Colonial Victoria: A Directory* (2023) is his most recent publication.

Judy Donnelly was Project Manager for a *History of the Book in Canada/Histoire du livre et de l'imprimé au Canada* (2002–2007), and Director and Co-editor of *Historical Perspectives on Canadian Publishing*, https://digitalcollections.mcmaster.ca/historical-perspectives-canadian-publishing. She completed a Master of Library & Information Science at the University of Toronto, studying under Patricia Lockhart Fleming, and has written about Canadian almanacs and print culture. After moving to Melbourne, she worked as an archivist/historian and editor prior to joining *HOBA* 1.

Raelene Frances is Emeritus Professor of History at the Australian National University. She has been writing labour history for over four decades and is currently the President of the Australian Society for the Study of Labour History. Her research on workers in the printing industries has appeared in journal articles and book chapters and in her prize-winning book, *The Politics of Work: Gender and Labour in Victoria: Case Studies of Three Victorian Industries, 1880–1939* (1993).

Stephen James Herrin was formerly Rare Book Librarian at Monash University. In the 1990s he was the Melbourne research assistant for *HOBA*. Both his theses for Monash University's Graduate School of Librarianship were on the history of printing in Australia. The first was published under the title *The Development of Printing in Nineteenth-Century Ballarat* (2000).

†R. Ian Jack (1935–2019) came to the University of Sydney from Britain in 1961 to lecture in medieval history. At the end of his career he was Associate Professor of History and had served for a time as Dean of the Faculty of Arts. By then he had turned to research and publication in areas of heritage, local history and historical archaeology applied to industrial sites. In retirement he was associated with St Andrew's College at the University of Sydney as Archivist and Librarian. He was President of the Royal Australian Historical Society from 2003 to 2010.

David J. Jones MA (Oxon) Dip Lib PhD (UNSW) FALIA, worked at the State Library of NSW, coordinating its recent building project and consulting on library projects in Australia and overseas, including Pustaka Negeri Sarawak in Kuching, Malaysia. He has been an interviewer for the National Library of Australia, Pustaka Negeri Sarawak and the National Trust of Australia (NSW). A Fellowship of the Australian Library and Information Association in 2003 was followed by its H. C. L. Anderson Award in 2017. That year the Library Council of New South Wales presented him with the Ifould Medal.

Wallace Kirsop is an Affiliate in the School of Languages, Literatures, Cultures and Linguistics at Monash University, where he taught French from 1962 to 1998. His research and publications are in the fields of physical bibliography and book history (*ancien régime* France and nineteenth-century Australia). Since 2010 he has been the Publisher of the Ancora Press.

Carol Mills was formerly Director of the Wagga Wagga Campus Library, Charles Sturt University. Her publications in bibliography and book history include the *Bibliography of the Northern Territory* (1977–1983) and *The New South Wales Bookstall Company as a Publisher* (1991).

Ian Morrison has worked as a librarian at state and university libraries in Victoria and Tasmania. He is a member of the Tasmanian working group for the *Australian Dictionary of Biography*. His publications include *Australian Almanacs 1806–1930: A Bibliography*, with Maureen Perkins and Tracey Caulfield (2003), and contributions to *The Oxford Companion to the Book,* edited by Michael F. Suarez and H. R. Woudhuysen (2010). His current projects include a reconstruction of the book collection willed to the Tasmanian Public Library by James Ebenezer Bicheno in 1851. He lives on the fringe of the Hobart CBD, not far from the final Hobart premises of Birchalls.

Maureen Perkins is the author of *Visions of the Future: Almanacs, Time, and Cultural Change 1775–1870* (1996) and *The Reform of Time: Magic and Modernity* (2001). She is the foundation and current editor of the Routledge literature journal *Life Writing*.

†Jeffrey Prentice (1940–2017), a long-time member of the book trade and a keenly purposeful collector, had a particular interest in and activity around children's books. This was reflected in various posts he occupied and in his many publications, for example, *The Little Bookroom: Fifty Years with Children's Books* (2010), his very substantial introduction to John Percy Holroyd, *The Australian Book Trade: A Bookseller's Contribution to its History* (2015), and the collection *Australian Children's Literature: Finding a Voice* (2016).

Graeme Skinner is an Australian music historian, author of the biography *Peter Sculthorpe: The Making of An Australian Composer* (2007; 2015), curator of *Australharmony*, an online resource toward the early history of music in colonial Australia, https://www.sydney.edu.au/paradisec/australharmony, and currently an Honorary Associate in musicology, Sydney Conservatorium of Music, University of Sydney.

Leonie Stevens is a novelist and ethnographic historian. Born on Wurundjeri land (Melbourne), she is descended from Irish and German settlers. She is the author of six novels, including *Nature Strip* and *The Marowack Two*, a range of short fiction, and has edited two anthologies. Her most recent book, based on her PhD thesis, is *Me Write Myself: The Free Aboriginal Inhabitants of Van Diemen's Land at Wybalenna* (2017). She is a Research Fellow at Monash Indigenous Studies Centre.

Clive Turner was formerly an Associate Professor of Law at the Law School, the University of Queensland. After graduating in law at the University of Birmingham (UK), he completed a PhD in the Department of Law, Research School of Social Sciences, Institute of Advanced Studies, Australian National University. He subsequently lectured in Commercial Law and Intellectual Property (including Copyright) at the University of Adelaide and Queensland University and conducted a course on International Intellectual Property Law at Marquette University, Milwaukee, Wisconsin, USA. He is joint author (with Dr John Trone) of *Australian Commercial Law*, 34th ed. (2023).

†**Penny van Toorn** (1952–2016), with degrees from the University of Sydney and the University of British Columbia, taught English in both institutions. Her work on Indigenous Australia was informed by experiences in the two countries. The collection of her papers in *Writing Never Arrives Naked: Early Aboriginal cultures of writing in Australia* (2006), demonstrates the reach and the quality of a career cut short.

†**Elizabeth Webby,** (1942–2023) spent all her tertiary teaching life at the University of Sydney, finishing up as Professor of Australian Literature. Her many publications, by no means all of them strictly relevant to book history, were of substance. The flow continued until her last two years of severe illness. She edited *Southerly* for more than a decade and later performed a similar role for the Australian Academy of the Humanities. *HOBA* 1 has benefited from the same skill and devotion to duty.

Susan Woodburn is a former archivist and Special Collections Librarian at the University of Adelaide and Manuscript Librarian at the National Library of Australia. Her interest in printing ventures, the Pacific Islands and colonial Australian history developed from custodianship of and private research into the rich collections of those institutions, further stimulated by professional association with colleagues through the Bibliographical Society of Australia and New Zealand.

List of Illustrations

Chapter 2: Printing Technology

Playbill: *Jane Shore*, Sydney, George Hughes, 1796. National Library of Australia. Bib ID: 4200235. Call no. RBRS N686.2099441 F692.

Photograph: Printing works of the *Border Post and Stannum Miner*, Stanthorpe, QLD, 1872. State Library of QLD. Negative no. 189991. Record no. 99183507692602061.

Wood engraving: Victory Rotary Press, *Illustrated Australian News*, 10 June 1878, p. 104. Melbourne, Ebenezer and David Syme, 1878. State Library Victoria. Accession no. IAN 10/06/78/104.

Chapter 3: Australian Print Workers to 1890

Photograph: Sewers' room, NSW Government Printing Office, c. 1890. State Archives & Records Authority of NSW; State Library of NSW. From 'Photographs of New South Wales Government Printing office, Sydney, c. 1871–1910 and Ultimo Office, 1959', Album Call no. PXD 792, Image 21. File Identifier pKyPbRMlM215X.

Chapter 4: Illustrations

Lithograph: F. McCoy. *Ranoidea aurea* in *Natural History of Victoria. Prodromus of the Zoology of Victoria; or, Figures and Descriptions of the living Species of all Classes of the Victorian Indigenous Animals*. Plate 53. Melbourne: Government Printer, 1881. Private collection.

Nature print: F. M. Bailey. *Lygodium reticulatum* in *Lithograms of the Ferns of Queensland*. Plate 7. Brisbane, Department of Agriculture, 1892. State Botanical Collection, Library, Royal Botanic Gardens, Melbourne. Call no. 587.309943 LIT.

Chapter 5: Australian Colonial Binding

Photograph: Worker, NSW Government Printing Office, c. 1890. State Archives & Records Authority of NSW; State Library of NSW. From 'Photographs of New South Wales Government Printing office, Sydney, c. 1871–1910 and Ultimo Office, 1959', Album. Call no. PXD 792, Image 18. File Identifier IX63da6zD7GVK.

Chapter 6: Paper in Nineteenth-Century Australian Publications

Photograph: Woman sorting rags at Barwon Paper Mills, c. 1880. J. H. (John Henry) Harvey, photographer. State Library Victoria. Accession no. H90.161/86, Record ID 9917556473607636.

Chapter 7: Colonial Type; Imported and Australian Made

Type specimen: Wm. Joseph Sayers Clarke, *Port Phillip Herald*, 29 April, 1845, p. 1. Melbourne, George Cavenagh, 1845. State Library Victoria. RARENSL-Melbourne-Reel no. 2 (14 Jan 1842-30 Dec 1843).

Title-page: L. E. Threlkeld, *A Key to the Structure of the Aboriginal Language*, Sydney, L.E. Threlkeld, 1850. National Library of Australia. https://nla.gov.au:443/tarkine/nla.obj-222915774 Image 5. [retrieved 7 August 2023].

Chapter 9: The Beginnings of Australian Publishing

Advertisement: J. Walch & Sons in *Tasmania Illustrated with Photographs*, Hobart, 1880. Tasmanian Archives. Agency no. NG 143. Series no. LPIC13. Item no. LPIC13/1/1.

Handbill: 'Mr Barnes of New York', 'Mystery of a Hansom Cab' and 'Lost in London', Bowen QLD, *Bowen Observer*, 1889. State Library Victoria. Call no. H81.287/81.

Chapter 10: The Significance of Colonial and Imperial Copyright

Cover: Charles Dickens, *The Posthumous Papers of the Pickwick Club*, no. 8, Launceston, Dowling, 1838. State Library Victoria. Call no. RARELT 823.83P. Record ID 99238053607636.

Chapter 11: 'The Land of Newspapers'

Lithographed sketch: S.T. Gill, 'Interior of John Alloo's Restaurant', Ballarat in *The Diggers and Diggings of Victoria as they are in 1855*, Melbourne, James J. Blundell & Co. 1855. State Library Victoria. 14.8 x 24.3 cm. Record ID: 1675453. Call no. PCLTFBOX; GILL DIGGERS 1.

Photograph: Exterior of *Argus* Newspaper & General Machine Printing Office, Gulgong, NSW, 1870–1875. Mitchell Library, State Library of NSW. Holtermann Collection, American and Australasian Photographic Company 1870–1875 ON 4/Box 1/no. 18137.

Case Study: Andrew Bent — Father of the Free Press

Masthead: *Hobart Town Gazette and Van Diemen's Land Advertiser*, 8 October 1824, p. 1. Hobart, Andrew Bent, 1824. Mitchell Library, State Library of NSW. Call no. F351.73/1, bound volume for 1824.

Chapter 12: Magazines

Cartoon: *Melbourne Punch*, 2 August 1855, p. 160. East Melbourne, Melbourne Punch, 1855. State Library of NSW. Call no. QA 827/ M4.v.1

Cartoon: *The Bulletin*, 19 June 1880, p. 9. Sydney, John Haynes and J.F. Archibald, 1880. State Library of NSW. Record ID: 74VvxjgzJ0qA.

Chapter 13: Bookselling

Photograph: Charles Platts's book and stationery shop, Adelaide, c. 1866. State Library of SA. Image B 1875. Acre 47 Collection.

Catalogue cover: *Catalogue of Books New and Old*. Melbourne, A. J. Smith, [1862], 28 pp; 21 cm. State Library Victoria. Call no. RARELT 010.4 B47. Record ID: 995940533607636.

Chapter 14: Australia's Public Libraries in Their Infancy

Photograph: Queen's Hall, Melbourne Public Library, 1859. Barnett Johnstone, photographer. State Library Victoria. Call no. PCLTAF 485 F.6. Record ID 9917228773607636.

Photograph: interior of Free Public Library, Sydney. Dixson Library, State Library of New South Wales. From album 'Photographs of New South Wales [1879-c.1891]', Sydney, Government Printing Office [1879-c. 1891]. Call no. DL PXX 63, Image 41.

Photograph: Adelaide Public Library, Museum and Art Gallery (now Mortlock Wing), c. 1885. Samuel White Sweet, photographer. State Library of SA. Call no. Public Library B 3720.

Chapter 15: Mechanics' Institutes

Photograph: Swan River Mechanics' Hall, 1861. Alfred Hawes Stone, photographer. State Library of Western Australia. Call no. 6923B/175.

Chapter 16: Commercial Circulating Libraries

Advertisement: T. M. Buzzard's Melbourne Circulating Library, in *Tanner's Melbourne Directory for 1859*. Melbourne, John Tanner, 1859. Private collection.

Chapter 17: Private Libraries

Catalogue: Book auction, library of Rev. Jas. Maughan, 16 May 1871. Adelaide, Parr & Luxmoore, 1871. Private collection.

Chapter 18: The Print Culture of Colonial Music from its Beginnings

Sheet music, J. H. Anderson, *The Lays of the Hebrews*, Sydney, F. Ellard, [1844]. Mitchell Library, State Library of NSW. Mitchell Sheet Music, MUSIC FILE/AND, Call no. 786.218992.

Chapter 19: Textbooks

Title-page: George and Alexander Sutherland, *The History of Australia from 1606 to 1876*, Melbourne, George Robertson, 1877. Monash University Library. Rare General Collection. Call no. Matheson 994 S966H.

Chapter 20: Australian Directories to 1890

Almanac cover: *Western Australian Almanack and Directory*, 2nd ed., Perth, Stirling, Sholl & Co., 1865. State Library of Western Australia. https://purl.slwa.wa.gov.au/slwa_b2072512_174 [accessed 24 April 2024].

Chapter 21: Australian Almanacs 1806–1890

Almanac: 'Hat almanac', Hobart, T. Browne, 1849. State Library of Tasmania. Call no. TL PQ 919.46 BRO.

Chapter 22: Australian Printing and Publishing in Pacific Islands and Indigenous Australian Languages 1814-1900

Title-page: J. G. Paton, transl. *Markus: Ta Fasao Erefia Iesu Kristo*, Melbourne, British Foreign and Bible Society (Melbourne Auxiliary), 1877. Mitchell Library, State Library of NSW. Call no. DSM/226.3/6A1.

Chapter 23: Official Printing

Title-page: G. A. Tucker, *Lunacy in Many Lands*, Sydney, Charles Potter, Government Printer, 1887. State Library Victoria. Call no. S 362.2 T79.

Chapter 24: After the 'toil of the long day': Reading in Colonial Australia

Photograph: Man reading newspaper in a Gympie garden, c. 1871. Edward H. Forster, photographer. State Library of Queensland. https://hdl.handle.net/10462/deriv/84275 [accessed 24 April 2024].

Photograph: Two boys reading in a garden, Sydney c. 1879–1882. [John Rae?], photographer. State Library of NSW. Call no. P1/2039.

Photograph: Hamilton Literary Society, 1889. Tasmanian Archives. Archives Series no. NS3688/1/1.

List of Abbreviations

AARL: *Australian Academic and Research Libraries*
ADB: *Australian Dictionary of Biography*
ALJ: *Australian Library Journal*
ANL: National Library of Australia. See also NLA.
ANU: Australian National University
BL: British Library
BLRCA Forum, 1984: Books, Libraries and Readers in Colonial Australia: Papers from the Forum on Australian Colonial Library History held at Monash University 1-2 June 1984
BSANZ: *Bulletin of the Bibliographical Society of Australia and New Zealand*
CUP: Cambridge University Press
JAHS: *Journal and Proceedings of the Australian Historical Society*. Became *JRAHS*.
JAPHS: *Journal of the Australian Printing Historical Society*
JRAHS: *Journal and Proceedings of the Royal Australian Historical Society*, formerly *JAHS*
LTJ: *La Trobe Journal*
LTLJ: *La Trobe Library Journal*
Monash UP: Monash University Publishing
MTS: Melbourne Typographical Society
MUP: Melbourne University Press
NHH: Museums of History NSW, Caroline Simpson Library & Research Collection, Historic Houses Trust of New South Wales
NLA: National Library of Australia (this form retained when call numbers are cited)
NSL: State Library of New South Wales
OUP: Oxford University Press
UQP: University of Queensland Press
PKIU: Printing and Kindred Industries Union
PBSA: *Papers of the Bibliographical Society of America*
QSL: State Library of Queensland
SLV: State Library Victoria (see also VSL)
SMH: *Sydney Morning Herald*
SSL: State Library of South Australia
SUP: Sydney University Press
TSL: Libraries Tasmania
UNSW: University of New South Wales
UQP: University of Queensland Press
VHJ: *Victorian Historical Journal*
VSL: State Library Victoria

Select Bibliography

The notes on sources provided at the end of each chapter offer a more comprehensive guide to the fields covered in the present volume than the following list. Essentially the select bibliography proposes a choice of separately published and accessible monographs with a limited number of online databases, significant journal articles and unpublished theses Many standard sources such as Ferguson have been digitised in recent years. The emphasis is on secondary works and on guides to sources, with no attempt to set out the vast extent of primary documents, notably in newspapers, manuscript collections and archives of all kinds. It is recognised that some of the works cited need updating in ways suggested in the various chapters. However, pending the new research our authors aspire to encourage, the existing serious literature has to be known and respected. It will be obvious that some subjects have received a lot more attention than others.

W.K.

Bibliographies and guides to sources

Adelaide, Debra, *Bibliography of Australian Women's Literature 1795–1990: A Listing of Fiction, Poetry, Drama and Non-Fiction*, Port Melbourne, D. W. Thorpe / Clayton, VIC, National Centre for Australian Studies, Monash University, 1991.

Arnold, John and John Hay, eds, *The Bibliography of Australian Literature*, Kew, VIC, Australian Scholarly Publishing, then St Lucia, QLD, UQP, 2001–2008, 4 vols.

———, and Terence O'Neill, *The Bibliography of Australian Literature Supplement*, Clayton, VIC, Monash University Publishing, 2022.

Austlit: The Resource for Australian Literature [www.austlit.edu.au]

Australian Dictionary of Biography, Carlton, VIC, MUP, 1966–2012, 18 volumes and *Index to volumes 1–12 & Supplement 1580–1980*. Online: https://adb.anu.edu.au/ [accessed 24 April 2024]

Borchardt, D. H., *Australian Bibliography: A Guide to Printed Sources of Information*, 3rd ed., Sydney, Pergamon, 1976.

———, ed., *Australian Official Publications*, Melbourne, Longman Cheshire, 1979.

———, with Victor Crittenden, eds, *Australians: A Guide to Sources*, Sydney, Fairfax, Syme & Weldon Associates, 1987.

Castles, Alex C., *Annotated Bibliography of Printed Materials on Australian Law 1788–1900*, Sydney, The Law Book Company Limited, 1994.

Ferguson, John Alexander, *Bibliography of Australia*, Sydney, Angus and Robertson, 1941–1969, 7 vols (reprint NLA, 1975), and *Addenda 1784–1850*, Canberra, NLA, 1986.

Ford, Edward, *Bibliography of Australian Medicine 1790–1900*, Sydney, SUP, 1976.

Gibbney, H. J. and Ann G. Smith, *A Biographical Register 1788–1939: Notes from the Name Index of the Australian Dictionary of Biography*, Canberra, ADB, 1987, 2 vols.

Herrin, Stephen, 'Sources for the History of the Book Located in the State Library of Victoria', *LTLJ*, no.59, Autumn 1997, pp. 15–26.

Kirsop, Wallace, 'The Literature on the History of the Book in Australia: A Survey', *Reference Australia*, no.7, July 1991, pp. 35–73.

Liberman, Serge, *The Bibliography of Australasian Judaica 1788–2008*, 3rd ed., Melbourne, Hybrid Publishers, 2011.

Macartney, Frederick T., *Australian Literature, a Bibliography to 1938 by E. Morris Miller, M.A., Litt. D. extended to 1950*, Sydney, Angus and Robertson, 1956.

Miller, E. Morris, *Australian Literature from its Beginnings to 1935 with Subsidiary Entries to 1938*, Carlton, VIC, MUP, 1940, 2 vols (reprint Sydney, SUP, 1973).

Morrison, Ian, *The Publishing Industry in Colonial Australia: A Name Index to John Alexander Ferguson's* Bibliography of Australia 1784–1900, Melbourne, BSANZ, 1996.

Muir, Marcie, *Australian Children's Books: A Bibliography, Volume One 1774–1972*, Carlton, VIC, MUP, 1992.

SouthHem, *Book Catalogues of the Colonial Southern Hemisphere* (BCCSH database), 2017. Website and digital archive. www.ucd.ie/southhem [accessed 24 April 2024]

Stuart, Lurline, *Australian Periodicals with Literary Content 1821–1925: An Annotated Bibliography*, Melbourne, Australian Scholarly Publishing, 2003.

Vamplew, Wray, ed., *Australians: Historical Statistics*, Sydney, Fairfax, Syme & Weldon Associates, 1987.

Webby, Elizabeth, *Early Australian Poetry: An Annotated Bibliography of Original Poems Published in Australian Newspapers, Magazines & Almanacks Before 1850*, Sydney, Hale & Iremonger, 1982.

General studies

Borchardt, D. H. and W. Kirsop, eds, *The Book in Australia: Essays Towards a Cultural & Social History*, Melbourne, Australian Reference Publications, 1988.

Green, H. M., *A History of Australian Literature Pure and Applied*, Sydney, Angus and Robertson, 1961, 2 vols.

Heath, Deana, *Purifying Empire: Obscenity and the Politics of Moral Regulation in Britain, India and Australia*, Cambridge, CUP, 2010.

Holroyd, John Percy, *The Australian Book Trade: A Bookseller's Contribution to Its History*, introduction by Jeff Prentice, Melbourne, Braidwood Press, 2015.

Johnston, Anna, *The Antipodean Laboratory: Making Colonial Knowledge, 1770–1870*, Cambridge, CUP, 2023.

Kirsop, Wallace, *Towards a History of the Australian Book Trade*, Sydney, Wentworth Books, 1969.

———, *Books for Colonial Readers — The Nineteenth-Century Australian Experience*, Melbourne, BSANZ, 1995.

Nadel, George, *Australia's Colonial Culture: Ideas, Men and Institutions in Mid-Nineteenth-Century Eastern Australia*, Melbourne, F. W. Cheshire, 1957.

Richards, Michael, *People, Print & Paper: A Catalogue of a Travelling Exhibition Celebrating the Books of Australia, 1788–1988*, Canberra, NLA, 1988.

Wantrup, Jonathan, *Australian Rare Books 1788–1900*, Potts Point NSW, Hordern House, 1987.

———, *Australian Rare Books 1788–1900*, 2nd ed. rev. and enlarged, Armadale, VIC, Australian Book Auctions, 2023, 2 vols.

Webby, Elizabeth, Literature and the Reading Public in Australia, 1800–1850, PhD thesis, University of Sydney, 1971.

Wilson, Ian J., *Collecting Old Tasmanian Books*, Melbourne, Boobook Press, 2010.

Chapter 1: A Book by Any Other Name? Towards a Social History of the Book in Aboriginal Australia

Finlay, Grant, *'Good people always crackney in heaven.' Mythic Conversations in Lutruwita/Tasmania*, Hobart, Fullers Publishing, 2019.

Heiss, Anita and Peter Minter, eds, [Nicholas Jose, gen. ed.], *Macquarie PEN Anthology of Aboriginal Literature*, Crows Nest, NSW, Allen & Unwin, 2008.

Stevens, Leonie, *'Me Write Myself': The Free Aboriginal Inhabitants of Van Diemen's Land at Wybalenna, 1832–47*, Clayton, VIC, Monash University Publishing, 2017.

van Toorn, Penny, *Writing Never Arrives Naked: Early Aboriginal Cultures of Writing in Australia*, Canberra, Aboriginal Studies Press, 2006.

Chapter 2: Printing Technology & Chapter 3: Australian Print Workers to 1890

Coupe, Sheena, *W. C. Penfold, Printer and Stationer, 1830-1980*, Kingsgrove, NSW, W. C. Penfold & Co., 1980.

Darragh, Thomas A., *Printer and Newspaper Registration in Victoria 1838-1924*, Wellington, NZ, Elibank Press, 1997.

Degotardi, Johann Nepomuk, *The Art of Printing (Sydney, 1861)*, 2 vols, Sydney, Brandywine Press, 1982.

Eckersall, Kenneth Eric, *Young Caxton: A History of the Aims in Printing Education in Melbourne 1870-1970*, North Melbourne, Melbourne College of Printing and Graphic Arts, 1980.

Finkelstein, David, *Movable Types: Roving Creative Printers of the Victorian World*, Oxford, OUP, 2018.

Fitzgerald, R. T., *The Printers of Melbourne: A History of a Union*, Melbourne, Pitman & Sons, in association with PKIU, 1967.

Fletcher, John, *John Degotardi: Printer, Publisher and Photographer*, Sydney, Book Collectors' Society of Australia, 1984.

Frances, Raelene, *The Politics of Work: Gender and Labour in Victoria 1880-1939*, Cambridge, CUP, 1993.

Hagan, James, *Printers and Politics: A History of the Australian Printing Unions 1850-1950*, Canberra, ANU Press in association with PKIU, 1966.

Hauser, Don, *Printers of the Streets and Lanes of Melbourne (1837-1975)*, Melbourne, The Nondescript Press, 2006.

Herrin, Stephen J., *The Development of Printing in Nineteenth-Century Ballarat*, Melbourne, BSANZ, 2000.

———, Printers and Printing in Australia to the Early Twentieth Century: Personal and Business Pursuits, PhD thesis, Monash University, 2004.

Hunt, Harold, *The Master Printers of Sydney: The Story of The Printing and Allied Trades Employers' Association of New South Wales, 1887-1971*, Sydney, PATEA NSW, 1976.

Kwasitsu, Lishi, Printing and the Book and Newspaper Press in Bendigo, PhD thesis, Monash University, 1989.

Marsh, Peter, *The Fawkner Press: Unravelling the Images*, Emerald Hill, Kitchen Table Press, 2018.

Chapter 4: Illustrations

Butler, Roger, *Printed Images in Colonial Australia 1801-1901*, Canberra, National Gallery of Australia, 2007.

Carroll, Alison, *Graven Images in the Promised Land: A History of Printmaking in South Australia 1836-1981*, Adelaide, Art Gallery of South Australia, 1981.

Craig, Clifford, *The Engravers of Van Diemen's Land*, Launceston, Tasmanian Historical Research Association, 1961.

———, *Old Tasmanian Prints*, Launceston, Foot & Playsted, 1964.

———, *More Old Tasmanian Prints*, Launceston, Foot & Playsted, 1984.

Darragh, Thomas A., *The Establishment and Development of Engraving and Lithography in Melbourne to the Time of the Gold Rush*, Willow Bend, Thumb Creek, NSW, Garravembi Press, 1990.

———, *Engravers and Lithographers in Colonial Victoria: A Directory*, Melbourne, Ancora Press, 2023.

Finney, Vanessa, *Transformations: Harriet and Helena Scott, Colonial Sydney's Finest Natural History Painters*, Sydney, NewSouth, 2018.

Holden, Robert, *Photography in Colonial Australia. The Mechanical Eye and the Illustrated Book*. Sydney, Hordern House, 1988.

Kerr, Joan, ed. *Dictionary of Australian Artists: Painters, Sketchers, Photographers and Engravers to 1870*, Melbourne, OUP, 1992.

Mahood, Marguerite, *The Loaded Line: Australian Political Caricature, 1788–1901*, Carlton, VIC, MUP, 1973.

Chapter 5: Australian Colonial Binding

Marsh, Peter, *Bookbinding Tools for the Government Printing Office of Victoria*, Melbourne, [the author], 2016.

Chapter 6: Paper in Nineteenth-Century Australian Publications

Rawson, Jacqueline, A History of the Australian Paper Making Industry, MA thesis, University of Melbourne, 1953.

Romanov-Hughes, Alexander, *Papermaking in Australasia to 1900*, 2017. Website. [As of May 2024, the URL of this website was no longer supported by its original host. The site could still be found by searching the author's name and website title.]

Sinclair, E. K., *The Spreading Tree: A History of APM and AMCOR, 1844–1989*, Sydney, Allen & Unwin, 1991.

Chapter 7: Colonial Type: Imported and Australian Made

Bryans, Dennis, *A Survey of Australian Typefounders' Specimens*, Blackburn South, VIC, Golden Point Press, 2014.

Chapter 8: 'The laurels in the pit were won': Authorship in Colonial Australia

Ackland, Michael, *Henry Kendall: The Man and the Myths*, Melbourne, MUP, 1995.

Carter, David and Roger Osborne, *Australian Books and Authors in the American Marketplace, 1840s–1960s*, Sydney, SUP, 2018.

Clarke, Patricia, *Pen Portraits: Women Writers and Journalists in Nineteenth-Century Australia*, Sydney, Allen & Unwin, 1988.

———, *Rosa! Rosa! A Life of Rosa Praed, Novelist and Spiritualist*, Melbourne, MUP, 1999.

Hergenhan, Laurie, gen. ed., *The Penguin New Literary History of Australia*, Ringwood, VIC, Penguin, 1988.

Stuart, Lurline, *James Smith. The Making of a Colonial Culture*, Sydney, Allen & Unwin, 1989.

Sussex, Lucy, ed., *The Fortunes of Mary Fortune*, Ringwood, VIC, Penguin Books, 1989.

Tiffin, Chris and Lynette Baer, *The Praed Papers*, Brisbane, The Library Board of Queensland, 1994.

Chapter 9: The Beginnings of Australian Publishing

Broinowski, Richard, *Under the Rainbow: The Life and Times of E. W. Cole*, Carlton, VIC, Miegunyah Press, 2020.

Clark, Laurel, *F. F. Baillière: Publisher in Ordinary, Publisher Extraordinary*, Canberra, Mulini Press, 2004.

Craig, Clifford, *The Van Diemen's Land Edition of the Pickwick Papers*, Hobart, Cat & Fiddle Press, 1973.

Holroyd, John, *George Robertson of Melbourne, 1825–1898: Pioneer Bookseller & Publisher*, Melbourne, Robertson & Mullens, 1968.

Hughes-d'Aeth, Tony, *Paper Nation: The Story of the Picturesque Atlas of Australasia, 1886–1888*, Carlton, VIC, MUP, 2001.

Robb, Gwenda, *George Howe: Australia's First Publisher*, Kew, VIC, Australian Scholarly Publishing, 2003.

Sussex, Lucy, *Blockbuster!: Fergus Hume and the Mystery of a Hansom Cab*, Melbourne, Text, 2015.

Chapter 10: Colonial and Imperial Copyright Law to 1890

Cantrell, Leon, ed., *Bards, Bohemians, and Bookmen: Essays in Australian Literature*, St Lucia, QLD, UQP, 1976.

Nowell-Smith, Simon, *International Copyright Law and the Publisher in the Reign of Queen Victoria*, Oxford, Clarendon Press, 1968.

Ricketson, Sam, *The Berne Convention for the Protection of Literary and Artistic Works: 1886–1986*, London, Centre for Commercial Law Studies and Kluwer, 1987.

Chapter 11: 'The Land of Newspapers'

Australian Newspaper History Group Newsletter, eds Victor Isaacs, then Rod Kirkpatrick, October 1999 to date.

Blair, Sandy, Newspapers and their Readers in early Eastern Australia. The *Sydney Gazette* and its contemporaries, 1803–1842, PhD thesis, UNSW, 1990.

Bloomfield, Sally and Craig Collins, *Andrew Bent: Father of the Free Press in Australia*, 2018. Website: andrew-bent-life [accessed 2 May 2023]

Bode, Katherine, *A World of Fiction: Digital Collections and the Future of Literary History*. Ann Arbor, University of Michigan Press, 2018.

———— and Carol Hetherington, eds, 'To Be Continued ...': The Australian Newspaper Fiction Database, 2017. Website: readallaboutit.com.au [accessed 20 August 2023]

Cryle, Denis, *The Press in Colonial Queensland: A Social and Political History 1845–1875*, St Lucia, QLD, UQP, 1989.

———— ed., *Disreputable Profession: Journalists and Journalism in Colonial Australia*, Rockhampton, Central Queensland University Press, 1997.

Curthoys, Ann and Julianne Schultz, eds, *Journalism: Print Politics and Popular Culture*, St Lucia, QLD, UQP, 1999.

Ferguson, J. A., Mrs A. G. Foster and H. M. Green, *The Howes and their Press*, Sydney, Sunnybrook Press, 1936.

Gilson, Miriam and Jerzy Zubrzycki, *The Foreign-language Press in Australia 1848–1964*, Canberra, ANU Press, 1967.

Griffen-Foley, Bridget, ed., *A Companion to the Australian Media*, North Melbourne, Australian Scholarly, 2014.

Isaacs, Victor, Rod Kirkpatrick and John Russell, *Australian Newspaper History: A Bibliography*, Middle Park, QLD, Australian Newspaper History Group, 2004, with a *First Supplement* in 2005.

———— and Rod Kirkpatrick, eds, *The Australian Press — A Bicentennial Retrospect*, Middle Park, QLD, Australian Newspaper History Group and State Library of NSW, 2003.

Johnson-Woods, Toni, *Index to Serials in Australian Periodicals and Newspapers: Nineteenth Century*, Canberra, Mulini Press, 2001.

Kirkpatrick, Rod, *The Bold Type: A History of Victoria's Country Newspapers, 1840–2010*, Ascot Vale, VIC, The Victorian Country Press Association Ltd, 2010.

————, *Country Conscience: A History of the New South Wales Provincial Press 1841–1995*, Canberra, Infinite Harvest Publishing Pty Ltd, 2000.

————, *Dailies in the Colonial Capitals: A Short History*, Newmarket, QLD, Rod Kirkpatrick, 2016.

————, *A Short History of the Australian Country Press*, Mount Pleasant, QLD, Australian Newspaper History Group, 2013.

————, *Sworn To No Master: A History of the Provincial Press in Queensland to 1930*, Toowoomba QLD, Darling Downs Institute Press, 1984.

Mayer, Henry, *The Press in Australia*, Melbourne, Lansdowne Press, 1964.

Miller, E. Morris, *Pressmen and Governors: Australian Editors and Writers in Early Tasmania*, Sydney, Angus and Robertson, 1952 (facsimile impression, SUP, 1973).

Morrison, Elizabeth, *David Syme: Man of The Age*, Melbourne, Monash UP and SLV, 2014.

———, *Engines of Influence: Newspapers of Country Victoria, 1840–1890*, Carlton, VIC, MUP, 2005.
Pitt, George H., *The Press in South Australia 1836 to 1850*, Adelaide, The Wakefield Press, 1946.
Porter, Muriel, ed., *The Argus: The Life and Death of a Great Melbourne Newspaper, 1846–1957: Papers from a Conference at RMIT University, 2001*, Melbourne, RMIT University, c. 2003.
Russell, John C., transcriber, *Bibliographical Notes for* The Press in Australia *and Related Subjects by Henry Mayer*, Middle Park, QLD, Australian Newspaper History Group, 2005.
Souter, Gavin, *Company of Heralds: A Century and a Half of Australian Publishing by John Fairfax Limited and its Predecessors 1831–1981*. Carlton, VIC, MUP, 1981.
Walker, R. B. *The Newspaper Press in New South Wales, 1803–1920*, Sydney, SUP, 1976.
Woodberry, Joan, *Andrew Bent and the Freedom of the Press in Van Diemen's Land*, Hobart, Fullers Bookshop, 1972.
Young, Sally, *Paper Emperors: The Rise of Australia's Newspaper Empires*, Sydney, UNSW Press, 2019.

Chapter 12: Magazines

Bennett, Bruce, ed., *Cross Currents: Magazines and Newspapers in Australian Literature*, Melbourne, Longman Cheshire, 1981.
Gelder, Ken and Rachael Weaver, *The Colonial Journals and the Emergence of Australian Literary Culture*, Crawley, UWA Publishing, 2014.
Greenop, Frank S., *History of Magazine Publishing in Australia*, Sydney, The K. G. Murray Publishing Co., 1947.
Lawson, Sylvia, *The Archibald Paradox: A Strange Case of Authorship*, Ringwood, VIC, Allen Lane, 1983.
Vann, J. Don and Rosemary T. VanArsdel, eds, *Periodicals of Queen Victoria's Empire*, Toronto, University of Toronto Press, 1996.

Chapter 13: Bookselling

Brodsky, Isadore, *Sydney's Phantom Book Shops*, Sydney University Co-operative Bookshop Limited, 1973.
The Early Australian Booksellers: The Australian Booksellers Association Memorial Book of Fellowship, Sydney, The Australian Booksellers Association, 1980.
Graetz, Joyce, *An Open Book: The Story of the Distribution and Production of Christian Literature by Lutherans in Australia*, Adelaide, Lutheran Publishing House, 1988.
Johanson, Graeme, *Colonial Editions in Australia, 1843–1972*, Wellington, NZ, Elibank Press, 2000.

McLaren, Ian F., *Henry Tolman Dwight, Bookseller and Publisher*, Parkville, University of Melbourne Library, 1989.

Ralph, Glen, comp., *Charles Platts (1813–1871), Adelaide's First Bookseller*, Lockleys, SA, Wilmar Library, 2013, 2 index vols + CD.

Rukavina, Alison, *The Development of the International Book Trade, 1870–1895: Tangled Networks*, Houndmills, Basingstoke, Hampshire, Palgrave Macmillan, 2010.

Turnley, Cole, *Cole of the Book Arcade: A Pictorial Biography of E. W. Cole*, Hawthorn, VIC, Cole Publications, 1974.

Webby, Elizabeth, 'A Checklist of Early Australian Booksellers' and Auctioneers' Catalogues and Advertisements: 1800–1849', *BSANZ Bulletin*, vol.3, no.4, 1978, pp. 123-48; vol.4, no.1, 1979, pp. 33-61; and no.2, pp. 95-150.

Chapter 14: Australia's Public Libraries in their Infancy

Atkin, Lara, Sarah Comyn, Porscha Fermanis and Nathan Garvey, *Early Public Libraries and Colonial Citizenship in the British Southern Hemisphere*, Cham, Palgrave Macmillan, 2019.

Biskup, Peter, with the assistance of Doreen M. Goodman, *Libraries in Australia*, Wagga Wagga, Centre for Information Studies, 1994.

Bridge, Carl, *A Trunk Full of Books: History of the State Library of South Australia and its Forerunners*, Netley, SA, Wakefield Press, 1986.

Gaunt, Heather, Identity and Nation in the Australian Public Library: The Development of Local and National Collections 1850s–1940s, using the Tasmanian Public Library as Case Study, PhD thesis, University of Tasmania, 2010.

Holgate, C. W., *An Account of the Chief Libraries of Australia and Tasmania*, London, C. Whittingham and Co., Chiswick Press, 1886 (facsimile reprint: Adelaide, Libraries Board of SA, 1971).

Jones, David J., *A Source of Inspiration and Delight: The Buildings of the State Library of New South Wales since 1826*, Sydney, Library Council of New South Wales, 1988.

McVilly, David, A History of the State Library of Victoria 1853–1974, MA thesis, Monash University, 1975.

Richardson, G. D., *The Colony's Quest for a National Library*, Sydney, Public Library of New South Wales, 1961.

Winter, Gillian, ed., *Tasmanian Insights: Essays in Honour of Geoffrey Thomas Stilwell*, Hobart, State Library of Tasmania, 1992.

Chapter 15: Mechanics' Institutes

Baragwanath, Pam and Ken James, *These Walls Speak Volumes: A History of Mechanics' Institutes in Victoria*, Melbourne, [the authors], 2015.

———, *Ubiquitous and Necessary: Australia's Mechanics' Institutes and Schools of Arts etc.: A Research Guide*, Melbourne, [the authors], 2016.

Candy, Philip and John Laurent, eds, *Pioneering Culture: Mechanics' Institutes and Schools of Arts*, Adelaide, Auslib Press, 1994.

Lowden, Bronwyn, *Mechanics' Institutes, Schools of Arts, Athenaeums, etc.* 3rd ed., Donvale, VIC, Lowden Publishing Co., 2010.

Marsden, Anne, *The Making of the Melbourne Mechanics' Institution: The 'movers and shakers' of Pre-goldrush Melbourne*, Melbourne, [the author] with the Melbourne Athenaeum Library, 2016.

Petrow, Stefan, *Going to the Mechanics: A History of the Launceston Mechanics' Institute 1842–1914*, Launceston, Historical Survey of Northern Tasmania, 1998.

Talbot, M. R., *A Chance to Read: a History of the Institutes Movement in South Australia*, Adelaide, Libraries Board of South Australia, 1992.

Worthington, Christine and Catherine Milward-Bason, eds, *Buildings, Books and Beyond: Mechanics' Worldwide Conference, 2004*, Windsor, VIC, Prahran Mechanics' Institute Press, 2004.

Chapter 16: Commercial Circulating Libraries

Spennemann, Dirk H.R., *The Ten-Mile Creek (Holbrook, NSW) Circulating Library*, Canberra, Mulini Press, 2002.

Chapter 17: Private Libraries

Chanin, Eileen, *Book Life: The Life and Times of David Scott Mitchell*, North Melbourne, Australian Scholarly, 2011.

Jordens, Ann-Mari, *The Stenhouse Circle: Literary Life in mid-Nineteenth Century Sydney*, Carlton, VIC, MUP, 1979.

Stitz, Charles, ed., *Australian Book Collectors: Some Noted Australian Book Collectors & Collections of the Nineteenth & Twentieth Centuries*, Bendigo, Bread Street Press in association with The Australian Book Auction Records, 2010.

———, *Australian Book Collectors*, Second Series, 2 parts, Melbourne, Books of Kells/Green Olive Press, 2013.

———, *Australian Book Collectors*, Third Series, 2 parts, Melbourne, Books of Kells, 2016.

Chapter 18: The Print Culture of Colonial Music from its Beginnings

Holmes, Robyn and Ruth Lee Martin, comps, *The Collector's Book of Sheet Music Covers*, Canberra, NLA, 2000.

Neidorf, Prue, A Guide to Dating Music Published in Sydney and Melbourne, 1800–1899, MA thesis, University of Wollongong, 1999.

Skinner, Graeme, *Australharmony (an online resource toward the early history of music in colonial Australia)*. Website: https://www.sydney.edu.au/paradisec/australharmony [accessed 24 April 2024]

Wafer, Jim and Myfany Turpin, eds, *Recirculating Songs: Revitalising the Singing Practices of Indigenous Australia*, Canberra, Asia-Pacific Linguistics, 2017.

Chapter 19: Textbooks

Clark, Anna, *Making Australian History*, Melbourne, Vintage Books, 2022.

Pescott, Edward Edgar, *James Bonwick: A Writer of School Books and Histories, with a Bibliography of his Writings*, Melbourne, H. A. Evans & Son, 1939.

Chapter 20: Australian Directories to 1890

Bartlett, Anne, *Local and Family History Sources in Tasmania*, 2nd ed., Launceston, Genealogical Society of Tasmania, 1994.

Down, H. P., *A Century of Printing: The Story of Sands & McDougall Pty Ltd During its First Hundred Years 1853–1953*, Melbourne, Sands & McDougall, 1956.

Hughes, Joy, *New South Wales Directories 1828–1950: A Bibliography*, bound with Christine Ealick, Joy Hughes and R. Ian Jack, *Bibliography of New South Wales Local History*, Kensington, NSWU Press, 1987.

Hyslop, Margot, *Victorian Directories, 1836–1974: A Checklist* bound with Carole Beaumont, with the assistance of Alice Zydower, *Local History in Victoria: An Annotated Bibliography*, Bundoora, VIC, La Trobe University Library, 1980.

Le Maistre, Barbara, *Using Directories in Local Historical Research*, Sydney, Royal Australian Historical Society, Technical Information Service 10, 1987.

Chapter 21: Australian Almanacs 1806–1890

Morrison, Ian, Maureen Perkins and Tracey Caulfield, *Australian Almanacs 1806–1930: A Bibliography*, Hawthorn East, VIC, Quiddlers Press, 2003.

Perkins, Maureen, *Visions of the Future: Almanacs, Time and Cultural Change 1775–1870*, Oxford, Clarendon Press, 1996.

Chapter 22: Australian Printing and Publishing in Pacific and Indigenous Australian Languages 1814-1900

Crowl, Linda S., Politics and Book Publishing in the Pacific Islands, PhD thesis, University of Wollongong, 2008.

Dance, D. G., *Oceanic Scriptures*, London, BFBS, 1963.

Darlow, T. H. and H. F. Moule, comps, *Historical Catalogue of the Printed Editions of Holy Scripture in the Library of the British and Foreign Bible Society*, London, The Bible House, 1903–1911.

Edridge, Sally, comp. *Solomon Islands Bibliography to 1980*, Suva, Fiji, Institute of Pacific Studies, University of the South Pacific/Wellington, NZ, The Alexander Turnbull Library/Honiara, The Solomon Islands National Library, 1985.

Ferguson, John A., *A Bibliography of the New Hebrides and a History of the Mission Press*, Sydney, [the author], 1917–1943.

Gunson, Niel, *Messengers of Grace: Evangelical Missionaries in the South Seas, 1797–1860*, Melbourne, OUP, 1978.

Harding, George L. and Bjarne Kroepelien, *The Tahitian Imprints of the London Missionary Society, 1810–1834*, Oslo, La Coquille qui chante, 1950.

Hilliard, David, *God's Gentlemen: A History of the Melanesian Mission 1849–1942*, St Lucia, UQP, 1978.

Johnston, Anna, *The Paper War: Morality, Print Culture, and Power in Colonial New South Wales*, Crawley, WA, UWA Publishing, 2011.

Krauss, N. L. H., *Bibliography of Niue, South Pacific*, Honolulu, [the author], 1970.

Laracy, Hugh, *Marists and Melanesians: A History of Catholic Missions in the Solomon Islands*, Canberra, ANU Press, 1975.

Lingenfelter, Richard, *Presses of the Pacific Islands 1817–1867*, Los Angeles, Plantin Press, 1967.

O'Reilly, Patrick, *Imprints of the Fiji Catholic Mission, Including the Loreto Press, 1864–1954*, London, F. Edwards, 1958.

Parkinson, Phil and Penny Griffith, *Books in Māori 1815–1900 Ngā tānga reo Māori*, Auckland, Reed Books, 2004.

Chapter 23: Official Printing

Marsh, Peter, *Establishment of the Government Printing Office, Melbourne: The Golden Fifties*, Emerald Hill, Kitchen Table Press, 2018.

———, *The Government Printing Office*, Melbourne, Kitchen Table Press, 2013–2014, 6 vols.

Chapter 24: 'After the toil of a long day': Reading in Colonial Australia

Adkins, Keith, *Reading in Colonial Tasmania: The Early Years of the Evandale Subscription Library*, Melbourne, Ancora Press, Monash University, 2010.

Bunn, Mary Anne, *The Lonely Pioneer: William Bunn, Diarist 1830–1901*, Braidwood, NSW, St Omer Pastoral Co., 2002.

Cleverley, John F., *The First Generation: School and Society in Early Australia*, Sydney, SUP, 1971.

Kirsop, Wallace, *The Bookshop as an 'Index of Civilisation': The Case of the Walches in the 1840s*, Melbourne, Chaskett Press, 2012.

Martin, Susan K. and Kylie Mirmohamadi, *Colonial Dickens: What Australians Made of the World's Favourite Writer*, North Melbourne, Australian Scholarly, 2011.

———, *Sensational Melbourne: Reading Sensation Fiction and* Lady Audley's Secret *in the Victorian Metropolis*, North Melbourne, Australian Scholarly, 2011.

Spedding, Patrick and Paul Tankard, *Marginal Notes: Social Reading and the Literal Margins*, Cham, Palgrave Macmillan, 2021.

Index

Note: References to Melbourne, Sydney, New South Wales and Victoria can be found in nearly every chapter of this volume, so it was not practical to include those locations in the index; all other States, cities and towns, when cited, are included. Similarly, the broad theme of publishing is mentioned throughout the volume so has not been exhaustively indexed. Literary and scientific works are listed under the author's name. Birth and death (or flourish) dates are included for individuals involved in the book trade who were born in, or lived in, Australia.

A
A.B. Fleming and Co. 130
A.T.A. (artist) 100
A Korao 390
Abbott, Edward (1801–1869) 165
a'Beckett, William (1806–1869) 229, 346, 427
Aborigines Friends Association 402
Ackerman, Rudolph 78, 91
Adams, Francis (1862–1893) 428
Adams, George (1839–1904) 116
Adams, John 362
Adelaide SA 30, 56, 71,104, 126, 130, 131, 161, 202, 244, 266, *273*, 283; almanacs 379; artists 188, *189*; bookbinders 105; booksellers and stationers 104, 105, 266, 268, 271, *273*, 280, 283; German language publishing 126-7, 131, 161, 163, 202; libraries: circulating 306, 333-4, private 342, *343*, 345, public/free 294, 300, 306, *307*, 308, 310, subscription 306; directories 374-5, 379; mechanics' institutes 320-1; music 349, 350, 352, 359; newspapers and magazines 30, 45, 53, 80, 131, 143, 161, 163-4, 202, 232-51 *passim*, 271, 430; printing and publishing 34, 53, 56, 82, 84, 100, 126, 130, 313, 373, 393. *See also* Germans in Australia; South Australia
Adelaide Circulating Library 306
Adelaide Mechanics' Institute 320
Adelaide Public Library, Museum and Art Gallery 306, *307*
Adey, Stephen (1781?–1860) 157
Africans, enslaved 264
Albany WA 379
Albert, Joseph 81-2

Albion Printing Office (Sydney) 44, 125
Albury NSW 379
Aldine Centennial History of New South Wales 118
Aldine History of Queensland 118
Aldine History of South Australia 118
Alexander Wilson's Letter Foundry 127
Allan and Co. 358
Allan, George Leavis (1826–1897) 358, 362
Allen family 345
Allen, George (1800–1877) 420, 421, 433
Allen, James (1806–1886) 173
Alloo, John (Chin Thum Lock) (1838?–1889) 188, *189*
almanacs 77, 91, 94, 104, 107, 113, 138, 152-3, 158-62 *passim*, 170, 212, 263, 372-91 *passim*, 382-7, 411, 433, 456. *See also* directories
almanacs by title
 Adelaide Almanack, Town and Country Directory, 1874-5, 379
 Australian Almanack and General Directory for the Year of our Lord 1835 375
 Australian Almanack and Sydney Directory for the Year of our Lord 1834 375
 Australian Handbook and Almanac and Shippers' and Importers' Directory 138
 Australian Pocket Almanac 385
 Border Post Almanac 379
 Calendar of All Days and Nights, Sabbaths and New Moons... 386
 Cole's Family Almanac 169
 Cooktown Almanac, Northern Queensland Directory and Miners and Settlers' Companion for 1876 432

Hat Almanack for 1849 384
Hobart Town Almanack 96, 383
Hopkins' Rockhampton Almanac 386
Kerr's Melbourne Almanac 162
Kerr's Melbourne Almanac, and Port Phillip Directory 374
Maryborough Almanac and Wide Bay and Burnett Business Directory, 1874-75; 379
New South Wales Pocket Almanack 104, 113, 411
New South Wales Pocket Almanack and Colonial Remembrancer 152-3, 382
Newcastle Business Directory and Hunter River District Almanac 378-9
Smith's Medical Almanac for 1863 76-7
South Australian Almanack and Town and Country Directory 161
Süd-Australische Deutsche Kalender 386
Tasmanian Almanack 384
Victorian Nautical and Commercial Almanack 161, 383
Western Australian Almanack 379, 386, 388
Western Australian Almanack and Directory 379, 380
Western Australian Calendar and Directory 380
Western Champion Almanac and Yearbook for 1890 432-3
Wood's Royal Southern Kalendar, Tasmanian Register...Australian & East Indian Official Directory 195
American & Australian Photographic Co. 438
American Board of Commissioners in Foreign Missions in Hawai'i 389
American Type Founders 128
Anderson, Alfred (c.1848–1876) 362
Anderson, James Henri (1823–1879) 358, *360-1*, 362
Andrews, James (fl. 1851) 94
Anglican New Guinea Mission 390
Angus & Robertson 110, 168, 278, 339, 453, 458
Angus, David M. (1855–1901) 110, 280. *See also* Angus & Robertson

Aniwa (language) 396
Anson Brothers *166*
Appleton, Frank (fl. 1877–1883) *Victoria in 1880* 95
Aranda (language) 393
Archer, William H. (1825–1909) 411, 413
Archibald, J.F. (1856–1919) 191, 249, 252-3
Arden, George (1814–1854) 30-31, 162, 232-3; *Latest Information with Regard to Australia Felix* 162
Arnhem Land 348
Arrernte 11 (people), 22 (language)
Art of Printing, The 50, 131
Art Union of Victoria 78
Arthur, Sir George (1784–1854) 152, 214-19 *passim*
Arthur, Walter George (c.1820–1861) 200
artists 11, 35, 79, 84-101 *passim*, 141, 171, 189, 239; music 352-7 *passim*; wood engravers 136, 179. *See also* cartoons and cartoonists; *names of individual artists*
Arts and Crafts Movement 108
Atkinson, Charles (1806?–1837) 96
auctions, book 258-91 *passim*, 341-46 *passim*, 421, 434-5, 439. *See also* catalogues
Auricht, J.C. (1832–1907) 399
Austin, J.G. (John Gardner) (fl. 1830s–1840s) 353; *Series of Lithographic Drawings of Sydney and its Environs* 158; *Series of Twelve Profile Portraits of Aborigines of New South Wales* 91
Austin, Robert (1825–1905) *Journal of an Expedition to Explore the Interior of Western Australia* 100
Australasia Illustrated 93
Australasian Bibliography 301
Australasian Wesleyan Methodist Missionary Society 399
Australian Circulating Library 333
Australian Dictionary of Dates and Men of the Time 171
Australian Men of Mark 110, 171
Australian Paper Company aka Australian Paper Mills (Collingwood) 116, 118
Australian Picture Pleasure Book 92
Australian Reading Books 370, 440

Australian Society of Compositors 66
Australian Stationery Warehouse 270, 332-3
Australian Subscription Library 154, 265, 293, 297-8, 319, 420, 426
Australian Type Founding Company 135
Australian Type Foundry 132-4
Australian Typographical Union 70
authorship 139-47, 222-57 *passim*; copyright 176-87 *passim*; Indigenous Australians 14-20, 24, 133, 200; self-publication 86, 169, 170; music 356, 358; women 16, 17-19, 25, 97, 143, 139-47 *passim*, 156-9 *passim*, 165, 168, 205, 242, 437. *See also names of individual authors*; wages and income
Auxiliary Bible Society of New South Wales 261
Awabakal (language) 392-3
Azzopardi & Markby 136
Azzopardi, Angelo (1846–1896) 136

B

Badham, Charles (1813–1884) 345, 365
Bagdad TAS 264
Bailey, F.M. (Frederick Manson) (1827–1915) *An Illustrated Monograph of the Grasses of Queensland* 97; *Lithograms of the Ferns of Queensland* 97, 98-99
Baillière, F.F. (Ferdinand François) (1838–1881) 167, 170, 257, 284, 345, 378
Baker, Horace (1833–1918) 93
Baker, William (c.1806–1857) 236, 267, 334, 354; *Heads of the People* 92, 160
Baker's gold-diggers 'Go-a-head Library and Registration Office for New Chums' 334
Balhannah SA 321
Ballarat VIC: artists 189; booksellers and stationers 286; directories 379; German club 324; libraries, public 196, 304; mechanics' institutes 326-7; music 351; newspapers and magazines 89, 117, 136, 164, 188, *189*, 203, 241, 351; printing and publishing 36-56 *passim*, 81, 89, 90, 135. *See also* gold rushes
Ballarat Public Library, Ballarat East, 196
Bank [paper] Mill 112
Banks Island 389, 392

Banks, Sir Joseph (1743–1820) 155
Bannister, Saxe (1790–1877) 218
Barak, William (1824–1903) 9, 10
Barcaldine QLD 432-3
Barfoot, U.B. 267
Barlow, David Edward 91
Barnard, James (1809?–1897) 115, 407, 408, 412
Barnes, Francis (c.1771–1842) 29, 407
Barrett, H. *Handbook to the City of Adelaide* 100
Barron, H.J.A. 84
Barry, Sir Redmond (1813–1880) 276, 294-310 *passim*, 338, 345, 453, 457; *Vocabulary of Dialects Spoken by Aboriginal Natives of Australia* 394
Bartholomew, Arthur *Prodromus of the Zoology of Victoria* 87-88
Bartholomew, E.R. 288
Barton, Charlotte (1796–1867) *A Mother's Offering to her Children; by a Lady, Long Resident in New South Wales* 439
Barton, G.B. (George Burnett) (1836–1901) 171, 431, 432; *Literature in New South Wales* 431
Barwon Paper Mill 114, 116, 117, *117*, 119
Bass, George (1771–1803) 420
Bathurst NSW 162, 266, 442
Batman, John (1801–1839) 162
Baudin, Nicolas 260
Beal, James C. (1830–1904) 408
Beaney, J.G. (James George) (1828–1891) 345
Beauvoir, de, Comte 163
Becker, Ludwig (1808?–1861) 85, 94, 95
Beechworth VIC 36, 326
Bell, Robert (fl. 1850s) 49, 55, 136
Bendigo VIC 36, 82, 192; booksellers and stationers 284, 287; Chinese in 45; directories 379; German club 196, 324; libraries: circulating 334, free/public 196, 304, private 344; mechanics' institutes 196, 327; music 351; newspapers and magazines 59, 117, 203, 251, 218; printing and publishing 36, 45, 59. *See also* gold rushes
Bendigo Deutscher Verein und Lesehalle 196

Bennelong aka Woollawarre Bennelong (1764?–1813) 348
Bent, Andrew (c.1790–1851) 29, 86, 107, 114, 125, 156, 157, 200, 211-21, 368, 373, 384, 385, 407, 439
Bent, Ellis (1783–1815) 262
Bentley (English publishers) 143, 192, 282
Berne Convention 183-4. *See also* copyright; piracy
Berry, Alexander (1781–1873) 345, 421
Berry and Wollstonecraft 421
Besley (foundry) 129
Bevan, David 262, 352
Bewick, Thomas 77
bibles and scriptures 6, 107, 151, 261, 307, 388-405 *passim*, 418, 422-39 *passim*
Biblical Library 293
Bigge Commission 104, 155, 215, 424
Biraban (fl. 1819–1842) *133*; *Specimens of a dialect of the Aborigines of New South Wales* 368-9, 392
Birchall, Andrew (1831–1893) *167*
Birds of Australia (Broinowski) 94
Birds of Australia (Gould) 296
Birtchnell, S.L. (fl. 1862–1875) 379
Bismarck Archipelago 389
Black and White List, or Electors' Handbook and Guide 170
Black War 150
Blackie and Co. 284, 288
Blackman, John 267
Blair, David (1820–1899) 143, 170, 171, 245; *Cyclopedia of Australasia* 142, 284; *History of Australasia* 142
Blake & Stephenson (later Stephenson Blake) 125, 130
Blake, Robert *166*
Blake, William 262
Bland, William (1789–1868) *Journey of Discovery to Port Phillip* 158
Blaxland, Gregory (1778–1853) 154
Bligh, Gov. William (1754–1817) 345
Boake, Barcroft (1866–1892) 140
Bock, Thomas (1790–1855) 96
Bohn, Henry G. 267
Boldrewood, Rolf (Thomas Browne, 1826–1915) 165, 181

Bonnard, Jean 89
Bonwick, James (1817–1906) 237; *Discovery and Settlement of Port Phillip* 167; *Geography for the use of Australian Youth* 369
bookbinding 35, 69, 70, 72, 103-11, 159, 171
booksellers and stationers 148-75 *passim*; 258-91, 439. *See also names of individual sellers and shops; individual cities and large towns*
Boothby, Guy (1867–1905) 145
Boothby, Josiah (1837–1916) 379
Borlase, James Skipp (1839–?) 242
Boston Type Foundry 128
Botany Bay 155
Bothwell TAS 318
Bothwell Literary Society 264, 445-6, 452
Boulanger, Edward 357, 358
Boullée, Étienne-Louis 151
Bourke, Sir Richard (1777–1855) 230
Bourne, Rev. Robert (1794–1871) 124
Bowden SA 321
Bowden, Thomas (1778–1834) 368
Bowden's Tables 368, 411
Boyd, Charles (c.1828–1897) 135
Boyes, G.T.W.B. (1787–1853) 266-7
Boyland, John 104
Brabazon, H.L. (Harry Lambert) 159
Brady, Matthew (1799–1826) 156
Braidwood Literary Institute 327, 442
Braidwood NSW 326-7
Braim, Rev. T.H. (1814–1891) 232
Brennan, Christopher (1870–1932) 453
Brennand, J. 266
Briggs, Jack (aka 'Tizz') 159, 179
Brisbane QLD 71, 283, 322, 435; artists 97, 99; bookbinding 105; booksellers and stationers 271, 280, 283, 435; libraries 266, 307; mechanics' institutes 325; music 362; newspapers and magazines 118, 134, 160, 203, 246, 251; printing 55, 71, 105, 129, 130; publishing 97, *98*, 99, 246; schools of arts 322, 326. *See also* Moreton Bay; Queensland; Townsville
Brisbane, Sir Thomas 91, 200, 211, 217
British and Foreign Bible Society 225, 397, 399, 400

Britton, Henry (1846–1890+) *Battle of Mordialloc, or How We Lost Australia* 168; *Fiji in 1870* 168; *Lolóma, or Two Years in Cannibal-land* 168
Broadford VIC 116, 119
Brodzky, Maurice (1847–1919) 203
Broinowski, G.J. (1837–1913) *Birds of Australia* 93-4; *Birds and Mammals of Australia* 93, 118
Brooks, John 344
Broughton, Thomas, *alias* William Smith (fl. 1800–1810) 104, 107
Brown, J.E. *Handbook to the City of Adelaide* 100
Browne, Thomas (1816–1870) 358, *384*
Browne, Thomas Alexander (1826–1915) see Boldrewood, Rolf
Brownrigg, Canon Marcus B. (1835–1890) *The Cruise of the Freak* 86
Bruce, Charles (1807–1851) 96
Bruce's New York Type Foundry 128
Brune, Thomas 200
Brush and MacDonnell 129
Bryant, James 116
Bryce Ross's Newspaper and General Agency Office 188
Bullen, H.L. (1857–1938) 45
Bundaberg QLD 326-7
Bunn, Anna Maria (1808–1889) *The Guardian* 156, 440-2
Bunn, William (1830–1901) 440-2, 452
Burke Museum 326
Burns, Robert 444; *Poetical Works of Robert Burns* 159
Busby, James (1801–1871) 412; *A Manual of Plain Directions for Planting and Cultivating Vineyards* 412; *Treatise on the Culture of the Vine* 412
bush: ballads 139, 164, 249, 254; reading in 159, 433-7, 435-6, 442-4, 450, 459; songs 351, 363
Buzzard and Vale 281
Buzzard, T.M. (Thomas M.) (fl. 1850s) 335, *336*
Byron, Lord 155, 440

C
cable link 192-3, 197, 458
Calder, J.E. (James Erskine) (1808–1882) 211-13

Callender, Caldwell & Co. 129-30
Callender, James 129-30
Calvert, Samuel (1828–1913) 90, 94, 95, 99; *Australian Home Companion* 237; *Queenslander* 99; *This is the Hut that Jack Built in Australia* 85; *Victoria in 1880* 95; *The Young Australian's Alphabet* 85
Calvert, W.S. (William) (1861–1923) 85, 93; *Australian Home Companion* 237
Cambridge, Ada (1844–1926) 144, 146, 205; *A Marked* Man 144; *Australasian* 144; *Manchester Weekly Times Supplement* 144; *Not All in Vain* 144; *Thirty Years in Australia* 205
Cameron, Rev. Andrew (1822–1877) 428
Campbell, Robert (music warehouse) 352
Campbell-Town Book Club 445
Canada 123, 318, 390, 456
Carfrae, John (fl. 1840s) 271
Carlyle, Thomas 160
Carmichael, John (c.1811–1857) 35, 355, 360
Carmichael, Rev. Henry (d.1862) 368
Carrington, Thomas (1843–1918) 100, 240
Carroll, T.V. (d.1936) 280
cartoons and cartoonists 47, 80, 101, 102, 236, 239-*240*, *250*, *253*, *255*. See also artists
Cartwright, Robert (1771–1856) 346
Carvosso, Rev. Benjamin (1789–1854) 293
Cassell & Co. 80, 171, 173, 288
Cassell's Picturesque Australasia 171
Castlemaine VIC 36, 286
Catalogue of Books Offered to the Trade 278
Catalogue of the Natural Science & Technical Periodicals in the Libraries in Melbourne 257
Catalogue of the Scientific Serial Literature in the following Libraries in Sydney 257
catalogues: auction, of private libraries 258-91 *passim*; booksellers' 258-91 *passim*, 287, 335, 339; commercial circulating libraries 331, 332, 333, 335; library 257, 301, 310, 319, 333; mechanics' institutes 318, 325; private libraries 338, 344

Catechism for the Use of Schools and Families 368
Catholic School Book, containing Easy and Familiar Lessons 368
Cavenagh, George (1808–1869) 35
Celtic (languages) 285, 286. *See also* Gaelic, Scots (language)
censorship: among families 440-3; government 200; by libraries, mechanics' institutes 295-6, 300-01, 306, 423-4, 447-8; novels, attitudes towards 156, 309, 418, 421, 423, 426-8, 431, 445; press freedom 211-21, 226
Central Type Foundry 128
Chambers, John 132
Champion Bay 380
Chapman, Abraham Western 358
Chapman, [Amy] 449
Charles Reed and Sons 129
Charlwood, Stephen 37
Charlwood and Son 351
Chatto & Hughes 275
Chatto & Windus 145
Chevalier, Nicholas (1828–1902) 84, 240
Chidley, W.J. (1860?–1916) 100
Child's First Book 365
children: circulating library 334; library access 303, 309; literacy 419; publications for 6, 85, 99, 169, 237, 242, 277, 365-71, 432-48 *passim*; reading 417-54 *passim*, 441; working in printing trades 51, 67-71 *passim*. *See also* textbooks
Chiltern VIC 327
Chinese (language and publications) 136, 164, 197, 205
Chinese (people) 455
Chippendale NSW 134
Chisholm, Caroline (1808–1877) *Female Immigration Considered* 158
Church Missionary Society 390
Church of England Missionary Society 392
circulation, newspapers and magazines 32, 34, 39-46 *passim*, 53, 61, 152, 200, 203, 243, 253, 431-2 *passim*. *See also* edition sizes or print runs
circulation, newspapers, imported 195-7, 201

Clark, George 29, 214, 407
Clark, Ralph (d.1794) 148
Clark(e), Charles 107
Clarke, J.R. (Jacob) (1821–1893) 164, 356
Clarke, Joseph Augustus (1840–1890) *Queensland Punch* 99; *Queenslander* 99
Clarke, Marcus (1846–1881) 140-1, 143, 144, 242, 245, 310, 346, 383; *Australian Journal* 141; *His Natural Life* 141, 170-1, 181, 187, 244, 247; *Humbug* 241; *Long Odds* 165
Clarke, William Joseph Sayers (1813–1855) *126*
Clarkson, Thomas 112
Clarson & Massina 165
Clarson, Shallard and Co. 359
Clarson, Shallard and Gibbs 48
Clayton, Robert (fl. 1830s) *Picture of Sydney* 92
Clayton, Thomas (fl. 1830–1840s) *Atlas* 92
Clint, Raphael (1797–1849) 91
Cobbett, William 213
Codrington, Rev. Dr Robert Henry 392
Coghlan, T.A. (1855–1926) 413
Cohen & Co. 285
Colac VIC 206
Cole, E.W. (Edward William) (1832–1918) 103, 167, 168-9, 173, 276-84 *passim*, 367; Cole's Book Arcade 169, 170, 280, 283-4; *Account of a Race of Human Beings with Tails* 169; *Cole's Edition of Saxon's Everybody's Pocket Cyclopedia of Things Worth Knowing* 169; *Cole's Family Almanac* 169; *Cole's Funny Picture Book* 103, 107, 169; *Cole's Handbook of Etiquette and Home Culture for Ladies and Gentlemen* 169; *The Real Place in History of Jesus and Paul* 168, 169
Collection of English Exercises, A 368
Collingridge, George (1847–1931) *Systematic Account of the Geology of Tasmania* 97
Collingwood VIC 303, 304
Collingwood Free Library 303, 304
Collins (publishers) 288, 369-70, 440
Collins, Lt-Gov. David (1756–1810) 28, 30, 151, 212, 348, 407

Collins, William 288
Colman and Piddington 435
Colman, W.A. (fl. 1840s & 1850s) 272, 435
Colonial and Home Library 269
Colonial Secretary's Office 128
Colonial Spelling Book 368
Colquhoun, Walter 260, 422
Compendious Latin Grammar for the use of the students of the Australian College 368
Conder, Charles (1868–1909) 254
Conner Type Foundry 128
Constable & Co. 267
Continuation of General Orders 411
convicts 66, 149, 154-5, 159, 160, 162, 261, 307; artists 91, 95, 96; authors 141, 157, 212; bookbinders 104, 105, 107, 108; literacy 423; papermakers 112, 115; printers 67; and theatre 28, 29, 149, 363. *See also* literacy; *names of individuals*; print workers
Conyber, James 105
Coo-e-e: An Illustrated Shorthand Magazine 79
Cook, Capt. James 10, 11, 22, 150, 155
Cook, Joseph (1825–1912) 399
Cook Islands 389, 398
cookery 165, 251, 252, 387, 434
Cooktown QLD 432
Coolgardie WA 101
Cooper, George 105
Coote, William (1822–1898) 238
Cope, R.W. 32
copyright 176-87, 310. *See also* piracy
Coranderrk Reserve VIC 9, 10, 21-2
Cornell, William 344
Corrangie, 'Harry' 348
Costin, John Thomas *Lithograms of the Ferns of Queensland* 97-98
costs: to booksellers 265, 268, 276, 279, 288, 367, 458; government printing 409-10; illustrations, to reproduce 84-6; magazines, to produce 234, 248; mission publications, to produce 397-8, 400; newspapers, to produce 234; paper 32, 113, 114, 118, 157; publishing (costs to authors/compilers) 143, 145-6, 156, 157, 386; printing equipment 33-61 *passim*, 125, 153; type 33, 130.
See also prices (consumer); wages and income
Cowan & Co. 49, 56, 129-30
Cox, James C. (1834–1912) *Monograph of Australian Land Shells* 92
Cox, W.C. (fl. 1849–1878) 407, 408
Cox, William (1764–1837) 262
Coxon, John 351
Crisp Photo Process 81, 82
Crocker, Samuel (1856–1936?) 88
Crook, William Pascoe (1775–1846) 439
Crowder, John 213
Cubbitt, Arthur (fl. 1850s–1860s) 129
Cundy, W.H. *Systematic Account of the Geology of Tasmania* 97
Cunningham, Allan (1791–1839) 154
Cunninghame, F. (fl. 1850s–1870s) 44, 399
Cumberland NSW 379
Cumberland Mutual Improvement Society 447
Curr, E.M. (Edward Micklethwaite) (1820–1889) *The Australian Race: Its Origins, Languages, Customs, Place of Landing in Australia* 413; *Recollections of Squatting in Victoria* 167, 436
Curtis, James 56
customs and tariffs 109, 114, 119, 135, 178, 183, 281

D

Dale, Robert (1815–1889) 134
Dalrymple, Capt. David 262
Daniyarri, Hobbles (c.1925–1988) 10, 22
Darke, W. Wedge (fl. 1830s–1850s) *Observations on Convicts and the Discipline to which They Have Hitherto Been Subjected* 159
Darling Downs 154, 160
Darling, Eliza, Lady (1798–1868) *Simple Rules for the Guidance of Persons in Humble Life* 158
Darling, Sir Ralph (1772–1858) 200, 349
Darlinghurst NSW *441*
Darrell, George (1851?–1921) 172
Darwin, Charles 272
Davenport, Harry, 50
Davey, Lt-Gov. Thomas (1758–1823) 214
Davies Brothers Australian Letter Foundry 134-5

Davies, John (foundry) (1819–1896) 134-5
Davies, John (Hobart *Mercury*) (1813–1872) 129
Davies, John (London Missionary Society) (1772–1855) 390
Davies, John J. (textbook author) 368
Davies, W.W. (fl. 1845–1854) 125, 132, 407
Davis, Rev. Richard 390
Davitt, Ellen (1820–1879) 165, 242
Dawbin, Annie Baxter (1816–1905) 443
Dawson, James (1806–1900) 7, 21; *The Australian Aborigines* 167
Deakin, Alfred (1856–1919) 191
Deane, John Philip (1796–1849) 270, 352
Deane, Rosalie (née Paine) 270
Degotardi, John (1823–1882) 82, 131, 395; *Art of Printing* 50, 359
Degotardi, Josephine (1846-?) 82
DeLittle of York 135-6
DeLittle, Robert Duncan 135-6
Demarr, James *Adventures in Australia Fifty Years Ago* 436
Deniehy, Daniel (1828–1865) 164, 346
Derwent Circulating Library 331, 333
Desroziers, Fernand 89
Detmold, William (1828–1884) 37, 48, 49, 103-10 *passim*, 277, 458
Deutsch, Hermann (1833–?) 50
Dickens, Charles 309, 332, 436-47 *passim*; *Pickwick Papers* (*The Posthumous Papers of the Pickwick Club*) 96, 159-60, 178-179, 187
Dicker, F.M. 379
Dickinson Type Foundry 128, 130
Diddams, H.J. & Co. 97
Dieri (language) 393, 397
Diggles, Silvester (1817–1880) 362; *The Ornithology of Australia* 97
directories 138, 160, 170, 283, 286, 372-81; New Zealand 377
directories by title
  Australian Almanack and General Directory for the Year of our Lord 1835 375
  Australian Almanack and Sydney Directory for the Year of our Lord 1834 375
  Adelaide Almanack, Town and Country Directory, 1864-83, 379
  Border Post Almanac 379
  Brabazon's New South Wales General Town Directory and Advertiser 375
  Cooktown Almanac, Northern Queensland Directory and Miners and Settlers' Companion...1876 432
  Directory of the City and District of Sydney for 1847 375
  Directory of the City and District of Sydney for MDCCCXLIV-V 374
  [Hobart, 1833] in *Memoir on the Practicability of Establishing a Permanent Communication...* 373
  Kerr's Melbourne Almanac, and Port Phillip Directory 1841 & 1842 162, 374
  Maryborough Almanac and Wide Bay and Burnett Business Directory 1874-75, 379
  New South Wales and Port Phillip General Post Office Directory for 1839 374
  New South Wales Calendar, and General Post Office Directory 1832-1836 373
  Newcastle Business Directory and Hunter River District Almanac 379
  Niven's Directory for Ballarat, & Ballarat East...1875 379
  Official Post Office Directory (New South Wales) 378
  Official Post Office Directory (Queensland) 378
  Official Post Office Directory of Victoria 378
  Sands, Sands and McDougall, Sands and Kenny directories [various titles] 375-88 *passim*
  Sands's Sydney and Suburban Directory 1889 283
  [South Australia, 1841] in *Report from Select Committee on South Australia, 1841* 374-5
  Squatters' Directory 1849 375
  Sydney Commercial Directory, compiled with the greatest of care... 375
  Tanner's Melbourne Directory 336
  Tasmania Post Office Directory 379
  Tasmanian Almanack 373
  Victoria Post Office Directory 378
  Victorian Directory 1851 375

Western Australian Almanack 379-80
Western Australian Almanack and Directory 380
Wood's Royal Southern Kalendar, Tasmanian Register...Australian & East Indian Official Directory 195. *See also* almanacs
Dolman, William 358
Domeny de Rienzi, G.L. 348
Douglass, Henry Grattan (1790–1865) 266
Dowling, Henry (1810–1885) 30, 96, 159-60, 178, 270, 369, 384
Dowling, Lilias 355
Dowling's First Book for Children: A Popular and Progressive Primer... 369
Drayton QLD 379
Drysdale, Robert 108, 111
Dubbo NSW 378
Duck Ponds VIC 304
Dudemain, Florentine 355
Duffy, James 267
Duncan Sinclair & Son 125
Duncan, John K. 432-3
Duncan, William Augustine (1811–1885) 159, 271; *Duncan's Weekly Register, of Politics, Facts and General Literature* 202, 322, 356, 363
Dunlop, Eliza Hamilton (1796–1880) *The Aboriginal Mother* 349-50, 356
Dunlop, James (1793–1848) 91
Dunolly, Thomas 9
Dürer, Albrecht 83
Dwight, H.T. (Henry Tolman) (1823–1871) 167, 168, 285, 286, 340, 344
Dwyer, E.J. (1864–1936) 280
Dymock, William (1861–1900) 280, 335, 339
Dyson, Edward (1865–1931) 118

E

Earle, Augustus (1793–1838) 352-3
Earnsey, John 434-5
Eaton & Wilson *The Ornithology of Australia* 97
Eaton, Henry Green (c.1811–1887) 97
Edgerton & Moore 37
edition sizes or print runs: 52, 76; books 53, 160, 161, 165, 170, 397; government publications 410-11;

job printing 37; magazines 228; mission presses 397, 400; newspapers 52, 61. *See also* circulation
Edmonds, J.B. 267
Edward, A.D. 82
Edwards Dunlop 49
Edwards, Ernest 81
Electric Photo Engraving Co. 80-81, 84, 88, 89
electrotype 48, 51-3, 97, 134, 136, 410
Ellard, Francis 354-5, 357, 358, 360
Ellard, Frederick 355-6
Ellery, R.L. (1827–1908) 413
Elliott, Joseph 345, 359
Ellis, Havelock (1859–1939) 308
Elliston, W.G. (William Gore) (1798–1872) 354, 407; *Views through Hobart Town* 96
Elvy, Robert Hammond (1830–1923) 359
emigrant guides 136, 286, 373, 374, 375, 379, 383, 384
Emmett, Henry James (1783–1848) 214-17 *passim*
Engel, J.A. 134
English and Australian Cookery Book 165
English Spelling Book, containing Easy and Familiar Lessons 368
engraving 74-102 *passim*; copperplate or steel line 75-7, 78, 83-4, 89, 90, 93, 97, 354; mezzotint 76-7; music-related 352-363 *passim*; process engraving 79-80; wood engraving and woodcuts 17-16, 75, 77-8, 85, 90-100 *passim. See also* illustrations, printing technology; printing, colour
Epitome of the Official History of New South Wales 411
Epworth Printing and Publishing House 399
Evandale TAS 318
Evandale Subscription Library 265, 327, 452
Evans, Benjamin S. 286
Evans, George William (1780–1852) 270
Evans and Campbell 109
exhibitions 408, 415; international 105, 115, 129, 132-*133*, 136, 201, 301, 408, 411; Launceston 324; Melbourne 43, 49, 52, 53, 107, 109, 131, 134-6 *passim*,

162, 163, 394, 411; Sydney 44, 92, 107, 163, 410, 411
exploration and expedition texts 100, 148, 151, 158, 260, 348, 353, 415
Eyre & Spottiswoode 173

F
F.B. Franklyn and Co. 43, 48, 127-8, 129. *See also* Franklyn, Francis Burnett
F.W. Niven & Co. 90. *See also* Niven, F.W.
Fairfax, John (1804–1877) 34, 42, 46, 57
Farmer, Little & Co. 128
Farquhar, George *Recruiting Officer* 148, 149
Fawkner, John Pascoe (1792–1869) 29, 30, 35, 126, 162, 200, 213, 270, 294, 333, 344
Ferguson, John (fl. 1866–1887) 369
Fergusson & Mitchell 82, 90
Fergusson & Moore 37
Fergusson, James (1829–1888) 37
Fergusson, M.W. (1848–1918) 54
Fernyhough, William Henry (1809–1849) 354
Ferres, John (1818–1898) 35, 128, 131, 408-11
Ffrench, Acheson (1810–1870) 446
Field, Barron (1786–1846) 349; *First Fruits of Australian Poetry* 155, 412; *Geographical Memoirs of New South Wales* 155; *Memoirs of James Hardy Vaux* 155
Fieldhouse, Samuel 116
Fiji 168; mission printing 389, 395
Fink, Theodore (1855–1942) 191
Finke River dialect 393
Fisher, Frederick 112
Fisher, James Churchill (c.1825–1891) 362
Fisher, Son & Co. 267
First Fleet 27, 122, 141, 151, 259, 261, 307
First lessons 390
First World War 116, 119
FitzRoy, Sir Charles (1796–1858) 162
Fiveash, Rosa (1854–1938) *Handbook to the City of Adelaide* 100
Flack, Alfred 105
Flierl, Johannes (1858–1947) 393
Flinders Island 200
fonts *see* type

Force and Fraud 165
Forest Creek, Mount Alexander Diggings VIC 188
Forster, Edward H. *438*
Forster, Thomas 356
Fortune, Mary (c.1833–c.1910) 143-4, 147, 164; *Australian Journal* 143-4, 165
foundries *see* type
Fourth Book of Lessons for the Use of Schools 369
Fowler, Frank (1833–1863) 238
France *see* French (language)
Franklin, Sir John (1786–1847) 412
Franklin, Miles (1879-1954) *My Brilliant Career* 450
Franklyn, Francis Burdett (c.1814–1869) 36, 48, 49, 127-9 *passim*,
Franklyn, H. Mortimer (1848?–1900) 245
Fraser and Cohen 341
Fraser, Robert Brown 45; *Handbook to the City of Adelaide* 100
Free Public Library (Sydney) 195, 292-315 *passim*, 320, 447. *See also* Public Library of NSW; State Library of NSW
Freemantle & Co. 49
Fremantle WA 37, 200, 279, 283, 357-8. *See also* Perth WA; Western Australia
French (language) 164, 196, 197, 205, 285, 286, 453, 459
French, C. (1842–1933) *A Handbook of the Destructive Insects of Victoria* 414
French Picpus Fathers 389
Fulton, John Walter 226
Furphy, Felix 437-8
Furphy, Joseph (1843–1912) 328; *Such is Life* 328, 426, 433, 437
Furse, Christopher (c.1832–1887) 135

G
Gaelic, Scots (language) 285. *See also* Celtic (languages)
Galbraith, William (1822–1911) 99
Gambier Islands 389
Gawler SA 321
Geelong VIC 90, 116, 117, *117*, 439; almanacs 162; booksellers and stationers 271, 280, 435; directories 336; libraries: free/public 304, private 266; mechanics' institutes 304, 321-2, 439;

newspapers and magazines 36, 201, 203, 205, 266, 271, 435, 443; paper mills 116, *117*,162, 200, 203; printing 55, 90
Geelong Free Library 304
Gemmell McCaul and Co. 281, 286
Gemmell, Tuckett, and Co. 342
Geography for the use of Australian Youth 369
George III, death 112
George Murray & Co Paper Mills Printing Works 94, 118
George Robertson & Co. 283, 458; *George Robertson's Books and Stationery List* 278; *George Robertson's Trade List of Goods to Arrive* 278. See also Robertson, George (1825–1898)
Geraldton WA 379
German (language) 126, 127, 130-1, 163-4, 196, 197, 202, 205, 213, 285, 386. *See also* Germans in Australia
Germans in Australia 90, 196, 263, 324, 459. *See also* German (language)
Gibbs, Shallard & Co. 37, 48, 54
Gilbert, G.A. (c. 1815–1877) *Port Phillip Magazine* 94
Gilbertese (language) 395
Gill, S.T. (Samuel Thomas) (1818–1880) 92, 94, 125, 188, *189*, 190; *Heads of the People* 99
Gillen, F.J. (Francis James) (1855–1912) 10
Ginibi, Ruby Langford (1934–2011) *Don't Take your Love to Town* 18; *Haunted by the Past* 17-19, 23
Ginn, Henry (1818–1892) 305
Gipps, Gov. George (1791–1847) 406
Gippsland VIC 6
Glasgow Book Warehouse 284
Glass, Charles E. (1833–1911) 286
Glenelg SA 34
gold rushes 36, 37, 68, 69, 91, 94, 99, 101, 109, 127, 136, 141, 162-3, 167, 188, *189*, 237, 444
Goode, Samuel (1818–1893) 35
Goodhugh & Hough 37
Goodwin, William Lushington (1798?–1862) 96
Gordon & Gotch 49, 55, 56, 129, 138, 195, 201

Gordon, Adam Lindsay (1833–1870) 139-40, 164, 167, 450; *Bush Ballads and Galloping Rhymes* 139; *Sea Spray and Smoke Drift* 167
Gordon, James (1779–1842) 262
Goulburn NSW 192, 266, 276, 379, 435
government printers 28, 29, 33, 35, 92, 99-100, 131, 152, 161, 406-16; list of all, to 1890, 407-8. *See also names of individual printers*
government printing 24, 27, 40, 50, 57, 72, 406-13; categories of publications 415; NSW 72, 80, 83, 84, 92, 106, 119, 124, 125, 131-4 *passim*, 371, 407, 410, 412; Queensland 97, 98, 408; South Australia 100, 161, 407; Tasmania/Van Diemen's Land 97, 115, 124, 212, 214, 407, 412, 413; Victoria 86, *87*, 95, 111, 128, 132, 371, 408, 410, 413, 414; Western Australia 407
Grange VIC 446
Grant, John (b.1776) 419-20
Greek (language) 44, 131, 135
Gregory, Rev. J.H. (1827–1897) 340
Greville & Co. 49, 378
Grey, Sir George (1812–1898) 340
Griffin, Benjamin Pitt 350
Griffith, Charles (1808–1863) *The Present State and Prospects of the Port Phillip District of New South Wales* 446
Griffith, Sir Samuel (1845–1920) 185
Griffiths, W.J. (1868–1945) 280
Grimstone, Mary Leman (1796?–1869) *Character, or Jew and Gentile* 157; *Cleone: A Tale of Married Life* 157; *Louisa Egerton* 157
Grocott, Alonzo 33
Grocott, James Turner 355-6
Gronau, Wilhelm 131
Grose, Major Francis (1758?–1814) 419
Grosse, Frederick (1828–1894) 88, 94; *Aborigines of Victoria* 95; *Gold Fields and Mineral Districts of Victoria* 95
Growth of Empire 118
Guildford WA 379
Guillaume, F.A. 265
Gunn, Ronald Campbell (1808–1881) 265
Gympie QLD *438*

H

Hailes, Nathaniel (1802–1879) 99
Halford, G.B. (1824–1910) *Thoughts, Observations, and Experiments on the Action of Snake Venom on the Blood* 82
Hall, Edward Smith (1786–1860) 33, 125
Hall, T.S. (1858–1915) 257
Halloran, Laurence (1765–1831)156
Ham, Thomas (1821–1870) *Atlas of Queensland* 97; *Port Phillip Magazine* 94
Hamel & Locher 85
Hamilton, George (1812–1883) *The Horse: Its Treatment in Australia* 84
Hamilton, Gov. Robert (1836–1895) 449
Hamilton, Teresa (1852–1932) 448, 449
Hand-colouring (illustrations) 85, 84, 86, 87, 113, 412. See also illustrations, printing technology; printing, colour
Handt, John (1794–1863) 393
Hansom Cab Publishing Company 171, *172*
Hanson, William (1816–1902) 134, 407
Harding, Robert Coupland (1849–1916) 131
Harpur, Charles (1813–1868) 140, 164; *Thoughts: A Series of Sonnets* 159
Harris, Alexander (1805–1874) 141
Harris, John (1754–1838) 421
Harrison, James (1816–1893) 36, 271, 435
Hart, W. (1840–1866) *Handbook to the City of Adelaide* 100
Harvey, J. H. (John Harvey) (1855–1938) *117*
Harwood, Charles 105
Hassall, Rowland (1768–1820) 439
Hatch, Henry John 232
Hauser, Miska 357
Hawai'i 389
Hawkesbury River 422
Hayes, Edward (1814–1870) 285
Haynes, John (1850–1917) 252
Hearn, William Edward (1826–1888) 346, 365
Hebrew (language) 127, 131, 164, 352, 356, 358, 386
Heinemann 144
heliotype 81-3
Hely, Frederick (1794–1836) 354-5
Hely, Mary (1818–1901) 354

Henriques, A. 36
Henry IV 49
Hermannsburg Mission 11, 393
Hermit in Van Diemen's Land, The 212
Hill, Alfred (fl. 1820s) 33, 156
Hill, Richard (1782–1836) 346
Hill, Samuel Prout (1821–1861) 236
Hillman, A. *Journal of an Expedition to Explore the Interior of Western Australia* 101
Hindmarsh SA 321
History of Australia 167, 366, 370
History of New South Wales from the Records 411
Hobart 211-21; almanacs 96, 263, 373, *384*; bookbinding 105; booksellers and stationers 157-8, *166*, 261, 283; directories 373; libraries: 298-9, 310, 317; circulating 331, lending 299, private 266, subscription 154, 424-5, 444; literary societies 426-7, 446, 448-50; mechanics' institutes 318, 425, 429, 444; music 270, 351, 352, 353-4, 358; newspapers and magazines 29, 156, 157, 161, 202, *218*, 219, 226-35 *passim*, 260, 263, 283, 417, 422, 426-35 *passim*; paper making 115; printing 28-9, 34, 96-7, 125, 157, 212, 214, *384*; publishing 96, 153, 156, 157, 165, 228, 230-1, 352, 354, 368; schools of arts 425. See also Tasmania/Van Diemen's Land
Hobart Mechanics' Institute 425, 431, 432, 429, 444
Hobart Town Book Society 425, 426-7, 446
Hobart Town Circulating Library 270
Hochkirch (Tarrington) VIC 285
Hodder & Stoughton 288
Hodgson, Arthur 358
Holtermann Collection *198*, 332
Home and Colonial Library 269
Hood, Robin Lloyd (1828–1916) 96
Hood, Robin Vaughan (1802–1888) 96, 105
Hopkins, Francis (1844–1913) 386
Hopkins, Livingstone aka Hop (1846–1927) 240
Horne, R.H. (Richard Henry) aka 'Orion' (1802–1884) 141, 346
Hornsby, Marryat 351

Horse, The: Its Treatment in Australia 84
Horsham VIC 204
Hovell, William (1786–1875) 154
Howe, Ann (1802–1842) 375, 385
Howe, George (1769–1821) 28, 32, 66, 107, 113, 122-3, 151-3, 155, 158, 199, 262-3, 368, 382, 388-90 *passim*, 411-12, 439. *See also* Sydney Gazette
Howe, George Terry (1806–1863) 407
Howe, Robert (1795–1829) 33, 263, 266, 385, 386, 388, 407, 412
Howitt, A.W. (1830–1908) *Native Tribes of South-East Australia* 21; *Notes on the contact of the metamorphic and sedimentary formations on the Upper Dargo River* 82
Howitt, William (1792–1879) 141
Hudson, Alice *Systematic Account of the Geology of Tasmania* 97
Hudson, George 356
Huggins, Jackie (1956–) 16-17, 23; *Auntie Rita* 16-17
Huggins, Rita (1921–1996) 16-17, 18, 23; *Auntie Rita* 16-17
Hughes, George (fl. 1795–1801) 28, 29, 122-3, 149, 151, 406, 407
Hughes, William Daniel 116
Hull, William *Remarks on the Probable Origin and Antiquity of the Aboriginal Natives* 94
Hullmandel, Charles 78
Hume, Fergus (1859–1932) *The Mystery of a Hansom Cab* 170-172
Hume, Hamilton (1797–1873) 154
Hunter, Gov. John (1737–1821) 123, 151, 348
Hunter River 379
Hunter Valley 434
Hutchi[n]son, John F. 112
Hutchinson, Matthew Leighton (1830–1913) 284
Huxtable & Co. 379
Huxtable and Deakin 357
Hyett, C.W. 287

I

Illustrated London News 194, 195, 196, 429, 432, 441, 446
illustrations, printing techniques 75-102; costs of reproducing 85-6. *See also* engraving; lithography; photography, printing techniques
ink 27, 28, 48, 125, 157, 171; Australian-made 52, 99, 129, 200, 212, 456; imported 55, 127, 130; shortages 32, 153, 212
Imperial Photographic Company 82
Indigenous Australians 1-26, 388-405 *passim*; authors 14-20, 24, 133, 200; Black War 150; early engagement with print 1-26, 161, 307, 388-405 *passim*; languages, publications in 388-405 *passim*: Aranda 393, Arrernte 22, Awabakal 392-3, Dieri 393, 397, Narrinyeri 393, Ngarigu 353, 356, 357, Wangkumara 11, Western Bundjalung 11, Wiradjuri 393; languages, publications about 132-*133*, 161, 227, 368-9, 387, 388-405 *passim*, 413; literacy (European) 2, 5; message sticks 4, 6, 7, 8, 10, 25; newspaper 200; oral culture 1-26 *passim*, 149, 150, 307, 450; peoples: Aranda 393, Arrernte 11, Awabakal 392-3, Dieri 393, 397, Mudburra 10, Ngarigu 353, 356, 357, Pindjarup 350, Wangal 348, Warlpiri 13-14, Woiwurrung 9, Wurundjeri 162; publications about 3-21 *passim*, 91, 94, 95, 156, 167, 227, 228, 239, 350, 368-9, 387, 388-405 *passim*; 413; publications for 260, 261, 368-9, 388-405 *passim*, 400; reserves and missions 388-405 *passim*, Coranderrk 9-10, 21-2, Hermannsburg 11, 393, Killalpaninna 393, 399, Norfolk Island 392, 395; songs about 350; songs of 348-9, 353, 356, 357
Innes, Annabella (1826–1916) 442
Innes, Sir George Long (1834–1896) 453
Introduction to Botanic Teachings in the Schools of Victoria 371
Ipswich QLD 322, 379
Ipswich Mechanics' School of Arts 322
Irish Readers 370
Isaacs, Sir Isaac (1855–1948) 457
Isom, F.R. 398
Ivimey, A.J. 379

J

J. and A. McKinley 256
J. & R.M. Woods Austin Type Foundry 128
J.G. Schelter und Giesecke 130-1
J.J. Moore and Co. 283. *See also* Moore, Jeremiah John
'J.M.' 156
'J.R.M.' 156
Jamison, Sir John (1776-1844) 262
Jane Shore, The Tragedy of 28, *29*, 122
Jemott, William 263
Jenny, Rudolph (1830-1905) 85, 88, 94; *Victoria in 1880* 95, 100
Jervis, Henry Cooper (1816-?) 99
jobbing trade 34-7 *passim*, 41, 44, 45, 48, 53-71 *passim*, *172*, 204
Johnson, Rev. Richard (1753-1827) 260, 261, 260, 307, 365, 438-9; *Address to the Inhabitants...Established in New South Wales and Norfolk Island...1792* 151
Johnson, W.J. 356, 357
Johnston, Robert M. (1843-1918) 413; *Systematic Account of the Geology of Tasmania* 97
Johnstone, Barnett (1832-1910) *297*
Jones, Edward 348
Jones, W. 267, 368
Jones, William 435 (bookseller, Goulburn)
Jose, Arthur (1863-1934) 118
Josephson, Joshua Frey (1815-1892) 353
Joubert, Leon 89
journalists and journalism 53, 60, 141-6 *passim*, 161, 164, 165, 189, 191, 199, 223-53 *passim*, 271, 322, 346, 366, 460
journals, professional and trade 255-7; reading of 428-33
journals, professional and trade, by title
Australasian Insurance and Banking Record 256
Australasian Typographical Journal 40, 59, 129
Australian Jurist 256
Australian Jurist and Notes of Cases 256
Australian Law Times 256
Australian Magazine, or Quarterly... Literature, Science, Philosophy, Agriculture, Morals...Religion 225
Australian Medical Journal 256, 336
Australian Quarterly Journal of Theology, Literature and Science 225
Journal of the Agricultural & Horticultural Society of Western Australia 256
Journal of the Bankers' Institute of Australasia 256
Medical Journal of Australia 256
New South Wales Medical Gazette 432
Papers and Proceedings of The Royal Society of Van Diemen's Land 256
Tasmanian Athenaeum, Or, Journal of Science, Literature and Arts 238
Tasmanian Journal of Agriculture 430
Tasmanian Journal of Natural Science, Agriculture, Statistics &c. 256, 412
Juvenile Circulating Library 334

K

Kalgoorlie WA 101
Kavanagh, Sgt Thomas 352
Keily, Eugene William 172
Kelly, John 86
Kemp & Boyce 170
Kemp and Fairfax 132
Kemp, Charles (1813-1864) 34
Kempe, Hermann 393
Kendall, Henry (1839-1882) 78, 140, 244, 440, 450; *Leaves from Australian Forests* 167; *Orana: An Illustrated Poem* 78; *Poems and Songs* 164
Kendall, Thomas (1778-1832) 390
Kenny, Thomas (1820-1866) 116
Kent, Capt. William (1751-1812) 262
Kerr, A.C. 379
Kerr and Curtis 36
Kerr, Nathaniel 117
Kerr, William (1812-1859) 35-6, 162, 229
Keystone Type Foundry 128
Khull, Edward (1805-1884) 132, 408
Killalpaninna Mission 393, 399
King, George 393
King, Gov. Philip Gidley (1758-1808) 29, 32, 66, 151, 406
Knaggs, R.C. (1809-1877) 379
Knopwood, Rev. Robert (1763-1838) 194
Koenig, Friedrich 39
Kopperamanna Mission 398

Kornhardt, Carl 386
Krebs, Benjamin 131
Krefft, Gerard (1830–1881) *Australian Mammals* 92; *Snakes of Australia* 92

L

L. Sharwood & Co. 49
La Trobe, Charles Joseph (1801–1875) 8
Lackington, James 284
Lady Hamilton Literary Society 448-9, *449*
Lajamanu NT 13
Lake Macquarie NSW 392
Lamb & Parbury General Merchants 125
Lambert, William V. (1818–1906) 135
Lang, John (1816–1864) *Aurora Australis* 227; *Legends of Australia* 158
Lang, John Dunmore (1799–1878) 132, 225, 266, 270, 346
Lang, Walter 262
Langford, Nobby 17, 18, 20
languages, foreign, availability of publications in 163-4, 170, 196-7, 185-6, 386, 453. See also *individual languages*
languages, Indigenous Australian *see* Indigenous Australians, languages
languages, Pacific Islands 107, 388-405 *passim*
Larra, James (1749–1839) 262
Latin (language) 341, 368
Launceston TAS 115; artists 96; booksellers and stationers *166-7*, 266, 267, 268, 271, 283; exhibition 324; libraries: 265, circulating 162, 333, public 319, subscription 265; literary societies 299; mechanics' institute 299, 318, 319, 327; newspapers and magazines 46, 53, 161, 201, 430; music 351, 352, 362; printing 29, 30, 34, 35, 46, 53, 86, *384*; publishing 86, 159-60, 178-*179*, 369. See also Hobart; Tasmania/Van Diemen's Land
Launceston Library Society 265
Launceston Mechanics' Institute 319, 327
Launceston Philharmonic Society 362
Launceston Public Library 319
Launceston Synagogue 352
Lavenu, Lewis Henry (1818–1859) 363
Law, Arthur 172

Lawson, Henry (1867–1922) 139, 142, 146, 249, 433
Lawson, Louisa (1848–1920) 252
Lawson, Lt William (1774–1850) 154
Le Plastrier, H.J. (Henry J.) *The Travels and Adventures of Mr Newchamp* 79
Lee & Ross 399
Lee, Alfred (1858–1923) 342
Lee, Edward 399
Lee, Richard 238
Lees, Samuel E. (1843–1916) 399
legal publishing *see* journals, professional and trade
Leichhardt, Ludwig (1813–1848) 126
Leigh, S.T. & Co. 89, 94
Lenakel (language) 398
Lever, Charles James *Charles O'Malley, the Irish Dragoon* 160
Levey and Robson 129
Levey, Oliver 49, 55, 128, 129
Levey, Robson and Franklyn 35
Levy, George William 89
Lewin, John (1770–1819) *Birds of New Holland* 91; *Birds of New South Wales with their Natural History* 107, 113, 412
Lewis (auctioneer) 262
Lewis, Leon *The Trapper's Last Trail* 244
Lhotsky, John (1800–1866?) 159, 229, 353
librarians 296, *297*, 298, 301, 309-11
libraries: commercial circulating 154, 265, 266, 267, 293, 297, 298, 306, 319, 320, 330-7, 420-4 *passim*; free/public 307-15 *passim*; funding 295-311 *passim*; lending 293-309, 333 *passim*, 423-5, 447; private 110, 266, 285-6, 293, 338-47, 420, 425, 429, 452, 457; rural services 302, 311; subscription 292-316 *passim*, 318, 320, 321, 327, 444, 446. See also *individual towns and cities*; literary and reading societies; mechanics' institutes; schools of arts
Library of New South Wales 297
Light, William (1786–1839) *Brief Journal* 161
Liley, Thomas 356
Lindsay, H.L. *Industrial Resources of Victoria* 167

Index

Linger, Carl (1810–1862) 359
Lingham, Henry (1819–1901) *Port Phillip Magazine* 94
linotype 27, 51, 58-9, 60, 61, 458. *See also* printing technology
Lipscomb, William (1841–1913) 434, 435, 439
literacy 419, 433, 436-37, 445, 450
literary and reading societies 264, 294, 299, 316, 425, 445-50. *See also* libraries; mechanics' institutes
Lithographic Drawings of Sydney and its Environs 91
lithography 48, 50, 55, 58, 70, 77, 79, 82-101 *passim*, 118, 127-36 *passim*, 158, 159, 168, 266-7, 395; chromolithography 84, 86, *87*; development of 78-9; examples of *87-88*, *189*, *384*; government usage of 410, 411; music 352-62 *passim*. *See also* engraving; illustrations, printing technology; photography
Liverpool NSW paper mill 116, 119
Loane and Hall 263
Lockwood, Douglas (1918–1980) *I, The Aboriginal* 15, 23
Logan, Maria 353-4
London Missionary Society 156, 389, 390, 392, 399, 439
London Typographical Society 48
Longman, Rees & Co. 267
Lord, Simeon (1771–1840) 262, 421
Lothian, John (1851–1940) 288
Low, Francis 375
Loyalty Islands (language and peoples) 389
Loyau, George (1835–1898) *The Gawler Handbook* 164; *Representative Men of South Australia* 164; *The Sydney Songster* (under alias 'George Chanson') 351
Lumley, Edward (1806?–1874) 267, 268-9, 338
Lyall, Scott & Co., 125
Lyall, William (1821–1888) 345
Lyceum for Literary and Scientific Discussion, Lectures, Etc. 322
Lyons, Samuel (1791–1851) 427
Lyster Opera Company 363

M

M. of Anambaba (pseud. of John McGarvie) 349
McCarron, Bird, Püttmann and Stewart 37
Macarthur, Elizabeth (1766–1850) 261, 339
Macarthur family 339
McCombie, Thomas (1819–1869) *Arabin* 436
McCoy, Sir Frederick (1817–1899) *Prodromus of the Palaeontology of Victoria* 95; *Prodromus of the Zoology of Victoria* 85, *87*, 95, 345
Macdonald, G.J. 228
Macdougall, Archibald 161, 407
McDougall, Dugald (1834–1885) 45
McDougall, James (1843–1909) 116
Macfaull, Charles (1800–1846) 34, 37, 387, 407
Macfaull, Elizabeth 407
McGarvie, John (1795–1853) 225, 269-70, 349, 417
McGarvie, William (1810–1841) 269-70, 332-3
McGarvie's circulating library *see* Australian Stationery Warehouse
Macgregor, John (1828–1884) 279, 342
Mack, Louise (1870–1935) 191
Mackay, George (1860–1948) *History of Bendigo* 82
Mackay, Robert (fl. 1850s–1860s) 284
MacKellar, Smiths & Jordan 128, 129, 130
Mackenzie, Kenneth *Master Tyll Owlglass* 168
Mackinolty, Chips (b.1954) 11, 22
McLean, Robert *New Atlas of Australia* 93
McLeay, Alexander (1767–1848) 266, 345
Maclehose, James (1811–1885) 374; *Picture of Sydney and Strangers' Guide to New South Wales* 92, 374
Macquarie, Gov. Lachlan (1762–1824) 2, 155, 214, 307
Macquarie Paper Mills 112, 113
Maddock, William (1835–1917) 280, 335
Mader, Frederick 358
magazines 222-57. *See also* costs; journals, professional and trade; prices

magazines, by title
　Adelaide Punch 241
　Adelaide's Miscellany of Useful and Entertaining Knowledge 234
　Advocate (Melbourne) 241, 428
　Arden's Sydney Magazine 232
　Austral-Asiatic Review (Hobart) 226
　Austral Review (Melbourne) 246
　Australian Cadeau (Sydney) 357
　Australian Churchman (Sydney) 399
　Australian Family Journal (Sydney) 237
　Australian Gold-Diggers' Monthly Magazine: Colonial family visitor (Melbourne) 237
　Australian Home Companion (Melbourne) 237
　Australian Journal (Melbourne) 141, 143, 165, 241, 242-4, 246, 431, 450
　Australian: A Monthly Magazine (Melbourne) 245-6
　Australian Magazine (Sons of Australia) (Sydney) 229-30
　Australian Magazine (Ralph Mansfield) (Sydney) 412
　Australian Magazine: or Compendium of Religious, Literary, and Miscellaneous Intelligence (Sydney) 225
　Australian Magazine, or Quarterly Journal of Literature, Science, Philosophy... (Melbourne) 225
　Australian Monthly Magazine (Melbourne) 242
　Australian News for Home Readers (Melbourne) 241
　Australian Penny Journal (Sydney) 233
　Australian Quarterly Journal of Theology, Literature and Science (Sydney) 225
　Australian Temperance Magazine (Sydney) 230
　Australian Weekly Magazine of Literature, Art and Fashion (Melbourne) 251
　Australian Women's Magazine and Domestic Journal (Melbourne) 251, 252
　Ballarat Punch 241
　Blossom (Sydney) 226
　Bulletin (Sydney) 44, 80, 191, 223-54 passim, 433, 450, 459
　Cole's Book Buyers' Guide (Melbourne) 280
　Colonial Advocate (Hobart) 212, 226
　Colonial Book Circular and Bibliographical Record (London) 280
　Colonial Literary Journal (Sydney) 233, 242
　Colonial Monthly Magazine (Melbourne) 241
　Crouch's Epitome of News (Sydney) 237
　Dawn: A Journal for Australian Women (Sydney) 252
　Evening News (Sydney) 252
　Freeman's Journal (Sydney) 237, 431
　George Robertson's Monthly Book Circular (Melbourne) 241, 278
　Harbinger of Light (Melbourne) 244, 281
　Heads of the People (Sydney) 235-6, 239
　Hobart Town Magazine 228, 230-1
　Hobart Town Monthly Magazine 157
　Humbug (Melbourne) 241
　Illustrated Australian Magazine (Melbourne) 94, 239
　Illustrated Journal of Australasia (Melbourne) 359
　Illustrated Sydney News 241, 432
　Illustrations of the Present State and Future Prospects of New South Wales (Sydney) 229
　Lantern: A Satirical Paper for Australians (Adelaide) 246
　Laughing Jackass (Melbourne) 241
　Life: Fun, Fact and Fiction (Melbourne) 252
　Literary News...Fact and Fiction; The Arts, Sciences and Belles Lettres (Sydney) 229, 427
　Lone Hand (Sydney) 252
　Melbourne Bulletin 250-1
　Melbourne Punch 203, 237, 239-240, 251, 363, 450
　Melbourne Review 168, 244-6, 247-9
　Melbourne Vocalist 358
　Miner and Weekly Star (Ballarat) 203
　Minstrelsy of the West (Fremantle) 357

Month, The (Sydney) 238
Monthly Book Circular (Melbourne) 167
Mullen's Monthly Circular of Literature, &c. (Melbourne) 279, 335, 460
Native Companion (Melbourne) 114
New South Wales Magazine (Sydney) 228, 232
New South Wales Sporting Magazine (Sydney) 235
Port Phillip Magazine 94
Quadrilateral: Moral, Social, Scientific and Artistic (Hobart) 246
Queensland Figaro...Society, Sport and the Drama (Brisbane) 146, 251
Queensland Punch (Brisbane) 246
Quiz: A Satirical, Social and Sporting Journal (Adelaide) 251
Rainbow (Melbourne) 280
Satirist and Sporting Chronicle (Sydney) 251
South-Asian Register (Sydney) 225, 226-8
South Australian Magazine (Adelaide) 234
South Australian Odd Fellows' Magazine (Adelaide) 235
Southern Euphrosyne (Sydney and London) 356, 357
Spirit of the Age (Sydney) 237
Sydney Harmonicon 357
Sydney Punch 92, 241
Tasmanian (Hobart) 425
Tasmanian Punch (Hobart) 241
Tegg's Monthly Magazine (Sydney) 229, 434
Touchstone (Melbourne) *241*
Tribune (Sydney) 252
Victorian Review (Melbourne) 245, 248
Walch's Literary Intelligencer and General Advertiser (Hobart) 237, 279, 282
Wide Awake: Illustrated Weekly of Pastimes, Fiction, Fashion, Science, Art, Drama (Melbourne) 251
Women's World: Australian Magazine of Literature and Art (Melbourne) 251
Magee, Charles 267
Maiden, J.H. (1859–1925) *The Flowering Plants and Ferns of New South Wales* 84
Maitland NSW 201, 320, 434-5
Maldon VIC 328
Mansfield, Ralph (1799–1880) 225, 228, 368, 385-6; *Analytical View of the Census of New South Wales for the Year 1846* 436
Māori (language, missions, peoples) 388, 390, 397, 412
maps and atlases 76-97 *passim*, 170, 171, 178, 182, 299, 374, 379, 410
marginalia 453
Marika, Wandjuk (1927–1987) 12, 13,14, 22; *Wandjuk Marika: Life Story* 14
Marist Fathers (Society of Mary) 389
Markby, John (1843–1920) 136
Markus. Ta Fasao Erefia O Iesu Kristo 396
Marsden, Rev. Samuel (1764–1838) 152, 155, 307-8, 390, 392, 423-4
Marsh, Henry 356, 357
Marsh, Stephen Hale (1805–1888) 355, 357, 363
Marston, Edward 173, 268
Martin, A. Patchett (1851–1902) 247
Maryborough QLD 438
Maryborough VIC 36
Mason, Charles 92
Mason, Cyrus 86, 94; *Australian Christmas Story Book* 86
Mason, Edward 92
Mason, Firth & McCutcheon 90
Mason, Frederick 92
Mason, George 92
Mason, Walter George 92
Massina, A.H. (1834–1917) 48
Matthew, William 136
Maughan, Rev. James (1826–1871) *343*
Maund, John (1823–1858) 345
Mavor, William 368
Maxwell, Charles (c.1849–1889) 256-7
May, John (1825–1898) 48, 52
May, Phil (1864–1903) 240
May, Thomas (1825–1905) 48
mechanics' institutes 163, 196-7, 294, 299, 303, 307, 308, 316-29, *323*, 425-7, 456; and women 193, 319, 326. *See also individual towns, cities and States*; libraries; schools of arts

Melanesia (languages and missions) 389-99 *passim*. *See also individual countries*
Melanesian Mission 399
Melanesian Mission Press 398
Melba, Dame Nellie (1861–1931) 459
Melbourne Athenaeum 321
Melbourne Circulating Library 335, *336*
Melbourne Mechanics' Institution 294, 321
Melbourne Philharmonic Society 363
Melbourne Photo Engraving Co. 90
Melbourne Public Library 83, 141, 163, 265, 275, 279, 292-321 *passim*, 339, 409
Melbourne Typographical Society 51, 68, 69
Melville, Adam Graham (1842–1921) 279, 335, 385
Melville, Henry (1799–1873) 96, 231, 385; *The Bushrangers, or Norwood Vale* 158
Menges, Henry 392, 398
message sticks 4, 6, 7, 8, 10, 25
Methodist Mission 399
Meyer, H.A.E. (1813–1862) 393
Michael, James Lionel (1824–1868) 164
Michael Howe, the Last and worst of the bushrangers of Van Diemen's Land 212
Michie, Archibald (1813–1899) 346; *Readings in Melbourne* 193
Micronesia 389. *See also individual countries*
Middleton & Maning 379
Middows, Frank 136
Miller & Richard 128, 129
Minchen, E.W. (1852–1913) 84
Minto NSW 201
mission presses 388-405
missions, religious 11, 136, 156, 388–405, 423. *See also names of individuals and individual societies*
Mitchell, David Scott (1836–1907) 341-2, 344, 452, 457. *See also* Mitchell Library
Mitchell Library 341-2
Mitchell, Sir Thomas (1792–1855) *Notes on the Cultivation of the Vine and the Olive* 159
Moffitt, William (1802–1874) 35, 104-5, 106, 111, 159, 270
Montagu, John (1797–1853) 216
Moore, J. (1803–1885) 128

Moore, Jeremiah John (c.1819–1883) 271, 358
Moore, J.S. (Joseph Sheridan) (1828–1891) 238
Moore, William (1824–1880) 37
Moore Theological College library 293
Moreton Bay QLD 36, 160, 322, 392
Morley, George 351
Morris, Edward E. (1843–1902) 171, 247
Morrison, W. Frederic (1837–1897+) 118
Mort, T.S. (1816–1878) 439
Mortimer, Benjamin (fl. 1850s) 281
Mortimer, William Henry 94
Moss, Phineas (1795–1866) 386
Mota (language) 392, 395
Mt Franklin VIC 8
Mudburra (people) 10
Mueller, Baron Sir Ferdinand von (1825–1896) 85, 115, 413; *Fragmenta phytographiae Australiae* 85; *Iconography of Australian Species of Acacia* 95; *Introduction to Botanic Teachings in the Schools of Victoria...* 371
Mullen, Samuel (1828–1890) 102, 167, 168, 170, 195, 205, 276-88 *passim*, 367, 370; *S. Mullen's Monthly Circular of Literature, &c.* 279, 335, 460
Mullen, William (c.1835–1903) 279
Mullen's Select Library 321, 327, 458
Müller, Oscar 285
Müller, William *Journal of an Expedition to Explore the Interior of Western Australia* 101
Murray, Andrew (1813–1880) 407; *Commerce: Its Laws, Their Anti-Christian Spirit...Their Demoralizing Tendency* 161; almanacs 161, 383-4, 386
Murray, Baldwin & Cradock 267
Murray, George (1832–1898) 94, 118
Murray, Gilbert (1866–1957) 276
Murray, H.N. 156
Murray, John III 269
Murray (publisher) 282
Murray, Robert Lathrop (1777–1850) 217, 417
Murray, Terence (1810–1873) 276
museums 83, 97, 257, 264, 298, 306, *307*, 313, 319, 325, 326, 409, 457

music 348-64; folksongs, Australian 350, 351; hymns 351, 358, 362, 388-95 passim, 400; Indigenous Australians, songs about 348-9, 350, 353, 356, 412; publishing and sales 273

music, by title: 'A collection of psalms and tunes...for the use of St George's Church, Hobart Town' 354; *The Aboriginal Mother* 350; *Adelaide Miscellany* 359; *Adelaide Musical Herald* 359; *Adoro te* 356; 'All around my hat' 355; *Ancient Hebrew Melodies* 358; *Australian Album* 357; 'Australian and Aboriginal Melodies' 356; *Australian Cadeau* 357; *Australian Harmonist* 351; *Australian Presentation Album* 357; *Australian Quadrilles* 351; *Australian Scrap Book* 351; *Bellini's Norma, at the New Theatre...Melbourne* 363; 'Billy Barlow in Australia' 351; *Boulanger's Keepsake for 1856* 358; *Catholic Hymns, Litanies, &c.* 358; *Collection of thirty standard psalm tunes* 362; *Coxon's Comic Songster* 351; *The Crown of Thorns* 359; *Currency Lasses* 353; *Delcourt Bouquet* 357; *Don John of Austria* 357; *Echo's Song* 353; *Emu* 359; 'The Exile of Erin on the Plains of Emu' 349; *Gentlemen in Black* 363; *Hebrew Melodies* 356; *Hymns for the eighth anniversary of the Parramatta Sunday School* 351; *Illustrated Journal of Australasia* 359; *Illustrated Melbourne Post* 359; 'The Jackets of Green' 350; *A Journey from Sydney to the Australian Alps* 351; *Kangaroo* 359; *Koorinda Braia* 356; *Kyrie* 256; 'La Engehurst' 354; 'La Wooloomooloo' 354; *The Lays of the Hebrews* 358, 360-1;*Long Live Victoria* 356; *Maritana* 363; *Mass in D* 359; *Melbourne Vocalist* 358; *Merry Freaks in Troublous Times* 356, 363; *The Minstrel Waltz* 354; *The Minstrelsy of the West* 357; *The Mock Catalani, in Little Puddleton* 363; *The Much Admired Australian Quadrilles* 354; 'Murdoch Delany's Description of the Races' 349; 'The Overlander' 351; *The Parting* 354; 'The Pretty Bark Hut in the Bush' 363; *The Queenslander's New Colonial Camp Fire Song Book* 351; *Select portions of the Psalms of David* 351; *The Separation Polka* 358; *Shaksperi Conglommorofunnidogammoniae* 363; *Singing Class Manual* 362; *Song* (Lhotsky) 353; *The Song of Australia* 359; *Song of Victoria* 358; 'South Australian Melody' 349; *The Southern Euphrosyne* 356; *Sydney Harmonicon* 357; *The Sydney Polka* 362; *The Sydney Songster* 351; *Tasmanian Lyre* 357; *Tasmanian Songster* 351; *Thatcher's Colonial Minstrel* 351; *Thatcher's Colonial Songster* 351; *Thatcher's Goldigger's Songster* 351; *Van Diemen's Land Quadrilles* 354; *Victoria Songster* 351; 'The Vow that Breathed in Solitudes' 354; *Walze favorite du Duc de Reichstadt* 354

Mutiny, The 119

N

N.S.W. Bookstall Company 283
Nagel, Charles 356, 363
Narrinyeri (language) 393
Nathan, Isaac (1790–1864) 350, 355, 356-7, 363
National Gallery (Melbourne) 409
National Museum (Melbourne) 409, 457
Native Book of Worship 393
Nayler, Benjamin Suggitt (1796–1875) 281; *Penny readings: institutions for elevating the unlettered masses* 444
Neild, James Edward (1824–1906) 335
Neilson, John Shaw (1872–1942) 328
Nettleton, Charles (1826–1902) 89
Neumayer, George (1826–1909) 413
New Books added to Maddock's Select Library, 383 George Street, Sydney 335
New Britain 389, 395
New Caledonia 289, 395
New Guinea 389, 390, 395
New Hebrides (Vanuatu) 389, 395, 398
New Norfolk Reading Association 445
New South Wales Album 84
New South Wales General Standing Orders and General Orders 123, 152, 411
New South Wales in 1881 411

Index

New South Wales Typographical Society 252

New Zealand 129-30; Cowan & Co.; circulating libraries 322; directories 377, 378; Māori (language and peoples) 388, 391; missions 388-391 *passim*, 397; printing 391; unions 70

Newbery, J. Cosmo (1843–1895) 117

Newcastle NSW 320

Newgate Calendar 422, 437, 443

newspapers 188-221. *See also* circulation; costs; edition sizes; journals; magazines; prices; wages and income

newspapers by title (Australian)
  Aboriginal or Flinders Island Chronicle 200
  Adelaide Daily Telegraph 143
  Adelaide Observer 80
  Adelaide Punch 100
  Advertiser (Adelaide) 53
  Age (Melbourne) 43, 53, 118, 119, 188, 194, 202, 203, 204, 458
  Alfred (Sydney) 425
  Argus (Melbourne) 37, 41-2, 127, 188, 189, 200, 204, 205, 274, 276, 460
  Armidale Express 46
  Atlas (Sydney) 92, 437
  Austral-Asiatic Review (Hobart) 417
  Australasian (Melbourne) 117, 143, 144, 189, 164, 192-3, 203, 205, 460
  Australasian Chronicle (Sydney) 202, 356, 427
  Australian (Sydney) 32, 154, 156, 201, 204, 211, 218
  Australian Graphic (Sydney) 89
  Australian Pictorial Weekly (Melbourne) 88
  Australian Sketcher (Melbourne) 88, 203
  Australian Town and Country Journal (Sydney) 118, 165, 203
  Australische Deutsche Zeitung (Sydney) 131
  Australische Zeitung (Adelaide) 131
  Ballarat Evening Mail 117
  Ballarat Star 89
  Ballarat Trumpeter 188, *189*
  Bell's Life 188
  Bendigo Advertiser 117, 281

Boomerang (Brisbane) 99
Border Post and Stannum Miner (Stanthorpe QLD) 38
Braidwood Dispatch and Mining Journal 442
Britannia and Trades' Advocate (Hobart) 202
Chinese Advertiser (Ballarat) 136. *See also English and Chinese Advertiser*
Colac Herald 206
Colonial Times (Hobart) 132, 212, 213, 219, 352
Colonist (Sydney) 34, 132
Courier (Brisbane) 118, 134. *See also Moreton Bay Courier*
Courier-Mail (Brisbane) 203
Courrier Australien, Le (Sydney) 459
Daily Telegraph (Adelaide) 143
Daily Telegraph (Melbourne) 203
Daily Telegraph (Sydney) 47, 53, 60
Derwent Star (Hobart) 29
Deutsche Post für die australischen Colonien/German Australian Post (Adelaide) 127, 163, 202
Diggers' Advocate (Melbourne) 194
Duncan's Weekly Register, of Politics, Facts and General Literature (Sydney) 202
Echo (Sydney) 118
Empire (Sydney) 35, 43, 118, 431
English and Chinese Advertiser (Ballarat) 136, 164. *See also Chinese Advertiser*
Evening Journal (Adelaide) 80
Evening News (Sydney) 203
Evening Star (Melbourne) 117
Fremantle Observer 37, *380*
Fremantle Observer, Perth Gazette and Western Australian Journal 380
Geelong Advertiser 36, 205, 271, 435, 443
Goldfields Courier (Coolgardie WA) 101
Goulburn Chronicle 44
Goulburn Herald 43-4, 435
Graphic News of Australasia (Melbourne) 88
Gympie Times and Mary River Mining Gazette 438

Herald (Melbourne), 49, 36, 127, 169, 188, 201, 203, 283
Hobart Mercury 128, 429
Hobart Town Courier 129, 352, 354, 426
Hobart Town Gazette 107, 114, 125, 126, 156, 212-21 *passim*, *218*, 260, 261, 263, 422
Horsham Times 204
Illustrated Australian News (Melbourne) 47
Illustrated Melbourne Post 203, 359
Illustrated Sydney News 81, 92, 102, 118, 203, 431
Inquirer (Perth) 101
Inquirer and Commercial News (Perth) 379-380
Journal de Melbourne 164
Launceston Examiner 46-7, 53
Leader (Melbourne) 203, 205
Maitland Mercury 43, 350, 432, 434-5, 439
Melbourne Advertiser 30, 162, 200
Melbourne Albion 36
Melbourne Church of England Messenger 237
Melbourne Courier 35
Melbourne Daily News 41
Melbourne Herald, 49, 127, 201, 283
Miner and Weekly Star (Ballarat) 203
Monitor (Sydney) 425
Moreton Bay Courier 36, 132, 160, 200-1. *See also Courier* (Brisbane)
News Letter of Australasia: A Narrative of Events, or a Letter to send to Friends (Melbourne) 194, 237-8
News of the Week (Geelong) 203
Observer (Adelaide) 45
Ovens Constitution 200
Perth Gazette 34, 350
Port Phillip Gazette 30, 135, 162
Port Phillip Herald 35, 126, 162
Port Phillip Patriot and Melbourne Advertiser 35, 105
Queensland Figaro (Brisbane) 99
Queensland Punch (Brisbane) 99
Queenslander (Brisbane) 99, 203
Register (Adelaide) 53, 105
South Australian Gazette and Colonial Register (London England, and Adelaide SA) 34, 161, 201
South Australian Register (Adelaide SA) 55, 161, 200
Southern Australian (Adelaide) 161, 349
Southern Cross (Sydney) 164
Sydney Gazette 66, 104, 107, 113, 123-4, 199, 218, 293, 351; advertisements in 260, 261, 262, 270, 339, 352, 368, 375, 439; almanac 152-3, 385; delivery of 201; fiction 155; music 349, 351, 352; poetry 155; printing for missions 388, 390; type 124
Sydney Herald 34, 41, 42, 200, 201, 270, 407, 425, 427
Sydney Mail 203, 431
Sydney Mercantile Advertiser 51
Sydney Monitor 124, 125, 156, 349
Sydney Morning Herald 39, 46, 53,118, 201, 204-5, 274, 431, 435
Table Talk (Melbourne) 203
Tasmanian (Hobart) 418, 425
True Colonist (Hobart) 354
Victoria Illustrated 76
Victoria Illustrated: Second Series 76
Victorian Miscellany and Wesleyan Chronicle 237
Voice of Jacob 127
Weekly Advertiser (Bendigo) 203
Weekly Mercury (Bendigo) 203
Weekly Times (Melbourne) 203
West Australian (Perth) 203
Western Mail (Perth) 101, 203
Yeoman and Australian Acclimatizer, The (Melbourne) 135
Yr Australydd (Melbourne) 164, 286
newspapers, manuscript 30, 146, 190, 191, 200
Newtown NSW 302
Ngarigu (people and language) 353, 357
Nhill VIC 328
Nichols, Isaac (1770–1819) 422
Nicholson, Sir Charles (1808–1903) 275, 341
Nil Desperandum Literary Society 448-9, *449*

Niven, F.W. (Francis Wilson) (1831–1905) 81, 82, 90, 379
Noone, John (1820–1893) 83
Norfolk Island 105, 149, 151; mission printing 389, 391, 394, 395
Norfolk Island Melanesian Mission 395
Norfolk Plains Book Society 445
Norman, W.C. 89
North Brisbane School of Arts 322, 326
North Melbourne Free Library & Mechanics' Institute 196
Northern Territory 9, 10, 11, 13, 21, 22
Northey, James (fl. 1889) 135
Note Book of Useful, Experimental and Entertaining Knowledge 368
Noufflard (Henri) (fl. 1850s–1860s) 345
novels, attitudes towards *See under* censorship

O

O'Shaughnessy, E.M. (1801–1840) 375
Oldfield, Roger 228
Orana: An Illustrated Poem 78
Orger and Meryon 265
Osborne, John Walter (1828–1902) 50, 83, 88
Oxford University Press 288
Oxley, John (1785?–1828) 154, 266, 421

P

Pacific Islands (languages) 107, 388-405 *passim*, 412. *See also individual languages and countries*
Packer, Charles Sandys (1810–1883) 357, 362
Palmer, Archdeacon John 392
paper and paper mills 27, 48, 112-21, 157; Australian-made, 109, 112-21 *passim*; price to purchase 157; imports 113, 114, 129; shortages 32, 113, 119, 152, 154, 199, 200, 212, 394
Papers and Proceedings of The Royal Society of Van Diemen's Land 256
Papua 389, 395
Papua New Guinea 389
Park, Archibald Alexander (fl. 1857–1861) 358
Parker, Edward Stone (1802–1865) 8-9
Parkes, Henry (1815–1896) 302-3

Parramatta NSW 266, 320, 351, 379, 392, 419, 447
Parramatta Literary Society 447
Patent Engraving Co. 85
Paterson, Banjo (Andrew Barton) (1864–1941) 249, 254; *The Man from Snowy River* 433
Paton, Frank (1870–1938) *396*, 398
Paton, John G. (1824–1907) *396*
Paul, Tempest Margaret 353
Pearson, Charles Henry (1830–1894) 346, 370
Pearson, James 353
Pedder, Sir John Lewes (1793–1859) 217, 318
Penfold *See* W.C. Penfold and Co.
Penman, John 99 (?–1900)
Penman and Galbraith 359
Perth WA 100, 105, 130, 266, 283, 379; almanacs 386, 387, 379-*380*; artists 100-101, 105; bookbinders 105; booksellers and stationers 266, 280, 283; directories 379, 386-88 *passim*; government printing 407; libraries 310, public 306-*323*; mechanics' institutes 307, *323*; music 350; newspapers and magazines 34, 200, 203, 350, 380; printing 34, 101, 130. *See also* Fremantle WA; Western Australia
Pether, Richard (fl. 1870–1901) 407, 408
Petherick, Edward Augustus (1847–1917) 277-9 *passim*, 282, 340
Philip, G.B. (1861–1940) 280
Phillip, Gov. Arthur (1738–1814) 425; *A Complete Account of the Settlement at Port Jackson* 151
Phillips-Stephan Photo-Litho and Typographic Company 83
Philosophical Society of Australasia 155, 293, 338, 345
photographers 50, 82, 171, *198*, *297*, 305, *307*, *323*, *384*, *395*, *438*, *441*. *See also* photography, printing techniques
photography, printing techniques 50, 76, 77, 79-93 *passim*, 99, 102, 408; collotype 81-3; photolithography 50, 81, 83, 88, 93, 395, 410. *See also* engraving; illustrations, printing technology; lithography; photographers

Photoline Printing Company 84
Picturesque Atlas Company 93
Picturesque Atlas of Australasia 76, 93, 171
Piddington, W.R. (William Richman) (1815–1887) 195, 272, 435
Pierssené, H. 380
Pillar, Joseph William 38
'Pindar Juvenal' 156
Pindjarup (people) 350
piracy 82, 96, 155-60, 176-87 *passim*, 180, 281, 354-9 *passim*. *See also* copyright
Pitt, E.R. (1877–1957) 257
Plain exhortations to prisoners 307
Platts, Charles (1813–1871) 104, 105, 271, *273*, 333
playbills 28-*29*, 122, 123, 149, 406. *See also* theatre
poetry 28, 68-9, 118, 139-47 *passim*, 155-60 *passim*, 164, 222, 225, 440, 449, 427, 450; in newspapers and magazines 119, 155-6, 164-5, 227-9, 230, 236, 245, 246, 252; publishing 2, 20, 139-47 *passim*, 152, 155-60, 164-5, 170, 227, 244, 349-50, 386, 412, 433. *See also individual poets*
Point Macleay Mission 393
Poitevin, Alphonse 81
Polynesia (languages, peoples) 389, 391, 399. *See also individual countries*
Pontville Reading Society 446
Poole, Mrs 86
Popular Penny Readings 459
population: Australia 155, 455, 458; individual States 163-4; Melbourne 456-7; NSW 26, 68
Port Augusta SA 82
Port Fairy VIC 162, 266, 268
Port Jackson NSW 28, 151, 307
Port Phillip VIC 8, 28, 154, 160, 162, 407
Port Phillip Association 160-1
Port Phillip District 321
Port Pirie SA 326-7
Porter's Yankee Circulating Library 334
Portland VIC 162, 266, 321-2, 439
Potter, Charles (1830–1901) 407, 411, *415*
Potter, Rev. Robert 247
Power, Matthew (c.1775–?) 38, 407
Praed, Rosa (1851–1935) 144-6 *passim*; *Christina Chard* 145; *The Scourge Stick* 145

Prahran VIC 326, 327
Preece, F.W. (Frederick William) (1857–1928) 280
press freedom *see* censorship
Preston, Walter (1777–?) *Views of New South Wales* 91
prices (consumer): almanacs 263, 379, *384*; books 160, 259-91 *passim*, *343*, 417-37 *passim*; commercial circulating libraries: catalogues 331-5 *passim*, fees 332-3, 335, *336*; directories 379; government printing and publications 409; magazines 224, 227, 228, 233-53 *passim*; mission publications 397; music 357, 362, 363; newspapers 33, 43, 46, 47, 200; pre-decimal currency xi. *See also* costs; wages and income
Primer for Children 368
Principles that underlie the Art of Teaching 370
print runs *see* edition sizes and print runs
print workers 66-74; apprenticeships 68, 69-70, 71, 73, 105, 132, 213, 403; artists, lithographic 89-94 *passim* (*See also names of individual artists*); children 51, 67-71 *passim*; convicts 66, 68, 104, 152, 213; customs and workplace culture 67, 71-3 *passim*; foreign-trained 47, 66-8 *passim*, 90, 93, 132, 213, 281; job loss due to technology 51, 68, 458; shortages of 31, 68, 304; strikes 37, 48, 51, 71; training 31; wages 43, 67, 68, 71; women 51, 66-74, 70-73 *passim*, 82, 96, 104, 132, 171, 352. *See also* jobbing trade; *names of individuals*; unions and trade societies
printers' brokers 49-50, 55
printers' furnishers 48-9, 127, 129
printing, colour 81, 84-5, *88*, 89, 90, 93-4, 135, 168; chromolithography 84, 86, *87*, 93. *See also* hand-colouring
printing, nature 97, *98-99*
printing equipment 27-65; repairing 37, 42, 43; second-hand 31, 44, 55, 57; shortages 31, 61, 200, 394; value 33, 37, 48, 57. *See also* government printing; jobbing trade; print workers; printing presses; type

printing presses: Albion 28, 32, 33, 34, 37, 38, 398; Applegath 41, 42, 43; Belper 41; Columbian 28, 33, 34, 36, 37, 39, 41, 398; Cowper 42, 43; cylinder 28, 37-57; electric-powered 46; gas-powered, 41, 44, 45, 46, 57; hand-presses 27-54 *passim*, 152, 212, 409, 410-11; Hoe & Co. 36, 42, 43, 46, 93; iron 31-2, 37, 61; Miehle 41; Napier 39-40; Quadrant 41, 56; Ramage 30, 36; rotary 42, 43, 47 (Victory), 52, 53; Ruthven 32, 37; Stanhope 28, 31, 32, 33, 34; steam-powered 56, 68, 410; treadle platen 36, 39, 54, 56, 57, 58, 60, 61; water-powered 45, 46 ; web-fed 27, 46-7, 53, 61; Wharfedale 40-1, 45, 56, 398; wooden 27, 28, *29*, 30, 31, 32, 34, 61
printing technology 28-65, 75-111. *See also* government printing; linotype; print workers; printing equipment; printing presses; type
Proceedings of the Royal Society of Victoria 86
Prout, John Skinner (1806–1876) 96
Public Library of New South Wales 297-8, 302. *See also* Free Public Library, Sydney; State Library of New South Wales
Public Library of Queensland 307
Public Library of South Australia 306
Public Library of Victoria *See* Melbourne Public Library
Public Library of Western Australia 306
publishing 148-75. *See also under individual States and cities*
Pugh, T.P. (1831–1896) 408
Püttmann, Hermann (1811–1874) 285
Pyke, W.T. (1859–1933) 280, 284

Q

Quaritch, Bernard 169, 275, 285, 338, 340, 342
Queanbeyan NSW 440
Queensland 34, 36, 99, 104, 144-5, 160, 259, 263, 285, 320, 324-5, 392, 459; almanacs and directories 378, 379, 386, 432; artists 97, 99; booksellers and stationers 432-3; copyright 185; government printing 97, 98, 408; Indigenous Australians 412; libraries 306, 307; magazines 246, 251, 252, 432-3; mechanics' institutes 322, 324-5; missions, religious 388-405, 412; music 351; newspapers 36, *38*, 160, 203, 432-3, 429, *438*; printing and publishing *38, 57,* 70, 71, 97-9, 99, 118, 129; schools of arts 322. *See also* Brisbane; *individual cities and towns*
Queensland Typographical Society 71

R

Rae, John (1813–1900) *441*
Rae, William (1823–1887) 344
Railway Guide to New South Wales 83, 92
Ralph, Thomas Shearman (1812–1891) *Elementary Botany (Australian Edition) for the Use of Beginners* 86
Ramsay, Robert (1842–1882) 369
Ramsden, Samuel (c. 1822–1877) 109, 116
Ramsey, Alfred George 438
Ratte, Felix August 89
Ravenscroft, Alison *Auntie Rita* 16-17, 23
Ray, Edgar 239
Raymond, James (1786?–1851) 374
readers and reading 417-53. *See also* bush, children, literacy, women
Reading & Wellbank 165
reading societies *see* literary and reading societies
readings, penny 326, 444, 459
Records of the Australian Museum 83
Redfern NSW 134
Redfern Literary Association 446
Reed & Fox 128, 129
Reed, Thomas 358
Reeves, J.G. 105
Reibey, Mary (1777–1855) 453
Reichenberg, Sgt Joseph (c.1790–1851) 352, 358
religion 11, 307, 325, 346
religious publishing, bookselling and libraries 388-405, 412, 423, 434; Anglican 225, 351, 392, 399, *See also* Church of England; Catholic 36, 127, 237, 241, 271, 277, 356, 358, 362, 368, 389, 395, 428, 431; Church of England (including Church Missionary Society) 237, 392, 399, *See also* Anglican;

Congregational (including London Missionary Society) 156, 389, 390, 439; Jewish 205, 356, 352, 358, 360; Lutheran 202, 263, 285, 390, 393, 399; Methodist, Wesleyan 225, 228, 235, 237, 343, 389, 390, 392, 393, 399; chapels 161, 293, 424-5; Presbyterian 136, 168, 170, 225, 270, 284, 349, 390, 392, 396, 399, 417; Protestant 391, 428. See also mission presses; names of individual religious societies
Remarks on the Probable Origin and Antiquity of the Aboriginal Natives 94
REMOS (pseud.) 351
Reyher, Oscar 359
Rhymes from the Mines 118
Richards, Thomas (1800–1877) 230-1
Richards, Thomas (1831–1898) 92, 134, 370-1, 407, 408, 410-11
Richmond NSW 201
Richmond VIC 135, 285, 303
Richmond Reading Society 445
Richardson, Henry Handel (Ethel) (1870–1946) 328
Rider & Mercer 90
Riegg, J. 86
Riley, Alexander (1778?–1833) 262
Riverina NSW 379, 437
Roberts, Philip (Waipuldanya) (c.1922–?) *I, The Aboriginal* 15, 23
Robertson & Mullens 458
Robertson, George (1825–1898) 95, 105, 109, 167, 168, 170, 248, 276-88 passim, 335, 367, 370, 456, 458; *George Robertson's Books & Stationery List* 278; *George Robertson's Monthly Book Circular* 278; *George Robertson's Trade List of Goods to Arrive* 278; *Select Catalogue of Books* 278
Robertson, George (1860–1933) 144, 168, 278, 280, 342, 458
Robertson, Jimmy Jampijimpa (c.1946–2002) 13
Robertson, William 367
Robinson, George 267
Robinson, George Augustus (1791–1866) 8, 21, 200, 318
Robinson, Michael Massey (1744–1826) 155

Robinson, T.W. 368
Robson, Levey & Franklyn, 127
Rockhampton QLD 326-7
Rockhampton School of Arts Museum 326
Rodius, Charles (1802–1860) 355
Roe, Capt. John Septimus (1797–1878) 323
Roeszler, Charles (1845–1912) 109
Rogers, Mrs 97
Rolfe, Thomas 356, 363
Rolwegan, George (1812–1866) 105, 111, 386
Roper, Edward (1833–1909) 88
Ross, James (1786–1838) 96, 318, 368, 373, 383, 407, 426-7
Rowcroft, Charles (1798–1856) 141
Royal Geographical Society of Australasia, South Australian Branch 340
Rudd, Steele (Davis, Arthur Hoey) (1868–1935) 254
Rules and Regulations for the Conduct and Management of the Bank of New South Wales 412
Rusden, Ann (1783–1860) 452
Rusden, Henry Keylock (1826–1910) 453
Russell, George (1812–1888) 345
Russell, H.C. (1836–1907) 413
Rutter, George Oswald 362

S

S. Cooke & Co. 49, 57
Sachs and Fischer 131
Sacred Heart Mission 389
Sadd, Henry (c. 1811–1893) 76-7
St Barnabas 391
St Luke, Gospel 397
St Matthew, Gospel 398
sales figures (books) 167-8, 169, 170-1
Salting, George (1835–1909) 341
Samoa (language and mission printing) 389, 395
Sandhurst VIC 326-7
Sands & Kenny 76, 374
Sands & McDougall 37, 45, 56, 57, 58, 90, 109, 374
Sands, John (1818–1873) 34, 89, 93, 136, 283, 375-6, 378, 380
Sanford, W.A. (1818–1902) *Journal of an Expedition to Explore the Interior of Western Australia* 100

Santa Cruz Islands 389
Sapsford, Newman 105
Savery, Henry (1791–1842) *The Hermit in Van Diemen's Land* 157, 212; *Quintus Servinton* 157
Sayers, John Nutt (1808–1891) 350
Schell, Frederic B. 93
Schoenfeldt, Friedrich (Fritz) (1810–1868) 85, 95
Schoknecht, Carl 393
schools of arts 197, 294, 303, 307, 319-26 *passim*, 425-6. *See also* libraries; mechanics' institutes
Schürmann, C.W. (1815–1893) 393
scientific publishing and publications 83, 86, 170, 225, 238, 255-7, 284; agriculture 159, 167, 256, 412, 414; anthropology 3, 6, 7, 9,13, 21, 91, 94, 95, 156, 167, 227, 228, 239, 350, 368-9, 387, 388-405 *passim*; 413; botany 79, 84, 85, 86, 95, 97, 98-99, 100, 115, 371; entomology 86, 414; geology 82, 95, 97, 411; medicine 76-7, 170, 256, 284, 336, 339, 345, 432, 469; ornithology 91, 93-4, 97, 107, 113, 296, 412; palaeontology 95; zoology 82-95 *passim*, 345. *See also* journals, professional and trade; *names of individual scientists/authors*
Scott, Alexander Walker (1800–1883) *Lepidoptera* 86, 92
Scott, Harriet (1830–1907) *Australian Mammals* 92; *Lepidoptera* 86; *Monograph of Australian Land Shells* 92; *Snakes of Australia* 92
Scott, Helena (1832–1910) *Australian Mammals* 92; *Lepidoptera* 86; *Monograph of Australian Land Shells* 92; *Snakes of Australia* 92
Sebastopol VIC 286
Senefelder, Alois 78
serialisation of fiction: in books 178-9; in magazines 141, 143, 144, 146, 228, 230, 236, 238, 245-6, 428; in newspapers 146, 178, 199, 204, 443
Seventh Day Adventists 399
Seward, Robert 377
Shakespeare-Tavern 267
Shanley, James (c. 1815–1857) 35-6
Shenton, Arthur (1816–1871) 386, 407

Shepparton VIC 328, 426
Shepparton Free Library and Workingmen's Club 328
Sholl, Robert John (1819–1886) 380
Short, Timothy (pseud.) 349
shorthand 79
Sidaway, Robert (1757?–1809) 149
Silver, S.W. 340
Sims, Walter C. (1841–1923) 359
Singleton NSW 320
Sinnett, Frederick (1830–1866) 239
Sippe, George (c.1793–1842) 353
Slade, Leonard (1859–1954) 279
Slater, George (1824–1886) 358-9
Smith, A.J. (Alfred James) (fl. 1850s–1880s) 279, 284, *287*
Smith, Elder and Co. 157
Smith, James (1820–1910) 142, 143, 239, 245, 346, 444
Smith, Joseph *172*
Smith, R.B. *Victoria in 1880* 95
Smith, William (alias of Thomas Broughton) 104, 107
Smyth, Robert Brough (1830–1889) *Aborigines of Victoria* 95, 413; *The Gold Fields and Mineral Districts of Victoria* 95, 411
Society for Promoting Christian Knowledge 155, 261, 392, 397, 423, 438-9
Society for the Propagation of the Gospel 392
Society of Mary 389
Solomon, Mrs John 267
Solomon Islands 389, 392, 395
Sorell, William (1775–1848) 214-16, 218
Sorrento VIC 28
South Australia 161, 163, 263, 306, 324, 406, 413, 460; almanacs and directories 374-5, 379; artists 100; bookbinding 105; bookselling 161, 259, *273*, 285; copyright in 183; government printing 407; Indigenous Australians 393, 398, 400; libraries and mechanics' institutes 294, 300, 302, 306, *307*, 320-1, 324; libraries, private 340, *343*; magazines 232, 234, 235; music 349, 359; newspapers 34, 46, 161, 200-1; printing 34, 44, 46, 55, 70, 99-100, 124, 163-4, 406; publishing 160, 163-4;

by religious missions 393, 398, 399; type imports 124, 126. *See also* Adelaide; *individual towns and cities*
South Australian Institute 294, 320
South Australian Literary Society 294, 320
South Australian Mechanics' Institute 294, 320
South Australian Subscription Library 320
South Australian Subscription Library and Mechanics' Institute 294
South Melbourne VIC 134
South Richmond VIC 303
Southern Phonographic Harmonia 79
Specimens of a dialect of the Aborigines of New South Wales 368-9, 392
Spelling Book (Dixon) 365, 438-9
Spelling Book (Howe) 368
Spelling Book for the Use of Schools in New South Wales 368
Spence, Catherine Helen (1825–1910) 143, 144, 245; *Clara Morison* 143; *Mr Hogarth's Will* 143; *Tender and True* 143; *Uphill Work* 143
Spencer, Sir Walter Baldwin (1860–1929) 10
Spicer (paper firm) 103
spiritualism 244, 281
sports publications 92, 235, 250, 251
Sprent, Mrs C.P. *Systematic Account of the Geology of Tasmania* 97
Springate aka Springquart, George 105
Staiger, K.T. 97
Stanley VIC 327
Stanley, William (1820–1902) 357
Stanthorpe QLD 38
State Library of New South Wales 297-8. *See also* Free Public Library, Sydney; Public Library of NSW
State Library of Queensland 307
State Library of South Australia 306
State Library of Tasmania 298. *See also* Tasmanian Public Library
State Library Victoria 295. *See also* Melbourne Public Library
State Library of Western Australia 306
Statistical Register of Victoria 411
steam-power: navigation 132; printing 56, 68, 410
Steele, Alexander 117

Steiglitz VIC 204
Stein, Bernard 105
Stenhouse, Nicol Drysdale (1806–1873) 164, 338
Stephens, E.J. (1846–1931) 204
Stephens, James Brunton (1835–1902) *Marsupial Bill* 99
Stephens, John (1806–1850) 407
Stephens, William (1833–1913) 188, 195, 367
Stephens and Stokes 368, 369, 407
Stephenson Blake (previously Blake & Stephenson) 125, 129, 130
stereotyping 46, 48, 51-3, 70, 77, 136, 397, 409
Stewart, Robert 353-4
Stilwell & Co. 82
Stirling, Edmund (1815–1897) 380
Stirling, Sir James (1791–1865) 34
Stirling Bros. 380
Stirling, Sholl & Co. 379, 380
Stokes, Frederick (c. 1811–1891) 39
Stokes, Thomas (1831–1910) 54, 55
Stone, Alfred Hawes (1801–1873) 323
Stone, John 377
Stoney, Henry Butler 357
Story, Edwin 195
Story, William (1801–1870) 195, 342
Stow, Rev. T.Q. (1801–1862) *Redemption Interesting to Angels* 161
Street, Philip 213
strikes, by printers 66, 69, 71. *See also* unions
Strode, Thomas (1812–1880) 30-1, 135, 162
Strode, William 31
Strong, H.A. (1841–1918) 370
Strother, G.H. 100
Strutt, William (1825–1915) 94
Strutt, William Thomas 407
Stuart, T.P. Anderson (1856–1920) 257
Stubbs, Thomas (composer) 354
Stubbs, Thomas (printers' broker) 50
Sturt, Charles (1795–1869) 154
Sullivan Bay VIC 28, 407
Supreme Court Library (Victoria) 265, 275, 295
Sutherland, Alexander (1852–1902) 247; *History of Australia* 366, 370

Sutherland, George (1855–1905) 80, 88; *History of Australia* 167, *366*, 370
Sutton, Henry (1856–1912) 89
Suttor, Beverley (fl. 1830s–1840s) *Original Poetry* 158
Swan, James (1811–1891) 132, 134
Swan River WA 307, 352, 393
Swan River Mechanics' Institute 307, 322, *323*, 327
Swan River Mission 393
Sydney Illustrated 96
Sydney Mechanics' School of Arts 294, 319, 325, 326, 425
Sydney Primer or Child's Manual 368
Sydney Synagogue 352, 358, *360*
Syme, David (1827–1908) 47, 202, 458
Syme, Ebenezer (1826–1860) *47*
synagogues 352, 358, *360*

T
Tables for the use of schools 368
Tahiti (language, missions, peoples) 388-92 *passim*, 397, 412
Talbot VIC 324
Tangye, George 308
Tangye, Richard 308
Tanner, John *336*
Tanunda SA 386, 398, 399
Taplin, Rev. George (1831–1879) 393
tariffs *see* customs and tariffs
Tarrington VIC 285
Tasmania 97, 155, 157, 163, 211, 263, 318, 324, 417-18, 440; almanacs 96, 212, 373, *384*; artists 96, 97; bookbinding 104, 105, 107-8; booksellers & stationers 165, 166, 195, 237, 259, 271-2, 279, 283; copyright 178-*179*; directories 195, 373, 379, 381; government printing 115, 407, 412; Indigenous Australians 150, 200; libraries 298-9: circulating 331-2, 426, 452; public 298-9; subscription 150, 265, 294-5, 298, 452; magazines 202, 226, 230, 231, 237, 238, 241, 246, 256, 430; mechanics' institutes 425; music 351, 354, 357, 359; newspapers 194, 226, 200, 231, 418; paper supplies and production 113-15 *passim*; printing 30, 48, 96-7, 124, 212, 412; publishing 96, 97, 142, 150, 156, 165, 178, *179*, 212, 256, 265, 352, 359, 412, 413; reading societies 264, 425, 445-6, 448-*449*. *See also* Bent, Andrew; Hobart; Launceston; *names of individual towns*
Tasmania Illustrated 96
Tasmanian Public Library 294-5, 298, 299
Tate, Ralph (1840–1901) 100
Taylor, Donald 82
Taylor, James 82
Taylor, Jessie 171
Tegg, James (1808–1845) 158, 271-2, 331, 362, 368, 434
Tegg, Samuel Augustus (1813–1872) 158, 160, *166*, 179, 271-2, 288, 334, 368
Tegg, Thomas 271-2; *Tegg's Handbook for Emigrants* 158
Teichelmann, Christian Gottlieb (1807–1888) *Aborigines of South Australia* 161, 393
Temple of the Muses 284
Tench, Watkin (1758–1833) 148, 307, 310, *Narrative of the Expedition to Botany Bay* 151
Terry, William Henry (1836–1913) 281
Testmenta Marra 393, 397, 398
textbooks 167, 365-71, 388, 392, 393, 411, 412, 424, 438-9, 440
Thatcher, Charles (1831–1878) 350-1
theatre 28, *29*, 122-3, 145, 146, 148-9, 158, 165, *172*, 222, 251, 254, 326, 433
This is the Hut that Jack Built in Australia 85
Thitchener, Henry James (1841–1911) 134-5
Thomas, Arnold Vivian 99
Thomas, Edmund (1827–1867) 92, 357
Thomas, Evan Henry (1801?–1837) 215-17 *passim*
Thomas, Robert (1781–1860) 34, 161, 407
Thompson, Alex 351
Thompson, Andrew (1773?–1810) 422
Thomson, Alexander (1814–1856) 132-4
Thomson, James (1805–1860) 96
Thomson, Richard (1858–1938) 280
Thomson, Sidney (?–1864) 134
Thorowgood and Besley 125. *See also* Besley
Thorpe, D.W. (1889–1976) 280

Threlkeld, L.E. (Lancelot Edward) (1788–1859) 227, 392-3; *Key to the Structure of the Aboriginal Language* 132, *133*; *Specimens of a Dialect of the Aborigines of New South Wales* 156, 392, 397; *An Australian Spelling Book, in the Language as spoken by the Aborigines...*368-9
Tingle, James 378
Todd, Sir Charles (1826–1910) 413
Tolmer, Alexander (1815–1890) 115
Tompson, Charles Jr 1807–1883) *Wild Notes from the Lyre of a Native Minstrel* 156, 263, 333, 412
Tompson, Charles Sr (1784?–1871) 263
Tonga (language, missions, people) 388, 389, 390, 395
Toowoomba QLD 379
Tough, William 262
Townson, Robert (1762–1827) 345
Townsville QLD 307, 432, 437
Townsville School of Arts Library 307
Tracy, Richard (1826–1874) 345
trade societies *See* unions and trade societies
Traill, W.H. (1843–1902) 80
Treeby, George *47*
Trischler, Frederick 170-1
Troedel & Co. 86, *87*
Troedel, Charles (1836–1906) 84, 135
Trollope, Anthony 295
Trood, Thomas 125
Tucker, George A. (fl. 1860s–1880s) *Lunacy in Many Lands* 414, *415*
Tulk, Augustus (1810–1873) 297, 301, 310
Tulloch, David (?–1869?) *Illustrated Australian Magazine* 94
Turner, Charles (1844–1913) *New Atlas of Australia* 93; *Victoria in 1880* 95; *Zoology and Things* 86
Turner, Ethel (1870–1958) 191
Turner, Henry Gyles (1831–1920) 246, 247-8
Turner, Nathaniel 390
Twopeny, Richard (1857–1915) 190, 204
type 122-38; agents, Australian, for overseas firms 125, 127-9, 131, 136; Australian made 131-6; costs 33, 130; early use in Australia 27, 29, 122, 123, 130; fonts (major): Caslon 28, 29, 123-29 *passim*; Clarendon 134; Figgins 28, 55, 123, 130, 135; German 126, 131; Greek 131; Hebrew 131; imported 125-36; mission presses 398-9; music 356, 359; poster 31, 54; typography *126*; wood, Australian-made 135-6. *See also* printing equipment; printing technology
Tyrrell, James R. (1875–1961) 282-3 *Old Books, Old Friends, Old Sydney* 282

U

Under the Holly 165
unions and trade societies 48, 51, 66-71 *passim*, 105, 252, 304, 450
United States of America 31-61 *passim*, 82, 90, 93
University of Melbourne 265, 295, 409
University of Sydney 341, 459
University of Tasmania 299, 324
Unwin, Henry Beauchamp (d.1874) *38*

V

V. & J. Figgins 129, 135. *See also* type, fonts (major)
Vale, William (1833–1895) 336
Van Diemen's Land *see* Tasmania/Van Diemen's Land
Van Diemen's Land Mechanics' Institute 294, 318
Van Diemen's Land Scientific Society 154
Van Diemen's Land Warriors, or the Heroes of Cornwall 156, 212
Vanuatu (formerly New Hebrides) 389, 390, 396, 398, 399
Vernon, Mr 443
Victoria and its Metropolis 96
Victoria Public Library (WA) 306
Victoria Subscription Library 321
Victoria Type Foundry 135
Victorian Parliamentary Library 265, 275, 295
Vidal, Maria Theresa (1815–1869) *Tales for the Bush* 159
Vocabulary of Dialects Spoken by Aboriginal Natives of Australia 394

W

W.C. Penfold and Co. 35, 104, 271
W.H. Paling and Co. 362
wages and income 70, 85-6, 152, 296; artists 77, 84-6; authors 139-47 *passim*, 162, 164, 248, 342; circulating library proprietors 331; post-gold rushes 69, 162, 163; printing trades 43, 67, 68, 71; publishing 382, 398. *See also* costs; prices (consumer)
'Waif Wanderer' *see* Fortune, Mary
Wainburranga, Paddy Fordham (c.1932–2006) 11, 22
Waipuldanya (Philip Roberts) (c.1922-?) *I, The Aboriginal* 15, 23
Walch, Charles Edward (1830–1915) 165, 279
Walch circulating library 452
Walch, Garnet (1843–1913) 142, 145, 165; *Victoria in 1880* 84, 95
Walch, J. and Sons 150, *166-7*, 195, 272-3, 276, 331-2, 359, 362; *Walch's Literary Intelligencer and General Advertiser* 237, 279, 282
Walch, James *166*
Walker, Alfred 99
Walker, George Edward 89
Walker, James Backhouse (1841–1899) 299, 344
Walker, May & Co. 37, 39, 47-8, 52
Walker, Robert Cooper (1833–1897) 298, 301, *305*, 310
Walker, Thomas 232
Wallace, William Vincent (1812–1865) 353, 354, 363
Wallis and Futuna Islands 389
Walter Scott Publishing Co. 282, 288
Wangkumara (language) 11, 22
Ward Lock 288
Wardell, Robert (1793–1834) 33, 154, 211, 219
Warning Voice, and Some Important Considerations on Observance of the Lord's Day 94
Warren VIC 446
Warwick & Sapsford 97, 99
Watling, Thomas (b. 1762) *Letters from an Exile at Botany-Bay, to his Aunt in Dumfries* 141

Watson, William (1793–1866) 393
Waugh & Cox 195, 375
Wearne, Joseph (1832–1884) 116
Weavell, Mr 37
Webb, Beatrice 205, 257
Webb, Sidney 205
Webster, John Campbell 358
Welch, Daniel Lovett 159
Wellington Vale NSW 393
Wells, Thomas (1782–1833) 214; *Michael Howe, the Last and worst of the bushrangers of Van Diemen's Land* 212
Welsh, Edward 104
Welsh (language) 164, 285, 286
Wenborn, W.A.J. (1842–1891) 287
Wendel, Richard (1851–1926) 84
Wentworth, William Charles (1790–1872) 33, 154, 211, 219, 220, 349
Wesleyan Chapel (Adelaide) 161
Wesleyan Chapel (Hobart) 293
Wesleyan Library (Hobart) 424-5
Wesleyan Methodist Society 389, 399
Wesleyan Tongan Mission 390
West, Absalom 91
West, John (1809–1873) 220
West Maitland NSW 116
Westcott, William (1813–1876) 332, 335
Western Australia 160-1, 163, 263, 458, 460; almanacs and directories 379-80, *380*, 386, 387, 388, 432-3; bookbinding 104,105; booksellers and stationers 259, 266, 367; copyright 185; government printing 407; Indigenous Australians 21, 387, 393; libraries and mechanics' institutes 294, 302, 306, 307, 322, 324; magazines 231, 235, 256; music 352, 357-8; newspapers 37, 203, 380; printing 34, 37, 57, 70, 90-1, 100-101, 124, 160, 406; publishing 160. *See also individual cities and towns*
Western Australian Book Society 266
Western Australian Institution 266
Western District VIC 435-36, 446
White, Surgeon John (1756?–1832) 151
Whitehead, Charles (1804–1862) 142
Whitehead, E. and Co. 136
Whitworth, R.P. (1831–1901) *Mary Summers* 165
Wickes, Edward Walter 370

Wide Bay QLD 379
Wigg, E.S. (1818–1899) 105, 273
Wild, J.J. (1828–1900) 85, 86
Wilkie, Joseph (1828–1875) 358
Wilkins, William (1827–1892) 370, 439-40
William Brooks and Co. 399
Williams, George 33
Williams, J. 100
Williams, W.H. (William Henry) (c. 1831–1910) 48, 358-9, 362-3
Williams, William *Vocabulary of the Aborigines of South Australia* 161
Williamstown VIC 30
Wills, Sarah (d.1823) 262
Willmett, T. 432, 437
Wilson, William (c. 1795–?) 92, 374; *Bell's Life in Sydney and Sporting Reviewer* 92; *Picture of Sydney and Strangers' Guide to New South Wales* 374
Wilson, Mackinnon & Fairfax 363
Wilton, Rev. C.P.N. (1795–1859) 225
Wimble, F.T. & Co. 30, 49, 57, 128, 130, 131, 135, 136
Windle, John 379
Windsor NSW 201
Winstanley, Eliza (1818–1882) 437
Winston, Charles (1825–1893) 94, 99
Winter Cooke family 339
Wiradjuri (language and people) 357, 393
Wise, Edward (1818–1865) 298, 344
Wise, Henry 377-80 *passim*
Woellmer, Wilhelm 131
Woiwurrung (people) 9-10
Wollstonecraft, Edward (1783–1832) 345, 421
women: access to libraries, mechanics' institutes 293, 296, 301, 306, 326; artists 86, 92, 93, 97, 100; authors 16, 17-19, 25, 97, 143, 139-47 *passim*, 156-9 *passim*, 165, 168, 205, 242, 437; circulating libraries and, 267, 273, 331; franchise 460; mechanics' institutes, support of 193, 319, 326; music 353, 354, 355; editors and journalists 143, 191, 199, 243, 251; private libraries of 267, 427; publications aimed at 165, 231, 236, 237, 240, 249-54 *passim*, 432, 440; reading 193, 250, 417-54 *passim*;

science 97; type founders 134; working in printing trades 66-74, 70, 71, 72, 73, 82, 96, 104, 132, 171, 352. *See also names of individual women*; literacy
Women's Love 157
Wood, Eulalie (fl. 1820s–1840s) 96, 352
Wood, James (c.1802–1854)) 96
Wood, Mrs Nugent *Women's Work in Australia* 168
wood type *See under* type
Woodbury, Walter (1834–1885) 82-3
woodcuts and wood engraving. *See under* engraving
Woodhouse, Frederick, Sr (1820–1909) and Jr (1846–1927) *Record of the Melbourne Cup* 86
Woodhouse, H.J. (Herbert J.) (1854–1937) *Victoria in 1880* 95
Woolcott and Clarke 356, 357
Woollahra Literary and Debating Society 447
Woolley, John (1816–1866) 164
Work, Thomas L. 131
Wright, Archibald 134
Wright, Hugh 309, 447
Wrigley, James and William 105
Wurundjeri (people) 162
Wybalenna Aboriginal settlement TAS 200

Y
Yate, Rev. William 390
yellowbacks 339, 437
Yemmerrawanne (1775–1794) 348
York (England) 135
York Gate Library 340
Young Australian's Alphabet, The 85